WILEY SERIES ON PARALLEL AND DISTRIBUTED COMPUTING

Series Editor: Albert Y. Zomaya

Parallel and Distributed Simulation Systems / Richard Fujimoto

Mobile Processing in Distributed and Open Environments / Peter Sapaty

Introduction to Parallel Algorithms / C. Xavier and S. S. Iyengar

Solutions to Parallel and Distributed Computing Problems: Lessons from Biological Sciences / Albert Y. Zomaya, Fikret Ercal, and Stephan Olariu (*Editors*)

Parallel and Distributed Computing: A Survey of Models, Paradigms, and Approaches / Claudia Leopold

Fundamentals of Distributed Object Systems: A CORBA Perspective / Zahir Tari and Omran Bukhres

Pipelined Processor Farms: Structured Design for Embedded Parallel Systems / Martin Fleury and Andrew Downton

Handbook of Wireless Networks and Mobile Computing / Ivan Stojmenović (*Editor*)

Internet-Based Workflow Management: Toward a Semantic Web / Dan C. Marinescu

Parallel Computing on Heterogeneous Networks / Alexey L. Lastovetsky

Performance Evaluation and Characteization of Parallel and Distributed Computing Tools / Salim Hariri and Manish Parashar

Distributed Computing: Fundamentals, Simulations and Advanced Topics, *Second Edition* / Hagit Attiya and Jennifer Welch

Smart Environments: Technology, Protocols, and Applications / Diane Cook and Sajal Das

Fundamentals of Computer Organization and Architecture / Mostafa Abd-El-Barr and Hesham El-Rewini

Advanced Computer Architecture and Parallel Processing / Hesham El-Rewini and Mostafa Abd-El-Barr

UPC: Distributed Shared Memory Programming / Tarek El-Ghazawi, William Carlson, Thomas Sterling, and Katherine Yelick

Handbook of Sensor Networks: Algorithms and Architectures / Ivan Stojmenović (*Editor*)

Parallel Metaheuristics: A New Class of Algorithms / Enrique Alba (*Editor*)

Design and Analysis of Distributed Algorithms / Nicola Santoro

DESIGN AND ANALYSIS
OF DISTRIBUTED
ALGORITHMS

THE WILEY BICENTENNIAL–KNOWLEDGE FOR GENERATIONS

*E*ach generation has its unique needs and aspirations. When Charles Wiley first opened his small printing shop in lower Manhattan in 1807, it was a generation of boundless potential searching for an identity. And we were there, helping to define a new American literary tradition. Over half a century later, in the midst of the Second Industrial Revolution, it was a generation focused on building the future. Once again, we were there, supplying the critical scientific, technical, and engineering knowledge that helped frame the world. Throughout the 20th Century, and into the new millennium, nations began to reach out beyond their own borders and a new international community was born. Wiley was there, expanding its operations around the world to enable a global exchange of ideas, opinions, and know-how.

For 200 years, Wiley has been an integral part of each generation's journey, enabling the flow of information and understanding necessary to meet their needs and fulfill their aspirations. Today, bold new technologies are changing the way we live and learn. Wiley will be there, providing you the must-have knowledge you need to imagine new worlds, new possibilities, and new opportunities.

Generations come and go, but you can always count on Wiley to provide you the knowledge you need, when and where you need it!

WILLIAM J. PESCE
PRESIDENT AND CHIEF EXECUTIVE OFFICER

PETER BOOTH WILEY
CHAIRMAN OF THE BOARD

DESIGN AND ANALYSIS OF DISTRIBUTED ALGORITHMS

Nicola Santoro
Carleton University, Ottawa, Canada

WILEY-INTERSCIENCE
A JOHN WILEY & SONS, INC., PUBLICATION

Library of Congress Cataloging-in-Publication Data:

Santoro, N. (Nicola), 1951-
   Design and analysis of distributed algorithms / by Nicola Santoro.
      p. cm. – (Wiley series on parallel and distributed computing)
   Includes index.
   ISBN-13: 978-0-471-71997-7
1. Electronic data processing–Distributed processing.   2. Computer algorithms.   I. Title.   II. Series.
   QA76.9.D5.S26 2007
   005.1–dc22

                                                                2006011214

To my favorite distributed environment: My children
Monica, Noel, Melissa, Maya, Michela, Alvin.

CONTENTS

The computational universe surrounding us is clearly quite different from that envisioned by the designers of the large mainframes of half a century ago. Even the subsequent most futuristic visions of *supercomputing* and of *parallel machines,* which have guided the research drive and absorbed the research funding for so many years, are far from today's computational realities.

These realities are characterized by the presence of communities of networked entities communicating with each other, cooperating toward common tasks or the solution of a shared problem, and acting autonomously and spontaneously. They are *distributed computing environments.*

It has been from the fields of network and of communication engineering that the seeds of what we now experience have germinated. The growth in understanding has occurred when computer scientists (initially very few) started to become aware of and study the computational issues connected with these new network-centric realities. The internet, the web, and the grids are just examples of these environments. Whether over wired or wireless media, whether by static or nomadic code, computing in such environments is inherently decentralized and distributed.[1] To compute in distributed environments one must understand the basic principles, the fundamental properties, the available tools, and the inherent limitations.

This book focuses on the *algorithmics* of distributed computing; that is, on how to solve problems and perform tasks efficiently in a distributed computing environment. Because of the multiplicity and variety of distributed systems and networked environments and their widespread differences, this book does not focus on any single one of them. Rather it describes and employes a distributed computing *universe* that captures the nature and basic structure of those systems (e.g., distributed operating systems, data communication networks, distributed databases, transaction processing systems, etc.), allowing us to discard or ignore the system-specific details while identifying the general principles and techniques.

This universe consists of a finite collection of computational *entities* communicating by means of *messages* in order to achieve a common goal; for example, to perform a given task, to compute the solution to a problem, to satisfy a request either from the user (i.e., outside the environment) or from other entities. Although each entity is capable of performing computations, it is the collection

---

[1] Incredibly, the terms "distributed systems" and "distributed computing" have been for years highjacked and (ab)used to describe very limited systems and low-level solutions (e.g., client server) that have little to do with distributed computing.

of all these entities that together will solve the problem or ensure that the task is performed.

In this universe, to solve a problem, we must discover and design a *distributed algorithm* or *protocol* for those entities: A set of rules that specify what each entity has to do. The collective but autonomous execution of those rules, possibly without any supervision or synchronization, must enable the entities to perform the desired task to solve the problem.

In the design process, we must ensure both *correctness* (i.e., the protocol we design indeed solves the problem) and *efficiency* (i.e., the protocol we design has a "small" cost).

As the title says, this book is on the *Design and Analysis of Distributed Algorithms.* Its goal is to enable the reader to learn how to *design* protocols to solve problems in a distributed computing environment, not by listing the results but rather by teaching how they can be obtained. In addition to the "how" and "why" (necessary for problem solution, from basic building blocks to complex protocol design), it focuses on providing the *analytical tools* and skills necessary for complexity evaluation of designs.

There are several *levels* of use of the book. The book is primarily a senior-undergraduate and graduate textbook; it contains the material for two one-term courses or alternatively a full-year course on Distributed Algorithms and Protocols, Distributed Computing, Network Computing, or Special Topics in Algorithms. It covers the "distributed part" of a graduate course on Parallel and Distributed Computing (the chapters on Distributed Data, Routing, and Synchronous Computing, in particular), and it is the theoretical companion book for a course in Distributed Systems, Advanced Operating Systems, or Distributed Data Processing.

The book is written for the students from the students' point of view, and it follows closely a well defined teaching path and method (the "course") developed over the years; both the path and the method become apparent while reading and using the book. It also provides a self-contained, self-directed guide for system-protocol designers and for communication software and engineers and developers, as well as for researchers wanting to enter or just interested in the area; it enables hands-on, head-on, and in-depth acquisition of the material. In addition, it is a serious sourcebook and referencebook for investigators in distributed computing and related areas.

Unlike the other available textbooks on these subjects, the book is based on a very simple *fully reactive* computational model. From a learning point of view, this makes the explanations clearer and readers' comprehension easier. From a teaching point of view, this approach provides the instructor with a natural way to present otherwise difficult material and to guide the students through, step by step. The instructors themselves, if not already familiar with the material or with the approach, can achieve proficiency quickly and easily.

All protocols in the textbook as well as those designed by the students as part of the exercises are immediately programmable.[2] Hence, the subtleties of actual implementation can be employed to enhance the understanding of the theoretical

---

[2] An open source Java-based engine, *DisJ,* provides the execution and visualization environment for our reactive protocols.

design principles; furthermore, *experimental* analysis (e.g., performance evaluation and comparison) can be easily and usefully integrated in the coursework expanding the analytical tools.

The book is written so to require *no* prerequisites other than standard undergraduate knowledge of operating systems and of algorithms. Clearly, concurrent or prior knowledge of communication networks, distributed operating systems or distributed transaction systems would help the reader to ground the material of this course into some practical application context; however, none is necessary.

The book is structured into nine chapters of different lengths. Some are focused on a single problem, others on a class of problems. The structuring of the written material into chapters could have easily followed different lines. For example, the material of *election* and of *mutual exclusion* could have been grouped together in a chapter on *Distributed Control*. Indeed, these two topics can be taught one after the other: Although missing an introduction, this "hidden" chapter is present in a distributed way. An important "hidden" chapter is Chapter 10 on *Distributed Graph Algorithms* whose content is distributed throughout the book: *Spanning-Tree Construction* (Section 2.5), *Depth-First Traversal* (Section 2.3.1), *Breadth-First Spanning Tree* (Section 4.2.5), *Minimum-Cost Spanning Tree* (Section 3.8.1), *Shortest Paths* (Section 4.2.3), Centers and medians (Section 2.6), Cycle and Knot Detection (Section 8.2).

The suggested prerequisite structure of the chapters is shown in Figure 1. As suggested by the figure, the first three chapters should be covered sequentially and before the other material.

There are only two other prerequisite relationships. The relationship between *Synchronous Compution* (Chapter 6) and *Computing in Presence of Faults* (Chapter 7) is particular. The recommended sequencing is in fact the following: Sections 7.1–7.2 (providing the strong motivation for synchronous computing), Chapter 6 (describing fault-free synchronous computing) and the rest of Chapter 7 (dealing with fault-tolerant synchronous computing as well as other issues). The other suggested

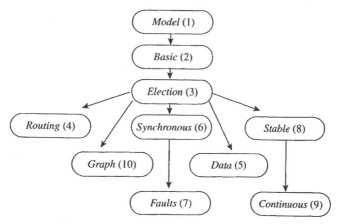

Figure 1: Prerequisite structure of the chapters.

prerequisite structure is that the topic of *Stable Properties* (Chapter 8) be handled before that of *Continuous Computations* (Chapter 9). Other than that, the sections can be mixed and matched depending on the instructor's preferences and interests. An interesting and popular sequence for a one-semester course is given by Chapters 1–6. A more conventional one-semester sequence is provided by Chapters 1–3 and 6–9.

The symbol ($\star$) after a section indicates noncore material. In connection with Exercises and Problems the symbol ($\star$) denotes difficulty (the more the symbols, the greater the difficulty).

Several important topics are not included in this edition of the book. In particular, this edition does not include algorithms on distributed coloring, on minimal independent sets, on self-stabilization, as well as on Sense of Direction. By design, this book does not include distributed computing in the *shared memory* model, focusing entirely on the message-passing paradigm.

This book has evolved from the teaching method and the material I have designed for the fourth-year undergraduate course *Introduction to Distributed Computing* and for the graduate course *Principles of Distributed Computing* at Carleton University over the last 20 years, and for the advanced graduate courses on *Distributed Algorithms* I have taught as part of the Advanced Summer School on Distributed Computing at the University of Siena over the last 10 years. I am most grateful to all the students of these courses: through their feedback they have helped me verify what works and what does not, shaping my teaching and thus the current structure of this book. Their keen interest and enthusiasm over the years have been the main reason for the existence of this book.

This book is very much work in progress. I would welcome any feedback that will make it grow and mature and change. Comments, criticisms, and reports on personal experience as a lecturer using the book, as a student studying it, or as a researcher glancing through it, suggestions for changes, and so forth: I am looking forward to receiving any. Clearly, reports on typos, errors, and mistakes are very much appreciated. I tried to be accurate in giving credits; if you know of any omission or mistake in this regards, please let me know.

My own experience as well as that of my students leads to the inescapable conclusion that

distributed algorithms are fun

both to teach and to learn. I welcome you to share this experience, and I hope you will reach the same conclusion.

NICOLA SANTORO

CHAPTER 1

Distributed Computing Environments

The universe in which we will be operating will be called a *distributed computing environment*. It consists of a finite collection $\mathcal{E}$ of computational *entities* communicating by means of *messages*. Entities communicate with other entities to achieve a common goal; for example, to perform a given task, to compute the solution to a problem, to satisfy a request either from the user (i.e., outside the environment) or from other entities. In this chapter, we will examine this universe in some detail.

1.1 ENTITIES

The computational unit of a distributed computing environment is called an *entity* . Depending on the system being modeled by the environment, an entity could correspond to a process, a processor, a switch, an agent, and so forth in the system.

Capabilities Each entity $x \in \mathcal{E}$ is endowed with local (i.e., private and nonshared) memory M_x. The *capabilities* of x include access (storage and retrieval) to local memory, local processing, and communication (preparation, transmission, and reception of messages). Local memory includes a set of *defined registers* whose values are always initially defined; among them are the *status register* (denoted by $status(x)$) and the *input value register* (denoted by $value(x)$). The register $status(x)$ takes values from a finite set of system states $\mathcal{S}$; the examples of such values are "Idle," "Processing," "Waiting,"... and so forth.

In addition, each entity $x \in \mathcal{E}$ has available a local *alarm clock* c_x which it can set and reset (turn off).

An entity can perform only four types of *operations*:

- local storage and processing
- transmission of messages
- (re)setting of the alarm clock
- changing the value of the status register

Design and Analysis of Distributed Algorithms, by Nicola Santoro
Copyright © 2007 John Wiley & Sons, Inc.

Note that, although setting the alarm clock and updating the status register can be considered as a part of local processing, because of the special role these operations play, we will consider them as distinct types of operations.

External Events   The behavior of an entity $x \in \mathcal{E}$ is *reactive*: x only responds to external stimuli, which we call *external events* (or just *events*); in the absence of stimuli, x is inert and does nothing. There are three possible external events: .

- arrival of a message
- ringing of the alarm clock
- spontaneous impulse

The arrival of a message and the ringing of the alarm clock are the events that are external to the entity but originate within the system: The message is sent by another entity, and the alarm clock is set by the entity itself.

Unlike the other two types of events, a spontaneous impulse is triggered by forces external to the system and thus outside the universe perceived by the entity. As an example of event generated by forces external to the system, consider an automated banking system: its entities are the bank servers where the data is stored, and the automated teller machine (ATM) machines; the request by a customer for a cash withdrawal (i.e., update of data stored in the system) is a spontaneous impulse for the ATM machine (the entity) where the request is made. For another example, consider a communication subsystem in the open systems interconnection (OSI) Reference Model: the request from the network layer for a service by the data link layer (the system) is a spontaneous impulse for the data-link-layer entity where the request is made. Appearing to entities as "acts of God," the spontaneous impulses are the events that start the computation and the communication.

Actions   When an external event e occurs, an entity $x \in \mathcal{E}$ will react to e by performing a finite, indivisible, and terminating sequence of operations called *action*.

An action is indivisible (or atomic) in the sense that its operations are executed without interruption; in other words, once an action starts, it will not stop until it is finished.

An action is terminating in the sense that, once it is started, its execution ends within finite time. (Programs that do not terminate cannot be termed as actions.)

A special action that an entity may take is the *null* action **nil**, where the entity does not react to the event.

Behavior   The nature of the action performed by the entity depends on the nature of the event e, as well as on which status the entity is in (i.e., the value of *status(x)*) when the events occur. Thus the specification will take the form

$$\text{Status} \times \text{Event} \longrightarrow \text{Action},$$

which will be called a *rule* (or a method, or a production). In a rule $s \times e \longrightarrow A$, we say that the rule is enabled by (s, e).

The behavioral specification, or simply *behavior*, of an entity x is the set $B(x)$ of all the rules that x obeys. This set must be *complete* and *nonambiguous*: for every possible event e and status value s, there is one and only one rule in $B(x)$ enabled by (s,e). In other words, x must always know exactly what it must do when an event occurs.

The set of rules $B(x)$ is also called *protocol* or *distributed algorithm* of x.

The behavioral specification of the entire distributed computing environment is just the collection of the individual behaviors of the entities. More precisely, the *collective behavior* $B(\mathcal{E})$ of a collection $\mathcal{E}$ of entities is the set

$$B(\mathcal{E}) = \{B(x): x \in \mathcal{E}\}.$$

Thus, in an environment with collective behavior $B(\mathcal{E})$, each entity x will be acting (behaving) according to its distributed algorithm and protocol (set of rules) $B(x)$.

Homogeneous Behavior   A collective behavior is *homogeneous* if all entities in the system have the same behavior, that is, $\forall x, y \in \mathcal{E},\ B(x) = B(y)$.

This means that to specify a homogeneous collective behavior, it is sufficient to specify the behavior of a single entity; in this case, we will indicate the behavior simply by B. An interesting and important fact is the following:

Property 1.1.1   *Every collective behavior can be made homogeneous.*

This means that if we are in a system where different entities have different behaviors, we can write a new set of rules, the *same* for all of them, which will still make them behave as before.

Example   Consider a system composed of a network of several identical workstations and a single server; clearly, the set of rules that the server and a workstation obey is not the same as their functionality differs. Still, a single program can be written that will run on both entities without modifying their functionality. We need to add to each entity an input register, *my_role*, which is initialized to either "workstation" or "server," depending on the entity; for each status–event pair (s, e) we create a new rule with the following action:

$$s \times e \longrightarrow \{\ \textbf{if } my\_role = \text{workstation } \textbf{then } A_{\text{workstation}} \textbf{ else } A_{\text{server}} \textbf{ endif }\},$$

where $A_{\text{workstation}}$ (respectively, A_{server}) is the original action associated to (s, e) in the set of rules of the workstation (respectively, server). If (s, e) did not enable any rule for a workstation (e.g., s was a status defined only for the server), then $A_{\text{workstation}} = \textbf{nil}$ in the new rule; analogously for the server.

It is important to stress that in a homogeneous system, although all entities have the same behavioral description (software), they do not have to act in the same way;

their difference will depend solely on the initial value of their input registers. An analogy is the legal system in democratic countries: the law (the set of rules) is the same for every citizen (entity); still, if you are in the police force, while on duty, you are allowed to perform actions that are unlawful for most of the other citizens.

An important consequence of the homogeneous behavior property is that we can concentrate solely on environments where all the entities have the same behavior. From now on, when we mention behavior we will always mean homogeneous collective behavior.

1.2 COMMUNICATION

In a distributed computing environment, entities communicate by transmitting and receiving *messages*. The *message* is the unit of communication of a distributed environment. In its more general definition, a message is just a *finite sequence of bits*.

An entity communicates by transmitting messages to and receiving messages from other entities. The set of entities with which an entity can communicate directly is not necessarily $\mathcal{E}$; in other words, it is possible that an entity can communicate directly only with a subset of the other entities. We denote by $N_{out}(x) \subseteq \mathcal{E}$ the set of entities to which x can transmit a message directly; we shall call them the *out-neighbors* of x. Similarly, we denote by $N_{in}(x) \subseteq \mathcal{E}$ the set of entities from which x can receive a message directly; we shall call them the *in-neighbors* of x.

The neighborhood relationship defines a directed graph $\vec{G} = (V, \vec{E})$, where V is the set of vertices and $\vec{E} \subseteq V \times V$ is the set of edges; the vertices correspond to entities, and $(x, y) \in \vec{E}$ if and only if the entity (corresponding to) y is an out-neighbor of the entity (corresponding to) x.

The directed graph $\vec{G} = (V, \vec{E})$ describes the *communication topology* of the environment. We shall denote by $n(\vec{G})$, $m(\vec{G})$, and $d(\vec{G})$ the number of vertices, edges, and the diameter of $\vec{G}$, respectively. When no ambiguity arises, we will omit the reference to $\vec{G}$ and use simply n, m, and d.

In the following and unless ambiguity should arise, the terms vertex, node, site, and entity will be used as having the same meaning; analogously, the terms edge, arc, and link will be used interchangeably.

In summary, an entity can only receive messages from its in-neighbors and send messages to its out-neighbors. Messages received at an entity are processed there in the order they arrive; if more than one message arrive at the same time, they will be processed in arbitrary order (see Section 1.9). Entities and communication may fail.

1.3 AXIOMS AND RESTRICTIONS

The definition of distributed computing environment with point-to-point communication has two basic *axioms*, one on communication delay, and the other on the local orientation of the entities in the system.

Any additional assumption (e.g., property of the network, a priori knowledge by the entities) will be called a *restriction*.

1.3.1 Axioms

Communication Delays   Communication of a message involves many activities: preparation, transmission, reception, and processing. In real systems described by our model, the time required by these activities is unpredictable. For example, in a communication network a message will be subject to queueing and processing delays, which change depending on the network traffic at that time; for example, consider the delay in accessing (i.e., sending a message to and getting a reply from) a popular web site.

The totality of delays encountered by a message will be called the *communication delay* of that message.

Axiom 1.3.1   Finite Communication Delays
In the absence of failures, communication delays are finite.

In other words, in the absence of failures, a message sent to an out-neighbor will eventually arrive in its integrity and be processed there. Note that the Finite Communication Delays axiom does not imply the existence of any bound on transmission, queueing, or processing delays; it only states that in the absence of failure, a message will arrive after a finite amount of time without corruption.

Local Orientation   An entity can communicate directly with a subset of the other entities: its neighbors. The only other axiom in the model is that an entity can distinguish between its neighbors.

Axiom 1.3.2   Local Orientation
An entity can distinguish among its in-neighbors.
An entity can distinguish among its out-neighbors.

In particular, an entity is capable of sending a message only to a specific out-neighbor (without having to send it also to all other out-neighbors). Also, when processing a message (i.e., executing the rule enabled by the reception of that message), an entity can distinguish which of its in-neighbors sent that message.

In other words, each entity x has a local function λ_x associating labels, also called *port numbers*, to its incident links (or *ports*), and this function is injective. We denote port numbers by $\lambda_x(x, y)$, the label associated by x to the link (x, y). Let us stress that this label is local to x and in general has no relationship at all with what y might call this link (or x, or itself). Note that for each edge $(x, y) \in \vec{E}$, there are two labels: $\lambda_x(x, y)$ local to x and $\lambda_y(x, y)$ local to y (see Figure 1.1).

Because of this axiom, we will always deal with *edge-labeled graphs* $(\vec{G}, \lambda)$, where $\lambda = \{\lambda_x : x \in V\}$ is the set of these injective labelings.

FIGURE 1.1: Every edge has two labels

1.3.2 Restrictions

In general, a distributed computing system might have additional properties or capabilities that can be exploited to solve a problem, to achieve a task, and to provide a service. This can be achieved by using these properties and capabilities in the set of rules.

However, any property used in the protocol limits the applicability of the protocol. In other words, any additional property or capability of the system is actually a *restriction* (or submodel) of the general model.

WARNING. When dealing with (e.g., designing, developing, testing, employing) a distributed computing system or just a protocol, it is crucial and imperative that *all restrictions are made explicit*. Failure to do so will invalidate the resulting communication software.

The restrictions can be varied in nature and type: they might be related to communication properties, reliability, synchrony, and so forth. In the following section, we will discuss some of the most common restrictions.

Communication Restrictions   The first category of restrictions includes those relating to communication among entities.

Queueing Policy   A link (x, y) can be viewed as a channel or a queue (see Section 1.9): x sending a message to y is equivalent to x inserting the message in the channel. In general, all kinds of situations are possible; for example, messages in the channel might overtake each other, and a later message might be received first. Different restrictions on the model will describe different disciplines employed to manage the channel; for example, first-in-first-out (FIFO) queues are characterized by the following restriction.

- *Message Ordering:* In the absence of failure, the messages transmitted by an entity to the same out-neighbor will arrive in the same order they are sent.

Note that Message Ordering does not imply the existence of any ordering for messages transmitted to the same entity from different edges, nor for messages sent by the same entity on different edges.

Link Property   Entities in a communication system are connected by physical links, which may be very different in capabilities. The examples are simplex and full-duplex links. With a fully duplex line it is possible to transmit in both directions. Simplex lines are already defined within the general model. A duplex line can obviously be described as two simplex lines, one in each direction; thus, a system where all lines are fully duplex can be described by the following restriction:

- *Reciprocal communication:* $\forall x \in \mathcal{E}$, $N_{in}(x) = N_{out}(x)$. In other words, if $(x, y) \in \vec{E}$ then also $(y, x) \in \vec{E}$.

Notice that, however, $(x, y) \neq (y, x)$, and in general $\lambda_x(x, y) \neq \lambda_x(y, x)$; furthermore, x might not know that these two links are connections to and from the same entity. A system with fully duplex links that offers such a knowledge is defined by the following restriction.

- *Bidirectional links:* $\forall x \in \mathcal{E}$, $N_{in}(x) = N_{out}(x)$ **and** $\lambda_x(x, y) = \lambda_x(y, x)$.

IMPORTANT. The case of Bidirectional Links is special. If it holds, we use a simplified terminology. The network is viewed as an *undirected* graph $G = (V, E)$ (i.e., $\forall x, y \in \mathcal{E}$, $(x, y) = (y, x)$), and the set $N(x) = N_{in}(x) = N_{out}(x)$ will just be called the set of *neighbors* of x. Note that in this case, $m(\vec{G}) = |\vec{E}| = 2|E| = 2m(G)$.

For example, in Figure 1.2 a graph $\vec{G}$ is depicted where the *Bidirectional Links* restriction and the corresponding undirected graph G hold.

Reliability Restrictions   Other types of restrictions are those related to reliability, faults, and their detection.

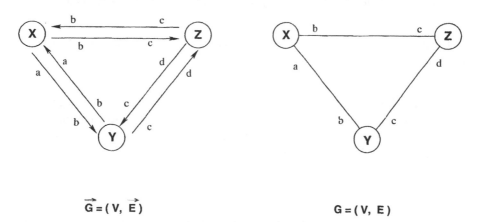

$$\vec{G} = (V, \vec{E})\qquad\qquad G = (V, E)$$

FIGURE 1.2: In a network with Bidirectional Links we consider the corresponding undirected graph.

Detection of Faults   Some systems might provide a reliable fault-detection mechanism. Following are two restrictions that describe systems that offer such capabilities in regard to *component* failures:

- *Edge failure detection:* $\forall (x, y) \in \vec{E}$, both x and y will detect whether (x, y) has failed and, following its failure, whether it has been reactivated.
- *Entity failure detection:* $\forall x \in V$, all in- and out-neighbors of x can detect whether x has failed and, following its failure, whether it has recovered.

Restricted Types of Faults   In some systems only some types of failures can occur: for example, messages can be lost but not corrupted. Each situation will give rise to a corresponding restriction. More general restrictions will describe systems or situations where there will be no failures:

- *Guaranteed delivery:* Any message that is sent will be received with its content uncorrupted.

Under this restriction, protocols do not need to take into account omissions or corruptions of messages during transmission. Even more general is the following:

- *Partial reliability:* No failures will occur.

Under this restriction, protocols do not need to take failures into account. Note that under Partial Reliability, failures might have occurred *before* the execution of a computation. A totally fault-free system is defined by the following restriction.

- *Total reliability:* Neither have any failures occurred nor will they occur.

Clearly, protocols developed under this restriction are *not* guaranteed to work correctly if faults occur.

Topological Restrictions   In general, an entity is not directly connected to all other entities; it might still be able to communicate information to a remote entity, using others as relayer. A system that provides this capability for all entities is characterized by the following restriction:

- *Connectivity:* The communication topology $\vec{G}$ is strongly connected.

That is, from every vertex in $\vec{G}$ it is possible to reach every other vertex. In case the restriction "Bidirectional Links" holds as well, connectedness will simply state that G is connected.

Time Restrictions   An interesting type of restrictions is the one relating to *time*. In fact, the general model makes no assumption about delays (except that they are finite).

- *Bounded communication delays:* There exists a constant Δ such that, in the absence of failures, the communication delay of any message on any link is at most Δ.

A special case of bounded delays is the following:

- *Unitary communication delays:* In the absence of failures, the communication delay of any message on any link is one unit of time.

The general model also makes no assumptions about the local clocks.

- *Synchronized clocks:* All local clocks are incremented by one unit simultaneously and the interval of time between successive increments is constant.

1.4   COST AND COMPLEXITY

The computing environment we are considering is defined at an abstract level. It models rather different systems (e.g., communication networks, distributed systems, data networks, etc.), whose performance is determined by very distinctive factors and costs.

The efficiency of a protocol in the model must somehow reflect the realistic costs encountered when executed in those very different systems. In other words, we need abstract cost measures that are general enough but still meaningful.

We will use two types of measures: the *amount of communication activities* and the *time* required by the execution of a computation. They can be seen as measuring costs from the system point of view (how much traffic will this computation generate and how busy will the system be?) and from the user point of view (how long will it take before I get the results of the computation?).

1.4.1   Amount of Communication Activities

The transmission of a message through an out-port (i.e., to an out-neighbor) is the basic *communication activity* in the system; note that the transmission of a message that will not be received because of failure still constitutes a communication activity. Thus, to measure the amount of communication activities, the most common function used is the number of message transmissions M, also called *message cost*. So in general, given a protocol, we will measure its communication costs in terms of the number of transmitted messages.

Other functions of interest are the *entity workload* $L_{node} = M/|V|$, that is, the number of messages per entity, and the *transmission load* $L_{link} = M/|E|$, that is, the number of messages per link.

Messages are sequences of bits; some protocols might employ messages that are very short (e.g., $O(1)$ bit signals), others very long (e.g., .gif files). Thus, for a more accurate assessment of a protocol, or to compare different solutions to the same problem that use different sizes of messages, it might be necessary to use as a cost measure the number of transmitted bits **B** also called *bit complexity*.

In this case, we may sometimes consider the bit-defined load functions: the *entity bit-workload* $\mathbf{Lb_{node}} = \mathbf{B}/|V|$, that is, the number of bits per entity, and the *transmission bit-load* $\mathbf{Lb_{link}} = \mathbf{B}/|E|$, that is, the number of bits per link.

1.4.2 Time

An important measure of efficiency and complexity is the total execution delay, that is, the delay between the time the first entity starts the execution of a computation and the time the last entity terminates its execution. Note that "time" is here intended as the one measured by an observer external to the system and will also be called real or physical time.

In the general model there is no assumption about time except that communication delays for a single message are finite in absence of failure (Axiom 1.3.1). In other words, communication delays are in general unpredictable. Thus, even in the absence of failures, the total execution delay for a computation is totally unpredictable; furthermore, two distinct executions of the same protocol might experience drastically different delays. In other words, we cannot accurately measure time.

We, however, can measure time assuming particular conditions. The measure usually employed is the *ideal execution delay* or *ideal time complexity*, **T**: the execution delay experienced under the restrictions "Unitary Transmission Delays" and "Synchronized Clocks;" that is, when the system is synchronous and (in the absence of failure) takes one unit of time for a message to arrive and to be processed.

A very different cost measure is the *causal time complexity*, $\mathbf{T_{causal}}$. It is defined as the length of the longest chain of causally related message transmissions, over all possible executions. Causal time is seldom used and is very difficult to measure exactly; we will employ it only once, when dealing with synchronous computations.

1.5 AN EXAMPLE: BROADCASTING

Let us clarify the concepts expressed so far by means of an example. Consider a distributed computing system where one entity has some important information unknown to the others and would like to share it with everybody else.

This problem is called *broadcasting* and it is part of a general class of problems called *information diffusion*. To solve this problem means to design a set of rules that, when executed by the entities, will lead (within finite time) to all entities knowing the information; the solution must work regardless of which entity had the information at the beginning.

Let $\mathcal{E}$ be the collection of entities and $\vec{G}$ be the communication topology.

To simplify the discussion, we will make some additional assumptions (i.e., restrictions) on the system:

1. Bidirectional links; that is, we consider the undirected graph G. (see Section 1.3.2).
2. Total reliability, that is, we do not have to worry about failures.

Observe that, if G is disconnected, some entities can never receive the information, and the broadcasting problem will be unsolvable. Thus, a restriction that (unlike the previous two) we *need* to make is as follows:

3. Connectivity; that is, G is connected.

Further observe that built in the definition of the problem, there is the assumption that only the entity with the initial information will start the broadcast. Thus, a restriction built in the definition is as follows:

4. Unique Initiator, that is, only one entity will start.

A simple strategy for solving the broadcast problem is the following:

"if an entity knows the information, it will share it with its neighbors."

To construct the set of rules implementing this strategy, we need to define the set S of status values; from the statement of the problem it is clear that we need to distinguish between the entity that initially has the information and the others: {*initiator, idle*} $\subseteq$ S. The process can be started only by the *initiator*; let I denote the information to be broadcasted. Here is the set of rules $B(x)$ (the same for all entities):

1. *initiator* $\times \iota \longrightarrow$ {**send**(I) **to** $N(x)$}
2. *idle* $\times$ *Receiving*(I) $\longrightarrow$ {Process(I); **send**(I) **to** $N(x)$}
3. *initiator* $\times$ *Receiving*(I) $\longrightarrow$ **nil**
4. *idle* $\times \iota \longrightarrow$ **nil**

where ι denotes the *spontaneous impulse* event and **nil** denotes the *null* action.

Because of connectivity and total reliability, every entity will eventually receive the information. Hence, the protocol achieves its goal and solves the broadcasting problem.

However, there is a serious problem with these rules:

the activities generated by the protocol never terminate.

Consider, for example, the simple system with three entities x, y, z connected to each other (see Figure 1.3). Let x be the *initiator*, y and z be *idle*, and all messages travel at the same speed; then y and z will be forever sending messages to each other (as well as to x).

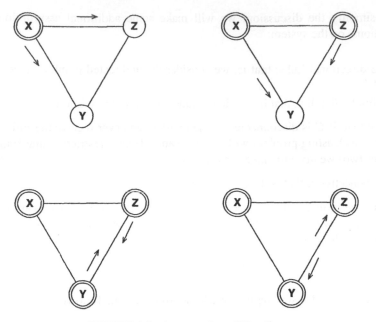

FIGURE 1.3: An execution of Flooding.

To avoid this unwelcome effect, an entity should send the information to its neighbors only once: the first time it acquires the information. This can be achieved by introducing a new status *done*; that is S ={*initiator, idle, done*}.

1. *initiator* $\times \iota \longrightarrow$ {**send**(I) **to** $N(x)$; **become** done}
2. *idle* $\times$ *Receiving*(I) $\longrightarrow$ {Process(I); **become** *done*; **send**(I) **to** $N(x)$}
3. *initiator* $\times$ *Receiving*(I) $\longrightarrow$ **nil**
4. *idle* $\times$ ι $\longrightarrow$ **nil**
5. *done* $\times$ *Receiving*(I) $\longrightarrow$ **nil**
6. *done* $\times$ ι $\longrightarrow$ **nil**

where **become** denotes the operation of changing status.

This time the communication activities of the protocol terminate: Within finite time all entities become *done*; since a *done* entity knows the information, the protocol is correct (see Exercise 1.12.1). Note that depending on transmission delays, different executions are possible; one such execution in an environment composed of three entities x, y, z connected to each other, where x is the initiator as depicted in Figure 1.3.

IMPORTANT. Note that entities terminate their execution of the protocol (i.e., become *done*) at different times; it is actually possible that an entity has terminated while others have not yet started. This is something very typical of distributed computations: There is a difference between *local termination* and *global termination*.

IMPORTANT. Notice also that in this protocol nobody ever knows when the entire process is over. We will examine these issues in details in other chapters, in particular when discussing the problem of *termination detection*.

The above set of rules correctly solves the problem of broadcasting. Let us now calculate the communication costs of the algorithm.

First of all, let us determine the number of *message transmissions*. Each entity, whether *initiator* or not, sends the information to all its neighbors. Hence the total number of messages transmitted is exactly

$$\sum_{x \in \mathcal{E}} |N(x)| = 2 |E| = 2 \, m.$$

We can actually reduce the cost. Currently, when an *idle* entity receives the message, it will broadcast the information to *all* its neighbors, including the entity from which it had received the information; this is clearly unnecessary. Recall that, by the Local Orientation axiom, an entity can distinguish among its neighbors; in particular, when processing a message, it can identify from which port it was received and avoid sending a message there. The final protocol is as before with only this small modification.

Protocol *Flooding*

1. *initiator* $\times \iota \longrightarrow$ {**send**(I) **to** $N(x)$; **become** *done*}
2. *idle* $\times$ *Receiving*(I) $\longrightarrow$ {Process(I); **become** *done*; **send**(I) **to** $N(x)$-**sender**}
3. *initiator* $\times$ *Receiving*(I) $\longrightarrow$ **nil**
4. *idle* $\times \iota \longrightarrow$ **nil**
5. *done* $\times$ *Receiving*(I) $\longrightarrow$ **nil**
6. *done* $\times \iota \longrightarrow$ **nil**

where **sender** is the neighbor that sent the message currently being processed.

This algorithm is called *Flooding* as the entire system is "flooded" with the message during its execution, and it is a basic algorithmic tool for distributed computing. As for the number of message transmissions required by flooding, because we avoid transmitting some messages, we know that it is less than $2m$; in fact, (Exercise 1.12.2):

$$M[Flooding] = 2m - n + 1. \tag{1.1}$$

Let us examine now the ideal time complexity of flooding.

Let $d(x, y)$ denote the distance (i.e., the length of the shortest path) between x and y in G. Clearly the message sent by the initiator has to reach every entity in the system, including the furthermost one from the *initiator*. So, if x is the initiator, the ideal time complexity will be $r(x) = \text{Max } \{d(x, y) : y \in \mathcal{E}\}$, which is called the *eccentricity* (or *radius*) of x. In other words, the total time depends on which entity is the initiator and thus cannot be known precisely beforehand. We can, however, determine exactly the ideal time complexity in the worst case.

Since any entity could be the initiator, the ideal time complexity in the worst case will be $d(G) = \text{Max } \{r(x) : x \in \mathcal{E}\}$, which is the *diameter* of G. In other words, the ideal time complexity will be at most the diameter of G:

$$T[Flooding] \leq d(G). \qquad (1.2)$$

1.6   STATES AND EVENTS

Once we have defined the behavior of the entities, their communication topology, and the set of restrictions under which they operate, we must describe the initial conditions of our environment. This is done first of all by specifying the initial condition of all the entities. The initial content of all the registers of entity x and the initial value of its alarm clock c_x at time t constitute the *initial internal state* $\sigma(x, 0)$ of x. Let $\Sigma(0) = \{\sigma(x, 0) : x \in \mathcal{E}\}$ denote the set of all the initial internal states.

Once $\Sigma(0)$ is defined, we have completed the *static* specification of the environment: the description of the system *before* any event occurs and before any activity takes place.

We are, however, also interested in describing the system *during* the computational activities, as well as *after* such activities. To do so, we need to be able to describe the changes that the system undergoes over time. As mentioned before, the entities (and, thus the environments) are *reactive*. That is, any activity of the system is determined entirely by the external events. Let us examine these facts in more detail.

1.6.1   Time and Events

In distributed computing environments, there are only three types of external events: spontaneous impulse (*spontaneously*), reception of a message (*receiving*), and alarm clock ring (*when*).

When an external event occurs at an entity, it triggers the execution of an action (the nature of the action depends on the status of the entity when the event occurs). The executed action may generate new events: The operation **send** will generate a *receiving* event, and the operation **set_alarm** will generate a *when* event.

Note first of all that the events so generated might not occur at all. For example, a link failure may destroy the traveling message, destroying the corresponding *receiving* event; in a subsequent action, an entity may turn off the previously set alarm destroying the *when* event.

Notice now that if they occur, these events will do so at a later time (i.e., when the message arrives, when the alarm goes off). This delay might be known precisely in the case of the alarm clock (because it is set by the entity); it is, however, unpredictable in the case of message transmission (because it is due to the conditions external to the entity). Different delays give rise to different *executions* of the same protocols with possibly different outcomes.

Summarizing, each event e is "generated" at some time $t(e)$ and, if it occurs, it will happen at some time later.

By definition, all spontaneous impulses are already generated before the execution starts; their set will be called the set of *initial events*. The execution of the protocol starts when the first spontaneous impulses actually happen; by convention, this will be time $t = 0$.

IMPORTANT. Notice that "time" is here considered as seen by an external observer and is viewed as *real time*. Each real time instant t separates the axis of time into three parts: *past* (i.e., $\{t' < t\}$), *present* (i.e., t), and *future* (i.e., $\{t' > t\}$). All events generated before t that will happen after t are called the *future at t* and denoted by *Future(t)*; it represents the set of future events determined by the execution so far.

An execution is fully described by the sequence of events that have occurred. For small systems, an execution can be visualized by what is called a *Time × Event Diagram* (TED) . Such a diagram is composed of temporal lines, one for each entity in the system. Each event is represented in such a diagram as follows:

A *Receiving* event r is represented as an arrow from the point $t_x(r)$ in the temporal line of the entity x generating e (i.e., sending the message) to the point $t_y(r)$ in the temporal line of the entity y where the events occur (i.e., receiving the message).

A *When* event w is represented as an arrow from point $t'_x(w)$ to point $t''_x(w)$ in the temporal line of the entity setting the clock.

A *Spontaneously* event ι is represented as a short arrow indicating point $t_x(\iota)$ in the temporal line of the entity x where the events occur.

For example, in Figure 1.4 is depicted the TED corresponding to the execution of Protocol *Flooding* of Figure 1.3.

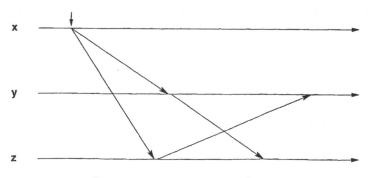

FIGURE 1.4: Time × Event Diagram

1.6.2   States and Configurations

The private memory of each entity, in addition to the behavior, contains a set of registers, some of them already initialized, others to be initialized during the execution. The content of all the registers of entity x and the value of its alarm clock c_x at time t constitute what is called the *internal state of x at t* and is denoted by $\sigma(x, t)$. We denote by $\Sigma(t)$ the set of the internal states at time t of all entities. Internal states change with time and the occurrence of events.

There is an important fact about internal states. Consider two different environments, E_1 and E_2, where, by accident, the internal state of x at time t is the same. Then x *cannot distinguish* between the two environments, that is, x is unable to tell whether it is in environment E_1 or E_2.

There is an important consequence. Consider the situation just described: At time t, the internal state of x is the same in both E_1 and E_2. Assume now that also by accident, exactly the same event occurs at x (e.g., the alarm clock rings or the same message is received from the same neighbor). Then x will perform exactly the same action in both cases, and its internal state will continue to be the same in both situations.

Property 1.6.1   *Let the same event occur at x at time t in two different executions, and let σ_1 and σ_2 be its internal states when this happens. If $\sigma_1 = \sigma_2$, then the new internal state of x will be the same in both executions.*

Similarly, if two entities have the same internal state, they *cannot distinguish* between each other. Furthermore, if by accident, exactly the same event occurs at both of them (e.g., the alarm clock rings or the same message is received from the same neighbor), then they will perform exactly the same action in both cases, and their internal state will continue to be the same in both situations.

Property 1.6.2   *Let the same event occur at x and y at time t, and let σ_1 and σ_2 be their internal states, respectively, at that time. If $\sigma_1 = \sigma_2$, then the new internal state of x and y will be the same.*

Remember: Internal states are local and an entity might not be able to infer from them information about the status of the rest of the system. We have talked about the internal state of an entity, initially (i.e., at time $t = 0$) and during an execution. Let us now focus on the state of the entire system during an execution.

To describe the *global* state of the environment at time t, we obviously need to specify the internal state of all entities at that time; that is, the set $\Sigma(t)$. However, this is *not enough*. In fact, the execution so far might have already generated some events that will occur *after* time t; these events, represented by the set *Future(t)*, are integral part of this execution and must be specified as well. Specifically, the global state, called *configuration*, of the system during an execution is specified by the couple

$$C(t) = (\Sigma(t), Future(t))$$

The *initial* configuration $C(0)$ contains not only the initial set of states $\Sigma(0)$ but also the set *Future*(0) of the spontaneous impulses. Environments that differ only in their initial configuration will be called *instances* of the same system.

The configuration $C(t)$ is like a snapshot of the system at time t.

1.7 PROBLEMS AND SOLUTIONS (⋆)

The topic of this book is how to design distributed algorithms and analyze their complexity. A distributed algorithm is the set of rules that will regulate the *behaviors* of the entities. The reason why we may need to design the *behaviors* is to enable the entities to solve a given problem, perform a defined task, or provide a requested service.

In general, we will be given a problem, and our task is to design a set of rules that will always solve the problem in finite time. Let us discuss these concepts in some details.

Problems   To give a problem (or task, or service) $\mathcal{P}$ means to give a description of *what* the entities must accomplish. This is done by stating what the initial conditions of the entities are (and thus of the system), and what the final conditions should be; it should also specify all given restrictions. In other words,

$$\mathcal{P} = \langle P_{\text{INIT}}, P_{\text{FINAL}}, R \rangle,$$

where P_{INIT} and P_{FINAL} are *predicates* on the values of the registers of the entities, and R is a set of restrictions. Let $w_t(x)$ denote the value of an input register $w(x)$ at time t and $\{w_t\} = \{w_t(x) : x \in \mathcal{E}\}$ the values of this register at all entities at that time. So, for example, $\{status_0\}$ represents the initial value of the status registers of the entities.

For example, in the problem *Broadcasting (I)* described in Section 1.5, the initial and final conditions are given by the predicates

$P_{\text{INIT}}(t) \equiv$ " *only one entity has the information at time t* " $\equiv$
$\quad \exists x \in \mathcal{E} \ (value_t(x) = I \ \wedge \forall y \neq x \ (value_t(y) = \emptyset)),$

$P_{\text{FINAL}}(t) \equiv$ " *every entity has the information at time t* " $\equiv$
$\quad \forall x \in \mathcal{E} \ (value_t(x) = I).$

The restrictions we have imposed on our solution are BL (Bidirectional Links), TR (Total Reliability), and CN (Connectivity). Implicit in the problem definition there is also the condition that only the entity with the information will start the execution of the solution protocol; denote by UI the predicate describing this restriction, called *Unique Initiator*. Summarizing, for *Broadcasting*, the set of restrictions we have made is {BL, TR, CN, UI}.

Status   A solution protocol B for $\mathcal{P} = \langle P_{INIT}, P_{FINAL}, R \rangle$ will specify *how* the entities will accomplish the required task. Part of the design of the set of rules $B(x)$ is the definition of the set of status values $\mathcal{S}$, that is, the values that can be held by the status register *status(x)*.

We call *initial* status values those values of $\mathcal{S}$ that can be held at the start of the execution of $B(x)$ and we shall denote their set by $\mathcal{S}_{INIT}$. By contrast, *terminal* status values are those values that once reached, cannot ever be changed by the protocol; their set shall be denoted by $\mathcal{S}_{TERM}$. All other values in $\mathcal{S}$ will be called *intermediate* status values.

For example, in the protocol *Flooding* described in Section 1.5, $\mathcal{S}_{INIT}=\{initiator, idle\}$ and $\mathcal{S}_{TERM}=\{done\}$.

Depending on the restrictions of the problem, only entities in specific initial status values will start the protocol; we shall denote by $\mathcal{S}_{START} \subseteq \mathcal{S}_{INIT}$ the set of those status values. Typically, $\mathcal{S}_{START}$ consists of only one status; for example, in *Flooding*, $\mathcal{S}_{START}=\{initiator\}$. It is possible to rewrite a protocol so that this is always the case (see Exercise 1.12.5).

Among terminal status values we shall distinguish those in which no further activity can take place; that is, those where the only action is **nil**. We shall call such status values *final* and we shall denote by $\mathcal{S}_{FINAL} \subseteq \mathcal{S}_{TERM}$ the set of those status values. For example, in *Flooding*, $\mathcal{S}_{FINAL}=\{done\}$.

Termination   Protocol B terminates if, for all initial configurations $C(0)$ satisfying P_{INIT}, and for all executions starting from those configurations, the predicate

$$\textit{Terminate}\,(t) \equiv (\{status_t\} \subseteq \mathcal{S}_{TERM}) \wedge (\textit{Future}(t) = \emptyset)$$

holds for some $t > 0$, that is, all entities enter a terminal status after a finite time and all generated events have occurred.

We have already remarked on the fact that entities might not be aware that the termination has occurred. In general, we would like each entity to know at least of its termination. This situation, called *explicit termination*, is said to occur if the predicate

$$\textit{Explicit-Terminate}\,(t) \equiv (\{status_t\} \subseteq \mathcal{S}_{FINAL})$$

holds for some $t > 0$, that is, all entities enter a final status after a finite time.

Correctness   Protocol B is correct if, for all executions starting from initial configurations satisfying P_{INIT},

$$\exists t > 0 : \textit{Correct}(t)$$

holds, where $\textit{Correct}(t) \equiv (\forall t' \geq t, P_{FINAL}(t))$; that is, the final predicate eventually holds and does not change.

Solution Protocol The set of rules B solves problem $\mathcal{P}$ if it always correctly terminates under the problem restrictions R. As there are two types of termination (simple and explicit), we will have two types of solutions:

Simple Solution$[B,\mathcal{P}]$ where the predicate

$$\exists t > 0 \; (Correct(t) \wedge Terminate(t))$$

holds, under the problem restrictions R, for all executions starting from initial configurations satisfying P_{INIT}; and

Explicit Solution$[B,\mathcal{P}]$ where the predicate

$$\exists t > 0 \; (Correct(t) \wedge Explicit\text{-}Terminate(t))$$

holds, under the problem restrictions R, for all executions starting from initial configurations satisfying P_{INIT}.

1.8 KNOWLEDGE

The notions of information and knowledge are fundamental in distributed computing. Informally, any distributed computation can be viewed as the process of acquiring information through communication activities; conversely, the reception of a message can be viewed as the process of transforming the state of knowledge of the processor receiving the message.

1.8.1 Levels of Knowledge

The content of the local memory of an entity and the information that can be derived from it constitute the *local knowledge* of an entity. We denote by

$$p \in \text{LK}_t[x]$$

the fact that p is local knowledge at x at the global time instant t. By definition, $\lambda_x \in \text{LK}_t[x]$ for all t, that is, the (labels of the) in- and out-edges of x are time-invariant local knowledge of x.

Sometimes it is necessary to describe knowledge held by more than one entity at a given time. Information p is said to be *implicit knowledge* in $W \subseteq \mathcal{E}$ at time t, denoted by $p \in \text{IK}_t[W]$, if at least one entity in W knows p at time t, that is,

$$p \in \text{IK}_t[W] \text{ iff } \exists x \in W \; (p \in \text{LK}_t[x]).$$

A stronger level of knowledge in a group W of entities is held when, at a given time t, p is known to every entity in the group, denoted by $p \in \text{EK}_t[W]$, that is

$$p \in \text{EK}_t[W] \text{ iff } \forall x \in W \; (p \in \text{LK}_t[x]).$$

In this case, p is said to be *explicit knowledge* in $W \subseteq \mathcal{E}$ at time t.

Consider for example *broadcasting* discussed in the previous section. Initially, at time $t = 0$, only the initiator s knows the information I; in other words, $I \in LK_0[s]$. Thus, at that time, I is implicitly known to all entities, that is, $I \in IK_0[\mathcal{E}]$. At the end of the broadcast, at time t', every entity will know the information; in other words, $I \in EK_{t'}[\mathcal{E}]$.

Notice that, in the absence of failures, knowledge cannot be lost, only gained, that is, for all $t' > t$ and all $W \subseteq \mathcal{E}$, if no failure occurs, $IK_t[W] \subseteq IK_{t'}[W]$ and $EK_t[W] \subseteq EK_{t'}[W]$.

Assume that a fact p is explicit knowledge in W at time t. It is possible that some (maybe all) entities are not aware of this situation. For example, assume that at time t, entities x and y know the value of a variable of z, say its ID; then the ID of z is explicit knowledge in $W=\{x, y, z\}$; however, z might not be aware that x and y know its ID. In other words, when $p \in EK_t[W]$, the fact "$p \in EK_t[W]$" might not be even locally known to any of the entities in W.

This gives rise to the highest level of knowledge within a group: common knowledge. Information p is said to be *common knowledge* in $W \subseteq \mathcal{E}$ at time t, denoted by $p \in CK_t[W]$, if and only if at time t every entity in W knows p, and knows that every entity in W knows p, and knows that entity in W knows that every entity in W knows p, and ..., etcetera, that is,

$$p \in CK_t[W] \text{ iff } \bigwedge_{1 \leq i \leq \infty} P_i,$$

where the P_i's are the predicates defined by: $P_1 = [p \in ES_t[W]]$ and $P_{i+1} = [P_i \in EK_t[W]]$.

In most distributed problems, it will be necessary for the entities to achieve common knowledge. Fortunately, we do not always have to go to ∞ to reach common knowledge, and a finite number of steps might actually do, as indicated by the following example.

Example (muddy forehead): Imagine n perceptive and intelligent school children playing together during recess. They are forbidden to play in the mud puddles, and the teacher has told them that if they do, there will be severe consequences. Each child wants to keep clean, but the temptation to play with mud is too great to resist. As a result, k of the children get mud on their foreheads. When the teacher arrives, she says, "I see that some of you have been playing in the mud puddle: the mud on your foreheads is a dead giveaway !" and then continues, "The guilty ones who come forward spontaneously will be given a small penalty; those who do not, will receive a punishment they will not easily forget." She then adds, "I am going to leave the room now, and I will return periodically; if you decide to confess, you must all come forward together when I am in the room. In the meanwhile, everybody must sit absolutely still and without talking."

Each child in the room clearly understands that those with mud on their foreheads are "dead meat," who will be punished no matter what. Obviously, the children do not want to confess if the foreheads are clean, and clearly, if the foreheads are dirty, they want to go forward so as to avoid their terrible punishment for those who do not confess. As each child shares the same concern, the collective goal is for the children with clean foreheads not to confess and for those with muddy foreheads to go forward simultaneously, and all of this without communication.

Let us examine this goal. The first question is as follows: can a child x find out whether his/her forehead is dirty or not ? She/he can see how many, say f_x, of the other children are dirty; thus, the question is if x can determine whether $k = f_x$ or $k = f_x + 1$.

The second, more complex question is as follows: can *all* the children with mud on their foreheads find out at the same time so that they can go forward together ? In other words, can the exact value of k become *common knowledge* ?

The children, being perceptive and intelligent, determine that the answer to both the questions is positive and find the way to achieve the common goal and thus common knowledge without communication (Exercise 1.12.6).

IMPORTANT. When working in a submodel, all the restrictions defining the sub-model are common knowledge to all entities (unless otherwise specified).

1.8.2 Types of Knowledge

We can have various types of knowledge, such as knowledge about the communication topology, about the labeling of the communication graph, about the input data of the communicating entities. In general, if we have some knowledge of the system, we can exploit it to reduce the cost of a protocol, although this may result in making the applicability of the protocol more limited.

A type of knowledge of particular interest is the one regarding the communication topology (i.e., the graph $\vec{G}$). In fact, as will be seen later, the complexity of a computation may vary greatly depending on what the entities know about $\vec{G}$. Following are some elements that, if they are common knowledge to the entities, may affect the complexity.

1. *Metric Information*: numeric information about the network; for example, number $n = |V|$ of nodes, number $m = |E|$ of links, diameter, girth, etcetera. This information can be *exact* or *approximate*.
2. *Topological Properties*: knowledge of some properties of the topology; for example, "$\vec{G}$ is a ring network," "$\vec{G}$ does not have cycles," "$\vec{G}$ is a Cayley graph," etcetera.
3. *Topological Maps*: a map of the neighborhood of the entity up to distance d, a complete "map" of $\vec{G}$ (e.g., the adjacency matrix of $\vec{G}$); a complete "map" of $(\vec{G}, \lambda)$ (i.e., it contains also the labels), etcetera.

Note that some types of knowledge imply other knowledge; for example, if an entity with k neighbors knows that the network is a complete undirected graph, then it knows that $n = k + 1$.

As a topological map provides all possible metric and structural information, this type of knowledge is very powerful and important. The strongest form of this type is *full topological knowledge*: availability at each entity of a labeled graph isomorphic to $(\vec{G}, \lambda)$, the isomorphism, and its own image, that is, every entity has a complete map of (v, λ) with the indication, "You are here."

Another type of knowledge refers to the labeling λ. What is very important is whether the labeling has some global consistency property.

We can distinguish two other types, depending on whether the knowledge is about the (input) data or the status of the entities and of the system, and we shall call them type-D and type-S, respectively.

Examples of type-D knowledge are the following: *Unique identifiers*: all input values are distinct; *Multiset*: input values are not necessarily identical; *Size*: number of distinct values.

Examples of type-S knowledge are the following: *System with leader*: there is a unique entity in status "leader"; *Reset*: all nodes are in the same status; *Unique initiator*: there is a unique entity in status "initiator." For example, in the broadcasting problem we discussed in Section 1.5, this knowledge was assumed as a part of the problem definition.

1.9   TECHNICAL CONSIDERATIONS

1.9.1   Messages

The content of a message obviously depends on the application; in any case, it consists of a finite (usually bounded) sequence of bits.

The message is typically divided into subsequences, called *fields*, with a predefined meaning ("type") within the protocol.

The examples of field types are the following: *message identifier* or *header* used to distinguish between different types of messages; *originator* and *destination* fields used to specify the (identity of the) entity originating this message and of the entity to whom the message is intended for; *data* fields used to carry information needed in the computation (the nature of the information obviously depends on the particular application under consideration).

Thus, in general, a message M will be viewed as a tuple $M = \langle f_1, f_2, \ldots f_k \rangle$ where k is a (small) predefined constant, and each f_i $(1 \leq i \leq k)$ is a field of a specified type, each type of a fixed length.

So, for example, in protocol *Flooding*, there is only one type of message; it is composed of two fields $M = \langle f_1, f_2 \rangle$ where f_1 is a message identifier (containing the information: "this is a broadcast message"), and f_2 is a data field containing the actual information I being broadcasted.

If (the limit on) the size of a message is a system parameter (i.e., it does not depend on the particular application), we say that the system has *bounded messages*. Such is, for example, the limit imposed on the message length in packet-switching networks, as well as on the length of control messages in circuit-switching networks (e.g., telephone networks) and in message-switching networks.

Bounded messages are also called *packets* and contain at most $\mu(G)$ bits, where $\mu(G)$ is the system-dependent bound called *packet size*. Notice that, to send a sequence of K bits in G will require the transmission of at least $\lceil K/\mu(G) \rceil$ packets.

1.9.2 Protocol

Notation   A protocol $B(x)$ is a set of rules. We have already introduced in Section 1.5 most of the notation for describing those rules. Let us now complete the description of the notation we will use for protocols. We will employ the following conventions:

1. Rules will be grouped by *status*.
2. If the action for a (*status,event*) pair is **nil**, then, for simplicity, the corresponding rule will be *omitted* from the description. As a consequence, if no rule is described for a (*status,event*) pair, the *default* will be that the pair enables the Null action.

WARNING. Although convenient (it simplifies the writing), the use of this convention must generate extra care in the description: If we forget to write a rule for an event occurring in a given status, it will be assumed that a rule exists and the action is nil.

3. If an action contains a change of status, this operation will be the last one before exiting the action.
4. The set of status values of the protocol, and the set of restrictions under which the protocol operates will be explicit.

Using these conventions, the protocol Flooding defined in Section 1.5 will be written as shown in Figure 1.5.

Precedence   The external events are as follows: spontaneous impulse (*Spontaneously*), reception of a message (*Receiving*), and alarm clock ring (*When*). Different types of external events can occur simultaneously; for example, the alarm clock might ring at the same time a message arrives. The simultaneous events will be processed sequentially. To determine the order in which they will be processed, we will use the following *precedence* between external events:

$$Spontaneously > When > Receiving;$$

that is, the spontaneous impulse takes precedence over the alarm clock, which has precedence over the arrival of a message.

At most one spontaneous impulse can always occur at an entity at any one time. As there is locally only one alarm clock, at any time there will be at most one *When* event. By contrast, it is possible that more than one message arrive at the same time to an entity from different neighbors; should this be the case, these simultaneous

PROTOCOL Flooding .

- Status Values: $S = \{\text{INITIATOR, IDLE, DONE}\}$;
  $S_{\text{INIT}} = \{\text{INITIATOR, IDLE}\}$;
  $S_{\text{TERM}} = \{\text{DONE}\}$.
- Restrictions: Bidirectional Links, Total Reliability, Connectivity, and Unique Initiator.

```
INITIATOR
      Spontaneously
      begin
            send (M) to N(x);
            become DONE;
      end

IDLE
      Receiving (I)
      begin
            Process(M);
            send (M) to N(x) − {sender};
            become DONE;
      end
```

FIGURE 1.5: Flooding Protocol

Receiving events have all the same precedence and will be processed sequentially in an arbitrary order.

1.9.3 Communication Mechanism

The communication mechanisms of a distributed computing environment must handle transmissions and arrivals of messages. The mechanisms at an entity can be seen as a system of queues.

Each link $(x, y) \in \vec{E}$ corresponds to a queue, with access at x and exit at y; the access is called *out-port* and the exit is called *in-port*.

Each entity has thus two types of ports: *out-ports*, one for each out-neighbor (or out-link), and *in-port*, one for each in-neighbor (or in-link). At an entity, each out-port has a distinct label (recall the Local Orientation axiom (Axiom 1.3.2)) called port number: the out-port corresponding to (x, y) has label $\lambda_x(x, y)$; similarly for the in-ports.

The sets N_{in} and N_{out} will in practice consist of the port numbers associated to those neighbors; this is because an entity has no other information about its neighbors (unless we add restrictions).

The command "**send** *M* **to** *W*" will have a copy of the message *M* sent through each of the out-ports specified by *W*.

When a message *M* is sent through an out-port *l*, it is inserted in the corresponding queue. In absence of failures (recall the Finite Communication Delays axiom), the communication mechanism will eventually remove it from the queue and deliver it to the other entity through the corresponding in-port, generating the *Receiving* (*M*) event; at that time the variable **sender** will be set to *l*.

1.10 SUMMARY OF DEFINITIONS

Distributed Environment: Collection of communicating computational entities.

Communication: Transmission of message.

Message: Bounded sequence of bits.

Entity's Capability: Local processing, local storage, access to a local clock, and communication.

Entity's Status Register: At any time an entity status register has a value from a predefined set of status values.

External Events: Arrival of a message, alarm clock ring, and spontaneous impulse.

Entity's Behavior: Entities react to external events. The *behavior* is dictated by a set of rules. Each rule has the form

$$STATUS \times EVENT \rightarrow Action$$

specifying what the entity has to do if a certain external event occurs when the entity is in a given status. The set of rules must be nonambiguous and complete.

Actions: An action is an indivisible (i.e., uninterruptible) finite sequence of operations (local processing, message transmission, change of status, and setting of alarm clock).

Homogeneous System: A system is homogeneous if all the entities have the same behavior. Every system can be made homogeneous.

Neighbors: The in-neighbors of an entity are those entities from which x can receive a message directly; the out-neighbors are those to which x can send a message directly.

Communication Topology: The directed graph $G = (V, E)$ defined by the neighborhood relation. If the Bidirectional Links restriction holds, then G is undirected.

Axioms: There are two axioms: local orientation and finite communication delays.

Local Orientation: An entity can distinguish between its out-neighbors and its in-neighbors.

Finite Communication Delays: In absence of failures, a message eventually arrives.

Restriction: Any additional property.

1.11 BIBLIOGRAPHICAL NOTES

Several attempts have been made to derive formalisms capable of describing both distributed systems and computations performed in such systems. A significant amount of study has been devoted to defining formalisms, which would ease the task of formally proving properties of distributed computation (e.g., absence of deadlock, liveness, etc.). The models proposed for systems of concurrent processes do provide both a formalism for describing a distributed computation and a proof system that can be employed within the formalism; such is, for example, the *Unity* model of Mani Chandi and Jayadev Misra [1]. Other models, whose intended goal is still to provide a proof system, have been specifically tailored for distributed computations. In particular, the *Input–Output Automata* model of Nancy Lynch and Mark Tuttle [4] provides a powerful tool that has helped discover and fix "bugs" in well-known existing protocols.

For the investigators involved in the design and analysis of distributed algorithms, the main concern rests with efficiency and complexity; proving correctness of an algorithm is a compulsory task, but it is usually accomplished using traditional mathematical tools (which are generally considered informal techniques) rather than with formal proof systems. The formal models of computation employed in these studies, as well as in the one used in this book, mainly focus on those factors that are directly related to efficiency of a distributed computation and complexity of a distributed problem: the underlining communication network, the communication primitives, the amount and type of knowledge available to the processors, etcetera.

Modal logic, and in particular the notion of common knowledge, is a useful tool to reason about distributed computing environments in presence of failures. The notion of knowledge used here was developed independently by Joseph Halpern and Yoram Moses [2], Daniel J. Lehmann [3], and Stanley Rosenschein [5].

The model we have described and will employ in this book uses *reactive* entities (they react to external stimuli). Several formal models (including *input–output Automata*) use instead *active* entities. To understand this fundamental difference, consider a message in transit toward an entity that is expecting it, with no other activity in the system. In an active model, the entity will attempt to receive the message, even while it is not there; each attempt is an event; hence, this simple situation can actually cause an unpredictable number of events. By contrast, in a reactive model, the entity does nothing; the only event is the arrival of the message that will "wake up" the entity and trigger its response.

Using the analogy of waiting for the delivery of a pizza, in the *active* model, you (the entity) must repeatedly open the door (i.e., act) to see if the person supposed to deliver the pizza has arrived; in the *reactive* model, you sit in the living room until the bell rings and then go and open the door (i.e., react).

The two models are equally powerful; they just represent different ways of looking at and expressing the world. It is our contention that at least for the description and the complexity analysis of protocols and distributed algorithms, the reactive model is more expressive and simpler to understand, to handle, and to use.

1.12 EXERCISES, PROBLEMS, AND ANSWERS

1.12.1 Exercises and Problems

Exercise 1.12.1 Prove that the flooding technique introduced in Section 1.5 is correct, that is, it terminates within finite time, and all entities will receive the information held by the initiator.

Exercise 1.12.2   Determine the exact number of message transmissions required by the protocol *Flooding* described in Section 1.5.

Exercise 1.12.3   In Section 1.5 we have solved the broadcasting problem under the restriction of Bidirectional Links. Solve the problem using the Reciprocal Communication restriction instead.

Exercise 1.12.4   In Section 1.5 we have solved the broadcasting problem under the restriction of Bidirectional Links. Solve the problem *without* this restriction.

Exercise 1.12.5   Show that any protocol B can be rewritten so that S_{START} consists of only one status. (*Hint: Introduce a new input variable.*)

Exercise 1.12.6   Consider the *muddy children* problem discussed in Section 1.8.1. Show that, within finite time, all the children with a muddy forehead can simultaneously determine that they are not clean. (*Hint: Use induction on k.*)

Exercise 1.12.7   *Half-duplex* links allow communication to go in both directions, but not simultaneously. Design a protocol that implements half-duplex communication between two connected entities, a and b. Prove its correctness and analyze its complexity.

Exercise 1.12.8   *Half-duplex* links allow communication to go in both directions, but not simultaneously. Design a protocol that implements half-duplex communication between three entities, a, b and c, connected to each other. Prove its correctness and analyze its complexity.

1.12.2   Answers to Exercises

Answer to Exercise 1.12.1
Let us prove that every entity will indeed receive the message. The proof is by induction on the distance d of an entity from the initiator s. The result is clearly true for $d = 0$. Assume that it is true for all entities at most at distance d. Let x be a process at distance $d + 1$ from s. Consider a shortest path $s \to x_1 \to \ldots \to x_{d-1} \to x$ between s and x. As process x_{d-1} is at distance $d - 1$ from s, then by the induction assumption it receives the message. If x_{d-1} received the message from x, then this means that x already received the message and the proof is completed. Otherwise, x_{d-1} received the message from a different neighbor, and it then sends the message to all its neighbors, including x. Hence x will eventually receive the message.

Answer to Exercise 1.12.2
The total number of messages sent without the improvement was $\sum_{x \in \mathcal{E}} |N(x)| = 2|E| = 2m$; in Flooding, every entity (except the initiator) will send one message less. Hence the total number of messages is $2m - (|V| - 1) = 2m - n + 1$.

Answer to Exercise 1.12.6 (Basis of Induction only)

Consider first the case $k = 1$: Only one child, say z, has a dirty forehead. In this case, z will see that everyone else has a clean forehead; as the teacher has said that at least one child has a dirty forehead, z knows that he/she must be the one. Thus, when the teacher arrives, he/she comes forward. Notice that a clean child sees that z is dirty but finds out that his/her own forehead is clean only when z goes forward.

Consider now the case $k = 2$: There are two dirty children, a and b; a sees the dirty forehead of b and the clean one of everybody else. Clearly he/she does not know about his status; he/she knows that if he/she is clean, b is the only one who is dirty and will go forward when the teacher arrives. So, when the teacher comes and b does *not* go forward, a understands that his/her forehead is also dirty. (A similar reasoning is carried out by b.) Thus, when the teacher returns the second time, both a and b go forward.

BIBLIOGRAPHY

[1] K.M. Chandi and J. Misra. *Parallel Program Design: A Foundation*. Addison-Wesley, 1988.

[2] J.Y. Halpern and Y. Moses. Knowledge and common knowledge in a distributed environment. *Journal of the A.C.M.*, 37(3):549–587, 1987.

[3] D.J. Lehmann. Knowledge, common knowledge and related puzzles. In *3rd ACM Symposium on Principles of Distributed Computing*, pages 62–67, Vancouver, 1984.

[4] N.A. Lynch and M.R. Tuttle. Hierarchical correctness proofs of distributed algorithms. In *6th ACM Symposium on Principles of Distributed Computing (PODC)*, pages 137–151, Vancouver, 1987.

[5] S.J. Rosenschein. Formal theories of AI in knowledge and robotics. *New Generation Computing*, 3:345–357, 1985.

CHAPTER 2

Basic Problems and Protocols

The aim of this chapter is to introduce some of the basic, primitive, computational problems and solution techniques. These problems are basic in the sense that their solution is commonly (sometimes frequently) required for the functioning of the system (e.g., *broadcast* and *wake-up*); they are primitive in the sense that their computation is often a preliminary step or a module of complex computations and protocols (e.g., *traversal* and *spanning-tree construction*).

Some of these problems (e.g., *broadcast* and *traversal*), by their nature, are started by a single entity; in other words, these computational problems have, in their definition, the restriction *unique initiator* (UI). Other problems (e.g., *wake-up* and *spanning-tree construction*) have no such restriction. The computational differences created by the additional assumption of a single initiator can be dramatic.

In this chapter we have also included the discussions on the (multiple-initiators) computations in tree networks. Their fundamental importance derives from the fact that most *global* problems (i.e., problems that, to be solved, require the involvement of all entities), oftentimes can be correctly, easily, and efficiently solved by designing a protocol for trees and executing it on a spanning-tree of the network.

All the problems considered here require, for their solution, the *Connectivity* (CN) restriction (i.e., every entity must be reachable from every other entity). In general, and unless otherwise stated, we will also assume *Total Reliability* (TR) and *Bidirectional Links* (BL). These three restrictions are commonly used together, and the set $\mathbf{R} = \{$BL, CN, TR$\}$ will be called the set of *standard* restrictions.

The techniques we introduce in this chapter to solve these problems are basic ones; once properly understood, they form a powerful and an essential *toolset* that can be effectively employed by every designer of distributed algorithms.

2.1 BROADCAST

2.1.1 The Problem

Consider a distributed computing system where only one entity, x, knows some important information; this entity would like to share this information with *all* the other entities in the system; see Figure 2.1. This problem is called *broadcasting* (**Bcast**),

Design and Analysis of Distributed Algorithms, by Nicola Santoro
Copyright © 2007 John Wiley & Sons, Inc.

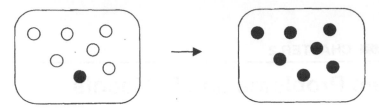

FIGURE 2.1: Broadcasting Process.

and already we have started its examination in the previous chapter. To solve this problem means to design a set of rules that, when executed by the entities, will lead (within finite time) to a configuration where all entities will know the information; the solution must work regardless of which entity has the information at the beginning.

Built-in the definition of the problem, there is the assumption, *Unique Initiator* (UI), that only one entity will start the task. Actually, this assumption is further restricted, because the unique initiator must be the one with the initial information; we shall denote this restriction by UI+.

To solve this problem, every entity must clearly be involved in the computation. Hence, for its solution, broadcasting requires the *Connectivity* (CN) restriction (i.e., every entity must be reachable from every other entity) otherwise some entities will never receive the information. We have seen a simple solution to this problem, *Flooding*, under two additional restrictions: Total Reliability (TR) and Bidirectional Links (BL). Recall that the set **R** = {BL, CN, TR} is the set of *standard* restrictions .

2.1.2 Cost of Broadcasting

As we have seen, the solution protocol *Flooding* uses $O(m)$ messages and, in the worst case, $O(d)$ ideal time units, where d is the diameter of the network.

The first and natural question is whether these costs could be reduced significantly (i.e., in order of magnitude) using a different approach or technique, and if so, by how much. This question is equivalent to ask what is the *complexity* of the broadcasting problem. To answer this type of questions we need to establish a *lower bound*: to find a bound f (typically, a function of the size of the network) and to prove that the cost of *every* solution algorithm is *at least f*. In other words, a lower bound is needed irrespective of the protocol, and it depends solely on the problem; hence, it is an indication of how complex the problem really is.

We will denote by $\mathcal{M}(\textbf{Bcast}/\textbf{RI+})$ and $\mathcal{T}(\textbf{Bcast}/\textbf{RI+})$ the message and the time complexity of broadcasting under $\textbf{RI+} = \textbf{R} \cup \text{UI+}$, respectively.

A lower bound on the amount of ideal time units required to perform a broadcast is simple to derive: Every entity must receive the information regardless of how distant they are from the initiator, and any entity could be the initiator. Hence, in the worst case,

$$\mathcal{T}(\textbf{Bcast}/\textbf{RI+}) \geq \text{Max}\{d(x, y) : x, y \in V\} = d. \tag{2.1}$$

The fact that *Flooding* performs the broadcast in d ideal time units means that the lower bound is *tight* (i.e., it can be achieved) and that *Flooding* is *time optimal*. In other words, we know exactly the ideal time complexity of broadcasting:

Property 2.1.1 *The ideal time complexity of broadcasting under* **RI+** *is* $\Theta(d)$.

Let us now consider the message complexity. An obvious lower bound on the number of messages is also easy to derive: in the end, every entity must know the information; thus a message must be received by each of the $n-1$ entities, which initially did not have the information. Hence,

$$\mathcal{M}(\text{Bcast/RI+}) \geq n-1.$$

With a little extra effort, we can derive a more accurate lower bound:

Theorem 2.1.1 $\mathcal{M}(\text{Bcast/RI+}) \geq m.$

Proof. Assume that there exists a correct broadcasting protocol A which, in each execution, under **RI+** on every G, uses fewer than $m(G)$ messages. This means that there is at least one link in G where no message is transmitted in any direction during an execution of the algorithm. Consider an execution of the algorithm on G, and let $e = (x, y) \in E$ be the link where no message is transmitted by A. Now construct a new graph G' from G by removing the edge e, and adding a new node z and two new edges $e_1 = (x, z)$ and $e_2 = (y, z)$ (see Fig. 2.2). Set z in a noninitiator status. Run exactly the same execution of A on the new graph G': since no message was sent along (x, y), this is possible. But since no message was sent along (x, y) in the original execution, x and y never send a message to z in the current execution. As a result, z will never receive the information (i.e., change status). This contradicts the fact that A is a correct broadcasting protocol. ∎

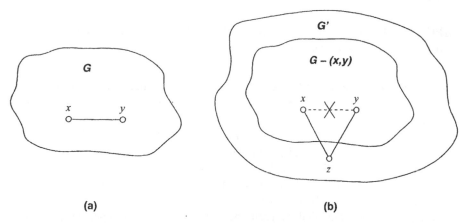

(a)   **(b)**

FIGURE 2.2: A message must be sent on each link.

This means that any broadcasting algorithm requires $\Omega(m)$ messages.

Since *Flooding* solves broadcasting with $2m - n + 1$ messages (see Exercise 2.9.1), this implies $\mathcal{M}(\text{Bcast/RI}+) \leq 2m - n + 1$. Since the upper bound and the lower bound are of the same order of magnitude, we can summarize

Property 2.1.2   *The message complexity of broadcasting under* **RI**+ *is* $\Theta(m)$.

The immediate consequence is that, in order of magnitude, *Flooding* is a *message-optimal* solution. Thus, if we want to design a new protocol to improve the $2m - n + 1$ cost of *Flooding*, the best we can hope to achieve is to reduce the constant 2; in any case, because of Theorem 2.1.1, the reduction cannot bring the constant below 1.

2.1.3 Broadcasting in Special Networks

The results we have obtained so far apply to *generic* solutions; that is, solutions that do not depend on G and can thus be applied regardless of the communication topology (provided it is undirected and connected).

Next, we will consider performing the broadcast in special networks. Throughout we will assume the standard restrictions plus UI+.

Broadcasting in Trees   Consider the case when G is a tree; that is, G is connected and contains no cycles. In a tree, $m = n-1$; hence, the use of protocol *Flooding* for broadcasting in a tree will cost $2m - (n - 1) = 2(n - 1) - (n - 1) = n - 1$ messages.

IMPORTANT. This cost is achieved even if the entities do *not know* that the network is a tree.

IMPORTANT. An interesting side effect of broadcasting on a tree is that the tree becomes *rooted* in the initiator of the broadcast.

Broadcasting in Oriented Hypercubes   A communication topology that is commonly used as an interconnection network is the (k-dimensional) labeled *hypercube*, denoted by H_k.

A oriented hypercube H_1 of dimension $k = 1$ is just a pair of nodes called (in binary) "0" and "1," connected by a link labeled "1" at both nodes.

A hypercube H_k of dimension $k > 1$ is obtained by taking two hypercubes of dimension $k - 1$–H'_{k-1} and H_{k-1}–and connecting the nodes with the same name with a link labeled k at both nodes; the name of each node in H'_{k-1} (respectively H''_{k-1}) is then modified by prefixing it with the bit 0 (respectively, 1); see Figure 2.3.

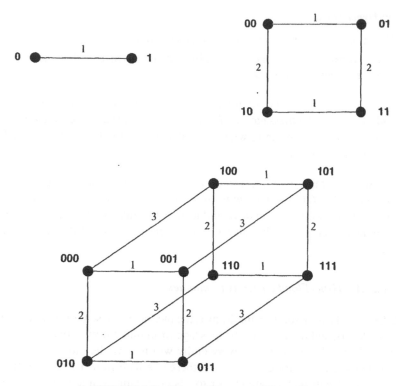

FIGURE 2.3: Oriented Hypercube Networks

So, for example, node "0010" in H_4' will be connected to node "0010" in H_4'' by a link labeled $l = 5$, and their names will become "00010" and "10010," respectively.

This labeling λ of the links is symmetric (i.e., $\lambda_x(x, y) = \lambda_y(x, y)$) and is called the *dimensional* labeling of a hypercube.

IMPORTANT. These names are used only for descriptive purposes; they are *not* known to the entities. By contrast, the labels of the links (i.e., the port numbers) are known to the entities by the Local Orientation axiom.

A hypercube of dimension k has $n = 2^k$ nodes; each node has k links, labeled $1, 2, \ldots, k$. Hence the total number of links is $m = nk/2 = (n/2) \log n = O(n \log n)$.

A straightforward application of *Flooding* in a hypercube will cost $2m - (n - 1) = n \log n - (n - 1) = n \log n/2 + 1 = O(n \log n)$ messages. However, hypercubes are highly structured networks with many interesting properties. We can exploit these special properties to construct a more efficient broadcast. Obviously, if we do so, the protocol cannot be used in other networks.

Consider the following simple strategy.

Strategy *HyperFlood*:

1. The initiator sends the message to all its neighbors.
2. A node receiving a message from the link labeled l will send the messages only to those neighbors with label $l' < l$.

NOTE. The only difference between *HyperFlood* and the normal *Flooding* is in step 2: Instead of sending the message to *all* neighbors except the sender, the entity will forward it only to some of them, which will depend on the label of the port from where the message is received.

As we will see, this strategy correctly performs the broadcast using only $n - 1$ messages (instead of $O(n \log n)$). Let us first examine termination and correctness.

Let $H_k(x)$ denote the subgraph of H_k induced by the links where messages are sent by *HyperFlood* when x is the initiator. Clearly every node in $H_k(x)$ will receive the information.

Lemma 2.1.1 *HyperFlood correctly terminates.*

Proof. Let x be the initiator; starting from x, the messages are sent only on links with *decreasing* labels, and if y receives the message from link 4 it will forward it only to the ports 1, 2, and 3. To prove that every entity will receive the information sent by x, we need to show that, for every node y, there is a path from x to y such that the sequence of the labels on the path from x to y is decreasing. (Note that the labels on the path do not need to be consecutive integers.) To do so we will use the following property of hypercubes.

Property 2.1.3 *In a k-dimensional hypercube H_k, any node x is connected to any other node y by a path $\pi \in \ ^\cdot[x, y]$ such that $\Lambda(\pi)$ is a decreasing sequence.*

Proof. Consider the k-bit names of x and of y in H_k: $\langle x_k, x_{k-1}, \ldots, x_1, x_0 \rangle$ and $\langle y_k, y_{k-1}, \ldots, y_1, y_0 \rangle$. If $x \neq y$, these two strings will differ in $t \geq 1$ positions. Let $j_1, j_2, \ldots, j_t$ be the positions in decreasing order; that is, $j_i > j_{i+1}$. Consider now the nodes $v_0, v_1, v_2, \ldots, v_t$, where $v_0 = x$, and the name of v_i differs from the name of v_{i+1} only in the j_{i+1}-th position. Thus, there is a link labeled j_{i+1} connecting v_i to v_{i+1}, and clearly $v_t = y$. But this means that $\langle v_0, v_1, v_2, \ldots, v_t \rangle$ is a path from x to y, and the sequence of labels on this path is $\langle j_1, j_2, \ldots, j_t \rangle$, which is decreasing. ∎

Thus, $H_k(x)$ is connected and spans (i.e., it contains all the nodes of) H_k, regardless of x. In other words, within finite time, every entity will have the information. ∎

Let us now concentrate on the cost of *HyperFlood*. First of all observe that

$$\mathbf{M}[HyperFlood/H_k] = n - 1. \tag{2.2}$$

To prove that only $n - 1$ messages will be sent during the broadcast, we just need to show that every entity will receive the information only once. This is true because, for every x, $H_k(x)$ contains no cycles (see Exercise 2.9.9).

Also as an exercise it is left the proof that for every x, the eccentricity of x in $H_k(x)$ is k (see Exercise 2.9.10); this implies that the ideal time delay of *HyperFlood* in H_k is always k. That is,

$$\mathbf{T}[HyperFlood/H_k] = k \tag{2.3}$$

These costs are the best that any broadcast algorithm can perform in a hypercube regardless of how much more knowledge they have. However, they are obtained here under the additional restriction that *the network is a k-dimensional hypercube with a dimensional labeling*; that is, under $H = \{(G, \lambda) = H_k\}$. Summarizing, we have

Property 2.1.4   *The ideal time complexity of broadcasting in a k-dimensional hypercube with a dimensional labeling under* **RI+** *is* $\Theta(k)$.

Property 2.1.5   *The message complexity of broadcasting in a k-dimensional hypercube with a dimensional labeling under* **RI+** *is* $\Theta(n)$.

IMPORTANT. The reason why we are able to "bypass" the $\Omega(m)$ lower bound expressed by Theorem 2.1.1 is because we are restricting the applicability of the protocol.

Broadcasting in Complete Graphs   Among all network topologies, the *complete graph* is the one with the most links: Every entity is connected to all others; thus $m = n(n - 1)/2 = O(n^2)$ (recall we are considering bidirectional links), and $d = 1$.

The use of a generic protocol will require $O(n^2)$ messages. But this is really unnecessary.

Broadcasting in a complete graph is easily accomplished: Because everybody is connected to everybody else, the initiator just needs to send the information to its neighbors (i.e., execute the command "**send**(I) **to** $N(x)$") and the broadcast is completed. This uses only $n - 1$ messages and $d = 1$ ideal time.

Clearly this protocol, *KBcast*, works only in a complete graph, that is under the additional restriction $K \equiv$ "*G is a complete graph*." Summarizing

Property 2.1.6   *The message and the ideal time complexity of broadcasting in a complete graph under* **RI+** *is* $\Theta(k)$ *are* $\mathcal{M}(\mathbf{Bcast/RI+} ; K) = n - 1$ *and* $\mathcal{T}(\mathbf{Bcast/RI+} ; K) = 1$, *respectively*.

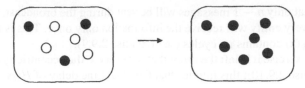

FIGURE 2.4: Wake-Up Process.

2.2   WAKE-UP

2.2.1   Generic Wake-Up

Very often, in a distributed environment, we are faced with the following situation: A task must be performed in which all the entities must be involved; however, only some of them are independently active (because of a spontaneous event, or having finished a previous computation) and ready to compute, the others are inactive, not even aware of the computation that must take place. In these situations, to perform the task, we must ensure that all the entities become active. Clearly, this preliminary step can only be started by the entities that are active already; however, they do *not* know which other entities (if any) are already active.

This problem is called *Wake-up* (**Wake-Up**): An active entity is usually called *awake*, an inactive (still) one is called *asleep*; the task is to wake all entities up; see Figure 2.4.

It is not difficult to see the relationship between broadcasting and wake-up: *Broadcast* is a *wake-up* with only one initially awake entity; conversely, *wake-up* is a broadcast with possibly many initiators (i.e., initially more than one entity has the information). In other words, broadcast is just a special case of the wake-up problem.

Interestingly, but not surprisingly, the flooding strategy used for broadcasting actually solves the more general **Wake-Up** problem. The modified protocol, called *WFlood*, is described in Figure 2.5. Initially all entities are *asleep*; any *asleep* entity can become spontaneously *awake* and start the protocol.

It is not difficult to verify that the protocol correctly terminates under the standard restrictions (Exercise 2.9.7).

Let us concentrate on the cost of protocol *WFlood*. The number of messages is at least equal to that of broadcast; actually, it is not much more (see Exercise 2.9.6):

$$2m \geq \mathbf{M}[WFlood] \geq 2m - n + 1. \tag{2.4}$$

As broadcast is a special case of wake-up, not much improvement is possible (except perhaps in the size of the constant):

$$\mathcal{M}(\mathbf{Wake\text{-}Up/R}) \geq \mathcal{M}(\mathbf{Bcast/RI+}) = \Omega(m)$$

The ideal time will, in general, be smaller than the one for broadcast:

$$\mathcal{T}(\mathbf{Bcast/RI+}) \geq \mathcal{T}(\mathbf{Wake\text{-}Up/R})$$

PROTOCOL WFlood .

- Status Values: $S = \{$ASLEEP,AWAKE$\}$;
  $S_{INIT} = \{$ASLEEP$\}$;
  $S_{TERM} = \{$AWAKE$\}$.
- Restrictions: **R**.

ASLEEP

> *Spontaneously*
> **begin**
>> send(W) **to** $N(x)$;
>> **become** AWAKE;
> **end**
>
> *Receiving* (W)
> **begin**
>> send (W) **to** $N(x) - \{$sender$\}$;
>> **become** AWAKE;
> **end**

FIGURE 2.5: Wake-Up by Flooding

However, in the case of a single initiator, the two cases coincide. As upper and lower bounds coincide in order of magnitude, we can conclude that protocol *WFlood* is both *message* and, worst case in the *time optimal*.

The complexity of **Wake-Up** is summarized by the following two properties,

Property 2.2.1 *The message complexity of Wake-up under* **R** *is* $\Theta(m)$.

Property 2.2.2 *The worst case ideal time complexity of Wake-up under* **R** *is* $\Theta(d)$.

2.2.2 Wake-Up in Special Networks

Trees The cost of using protocol *WFlood* for wake-up will depend on the number of initiators. In fact, if there is only one initiator, then this is just a broadcast and costs only $n - 1$ messages. By contrast, if every entity starts independently, there will be a total of $2(n - 1)$ messages. Let $k_{\star}$ denote the number of initiators; note that this number is *not* a system parameter like n or m, it is, however, bounded by a system parameter: $k_{\star} \leq n$. Then the total number of messages when executing *WFlood* in a tree will be exactly

$$\mathbf{M}[WFlood/Tree] = n + k_{\star} - 2. \tag{2.5}$$

Labeled Hypercubes In Section 2.1, by exploiting the properties of the hypercube and of the dimensional labeling, we have been able to construct a broadcast protocol, which uses only $O(n)$ messages, instead of the $\Omega(n \log n)$ messages required by any generic protocol.

Let us see if we can achieve a similar result also for the wake-up. In other words, can we exploit the properties of a labeled hypercube to do better than generic protocols? The answer is, unfortunately, *NO*.

Lemma 2.2.1 $\mathcal{M}(\textbf{Wake-Up/R} \; ; H) = \Omega(n \log n)$.

As a consequence, we might as well employ the generic protocol *WFlood*, which uses $O(n \log n)$ messages. Summarizing,

Property 2.2.3   *The message complexity of wake-up under* **R** *in a k-dimensional hypercube with a dimensional labeling is* $\Theta(n \log n)$.

Complete Graphs   Let us focus on wake-up in a complete graph. The use of the generic protocol*WFlood* will require $O(n^2)$ messages. We can obviously use the simplified broadcast protocol *KBcast* we developed for complete graphs. The number of messages transmitted will be $k_*(n-1)$, where k_* denotes the number of initiators. Even in the worst case (when every entity is independently awake and they all simultaneously start the protocol) $O(n^2)$ messages will be transmitted.

Let us see if, by exploiting the properties of complete graphs, we have been able to construct a wake-up protocol that uses only $O(n)$ messages, instead of the $O(n^2)$ we have achieved so far. (After all, we have been able to do it in the case of the broadcast problem.)

Surprisingly, also in this case, the answer is *NO*.

Lemma 2.2.2 $\mathcal{M}(\textbf{Wake-Up/R} \; ; K) = \Omega(n^2)$.

This implies that the use of *WFlood* for wake-up is a *message-optimal* solution. In other words,

Property 2.2.4   *The message complexity of wake-up under* **R** *in a complete network is* $\Theta(n^2)$.

Complete Graphs with ID   To reduce the number of messages, a more restricted environment is required; that is, we need to make additional assumptions.

For example, if we add the restriction that the entities have unique names (restriction Initial Distinct values (ID)), then there are protocols capable of performing wake-up with $O(n \log n)$ messages in a complete graph; they are not simple and actually solve a much more complex problem, *Election*, which we will discuss at length in Chapter 3. Strangely, nothing better than that can be accomplished. In fact, let IR + K = **R** ∪ K; then the worst case *message complexity* of wake-up in a complete graph under the standard restrictions **R** plus ID is as follows:

Property 2.2.5 $\mathcal{M}(\textbf{Wake-Up/R}; \text{ID}; K) \geq 0.5n \log n$.

To see why this is true, we will construct a "bad" but possible case, which any protocol can encounter, and show that, in such a case, $O(n \log n)$ messages will be exchanged. The lower bound will hold even if there is message ordering. For simplicity of discussion and calculation, we will assume that n is a power of 2; the results hold also if this is not the case.

To construct the "bad" case for an (arbitrary) solution protocol A, we will consider a *game* between the entities on one side and an *adversary* on the other: the entities obey the rules of the protocol; the adversary will try to make the worst possible scenario occur, so, to force the use of as many messages as possible.

The adversary has the following four powers:

1. it decides the initial values of the entities (they must be distinct);
2. it decides which entities spontaneously start the execution of A, and when;
3. it decides when a transmitted message arrives (it must be within finite time); and
4. importantly, it decides the matching between links and labels: Let $e_1, e_2, \ldots, e_k$ be the links incident on x, and let $l_1, l_2, \ldots, l_k$ be the port labels to be used by x for those links; during the execution, when x performs a "**send to** l" command, and l has not been assigned yet, the adversary will choose which of the unused links (i.e., through which no messages has been sent nor received) the label l will be assigned to.

NOTE. Sending a message to more than one port will be treated as sending the message to each of those ports one at a time (in an arbitrary order).

Whatever the adversary decides, it can happen in a real execution. Let us see how bad a case can the adversary create for A.

Two sets of entities will be said to be *connected* at a time t if at least a message has been transmitted from an entities of one set to an entity of the other.

Adversary's Strategy.

1. Initially, the adversary will wake up only one entity s, which we will call the *seed*, and which will start the execution of the protocol. When s decides to send a message to port number l, the adversary will wake up another entity y and assign label l to the edge from s to y. It will then delay the transmission on that link until also y decides to send a message to some port number l'; the adversary will then assign label l' to the link from y to s and let the two messages arrive to their destination simultaneously. In this way, each message will reach an awake node, and the two entities are connected.

   From now on, the adversary will act in a similar way; always ensure that messages are sent to already-awake nodes, and that the set of awake nodes is connected.

2. Consider an entity x executing a **send** operation to an unassigned label a.

   (a) If x has an unused link (i.e., a link on which no messages have been sent so far) connecting it to an awake node, the adversary will assign a to that link. In other words, the adversary will always try to make the awake entities send messages to other awake entities.

   (b) If all links between x and the awake nodes have been used, then the adversary will create another set of awake nodes and connect the two sets.

      i. Let $x_0, \ldots, x_{k-1}$ be the currently awake nodes, ordered according to their wake-up time (thus, $x_0 = s$ is the seed, and $x_1 = y$). The adversary will perform the following function: choose k inactive nodes $z_0, \ldots, z_{k-1}$; establish a logical correspondence between x_j and z_j; assign initial values to the new entities so that the order among them is the same as the one among the values of the corresponding entities; wake up these entities and force them to have the "same" execution (same scheduling and same delays) as already did the corresponding ones. (So, z_0 will be woken up first, its first message will be sent to z_1, which will be woken up next and will send a message to z_0, and so forth)

      ii. The adversary will then assign label a to the link connecting x to its corresponding entity z in the new set; the message will be held in transit until z (like x did) will need to transmit a message on an unused link (say, with label b) but all the edges connecting it to its set of awake entities have already been used.

      iii. When this happens, the adversary will assign the label b to the link from z to x and make the two messages between x and z arrive and be processed.

Let us summarize the strategy of the adversary: The adversary tries to force the protocol to send messages only to already-awake entities and awakens new entities only when it cannot do otherwise; the newly awake entities are equal in number to the already awake entities; and they are forced by the adversary to have the same execution between them as did the other entities before any communication takes place between the two sets. When this happens, we will say that the adversary has started a new *stage*.

Let us now examine the situations created by the adversary with this strategy and analyze the cost of the protocol in the corresponding executions.

Let $Active(i)$ denote the awake entities in stage i and $New(i) = Active(i) - Active(i-1)$ the entities that the adversary woke up in this stage; initially, $Active(0)$ is just the seed. The newly awake entities are equal in number to the already awake entities; that is, $|New(i)| = |Active(i-1)|)$.

Let $\mu(i-1)$ denote the *total* number of messages, which have been exchanged before the activation of the new entities. The adversary forces the new entities to have the same execution as did the entities in $Active(i-1)$, thus exchanging $\mu(i-1)$ of messages, before allowing the two sets to become connected. Thus, the total number of messages until the communication between the two sets takes place is $2\mu(i-1)$.

Once the communication takes place, how many messages (including those two) are transmitted before the next stage?

The exact answer will depend on the protocol A, but regardless of which protocol we are using, the adversary will not start a new stage $i + 1$ unless it is forced to; this will happen only if an entity x issues a **"send to** l**"** command (where l is an unassigned label) and all the links connecting x to the other awake entities have already been used. This means that x must have either sent to or received from all the entities in $Active(i) = Active(i - 1) \cup New(i)$. Assume that $x \in Active(i - 1)$; then, of all these messages, the ones between x and $New(i)$ have only occurred in stage i (since those entities were not active before); this means that at least $|New(i)| = |Active(i - 1)|$ additional messages are sent before stage $i + 1$. If instead $x \in New(i)$, these messages have all been transmitted in this stage (as x was not awake before); in other words, even in this case, $|New(i)| = |Active(i - 1)|$ additional messages are sent before stage $i + 1$.

Summarizing, the total cost $\mu(i - 1)$ before stage i is thus doubled and *at least* additional $|Active(i - 1)|$ messages are sent before stage $i + 1$. In other words,

$$\mu(i) \geq 2\, \mu(i - 1) + |Active(i - 1)|.$$

As the awake entities double in each stage, and initially only the seed is active, then $|Active(i)| = 2^i$. Hence, observing that $\mu(0) = 0$,

$$\mu(i) \geq 2\, \mu(i - 1) + 2^{i-1} \geq i\, 2^{i-1}.$$

The total number of stages is exactly $\log n$ as the awake processes double every stage. Hence, with this strategy, the adversary can force any protocol to transmit *at least* $\mu(\log n)$ messages. As

$$\mu(\log n) \geq 0.5\, n \log n$$

it follows that *any* wake-up protocol will transmit $\Omega(n \log n)$ messages in the worst case even if the entities have distinct identifiers (ids).

More efficient wake-up protocols can be derived if we have in our system a "good" labeling of the links instead.

2.3 TRAVERSAL

Traversal of the network allows every entity in the network to be "visited" sequentially (one after the other). Its main uses are in the control and management of a shared resource and in sequential search processes. In abstract terms, the *traversal problem* starts with an initial configuration where all entities are in the same state (say *unvisited*) except the one that is *visited* and is the sole initiator; the goal is to render all the entities visited but sequentially (i.e., one at the time).

A *traversal protocol* is a distributed algorithm that, starting from the single initiator, allows a special message called "traversal token" (or simply, *token*), to reach every entity *sequentially* (i.e., one at the time). Once a node is reached by the token, it is marked as "visited." Depending on the traversal strategy employed, we will have different traversal protocols.

2.3.1 Depth-First Traversal

A well known strategy is the *depth-first traversal* of a graph. According to this strategy, the graph is visited (i.e., the token is forwarded) trying to go forward as long as possible; if it is forwarded to an already visited node, it is sent back to the sender, and that link is marked as a *back-edge*; if the token can no longer be forwarded (it is at a node where all its neighbors have been visited), the algorithm will "backtrack" until it finds an unvisited node where the token can be forwarded to.

The distributed implementation of depth-first traversal is straightforward.

1. When first visited, an entity remembers who sent the token, creates a list of all its still unvisited neighbors, forwards the token to one of them (removing it from the list), and waits for its reply returning the token.

2. When the neighbor receives the token, it will return the token immediately if it had been visited already by somebody else, notifying that the link is a back-edge; otherwise, it will first forward the token to each of its unvisited neighbors sequentially, and then reply returning the token.

3. Upon the reception of the reply, the entity forwards the token to another unvisited neighbor.

4. Should there be no more unvisited neighbors, the entity can no longer forward the token; it will then send the reply, returning the token to the node from which it first received it.

NOTE. When the neighbor in step (2) determines that a link is a back-edge , it knows that the sender of the token is already visited; thus, it will remove it from the list of unvisited neighbors.

We will use three types of messages: "T" to forward the token in the traversal, "Backedge" to notify the detection of a back-edge, and "Return" to return the token upon local termination.

Protocol *DF_Traversal* is shown in Figure 2.6, where the operation of extracting an element from a set B and assigning it to variable a is denoted by $a \Leftarrow B$. Let us examine its costs.

Focus on a link $(x,y) \in E$. What messages can be sent on it? Suppose x sends T to y; then y will only send to x either Return (if it was *idle* when the T arrived) or Backedge (otherwise). In other words, on each link there will be exactly two messages transmitted. Since the traversal is sequential, $\mathbf{T}[DF\_Traversal] = \mathbf{M}[DF\_Traversal]$; hence

$$\mathbf{T}[DF\_Traversal] = \mathbf{M}[DF\_Traversal] = 2m. \tag{2.6}$$

PROTOCOL DF_Traversal.

- Status: $\mathcal{S} = \{$INITIATOR,IDLE,VISITED,DONE$\}$;
  $\mathcal{S}_{INIT} = \{$INITIATOR,IDLE$\}$; $\mathcal{S}_{TERM} = \{$DONE$\}$.

- Restrictions: **R** ;UI.

```
INITIATOR
              Spontaneously
              begin
                    Unvisited:= N(x);
                    initiator:= true;
                    VISIT;
              end

IDLE
              Receiving (T)
              begin
                    entry: = sender;
                    Unvisited: = N(x) − {sender};
                    initiator: = false;
                    VISIT;
              end

VISITED
              Receiving (T)
              begin
                    Unvisited: = Unvisited −{sender};
                    send (Backedge) to {sender};
              end

              Receiving (Return)
              begin
                    VISIT;
              end

              Receiving (Backedge)
              begin
                    VISIT;
              end

Procedure VISIT
begin
     if Unvisited ≠ ∅ then
        next ⇐ Unvisited;
        send (T) to next;
        become VISITED
     else
        if not (initiator) then send (Return) to entry; endif
        become DONE;
     endif
end
```

FIGURE 2.6: DF_Traversal

To determine how efficient is the protocol, we are going to determine what is the complexity of the problem.

Using exactly the same technique we employed in the proof of Theorem 2.1.1, we have (Exercise 2.9.11):

Theorem 2.3.1 $\mathcal{M}(\text{DFT/R}) \geq m$.

Therefore, the $2m$ message cost of protocol *DF_Traversal* is indeed excellent, and the protocol is *message optimal*.

Property 2.3.1 *The message complexity of depth-first traversal under* **R** *is* $\Theta(m)$.

The time requirements of a depth-first traversal are quite different from those of a broadcast. In fact, since each node must be visited sequentially, starting from the sole initiator, the time complexity is at least the number of nodes:

Theorem 2.3.2 $\mathcal{T}(\text{DFT/R}) \geq n - 1$.

The time complexity of protocol *DF_Traversal* is dreadful. In fact, the upper bound $2m$ could be several order of magnitude larger than the lower bound $n - 1$. For example, in a complete graph, $2m = n^2 - n$. Some significant improvements in the time complexity can, however, be made by going into a finer granularity. We will discuss this topic in greater details next.

2.3.2 Hacking (*)

Let us examine protocol *Protocol DF_Traversal* to see if it can be improved, especially its time cost.

IMPORTANT. When measuring ideal time, we consider only *synchronous* executions; however, when measuring messages and establishing correctness we must consider *every* possible schedule of events, especially the nonsynchronous executions.

Basic Hacking The protocol we have constructed is totally sequential: in a synchronous execution, at each time unit only one message will be sent, and every message requires one unit of time. So, to improve the time complexity, we need to (1) reduce the number of messages and/or (2) introduce some concurrency.

By definition of traversal, each entity must receive the token (message T) at least once. In the execution of our protocol, however, some entities receive it more than once; those links from which these other T messages arrive are precisely the back-edges.

Question. Can we avoid sending T messages on back-edges?

To answer this question we must understand why T messages are sent on back-edges. When an entity x sends a T message to y, it does not know whether the link is a back-edge or not; that is, whether y has already been visited by somebody else or not. If x knew which of its neighbors are already visited, it would not send a T message to them, there would be no need for Backedge messages from them, and we would be saving messages and time. Let us examine how to achieve such a condition.

Suppose that, whenever a node is visited (i.e., it receives T) for the first time, it notifies all its (other) neighbors of this event (e.g., sending a "Visited" message) and waits for an acknowledgment (e.g., receiving an "Ack" message) from them before forwarding the token.

The consequence of such a simple act is that now an entity ready to forward the token (i.e., to send a T message) really knows which of its neighbors have already been visited.

This is exactly what we wanted. The price we have to pay is the transmission of the Visited and Ack messages.

Notice that now an *idle* entity (that is an entity that has not yet been involved in the traversal) might receive a Visited message as its first message. In the revised protocol, we will make such an entity enter a new status, *available*.

Let us examine the effects of this change on the overall *time cost* of the protocol; call DF+ the resulting protocol. The time is really determined by the number of sequential messages. There are four types of messages that are sent: T, Return, Visited, and Ack.

Each entity (except the initiator) will receive only one T message and send only one Return message; the initiator does not receive any T message and does not send any Return; thus, in total there will be $2(n-1)$ such messages. Since all these communications occur sequentially (i.e., without any overlap), the time taken by sending the T and Return messages will be $2(n-1)$.

To determine how many ideal time units are added by the transmission of Visited and Ack messages, consider an entity: its transmission of all the Visited messages takes only a single time unit, since they are sent concurrently; the corresponding Ack messages will also be sent concurrently, adding an additional time unit. Since every node will do it, the sending of the Visited messages and receiving the Ack messages will increase the ideal time of the original algorithm by exactly $2n$.

This will give us a time cost of

$$T[DF+] = 4n - 2. \tag{2.7}$$

It is also easy to compute how many *messages* this will cost. As mentioned above, there is a total of $2(n-1)$ T and Return messages. In addition, each entity (except the initiator) sends a Visited message to all its neighbors except the one from which it received the token; the initiator will send it to all its neighbors. Thus, denoting by s the initiator, the total number of Visited messages is $|N(s)| + \sum_{x \neq s}(|N(x)| - 1) = 2m - (n-1)$. Because for each Visited message there will be an Ack, the total message cost will be

$$M[DF+] = 4m - 2(n-1) + 2(n-1) = 4m. \tag{2.8}$$

Summarizing, we have been able to reduce the time costs from $O(m)$ to $O(n)$ that, because of Theorem 2.3.2, is *optimal*. The price has been the doubling of the number of messages.

Property 2.3.2 *The ideal time complexity of depth-first traversal under* **R** *is* $\Theta(n)$.

Advanced Hacking   Let us see if the number of messages can be decreased without significantly increasing the time costs.

Question. Can we avoid sending the Ack messages?

To answer this question we must understand what would happen if we do *not* send Ack messages. Consider an entity x that sends Visited to its neighbors; (if we no longer use Ack) x will proceed immediately with forwarding the token. Assume that, after some time, the token arrives, for the first time, to a neighbor z of x (see Fig. 2.7); it is possible that the Visited message sent by x to z has not arrived yet (due to communication delays). In this case, z would not know that x has already been visited and would send the T message to it. That is, we will again send a T message on a back-edge undoing what we had accomplished with the previous change to the protocol.

But the algorithm now is rather different (we are using Visited messages, no longer Backedge messages) and this situation might not happen all the time.

Still, if it happens, z will eventually receive the Visited message from x (recall we are operating under total reliability); z can then understand its mistake, pretend nothing happened (just the waste of a T message), and continue like T message was never really sent. On its side, x upon receiving the token will also understand that z made a mistake and ignore the message; x also realizes (if it did not know already) that z is visited and will remove it from its list of unvisited neighbors.

Although the correctness will not be affected (Exercise 2.9.15), mistakes cost additional messages. Let us examine what is really the cost of this modified protocol, which we shall call DF++.

As before, the "correct" T and Return yield a total of $2n - 2$ messages, and the Visited messages are $2m - n + 1$ in total.

Then there are the "mistakes"; each mistake costs one message. The number of mistakes can be very large. In fact, unfriendly time delays can force mistakes to

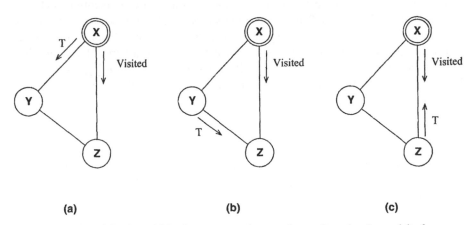

(a)   **(b)**   **(c)**

FIGURE 2.7: Slow *Visited* message : z does not know that x has been visited.

occur on *every* back-edge; on some back-edges, there can be two mistakes, one in each direction. (Exercise 2.9.16). In other words, there will be at most $2(m - n + 1)$ incorrect T messages. Summing up all, this yields

$$M[DF++] \leq 4m - n + 1. \tag{2.9}$$

Let us consider now the time. We have an improvement in that the Ack messages are no longer sent, saving n time units.

As there are no more Ack to wait for, an entity can forward the token at the same time as the transmission of the Visited messages; if it does not have any unvisited neighbor to send the T to, the entity will send the Return at the same time as the Visited. Hence, the sending of the Visited is done in overlap with the sending of either a T or a Return message, saving another n time units.

In other words, without considering the mistakes, the total time will be $2n - 2$. Let us now also consider the mistakes and evaluate the ideal time of the protocol.

Strange as it might sound, when we attempt to measure the ideal execution time of this protocol, in the execution *no mistakes will ever occur*. This is because mistakes can only occur owing to *arbitrarily long* communication delays; on the contrary, ideal time is only measured under *unitary* delays. But under unitary delays there are no mistakes. Therefore,

$$T[DF++] = 2n - 2. \tag{2.10}$$

IMPORTANT. It is crucial to understand this inherent limit of the cost measure we call *ideal time*. Unlike the number of messages, ideal time is not a "neutral" measure; it influences (thus limiting) the nature of what we want to measure. In other words, it should be treated and handled with caution. Even greater caution should be employed in interpreting the results it gives.

Extreme Hacking As we are on a roll, let us observe that we could actually use the T message as an implicit Visited, saving some additional messages.

This saving will happen at every entity except those that, when they are reached for the first time by a T message, do not have any unvisited neighbor. Let $f_\star$ denote the number of these nodes; thus the number of Visited messages we save is $n - f_\star$. Hence, the total number of messages is $4m - n + 1 - n + f_\star$.

Summarizing, the cost of the optimized protocol, called DF* and described in Figures 2.8 and 2.9, is as follows:

$$T[DF\star] = 2n - 2. \tag{2.11}$$

$$M[DF\star] = 4m - 2n + f_\star + 1. \tag{2.12}$$

PROTOCOL DF*

- Status: S = {INITIATOR,IDLE,AVAILABLE,VISITED,DONE};
  S_{INIT} = {INITIATOR,IDLE}; S_{TERM} = {DONE}.
- Restrictions: **R** ;UI.

INITIATOR

> *Spontaneously*
> **begin**
> > initiator:= true;
> > Unvisited:= $N(x)$;
> > next $\Leftarrow$ Unvisited;
> > **send**(T) **to** next;
> > **send**(Visited) **to** $N(x)$-{next};
> > **become** VISITED
> **end**

IDLE

> *Receiving*(T)
> **begin**
> > Unvisited:= $N(x)$;
> > FIRST-VISIT;
> **end**

> *Receiving*(*Visited*)
> **begin**
> > Unvisited:= $N(x)$ − {**sender**};
> > **become** AVAILABLE
> **end**

AVAILABLE

> *Receiving*(T)
> FIRST-VISIT;

> *Receiving*(Visited)
> **begin**
> > Unvisited:= *Unvisited* − {**sender**};
> **end**

VISITED

> *Receiving*(Visited)
> **begin**
> > Unvisited:= Unvisited −{**sender**};
> > **if** next = **sender then** VISIT; **endif**
> **end**

> *Receiving*(T)
> **begin**
> > Unvisited:= Unvisited −{**sender**};
> > **if** next = **sender then** VISIT; **endif**
> **end**

> *Receiving*(Return)
> **begin**
> > VISIT;
> **end**

FIGURE 2.8: Protocol DF*

```
Procedure FIRST-VISIT
begin
    initiator:= false;
    entry:=sender;
    Unvisited:= Unvisited-{sender};

    if Unvisited ≠ ∅ then
       next ⇐ Unvisited;
       send(T) to next;
       send(Visited) to N(x)−{entry,next};
       become VISITED;
    else
       send(Return) to {entry};
       send(Visited) to N(x)−{entry};
       become DONE;
    endif
end

Procedure VISIT
begin
    if Unvisited ≠ ∅ then
       next ⇐ Unvisited;
       send(T) to next;
    else
       if not(initiator) then send(Return) to entry; endif
       become DONE;
    endif
end
```

FIGURE 2.9: Routines used by Protocol DF*

IMPORTANT. The value of $f_\star$, unlike n and m, is *not* a system parameter. In fact, it is *execution-dependent.*: it may change at each execution value. We shall indicate this fact (for f as well as for any other execution-dependent value) by the use of the subscript $\star$.

2.3.3 Traversal in Special Networks

Trees In a tree network, depth-first traversal is particularly efficient in terms of messages, and there is no need of any optimization effort (hacking). In fact, in any execution of *DF_Traversal* in a tree, no Backedge messages will be sent (Exercise 2.9.12). Hence, the total number of messages will be exactly $2(n - 1)$. The time complexity is the same as the optimized version of the protocol: $2(n - 1)$.

$$\mathbf{M}[DF\_Traversal/Tree] = \mathbf{T}[DF\_Traversal/Tree] = 2n - 2 \qquad (2.13)$$

An interesting side effect of a depth-first traversal of a tree is that it constructs a *virtual ring* on the tree (Figure 2.10). In this ring some nodes appear more than once; in fact the ring has size $2n - 2$ (Exercise 2.9.13). This fact will have useful consequences.

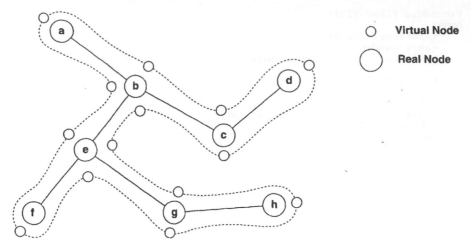

FIGURE 2.10: Virtual ring created by DF_Traversal.

Rings In a ring network, every node has exactly two neighbors. Depth-first traversal in a ring can be achieved in a simple way: the initiator chooses one direction and the token is just forwarded along that direction; once the token reaches the initiator, the traversal is completed. In other words, each entity will send and receive a single T message. Hence both the time and the message costs are exactly n. Clearly this protocol can be used only in rings.

Complete Graph In a complete graph, execution of DF* will require $O(n^2)$ messages. Exploiting the knowledge of being in a complete network, a better protocol can be derived: the initiator sequentially will send the token to all its neighbors (which are the other entities in the network); each of this entities will return the token to the initiator without forwarding it to anybody else. The total number of messages is $2(n-1)$, and so is the time.

2.3.4 Considerations on Traversal

Traversal as Access Permission The main use of a traversal protocol is in the control and management of shared resources. For example, access to a shared transmission medium (e.g., bus) must be controlled to avoid *collisions* (simultaneous frame transmission by two or more entities). A typical mechanism to achieve this is by the use of a *control* (or *permission*) *token*. This token is passed from one entity to another according to the same set of rules. An entity can only transmit a frame when it is in possession of the token; once the frame has been transmitted, the token is passed to another entity. A traversal protocol by definition "passes" the token sequentially through all the entities and thus solves the access control problem. The only proviso is that, for the access permission problem, it must be made *continuous*: once a traversal is terminated, another must be started by the initiator.

The access permission problem is part of a family of problems commonly called *Mutual Exclusion*, which will be discussed in details later in the book.

Traversal as Broadcast It is not difficult to see that *any traversal protocol solves the broadcast problem*: the initiator puts the information in the token message; every entity will be visited by the token and thus will receive the information. The converse is not necessarily true; for example, *Flooding* violates the *sequentiality* requirement since the message is sent to all (other) neighbors simultaneously.

The use of traversal to broadcast does not lead to a more efficient broadcasting protocol. In fact, a comparison of the costs of *Flooding* and DF* (Expressions 1.1 and 2.12) shows that *Flooding* is more efficient in terms of both messages and ideal time. This is not surprising since a traversal is constrained to be sequential; flooding, by contrast, exploits concurrency at its outmost.

2.4 PRACTICAL IMPLICATIONS: USE A SUBNET

We have considered three basic problems (*broadcast, wake-up*, and *depth-first traversal*) and studied their complexity, devised solution protocols and analyzed their efficiency. Let us see what the *theoretical* results we have obtained tell us about the situation from a *practical* point of view.

We have seen that generic protocols for broadcasting and *wake-up* require $\Omega(m)$ messages (Theorem 2.1.1). Indeed, in some special networks, we can sometimes develop topology-dependent solutions and obtain some improvements.

A similar situation exists for generic traversal protocols: They all require $\Omega(m)$ messages (Theorem 2.3.1); this cost cannot be reduced (in order of magnitude) unless we make additional restrictions, for example, exploiting some special properties of G of which we have a priori (i.e., at design time) knowledge.

In any connected, undirected graph G, we have

$$(n^2 - n)/2 \geq m \geq n - 1,$$

and, for every value in that range, there are networks with those many links; in particular, $m = (n^2 - n)/2$ occurs when G is the *complete* graph, and $m = n - 1$ when G is a *tree*.

Summarizing, the cost of broadcasting, wake-up, and traversal depends on the number of links: The more links the greater the cost; and it can be as bad as $O(n^2)$ messages per execution of any of the solution protocols.

This result is punitive for networks where a large investment has been made in the construction of communication links. As broadcast is a basic communication tool (in some systems, it is a primitive one) dense networks are penalized continuously. Similarly, larger operating costs will be incurred by dense networks every time a wake-up (a very common operation, used as preliminary step in most computations) or a traversal (fortunately, not such a common operation) is performed.

The theoretical results, in other words, indicate that *investments in communication hardware* will result in *higher operating communication costs*.

Obviously, this is not an acceptable situation, and it is necessary to employ some "lateral thinking."

The strategy to circumvent the obstacle posed by these lower-bounds (Theorems 2.1.1 and 2.3.1) without restricting the applicability of the protocol is fortunately simple:

1. construct a subnet G' of G and
2. perform the operations only on the subnet.

If the subnet G' we construct is *connected* and *spans* G (i. e., contains all nodes of G), then doing broadcast on G' will solve the broadcasting problem on G: Every node (entity) will receive the information. Similarly, performing a traversal on G' will solve that problem on G.

The important consequence is that, if G' is a proper subnet, it has fewer links than G; thus, the cost of performing those operations on G' will be lower than doing it in G.

Which connected spanning subnet of G should we construct?

If we want to minimize the message costs, we should choose the one with the fewest number of links; thus, the answer is: a *spanning tree* of G. So, the strategy for a general graph G will be

Strategy *Use-a-Tree*:

1. construct a spanning tree of G and
2. perform the operations only on this spanning tree.

This strategy has two costs. First, there is the cost of constructing the spanning tree; this task will have to be carried out only once (if no failures occur). Then there are the operating costs, that is the costs of performing broadcast, wake-up, and traversal on the tree. Broadcast will cost exactly $n - 1$ messages, and the cost of wake-up and traversal will be twice that amount. These costs are *independent* of m and thus do not inhibit investments in communication links (which might be useful for other reasons).

2.5 CONSTRUCTING A SPANNING TREE

Spanning-tree construction (**SPT**) is a classical problem in computer science. In a distributed computing environment, the solution of this problem has, as we have seen, strong practical motivations. It also has distinct formulation and requirements.

In a distributed computing environment, to construct a spanning tree of G means to move the system from an initial system configuration, where each entity is just aware of its own neigbors, to a system configuration where

1. each entity x has selected a subset Tree-neighbors$(x) \subseteq N(x)$ and
2. the collection of all the corresponding links forms a spanning tree of G.

What is wanted is a distributed algorithm (specifying what each node has to do when receiving a message in a given status) such that, once executed, it guarantees that a spanning tree $T(G)$ of G has been constructed; in the following we will indicate $T(G)$ simply by T, if no ambiguity arises.

Note that T is not known a priori to the entities and might not be known after it has been constructed: an entity needs to know only which of its neighbors are also its neighbors in the spanning tree T.

As before, we will restrict ourselves to connected networks with bidirectional links and further assume that no failure will occur.

We will first assume that the construction will be started by only one entity (i.e., Unique Initiator (UI) restriction); that is, we will consider spanning-tree construction under restrictions **RI**.

We will then consider the general problem when any number of entities can independently start the construction. As we will see, the situation changes dramatically from the single-initiator scenario.

2.5.1 SPT Construction with a Single Initiator: Shout

Consider the entities; they do not know G, not even its size. The only things an entity is aware of are the labels on the ports leading to its neighbors (because of the Local Orientation axiom) and the fact that, if it sends a message to a neighbor, the message will eventually be received (because of the Finite Communication Delays axiom and the Total Reliability restriction).

How, using just this information, can a spanning tree be constructed?

The answer is surprisingly simple. Each entity needs to know which of its neighbors are also neighbors in the spanning tree. The solution strategy is *just "ask:"*

Strategy *Ask-Your-Neighbors*:

1. The initiator s will "ask" its neighbors; that is, it will send a message $Q = ($ *"Are you my neighbor in the spanning tree"?* $)$ to all its neighbors.
2. An entity $x \neq s$ will reply *"Yes"* only the first time it is asked and, in this occasion, it will ask all its other neighbors; otherwise, it will reply *"No."* The initiator s will always reply *"No."*
3. Each entity terminates when it has received a reply from all neighbors to which it asked the question.

For an entity x, its neighbors in the spanning tree T are the neighbors that have replied *"Yes"* and, if $x \neq s$, also the neighbor from which the question was first asked.

The corresponding set of rules is depicted in Figure 2.11 where in bold are shown the tree links and in dotted lines the nontree links. The protocol *Shout* implementing this strategy is shown in Figure 2.12. Initially, all nodes are in status *idle* except the sole *initiator*.

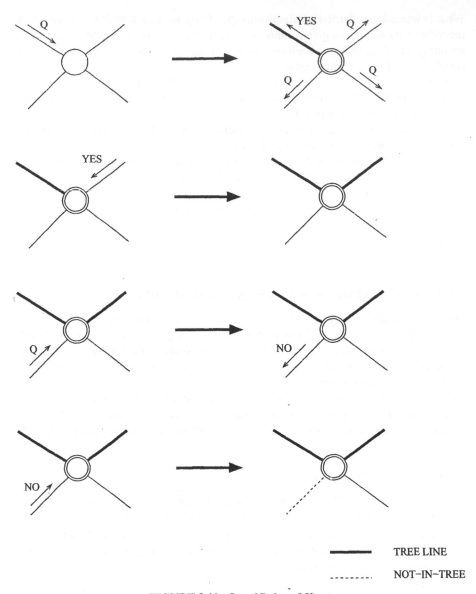

FIGURE 2.11: Set of Rules of Shout.

Before we discuss the correctness and the efficiency of the protocol, consider how it is structured and operates. First of all observe that, in *Shout* the question Q is broadcasted through the network (using flooding). Further observe that, when an entity receives Q, it always sends a reply (either *Yes* or *No*). Summarizing, the structure of this protocol is a flood where every information message is acknowledged. This type of structure will be called *Flood + Reply*.

PROTOCOL Shout

- Status: $S = \{\text{INITIATOR,IDLE,ACTIVE,DONE}\}$;
  $S_{INIT} = \{\text{INITIATOR,IDLE}\}$;
  $S_{TERM} = \{\text{DONE}\}$.
- Restrictions: **R** ;UI.

INITIATOR
        Spontaneously
        begin
            root:= **true**;
            Tree-neighbors:=$\emptyset$;
            send(Q) **to** $N(x)$;
            counter:=0;
            become ACTIVE;
        end

IDLE
        Receiving (Q)
        begin
            root:= **false**;
            parent:= **sender**;
            Tree-neighbors:={sender};
            send(Yes) **to** {sender};
            counter:=1;
            if counter=$|N(x)|$ **then**
               become DONE
            else
               send(Q) **to** $N(x) - $ {sender};
               become ACTIVE;
            endif
        end

ACTIVE
        Receiving (Q)
        begin
            send(No) **to** {sender};
        end

        Receiving (Yes)
        begin
            Tree-neighbors:=Tree-neighbors U{sender};
            counter:=counter+1;
            if counter=$|N(x)|$ **then become** DONE; **endif**
        end

        Receiving (No)
        begin
            counter:=counter+1;
            if counter=$|N(x)|$ **then become** DONE; **endif**
        end

FIGURE 2.12: Protocol Shout

Correctness   Let us now show that *Flood + Reply*, as used above, always constructs a spanning tree; that is, the graph defined by all the *Tree-neighbors* computed by the entities forms a spanning tree of G; furthermore, this tree is *rooted* in the initiator s.

Theorem 2.5.1 *Protocol Shout correctly terminates.*

Proof. This protocol consists of the flooding of Q, where every Q message is acknowledged. Because of the correctness of flooding, we are guaranteed that every entity will receive Q and by construction will reply (either *Yes* or *No*) to each Q it receives. Termination then follows.

To prove correctness we must show that the subnet G' defined by all the *Tree-neighbors* is a spanning tree of G. First observe that, if x is in *Tree-neighbors* of y, then y is in *Tree-neighbors* of x (see Exercise 2.9.18). If an entity x sends a *Yes* to y, then it is in *Tree-neighbors* of y; furthermore, it is connected to s by a path where a *Yes* is sent on each link (see Exercise 2.9.19). Since every $x \neq s$ sends exactly one *Yes*, the subnet G' defined by all the *Tree-neighbors* contains all the entities (i.e., it spans G), it is connected, and contains no cycles (see Exercise 2.9.20). Therefore, it is a spanning tree of G. ∎

Note that G' is actually a tree *rooted* in the initiator. Recall that, in a rooted tree , every node (except the root) has one *parent*: the neighbor closest to the root; all its other neighbors are called *children*. The neighbor to which x sends a *Yes* is its *parent*; all neighbors from which it receives a *Yes* are its *children*. This fact can be useful in subsequent operations.

IMPORTANT. The execution of protocol *Shout* ends with *local termination*: each entity knows when its own execution is over; this occurs when it enters status *done*. Notice however that no entity, including the initiator, is aware of *global termination* (i.e., every entity has locally terminated). This situation is fairly common in distributed computations. Should we need the initiator to know that the execution has terminated (e.g., to start another task), *Flood + Reply* can be easily modified to achieve this goal (Exercise 2.9.24).

Costs The message costs of *Flood+Reply*, and thus of *Shout*, are simple to analyze. As mentioned before, *Flood+Reply* consists of an execution of *Flooding(Q)* with the addition of a reply (either *Yes* or *No*) for every Q. In other words,

$$\mathbf{M}[Flood+Reply] = 2\,\mathbf{M}[Flooding].$$

The time costs of *Flood+Reply*, and thus of *Shout*, are also simple to determine; in fact (Exercise 2.9.21):

$$\mathbf{T}[Flood+Reply] = \mathbf{T}[Flooding]+1.$$

Thus

$$\mathbf{M}[Shout] = 4m - 2n + 2 \tag{2.14}$$

$$\mathbf{T}[Shout] = r(s_\star) + 1 \leq d + 1 \tag{2.15}$$

The efficiency of protocol Shout can be evaluated better taking into account the complexity of the problem it is solving.

Since every node must be involved, using an argument similar to the proof of Theorem 2.1.1, we have:

Theorem 2.5.2 $\mathcal{M}(\text{SPT}/\text{RI}) \geq m$.

Proof. Assume that there exists a correct SPT protocol A that, in each execution under **RI** on every G, uses fewer than $m(G)$ messages. This means that there is at least one link in G where no message is transmitted in any direction during an execution of the algorithm. Consider an execution of the algorithm on G, and let $e = (x, y) \in E$ be the link where no message is transmitted by A. Now construct a new graph G' from G by removing the edge e and adding a new node z and two new edges $e_1 = (x, z)$ and $e_2 = (y, z)$ (see Fig. 2.2). Set z in a noninitiator status. Run exactly the same execution of A on the new graph G': since no message was sent along (x,y), this is possible. But since no message was sent along (x,y) in the original execution in G, x and y never send a message to z in the current execution in G'; and since z is not the initiator and does not receive any message, it will not send any message. Within finite time, protocol A terminates claiming that a spanning-tree T of G' has been constructed; however, z is not part of T, and hence T does not span G'.   ∎

And similarly to the broadcast problem we have

Theorem 2.5.3 $\mathcal{T}(\text{SPT}/\text{RI}) \geq d$.

This implies that protocol *Shout* is both *time optimal* and *message optimal* with respect to order of magnitude. In other words,

Property 2.5.1 *The message complexity of spanning-tree construction under* **RI** *is* $\Theta(m)$.

Property 2.5.2 *The ideal time complexity of spanning-tree construction under* **RI** *is* $\Theta(d)$.

In the case of the number of messages some improvement might be possible in terms of the constant.

Hacking Let us examine protocol *Shout* to see if it can be improved, thereby, helping us to save some messages.

Question. Do we have to send *No* messages?

When constructing the spanning tree, an entity needs to know who its tree-neighbors are; by construction, they are the ones that reply *Yes* and, except for the initiator, also the ones that first asked the question. Thus, for this determination, the *No* messages are not needed.

On the contrary hand, the *No* messages are used by the protocol to terminate in finite time. Consider an entity x that just sent Q to neighbor y; it is now waiting for a reply. If the reply is *Yes*, it knows y is in the tree; if the reply is *No*, it knows y is not. Should we remove the sending of *No*–how can x determine that y would have sent *No*?

More clearly: Suppose x has been waiting for a reply from y for a (very) long time; it does not know if y has sent *Yes* and the delays are very long, or y would have sent *No* and thus will send nothing. Because the algorithm must terminate, x cannot wait forever and has to make a decision. How can x decide?

The question is relevant because communication delays are finite but unpredictable.

Fortunately, there is a simple answer to the question that can be derived by examining how protocol *Shout* operates.

Focus on a node x that just sent Q to its neighbor y. Why would y reply *No* ? It would do so only if it had already said *Yes* to somebody else; if that happened, y sent Q at the same time to all its other neighbors, including x. Summarizing, if y replies *No* to x, it must have already sent Q to x. We can clearly use this fact to our advantage: after x sent Q to y, if it receives *Yes* it knows that y is its neighbor in the tree; if it receives Q, it can deduce that y will definitely reply *No* to x's question. All of this can be deduced by x without having received the *No*.

In other words: a message Q that arrives at a node waiting for a reply can act as an *implicit negative acknowledgment*; therefore, we can avoid sending *No* messages.

Let us now analyze the message complexity of the resulting protocol *Shout+*. The time complexity is clearly unchanged; hence

$$\mathbf{T}[Shout]+ = r(s_\star) + 1 \leq d + 1. \tag{2.16}$$

On each link $(x, y) \in E$ there will be exactly a pair of messages: either Q in one direction and *Yes* in the other, or two Q messages, one in each direction. Thus

$$\mathbf{M}[Shout+] = 2m. \tag{2.17}$$

2.5.2 Other SPT Constructions with Single Initiator

SPT Construction by Traversal   It is well known that a depth-first traversal of a graph G actually constructs a spanning tree (*df-tree*) of that graph. The df-tree is obtained by removing the back-edges from G (i.e., the edges where a Back-edge message was sent in *DF_Traversal*). In other words, the tree-neighbors of an entity x will be those from which it receives a Return message and, if x is not the initiator, the one from which x received the first T.

Simple modifications to protocol DF* will ensure that each entity will correctly compute their neighbors in the df-tree and locally terminate in finite time (Exercise 2.9.25). Notice that these modifications involve just local bookkeeping and no additional communication. Hence the time and message costs are unchanged. The resulting protocol is denoted by $df - SPT$; then

$$\mathbf{M}[df - SPT] = 4m - 2n + f_* + 1. \tag{2.18}$$

$$\mathbf{T}[df - SPT] = 2n - 2. \tag{2.19}$$

We can now better characterize the variable f_*, which appears in the cost above. In fact, f_* is exactly the number of *leaves* of the df-tree constructed by $df - SPT$ (Exercise 2.9.26).

Expressions 2.18 and 2.19, when compared with the costs of protocol *Shout*, indicate that depth-first traversal is *not* an efficient tool for constructing a spanning tree; this is particularly true for its very high time costs.

Notice that, like in protocol *Shout*, all entities will become aware of their local termination, but only the initiator will be aware of *global termination*, that is, that the construction of the spanning tree has been completed (Exercise 2.9.27).

SPT Construction by Broadcasting   We have just seen how, with simple modifications, the techniques of flooding and of df-traversal can be used to construct a spanning tree, if there is a unique initiator. This fact is part of a very interesting and more general phenomenon: under **RI**,

> *the execution of any broadcast protocol constructs a spanning tree.*

Let us examine this statement in more details. Take any broadcast protocol B; by definition of broadcast, its execution will result in all entities receiving the information initially held by the initiator. For each entity x different from the initiator, call *parent* the neighbor from which x received the information for the first time; clearly, everybody except the initiator will have only one parent, and the initiator has none. Denote by $x \succ y$ the fact that x is the parent of y; then we have the following property whose proof is left as an exercise (Exercise 2.9.28):

Theorem 2.5.4 *The parent relationship* $\succ$ *defines a spanning tree rooted in the initiator.*

As a consequence, it would appear that, to solve **SPT**, we just need to execute a broadcast algorithm without any real modification, just adding some local variables (Tree-neighbors) and doing some local bookkeeping.

This is generally not the case; in fact, knowing its *parent* in the tree is not enough for an entity. To solve **SPT**, when an entity x terminates its execution, it must explicitly know which neighbors are its *children* as well as which neighbor are *not* its tree-neighbors.

If not provided already by the protocol, this information can obviously be acquired. For example, if every entity sends a notification message to its parent, the parents will know their children. To find out which neighbors are *not* children is more difficult and will depend on the original broadcast protocol.

In protocol *Shout* this is achieved by adding the "Yes" (I am your child) and "No" (I am not your child) messages to *Flooding*. In *DF_Traversal* protocol this is already achieved by the "Return" (I am your child) and the "Backedge" (I am not your child) messages; so, no additional communication is required.

This fact establishes a *computational* relationship between the broadcasting problem and the spanning-tree construction problem. If I know how to broadcast, then (with minor modifications) I know how to construct a spanning tree with a unique initiator. The converse is also trivially true: Every protocol that constructs a spanning tree solves the broadcasting problem. We shall say that these two problems are *computationally equivalent* and denote this fact by

$$\textbf{Bcast} \equiv \textbf{SPT(UI)}. \tag{2.20}$$

Since, as we have discussed in section 2.3.4, every traversal protocol performs a broadcast, it follows that, under **RI**, the execution of any traversal protocol constructs a spanning tree.

SPT Construction by Global Protocols   Actually, we can make a much stronger statement. Call a problem *global* if every entity must participate in its solution; participation implies the execution of a communication activity: transmission of a message and/or arrival of a message (even if it triggers only the Null action, i.e., no action is taken). Both broadcast and traversal are global problems. Now, every single-initiator protocol that solves a *global problem* **P** solves also **Bcast**; thus, from Equation 2.20, it follows that, under **RI**,

the execution of any solution to a global problem **P** *constructs a spanning tree.*

2.5.3   Considerations on the Constructed Tree

We have seen how, with few more messages than those required by *flooding* and the same messages as a *df-traversal*, we can actually construct a spanning tree.

As discussed previously, once such a tree is constructed, we can from now on perform broadcast and traversal using only $O(n)$ messages (which is optimal) instead of $O(m)$ (which could be as bad as $O(n^2)$).

IMPORTANT. Different techniques construct different spanning trees. It is even possible that the same protocol constructs different spanning trees when executed at different times.

This is for example the case of *Shout*: Because communication delays are unpredictable, subsequent executions of this algorithm on the same graph may result in different spanning trees. In fact (Exercise 2.9.23)

every possible spanning tree of G could be constructed by Shout.

Prior to its execution, it is impossible to predict which spanning tree will be constructed; the only guarantee is that *Shout* will construct *one*.

This has implications for the time costs of the strategy *Use-a-Tree* of broadcasting on the spanning tree T instead of the entire graph G. In fact, the broadcast time will be $d(T)$ instead of $d(G)$; but $d(T)$ could be much greater than $d(G)$.

For example, if G is the complete graph, the df-tree constructed by any depth-first traversal will have $d(T) = n - 1$; but $d(G) = 1$.

In general, the trees constructed by depth-first traversal have usually terrible diameters. The ones generated by *Shout* usually perform better, but there is no guarantee on the diameter of the resulting tree.

This fact poses the problem of constructing spanning trees that have a good diameter; that is, to find a spanning tree T' of G such that $d(T')$ is not *much more* than $d(G)$. For obvious reasons, such a tree is traditionally called a *broadcast tree*. To construct a broadcast tree we must first understand the relationship between *radius* and *diameter*. The *eccentricity* (or radius) of a node x in G is the longest of its *distances* to the other nodes:

$$r_G(x) = \text{Max}\{d_G(x, y) : y \in_V\}.$$

A node c with minimum radius (or eccentricity) is called a *center*; that is, $\forall x \in V$, $r_G(c) \leq r_G(x)$. There might be more than one center; they all, however, have the same eccentricity, denoted by $r(G)$ and are called the *radius of G*:

$$r(G) = \text{Min}\{r_G(x) : x \in V\}.$$

There is a strong relationship between the radius and the diameter of a graph; in fact, in every graph G,

$$r(G) \leq d(G) \leq 2r(G). \tag{2.21}$$

The other ingredient we need is a *breadth-first spanning tree (bf-tree)*. A breadth-first spanning tree of G rooted in a node u, denoted by BFT(u, G), has the following property: The distance between a node v and the root in the tree is the same as their distance in the original graph G.

The strategy to construct a broadcast tree with diameter $d(T') \leq 2d(G)$ is then simple to state:

Strategy *Broadcast-Tree Construction*:

1. determine a *center* c of G;
2. construct a breadth-first spanning tree BFT(c, G) rooted in c.

This strategy will construct the desired broadcast tree (Exercise 2.9.29):

Theorem 2.5.5 BFT(c, G) *is a broadcast tree of G.*

To be implemented, this strategy requires that we solve two problems: Center Finding and Breadth-First Spanning-Tree Construction. These problems, as we will see, are *not* simple to solve efficiently; we will examine them in later chapters.

2.5.4 Application: Better Traversal

In Section 2.4, we have discussed the general strategy *Use-a-Tree* for problem solving. Now that we know how to construct a spanning tree (using a single initiator), let us apply the strategy to a known problem.

Consider again the traversal problem. Using the *Use-a-Tree* strategy, we can produce an efficient traversal protocol that is much simpler than all the algorithms we have considered before:

Protocol *Smart Traversal*:

1. Construct, using *Shout+*, a spanning-tree T rooted in the initiator.
2. Perform a traversal of T, using *DF_Traversal*.

The number of messages of *SmartTraversal* is easy to compute: *Shout+* uses $2m$ messages (Equation 2.17), while *DF_Traversal* on a tree uses exactly $2(n-1)$ messages (Equation 2.13). In other words,

$$\mathbf{M}[SmartTraversal] = 2(m + n - 1). \tag{2.22}$$

The problem with *DF_Traversal* was its time complexity: It was to reduce time in which we developed more complex protocols. How about the time costs of this simple new protocol? The ideal time of *Shout+* is exactly $d + 1$. The ideal time of *DF_Traversal* in a tree is $2(n-1)$. Hence the total is

$$\mathbf{T}[SmartTraversal] \leq 2n + d - 1. \tag{2.23}$$

In other words, *SmartTraversal* not only is simple but also has optimal time and message complexity.

2.5.5 Spanning-Tree Construction with Multiple Initiators

We have started examining the *spanning-tree construction* problem in Section 2.5 assuming that there is a unique initiator. This is unfortunately a very strong (and "unnatural") assumption to make, as well as difficult and expensive to guarantee.

What happens to the single-initiator protocols *Shout* and *df-SPT* if there is more than one initiator?

Let us examine first protocol *Shout*. Consider the very simple case (depicted in Fig. 2.13) of three entities, x, y, and z, connected to each other. Let both x and y be initiators and start the protocol, and let the Q message from x to z arrive there before the one sent by y.

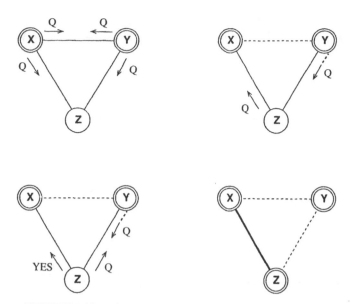

FIGURE 2.13: With multiple initiators, *Shout* creates a forest.

In this case, neither the link (x,y) nor the link (y,z) will be included in the tree; hence, the algorithm creates not a spanning tree but a *spanning forest*, which is not connected.

Consider now protocol *df-SPT*, discussed in Section 2.5.2. Let us examine its execution in the simple network depicted in Figure 2.14 composed of a chain of four nodes x, y, z, and w. Let y and z be both initiators, and start the traversal by sending the T message to x and w, respectively.

Also in this case, the algorithm will create a disconnected *spanning forest* of the graph. It is easy to verify that the same situation will occur also with the optimized versions (DF+ and DF*) of the protocol (Exercise 2.9.30).

The failure of these algorithms is not surprising, as they were developed specifically for the restricted environment of a Unique Initiator.

Removing the restriction brings out the true nature of the problem, which, as we will now see, has a formidable obstacle.

2.5.6 Impossibility Result

Our goal is to design a spanning-tree protocol, which works solely under the standard assumptions and thus is independent of the number of initiators. Unfortunately, any design effort to this end is destined to *fail*. In fact

Theorem 2.5.6 *The* **SPT** *problem is deterministically* unsolvable *under* **R**.

Deterministically unsolvable means that there is *no deterministic protocol that always correctly terminates within finite time.*

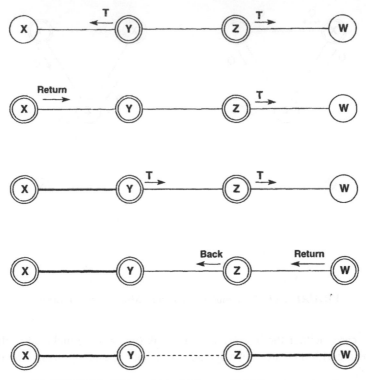

FIGURE 2.14: With multiple initiators, *df-SPT* creates a forest.

Proof. To see why this is the case, consider the simple system composed of three entities x, y, and z connected by links labeled as shown in Figure 2.15. Let the three entities have identical initial values (the symbols x, y, z are used only for description purposes). If a solution protocol A exists, it must work under any conditions of message delays (as long as they are finite) and regardless of the number of initiators. Consider a *synchronous schedule* (i.e., an execution where communication delays are unitary) and let *all* three entities start the execution of A simultaneously. Since they are in identical states (same initial status and values, same port labels), they will execute the

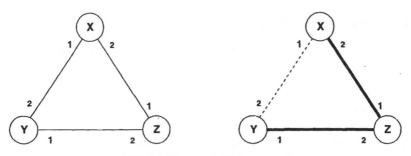

FIGURE 2.15: Proof of Theorem 2.5.6.

same rule, obtain the same results (thus, continuing to have the same local values), compose and send (if any) the same messages, and enter the same (possibly new) status. In other words, by Property 1.6.2, they will remain in identical states. In the next time unit, all sent messages (if any) will arrive and be processed. If one entity receives a message, the others will receive the same message at the same time, perform the same local computation, compose and send (if any) the same messages, and enter the same (possibly new) status. And so on. In other words, the entities will continue to be in identical states.

If A is a solution protocol, it must terminate within finite time. A spanning tree of our simple system is obtained by removing one of the three links, let us say (x,y). In this case, Tree-neigbors will be the port label 2 for entity x and the port label 1 for entity y; instead, z has in Tree-neighbors both port numbers. In other words, when they all terminate, they have *distinct* values for their local variable Tree-neighbors. But this is impossible, since we just said that the states of the entities are always identical.

Thus, no such a solution algorithm A exists.   ∎

A consequence of this very negative result is that, to construct a spanning tree without constraints on the number of initiators, we need to impose additional restrictions. To determine the "minimal" restrictions that, added to **R**, will enable us to solve **SPT** is an interesting research problem still open. The restriction that is commonly used is a very powerful one, Initial Distinct Values, and we will discuss it next.

2.5.7 SPT with Initial Distinct Values

The impossibility result we just witnessed implies that, to solve the SPT problem, we need an additional restriction. The one commonly used is *Initial Distinct Values* (ID): *Each entity has a distinct initial value*. Distinct initial values are sometimes called *identifiers* or *ids* or *global names*.

We will now examine some ways in which **SPT** can be solved under **IR = R** ∪ {ID}.

Multiple Spanning Trees   As in most software design situations, once we have a solution for a problem and are faced with a more general one, one approach is to try to find ways to re-use and re-apply the already existing solution. The solutions we already have are unique-initiator ones and, as we know, they fail in presence of multiple initiators. Let us see how can we mend their shortcomings using distinct values.

Consider the execution of *Shout* in the example of Figure 2.13. In this case, the reason why the protocol fails is because the entities do not realize that there are two different requests (e.g., when x receives Q from y) for spanning-tree construction.

But we can now use the entities' ids to *distinguish* between requests originating from different initiators.

The simplest and most immediate application of this approach is to have each initiator construct "its own" spanning tree with a single-initiator protocol and to use the ids of the initiators to distinguish among different constructions. So, instead of cooperating to construct a single spanning tree, we will have several spanning trees concurrently and independently built.

This implies that all the protocol messages (e.g., Q and Yes in $Shout+$) must contain also the id of the initiator. It also requires additional variables and bookkeeping; for example, at each entity, there will be several instances of the variable tree-neighbors, one for each spanning tree being constructed (i.e., one for each initiator). Furthermore, each entity will be in possibly different status values for each of these independent SPT-constructions. Recall that the number k_* of initiators is not known a priori and can change at every execution.

The message cost of this approach depends solely on the number of initiators and on the type of unique-initiator protocol used. But it is in any case very expensive. In fact, if we employ the most efficient SPT-construction protocol we know, $Shout+$, we will use $2mk_*$ messages, which could be as bad as $O(n^3)$.

Selective Construction   The large message cost derives from the fact that we construct not one but k_* spanning trees. Since our goal is just to construct one, there is clearly a needless amount of communication and computation being performed.

A better approach consists of letting every initiator start the construction of its own uniquely identified spanning tree (as before), but then suppressing some of these constructions, allowing only one to complete. In this approach, an entity faced with two different SPT-constructions will select and act on only one, "killing" the other; the entity continues this selection process as long as it receives conflicting requests.

The criterion an entity uses to decide which SPT-construction to follow and which one to terminate must be chosen very carefully. In fact, the danger is to "kill" all constructions.

The criterion commonly used is based on *min-id*: Since each SPT-construction has a unique id (that of its initiator), when faced with different SPT-constructions, an entity will choose the one with the *smallest* id and terminate all the others. (An alternative criterion would be the one based on *max-id*.)

The solution obtained with this approach has some very clear advantages over the previous solution. First of all, each entity is at any time involved only in one SPT-construction; this fact greatly simplifies the internal organization of the protocol (i.e., the set of rules), as well as the local storage and bookkeeping of each entity. Second, upon termination, all entities have a single shared spanning tree for subsequent uses.

However, there is still competitive concurrency: An entity involved in one SPT-construction might receive messages from another construction; in our approach, it will make a choice between the two constructions. If the entity chooses the new one, it will give up all the knowledge (variables, etc) acquired so far and start from scratch. The message cost of this approach depends again on the number of initiators and on the unique-initiator protocol used.

Consider a protocol developed using this approach, using $Shout+$ as the basic tool.

Informally, an entity u, at any time, participates in the construction of just one spanning tree rooted in some initiator, x. It will ignore all messages referring to the construction of other spanning trees where the initiators have larger ids than x. If instead u receives a message referring to the construction of a spanning tree rooted in an initiator y with an id smaller than x's, then u will stop working for x and start working for y. As we will see, these techniques will construct a spanning tree rooted in the initiator with the smallest initial value.

IMPORTANT. It is possible that an entity has already terminated its part of the construction of a spanning tree when it receives a message from another initiator (possibly, with a smaller id).

In other words, when an entity has terminated a construction, it does not know whether it might have to restart again. Thus, it is *necessary* to include in the protocol a mechanism that ensures an effective local termination for each entity.

This can be achieved by ensuring that we use, as a building block, a unique-initiator SPT-protocol in which the initiator will know when the spanning tree has been completely constructed (see Exercise 2.9.24). In this way, when the spanning tree rooted in the initiator s with the smallest initial value has been constructed, s will become aware of this fact (as well as that all other constructions, if any, have been "killed"). It can then notify all other entities so that they can enter a terminal status. The notification is just a broadcast; it is appropriate to perform it on the newly constructed spanning-tree (so we start taking advantage of its existence).

Protocol *MultiShout*, depicted in Figures 2.16 and 2.17, uses *Shout+* appropriately modified so to ensure that the root of a constructed tree becomes aware of termination and includes a final broadcast (on the spanning tree) to notify all entities that the task has been indeed completed. We denote by $v(x)$ the id of x; initially all entities are *idle* and any of them can spontaneously start the algorithm.

Theorem 2.5.7 *Protocol* MultiShout *constructs a spanning tree rooted in the initiator with the smallest initial value.*

Proof. Let s be the initiator with the smallest initial value. Focus on an initiator $x \neq s$; its initial execution of the protocol will start the construction of a spanning tree T_x rooted in x. We will first show that the construction of T_x will *not* be completed. To see this, observe that T_x must include every node, including s; but when s receives a message relating to the construction of somebody's else tree (such as T_x), it will ignore it, killing the construction of that tree. Let us now show that T_s will instead be constructed. Since the id of s is smaller than all other ids, *no* entity will ignore the messages related to the construction of T_s started by s; thus, the construction will be completed. ∎

Let us now consider the message costs of protocol *MultiShout*. It is clearly more efficient than protocols obtained with the previous approach. However, in the worst case, it is not much better in order of magnitude. In fact, it can be as bad as $O(n^3)$.

Consider for example the graph, shown in Figure 2.18, where $n - k$ of the nodes are fully connected among themselves (the subgraph K_{n-k}), and each of the other

PROTOCOL MultiShout

- Status: S = {IDLE, ACTIVE, DONE}; S_{INIT} = {IDLE}; S_{TERM} = {DONE}.
- Restrictions: **R** ;ID.

```
IDLE
    Spontaneously
    begin
            root:= true;
            root_id:=v(x);
            Tree_neighbors:=∅;
            send (Q,root_id) to N(x);
            counter:=0;
            check_counter:=0;
            become ACTIVE;
    end

    Receiving (Q, id)
    begin
            CONSTRUCT;
    end

ACTIVE
    Receiving (Q, id)
    begin
            if root_id = id then
                counter:=counter+1;
                if counter=|N(x)| then done:= true; CHECK; endif
            else
                if root_id > id then CONSTRUCT;
            endif
    end

    Receiving (Yes, id)
    begin
            if root_id = id then
                Tree-neighbors:=Tree-neighbors ∪{sender};
                counter:=counter+1;
                if counter=|N(x)| then done:= true; CHECK; endif
            endif
    end

    Receiving (Check, id)
    begin
            if root_id = id then
                check_counter:=check_counter+1;
                if (done ∧ check_counter=|Children|) then TERM; endif
            endif
    end

    Receiving (Terminate)
    begin
            send(Terminate) to Children;
            become DONE;
    end
```

FIGURE 2.16: Protocol MultiShout

```
Procedure CONSTRUCT
begin
      root:= false;
      root_id:= id;
      Tree_neighbors:={sender};
      parent:= sender;
      send(Yes,root_id) to {sender};
      counter:=1;
      check_counter:=0;
      if counter=|N(x)| then
        done:= true;
        CHECK;
      else
        send(Q,root-id) to N(x) - {sender};
      endif
      become ACTIVE;
end



Procedure CHECK
begin
      Children:= Tree_neighbors-{parent};
      if Children = ∅ then
        send(Check,root_id) to parent;
      endif
end



Procedure TERM
begin
      if root then
        send(Terminate) to Tree-neighbors;
        become DONE;
      else
        send(Check,root-id) to parent;
      endif
end
```

FIGURE 2.17: Routines of MultiShout

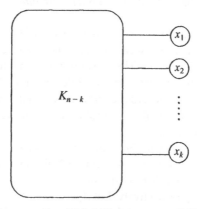

FIGURE 2.18: The execution of MultiShout can cost $O(k(n - k)^2)$ messages.

k (nodes $x_1, x_2, \ldots, x_k$) is connected only to a node in K_{n-k}. Suppose that these k "external" nodes are the initiators and that $v(x_1) > v(x_2) > \cdots > v(x_k)$,

Consider now an execution where the Q messages from the external entities arrive to K_{n-k} in order, according to the indices (i.e., the one from x_1 arrives first).

When the Q message from x_1 arrives to K_{n-k} it will trigger the SPT-construction there. Notice that the *Shout+* component of our protocol with a unique initiator will use $O((n-k)^2)$ messages inside the subgraph K_{n-k}. Assume that the entire computation inside K_{n-k} triggered by x_1 is practically completed (costing $O((n-k)^2)$ messages) by the time the Q message from x_2 arrives to K_{n-k}. Since $v(x_1) > v(x_2)$, all the work done in K_{n-k} has been wasted and every entity there must start the construction of the spanning tree rooted in x_2.

In the same way, assume that the time delays are such that the Q message from x_i arrives to K_{n-k} only when the computation inside K_{n-k} triggered by x_{i-1} is practically completed (costing $O((n-k)^2)$ messages).

Then, in this case (which is possible), work costing $O((n-k)^2)$ messages will be repeated k times, for a total of $O(k(n-k)^2)$ messages. If k is a linear fraction of n (e.g., $k = n/2$), then the cost will be $O(n^3)$.

The fact that this solution is not very efficient does not imply that the approach of *selective construction* it uses is not effective. On the contrary, it can be made efficient at the expenses of simplicity. We will examine it in great details later in the book when studying the *leader election* problem.

2.6 COMPUTATIONS IN TREES

In this section, we consider computations in *tree* networks under the standard restrictions **R** plus clearly the common knowledge that the network is tree.

Note that the knowledge of being in a tree implies that each entity can determine whether it is a *leaf* (i.e., it has only one neighbor) or an *internal node* (i.e., it has more than one neighbor).

We have already seen how to solve the Broadcast, the Wake-Up, and the Traversal problems in a tree network. The first two are optimally solved by protocol *Flooding*, the latter by protocol *DF_Traversal*. These techniques constitute the first set of algorithmic tools for computing in trees with multiple initiators. We will now introduce another very basic and useful technique, *saturation*, and show how it can be employed to efficiently solve many different problems in trees regardless of the number of initiators and of their location.

Before doing so, we need to introduce some basic concepts and terminology about trees. In a tree T, the removal of a link (x,y) will disconnect T into two trees, one containing x (but not y), the other containing y (but not x); we shall denote them by $T[x - y]$ and $T[y - x]$, respectively. Let $d[x, y] = \text{Max}\{d(x, z) : z \in T[y - x]\}$ be the longest distance between x and the nodes in $T[y - x]$. Recall that the longest distance between any two nodes is called *diameter*, and it is denoted by d. If $d[x, y] = d$, the path between x and y is said to be *diametral*.

2.6.1   Saturation: A Basic Technique

The technique, which we shall call *Full Saturation*, is very simple and can be autonomously and independently started by *any* number of initiators.

It is composed of three stages:

1. the *activation* stage, started by the initiators, in which all nodes are activated;
2. the *saturation* stage, started by the leaf nodes, in which a unique couple of neighboring nodes is selected; and
3. the *resolution* stage, started by the selected pair.

The *activation* stage is just a wake-up: each initiator sends an activation (i.e., wake-up) message to all its neighbors and becomes *active*; any noninitiator, upon receiving the activation message from a neighbor, sends it to all its other neighbors and becomes *active*; *active* nodes ignore all received activation messages. Within finite time, all nodes become *active*, including the leaves. The leaves will start the second stage.

Each active leaf starts the *saturation* stage by sending a message (call it M) to its only neighbor, referred now as its "parent," and becomes *processing*. (Note: M messages will start arriving within finite time to the internal nodes.) An internal node waits until it has received an M message from all its neighbors *but one*, sends a M message to that neighbor that will now be considered its "parent," and becomes *processing*. If a *processing* node receives a message from its parent, it becomes *saturated*.

The *resolution* stage is started by the *saturated* nodes; the nature of this stage depends on the application. Commonly, this stage is used as a *notification* for all entities (e.g., to achieve local termination).

Since the nature of the final stage will depend on the application, we will only describe the set of rules implementing the first two stages of Full Saturation.

IMPORTANT. A "truncated" protocol like this will be called a **"plug-in"**. In its execution, not all entities will enter a terminal status. To transform it into a full protocol, some other action (e.g., the resolution stage) must be performed so that eventually all entities enter a terminal status.

It is assumed that initially all entities are in the same status *available*.

Let us now discuss some properties of this basic technique.

Lemma 2.6.1 *Exactly two* processing *nodes will become* saturated; *furthermore, these two nodes are neighbors and are each other's parent.*

Proof. From the algorithm, it follows that an entity sends a message M only to its parent and becomes *saturated* only upon receiving an M message from its parent. Choose an arbitrary node x, and traverse the "up" edge of x (i.e., the edge along which the M message was sent from x to its parent). By moving along "up" edges, we must meet a *saturated* node s_1 since there are no cycles in the graph. This node has become *saturated* when receiving an M message from its parent s_2. Since s_2

PLUG-IN Full Saturation .

- Status: $S = \{$AVAILABLE, ACTIVE, PROCESSING, SATURATED$\}$;
  $S_{INIT} = \{$AVAILABLE$\}$;
- Restrictions: $R \cup T$.

AVAILABLE
     Spontaneously
     begin
          send (*Activate*) **to** $N(x)$;
          Initialize;
          Neighbors:= $N(x)$;
          if |Neighbors| =1 **then**
           Prepare_Message;
           parent $\Leftarrow$ Neighbors;
           send (M) **to** parent;
           become PROCESSING;
          else become ACTIVE;
          endif
     end

     Receiving (Activate)
     begin
          send (Activate) **to** $N(x) - \{$sender$\}$;
          Initialize;
          Neighbors:= $N(x)$;
          if |Neighbors| =1 **then**
           Prepare_Message;
           parent $\Leftarrow$ Neighbors;
           send (M) **to** parent;
           become PROCESSING;
          else become ACTIVE;
          endif
     end

ACTIVE
     Receiving(M)
     begin
          Process_Message;
          Neighbors:= Neighbors-$\{$sender$\}$;
          if |Neighbors| =1 **then**
           Prepare_Message;
           parent $\Leftarrow$ Neighbors;
           send (M) **to** parent;
           become PROCESSING;
          endif
     end

PROCESSING
     Receiving(M)
     begin
          Process_Message;
          Resolve;
     end

FIGURE 2.19: Full Saturation

```
Procedure Initialize
begin
    nil;
end

Procedure Prepare_Message
begin
    M:=("Saturation");
end

Procedure Process_Message
begin
    nil;
end

Procedure Resolve
begin
    become SATURATED;
    Start Resolution stage;
end
```

FIGURE 2.20: Procedures used by Full Saturation

has sent an M message to s_1, this implies that s_2 must have been *processing* and must have considered s_1 its parent; thus, when the M message from s_1 will arrive at s_2, s_2 will become *saturated* also. Thus, there exist at least two nodes that become *saturated*; furthermore, these two nodes are each other's parent. Assume that there are more than two *saturated* nodes; then there exist two *saturated* nodes, x and y, such that $d(x, y) \geq 2$. Consider a node z on the path from x to y; z could not send am M message toward both x and y; therefore, one of the nodes cannot be *saturated*. Therefore, the lemma holds.   ■

IMPORTANT. It depends on the communication delays which entities will become saturated and it is therefore totally unpredictable. Subsequent executions with the same initiators might generate different results. In fact

any pair of neighbors could become saturated.

The only guarantee is that *a* pair of neighbors will be selected; since a pair of neighbors uniquely identifies an edge, the one connecting them; this result is also called *edge election*.

To determine the number of message exchanges, observe that the activation stage is a wake-up in a tree and hence it will use $n + k_\star - 2$ messages (Equation 2.5), where $k_\star$ denotes the number of initiators. During the saturation stage, exactly one message is transmitted on each edge, except the edge connecting the two *saturated* nodes on which two M messages are transmitted, for a total of $n - 1 + 1 = n$ messages. Thus,

$$\mathbf{M}[\textit{Full Saturation}] = 2n + k_\star - 2. \tag{2.24}$$

Notice that only n of those messages are due to the saturation stage.

To determine the ideal time complexity, let $I \subseteq V$ denote the set of initiator nodes, $L \subseteq V$ denote the set of leaf nodes; $t(x)$ the time delay, from the initiation of the algorithm, until node x becomes *active*. To become *saturated*, node s must have waited until all the leafs have become *active* and the M messages originated from them have reached s; that is, it must have waited $\text{Max}\{t(l) + d(l, s) : l \in L\}$. To become *active*, a noninitiator node x must have waited for an "Activation" message to reach it, while there is no additional waiting time for an initiator node; thus, $t(x) = \text{Min}\{d(x, y) + t(y) : y \in I\}$. Therefore, the total delay, from the initiation of the algorithm, until s becomes *saturated* (and, thus, the ideal execution delay of the algorithm) is

$$\mathbf{T}[\textit{Full Saturation}] = \text{Max}\{\text{Min}\{d(l, y) + t(y)\} + d(l, y) : y \in I, l \in L\}. \quad (2.25)$$

We will now discuss how to apply the saturation technique to solve different problems.

2.6.2 Minimum Finding

Let us see how the saturation technique can be used to compute the smallest among a set of values distributed among the nodes of the network. Every entity x has an input value $v(x)$ and is initially in the same status; the task is to determine the minimum among those input values. That is, in the end, each entity must know whether or not its value is the smallest and enter the appropriate status, *minimum* or *large*, respectively.

IMPORTANT. Notice that these values are *not* necessarily distinct. So, more than one entity can have the minimum value; all of them must become *minimum*. This problem is called *Minimum Finding* (**MinFind**) and is the simplest among the class of *Distributed Query Processing* problems that we will examine in later chapters: a set of data (e.g., a file) is distributed among the sites of a communication network; *queries* (i.e., external requests for information about the set) can arrive at any time at any site (which becomes an initiator of the processing), triggering computation and communication activities. A stronger version of this problem requires all entities to *know* the minimum value when they enter the final status.

Let us see how to solve this problem in a tree network. If the tree was *rooted*, then this task can be trivially performed. In fact, in a rooted tree not only is there a special node, the root, but also a logical orientation of the links: "up" toward the root and "down" away from the root; this corresponds to the "parent" and "children" relationship, respectively. In a rooted tree, to find the minimum, the root would broadcast down the request to compute the minimum value; exploiting the orientation of the links, the entities will then perform a *convergecast* (described in more details in Section 2.6.7): starting from the leaves, the nodes determine the smallest value among the values "down" and send it "up." As a result of this process, the minimum value is then determined at the root, which will then broadcast it to all nodes.

```
PROCESSING
            Receiving (Notification)
            begin
                send (Notification) to N(x)−parent;
                if   v(x) =Received_Value then
                     become MINIMUM;
                else
                        become LARGE;
                endif
            end


Procedure  Initialize
begin
     min:=v(x);
end


Procedure  Prepare_Message
begin
     M:=("Saturation", min);
end


Procedure  Process_Message
begin
     min:= MIN{min, Received_Value};
end


Procedure  Resolve
begin
     Notification:= ("Resolution", min);
     send (Notification) to N(x)−parent;
     if   v(x) =min then
          become MINIMUM;
     else
             become LARGE;
     endif
end
```

FIGURE 2.21: New Rule and Procedures used for Minimum Finding

Notice that convergecast can be used only in rooted trees. The existence of a root (and the additional information existing in a rooted tree) is, however, a very strong assumption; in fact, it is equivalent to assuming the existence of a *leader* (which, as we will see, might not be computable).

Full Saturation allows to achieve the same goals *without* a root or any additional information. This is achieved simply by including in the M message the smallest value known to the sender. Namely, in the saturation stage the leaves will send their value with the M message, and each internal node sends the smallest among its own value and all the received ones. In other words, *MinF-Tree* is just protocol *Full Saturation* where the procedures Initialize, Prepare_Message, and Process_Message are as shown in Figure 2.21 and where the *resolution* stage is just a notification started by the two saturated nodes, of the minimum value they have computed. This is obtained by simply modifying procedure *Resolve* accordingly and adding the rule for handling the reception of the notification.

The correctness follows from the fact that both saturated nodes know the minimum value (Exercise 2.9.31).

The number of message transmission for the minimum-finding algorithm *MinF-Tree* will be exactly the same as the one experienced by *Full Saturation* plus the ones performed during the notification. Since a notification message is sent on every link *except* the one connecting the two *saturated* nodes, there will be exactly $n - 2$ such messages. Hence

$$\mathbf{M}[MinF - Tree] = 3n + k_* - 4. \tag{2.26}$$

The time costs will be the one experienced by Full Saturation plus the ones required by the notification. Let *Sat* denote the set of the two saturated nodes; then

$$\mathbf{T}[MinF - Tree] = \mathbf{T}[Full\ Saturation] + \text{Max}\{d(s, x) : s \in Sat, x \in V\}. \tag{2.27}$$

2.6.3 Distributed Function Evaluation

An important class of problems are those of *Distributed Function Evaluation*; that is, where the task is to compute a function whose arguments are distributed among the processors of a distributed memory system (e.g., the sites of a network). An instance of this problem is the the one we just solved: Minimum Finding. We will now discuss how the saturation technique can be used to evaluate a large class of functions.

Semigroup Operations   Let f be an *associative* and *commutative* function defined over all subsets of the input values. Examples of this type of functions are: minimum, maximum, sum, product, and so forth, as well as logical predicates. Because of their algebraic properties, these functions are called *semigroup operations*.

IMPORTANT. It is possible that some entities do not have an argument (i.e., initial value) or that the function must only be evaluated on a subset of the arguments. We shall denote the fact that x does not have an argument by $v(x) = \text{nil}$.

The same approach that has led us to solve Minimum Finding can be used to evaluate f.

The protocol *Function Tree* is just protocol *Full Saturation* where the procedures Initialize, Prepare_Message, and Process_Message are as shown in Figure 2.22 and where the *resolution* stage is just a notification started by the two saturated nodes, of the final result of the function they have computed. This is obtained by simply modifying procedure *Resolve* accordingly and adding the rule for handling the reception of the notification.

The correctness follows from the fact that both saturated nodes know the result of the function (Exercise 2.9.32). For particular types of functions, see Exercises 2.9.33, 2.9.34, and 2.9.35.

```
PROCESSING
            Receiving (Notification)
            begin
                result:= received_value;
                send(Notification) to N(x)—parent;
                become DONE;
            end
```

```
Procedure Initialize
begin
    if v(x) ≠ nil then
    result:=f(v(x));
    else
    result:=nil;
end
```

```
Procedure Prepare_Message
begin
    M:=("Saturation", result);
end
```

```
Procedure Process_Message
begin
    if  received_value ≠ nil then
        if      result ≠ nil then
            result:= f(result, received_value);
        else
            result:= f(received_value);
        endif
    endif
end
```

```
Procedure Resolve
begin
    Notification:= ("Resolution", result);
    send(Notification) to N(x)—parent;
    become DONE;
end
```

FIGURE 2.22: New Rule and Procedures used for Function Tree

The time and message costs of the protocol are exactly the same as the one for Minimum Finding. Thus, semigroup operations can be performed *optimally* on a tree with any number of initiators and without a root or additional information.

Cardinal Statistics   A useful class of functions are *statistical* ones, such as *average*, *standard deviation*, and so for. These functions are not semigroup operation but can nevertheless be optimally solved using the saturation technique.

We will just examine, as an example, the computation of *Ave*, the average of the (relevant) entities' values. Observe that *Ave* ≡ *Sum* / *Size* where *Sum* is the the the sum of all (relevant) values, and *Size* is the number of those values. Since *Sum* is a semigroup operation, we already know how to compute it. Also *Size* is trivially computed using saturation (Exercises 2.9.36 and 2.9.37).

We can collect at the two saturated nodes *Sum* and *Size* with a single execution of Saturation: the *M* message will contain two data fields *M*=("Saturation," sum,size), which are initialized by each leaf node and *updated* by the internal ones. The *resolution* stage is just a notification started by the two saturated nodes, of the average they can have computed.

Similarly, a single execution of *Full Saturation* with a final notification of the result will allow the entities to compute *cardinal* statistics on the input values.

Notice that *ordinal* statistics (e.g., median) are in general more difficult to resolve. We will discuss them in the chapter on selection and sorting of distributed data.

2.6.4 Finding Eccentricities

The basic technique has been so far used to solve single-valued problems; that is, problems whose solution requires the identification of a single value. It can also be used to solve multi-valued problems such as the problem of determining the eccentricities of all the nodes.

```
PROCESSING
            Receiving (Notification)
            begin
                result:= received_value;
                send(Notification) to N(x)−parent;
                become DONE;
            end


Procedure Initialize
begin
    sum:=v(x);
    size:=1;
end


Procedure Prepare_Message
begin
    M:=("Saturation", sum,size);
end


Procedure Process_Message
begin
    sum:= sum + Received_sum;
    size:=size + Received_size;
end


Procedure Resolve
begin
    result := sum / size;
    Notification:= ("Resolution", result);
    send(Notification) to N(x)−parent;
    become DONE;
end
```

FIGURE 2.23: New Rule and Procedures used for computing the Average

The *eccentricity* of a node x, denoted by $r(x)$, is the largest distance between x and any other node in the tree: $r(x) = \text{Max}\{d(x, y) : y \in V\}$; note that a *center* is a node with the smallest eccentricity. (We briefly discussed center and eccentricity already in Section 2.5.3.)

To compute its own eccentricity, a node x needs to determine the maximum distance from all other nodes in the tree. To accomplish this, x needs just to broadcast the request, making itself the root of the tree, and, using convergecast on this rooted tree, collect the maximum distance to itself. This approach would require $2(n - 1)$ messages and it is clearly optimal with respect to order of magnitude. If we want *every* entity to compute its eccentricity, this however would lead to a solution that requires $2(n^2 - n)$ messages.

We will now show that saturation will yield instead a $O(n)$, and thus optimal, solution.

The first step is to use saturation to compute the eccentricity of the two saturated nodes. Notice that we do not know a priori which pair of neighbors will become saturated. We can nevertheless ensure that when they become saturated they will know their eccentricity. To do so, it is enough to include, in the M message sent by an entity x to its neighbor y, the maximum distance from x to the nodes in $T[x - y]$, increased by 1. In this way, a saturated node s will know $d[s, y]$ for each neighbor y; thus, it can determine its eccentricity (Exercise 2.9.38).

Our goal is to have *all* nodes determine their eccentricity, not just the saturated ones. The interesting thing is that the information available at each entity at the end of the saturation stage is *almost* sufficient to make them compute their own eccentricity.

Consider an entity u; it sent the M message to its parent v, after it received one from all its other neighbors; the message from $y \neq v$ contained $d[u, y]$. In other words, u knows already the maximum distance from all the entities *except* the ones in the tree $T[v - u]$. Thus, the only information u is missing is $d[u, v] = \text{Max}\{d(u, y) : y \in T[v - u]\}$. Notice that (Exercise 2.9.39)

$$d[u, v] = \text{Max}\{d(u, y) : y \in T[v - u]\} = 1 + \text{Max}\{d[v, z] : z \neq u \in N(v)\}. \tag{2.28}$$

Summarizing, every node, except the saturated ones, is missing one piece of information: the maximum distance from the nodes on the other side of the link connecting it to its parent. If the parents could provide this information, the task can be completed. Unfortunately, the parents are also missing the information, unless they are the saturated nodes.

The saturated nodes have all the information they need. They also have the information their neighbors are missing: let s be a saturated node and x be an unsaturated neighbor; x is missing the information $d[x, s]$; by Equation 2.28, this is exactly $d[x, s] = 1 + \text{Max}\{d[s, z] : x \neq z \in N(s)\}$, and s knows all the $d[s, z]$ (they were included in the M messages it received). So, the saturated nodes s can provide the needed information to their neighbors, who can then compute their eccentricity. The nice property is that now these neighbors have the information required by their own neighbors (further away from the saturated nodes). Thus, the resolution stage of *Full*

```
PROCESSING
              Receiving ("Resolution", dist)
              begin
                       Resolve;
              end

Procedure Initialize
begin
     Distance[x] := 0;
end

Procedure Prepare_Message
begin
     maxdist := 1+ Max{Distance[*]};
     M := ("Saturation", maxdist);
end

Procedure Resolve
begin
     Process_Message;
     Calculate_Eccentricity;
     forall  y ∈ N(x) − {parent} do
        maxdist := 1 + Max{Distance[z] : z ∈ N(x) − {parent, y}};
        send("Resolution", maxdist) to y;
     endfor
     become DONE;
end

Procedure Process_Message
begin
     Distance[sender] := Received_distance;
end

Procedure Calculate_Eccentricity
begin
     r(x) := Max{Distance[z] : z ∈ N(x)};
end
```

FIGURE 2.24: New Rule and Procedures used for computing the Eccentricities

Saturation can be used to provide the missing information: starting from the saturated nodes, once an entity receives the missing information from a neighbor, it will compute its eccentricity and provide the missing information to all its other neighbors.

IMPORTANT. Notice that, in the resolution stage, an entity sends *different* information to each of its neighbors. Thus, unlike the resolution we used so far, it is *not* a notification.

The protocol *Eccentricities* will thus be a *Full Saturation* where the procedures *Initialize*, *Prepare_Message*, and *Process_Message* are as shown in Figure 2.24. The rules for handling the reception of the message, the procedure *Resolve*, and the procedure to calculate the eccentricity are also shown in Figure 2.24.

Notice that, even though each node receives a different message in the resolution stage, only one message will be received by each node in that stage, except the saturated nodes, which will receive none. Thus, the message cost of protocol *Eccentricities* will be exactly as the one of *MinF-Tree* and so will the time cost:

$$M[Eccentricities] = 3n + k_\star - 4 \leq 4n - 4. \tag{2.29}$$

$$T[Eccentricities] = T[MinF - Tree]. \tag{2.30}$$

2.6.5 Center Finding

A *center* is a node from which the maximum distance to all other nodes is minimized. A network might have more than one center. The Center Finding problem (**Center**) is to make each entity aware of whether or not it is a center by entering the appropriate terminal status *center* or *not-center*, respectively.

A Simple Protocol To solve **Center** we can use the fact that a center is exactly a node with the smallest eccentricity. Thus a solution protocol consists of finding the minimum among all eccentricities, combining the protocols we have developed so far:

1. Execute protocol *Eccentricities*;
2. Execute the last two stages (saturation and resolution) of *MinF-Tree*.

Part (1) will be started by the initiators; part (2) will be started by the leaves once, upon termination of their execution of *Eccentricities*, they know their eccentricity; the saturation stage of *MinF-Tree* will determine at two new saturated nodes the minimum overall eccentricity and will be broadcasted in the notification stage by them. At that time, an entity can determine if it is a center or not.

This approach will cost $3n + k_\star - 4$ messages for part (1) and $n + n - 2 = 2n - 2$ for part (2), for a total of $5n + k_\star - 6 \leq 6n - 6$ messages.

The time costs are no more than $T[Eccentricities] + 2d \leq 4d$.

A Refined Protocol An improvement can be derived by exploiting the structure of the problem in more details. Recall that $d[x, y] = Max\{d(x, z) : z \in T[y - x]\}$ is the longest distance between x and the nodes in $T[y - x]$. Let $d_1[x]$ and $d_2[x]$ be the largest and second-largest of all $\{d[x, y] : y \in N(x)\}$, respectively. The centers of a tree have some very interesting properties. Among them

Lemma 2.6.2 *In a tree either there is a unique center or there are two centers and they are neighbors.*

Lemma 2.6.3 *In a tree all centers lie on all diametral paths.*

Lemma 2.6.4 *A node x is a center if and only if $d_1[x] - d_2[x] \leq 1$; if strict inequality holds, then x is the only center.*

Lemma 2.6.5   *Let y and z be neighbors of x such that $d_1[x] = d[x, y]$ and $d_2[x] = d[x, z]$. If $d[x, y] - d[x, z] > 1$, then all centers are in $T[y - x]$.*

Lemma 2.6.4 gives us the tool we need to devise a solution protocol: an entity x can determine whether or not it is a center, provided it knows the value $d[x, y]$ for each of its neighbors y. But this is exactly the information that was provided to x by protocol *Eccentricities* so it could compute $r(x)$.

This means that to solve **Center** it suffices to execute *Eccentricities*. Once an entity has all the information to compute its radius, it will check whether the largest and the second largest received values differ at most by one; if so, it becomes *center*, otherwise *not-center*. Thus, the solution protocol *Center_Tree* is obtained from *Eccentricities* adding this test and some bookkeeping (Exercise 2.9.40).

The time and message costs of *Center_Tree* will be exactly the same as that of *Eccentricities*.

$$\mathbf{M}[Center\_Tree] = 3n + k_\star - 4 \leq 4n - 4. \tag{2.31}$$

$$\mathbf{T}[Center\_Tree] = \mathbf{T}[FullSaturation]. \tag{2.32}$$

An Efficient Plug-In   The solutions we have discussed are *full protocols*. In some circumstances, however, a *plug-in* is sufficient; that is, when the centers must start another global task. In these circumstances, the goal is just for the centers to know that they are centers.

In such a case, we can construct a more efficient mechanism, always based on saturation, using the resolution stage in a different way.

The properties expressed by Lemmas 2.6.4 and 2.6.5 give us the tools we need to devise the plug-in.

In fact, by Lemma 2.6.4, x can determine whether or not it is a center once it knows the value $d[x, y]$ for each of its neighbors y. Furthermore, if x is not a center, by Lemma 2.6.5, this information is sufficient to determine in which subtree $T[y - x]$ a center resides.

Thus, the solution is to collect such values at a node x; determine whether x is a center; and, if not, *move toward* a center until it is reached.

In order to collect the information needed, we can use the first two stages (Wake-up and Saturation) of protocol *Eccentricities*. Once a node becomes saturated, it can determine whether it is a center by checking whether the largest and the second largest received values differ at most by one. If it is not a center, it will know that the center(s) must reside in the direction from which the largest value has been received. By keeping track at each node (during the saturation stage) of which neighbor has sent the largest value, the direction of the center can also be determined. Furthermore, a saturated node can decide whether it is closest to a center or its parent.

The saturated node, say x, closest to a center will then send a "Center" message, containing the second largest received value increased by one, in the direction of the center. A processing node receiving such a message will, in turn, be able to determine whether it is a center and, if not, the direction toward the center(s).

Once the message arrives at a center c, c will be able to determine if it is the only center or not (using Lemma 2.6.4); in this case, it will know which neighbor is the other center and will notify it.

The *Center Finding* plug-in will then be the *Full Saturation* plug-in with the addition of the "Center" message traveling from the saturated nodes to the centers. In particular, the routines *Initialize*, *Process_Message*, *Prepare_Message*, *Resolve*, and the new rules governing the reception of the "Center" messages are shown in Figure 2.25.

```
PROCESSING
            Receiving("Center", value)
            begin
                Process_Message;
                Resolve;
            end

Procedure Initialize
begin
    Max_Value := 0;
    Max2_Value := 0;
end

Procedure Prepare_Message
begin
    M:=("Saturation", Max_Value+1);
end

Procedure Process_Message
begin
    if Max_Counter < Received_value then
       Max2_Value := Max_Value;
       Max_Value := Received_Value;
       Max_Neighbor := sender;
    else
       if Max2_Value < Received_value then
          Max2_Value := Received_value;
       endif
    endif
end

Procedure Resolve
begin
    if Max_Value - Max2_Value = 1 then
       if Max_Neighbor ≠ parent then
          send(Center,Max2_Value) to Max_Neighbor;
       endif
       become CENTER;
    else
       if Max_Value - Max2_Value > 1 then
          send(Center,Max2_Value) to Max_Neighbor;
       else
          become CENTER;
       endif
    endif
end
```

FIGURE 2.25: Transforming Saturation into an efficient Plug-In for Center Finding

The message cost of this plug-in is easily determined by observing that, after the *Full Saturation* plug-in is applied, a message will travel from the saturated node s (closest to a center) to its furthermost center c; hence, $d(s, c)$ additional messages are exchanged. Since $d(s, c) \leq n/2$, the total number of message exchanges performed is

$$\mathbf{M}[Center - \text{Finding}] = 2.5n + k_{\star} - 2 \leq 3.5n - 2. \qquad (2.33)$$

2.6.6 Other Computations

The simple modifications to the basic technique that we have discussed in the previous sections can be applied to solve a variety of other problems efficiently.

Following is a sample of them and the key properties employed toward their solution.

Finding a Median   A *median* is a node from which the average distance to all nodes in the network is minimized. Since a median obviously minimizes the sum of the distances to all other nodes, it is also called a *communication center* of the network.

In a tree, the key properties are:

Lemma 2.6.6   *In a tree either there is a unique median or there are two medians and they are neighbors.*

Given a node x, and a sub-tree T', let $g[T, x] = \sum_{y \in T} d(x, y)$ denote the sum of all distances between x and the nodes in T, and let $G[x, y] = g[T, x] - g[T, y] = n + 2 - 2 * |T[y - x]|$; then

Lemma 2.6.7   *Entity x is a median if and only if $G[x, y] \geq 0$ for all neighbors y.*

Furthermore,

Lemma 2.6.8   *If x is not the median, there exists a unique neighbor y such that $G[y, x] < 0$; such a neighbor lies in the path from x to the median.*

Using these properties, it is simple to construct a full protocol as well as an efficient plug-in, following the same approaches used for center finding (Exercise 2.9.41).

Finding Diametral Paths   A diametral path is a path of the longest length. In a network there might be more than one diametral path. The problem we are interested in is to identify all these paths. In distributed terms, this means that each entity needs to know if it is part of *a* diametral path or not, entering an appropriate status (e.g., *on-path* or *off-path*).

The key property to solve this problem is

Lemma 2.6.9   *A node x is on a diametral path if and only if $d_1[x] + d_2[x] = d$.*

Thus, a solution strategy will be to determine d, $d_1[x]$, and $d_2[x]$ at every x and then use Lemma 2.6.9 to decide the final status. A full protocol efficiently implementing this strategy can be designed using the tools developed so far (Exercise 2.9.45).

Consider now designing a plug-in instead of a full protocol; that is, we are only interested in that the entities on diametral paths (and only those) become aware of it.

In this case, the other key property is Lemma 2.6.4: every center lies on every diametral path. This gives us a starting point to find the diametral paths: the centers. To continue, we can then use Lemma 2.6.9. In other words, we first find the centers (note: they know the diameter) and then propagate the information along the diametral paths. A center (or for that matter, a node on a diametral path) does not know a priori which one of its neighbors is also on a diametral path. It will thus send the needed information to *all* its neighbors which, upon receiving it, will determine whether or not they are on such a path; if so, they continue the execution (Exercise 2.9.46).

2.6.7 Computing in Rooted Trees

Rooted Trees   In some cases, the tree T is actually *rooted*; that is, there is a distinct node, r, called the *root*, and all links are oriented toward r. In this case, the tree T will be denoted by $T_{[r]}$.

If link (x,y) is oriented from y to x, x is called the *parent* of y and y is said to be a *child* of x. Similarly, a *descendant* of x is any entity z for which there is a directed path from z to x, and an *ancestor* of x is any entity z for which there is a directed path from x to z.

Two important properties of a rooted tree are that the root has no parent, while every other node has only one parent (see Fig. 2.26).

Before examining how to compute in rooted trees, let us first observe the important fact that transforming a tree into a rooted one might be an *impossible* task.

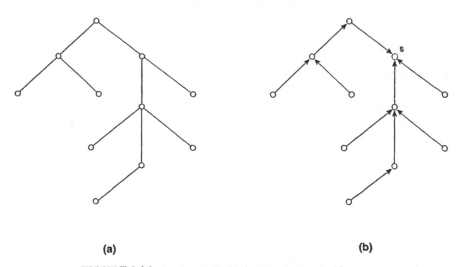

(a)   (b)

FIGURE 2.26: (a) A tree T; (b) the same tree rooted in s: $T_{[s]}$.

FIGURE 2.27: It is impossible to transform this tree into a rooted one.

Theorem 2.6.1 The problem of transforming trees into rooted ones is deterministically *unsolvable* under **R**.

Proof. Recall that deterministically unsolvable means that there is no deterministic protocol that always correctly terminates within finite time. To see why this is true, consider the simple tree composed of two entities x and y connected by links labeled as shown in Figure 2.27. Let the two entities have identical initial values (the symbols x, y are used only for description purposes). If a solution protocol A exists, it must work under any conditions of message delays (as long as they are finite) and regardless of the number of initiators. Consider a *synchronous schedule* (i.e., an execution where communication delays are unitary) and let both entities start the execution of A simultaneously. Since they are identical (same initial status and values, same port labels), they will execute the same rule, obtain the same results (thus, continuing to have the same local values), compose and send (if any) the same messages, and enter the same (possibly new) status. In other words, they will remain identical. In the next time unit, all sent messages (if any) will arrive and be processed. If one entity receives a message, the other will receive the same message at the same time, perform the same local computation, compose and send (if any) the same messages, and enter the same (possibly new) status. And so on. In other words, the two entities will continue to be identical. If A is a solution protocol, it must terminate within finite time; when this occurs, one entity, say x, becomes the root. But since both entities will always have the same state in this execution, y will also become root, contradicting the fact that A is correct. Thus, no such a solution algorithm A exists. ■

This means that being in a rooted tree is considerably different from being in a tree. Let us see how to exploit this difference.

Convergecast   The orientation of the links in a rooted tree is such that each entity has a notion of "up" (i.e., towards the root) and "down" (i.e., away from the root). If we are in a rooted tree, we can obviously exploit the availability of this globally consistent orientation. In particular, in the *saturation* technique, the process performed in the saturation stage can be simplified as follows:

Convergecast

1. a leaf sends its message to its parent;
2. each internal node waits until it receives a message from all its children; it then sends a message to its parent.

In this way, the root (that does not have a parent) will be the sole *saturated* node and will start the resolution stage.

This simplified process is called *convergecast*. If we are in a rooted tree, we can solve all the problems we discussed in the previous section (minimum finding, center finding, etc.) using convergecast in the saturation stage.

In spite of its greater simplicity, the savings in cost due to convergecast is only 1 message (Exercise 2.9.47). Clearly, such an amount alone does not justify the difference between general trees and rooted ones. There are however other advantages in rooted trees, as we will see later.

Totally Ordered Trees In addition to the globally consistent orientation "up and down," a rooted tree has another powerful property. In fact, the port numbers at a node are distinct; thus, they can be sorted, for example, in increasing order, and the corresponding links can be ordered accordingly. This means that the entire tree is *ordered*. As a consequence, also the nodes can be totally ordered, for example, according to a preorder traversal (see Fig. 2.28).

Note that a node might not be aware of its order number in the tree, although this information can be easily acquired in the entire tree (Exercise 2.9.49). This means that, *in a rooted tree the root assigns unique ids to the entities*. This fact shows indeed the power of rooted trees.

The fact that a rooted tree is totally ordered can be exploited also in other computations. Following are two examples.

Example: Choosing a Random Entity. In many systems and applications, it is necessary to occasionally select an entity at random. This occurs for instance in routing systems where, to reduce congestion, a message is first sent to an intermediate destination chosen at random and then delivered from there to the final destination. The same random selection is made, for example, for coordination of a computation, for control of a resource, etc. The problem is how to determine an entity at random. Let us concentrate on *uniform* choice; that is, every entity must have the same probability, $1/n$, of being selected.

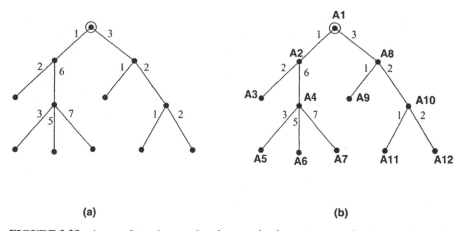

(a)   (b)

FIGURE 2.28: A rooted tree is an ordered tree and unique names can be given to the nodes.

In a rooted tree, it becomes easy for the root to select uniformly an entity at random. Once unique names have been assigned in preorder to the nodes and the root knows the number n of entities, the root needs only to choose locally a number uniformly at random between 1 and n; the entity with such a name will be the selected one. At this point, the only thing that the root r still has to do is to communicate efficiently to the selected entity x the result of the selection.

Actually, it is not necessary to assign unique names to the identities; in fact, it suffices that each entity knows the number of descendents of each of its children, and the entire process (from initial notification to all to final notification to x) can be performed with at most $2(n-1) + d_T(s, x)$ messages and $2r(s) + d_T(s, x)$ ideal time units (Exercise 2.9.50).

Example: Choosing at Random from a Distributed Set. An interesting computation is the one of choosing at random an element of a set of data distributed (without replication) among the entities. The setting is that of a set D partitioned among the entities; that is, each entity x has a subset $D_x \subseteq D$ of the data where $\cup_x D_x = D$ and, for $x \neq y$, $D_x \cap D_y = \emptyset$.

Let us concentrate again on *uniform* choice; that is, every data item must have the same probability, $1/|D|$ of being selected. How can this be achieved?

IMPORTANT. Choosing first an entity uniformly at random and then choosing an item uniformly at random in the set stored there will NOT give a uniformly random choice from the entire set (Exercise2.9.51).

Interestingly, this problem can be solved with a technique similar to that used for selecting an entity at random and with the same cost (Exercise 2.9.52).

Application: Broadcast with Termination Detection

Convergecast can be used whenever there is a rooted spanning tree. We will now see an application of this fact.

It is a "fact of life" in distributed computing that entities can terminate the execution of a protocol at different times; furthermore, when an entity terminates, it is usually unaware of the status of the other entities. This is why we differentiate between *local* termination (i.e., of the entity) and *global* termination (i.e., of the entire system).

For example, with the broadcast protocol *Flooding* the initiator of the broadcast does not know when the broadcast is over. To ensure that the initiator of the broadcast becomes aware of when global termination occurs, we need to use a different strategy.

To develop this strategy, recall that, if an entity s performs a *Flood+Reply* (e.g., protocol *Shout*) in a tree, the tree will become rooted in s: the initiator is the root; for every other node y, the neighbor x from which it receives the first broadcasted message is its parent, and all the neighbors that send the positive reply (e.g., "YES" in *Shout* and *Shout+*) are its children. This means that *convergecast* can be "appended" to any *Flood+Reply* protocol.

Strategy Broadcast with Termination Detection:

1. The initiator s uses any *Flood+Reply* protocol to broadcast and construct a spanning tree $T_{[s]}$ of the network;
2. Starting from the leaves of $T_{[s]}$, the entities perform a *convergecast* on T.

At the end of the convergecast, s becomes aware of the global termination of the broadcast (Exercise 2.9.48).

As for the cost, to broadcast with termination detection we need just to add the cost of the convergecast to the one of the *Flood+Reply* protocol used. For example, if we use *Shout+*, the resulting protocol that we shall call *TDCast* will then use $2m + n - 1$ messages. The ideal time of *Shout+* is exactly $r(s) + 1$; the ideal time of *convergecast* is exactly the height of the tree $T_{[s]}$, that is $r(s)$; thus, protocol *TDCast* has ideal time complexity $2r(s) + 1$. This means that termination detection can be added to broadcast with less than twice the cost of broadcasting alone.

2.7 SUMMARY

2.7.1 Summary of Problems

Broadcast [Information problem] $\Longrightarrow$ A single entity has special information that everybody must know.

- Unique Initiator
- *Flooding*: Messages $= \Theta(m)$; Time $= \Theta(d)$

Wake-Up [Information/Synchronization problem] $\Longrightarrow$ Some entities are awake; everybody must wake-up.

- Wake-Up $\equiv$ (Broadcast with multiple initiators)
- *WFlood*: Messages $= \Theta(m)$; Time $= \Theta(d)$

Traversal [Network problem] $\Longrightarrow$ Starting form the initiator, each entity is visited sequentially.

- Unique Initiator
- *DF-Traversal*: Messages $= \Theta(m)$; Time $= \Theta(n)$

Spanning-Tree Construction [Network problem] $\Longrightarrow$ Each entity identifies the subset of neighbors in the spanning tree.

- SPT with unique initiator $\equiv$ Broadcast
- Unique Initiator: *Shout*: Messages $= \Theta(m)$; Time $= \Theta(d)$
- Multiple Initiators: assume Distinct Initial Values

Election [Control problem] $\Longrightarrow$ One entity becomes leader, all others enter different special status.

- Distinct Initial Values

Minimum Finding [Data problem] $\Longrightarrow$ Each entity must know whether its initial value is minimum or not.

Center Finding [Network problem] $\Longrightarrow$ Each entity must know whether or not it is a center of the network.

2.7.2 Summary of Techniques

Flooding: with single initiator = broadcast; with multiple initiators = wake-up.

Flooding with Reply (*Shout*): with single initiator, it creates a spanning tree rooted in the initiator.

Convergecast: in rooted trees only.

Flooding with Replies plus Convergecast (TDCast): single initiator only, initiator finds out that the broadcast has globally terminated.

Saturation: in trees only.

Depth-first traversal: single initiator only.

2.8 BIBLIOGRAPHICAL NOTES

Of the basic techniques, *flooding* is the oldest one, still currently and frequently used. The more sophisticated refinements of adding reply and a convergecast were discussed and employed independently by Adrian Segall [11] and Ephraim Korach, Doron Rotem and Nicola Santoro [8]. Broadcasting in a linear number of messages in unoriented hypercubes is due to Stefan Dobrev and Peter Ruzicka [6]. The use of broadcast trees was first discussed by David Wall [12].

The depth-first traversal protocol was first described by Ernie Chang [3]; the first hacking improvement is due to Baruch Awerbuch [2]; the subsequent improvements were obtained by Kadathur Lakshmanan, N. Meenakshi, and Krishnaiyan Thulasiraman [9] and independently by Israel Cidon [4].

The difficulty of performing a wake-up in labeled hypercubes and in complete graphs has been proved by Stefan Dobrev, Rastislav Kralovic, and Nicola Santoro [5].

The first formal argument on the impossibility of some global computations under **R** (e.g., the impossibility result for spanning-tree construction with multiple initiators) is due to Dana Angluin [1].

The saturation technique is originally due to Nicola Santoro [10]; its application to center and median finding was developed by Ephraim Korach, Doron Rotem, and Nicola Santoro [8]. A decentralized solution to the ranking problem (Problem 2.9.4) was designed by Ephraim Korach, Doron Rotem, and Nicola Santoro [7]; a less efficient centralized one is due to Shmuel Zaks [13].

2.9 EXERCISES, PROBLEMS, AND ANSWERS

2.9.1 Exercises

Exercise 2.9.1 Show that protocol *Flooding* uses exactly $2m - n + 1$ messages.

Exercise 2.9.2 Design a protocol to broadcast without the restriction that the unique initiator must be the entity with the initial information. Write the new problem definition. Discuss the correctness of your protocol. Analyze its efficiency.

Exercise 2.9.3 Modify *Flooding* so to broadcast under the restriction that the unique initiator *must* be an entity *without* the initial information. Write the new problem definition. Discuss the correctness of your protocol. Analyze its efficiency.

Exercise 2.9.4 We want to move the system from an initial configuration where every entity is in the same status *ignorant* except the one that is *knowledgeable* to a final configuration where every entity is in the same status. Consider this problem under the standard assumptions plus Unique Initiator.

(a) Prove that, if the unique initiator is restricted to be one of the *ignorant* entities, this problem is the same as broadcasting (same solution, same costs).
(b) Show how, if the unique initiator is restricted to be the *knowledgeable* entity, the problem can be solved without any communication.

Exercise 2.9.5 Design a protocol to broadcast without the Bidirectional Link restriction. Discuss its correctness. Analyze its efficiency.

Exercise 2.9.6 Prove that, in the worst case, the number of messages used by protocol *WFlood* is at most $2m$. Show under what conditions such a bound will be achieved. Under what conditions will the protocol use only $2m - n + 1$ messages?

Exercise 2.9.7 Prove that protocol *WFlood* correctly terminates under the standard set of restrictions BL,C, and TR.

Exercise 2.9.8 Write the protocol that implements strategy *HyperFlood*.

Exercise 2.9.9 Show that the subgraph $H_k(x)$, induced by the messages sent when using *HyperFlood* on the k-dimensional hypercube H_k with x as the initiator, contains no cycles.

Exercise 2.9.10 Show that for every x the eccentricity of x in $H_k(x)$ is k.

Exercise 2.9.11 Prove that the message complexity of traversal under **R** is at least m. *(Hint: use the same technique employed in the proof of Theorem 2.1.1.)*

Exercise 2.9.12 Let G be a *tree*. Show that, in this case, no Backedge messages will be sent in any execution of *DF_Traversal*.

Exercise 2.9.13 Characterize the *virtual ring* formed by an execution of *DF_Traversal* in a tree network. Show that the ring has $2n - 2$ virtual nodes.

Exercise 2.9.14 Write the protocol *DF++*.

Exercise 2.9.15 Prove that protocol *DF++* correctly performs a depth-first traversal.

Exercise 2.9.16 Show that, in the execution of *DF++*, on some back-edges there might be two "mistakes."

Exercise 2.9.17 Determine the exact number of messages transmitted in the worst case when executing *DF** in a *complete graph*.

Exercise 2.9.18 Prove that in protocol *Shout*, if an entity x is in *Tree-neighbors* of y, then y is in *Tree-neighbors* of x.

Exercise 2.9.19 Prove that in protocol *Shout*, if an entity sends *Yes*, then it is connected to the *initiator* by a path where on every link a *Yes* has been transmitted. *(Hint: use induction.)*

Exercise 2.9.20 Prove that the subnet constructed by protocol *Shout* contains no cycles.

Exercise 2.9.21 Prove that $\mathbf{T}[Flood+Reply] = \mathbf{T}[Flooding]+1$.

Exercise 2.9.22 Write the set of rules for protocol *Shout+*.

Exercise 2.9.23 Determine under what conditions on the communication delays, protocol *Shout* will construct a breadth-first spanning tree.

Exercise 2.9.24 Modify protocol *Shout* so that the initiator can determine when the broadcast is *globally* terminated. *(Hint: integrate in the protocol the convergecast operation for rooted trees.)*

Exercise 2.9.25 Modify protocol *DF** so that every entity determines its neighbors in the df-tree it constructs.

Exercise 2.9.26 Prove that f_* is exactly the number of *leaves* of the df-tree constructed by *df-SPT*.

Exercise 2.9.27 Prove that, in the execution of *df-SPT*, when the initiator becomes *done*, a df-tree of the network has already been constructed.

Exercise 2.9.28   Prove that, for any broadcast protocol, the graph induced by relationship "parent" is a spanning tree of the network.

Exercise 2.9.29   Prove that the bf-tree of G rooted in a center is a broadcast tree of G.

Exercise 2.9.30   Verify that, with multiple initiators, the optimized version $DF+$ and $DF*$ of protocol df-SPT will always create a spanning forest of the graph depicted in Figure 2.14.

Exercise 2.9.31   Prove that when a node becomes *saturated* in the execution of protocol *MinF-Tree*, it knows the minimum value in the network.

Exercise 2.9.32   Prove that when a node becomes *saturated* in the execution of protocol *Funct-Tree*, it knows the value of f.

Exercise 2.9.33   Design a protocol to determine if all the entities of a tree network have positive initial values. Any number of entities can independently start.

Exercise 2.9.34   Consider a tree system where each entity has a *salary* and a *gender*. Some external investigators want to know if all the entities with a salary below $50,000$ are *female*. Design a solution protocol that can be started by any number of entities independently.

Exercise 2.9.35   Consider the same tree system of Question 2.9.34. The investigators now want to know if there is at least one *female* with a salary above $50,000$. Design a solution protocol that can be started by any number of entities independently.

Exercise 2.9.36   Design an efficient protocol to compute the number of entities in a tree network. Any number of entities can independently start the protocol.

Exercise 2.9.37   Consider the same tree system of Question 2.9.34. The investigators now want to know how many *female* entities are in the system. Design a solution protocol that can be started by any number of entities independently.

Exercise 2.9.38   Consider the following use of the M message: a leaf will include a value $v = 1$; an internal node will include one plus the maximum of all the received values. Prove that the saturated nodes will compute their maximum distance from all other nodes.

Exercise 2.9.39   Prove that for any link (u, v), $d[u, v] = \text{Max} \{d(u, y) : y \in T[v - u]\} = 1 + \text{Max}\{d(v, y) : y \in T[u - v]\} = \text{Max}\{d[v, z] : z \neq u \in N(v)\}$.

Exercise 2.9.40   Modify protocol *Eccentricities* so it can solve **Center**, as discussed in Section 2.6.5.

Exercise 2.9.41 Median Finding. Construct an efficient plug-in so that the median nodes know that they are such.

Exercise 2.9.42 Diameter Finding. Design an efficient protocol to determine the *diameter* of the tree. (*Hint: use Lemma 2.6.2.*)

Exercise 2.9.43 Rank Finding in Tree. Consider a tree where each entity x has an initial value $v(x)$; these values are not necessarily distinct. The *rank* of an entity x will be the rank of its value; that is, $rank(x) = 1 + |\{y \in V : v(y) < v(x)\}|$. So, whoever has the smallest value, it has rank 1. Design an efficient protocol to determine the rank of a *unique initiator* (i.e., under the additional restriction UI).

Exercise 2.9.44 Generic Rank Finding. Consider the *ranking problem* described in Exercise 2.9.43. Design an efficient solution protocol that is *generic*; that is, it works in an arbitrary connected graph.

Exercise 2.9.45 Diametral Paths. A path whose length is d is called *diametral*. Design an efficient protocol so that each entity can determine whether or not it lies on a diametral path of the tree.

Exercise 2.9.46 A path whose length is d is called *diametral*. Design an efficient plug-in so that all and only the entities on a diametral path of the tree become aware of this fact.

Exercise 2.9.47 Show that convergecast uses only 1 (one) message less than the saturation stage in general trees.

Exercise 2.9.48 Prove that, when an initiator of a *TDCast* protocol receives the convergecast message from all its children, the initial broadcast is globally terminated.

Exercise 2.9.49 Show how to assign efficiently a unique id to the entities in a rooted tree.

Exercise 2.9.50 Random Entity Selection $(\star)$ Consider the task of selecting uniformly at random an entity in a tree rooted at s. Show how to perform this task, started by the root, with at most $2(n-1) + d_T(s, x)$ messages and $2r(s) + d_T(s, x)$ ideal time units. Prove both correctness and complexity.

Exercise 2.9.51 Show why choosing uniformly at random a site and then choosing uniformly at random an element from that site is not the same as choosing uniformly at random an element from the entire set.

Exercise 2.9.52 Random Item Selection $(\star\star)$ Consider the task of selecting uniformly at random an item from a set of data partitioned among the nodes of a tree rooted at s. Show how to perform this task, started by the root, with at most

$2(n-1) + d_T(s, x)$ messages and $2r(s) + d_T(s, x)$ ideal time units. Prove both correctness and complexity.

2.9.2 Problems

Problem 2.9.1 Develop an efficient solution to the Traversal problem without the Bidirectional Links assumption.

Problem 2.9.2 Develop an efficient solution to the Minimum Finding problem in a *hypercube* with a *unique initiator* (i.e., under the additional restriction UI). Note that the values might not be distinct.

Problem 2.9.3 Solve the Minimum Finding problem is a system where there is already a leader; that is, under restrictions $\mathbf{R} \cup \mathrm{UI}$. Note that the values might not be distinct. Prove the correctness of your solution, and analyze its efficiency.

Problem 2.9.4 Ranking. ($\star$) Consider a tree where each entity x has an initial value $v(x)$; these values are not necessarily distinct. The *rank* of an entity x will be the rank of its value; that is, $rank(x) = 1 + |\{y \in v : v(y) < v(x)\}|$. So, whoever has the smallest value, has rank 1. Design an efficient protocol to determine the rank of all entities. prove the correctness of your protocol and analyze its complexity.

2.9.3 Answers to Exercises

Answer to Exercise 2.9.13
A node appears several times in the virtual ring; more precisely, there is an instance of node z in R for each time z has received a Token or a Finished message. Let x be the initiator; node x sends a Token to each of its neighbors sequentially and receives a Finished message from each. Every node $y \neq x$ receives exactly one Token (from its parent) and sends one to all its other neighbors (its children); it will also receive a Finished message from all its children and send one to its parent. In other words every node z, including the initiator x, will appear $n(z) = |N(z)|$ times in the virtual ring. The total number of (virtual) nodes in the virtual ring is therefore $\sum_{z \in V} |N(z)| = 2m = 2(n-1)$.

Answer to Exercise 2.9.16
Consider a ring network with the three nodes $x, y,$ and z. Assume that entity x holds the *Token* initially. Consider the following sequence of events that take place successively in time as a result of the execution of the $DF++$ protocol: x sends *Visited* messages to y and z, sends the *Token* to y, and waits for a (*Visited* or *Return*) reply from y. Assume that the link (x, z) is extremely slow.

When y receives the *Token* from x, it sends to z a *Visited* message and then the *Token*. Assume that when z receives the *Token*, the *Visited* message from x has not arrived yet; hence z sends *Visited* to x followed by the *Token*. This is the first mistake: *Token* is sent on a back-edge to x, which has already been visited.

When z finally receives the *Visited* message from x, it realizes the *Token* it sent to x was a mistake. Since it has no other unvisited neighbors, z sends a *Return* message back to y. Since y has no other unvisited neighbors, it will then send a *Return* message back to x. Assume that when x receives the *Return* message from y, x has not received yet neither the *Visited* nor the *Return* messages sent by z. Hence, x considers z as an unvisited neighbor and sends the *Token* to z. This is the second mistake on the back-edge between x and z.

Answer to Exercise 2.9.19

Suppose some node x is not reachable from s in the graph T induced by the "parent" relationship. This means that x never sent the Yes messages; this implies that x never received the question Q. This is impossible because, since flooding is correct, every entity will receive Q; thus, no such x exists.

Answer to Exercise 2.9.20

Suppose the graph T induced by the "parent" relationship (i.e., the Yes messages) contains a directed cycle $x_0, x_1, \ldots, x_{k-1}$; that is, x_i is the parent of x_{i+1} (operations on the indices are modulo k). This cycle cannot contain the initiator s (because it does not send any Yes). We know (Exercise 2.9.19) that in T there is a path from s to each node, including those in the cycle. This means that there will be in T a node y not in the cycle that is connected to a node x_i in the cycle. This means that x_i sent a Yes message to y; but since it is in the cycle, it also sent a Yes message to x_{i-1} (operations on the indices are modulo k). This is impossible because an entity sends no more than one Yes message.

Answer to Exercise 2.9.31

First show that if a node x sends M to neighbor y, N contains the smallest value in $T[x - y]$; then, since a saturated node receives by definition a M message from all neighbors, it knows the minimum value in the network. Prove that value sent by x to y in M is the minimum value in $T[x - y]$ by induction on the height h of $T[x - y]$. Trivially true if $h = 1$, that is, x is a leaf. Let it be true up to $k \geq 1$; we will now show it is true for $h = k + 1$. x sends M to y because it has received a value from all its other neighbors $y_1, y_2, \ldots$; since the height of $(T[y_i - x])$ is less than h, then by inductive hypothesis the value sent by y_i to x is the minimum value in $(T[y_i - x])$. This means that the smallest among $v(x)$ and all the values received by x is the minimum value in $T[x - y]$; this is exactly what x sends to y.

Answer to Exercise 2.9.41

It is clear that if node x knows $|T[y - x]|$ for all neighbors y, then it can compute $G[y, x]$ and decide whether x is itself a median and, if not, determine the direction of the median. Thus, to find a median is sufficient to modify the basic technique to supply this information to the elected node from which the median is approached. This is done by providing two counters, m_1 and m_2, with each M message: When a node x sends a M message to y, then $m_1 = g[T[y - x], y] - 1$ and $m_2 = |T[y - x]| - 1$. An active node x processes all received M messages so that, before it sends M to the last neighbor y, it knows $G[T[x-z],x]$ and $|T[z-x]|$ for all other neighbors z. In particular, the elected node can determine whether it is the median and, if not, can send a message toward it; a node receiving such a message will, in turn, perform the same operations until a median is located. Once again, the total number of exchanged messages is the ones of the *Full Saturation* plug-in plus $d(s,med)$, where s is the saturated node closer to the medians, and *med* is the median furthermost from x.

Partial Answer to Exercise 2.9.48
By induction on the height of the rooted tree, prove that, in a *TDCast* protocol, when an entity x receives the convergecast message from all its children, all its descendants have locally terminated the broadcast.

Partial Answer to Exercise 2.9.49
Perform first a broadcast from the root to notify all entities of the start of the protocol, and then a convergecast to collect at each entity the number of its descendents. Afterwards use this information to assign distinct values to the entities according to a preorder traversal of the tree.

Partial Answer to Exercise 2.9.51
Show that the data items from smaller sets will be chosen with higher probability than that of the items from larger sets.

BIBLIOGRAPHY

[1] D. Angluin. Local and global properties in networks of processors. In *Proc. of the 12th ACM STOC Symposium on Theory of Computing*, pages 82–93, 1980.

[2] B. Awerbuch. A new distributed depth-first search algorithm. *Information Processing Letters*, 20:147–150, 1985.

[3] E.J.H. Chang. Echo algorithms: Depth parallel operations on general graphs. *IEEE Transactions on Software Engineering*, SE-8(4):391–401, July 1982.

[4] I. Cidon. Yet another distributed depth-first search algorithm. *Information Processing Letters*, 26:301–305, 1987.

[5] S. Dobrev, R. Kralovic, and N. Santoro. On the difficulty of waking up. In *print*, 2006.

[6] S. Dobrev and P. Ruzicka. Linear broadcasting and $O(n \log \log n)$ election in unoriented hypercubes. In *Proc. of the 4th International Colloquium on Structural Information and Communication Complexity, (Sirocco'97)*, Ascona, July 1997. To appear.

[7] E. Korach, D. Rotem, and N. Santoro. Distributed algorithms for ranking the nodes of a network. In *13th SE Conf. on Combinatorics, Graph Theory and Computing*, volume 36 of *Congressus Numeratium*, pages 235–246, Boca Raton, February 1982.

[8] E. Korach, D. Rotem, and N. Santoro. Distributed algorithms for finding centers and medians in networks. *ACM Transactions on Programming Languages and Systems*, 6(3):380–401, July 1984.

[9] K.B. Lakshmanan, N. Meenakshi, and K. Thulasiraman. A time-optimal message-efficient distributed algorithm for depth-first search. *Information Processing Letters*, 25:103–109, 1987.

[10] N. Santoro. Determining topology information in distributed networks. In *Proc. 11th SE Conf. on Combinatorics, Graph Theory and Computing*, Congressus Numeratium, pages 869–878, Boca Raton, February 1980.

[11] A. Segall. Distributed network protocols. *IEEE Transactions on Information Theory*, IT-29(1):23–35, Jan 1983.

[12] D. Wall. *Mechanisms for broadcast and selective broadcast*. PhD thesis, Stanford University, June 1980.

[13] Shmuel Zaks. Optimal distributed algorithms for sorting and ranking. *IEEE Transactions on Computers*, 34:376–380, 1985.

CHAPTER 3

Election

3.1 INTRODUCTION

In a distributed environment, most applications often require a single entity to act temporarily as a central controller to coordinate the execution of a particular task by the entities. In some cases, the need for a single coordinator arises from the desire to simplify the design of the solution protocol for a rather complex problem; in other cases, the presence of a single coordinator is required by the nature of the problem itself.

The problem of choosing such a coordinator from a population of autonomous symmetric entities is known as *Leader Election* (**Elect**). Formally, the task consists in moving the system from an initial configuration where all entities are in the same state (usually called *available*) into a final configuration where all entities are in the same state (traditionally called *follower*), except one, which is in a different state (traditionally called *leader*). There is no restriction on the number of entities that can start the computation, nor on which entity should become *leader*.

We can think of the Election problem as the problem of enforcing restriction *Unique Initiator* in a system where actually no such restriction exists: The multiple initiators would first start the execution of an Election protocol; the sole *leader* will then be the unique initiator for the subsequent computation.

As election provides a mechanism for breaking the symmetry among the entities in a distributed environment, it is at the base of most control and coordination processes (e.g., *mutual exclusion, synchronization, concurrency control*, etc.) employed in distributed systems, and it is closely related to other basic computations (e.g., *minimum finding, spanning-tree construction, traversal*).

3.1.1 Impossibility Result

We will start considering this problem under the standard restrictions **R**: Bidirectional Links, Connectivity, and Total Reliability. There is unfortunately a very strong *impossibility* result about election.

Theorem 3.1.1 *Problem* **Elect** *is deterministically unsolvable under* **R**.

Design and Analysis of Distributed Algorithms, by Nicola Santoro
Copyright © 2007 John Wiley & Sons, Inc.

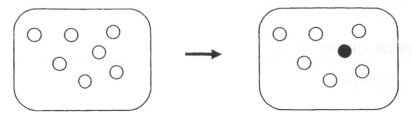

FIGURE 3.1: Electing a leader.

In other words, there is no deterministic protocol that will always correctly terminate within finite time if the only restrictions are those in **R**.

To see why this is the case, consider a simple system composed of two entities, x and y, both initially *available* and with no different initial values; in other words, they are initially in identical states. If a solution protocol P exists, it must work under any conditions of message delays. Consider a *synchronous schedule* (i.e., an execution where communication delays are unitary) and let the two entities start the execution of P simultaneously. As they are in identical states, they will execute the same rule, obtain the same result, and compose and send (if any) the same message; thus, they will still be in identical states. If one of them receives a message, the other will receive the same message at the same time and, by Property 1.6.2, they will perform the same computation, and so on. Their state will always be the same; hence if one becomes *leader*, so will the other. But this is against the requirement that there should be *only one* leader; in other words, P is *not* a solution protocol.

3.1.2 Additional Restrictions

The consequence of Theorem 3.1.1 is that to break symmetry, we need additional restrictions and assumptions.

Some restrictions are not powerful enough. This is the case, for example, with the assumption that there is already available a spanning tree (i.e., restriction *Tree*). In fact, the two-node network in which we know election is impossible is a tree.

To determine which restrictions, added to **R**, will enable us to solve **Elect**, we must consider the nature of the problem. The entities have an inherent behavioral symmetry: They all obey the same set of rules plus they have an initial state symmetry (by definition of election problem). To elect a leader means to break these symmetries; in fact, election is also called *symmetry breaking*. To be able to do so, from the start there must be something in the system that the entities can use, something that makes (at least one of) them different. Remember that any restriction limits the applicability of the protocol.

The most obvious restriction is *Unique Initiator* (UI): The unique initiator, known to be unique, becomes the *leader*. This is, however, "sweeping the problem under the carpet," saying that we can elect a leader if there is already a leader and it knows about it. The problem is to elect a leader when many (possibly, all) entities are initiators; thus, without UI.

The restriction that is commonly used is a very powerful one, *Initial Distinct Values* (ID), which we have already employed to circumvent a similar impossibility result for constructing a spanning tree with multiple initiators (see Section 2.5.5). Initial distinct values are sometimes called *identifiers* or *ids* or *global names* and, as we will see, their presence will be sufficient to elect a leader; let id(x) denote the distinct value of x. The use of this additional assumption is so frequent that the set of restrictions $\mathbf{IR} = \mathbf{R} \cup \{\mathrm{ID}\}$ is called the *standard set for election*.

3.1.3 Solution Strategies

How can the difference in initial values be used to break the symmetry and to elect a leader?

According to the election problem specifications, it does not matter which entity becomes the leader. Using the fact that the values are distinct, a possible strategy is to choose as a leader the entity with the *smallest* value; in other words, an election strategy is as follows:

Strategy *Elect Minimum*:

1. find the smallest value;
2. elect as a leader the entity with that value.

IMPORTANT. Finding the minimum value is an important problem of its own, which we have already discussed for tree networks (Section 2.6.2). Notice that in that occasion, we found the minimum value *without* unique identifiers; it is the election problem that needs them.

A useful variant of this strategy is the one restricting the choice of the leader to the set of entities that initiate the protocol. That is,

Strategy *Elect Minimum Initiator*:

1. find the smallest value among the initiators;
2. elect as a leader the entity with that value.

IMPORTANT. Notice that any solution implementing the strategy *Elect Minimum* solves **Min** as well as **Elect**, not so the ones implementing *Elect Minimum Initiator*.

Similarly, we can define the *Elect Maximum* and the *Elect Maximum Initiator* strategies.

Another strategy is to use the distinct values to construct a rooted spanning tree of the network and to elect the root as the leader. In other words, an election strategy is as follows:

Strategy *Elect Root*:

1. construct a rooted spanning tree;
2. elect as the leader the root of the tree.

IMPORTANT. Constructing a (rooted) spanning tree is an important problem of its own, which we have already discussed among the basic problems (Section 2.5). Recall that **SPT**, like **Elect**, is *unsolvable* under **R**.

In the rest of this chapter, we will examine how to use these strategies to solve **Elect** under election's standard set of restrictions $IR = R \cup \{ID\}$. We will do so by first examining special types of networks and then focusing on the development of topology-independent solutions.

3.2   ELECTION IN TREES

The tree is the connected graph with the "sparsest" topology: $m = n - 1$.

We have already seen how to optimally find the smallest value using the saturation technique: protocol *MinF-Tree* in Section 2.6.2. Hence the strategy *Elect Minimum* leads to an election protocol *Tree:Elect_Min* where the number of messages in the worst case is as follows:

$$\mathbf{M}[Tree:Elect\_Min] = 3n + k_* - 4 \leq 4n - 4.$$

Interestingly, also the strategy *Elect Minimum Initiator* will have the same complexity (Exercise 3.10.1).

Consider now applying the strategy *Elect Root*. As the network *is* a tree, the only work required is to transform it into a *rooted* tree. It is not difficult to see how saturation can be used to solve the problem. In fact, if *Full Saturation* is applied, then a *saturated* node knows that it itself and its parent are the only *saturated* nodes; furthermore, as a result of the saturation stage, every nonsaturated entity has identified as its parent the neighbor closest to the saturated pair. In other words, saturation will root the tree not in a single node but in a pair of neighbors: the saturated ones.

Thus, to make the tree rooted in a single node we just need to choose only one of the two saturated nodes. In other words, the "Election" among *all* the nodes is reduced to an "election" between the *two* saturated ones. This can be easily accomplished by having the *saturated* nodes communicate their identities and by having the node with the smallest identity become elected, while the other stays processing.

Thus, the *Tree:Elect_Root* protocol will be *Full Saturation* with the new rules and the routine *Resolve* shown in Figure 3.2.

The number of message transmissions for the election algorithm *Tree_Election* will be exactly the same as the one experienced by *Full Saturation* with notification

```
SATURATED
            Receiving (Election, id*)
            begin
                if  id(x) < id* then
                    become LEADER;
                else
                    become FOLLOWER;
                endif
                send("Termination") to N(x) − {parent};
            end

PROCESSING
            Receiving ("Termination")
            begin
                become FOLLOWER;
                send("Termination") to N(x) − {parent};
            end

Procedure Resolve
begin
    send("Election",id(x)) to parent;
    become SATURATED;
end
```

FIGURE 3.2: New rules and routine Resolve used for Tree:Elect_Root.

plus two "Election" messages, that is,

$$\mathbf{M}[\textit{Tree:Elect\_Root}]= 3n + k_* - 2 \le 4n - 2.$$

In other words, it uses two messages more than the solution obtained using the strategy *Elect Minimum*.

Granularity of Analysis: Bit Complexity

From the discussion above, it would appear that the strategy *Elect Minimum* is "better" because it uses two messages less than the strategy *Elect Root*. This assessment is indeed the only correct conclusion obtainable using the number of messages as the cost measure. Sometimes, this measure is too "coarse" and does not really allow us to see possibly important details; to get a more accurate picture, we need to analyze the costs at a "finer" level of granularity.

Let us re-examine the two strategies in terms of the number of *bits*. To do so, we have to distinguish between different types of messages because some contain counters and values, while others contain only a message identifier.

IMPORTANT. Messages that do not carry values but only a constant number of bits are called *signals* and in most practical systems, they have significantly less communication costs than *value messages*.

In *Elect Minimum*, only the n messages in the saturation stage carry a value, while all the others are signals; hence, the total number of *bits* transmitted will be

$$\mathbf{B}[\textit{Tree:Elect\_Min}] = n (c + \log \mathbf{id}) + c (2n + k_* - 2), \qquad (3.1)$$

where **id** denotes the largest value sent in a message, and $c = O(1)$ denotes the number of bits required to distinguish among the different messages.

In *Elect Root*, only the "Election" message carries a node identity; thus, the total number of *bits* transmitted is

$$\mathbf{B}[\textit{Tree:Elect\_Root}] = 2\,(c\ +\log\mathbf{id}) + c\,(3n + k_* - 2). \tag{3.2}$$

That is, in terms of number of bits, *Elect Root* is an order of magnitude better than *Elect Minimum*. In terms of signals and value messages, with *Elect Root* strategy we have only two value messages and with *Elect Minimum* strategy we have n value messages.

Remember: Measuring the number of bits gives us always a "picture" of the efficiency at a more refined level of granularity. Fortunately, it is not always necessary to go to such a level.

3.3 ELECTION IN RINGS

We will now consider a network topology that plays a very important role in distributed computing: the *ring*, sometimes called *loop* network.

A ring consists of a single cycle of length n. In a ring, each entity has exactly two neighbors, (whose associated ports are) traditionally called *left* and *right* (see Figure 3.3).

IMPORTANT. Note that the labeling might, however, be globally *inconsistent*, that is, 'right' might not have the same meaning for all entities. We will return to this point later.

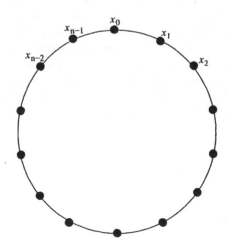

FIGURE 3.3: A ring network.

After trees, rings are the networks with the sparsest topology: $m = n$; however, unlike trees, rings have a complete structural symmetry (i.e., all nodes look the same).

We will denote the ring by $R = (x_0, x_1, \ldots, x_{n-1})$. Let us consider the problem of electing a leader in a ring R, under the standard set of restrictions for election, $\mathbf{IR} =$ {Bidirectional Links, Connectivity, Total Reliability, Initial Distinct Values}, as well as the knowledge that the network is a ring (*Ring*). Denote by id(x) the unique value associated to x.

Because of its structure, in a ring we will use almost exclusively the approach of minimum finding as a tool for leader election. In fact we will consider both the *Elect Minimum* and the *Elect Minimum Initiator* approaches. Clearly the first solves both **Min** and **Elect**, while the latter solves only **Elect**.

NOTE. Every protocol that elects a leader in a ring can be made to find the minimum value (if it has not already been determined) with an additional n message and time (Exercise 3.10.2). Furthermore, in the worst case, the two approaches coincide: All entities might be initiators.

Let us now examine how minimum finding and election can be efficiently performed in a ring.

As in a ring each entity has only two neighbors, for brevity we will use the notation **other** to indicate $N(x)-$**sender** at an entity x.

3.3.1 All the Way

The first solution we will use is rather straightforward: When an entity starts, it will choose one of its two neighbors and send to it an "Election" message containing its id; an entity receiving the id of somebody else will send its id (if it has not already done so) and forward the received message along the ring (i.e., send it to its other neighbor) keeping track of the smallest id seen so far (including its own).

This process can be visualized as follows: Each entity originates a message (containing its id), and this message travels "all the way" along the ring (forwarded by the other entities) (see Figure 3.4). Hence, the name *All the Way* will be used for the resulting protocol.

Each entity will eventually see the id of everybody else id (finite communication delays and total reliability ensure that) including the minimum value; it will, thus, be able to determine whether or not it is the (unique) minimum and, thus, the leader. When will this happen ? In other words,

Question. *When will an entity terminate its execution?*

Entities only forward messages carrying values other than their own: Once the message with $id(x)$ arrives at x, it is no longer forwarded. Thus, each value will travel "All the Way" along the ring only once. So, the communication activities will eventually terminate. But how does an entity know that the communication activities

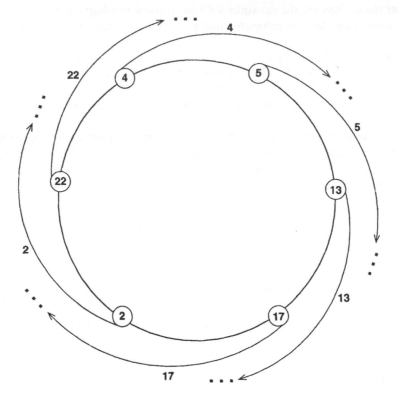

FIGURE 3.4: All the Way: Every id travels along the ring.

have terminated, that no more messages will be arriving, and, thus, the smallest value seen so far is really the minimum id?

Consider a "reasonable" but unfortunately *incorrect* answer:

> *An entity knows that it has seen all values once it receives its value back.*

The "reason" is that the message with its own id has to travel longer along the ring to reach x than those originated by other entities; thus, these other messages will be received first. In other words, reception of its own message can be used to detect termination.

This reasoning is incorrect because it uses the (hidden) additional assumption that the system has first in first out (FIFO) communication channels, that is, the messages are delivered in the order in which they arrive. This restriction, called *Message Ordering*, is not a part of election's standard set; few systems actually have it built in, and the costs of offering it can be formidable.

So, whatever the answer, it must not assume FIFO channels. With this proviso, a "reasonable" but unfortunately still *incorrect* answer is the following:

> *An entity counts how many different values it receives; when the counter is equal to n, it knows it can terminate.*

PROTOCOL All the Way.

- States: $S = \{$ASLEEP, AWAKE, FOLLOWER, LEADER$\}$;
  $S_{\text{INIT}} = \{$ASLEEP$\}$;
  $S_{\text{TERM}} = \{$FOLLOWER, LEADER$\}$.
- Restrictions: **IR** $\cup Ring$.

```
ASLEEP
        Spontaneously
        begin
            INITIALIZE;
            become AWAKE;
        end

        Receiving("Election", value*, counter*)
        begin
            INITIALIZE;
            send("Election", value*, counter*+1) to other;
            min:= Min{ min, value};
            count:= count+1;
            become AWAKE;
        end


AWAKE
        Receiving("Election", value*, counter*)
        begin
            if value ≠ id(x) then
                send("Election", value*, counter*+1) to other;
                min:= MIN{min,value*};
                count:= count+1;
                if known then CHECK endif;
            else
                ringsize:= counter*;
                known:= true;
                CHECK;
            endif
        end
```

FIGURE 3.5: Protocol *All the Way.*

The problem is that this answer assumes that the entity knows *n*, but a priori knowledge of the ring size is *not* a part of the standard restrictions for election. So it cannot be used.

It is indeed strange that the termination should be difficult for such a simple protocol in such a clear setting. Fortunately, the last answer, although incorrect, provides us with the way out. In fact, although *n* is not known a priori, it can be *computed*. This is easily accomplished by having a counter in the Election message, initialized to 1 and incremented by each entity forwarding it; when an entity receives its id back, the value of the counter will be *n*.

Summarizing, we will use a counter at each entity, to keep track of how many different ids are received and a counter in each message, so that each entity can determine *n*. The protocol is shown in Figures 3.5 and 3.6.

The message originated by each entity will travel along the ring exactly once. Thus, there will be exactly n^2 messages in total, each carrying a counter and a value,

```
Procedure INITIALIZE
begin
    count:= 0;
    size:= 1;
    known:= false;
    send("Election", id(x), size) to right;
    min:= id(x);
end


Procedure CHECK
begin
    if count = ringsize then
        if min = id(x) then
            become LEADER;
        else
            become FOLLOWER;
        endif
    endif
end
```

FIGURE 3.6: Procedures of protocol *All the Way.*

for a total of $n^2 \log(\mathbf{id} + n)$ bits. The time costs will be at most $2n$ (Exercise 3.10.3). Summarizing,

$$\mathbf{M}[Allthe Way] = n^2 \tag{3.3}$$

$$\mathbf{T}[Allthe Way] \leq 2n - 1. \tag{3.4}$$

The solution protocol we have just designed is very expensive in terms of communication costs (in a network with 100 nodes it would cause 10, 000 message transmissions).

The protocol can be obviously modified so as to follow strategy *Elect Minimum Initiator*, finding the smallest value only among the initiators. In this case, those entities that do not initiate will not originate a message but just forward the others'. In this way, we would have fewer messages whenever there are fewer initiators.

In the modification we must be careful. In fact, in protocol *All the Way*, we were using an entity's own message to determine n so as to be able to determine local termination. Now some entities will not have this information. This means that termination is again a problem. Fortunately, this problem has a simple solution requiring only n additional messages and time (Exercise 3.10.4). Summarizing, the costs of the modified protocol, *All the Way:Minit*, are as follows:

$$\mathbf{M}[Allthe Way : Minit] = nk_* + n \tag{3.5}$$

$$\mathbf{T}[Allthe Way : Minit] \leq 3n - 1 \tag{3.6}$$

The modified protocol *All the Way:Minit* will in general use fewer messages than the original one. In fact, if only a constant number of entities initiate, it will use only

$O(n)$ messages, which is excellent. By contrast, if *every* entity is an initiator, this protocol uses n messages *more* than the original one.

IMPORTANT. Notice that *All the Way* (in its original or modified version) can be used also in *unidirectional* rings with the same costs. In other words, it does not require the Bidirectional Links restriction. We will return to this point later.

3.3.2 As Far As It Can

To design an improved protocol, let us determine the drawback of the one we already have: *All the Way*. In this protocol, each message travels all along the ring.

Consider the situation (shown in Figure 3.7) of a message containing a large id, say 22, arriving at an entity x with a smaller id, say 4. In the existing protocol, x will forward this message, even though x knows that 22 is not the smallest value.

But our overall strategy is to determine the smallest id among all entities; if an entity determines that an id is not the minimum, there is no need whatsoever for the message containing such an id to continue traveling along the ring.

We will thus modify the original protocol *All the Way* so that an entity will only forward Election messages carrying an id *smaller* than the smallest seen so far by

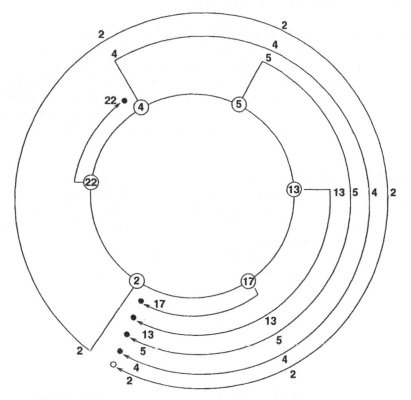

FIGURE 3.7: Message with a larger id does not need to be forwarded.

that entity. In other words, an entity will become an insurmountable obstacle for all messages with a larger id "terminating" them.

Let us examine what happens with this simple modification. Each entity will originate a message (containing its id) that travels along the ring "as far as it can": until it returns to its originator or arrives at a node with a smaller id. Hence the name *AsFar* (As It Can) will be used for the resulting protocol.

Question. *When will an entity terminate its execution?*

The message with the smallest id will always be forwarded by the other entities; thus, it will travel all along the ring returning to its originator. The message containing another id will instead be unable to return to its originator because it will find an entity with a smaller id (and thus be terminated) along the way. In other words, only the message with the smallest id will return to its originator. This fact provides us with a termination detection mechanism.

If an entity receives a message with its own id, it knows that its id is the minimum, that is, it is the leader; the other entities have all seen that message pass by (they forwarded it) but they still do not know that there will be no smaller ids to come by. Thus, to ensure their termination, the newly elected leader must *notify* them by sending an additional message along the ring.

Message Cost   This protocol will definitely have fewer messages than the previous one. The exact number depends on several factors. Consider the cost caused by the *Election* message originated by x. This message will travel along the ring until it finds a smaller id (or complete the tour). Thus, the cost of its travel depends on how the ids are allocated on the ring. Also notice that what matters is whether an id is smaller or not than another and not their actual value. In other words, what is important is the rank of the ids and how those are situated on the ring. Denote by #i the id whose rank is i.

Worst Case   Let us first consider the *worst possible case*. Id #1 will always travel all along the ring costing n messages. Id #2 will be stopped only by id #1; so its cost in the worst case is $n - 1$, achievable if id #2 is located immediately after id #1 in the direction it travels. In general, id #$(i + 1)$ will be stopped by any of those with smaller rank, and, thus, it will cost at most $n - i$ messages; this will happen if all those entities are next to each other, and id #$(i + 1)$ is located immediately after them in the direction it will travel. In fact, all the worst cases for each of the ids are *simultaneously* achieved when the ids are arranged in an (circular) order according to their rank and all messages are sent in the "increasing" direction (see Figure 3.9).

In this case, including also the n messages required for the final notification, the total cost will be

$$\mathbf{M}[\textit{AsFar}] = n + \sum_{i=1}^{n} i = \frac{n(n+3)}{2}. \tag{3.7}$$

PROTOCOL AsFar.

- States: S = {ASLEEP, AWAKE, FOLLOWER, LEADER};
  S_{INIT} = {ASLEEP};
  S_{TERM} = {FOLLOWER, LEADER}.
- Restrictions: **IR** ∪*Ring*.

```
ASLEEP
        Spontaneously
        begin
            INITIALIZE;
            become AWAKE;
        end

        Receiving("Election", value)
        begin
            INITIALIZE;
            if value < min then
              send("Election", value) to other;
              min:= value;
            endif
            become AWAKE;
        end


AWAKE
        Receiving("Election", value)
        begin
            if value < min then
              send("Election", value) to other;
              min:= value;
            else
              if value min then NOTIFY endif;
            endif
        end

        Receiving(Notify)
            send(Notify) to other;
            become FOLLOWER;
        end
```

where the procedures *Initialize* and *Notify* are as follows:

```
Procedure INITIALIZE
begin
    send("Election", id(x)) to right;
    min:= id(x);
end


Procedure NOTIFY
begin
    send(Notify) to right;
    become LEADER;
end
```

FIGURE 3.8: Protocol *AsFar.*

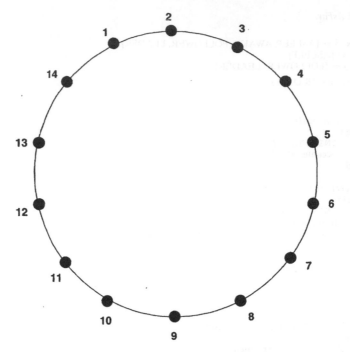

FIGURE 3.9: Worst case setting for protocol *AsFar.*

That is, we will cut the number of messages *at least to half*. From a theoretical point of view, the improvement is not significant; from a practical point of view, this is already a reasonable achievement. However we have so far analyzed only the worst case. In general, the improvement will be much more significant. To see precisely how, we need to perform a more detailed analysis of the protocol's performance.

IMPORTANT. Notice that *AsFar* can be used in *unidirectional rings*. In other words, it does not require the Bidirectional Links restriction. We will return to this point later.

The worst case gives us an indication of how "bad" things could get when the conditions are really bad. But how likely are such conditions to occur? What costs can we generally expect? To find out, we need to study the *average case* and determine the mean and the variance of the cost of the protocol.

Average Case: Oriented Ring   We will first consider the case when the ring is *oriented*, that is, "right" means the same to all entities. In this case, all messages will travel in only one direction, say clockwise.

IMPORTANT. Because of the unique nature of the ring network, this case *coincides* with the execution of the protocol in a *unidirectional* ring. Thus, the results we will obtain will hold for those rings.

To determine the average case behavior, we consider all possible arrangements of the ranks $1, \ldots, n$ in the ring as equally likely. Given a set of size a, we denote by $C(a, b)$ the number of subsets of size b that can be formed from it.

Consider the id $\#i$ with rank i; it will travel clockwise exactly k steps if and only if the ids of its $k - 1$ clockwise neighbors are larger than it (and thus will forward it), while the id of its kth clockwise neighbor is smaller (and thus will terminate it).

There are $i - 1$ ids smaller than id $\#i$ from which to choose those $k - 1$ smaller clockwise neighbors, and there are $n - i$ ids larger than id $\#i$ from which to choose the kth clockwise neighbor. In other words, the number of situations where id $\#i$ will travel clockwise exactly k steps is $C(i - 1, k - 1)C(n - i, 1)$, out of the total number of $C(n - 1, k - 1)C(n - k, 1)$ possible situations.

Thus, the probability $P(i, k)$ that id $\#i$ will travel clockwise exactly k steps is

$$P(i, k) = \frac{C(i - 1, k - 1)C(n - i, 1)}{C(n - 1, k - 1)C(n - k, 1)}. \tag{3.8}$$

The smallest id, $\#1$, will travel the full length n of the ring. The id $\#i, i > 1$, will travel less; the expected distance will be

$$E_i = \sum_{k=1}^{n-1} k\, P(i, k). \tag{3.9}$$

Therefore, the overall expected number of message transmissions is

$$E = n + \sum_{i=1}^{n-1}\sum_{k=1}^{n-1} k\, P(i, k) = n + \sum_{k=1}^{n-1} \frac{n}{k+1} = nH_n, \tag{3.10}$$

where $H_n = 1 + \frac{1}{2} + \frac{1}{3} + \ldots + \frac{1}{n}$ is the *nth Harmonic* number.

To obtain a close formula, we use the fact that the function $f(x) = \frac{1}{x}$ is continuous, linear, and decreasing; thus $\int_1^\infty \frac{1}{x}\,dx = \lim_{n\to\infty}\int_1^n \frac{1}{x}\,dx = \lim_{n\to\infty} \ln x \Big|_n^1 = \lim_{n\to\infty}(\ln n - \ln 1 + c) = \ln n + c$. Hence, $H_n = \ln n + O(1) \approx .69 \log n + O(1)$; thus

Theorem 3.3.1 *In oriented and in unidirectional rings, protocol* AsFar *will cost* $nH_n \approx .69n \log n + O(n)$ *messages on an average.*

This is indeed great news: On an average, the message cost is an order of magnitude less than that in the worst case. For $n = 1024$, this means that on an average we have 7066 messages instead of $525, 824$, which is a considerable difference.

If we use the strategy of electing the *Minimum Initiator* instead, we obtain the same bound but as a function of the number k_* of initiators:

Theorem 3.3.2   *In oriented and in unidirectional rings, protocol* AsFar-Minit *will cost* $n H_{k_*} \approx .69n \log k_*$ *messages on an average.*

Average Case: Unoriented Ring   Let us now consider what will happen on an average in the general case, when the ring is *unoriented*. As before, we consider all possible arrangements of the ranks $1, \ldots, n$ of the values in the ring as equally likely. The fact that the ring is not oriented means that when two entities send a message to their "right" neighbors, they might send it in different directions.

Let us assume that at each entity the probability that "right" coincides with the clockwise direction is $\frac{1}{2}$. Alternatively, assume that an entity, as its first step in the protocol, flips a fair coin (i.e., probability $\frac{1}{2}$) to decide the direction it will use to send its value. We shall call the resulting probabilistic protocol *ProbAsFar*.

Theorem 3.3.3   *In unoriented rings, Protocol* ProbAsFar *will cost* $\frac{\sqrt{(2)}}{2} n H_n \approx .49n \log n$ *messages on an average.*

A similar bound holds if we use the strategy of electing the *Minimum Initiator*:

Theorem 3.3.4   *In unoriented rings, protocol* ProbAsFar-Minit *will cost* $\frac{\sqrt{(2)}}{2} n H_{k_*} \approx .49n \log k_*$ *messages on an average.*

What is very interesting about the bound expressed by Theorem 3.3.3 is that it is *better* (i.e., smaller) than the one expressed by Theorem 3.3.1. The difference between the two bounds is restricted to the constant and is rather limited. In numerical terms, the difference is not outstanding: 5018 instead of 7066 messages on an average when $n = 1024$.

In practical terms, from the algorithm design point of view, it indicates that we should try to have the entities send their initial message in different directions (as in the probabilistic protocol) and not all in the same one (like in the oriented case). To simulate the initial "random" direction, different means can be used. For example, each entity x can choose (its own) "right" if $id(x)$ is even, (its own) "left" otherwise.

This result has also a theoretical relevance that will become apparent later, when we will discuss lower bounds and will have a closer look at the nature of the difference between oriented and unoriented rings.

Time Costs   The time costs are the same as the ones of *All the Way* plus an additional $n - 1$ for the notification. This can, however, be halved by exploiting the fact that the links are bidirectional and by broadcasting the notification; this will require an extra message but halve the time.

Summary   The main drawback of protocol *AsFar* is that there still exists the possibility that a very large number of messages ($O(n^2)$) will be exchanged. As we have seen, on an average, the use of the protocol will cost only $O(n \log n)$ messages. There is, however, no guarantee that this will happen the next time the protocol will be used. To give such a guarantee, a protocol must have a $O(n \log n)$ worst case complexity.

3.3.3 Controlled Distance

We will now design a protocol that has a *guaranteed* $O(n \log n)$ message performance.

To achieve this goal, we must first of all determine what causes the previous protocol to use $O(n^2)$ messages and then find ways around it.

The first thing to observe is that in *AsFar* (as well as in *All the Way*), an entity makes only one attempt to become leader and does so by originating a message containing its id. Next observe that, once this message has been created and sent, the entity has no longer any control over it: In *All the Way* the message will travel all along the ring; in *AsFar* it will be stopped if it finds a smaller id.

Consider now the situation that causes the worst case for protocol *AsFar*: this is when the ids are arranged in an increasing order along the ring, and all entities identify "right" with the clockwise direction (see Figure 3.9). The entity x with id 2 will originate a message that will cause $n - 2$ transmissions. When x receives the message containing id 1, x finds out that its own value is not the smallest, and thus its message is destined to be wasted. However, x has no means to stop it as it has no longer any control over that message.

Let us take these observations into account to design a more efficient protocol. The key design goal will be to make an entity retain some control over the message it originates. We will use several ideas to achieve this:

1. *limited distance:* The entity will impose a *limit* on the distance its message will travel; in this way, the message with id 2 will not travel "as far as it can" (i.e., at distance $n - 2$) but only up to some predefined length.

2. *return* (or *feedback*) *messages:* If, during this limited travel, the message is *not* terminated by an entity with smaller id, it will *return* back to its originator to get authorization for further travel; in this way, if the entity with id 2 has seen id 1, it will abort any further travel of its own message.

Summarizing, an entity x will originate a message with its own id, and this message will travel until it is terminated or it reaches a certain distance *dis*; if it is not terminated, the message returns to the entity. When it arrives, x knows that on this side of the ring, there are no smaller ids within the traveled distance *dis*.

The entity must now decide if to allow its message to travel a further distance; it will do so only if it knows for sure that there are no smaller ids within distance *dis* on the other side of the ring as well. This can be achieved as follows:

3. *check both sides:* The entity will send a message in both directions; only if they both return, they will be allowed to travel a further distance.

As a consequence, instead of a single global attempt at leadership, an entity will go through several attempts, which we shall call *Electoral Stages*: An entity enters the

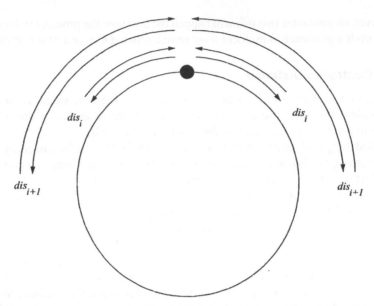

FIGURE 3.10: Controlled distances: A message travels no more than *dis(i)*; if it is not discarded, a feedback is sent back to the originator. A *candidate* that receives a feedback from both sides starts the next stage.

next stage only if it passes the current one (i.e., both messages return) (see Fig. 3.10). If an entity is *defeated* in an electoral stage (i.e., at least one of its messages does not return), it still will have to continue its participation in the algorithm forwarding the messages of those entities that are still undefeated.

Although the protocol is almost all outlined, some fundamental issues are still unresolved. In particular, the fact that we now have several stages can have strange consequences in the execution.

IMPORTANT. Because of variations in communication delays, it is possible that at the same time instant, entities in different parts of the ring are in different electoral stages. Furthermore, as we are only using the standard restrictions for elections, messages can be delivered out of order; thus, it might be possible that messages from a higher stage will arrive at an entity before the ones from the current one.

We said that an entity is defeated if it does not receive one of its messages back. Consider now an entity x; it has sent its two messages and it is now waiting to know the outcome. Let us say that one of its messages has returned but the other has not yet. It is possible that the message is coming very slowly (e.g., experiencing long transmission delays) or that it is not coming at all (i.e., it found a smaller id on the way). How can x know ? How long will x have to wait before taking a decision (a decision *must* be taken within finite time)? More specifically, what will x do if, in the meanwhile, it receives a message from a higher stage ? The answer to all these questions is fortunately simple:

4. *the smallest id wins:* If, at any time, a candidate entity receives message with a *smaller* id, it will become *defeated*, regardless of the stage number.

Notice that this creates a new situation: A message returns to its originator and finds it *defeated*; in this case, the message will be terminated.

The final issue we need to address is termination. The limit to the travel distance for a message in a given stage will depend on the stage itself; let dis_i denote the limit in stage i. Clearly, these distances must be monotonically increasing, that is, $dis_i > dis_{i-1}$. The messages from an entity whose id is not the minimum will sooner or later encounter a smaller id in their travel and will not return to their originator.

Consider now the entity s with the smallest id. In each stage, both of its messages will travel the full allocated distance (as no entity can terminate them) and return, making s enter the next stage. This process will continue until $dis_i \geq n$; at this time, each message will complete a full tour of the ring reaching s *from the other side*. When this happens, s will know that it has the smallest value and, thus, it is the leader. It will then start a notification process so that all the other entities can enter a terminal state.

A synthetic description of the protocol will thus be as follows:

- in each electoral stage there are some *candidates*;
- each *candidate* sends a message in both directions carrying its own id (as well as the stage number);
- a message travels until it encounters a smaller id or it reaches a certain distance (whose value depends on the stage);
- if a message does not encounter a smaller id, it will return back to its originator;
- a *candidate* that receives both of its own messages back survives this stage and starts the next one;

with three *meta* rules:

- if a *candidate* receives its message from the opposite side it sent to, it becomes the *leader* and notifies all the other entities of termination;
- if a *candidate* receives a message with a smaller id, it becomes *defeated*, regardless of the stage number;
- a *defeated* entity forwards the messages originating from the other entities; if the message is notification of termination, it will terminate.

The fully specified protocol *Control* is shown in Figures 3.11 and 3.12, where *dis* is a monotonically increasing function.

Correctness   The correctness of the algorithm follows from the dynamics of the rules: The messages containing the smallest id will always travel all the allocated

PROTOCOL Control.

- States: $S = \{$ASLEEP, CANDIDATE, DEFEATED, FOLLOWER, LEADER$\}$;
  $S_{INIT} = \{$ASLEEP$\}$;
  $S_{TERM} = \{$FOLLOWER, LEADER$\}$.
- Restrictions: **IR** $\cup Ring$.

```
ASLEEP
        Spontaneously
        begin
            INITIALIZE;
            become CANDIDATE;
        end

        Receiving("Forth", id*, stage*, limit*)
        begin
            if id* < id(x) then
                PROCESS-MESSAGE;
                become DEFEATED
            else
                INITIALIZE;
                become CANDIDATE;
            endif
        end


CANDIDATE
        Receiving("Forth", id*, stage*, limit*)
        begin
            if id* < id(x) then
                PROCESS-MESSAGE;
                become DEFEATED
            else
                if id* = id(x) then NOTIFY endif;
            endif
        end

        Receiving("Back", id*)
        begin
            if id* = id(x) then CHECK endif;
        end

        Receiving(Notify)
        begin
            send(Notify) to other;
            become FOLLOWER;
        end


DEFEATED
        Receiving(*)
        begin
            send(*) to other;
            if * = Notify then become FOLLOWER endif;
        end
```

FIGURE 3.11: Protocol *Control.*

```
Procedure INITIALIZE
begin
    stage:= 1;
    limit:= dis(stage);
    count:= 0;
    send("Forth", id(x), stage, limit) to N(x);
end


Procedure PROCESS-MESSAGE
begin
    limit*:=limit*-1;
    if limit* =0 then
      send("Back",id*, stage*) to sender;
    else
      send("Forth", id*, stage*, limit*) to other;
    endif
end


Procedure CHECK
begin
    count:=count+1;
    if count = 1 then
      count:= 0
      stage:= stage+1
      limit:= dis(stage);
      send("Forth", id(x), stage, limit) to N(x);
    endif
end


Procedure NOTIFY
begin
    send(Notify) to right;
    become LEADER;
end
```

FIGURE 3.12: Procedures used by protocol *Control.*

distance, and every entity still *candidate* they encounter will be transformed in *defeated*; the distance is monotonically increasing in the number of stages; hence, eventually, the distance will be at least *n*. When this happens, the messages with the smallest value will travel all along the ring; as a result, their originator becomes *leader* and all the others are already *defeated*.

Costs The costs of the algorithm depend totally on the choice of the function *dis* used to determine the maximum distance a "Forth" message can travel in a stage.

Messages If we examine the execution of the protocol at some global time *t*, because communication delays are unpredictable, we can find not only that entities in different parts of the ring are in different states (which is expected) but also that entities in the *candidate* state are in different stages. Moreover, because there is no Message Ordering, messages from high stages (the "future") might overtake messages from lower stages and arrive at an entity still in a lower stage (the "past").

Still, we can visualize the execution as proceeding in *logical* stages; it is just that different entities might be executing the same stage at different times.

Focus on stage $i > 1$ and consider the entities that will start this stage; these n_i entities are those that survived stage $i - 1$.

To survive stage $i - 1$, the id of x must be smaller than the ids of its neighbors at distance up to dis(i) on each side of the ring. Thus, within any group of dis$(i) + 1$ consecutive entities, at most one can survive stage $i - 1$ and start stage i. In other words,

$$n_i \leq \left\lfloor \frac{n}{\text{dis}(i-1) + 1} \right\rfloor. \tag{3.11}$$

An entity starting stage i will send "Forth" messages in both directions; each message will travel at most dis(i), for a total of $2n_i$ dis(i) message transmissions.

Let us examine now the "Back" messages. Each entity that survives this stage will receive such a message from both sides; as n_{i+1} entities survive this stage, this gives an additional $2n_{i+1}$ dis(i) messages. Each entity that started but did *not* survive stage i will receive either no or at most one "Back" message, causing a cost of *at most* dis(i); as there are $n_i - n_{i+1}$ such entities, they will cost no more than an additional $(n_i - n_{i+1})dis(i)$ messages in total. So, in total, the transmissions for "Back" messages are at most $2n_{i+1}dis(i) + (n_i - n_{i+1})dis(i)$.

Summarizing, the total number of messages sent in stage $i > 1$ will be no more than

$$2\, n_i\, \text{dis}(i) + 2\, n_{i+1}\, \text{dis}(i) + (n_i - n_{i+1})\, \text{dis}(i) = (3\, n_i + n_{i+1})\, \text{dis}(i)$$

$$\leq \left(3 \left\lfloor \tfrac{n}{\text{dis}(i-1)+1} \right\rfloor + \left\lfloor \tfrac{n}{\text{dis}(i)+1} \right\rfloor \right) \text{dis}(i) < n \left(3 \tfrac{\text{dis}(i)}{\text{dis}(i-1)} + 1\right).$$

The first stage is a bit different, as every entity starts; the n_2 entities that survive this stage will have caused the messages carrying their id to travel to distance $dis(1)$ and back on both sides, for a total of $4n_2\, dis(1)$ messages. The $n - n_2$ entities that will not survive will cause at most three messages each (two "Forth" and one "Back") to travel distance dis(1), for a total of $3(n_1 - n_2)$ dis(1) messages. Hence the first stage will cost no more than

$$\left(3n + n_2\right) \text{dis}\left(1\right) \leq \left(3n + \tfrac{n}{\text{dis}(1)+1}\right) \text{dis}\left(1\right) < n\,(3\, \text{dis}\left(1\right) + 1).$$

To determine the total number of messages, we then need to know the total number k of stages. We know that a leader is elected as soon as the message with the smallest value makes a complete tour of the ring, that is, as soon as dis(i) is greater or equal to n. In other words, k is the smallest integer such that dis$(k) \geq n$; such an integer is called the *pseudo-inverse* of n and denoted by $\text{dis}^{-1}(n)$.

So, the total number of messages used by protocol *Control* will be at most

$$\mathbf{M}[Control] \leq n \sum_{i=1}^{\text{dis}^{-1}(n)} \left(3 \frac{\text{dis}(i)}{\text{dis}(i-1)} + 1\right) + n, \tag{3.12}$$

where dis$(0) = 1$ and the last n messages are those for the final notification.

To really finalize the design, we must choose the function *dis*. Different choices will result in different performances.

Consider, for example, the choice $dis(i) = 2^{i-1}$; then $\frac{dis(i)}{dis(i-1)} = 2$ (i.e., we double the distance every time) and $dis^{-1}(n) = \lceil \log n \rceil + 1$, which in Expression 3.12 yields

$$\mathbf{M}[Control] \leq 7 \, n \log n + O(n),$$

which is what we were aiming for: a $O(n \log n)$ worst case.

The constant can be, however, further improved by carefully selecting *dis*. It is rather difficult to determine the best function. Let us restrict the choice to among the functions where, like the one above, the ratio between consecutive values is constant, that is, $\frac{dis(i)}{dis(i-1)} = c$. For these functions, $\mathrm{dis}^{-1}(n) = \lceil \log_c(n) \rceil + 1$; thus, Expression 3.12 becomes

$$\tfrac{3c+1}{\log c} n \log n + O(n).$$

Thus, with all of them, protocol *Control* has a guaranteed $O(n \log n)$ performance.

The "best" among those functions will be the one where $\frac{3c+1}{\log c}$ is minimized; as distances must be integer quantities, also c must be an integer. Thus such a best choice is $c = 3$ for which we obtain

$$\mathbf{M}[Control] \leq 6.309 \, n \log n + O(n). \tag{3.13}$$

Time   The ideal time complexity of procedure *Control* is easy to determine; the time required by stage i is the time needed by the message containing the smallest id to reach its assigned distance and come back to its originator; hence exactly $2dis(i)$ time units. An additional n time units are needed for the final notification, as well as for the initial wake-up of the entity with the smallest id. This means that the total time costs will be at most

$$\mathbf{T}[Control] \leq 2n + \sum_{i=1}^{\mathrm{dis}^{-1}(n)} 2 \, \mathrm{dis}(i). \tag{3.14}$$

Again, the choice of dis will influence the complexity. Using any function of the form $\mathrm{dis}(i) = c^{i-1}$, where c is a positive integer, will yield $O(n)$ time. The determination of the best choice from the time costs point of view is left as an exercise.

Electing Minimum Initiator $(\star)$ Let us use the strategy of electing a leader only among the initiators. Denote as usual by $k_\star$ the number of initiators. Let us analyze the worst case.

In the analysis of protocol *Control*, we have seen that those that survive stage i contribute $4 \, \mathrm{dis}(i)$ messages each to the cost, while those that do not survive contribute at most $3 \, \mathrm{dis}(i)$ messages each. This is still true in the modified version *Control-Minit*;

what changes is the values of the number n_i of entities that will start that stage. Initially, $n_1 = k_*$. In the worst case, the k_* initiators are placed far enough from each other in the ring that each completes the stage without interfering with the others; if the distances between them are large enough, each can continue to go to higher stages without coming into contact with the others, thus, causing $4 \, \mathrm{dis}(i)$ messages.

For how many stages can this occur ? This can occur as long as $\mathrm{dis}(i) < \frac{n}{k_*+1}$. That is, in the worst case, $n_i = k_*$ in each of the first $l = \mathrm{dis}^{-1}\left(\frac{n}{k_*+1} - 1\right)$ stages, and the cost will be $4 \, k_* \mathrm{dis}(i)$ messages. In the following stages instead, the initiators will start interfering with each other, and the number of survivors will follow the pattern of the general algorithm: $n_i \leq \left\lfloor \frac{n_1}{\mathrm{dis}(i-1)+1} \right\rfloor$.

Thus, the total number $\mathbf{M}[\textit{Control-Minit}]$ of messages in the worst case will be at most

$$\mathbf{M}[\textit{Control-Minit}] \leq 4 \, k_* \sum_{i=1}^{l} \mathrm{dis}(i) + n \sum_{i=l+1}^{\mathrm{dis}^{-1}(n)} \left(3 \, \frac{\mathrm{dis}(i)}{\mathrm{dis}(i-1)} + 1 \right) + n.$$

$$(3.15)$$

3.3.4 Electoral Stages

In the previous protocol, we have introduced and used the idea of *limiting the distances* to control the complexity of the original "as far as it can" approach. This idea requires that an entity makes several successive attempts (at increasing distances) to become a leader.

The idea of not making a single attempt to become a leader (as it was done in *All the Way* and in *AsFar*), instead of proceeding in stages, is a very powerful algorithmic tool of its own. It allows us to view the election as a sequence of *electoral stages* : At the beginning of each stage, the "candidates" run for election; at the end of the stage, some "candidates" will be defeated, the others will start the next stage. Recall that "stage" is a logical notion, and it does not require the system to be synchronized; in fact, parts of the system may run very fast while other parts may be slow in their operation, so different entities might execute a stage at totally different times.

We will now see how the proper use of this tool allows us to achieve even better results, *without* controlling the distances and *without* return (or feedback) messages.

To simplify the presentation and the discussion, we will temporarily assume that there is *Message Ordering* (i.e., the links are FIFO); we will remove the restriction immediately after.

As before, we will have each *candidate* send a message carrying its own id in both directions. Without setting an a priori fixed limit on the distance these messages can travel, we still would like to avoid them to travel unnecessarily far (costing too many transmissions). The strategy to achieve this is simple and effective:

- A message will travel until it reaches another candidate in the same (or higher) stage.

The consequence of this simple strategy is that in each stage, *a candidate will receive a message from each side*; thus, it will know the ids of the neighboring candidate on each side. We will use this fact to decide whether a candidate x enters the next stage: x will survive this stage only if the two received ids are not smaller than its own $id(x)$ (recall we are electing the entity with the smallest id); otherwise, it becomes *defeated*. As before, we will have *defeated* entities continue to participate by forwarding received messages.

Correctness and termination are easy to verify. Observe that the initiator with the smallest identity will never become *defeated*; by contrast, at each stage, its message will transform into *defeated* the neighboring *candidate* on each side (regardless of their distance). Hence, the number of *candidates* decreases at each stage. This means that eventually, the only *candidate* left is the one with the minimum id. When this happens, its messages will travel all along the ring (forwarded by the *defeated* entities) and reach it. Thus, a *candidate* receiving its own messages back knows that all other entities are *defeated*; it will then become *leader* and notify all other entities of termination.

Summarizing (see also Figure 3.13):

- A candidate x sends a message in both directions carrying its identity; these messages will travel until they encounter another candidate node.
- By symmetry, entity x will receive two messages, one from the "left" and one from the "right" (independently of any sense of direction); it will then become *defeated* if at least one of them carries an identity smaller than its own; if both the received identities are larger than its own, it starts the next stage; finally, if the received identities are its own, it becomes *leader* and notifies all entities of termination.
- A *defeated* node will forward any received election message, and each noninitiator will automatically become defeated upon receiving an election message.

The protocol is shown in Figure 3.14, where **close** and **open** denote the operation of closing a port (with the effect of enqueueing incoming messages) and opening a closed port (dequeueing the messages), respectively, and where procedure Initialize is shown in Figure 3.15.

$x > Min\{y,z\} \implies x$ *defeated*

$x < Min\{y,z\} \implies x$ *candidate next stage*

$x = Min\{y,z\} \implies x$ *leader*

FIGURE 3.13: A *candidate* x in an electoral stage.

PROTOCOL Stages.

- States: S = {ASLEEP, CANDIDATE, WAITING, DEFEATED, FOLLOWER, LEADER};
  S_{INIT} = {ASLEEP}; S_{TERM} $\doteq$ {FOLLOWER, LEADER}.
- Restrictions: **IR** $\cup Ring$.

```
ASLEEP
        Spontaneously
        begin
              INITIALIZE;
              become CANDIDATE;
        end

        Receiving("Election", id*, stage*)
        begin
              INITIALIZE;
              min:= Min(id*,min);
              close(sender);
              become WAITING;
        end

CANDIDATE
        Receiving("Election", id*, stage*)
        begin
              if id* ≠ id(x) then
                    min:= Min(id*,min);
                    close(sender);
                    become WAITING;
              else
                    send(Notify) to N(x);
                    become LEADER;
        end

WAITING
        Receiving("Election", id*, stage*)
              open(other);
              stage:= stage+1;
              min:= Min(id*,min);
              if min= id(x) then
                    send("Election", id(x), stage) to N(x);
                    become CANDIDATE;
              else
                    become DEFEATED;
              endif
        end

DEFEATED
        Receiving(*)
        begin
              send(*) to other;
              if * = Notify then become FOLLOWER endif;
        end
```

FIGURE 3.14: Protocol *Stages.*

Messages It is not so obvious that this strategy is more efficient than the previous one.

Let us first determine the number of messages exchanged during a stage. Consider the segment of the ring between two neighboring *candidates* in stage i, x, and

```
Procedure INITIALIZE
begin
     stage:= 1;
     count:= 0;
     min:= id(x);
     send("Election", id(x), stage) to N(x);
end
```

FIGURE 3.15: Procedure Initialize used by protocol *Stages*.

$y = r(i, x)$; in this stage, x will send a message to y and y will send one to x. No other messages will be transmitted during this stage in that segment. In other words, on each link, only *two* messages will be transmitted (one in each direction) in this stage. Therefore, in total, $2n$ message exchanges will be performed during each stage.

Let us determine now the number of stages. Consider a node x that is *candidate* at the beginning of stage i and is not defeated during this stage; let $y = r(i, x)$ and $z = l(i, x)$ be the first entity to the right and to the left of x, respectively, that are also *candidates* in stage i (Figure 3.16).

It is not difficult to see that if x survives stage i, both $r(i, x)$ and $l(i, x)$ will be *defeated*. Therefore, at least half of the candidates are *defeated* at each stage. In other words, at most half of them survive:

$$n_i \leq \tfrac{n_{i-1}}{2}.$$

As $n_1 = n$, the total number of stages is at most $\sigma_{Stages} \leq \lceil \log n \rceil + 1$.

Combining the two observations, we obtain,

$$\mathbf{M}[Stages] \leq 2\,n \log n + O(n). \tag{3.16}$$

That is, protocol *Stages* outperforms protocol *Control*.

Observe that equality is achievable in practice (Exercise 3.10.9). Further note that if we use the *Minimum Initiator* approach the bound will become

$$\mathbf{M}[Stages:Minit] \leq 2\,n \log k_* + O(n). \tag{3.17}$$

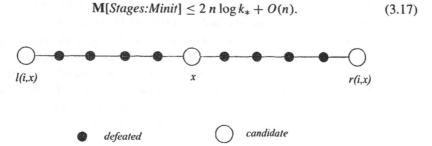

FIGURE 3.16: If x survives this stage, its neighboring *candidates* will not.

Removing Message Ordering   The correctness and termination of *Stages* are easy to follow also because we have assumed in our protocol that there is *Message*

Ordering. This assumption ensured that the two messages received by a *candidate* in stage *i* are originated by *candidates* also in stage *i*. If we remove the *Message Ordering* restriction, it is possible that messages arrive out of order and that a message sent in stage $j > i$ arrives *before* a message sent in stage *i*.

Simple Approach   The simplest way to approach this problem is by enforcing the "effects" of Message Ordering, without really having it.

1. First of all, each message will also carry the stage number of the entity originating it.
2. When a *candidate* node *x* in stage *i* receives a message $M*$ with stage $j > i$, it will not process it but will locally enqueue it until it has received from that side (and processed) all the messages from stages $i, i + 1, \ldots, j - 1$, which have been "jumped over" by $M*$; it will then process $M*$.

The only modification to protocol *Stages* as described in Figure 3.14 is the addition of the local enqueueing of messages (Exercise 3.10.6); as this is only local processing, the message and time costs are unchanged.

Stages*   An alternative approach is to keep a track of a message "jumping over" others but without enqueueing it locally. We shall describe it in some details and call *Stages** the corresponding protocol.

1. First of all, we will give a stage number to all the nodes: For a *candidate* entity, it is the current stage; for a *defeated* entity, it is the stage in which it was defeated. We will then have a *defeated* node forward only messages from higher stages.
2. A *candidate* node *x* in stage *i* receiving an Election message $M*$ with stage $j > i$ will use the id included in the message, id*, and will make a decision about the outcome of the stage *i* as if both of them were in the same stage.
   - If *x* is defeated in this round, then it will forward the message $M*$.
   - If *x* survives, it means that id(*x*) is smaller not only than id* in $M*$ but also than the ids in the messages "jumped over" by $M*$ (Exercise3.10.13).

     In this case, *x* can act because it has received already from that side all the messages from stages $i, i + 1, \ldots, j$, and they all have an id larger than id(*x*). We will indicate this fact by saying that *x* has now a *credit* of $j - i$ messages on that port. In other words, if a *candidate* *x* has a *credit* $c > 0$ associated with a port, it does not have to wait for a message from that port during the current stage. Clearly, the credit must be decreased in each stage.

To write the set of rules for protocol *Stages** is a task that, although not difficult, requires great care and attention to details (Exercise 3.10.12); similar characteristics has the task of proving the correctness of the protocol *Stages** (Exercise 3.10.14).

As for the resulting communication complexity, the number of messages is never more (sometimes less) than that with *Message Ordering* (Exercise 3.10.15).

Interestingly, if we attempt to measure the *ideal time* complexity, we will only see executions with *Message Ordering*. In other words,

the phenomenon of messages delivered out of order will disappear.

This is yet another case showing how biased and limited (and thus dangerous) *ideal time* is as a cost measure.

3.3.5 Stages with Feedback

We have seen how, with the proper use of electoral stages in protocol *Stages*, we can obtain a $O(n \log n)$ performance without the need of controlling the distance travelled by a message.

In addition to controlled distances, protocol *Control* uses also a "feedback" technique: If a message successfully reaches its target, it returns back to its originator, providing it with a "positive feedback" on the situation it has encountered. Such a technique is missing in *Stages*: A message always successfully reaches its target (the next candidate in the direction it travels), which could be at an unpredictable distance; however, the use of the message ends there.

Let us integrate the positive feedback idea in the overall strategy of *Stages*: When an "Election" message reaches its target, a positive *feedback* will be sent back to its originator if the id contained in the message is the smallest seen by the target in this stage.

More precisely, when a *candidate x* receives Election messages containing $id(y)$ and $id(z)$ from its neighboring *candidates*, $y = r(i, x)$ and $z = l(i, x)$, it will send a (positive) *"feedback"* message: to y if $id(y) < \text{Min}\{id(x), id(z)\}$, to z if $id(z) < \text{Min}\{id(x), id(y)\}$, and to none otherwise. A *candidate* will then survive this stage and enter the new one if and only if it receives a feedback from both sides.

In the example of Figure 3.17, *candidates* with ids 2, 5, and 8 will not send any feedback; of these three, only *candidate* with id 2 will enter next stage. The fate of entity with id 7 depends on its other neighboring *candidate*, which is not shown; so, we do not know whether it will survive or not.

If a node sends a "feedback" message, it knows that it will not survive this stage. This is the case, for example, of the entities with ids 6, 9, 10, and 11.

Some entities, however, do not send any "feedback" and wait for a "feedback" that will never arrive; this is, for example, the case of the entities with ids 5 and 8. How will such an entity discover that no "feedback" is forthcoming and it must become *defeated*? The answer is fortunately simple. Every entity that survives stage i (e.g.,

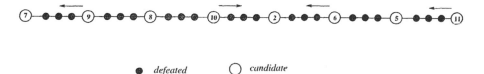

● *defeated*   ○ *candidate*

FIGURE 3.17: Only some *candidates* will send a feedback.

the node with id 2) will start the next stage; its Stage message will act as a *negative feedback* for those entities receiving the message while still waiting in stage i.

More specifically, if while waiting for a "feedback" message in stage i, an entity receives an "Election" message (clearly with a smaller id) in stage $i + 1$, it becomes *defeated* and forwards the message.

We shall call the protocol *Stages with Feedback*; our description was assuming message ordering. As for protocol *Stages*, this restriction can and will be logically enforced with just local processing.

Correctness   The correctness and termination of the protocol follows from the fact that the entity x_{min} with the smallest identity will always receive a positive feedback from both sides; hence, it will never be defeated. At the same time, x_{min} never sends a positive feedback; hence, its left and right neighboring candidates in that stage do not survive it. In other words, the number n_i of *candidates* in stage i is monotonically decreasing, and eventually only x_{min} will be in such a state. When this happens, its own "Election" messages will travel along the ring, and termination will be detected.

Messages   We are adding bookkeeping and additional messages to the already highly efficient protocol *Stages*. Let us examine the effect of these changes.

Let us start with the number of stages.

As in *Stages*, if a *candidate* x in stage i survives, it is guaranteed that its neighboring *candidates* in the same stage, $r(i, x)$ and $l(i, x)$, will become *defeated*. With the introduction of positive feedback, we can actually guarantee that if x survives, neither will the first *candidate* to the right of $r(i, x)$ survive nor will the first candidate to the left of $l(i, x)$ survive.

This is because if x survives, it must have received a "feedback" from both $r(i, x)$ and $l(i, x)$ (see Figure 3.18). But if $r(i, x)$ sends "feedback" to x, it does not send one to its neighboring *candidate* $r^2(i, x)$; similarly, $l(i, x)$ does not send a "Feedback" to $l^2(i, x)$. In other words,

$$n_i \le \frac{n_{i-1}}{3}.$$

That is, at most one third of the candidates starting a stage will enter the next one. As $n_1 = n$, the total number of stages is at most $\sigma_{Stages} \le \lceil \log_3 n \rceil + 1$. Note that there are initial configurations of the ids that will force the protocol to have exactly these many stages (Exercise 3.10.22).

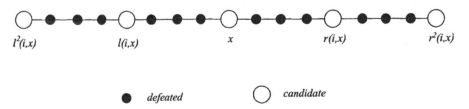

$l^2(i,x)$ $l(i,x)$ x $r(i,x)$ $r^2(i,x)$

● *defeated*   ○ *candidate*

FIGURE 3.18: If x survives, those other *candidates* do not.

In other words, the number of stages has *decreased* with the use of "feedback" messages. However, we are sending more messages in each stage.

Let us examine now how many messages will be sent in each stage. Consider stage i; this will be started by n_i candidates. Each candidate will send an "Election" message that will travel to the next *candidate* on either side. Thus, exactly like in *Stages*, two "Election" messages will be sent over each link, one in each direction, for a total of $2n$ "Election" messages per stage. Consider now the "feedback" messages; a candidate sends at most one "feedback" and only in one direction. Thus, in the segment of the ring between two candidates, there will be at most one "feedback" message on each link; hence, there will be no more than n "feedback" transmissions in total in each stage. This means that in each stage there will be at most $3n$ messages.

Summarizing,

$$\mathbf{M}[\textit{StagesFeedback}] \leq 3\,n\,\log_3 n + O(n) \leq 1.89\,n\log n + O(n). \qquad (3.18)$$

In other words, the use of feedback with the electoral stages allows us to reduce the number of messages in the worst case. The use of *Minimum Initiator* strategy yields the similar result:

$$\mathbf{M}[\textit{StagesFeedback–Minit}] \leq 1.89\,n\log k_* + O(n). \qquad (3.19)$$

In the analysis of the number of "feedback" messages sent in each stage, we can be more accurate; in fact, there are some areas of the ring (composed of consecutive *defeated* entities between two successive candidates) where no feedback messages will be transmitted at all. In the example of Figure 3.17, this is the case of the area between the candidates with ids 8 and 10. The number of these areas is exactly equal to the number n_{i+1} of candidates that survive this stage (Exercise 3.10.19). However, the savings are not enough to reduce the constant in the leading term of the message costs (Exercise 3.10.21).

Granularity of Analysis: Bit Complexity The advantage of protocol *Stages with Feedback* becomes more evident when we look at communication costs at a finer level of granularity, focusing on the actual *size* of the messages being used. In fact, while the "Election" messages contain values, the "feedback" messages are just *signals*, each containing $O(1)$ bits. (Recall the discussion in Section 3.2.)

In each stage, only the $2n$ "Election" messages carry a value, while the other n are signals; hence, the total number of *bits* transmitted will be at most

$$2\,n\,(c\,+\log\mathbf{id})\,\log_3 n + n\,c\,\log_3 n + l.o.t.,$$

where **id** denotes the largest value sent in a message, $c = O(1)$ denotes the number of bits required to distinguish among the different types of message, and *l.o.t.* stands for "lower order terms." That is,

$$\mathbf{B}[\textit{StageswithFeedback}] \leq 1.26\,n\log n\,\log\mathbf{id} + l.o.t. \qquad (3.20)$$

The improvement on the bit complexity of *Stages*, where every message carries a value, is, thus, in the reduction of the constant from 2 to 1.26.

Further Improvements? The use of electoral stages allows us to transform the election process into one of successive "eliminations," reducing the number of *candidates* at each stage. In the original protocol *Stages*, each surviving candidate will eliminate its neighboring candidate on each side, guaranteeing that at least half of the candidates are eliminated in each stage. By using feedback, protocol *Stages with Feedback* extends the "reach" of a candidate also to the second neighboring candidate on each side, ensuring that at least two third of the candidates are eliminated in each stage. Increasing the "reach" of a candidate during a stage will result in a larger proportion of the candidates in each stage, thus, reducing the number of stages. So, intuitively, we would like a candidate to reach as far as possible during a stage. Obviously the price to be paid is the additional messages required to implement the longer reach.

In general, if we can construct a protocol that guarantees a reduction rate of at least b, that is, $n_i \leq \frac{n_{i-1}}{b}$, then the total number of stages would be $\log_b(n)$; if the messages transmitted in each stage are at most an, then the overall complexity will be

$$a\,n\,\log_b(n) = \frac{a}{\log b}\,n\log n.$$

To improve on *Stages with Feedback*, the reduction must be done with a number of messages such that $\frac{a}{\log b} < 1.89$. Whether this is possible or not is an open problem (Problem 3.10.3).

3.3.6 Alternating Steps

It should be clear by now that the road to improvement, on which creative ingenuity will travel, is oftentimes paved by a deeper understanding of what is already available.

A way to achieve such an understanding is by examining the functioning of the object of our improvement in "slow motion," so as to observe its details.

Let us consider protocol *Stages*. It is rather simple and highly efficient. We have already shown how to achieve improvements by extending the "reach" of a candidate during a stage; in a sense, this was really "speeding up" the functioning of the protocol. Let us examine now *Stages* instead by "slowing down" its functioning.

In each stage, a candidate sends its id in both directions, receives an id from each direction, and decides whether to survive, be elected, or become defeated on the basis of its own value and the received ones.

Consider the example shown in Figure 3.19; the result of *stages* will result in candidates w, y, and v being eliminated and x and z surviving; the fate of u will depend on its right candidate neighbor, which is not shown.

We can obviously think of "sending in both directions" as two separate steps: send to one direction (say "right") and send to the other. Assume for the moment that the ring is *oriented*: "right" has the same meaning for all entities. Thus, the stage can be thought of having two steps: (1) The *candidate* sends to the "right" and receives from the "left"; (2) it will then send to the "left" and receive from the "right."

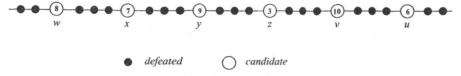

● *defeated*   ○ *candidate*

FIGURE 3.19: *Alternating Steps*: slowing down the execution of *Stages*.

Consider the first step in the same example as shown in Figure 3.19; both *candidates* y and v already know at this time that they would not survive. Let us take advantage of this "early" discovery. We will use each of these two steps to make an electoral decision, and we will eliminate a *candidate* after step (1) if it receives a smaller id in this step. Thus, a *candidate* will perform step (2) only if it is not eliminated in step (1).

The advantage of doing so becomes clear observing that by eliminating candidates in each step of a phase, we eliminate more than that in the original phase; in the example of Figure 3.19, also x will be eliminated.

Summarizing, the idea is that at each step, a candidate sends only one message with its value, waits for one message, and decides on the basis of its value and the received one; the key is to alternate at each step the direction in which messages are sent.

This protocol, which we shall call *Alternate*, is shown in Figure 3.20, where **close** and **open** denote the operation of closing a port (with the effect of enqueueing incoming messages) and opening a closed port (dequeueing the messages), respectively; and the procedures *Initialize* and *Process_Message* are shown in Figure 3.21.

Correctness   The correctness of the protocol follows immediately from observing that, as usual, the *candidate* x_{min} with the smallest value will never be eliminated and that, on the contrary, it will in each step eliminate a neighboring *candidate*. Hence, the number of *candidates* is monotonically decreasing in the steps; when only x_{min} is left, its message will complete the tour of the ring transforming it into the *leader*. The final notification will ensure proper termination of all entities.

Costs   To determine the cost is slightly more complex. There are exactly n messages transmitted in each step, so we need to determine the total number of steps $\sigma_{Alternate}$ (or, where no confusion arises, simply σ) until a single candidate is left, in the worst case, regardless of the placement of the ids in the ring, time delays, and so forth.

Let n_i be the candidate entities starting step i; clearly $n_1 = n$ and $n_\sigma = 1$. We know that two successive steps of *Alternate* will eliminate more candidates than a single stage of *Stages*; hence, the total number of steps will be less than twice the number of stages of *Stages*:

$$\sigma < 2 \log n.$$

We can, however, be more accurate regarding the amount of elimination performed in two successive steps.

PROTOCOL Alternate.

- States: $S = \{$ASLEEP, CANDIDATE, DEFEATED, FOLLOWER, LEADER$\}$;
  $S_{INIT} = \{$ASLEEP$\}$;
  $S_{TERM} = \{$FOLLOWER, LEADER$\}$.
- Restrictions: **IR** $\cup$ *OrientedRing* $\cup$ *MessageOrdering*.

ASLEEP
  Spontaneously
  begin
    INITIALIZE;
    become CANDIDATE;
  end

  Receiving("Election", id*, step*)
  begin
    INITIALIZE;
    become CANDIDATE;
    PROCESS_MESSAGE;
  end

CANDIDATE
  Receiving("Election", id*, step*)
  begin
    if id* $\neq id(x)$ **then**
      PROCESS_MESSAGE;
    else
      send(Notify) **to** $N(x)$;
      become LEADER;
  end

DEFEATED
  Receiving(*)
  begin
    send(*) **to** other;
    if * = Notify **then become** FOLLOWER **endif**;
  end

FIGURE 3.20: Protocol *Alternate.*

Assume that in step i, the direction is "right" (thus, it will be "left" in step $i + 1$). Let d_i denote the number of candidates that are eliminated in step i. Of those n_i candidates that start step i, d_i will be defeated and only n_{i+1} will survive that step. That is,

$$n_i = d_i + n_{i+1}$$

Consider a candidate x that survives both step i and step $i + 1$. First of all observe that the candidate to the right of x in step i will be eliminated in that step. (If not, it would mean that its id is smaller than id(x) and thus would eliminate x in step $i + 1$; but we know that x survives.)

This means that every candidate that, like x, survives both stages will eliminate one candidate in the first stage; in other words,

$$d_i \geq n_{i+2},$$

```
Procedure INITIALIZE
begin
     step:= 1;
     min:= id(x);
     send("Election", id(x), step) to right;
     close(right);
end


Procedure PROCESS_MESSAGE
begin
     if id*< min then
        open(other);
        become DEFEATED;
     else
        step:= step+1;
        send("Election", id(x), step) to sender;
        close(sender);
        open(other);
     endif
end
```

FIGURE 3.21: Procedures used by protocol *Alternate*.

but then

$$n_i \geq n_{i+1} + n_{i+2}. \tag{3.21}$$

The consequence of this fact is very interesting. In fact, we know that $n_\sigma = 1$ and, obviously, $n_{\sigma-1} \geq 2$. From Equation 3.21, we have $n_{\sigma-i} \geq n_{\sigma-i+1} + n_{\sigma-i+2}$.

Consider now the Fibonacci numbers F_j defined by $F_j = F_{j+1} + F_{j+2}$, where $F_{-1} = 0$ and $F_0 = 1$. Then, clearly

$$n_{\sigma-i} \geq F_{i+1}.$$

It follows that $n_1 \geq F_\sigma$, but $n_1 = n$; thus σ is the index of the largest Fibonacci number not exceeding n. This helps us in achieving our goal of determining σ, the number of steps until there is only one candidate left. As $F_j = b \left(\frac{1+\sqrt{5}}{2}\right)^j$, where b is a positive constant, we have

$$n \geq F_\sigma = b \left(\frac{1+\sqrt{5}}{2}\right)^\sigma$$

from where we get,

$$\sigma_{Alternate} \leq 1.44 \log n + O(1).$$

That means that after *at most* so many steps, there will be only one candidate left. Observe that what we have derived is actually *achievable*. In fact, there are allocations of the ids to the nodes or a ring that will force the protocol to perform $\sigma_{Alternate}$ steps before there is only one *candidate* left (Exercise 3.10.26). In the next step, this *candidate* will become *leader* and start the notification. These last two operations require *n* messages each.

Thus the total number of messages will be

$$M[Alternate] \leq 1.44\, n \log n + O(n). \tag{3.22}$$

In other words, protocol *Alternate* is not only simple but also more efficient than all other protocols seen so far.

Recall, however, that it has been described and analyzed assuming that the ring is *oriented*.

Question. *What happens if the ring is* not *oriented ?*

If the entities have different meaning for "right," when implementing the first step, some candidates will send messages clockwise while others in a counterclockwise direction.

Notice that in the implementation for oriented rings described above, this would lead to deadlock because we close the port we are not waiting to receive from; the implementation can be modified so that the ports are never closed (Exercise 3.10.24). Consider this to be the case.

It will then happen that a candidate waiting to receive from "left" will instead receive from "right." Call this situation a *conflict*.

What we need to do is to add to the protocol a *conflict resolution* mechanism to cope with such situations. Clearly this complicates the protocol (Problem 3.10.2).

3.3.7 Unidirectional Protocols

The first two protocols we have examined, *All the Way* and *AsFar*, did not really require the restriction Bidirectional Links; in fact, they can be used without any modification in a *directed* or a *unidirectional* ring. The subsequent protocols *Distances*, *Stages*, *Stages with Feedback*, and *Alternate* all used the communication links in both directions, for example, for obtaining feedback. It was through them that we have been able to reduce the costs from $O(n^2)$ to a guaranteed $O(n \log n)$ messages. The immediate and natural question is as follows:

Question. *Is "Bidirectional Links" necessary for a $O(n \log n)$ cost ?*

The question is practically relevant because if the answer is positive, it would indicate that an additional investment in communication hardware (i.e., full duplex lines) is necessary to reduce the operating costs of the election task. The answer is important also from a theoretical point of view because if positive, it would clearly indicate the "power" of the restriction Bidirectional Links. Not surprisingly, this question has attracted the attention of many researchers.

We are going to see now that the answer is actually *No*.

We are also going to see that, strangely enough, we know how to do better with unidirectional links than with bidirectional ones.

First of all, we are going to show how the execution of protocols *Stages* and *Alternate* can be *simulated* in unidirectional links yielding the same (if not better) complexity. Then, using the lessons learned in this process, we are going to develop a more efficient *unidirectional* solution.

Unidirectional Stages   What we are going to do is to show how to *simulate* the execution of protocol *Stages* in unidirectional rings $\vec{R}$, with the same message costs. Consider how protocol *Stages* works. In a stage, a *candidate* entity x

1. sends a message carrying a value (its id) in both directions and thus receives a message with the value (the id) of another *candidate* from each directions, and then,

2. on the basis of these three values (i.e., its own and the two received ones), makes a decision on whether it (and its value) should survive this stage and start the next stage.

Let us implement each of these two steps separately.

Step (1) is clearly the difficult one because, in a unidirectional ring, messages can only be sent in one direction. Decompose the operation "send in both directions" into two substeps: (I) "send in one direction" and then (II) "send in the other direction."

Substep (I) can be executed directly in $\vec{R}$; as a result, every *candidate* will receive a message with the value of its neighboring *candidate* from the opposite direction (see Figure 3.22 c). The problem is in implementing now substep (II); as we cannot send information in the other direction, *we will send information again in the same direction*, and, as it is meaningless to send again the same information, *we will send the information we just received*. As a result, every *candidate* will receive now the value of another candidate from the opposite direction (see Figure 3.22d).

Every entity in $\vec{R}$ has now three values at its disposal: the one it started with plus the two received ones. We can now proceed to implement Step (2). To simulate the bidirectional execution, we need that a *candidate* decides on whether to survive or to become *passive* on the basis of exactly *the same information* in $\vec{R}$ as in the bidirectional case. Consider the initial configuration in the example shown in Figure 3.22 and focus on the *candidate* x with starting value 7; in the bidirectional case, x decides that the value 7 should survive on the basis of the information: 7, 15, and 8. In the unidirectional case, after the implementation of Step (1), x knows now 4 and 15 in addition to 7. This is *not* the same information at all. In fact, it would lead to totally different decisions in the two cases, destroying the simulation.

There is, however, in $\vec{R}$ a *candidate* that, at the end of Step (1), has exactly the same information that x has at the end of Step (1) in the bidirectional case: This is the candidate that started with value 8. In fact, the information available in R exists in $\vec{R}$ (compare carefully Figures 3.22 (b) and (d)), but it is shifted to the "next" *candidate* in the ring direction. It is, thus, possible to make the same decisions in $\vec{R}$ as in R; they will just have to be made by different entities in the two cases.

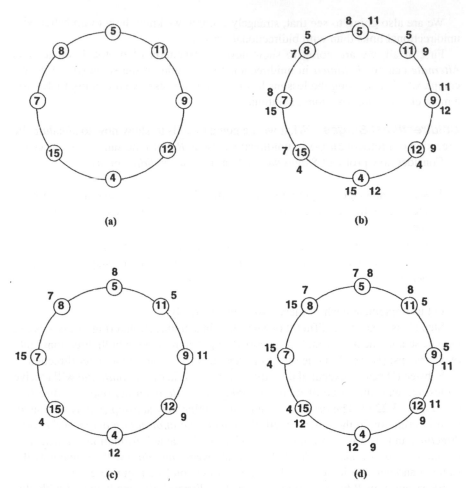

FIGURE 3.22: (a) Initial configuration; (b) information after the first full stage of *Stages* with Bidirectional Links; (c) information after first substep in the unidirectional simulation; (d) information after the second substep.

In each stage, a *candidate* makes a decision on a value. In protocol *Stages*, this value was always the *candidate*'s id. In the unidirectional algorithm, this value is not the id; it is *the first value sent by its neighboring candidate* in Step (1). We will call this value the *envelope*.

IMPORTANT. Be aware that unless we add the assumption *Message Ordering*, it is possible that the second value arrives before the envelope. This problem can be solved (e.g., by locally enqueueing out-of-order messages).

It is not difficult to verify that the simulation is *exact*: In each stage, exactly the same values survive in $\bar{R}$ as in R; thus, the number of stages is exactly the same.

PROTOCOL UniStages.

- States: $S = \{$ASLEEP, CANDIDATE, DEFEATED, FOLLOWER, LEADER$\}$;
  $S_{\text{INIT}} = \{$ASLEEP$\}$;
  $S_{\text{TERM}} = \{$FOLLOWER, LEADER$\}$.
- Restrictions: **IR** $\cup$ *Unidirectional Ring*.

ASLEEP
        Spontaneously
        begin
            INITIALIZE;
            become CANDIDATE;
        end

        Receiving ("Election", value*, stage*, order*)
        begin
            send ("Election", value*, stage*, order*);
            become DEFEATED;
        end

CANDIDATE
        Receiving ("Election", value*, stage*, order*)
        begin
            if   value* $\neq$ value1 **then**
                PROCESS_MESSAGE;
            else
                send (Notify);
                become LEADER;
        end

DEFEATED
        Receiving (*)
        begin
            send (*);
            if * = Notify **then become** FOLLOWER **endif**;
        end

FIGURE 3.23: Protocol *UniStages.*

The cost of each stage is also the same: $2n$ messages. In fact, each node will send (or forward) exactly two messages.

In other words,

$$\mathbf{M}[UniStages] \le 2\,n\log n + O(n). \tag{3.23}$$

This shows that $O(n\log n)$ guaranteed message costs can be achieved in ring networks also *without* Bidirectional Links.

The corresponding protocol *UniStages* is shown in Figure 3.23, described not as a unidirectional simulation of *Stages* (which indeed it is) but directly as a unidirectional protocol.

NOTES. In this implementation,

1. we elect a leader only among the initiators (using approach *Minimum Initiator*);
2. *Message Ordering* is not assumed; within a stage, we use a Boolean variable, in *order* to distinguish between value and envelope and to cope with messages

from different stages arriving out of order: If a *candidate* receives a message from the "future" (i.e., with a higher stage number), it will be transformed immediately into *defeated* and will forward the message.

Unidirectional Alternate We have shown how to simulate *Stages* in a unidirectional ring, achieving exactly the same cost. Let us focus now on *Alternate*; this protocol makes full explicit use of the full duplex communication capabilities of the bidirectional ring by alternating direction at each step. Surprisingly, it is possible to achieve an exact simulation also of this protocol in a unidirectional ring $\vec{R}$.

Consider how protocol *Alternate* works. In a "left" step,

1. a *candidate* entity x sends a message carrying a value $v(x)$ to the "left", and receives a message with the value of another *candidate* from the "right";

```
Procedure INITIALIZE
begin
    stage:= 1;
    count:= 0;
    order:= 0;
    value1:= id(x);
    send("Election", value1, stage, order);
end

Procedure PROCESS_MESSAGE
begin
    if  stage* = stage then
        if  order* = 0 then
            envelope:= value*;
            order:= 1;
            send ("Election", value*, stage*, order);
        else
            value2:= value*;
        endif
        count:=count+1;
        if count=2 then
            if  envelope < Min(value1, value2) then
                order:= 0;
                count:= 0;
                stage:= stage+1;
                value1:= envelope;
                send ("Election", value1, stage, order);
            else
                become DEFEATED;
            endif
        endif
    else
        if stage* > stage then
            send ("Election", value*, stage*, order*);
            become DEFEATED;
        endif
    endif
end
```

FIGURE 3.24: Procedures used by protocol *UniStages*.

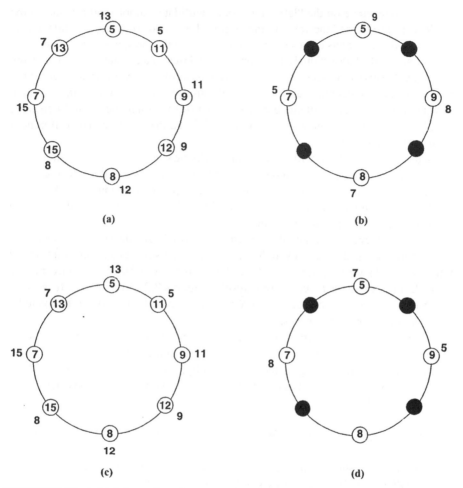

FIGURE 3.25: (a-b) Information after (a) the first step and (b) the second step of *Alternate* in an oriented bidirectional ring. (c-d) Information after (c) the first step and (d) the second step of the unidirectional simulation.

2. on the basis of these two values (i.e., its own and the received one), x makes a decision on whether it (and its value) should survive this step and start the next step.

The actions in a "right" step are the same except that "left" and "right" are interchanged.

Consider the ring $\vec{R}$ shown in Figure 3.25, and assume we can send messages only to "right". This means that the initial "right" step can be trivially implemented: Every entity will send a value (its own) and receive another; it starts the next step if and only if the value it receives is not smaller that its own.

Let us concentrate on the "left" step. As a candidate cannot send a value to the left, it will have to send the value to the "right". Let us do so. Every candidate in $\vec{R}$ has now two values at its disposal: the one it started with and the received one.

To simulate the bidirectional execution, we need that a candidate makes a decision on whether to survive or to become passive on the basis of exactly *the same information* in $\vec{R}$ as in the bidirectional case. Consider the initial configuration in the example shown in Figure 3.25. First of all observe that the information in the "right" step is the same both in the bidirectional (a) and in the unidirectional (c) case. The differences occur in the "left" step.

Focus on the candidate x with starting value 7; in the second step of the bidirectional case, x decides that the value 7 should not survive on the basis of the information: 5 and 7. In the unidirectional case, after the second step, x knows now 7 and 8. This is *not the same information* at all. In fact, it would lead to totally different decisions in the two cases, destroying the simulation.

There is, however, in $\vec{R}$ a candidate that, at the end of the second step, has exactly the same information that x has in the bidirectional case: This is the candidate that started with value 5. As we have seen already in the simulation of *Stages*, the information available in R exists in $\vec{R}$ (compare carefully Figures 3.25(b) and (d)). It is, thus, possible to make the same decisions in $\vec{R}$ as in R; they will just have to be made by different entities in the two cases.

Summarizing, in each step, a *candidate* makes a decision on a value. In protocol *Alternate*, this value was always the candidate's id. In the unidirectional algorithm, this value changes depending on the step. Initially, it is its own value; in the "left" step, it is the value it receives; in the "right" step, it is the value it already has.

In other words,

1. in the "right" step, a *candidate* x survives if and only if the received value is *larger* than $v(x)$;
2. in the "left" step, a *candidate* x survives if and only if the received value is *smaller* than $v(x)$, and if so, x will now play for that value.

Working out a complete example will help clarify the simulation process and dispel any confusion (Exercise 3.10.33).

IMPORTANT. Be aware that unless we add the assumption *Message Ordering*, it is possible that the value from step $i + 1$ arrives before the value for step i.

It is not difficult to verify that the simulation is *exact*: In each step, exactly the same values survive in $\vec{R}$ as in R; thus, the number of steps is exactly the same. The cost of each step is also the same: n messages. Thus,

$$\mathbf{M}[UniAlternate] \leq 1.44\, n \log n + O(n). \tag{3.24}$$

The unidirectional simulation of *Alternate* is shown in Figure 3.26; it has been simplified so that we elect a leader only among the initiators, and assuming *Message*

PROTOCOL UniAlternate.

- States: $S = \{$ASLEEP, CANDIDATE, DEFEATED, FOLLOWER, LEADER$\}$;
  $S_{INIT} = \{$ASLEEP$\}$;
  $S_{TERM} = \{$FOLLOWER, LEADER$\}$.
- Restrictions: **IR** $\cup Unidirectional\,Ring \cup Message\,Ordering$.

```
ASLEEP
        Spontaneously
        begin
            INITIALIZE;
            become CANDIDATE;
        end

        Receiving("Election", value*, stage*,order*)
        begin
            send ("Election", value*, stage*, order*);
            become DEFEATED;
        end


CANDIDATE
        Receiving("Election", value*, stage*)
        begin
            if    value* ≠ value then
                PROCESS_MESSAGE;
            else
                send(Notify);
                become LEADER;
        end

DEFEATED
        Receiving(*)
        begin
            send(*);
            if * = Notify then become FOLLOWER endif;
        end
```

FIGURE 3.26: Protocol *UniAlternate.*

Ordering. The protocol can be modified to remove this assumption without changes in its cost (Exercise 3.10.34). The procedures *Initialize* and *Prepare_Message* are shown in Figure 3.27.

An Alternative Approach

In all the solutions we have seen so far, both for unidirectional and bidirectional rings, we have used the same basic strategy of *minimum finding*; in fact in all of the protocols so far, we have elected as a leader the entity with the smallest value (either among all the entities or among just the initiators). Obviously, we could have used *maximum finding* in those solution protocols, just substituting the function *Min* with *Max* and obtaining the exact same performance.

A very different approach consists in mixing these two strategies. More precisely, consider the protocols based on *electoral stages*. In all of them, what we could do is to alternate strategy in each stage: In "odd" stages we use the function *Min*, and in "even" stages we use the function *Max*. Call this approach *min-max*.

```
Procedure INITIALIZE
begin
    step:= 1;
    direction:= "right";
    value:= id(x);
    send("Election", value, step, direction);
end

Procedure PROCESS_MESSAGE
begin
    if  direction = "right" then
        if  value < value* then
            step:= step+1;
            direction:= "left";
            send ("Election", value, step, direction);
        else
            become DEFEATED;
        endif
    else
        if  value > value* then
            step:= step+1;
            direction:= "right";
            send ("Election", value, step, direction);
        else
            become DEFEATED;
        endif
    endif
end
```

FIGURE 3.27: Procedures used by protocol *UniAlternate*.

It is not difficult to verify that all the stage-based protocols we have seen so far, both bidirectional and unidirectional, still correctly solve the election problem; moreover, they do so with the same costs as before (Exercises 3.10.11, 3.10.23, 3.10.28, 3.10.31, 3.10.36).

The interesting and surprising thing is that this approach can lead to the design of a more efficient protocol for unidirectional rings. -

The protocol we will construct has a simple structure. Let us assume that every entity starts and that there is *Message Ordering* (we will remove both assumptions later).

1. Each initiator x becomes *candidate*, prepares a message containing its own value id(x) and the stage number $i = 1$, and sends it (recall, we are in a unidirectional ring, so there is only one out-neighbor); x is called the *originator* of this message and remembers its content.

2. When a message with value b arrives at a *candidate* y, y compares the received value b with the value a it sent in its last message.

   (a) If $a = b$, the message originated by y has made a full trip around the ring; y becomes the *leader* and notifies all other entities of termination.

   (b) If $a \neq b$, the action y will take depends on the stage number j:

      (i) if j is "even," the message is *discarded* if and only if $a < b$ (i.e., b survives only if *max*);

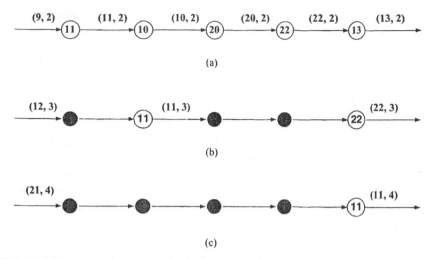

FIGURE 3.28: Protocol *MinMax*: (a) In an even stage, a *candidate* survives only if it receives an envelope with a larger value; (b) it then generates an envelope with that value and starts the next stage; (c) in an odd stage, a candidate survives only if it receives an envelope with a smaller value; if so, it generates an envelope with that value and starts the next stage.

      (ii) if j is "odd," the message is *discarded* if and only if $a > b$ (i.e., b survives only if min).

      If the message is discarded, y becomes *defeated*; otherwise, y will enter the next stage: Originate a message with content $(b, j + 1)$ and send it.

3. A *defeated* entity will, as usual, forward received messages.

For example, see Figure 3.28.

The correctness of the protocol follows from observing that,

    (a) in an even stage i, the *candidate* x receiving the largest of all values in that stage, $v_{max}(i)$, will survive and enter the next stage; by contrast, its "predecessor" $l(i, x)$ that originated that message will become *defeated* (Exercise 3.10.37), and

    (b) in an odd stage j, the *candidate* y receiving the smallest of all values in that stage, $v_{min}(j)$, will survive and enter the next stage; furthermore, its "predecessor" $l(j, y)$ that originated that message will become *defeated*.

    In other words, in each stage at least one *candidate* will survive that stage, and the number of *candidates* in a stage is monotonically decreasing with the number of stages. Thus, within finite time, there will be only one *candidate* left; when that happens, its message returns to it transforming it into a *leader*.

IMPORTANT. Note that the entity that will be elected *leader* will be neither the one with the smallest value nor the one with the largest value.

Let us now consider the costs of this protocol, which we will call *MinMax*. In a stage, each *candidate* sends a message that travels to the next *candidate*. In other words, in each stage there will be exactly n messages. Thus, to determine the total number of messages, we need to compute the number σ_{MinMax} of stages.

We can rephrase the protocol in terms of values instead of entities. Each value sent in a stage j travels from its originator to the next *candidate* in stage j. Of all these values, only some will survive and will be sent in the next stage: In an even stage, a value survives if it is *larger* than its "successor" (i.e., the next value in the ring in also this stage); similarly, in an odd stage, it survives if it is *smaller* than its successor. Let n_i be the number of *values* in stage i; of those, d_i will be *discarded* and n_{i+1} will be sent in the next stage. That is,

$$n_{i+1} = n_i - d_i.$$

Let i be an odd (i.e., *min*) stage, and let value v survive this stage; this means that the successor of v in stage i, say u, is larger than v that is, $u > v$. Let v survive also stage $i + 1$ (an even, i.e., *max*, stage). This implies v must have been discarded in stage i: If not, the entity that originates the message $(i + 1, u)$ would discard $(i + 1, v)$ because $u > v$, but we know that x survives this stage. This means that every value that, like v, survives both stages will eliminate one value in the first of the two stages; in other words,

$$n_{i+2} \leq d_i,$$

but then

$$n_i \geq n_{i+1} + n_{i+2}. \tag{3.25}$$

Notice that this is exactly the same equation as the one (Equation 3.21) we derived for protocol *Alternate*. We thus obtain that

$$\sigma_{MinMax} \leq 1.44 \log n + O(1).$$

After at most these many stages, there will be only one value left. Observe that this bound we have derived is actually *achievable*. In fact, there are allocations of the ids to the nodes or a ring, which will force the protocol to perform σ_{MinMax} steps before there is only one value left (Exercise 3.10.38). The *candidate* sending this value will receive its message back and become *leader*; it will then start the notification. These last two steps require n messages each; thus the total number of messages will be

$$\mathbf{M}[MinMax] \leq 1.44 \, n \log n + O(n). \tag{3.26}$$

PROTOCOL MinMax

- States: $S = \{$ASLEEP, CANDIDATE, DEFEATED, FOLLOWER, LEADER$\}$; $S_{INIT} = \{$ASLEEP$\}$; $S_{TERM} = \{$FOLLOWER, LEADER$\}$.
- Restrictions: **IR** $\cup$ *Unidirectional Ring* $\cup$ *Message Ordering*.

```
ASLEEP
        Spontaneously
        begin
            stage:= 1; value:= id(x);
            send("Envelope", value, stage);
            become ORIGINATOR;
        end


        Receiving("Envelope", value*, stage*)
        begin
            send ("Envelope", value*, stage*);
            become DEFEATED;
        end


CANDIDATE
        Receiving("Envelope", value*, stage*)
        begin
            if    value* ≠ value then
                  PROCESS_ENVELOPE;
            else
                  send(Notify);
                  become LEADER;
        end



DEFEATED
        Receiving("Envelope", value*, stage*)
        begin
            send("Envelope", value*, stage*);
        end


        Receiving("Notify")
        begin
            send ("Notify");
            become FOLLOWER;
        end
```

FIGURE 3.29: Protocol *MinMax*.

In other words, we have been able to obtain the same costs of *UniAlternate* with a very different protocol, *MinMax*, described in Figure 3.29.

We have assumed that all entities start. When removing this assumption we have two options: The entities that are not initiators can be (i) made to start (as if they were initiators) upon receiving their first message or (ii) transformed into *passive* and just act as relayers. The second option is the one used in Figure 3.29.

We have also assumed *Message Ordering* in our discussion. As with all the other protocols we have considered, this restriction can be enforced with just local book-keeping at each entity, without any increase in complexity (Exercise 3.10.39).

```
Procedure PROCESS_ENVELOPE
begin
    if   odd(stage*) then
        if  value* < value then
            stage= stage+1;
            value:= value*;
            send ("Envelope", value*, stage);
        else
            become DEFEATED;
    else
        if  value* > value then
            stage= stage+1;
            value:= value*;
            send ("Envelope", value, stage);
        else
            become DEFEATED;
        endif
    endif
end
```

FIGURE 3.30: Procedure Process_Envelope of Protocol *MinMax*.

Hacking: Employing the Defeated (⋆)   The different approach used in protocol *MinMax* has led to a different way of obtaining the same efficiency as we had already with *UniAlternate*. The advantage of *MinMax* is that it is possible to obtain additional improvements that lead to a significantly better performance.

Observe that like in most previous protocols, the *defeated* entities play a purely passive role, that is, they just forward messages. The key observation we will use to obtain an improvement in performance is that these entities can be exploited in the computation.

Let us concentrate on the even stages and see if we can obtain some savings for those steps. The message sent by a *candidate* travels (forwarded by the *defeated* entities) until it encounters the next *candidate*. This distance can vary and can be very large. What we will do is to control the maximum distance to which the message will travel, following the idea we developed in Section 3.3.3.

(I) in an even step j, a message will travel no more than a predefined distance $dis(j)$.

This is implemented by having in the message a counter (initially set to $dis(j)$) that will be decreased by one by each defeated node it passes. What is the appropriate choice of $dis(i)$ will be discussed next.

Every change we make in the protocol has strong consequences. As a consequence of (I), the message from x might not reach the next *candidate* y if it is too far away (more than $dis(j)$) (see Figure 3.31). In this case, the *candidate* y does *not* receive the message in this stage and, thus, does not know what to do for the next stage.

IMPORTANT. It is possible that *every* candidate is too far away from the next one in this stage, and hence *none* of them will receive a message.

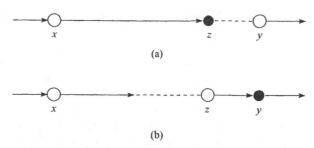

(a)

(b)

FIGURE 3.31: Protocol *MinMax+*. Controlling the distance: In even stage j, the message does not travel more than $dis(j)$ nodes. (a) If it does not reach the next *candidate* y, the *defeated* node reached last, z, will become *candidate* and start the next step; (b) in the next step, the message from z transforms into *defeated* the entity y still waiting for the stage j message.

However, if *candidate* y does *not* receive the message from x, it is because the counter of the message containing (v, j) reaches 0 at a *defeated* node z, on the way from x to y (see Figure 3.31). To ensure *progress* (i.e., absence of deadlock), we will make that *defeated* z become *candidate* and start the next stage $j + 1$ immediately, sending $(v, j+1)$. That is,

(II) in an even step j, if the counter of the message reaches 0 at a *defeated* node z, then z becomes *candidate* and starts stage $j + 1$ with *value* $= v^*$, where v^* is the value in the transfer message.

In other words, we are bringing some *defeated* nodes back into the game making them *candidates* again. This operation could be dangerous for the complexity of the protocol as the number of *candidates* appears to be increasing (and not decreasing). This is easily taken care of: The *originators*, like y, waiting for a transfer message that will not arrive will become *defeated*.

Question. *How will y know that it is* defeated?

The answer is simple. The *candidate* that starts the next stage (e.g., z in our example) sends a message; when this message reaches a *candidate* (e.g., y) still waiting for a message from the previous stage, that entity will understand, become *defeated*, and forward the message. In other words,

(III) when, in an even step, a *candidate* receives a message for the next step, it becomes *defeated* and forwards the message.

We are giving decisional power to the *defeated* nodes, even bringing some of them back to "life." Let us push this concept forward and see if we can obtain some other savings.

Let us concentrate on the odd stages.

Consider an even stage i in *MinMax* (e.g., Figure 3.28). Every *candidate* x sends its message containing the value and the stage number and receives a message; it becomes *defeated* if the received value is smaller than the one it sent. If it survives, x starts stage $i + 1$: It sends a message with the received value and the new stage number (see Figure 3.28(b)); this message will reach the next *candidate*.

Concentrate on the message $(11, 3)$ in Figure 3.28(b) sent by x. Once $(11, 3)$ reaches its destination y, as $11 < 22$ and we are in a odd (i.e., *min*) stage, a new message $(11, 4)$ will be originated. Observe that the fact that $(11, 4)$ must be originated can be discovered *before* the message reaches y (see Figure 3.32(c)). In fact, on its travel from x to y, message $(11, 3)$ will reach the *defeated* node z that originated $(20, 2)$ in the previous stage; once this happens, z knows that 11 will survive this stage (Exercise 3.10.40). What z will do is to become *candidate* again and immediately send $(11, 4)$.

(IV) When, in an even stage, a *candidate* becomes *defeated*, it will remember the stage number and the value it sent. If, in the next stage, it receives a message with a smaller value, it will become *candidate* again and start the next stage with that value.

In our example, this means that the message $(11, 3)$ from x will stop at z and never reach y; thus, we will save $d(z, y)$ messages. Notice that in this stage *every message with a smaller value will be stopped earlier*. We have, however, transformed a *defeated* entity into a *candidate*. This operation could be dangerous for the complexity of the

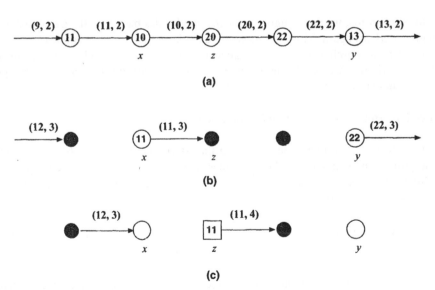

FIGURE 3.32: Protocol *MinMax+*. (a) Early promotion in odd stages. (b) The message $(11, 3)$ from x, on its way to y, reaches the *defeated* node z that originated $(20, 2)$. (c) Node z becomes *candidate* and immediately originates envelope $(11, 4)$.

protocol as the number of *candidates* appears to be increasing (and not decreasing). This is easily taken care of: This *candidates*, like y, waiting for a message of an odd stage that will not arrive will become *defeated*.

How will y know that is *defeated*? The answer again is simple. The *candidate* that starts the next stage (e.g., z in our example) sends the message; when this message reaches an entity still waiting for a message from the previous stage (e.g., y), that entity will understand, become *defeated*, and forward the message. In other words,

(V) When, in an odd step, a *candidate* receives a message for the next step, it becomes *defeated* and forwards the message.

The modifications to *MinMax* described by (I)–(V) generate a new protocol that we shall call *MinMax+* (Exercises 3.10.41 and 3.10.42).

Messages   Let us estimate the cost of protocol *MinMax+*. First of all observe that in protocol *MinMax*, in each stage a message (v, i) would always reach the next *candidate* in that stage. This is not necessarily so in *MinMax+*. In fact, in an even stage i no message will travel more than dis(i), and in an odd stage a message can be "promoted" by a *defeated* node on the way. We must concentrate on the savings in each type of stages.

Consider a message (v, i); denote by $h_i(v)$ the *candidate* that originates it, and if the message is discarded in this stage, denote by $g_i(v)$ the node that discards it. For the even stages, we must first of all choose the maximum distance dis(i) a message will travel. We will use

$$\text{dis}(i) = F_{i+2}$$

With this choice of distance, we have a very interesting property.

Property 3.3.1 *Let i be even.*
If message (v, i) is discarded in this stage, then $d(h_i(v), g_i(v)) \geq F_i$.
For any message $(v, i + 1)$, $d(h_i(v), h_{i+1}(v)) \geq F_{i+1}$.

This property allows us to determine the number of stages $\sigma_{MinMax+}$: In an even stage i, the distance traveled by any message is at least F_i; however, none of these messages travels beyond the next *candidate* in the ring. Hence, the distance between two successive *candidates* in an odd stage i is at least F_i; this means that the number n_i of *candidates* is at most $n_i \leq \frac{n}{F_i}$. Hence, the number of stages will be at most $F_n^{-1} + O(1)$, where F_n^{-1} is the smallest integer j such that $F_j \geq n$. Thus the algorithm will use at most

$$\sigma_{MinMax+} \leq 1.44 \log n + O(1)$$

stages. This is the same as protocol *MinMax*.

The property also allows us to measure the number of messages we save in the odd stages. In our example of Figure 3.32(b), message $(11, 3)$ from x will stop at z and never reach y; thus, we will save $d(z, y)$ transmissions. In general, a message with value v that reaches an even stage $i + 1$ (e.g., $(11, 4)$) saves at least F_i transmissions in stage i (Exercise 3.10.44). The total number of transmissions in an odd stage i is, thus, at most

$$n - n_{i+1} F_i,$$

where n_{i+1} denotes the number of *candidates* in stage $i + 1$.

The total number of messages in an even stage is at most n. As in an even stage $i + 1$ each message travels at most F_{i+3} (by Property 3.3.1), the total number of message transmissions in an even stage $i + 1$ will be at most $n_{i+1} F_{i+3}$. Thus, the total number of messages in an even stage $i + 1$ is at most

$$\text{Min}\{n, n_{i+1} F_{i+3}\}.$$

If we now consider an odd stage i followed by an even stage $i + 1$, the total number of message transmissions in the two stages will be at most

$$\text{Min}\{n + n_{i+1}(F_{i+3} - F_i), 2n - n_{i+1} F_i\} \leq 2n - n\frac{F_i}{F_{i+3}} < n(4 - \sqrt{5} + \phi^{-2i}),$$

where $\phi = \frac{1+\sqrt{5}}{2}$. Hence,

$$\mathbf{M}[MinMax+] \leq \frac{4 - \sqrt{5}}{2} n \log_\phi(n) + O(n) < 1.271\, n \log n + O(n). \tag{3.27}$$

Thus, protocol *MinMax+* is the most efficient protocol we have seen so far, with respect to the worst case.

3.3.8   Limits to Improvements (⋆)

Throughout the previous sections, we have reduced the message costs further and further using new tools or combining existing ones. A natural question is *how far we can go*. Considering that the improvements have only been in the multiplicative constant of the $n \log n$ factor, the next question becomes: Is there a tool or a technique that would allow us to reduce the message costs for election significantly, for example, from $O(n \log n)$ to $O(n)$?

These type of questions are all part of a larger and deeper one: *What is the message complexity of election in a ring* ? To answer this question, we need to establish a *lower bound*, a limit that no election protocol can improve upon, regardless of the amount and cleverness of the design effort.

In this section we will see different bounds, some for unidirectional rings and others for bidirectional ones, depending on the amount of a priori knowledge the entities have about the ring. As we will see, in all cases, the lower bounds are all of the form $\Omega(n \log n)$. Thus, any further improvement can only be in the multiplicative constant.

Unidirectional Rings   We want to know what is the number of messages that any election algorithm for unidirectional rings must transmit in the *worst case*. A subtler question is to determine the number of messages that any solution algorithm must transmit on the *average*; clearly, a lower bound on the average case is also a lower bound on the worst case[1].

We will establish a lower bound under the standard assumptions of Connectivity and Total Reliability, plus Initial Distinct Values (required for election), and obviously *Ring*. We will actually establish the bound assuming that there is Message Ordering; this implies that in systems without Message Ordering, the bound is at least as bad. The lower bound will be established for *minimum-finding* protocols; because of the Initial Distinct Values restriction, every minimum-finding protocol is also an election protocol. Also, we know that with the additional n messages, every election protocol becomes a minimum-finding protocol.

When a minimum-finding algorithm is executed in a ring of entities with distinct values, the total number of transmitted messages depends on two factors: communication delays and the assignment of initial values.

Consider the unidirectional ring $\vec{R} = (x_0, x_1, \ldots, x_{n-1})$; let $s_i = \mathrm{id}(x_i)$ be the unique value assigned to x_i. The sequence $\mathbf{s} = \langle s_1, s_2, \ldots, s_n \rangle$, thus, describes the assignment of ids to the entities.

Denote by S the set of all such assignments. Given a ring R of size n and an assignment $\mathbf{s} \in S$ of n ids, we will say that $\vec{R}$ is labeled by $\mathbf{s}$, and denote it by $\vec{R}(\mathbf{s})$.

Let A be a minimum-finding protocol under the restrictions stated above. Consider the executions of A started simultaneously by all entities and their cost. The average and the worst-case costs of these executions are possibly better but surely not worse than the average and the worst-case costs, respectively, over all possible executions; thus, if we find them, they will give us a lower bound.

Call *global state* of an entity x at time t, the content of all its local registers and variables at time t. As we know, the entities are *event driven*. This means that for a fixed set of rules A, their next global state will depend solely on the current one and on what event has occurred. In our case, once the execution of A is started, the only external events are the arrival of messages.

During an action, an entity might send one or more messages to its only out-neighbor; if it is more than one, we can "bundle" them together as they are all sent within the same action (i.e., before any new message is received). Thus, we assume that in A, only one message is sent in the execution of an action by an entity.

Associate to each message all the "history" of that message. That is, with each message M, we associate a sequence of values, called *trace*, as follows: (1) If the sender has id s_i and has not previously received any message, the trace will be just

---

[1] The converse is not true.

$\langle s_i \rangle$. (2) If the sender has id s_i and its last message previously received has trace $\langle l_1, \ldots, l_{k-1} \rangle, k > 1$, the trace will be $\langle l_1, \ldots, l_{k-1}, s_i \rangle$, which has length k.

Thus, a message M with trace $\langle s_i, s_{i+1}, \ldots, s_{i+k} \rangle$ indicates that a message was originally sent by entity x_i; as a reaction, the neighbor x_{i+1} sent a message; as a reaction, the neighbor x_{i+2} sent a message; ... ; as a reaction, x_{i+k} sent the current message M.

IMPORTANT. Note that because of our two assumptions (simultaneous start by all entities and only one message per action), messages are uniquely described by their associated trace.

We will denote by **ab** the concatenation of two sequences **a** and **b**. If $\mathbf{d} = \mathbf{abc}$, then **a**, **b**, and **c** are called *subsequences* of **d**; in particular, each of **a**, **ab**, and **abc** will be called a *prefix* of **d**; each of **c**, **bc**, and **abc** will be called a *suffix* of **d**. Given a sequence **a**, we will denote by len(**a**) the length of **a** and by $C(\mathbf{a})$ the set of cyclic permutations of **a**; clearly, $|C(\mathbf{a})| = \text{len}(\mathbf{a})$.

Example   If $\mathbf{d} = \langle 2, 15, 9, 27 \rangle$, then len(**d**) = 4; the subsequences $\langle 2 \rangle$, $\langle 2, 15 \rangle$, $\langle 2, 15, 9 \rangle$, and $\langle 2, 15, 9, 27 \rangle$ are prefixes; the sequences $\langle 27 \rangle$, $\langle 9, 27 \rangle$, $\langle 15, 9, 27 \rangle$, and $\langle 2, 15, 9, 27 \rangle$ are suffixes; and $C(\mathbf{d}) = \{\langle 2, 15, 9, 27 \rangle, \langle 15, 9, 27, 2 \rangle, \langle 9, 27, 2, 15 \rangle, \langle 27, 2, 15, 9 \rangle\}$.

The key point to understand is the following: If in two different rings, for example, in $\vec{R}(\mathbf{a})$ and in $\vec{R}(\mathbf{b})$, an entity executing A happens to have the same global state, and it receives the same message, then it will perform the same action in both cases, and the next global state will be the same in both executions. Recall Property 1.6.1.

Let us use this point.

Lemma 3.3.1   *Let* **a** *and* **b** *both contain* **c** *as a subsequence. If a message with trace* **c** *is sent in an execution of A on* $\vec{R}(\mathbf{a})$, *then* **c** *is sent in an execution of A on* $\vec{R}(\mathbf{b})$.

Proof. Assume that a message with trace $\mathbf{c} = \langle s_i, \ldots, s_{i+k} \rangle$ is sent when executing A on $\vec{R}(\mathbf{a})$. This means that when entity x_i started the trace, it had not received any other message, and so, the transmission of this message was part of its initial "spontaneous" action; as the nature of this action depends only on A, x_i will send the message both in $\vec{R}(\mathbf{a})$ and in $\vec{R}(\mathbf{b})$. This message was the first and only message x_{i+1} received from x_i both in $\vec{R}(\mathbf{a})$ and in $\vec{R}(\mathbf{b})$; in other words, its global state until it received the message with trace starting with $\langle s_i \rangle$ was the same in both rings; hence, it will send the same message with trace $\langle s_i, s_{i+1} \rangle$ to x_{i+2} in both situations. In general, between the start of the algorithm and the arrival of a message with trace $\langle s_i, \ldots, s_{j-1} \rangle$, entity x_j with id $s_j, i \langle j \leq i + k$ is in the same global state and sends and receives the same message in both $\vec{R}(\mathbf{a})$ and $\vec{R}(\mathbf{b})$; thus, it will send a message with trace $\langle s_i, \ldots, s_{j-1}, s_j \rangle$ regardless of whether the input sequence is **a** or **b**.

Thus, if an execution of A in $\vec{R}(\mathbf{a})$ has a message with trace **c**, then there is an execution of A in $\vec{R}(\mathbf{b})$ that has a message with trace **c**.   ∎

In other words, if $\vec{R}(\mathbf{a})$ and $\vec{R}(\mathbf{b})$ have a common segment $\mathbf{c}$ (i.e., a consecutive group of $len(\mathbf{c})$ entities in $\vec{R}(\mathbf{a})$ has the same ids as a consecutive group of entities in $\vec{R}(\mathbf{b})$), the entity at the end of the segment cannot distinguish between the two rings when it sends the message with trace $\mathbf{c}$.

As different assignments of values to rings may lead to different results (i.e., different minimum values), the protocol A must allow the entities to distinguish between those assignments. As we will see, this will be the reason $\Omega(n \log n)$ messages are needed. To prove it, we will consider a set of assignments on rings, which makes distinguishing among them "expensive" for the algorithm.

A set $E \subseteq S$ of assignments of values is called *exhaustive* if it has the following two properties:

1. *Prefix Property*: For every sequence belonging to E, its nonempty prefixes also belong to E, that is, if $\mathbf{ab} \in E$ and $len(\mathbf{a}) \geq 1$, then $\mathbf{a} \in E$.

2. *Cyclic Permutation Property*: Whether an assignment of values s belongs or not belongs to E, at least one of its cyclic permutations belongs to E, that is, if $s \in S$, then $C(s) \cap E \neq \phi$

Lemma 3.3.2   *A has an exhaustive set $E(A) \subseteq S$.*

Proof. Define $E(A)$ to be the set of all the arrangements $\mathbf{s} \in S$ such that a message with trace $\mathbf{s}$ is sent in the execution of A in $\vec{R}(\mathbf{s})$. To prove that this set is exhaustive, we need to show that the cycle permutation property and the prefix property hold.

To show that the prefix property is satisfied, choose an arbitrary $\mathbf{s} = \mathbf{ab} \in E(A)$ with $len(\mathbf{a}) \geq 1$; by definition of $E(A)$, there will be a message with trace $\mathbf{ab}$ when executing A in $\vec{R}(\mathbf{ab})$; this means that in $\vec{R}(\mathbf{ab})$ there will also be a message with trace $\mathbf{a}$. Consider now the (smaller) ring $\vec{R}(\mathbf{a})$; as $\mathbf{a}$ is a subsequence of both $\mathbf{ab}$ and (obviously) $\mathbf{a}$, and there was a message with that trace in $\vec{R}(\mathbf{ab})$, by Lemma 3.3.1 there will be a message with trace $\mathbf{a}$ also in $\vec{R}(\mathbf{a})$; but this means that $\mathbf{a} \in E(A)$. In other words, the suffix property holds.

To show that the cyclic permutation property is satisfied, choose an arbitrary $\mathbf{s} = \langle s_1, \ldots, s_k \rangle \in S$ and consider $\vec{R}(\mathbf{s})$. At least one entity must receive a message with a trace of length k, otherwise the minimum value could not have been determined; then $\mathbf{t}$ is a cyclic permutation of $\mathbf{s}$. Furthermore, as $\mathbf{t}$ is a trace in $\vec{R}(\mathbf{t})$, $\mathbf{t} \in E(A)$. Summarizing, $\mathbf{t} \in E(A) \cup S(\mathbf{s})$. In other words, the cyclic permutation property holds. ∎

Now we are going to measure how expensive it is for the algorithm A to distinguish between the elements of $E(A)$.

Let $m(\mathbf{s}, E)$ be the number of sequences in $E \subseteq S$, which are prefixes of some cyclic permutation of $\mathbf{s} \in S$, and $m_k(\mathbf{s}, E)$ denote the number of those that are of length $k > 1$.

Lemma 3.3.3   *The execution of A in $\vec{R}(\mathbf{s})$ costs at least $m(\mathbf{s}, E(A))$ messages.*

Proof. Let $\mathbf{t} \in E(A)$ be the prefix of some $\mathbf{r} \in C(\mathbf{s})$. That is, a message with trace $\mathbf{t}$ is sent in $\vec{R}(\mathbf{t})$ and because of Lemma 3.3.1, a message with trace $\mathbf{t}$ is sent also in $\vec{R}(\mathbf{r})$; as $\mathbf{r} \in C(\mathbf{s})$, a message with trace $\mathbf{t}$ is sent also in $\vec{R}(\mathbf{r})$. That is, for each prefix $\mathbf{t} \in E(A)$ of a cyclic permutation of $\mathbf{s}$, there will be a message sent with trace $\mathbf{t}$. The number of such prefixes $\mathbf{t}$ is by definition $m(\mathbf{s}, E(A))$. ∎

Let $I = \{s_1, s_2, \ldots, s_n\}$ be the set of ids, and $\text{Perm}(I)$ be the set of permutations of I. Assuming that all $n!$ permutations in $\text{Perm}(I)$ are equally likely, the average number $\text{ave}_A(I)$ of messages sent by A in the rings labeled by I will be the average message cost of A among the rings $\vec{R}(\mathbf{s})$, where $\mathbf{s} \in \text{Perm}(I)$. By Lemma 3.3.3, this means the following:

$$\text{ave}_A(I) \geq \frac{1}{n!} \sum_{\mathbf{s} \in \text{Perm}(I)} m(\mathbf{s}, E(A)).$$

By definition of $m_k(\mathbf{s}, E(A))$, we have

$$\text{ave}_A(I) \geq \frac{1}{n!} \sum_{\mathbf{s} \in \text{Perm}(I)} \sum_{k=1}^{n} m_k(\mathbf{s}, E(A)) = \frac{1}{n!} \sum_{k=1}^{n} \sum_{\mathbf{s} \in \text{Perm}(I)} m_k(\mathbf{s}, E(A)).$$

We need to determine what $\sum_{\mathbf{s} \in \text{Perm}(I)} m_k(\mathbf{s}, E(A))$ is. Fix k and $\mathbf{s} \in \text{Perm}(I)$. Each cyclic permutation $C(\mathbf{s})$ of $\mathbf{s}$ has only one prefix of length k. In total, there are n prefixes of length k among all the cyclic permutations of $\mathbf{s} \in \text{Perm}(I)$. As there are $n!$ elements in $\text{Perm}(I)$, there are $n! \, n$ instances of such prefixes for a fixed k. These $n! \, n$ prefixes can be partitioned in groups G_j^k of size k, by putting together all the cyclic permutations of the same sequence; there will be $q = \frac{n! \, n}{k}$ such groups. As $E(A)$ is exhaustive, by the cyclic permutation property, the set $E(A)$ intersects each group, that is, $|E(A) \cup G_j^k| \geq 1$.

$$\sum_{\mathbf{s} \in \text{Perm}(I)} m_k(\mathbf{s}, E(A)) \geq \sum_{j=1}^{q} |E(A) \cup G_j^k| \geq \frac{n! \, n}{k}.$$

Thus,

$$\text{ave}_A(I) \geq \frac{1}{n!} \sum_{k=1}^{n} \frac{n! \, n}{k} \geq n \sum_{k=1}^{n} \frac{1}{k} = n H_n,$$

where H_n is the nth harmonic number. This lower bound on the average case is also a lower bound on the number $\text{worst}_A(I)$ of messages sent by A in the worst case in the rings labeled by I:

$$\text{worst}_A(I) \geq \text{ave}_A(I) \geq n H_n \approx 0.69 \, n \log n + O(n). \tag{3.28}$$

This result states that $\Omega(n \log n)$ messages are needed in the worst case by *any* solution protocol (the bound is true for every A), even if there is Message Ordering. Thus, any improvement we can hope to obtain by clever design will at most reduce the constant; in any case, the constant cannot be smaller than 0.69. Also, we cannot expect to design election protocols that might have a bad worst case but cost dramatically less on an average. In fact, $\Omega(n \ log n)$ messages are needed on an average by any protocol.

Notice that the lower bound we have established can be achieved. In fact, protocol *AsFar* requires on an average $n H_n$ messages (Theorem 3.3.1). In other words, protocol *AsFar* is *optimal* on an average.

If the entities know n, it might be possible to develop better protocols exploiting this knowledge. In fact, the lower bound in this case leaves a little more room but again the improvement can only be in the constant (Exercise 3.10.45):

$$\text{worst}_A(I \,|\, n \text{ known}) \geq \text{ave}_A(I \,|\, n \text{ known}) \geq \left(\frac{1}{4} - \varepsilon\right) n \log n. \tag{3.29}$$

So far no better protocol is known.

Bidirectional Rings   In bidirectional rings, the lower bound is slightly different in both derivation and value (Exercise 3.10.46):

$$\text{worst}_A(I) \geq \text{ave}_A(I) \geq \frac{1}{2} n H_n \approx 0.345 \, n \log n + O(n). \tag{3.30}$$

Actually, we can improve this bound even if the entities know n (Exercise 3.10.47):

$$\text{worst}_A(I : n \text{ known}) \geq \text{ave}_A(I : n \text{ known}) \geq \frac{1}{2} n \log n. \tag{3.31}$$

That is, even with the additional knowledge of n, any improvement can only be in the constant. So far, no better protocol is known.

Practical and Theoretical Implications   The lower bounds we have discussed so far indicate that $\Omega(n \log n)$ messages are needed both in the worst case and on the average, regardless of whether the ring is unidirectional or bidirectional, and whether n is known or not. The only difference between these cases will be in the constant. In the previous sections, we have seen several protocols that use $O(n \log n)$ messages in the worst case (and are thus optimal); their cost provides us with upper bounds on the complexity of leader election in a ring.

If we compare the best upper and lower bounds for unidirectional rings with those for bidirectional rings, we notice the existence of a very surprising situation: The bounds for unidirectional rings are "better" than those for bidirectional ones; the upper bound is smaller and the lower bound is bigger (see Fig. 3.33 and 3.34). This fact has strange implications: As far as electing a leader in a ring is concerned, unidirectional rings seem to be better systems than bidirectional ones, which in turn implies that practically

half-duplex links are better than full-duplex links.

bidirectional	worst case	average	notes
All the Way	n^2	n^2	
AsFar	n^2	$0.69n \log n + O(n)$	
ProbAsFar	n^2	$0.49n \log n + O(n)$	
Control	$6.31n \log n + O(n)$		
Stages	$2n \log n + O(n)$		
StagesFbk	$1.89n \log n + O(n)$		
Alternate	$1.44n \log n + O(n)$		oriented ring
BiMinMax	$1.44n \log n + O(n)$		
lower bound		$0.5n \log n + O(n)$	$n = 2^p$ known

FIGURE 3.33: Summary of bounds for bidirectional rings.

This is clearly counterintuitive: In terms of communication hardware, Bidirectional Links are clearly more powerful than half-duplex links. On the contrary, the bounds are quite clear: Election protocols for unidirectional rings are more efficient than those for bidirectional ones.

A natural reaction to this strange status of affairs is to suggest the use in bidirectional rings of unidirectional protocols; after all, with Bidirectional Links we can send in both directions, "left" and "right," so we can just decide to use only one, say "right." Unfortunately, this argument is based on the hidden assumption that the bidirectional ring is also *oriented*, that is, "right" means the same to all processors. In other words, it assumes that the labeling of the port numbers, which is purely local, is actually *globally consistent*.

This explains why we cannot use the (more efficient) unidirectional protocol in a generic bidirectional ring. But why should we do better in unidirectional rings?

The answer is interesting—*In a unidirectional ring, there is orientation*: Each entity has only one out-neighbor; so there is no ambiguity as to where to send a message. In other words, we have discovered an important principle of the nature of distributed computing:

Global consistency is more important than hardware communication power.

unidirectional	worst case	average	notes
All the Way	n^2	n^2	
AsFar	n^2	$0.69n \log n + O(n)$	
UniStages	$2n \log n + O(n)$		
UniAlternate	$1.44n \log n + O(n)$		
MinMax	$1.44n \log n + O(n)$		
MinMax+	$1.271n \log n + O(n)$		
lower bound		$0.69n \log n + O(n)$	
lower bound		$0.25n \log n + O(n)$	$n = 2^p$ known

FIGURE 3.34: Summary of bounds for unidirectional rings.

This principle is quite general. In the case of rings, the difference is not much, just in the multiplicative constant. As we will see in other topologies, this difference can actually be dramatic.

If the ring is both bidirectional and oriented, then we can clearly use any unidirectional protocol as well as any bidirectional one. The important question is whether in this case we can do better than that. That is, the quest is for a protocol for bidirectional oriented rings that

1. fully exploits the power of both full-duplex links and orientation;
2. cannot be used or simulated in unidirectional rings, nor in general bidirectional ones; and
3. is more efficient than any unidirectional protocol or general bidirectional one.

We have seen a protocol for oriented rings, *Alternate*; however, it can be simulated in unidirectional rings (protocol *UniAlternate*). To date, no protocol with such properties is known. It is not even known whether it can exist (Problem 3.10.7).

3.3.9 Summary and Lessons

We have examined the design of several protocols for leader election in ring networks and analyzed the effects that design decisions have had on the costs.

When developing the election protocols, we have introduced some key strategies that are quite general in nature and, thus, can be used for different problems and for different networks. Among them are the idea of *electoral stages* and the concept of *controlled distances*. We have also employed ideas and tools, for example, *feedback* and *notification*, already developed for other problems.

In terms of costs, we have seen that $\Theta(n \log n)$ messages will be used both in the worst case and on the average, regardless of whether the ring is unidirectional or bidirectional, oriented or unoriented, and n is known or not. The only difference is in the multiplicative constant. The bounds are summarized in Figures 3.33 and 3.34. As a consequence of these bounds, we have seen that orientation of the ring is, so far, more powerful than presence of Bidirectional Links.

Both ring networks and tree networks have very sparse topologies: $m = n - 1$ in trees and $m = n$ in rings. In particular, if we remove any single link from a ring, we obtain a tree. Still, electing a leader costs $\Theta(n \log n)$ in rings but only $\Theta(n)$ in trees. The reason for such a drastic complexity difference has to be found not in the number of links but instead in the properties of the topological structure of the two types of networks. In a tree, there is a high level of *asymmetry*: We have two types of nodes internal nodes and leaves; it is by exploiting such asymmetry that election can be performed in a linear number of messages. On the contrary, a ring is a highly symmetrical structure, where every node is indistinguishable from another. Consider that the election task is really a task of breaking symmetry: We want one entity to become different from all others. The entities already have a behavioral symmetry: They all have the same set of rules and the same initial state, and potentially they are all initiators. Thus, the structural symmetry of the ring topology only makes the solution to the problem more difficult and more expensive. This observation reflects a more general principle: As far as election is concerned, structural asymmetry is to the protocol designer's advantage; on the contrary, *the presence of structural symmetry is an obstacle for the protocol designer.*

3.4 ELECTION IN MESH NETWORKS

Mesh networks constitute a large class of architectures that includes *meshes* and *tori*; this class is popular especially for parallel systems, redundant memory systems, and interconnection networks. These networks, like trees and rings, are sparse: $m = O(n)$. Using our experience with trees and rings, we will now approach the election problem in such networks. Unless otherwise stated, we will consider Bidirectional Links.

3.4.1 Meshes

A *mesh M* of dimensions $a \times b$ has $n = a \times b$ nodes, $x_{i,j}$, $1 \le i \le a, 1 \le j \le b$. Each node $x_{i,j}$ is connected to $x_{i-1,j}, x_{i,j-1}, x_{i+1,j}, x_{i,j+1}$ if they exist; let us stress that these names are used for descriptive purposes only and are not known to the entities. The total number of links is thus $m = a(b-1) + b(a-1) = 2ab - a - b$ (see Figure 3.35).

Observe that in a mesh, we have three types of nodes: *corner* (entities with only two neighbors), *border* (entities with three neighbors), and *interior* (with four neighbors) nodes. In particular, there are four corner nodes, $2(a + b)$ border nodes, and $n - 2(a + b - 2)$ interior nodes.

Unoriented Mesh   The asymmetry of the mesh can be exploited to our advantage when electing a leader: As it does not matter which entity becomes leader, we can elect one of the four corner nodes. In this way, the problem of choosing a leader among (possibly) n nodes is reduced to the problem of choosing a leader among the

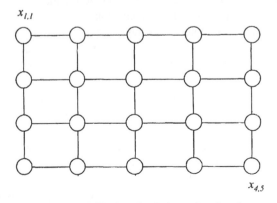

FIGURE 3.35: Mesh of dimension 4×5.

four corner nodes. Recall that any number of nodes can start (each unaware of when and where the others will start, if at all); thus, to achieve our goal, we need to design a protocol that first of all makes the corners aware of the election process (they might not be initiators at all) and then performs the election among them.

The first step, to make the corners aware, can be performed doing a *wake-up* of all entities. When an entity wakes up (spontaneously if it is an initiator, upon receiving a wake-up message otherwise), its subsequent actions will depend on whether it is a corner, a border, or an interior node.

In particular, the four corners will become awake and can start the actual election process.

Observe the following interesting property of a mesh: If we consider only the border and corner nodes and the links between them, they form a ring network. We can, thus, elect a leader among the corners by using a election protocol for rings: The corners will be the only *candidates*; the borders will act as relayers (*defeated* nodes). When one of the corner nodes is elected, it will notify all other entities of termination.

Summarizing, the process will consist of:

1. wake-up, started by the initiators;
2. election (on outer ring), among the corners;
3. notification (i.e., broadcast) started by the leader;

Let us consider these three activities individually.

(1) Wake up is straightforward. Each of the k_* initiators will send a wake-up to all its neighbors; a noninitiator will receive the wake-up message from a neighbor and forward it to all its other neighbors (no more than three); hence the number of messages (Exercise 3.10.48) will be no more than

$$3n + k_*.$$

(2) The election on the outer ring requires a little more attention. First of all, we must choose which ring protocol we will use; clearly, the selection is among the efficient ones we have discussed at great length in the preceding sections. Then we must ensure that the messages of the ring election protocol are correctly forwarded along the links of the outer ring.

Let us use protocol *Stages* and consider the first stage. According to the protocol, each *candidate* (in our case, a corner node) sends a message containing its value in both directions in the ring; each *defeated* entity (in our case, a border node) will forward the message along the (outer) ring.

Thus, in the mesh, each corner node will send a message to the only two neighbors. A border node y, however, has *three* neighbors, of which only two are in the outer ring; when y receives the message, it does not know to which of the other two ports it must forward the message. What we will do is simple; as we do not know to which port the message must be sent, we will forward it to *both*: One will be along the ring and proceed safely, and the other will instead reach an interior node z; when the interior node z receives such an election message, it will reply to the border node y "I am in the interior," so no subsequent election messages are sent to it. Actually, it is possible to avoid those replies without affecting the correctness (Exercise 3.10.50).

In *Stages*, the number of *candidates* is at least halved every time. This means that after the second stage, one of the corners will determine that it has the smallest id among the four candidates and will become *leader*.

Each stage requires $2n'$ messages, where $n' = 2(a + b - 2)$ is the dimension of the outer ring. An additional $2(a + b - 4)$ messages are unknowingly sent by the border to the interior in the first stage; there are also the $2(a + b - 4)$ replies from those interior nodes, that, however, can be avoided (Exercise 3.10.50). Hence, the number of messages for the election process will be at most

$$4(a + b - 2) + 2(a + b - 4) = 6(a + b) - 16.$$

IMPORTANT. Notice that in a *square* mesh (i.e., $a = b$), this means that the election process proper can be achieved in $O(\sqrt{n})$ messages.

(3) Broadcasting the notification can be performed using *Flood*, which will require less than $3n$ messages as it is started by a corner. Actually, with care, we can ensure that less than $2n$ messages are sent in total (Exercise 3.10.49).

Thus in total, the protocol *ElectMesh* we have designed will have cost

$$6(a + b) + 5n + k_\star - 16.$$

With a simple modification to the protocol, it is possible to save an additional $2(a + b - 4)$ messages (Exercise 3.10.51), achieving a cost of at most

$$\mathbf{M}[ElectMesh] \leq 4(a + b) + 5n + k_\star - 32. \tag{3.32}$$

NOTE. The most expensive operation is to wake up the nodes.

Oriented Mesh   A mesh is called *oriented* if the port numbers are the traditional *compass* labels (*north, south, east, west*) assigned in a globally consistent way. This assignment of labels has many important properties, in particular, one called *sense of direction* that can be exploited to obtain efficient solutions to problems such as broadcast and traversal (Problems 3.10.52 and 3.10.53). For the purposes of election,

in an oriented mesh, it is trivial to agree on a unique node.

For example, there is only one corner with link labels "south" and "west." Thus, to elect a leader in an oriented mesh, we must just ensure that that unique node knows that it must become *leader*.

In other words, the only part needed is a wake-up: Upon becoming awake, and participating in the wake-up process, an entity can immediately become *leader* or *follower* depending on whether or not it is southwest corner.

Notice that in an oriented mesh, we can exploit the structure of the mesh and the orientation to perform a wakeup with fewer than $2n$ messages (Problem 3.10.54).

Complexity   These results mean that regardless of whether the mesh is oriented or not, a leader can be elected with $O(n)$ messages, the difference being solely in the multiplicative constant. As no election protocol for any topology can use fewer than n messages, we have

Lemma 3.4.1 $\mathcal{M}(\text{Elect/IR} \; ; Mesh) = \Theta(n)$

3.4.2 Tori

Informally, the *torus* is a mesh with "wrap-around" links that transform it into a *regular* graph: Every node has exactly four neighbors.

A torus of dimensions $a \times b$ has $n = ab$ nodes $v_{i,j}$ ($0 \le i \le a - 1, 0 \le j \le b - 1$); each node $v_{i,j}$ is connected to four nodes $v_{i,j+1}$, $v_{i,j-1}$, $v_{i+1,j}$, and $v_{i-1,j}$, where all the operations on the first index are *modulo a*, while those on the second index are *modulo b* (e.g., see Figure 3.36). In the following sections, we will focus on *square* tori (i.e., where $a = b$).

Oriented Torus   We will first develop an election protocol assuming that there is the *compass* labeling (i.e., the links are consistently labeled as *north*, *south*, *east*, and *west*, and the dimensions are known); we will then see how to solve the problem also when the labels are arbitrary. A torus with such a labeling is said to be *oriented*.

In designing the election protocol, we will use the idea of *electoral stages* developed originally for ring networks and also use the *defeated* nodes in an active way. We will also employ a new idea, *marking of territory*.

(I) In stage i, each *candidate* x must "mark" the boundary of a territory T_i (a $d_i \times d_i$ region of the torus), where $d_i = \alpha^i$ for some fixed constant $\alpha > 1$; initially

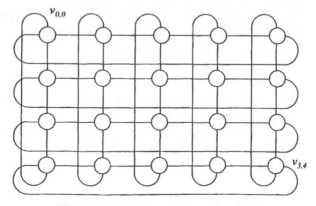

FIGURE 3.36: Torus of dimension 4×5.

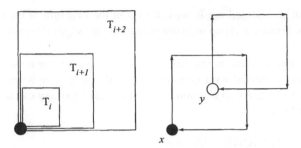

FIGURE 3.37: Marking the territory. If the territories of two *candidates* intersect, one of them will see the marking of the other.

the territory is just the single *candidate* node. The marking is done by originating a "Marking" message (with x's value) that will travel to distance[2] d_i first *north*, then *east*, then *south*, and finally *west* to return to x.

A very important fact is that if the territory of two *candidates* have some elements in common, the "Marking" message of at least one of them will encounter the marking of the other (Figure 3.37).

(II) If the "Marking" message of x does not encounters any other marking of the same stage, x survives this stage, enters stage $i + 1$, and starts the marking of a larger territory T_{i+1}.

(III) If the "Marking" message arrives at a node w already marked by another *candidate* y in the same stage, the following will occur:

1. If y has a larger id, the "Marking" message will continue to mark the boundary, setting a boolean variable SawLarger to *true*.

2. If the id of y is instead smaller, then w will terminate the "Marking" message from x; it will then originate a message "SeenbyLarger(x, i)" that will travel along the boundary of y' territory.

If *candidate* x receives both its "Marking" message with SawLarger $= true$ and a "SeenbyLarger" message, x survives this stage, enters stage $i + 1$, and starts the marking of a larger territory T_{i+1}.

Summarizing, for a *candidate* x to survive, it is necessary that it receives its "Marking" message back. If SawLarger $= false$, then that suffices; if SawLarger $= true$, x must also receive a "SeenbyLarger" message.

Note that if x receives a "SeenbyLarger(z, i)" message, then z did not finish marking its boundary; thus z does not survives this stage. In other words, if x survives, either its message found no other markings, or at least another *candidate* does not survive.

---

[2] Distances include the starting node.

(IV) A relay node w might receive several "Marking" messages from different *candidates* in the same stage. It will only be part of the boundary of the territory of the *candidate* with the smallest id.

This means that if w was part of the boundary of some *candidate* x and now becomes part of the boundary of y, a subsequent "SeenbyLarger" message intended for x will be sent along the boundary of y. This is necessary for correctness. To keep the number of messages small, we will also limit the number of "SeenbyLarger" messages sent by a relayer.

(V) A relay node will only forward one "SeenbyLarger" message.

The algorithm continues in this way until $d_i \geq \sqrt{n}$. In this case, a *candidate* will receive its "Marking" message from *south* instead of *east* because of, the "wrap-around" in the torus; it then sends the message directly *east*, and will wait for it to arrive from *west*.

(VI) When a wrap-around is detected (receive its "Marking" message from *south* rather than from *east*), a *candidate* x sends the message directly *east*, and waits for it to arrive from *west*.

If it survives, in all subsequent stages the marking becomes simpler.

(VII) In every stage after wrap-around, a *candidate* x sends its "Marking" message first *north* and waits to receive it from *south*, then it sends it *east*, and waits for it to arrive from *west*.

The situation where there is only one *candidate* left will be for sure reached after a constant number p of stages after the wrap-around occurs, as we will see later.

(VIII) If a *candidate* x survives p stages after wrap-around, it will become *leader* and notify all other entities of termination.

Let us now discuss the correctness and cost of the algorithm, protocol *MarkBoundary*, we have just described.

Correctness and Cost   For the correctness, we need to show *progress*, that is, at least one *candidate* survives each stage of the algorithm, and *termination*, that is, p stages after wrap-around there will be only one *candidate* left.

Let us discuss progress first. A *candidate* whose "Marking" message does not encounter any other boundary will survive this stage; so the only problem would be if, in a stage, every "Marking" message encounters another *candidate*'s boundary, and somehow none of them advances. We must show that this cannot happen. In fact, if every "Marking" message encounters another *candidate*'s boundary, the one with the largest id will encounter a smaller id; the *candidate* with this smaller id will go onto the next stage unless its message encounters the boundary with an even smaller id, and so on; however, the message of the *candidate* with the smallest id cannot encounter a larger id (because it is the smallest) and, thus, that entity would survive this stage.

For termination, the number of *candidates* does decrease overall, but not in a simple way. However, it is possible to bound the maximum number of *candidates* in each stage, and that bound strictly decreases. Let n_i be the maximum number of *candidates* in stage i. Up until wrap-around, there are two types of survivors: (a) those entities whose message did not encounter any border and (b) those whose message encountered a border with a larger id and whose border was encountered by a message with a larger id. Let a_i denote the number of the first type of survivors; clearly $a_i \leq n/d_i^2$. The number of the second type will be at most $(n_i - a_i)/2$ as each defeated one can cause at most one *candidate* to survive. Thus,

$$n_{i+1} \leq a_i + (n_i - a_i)/2 = (n_i + a_i)/2 \leq \left(n_i + \tfrac{n}{d_i^2}\right)/2.$$

As $d_i = \alpha^i$ is increasing each stage, the upper bound n_i on the number of *candidates* is decreasing. Solving the recurrence relation gives

$$n_{i+1} \leq n/\alpha^{2i}(2 - \alpha^2). \tag{3.33}$$

Wrap-around occurs when $\alpha^i \geq \sqrt{n}$; in that stage, only one *candidate* can complete the marking of its boundary without encountering any markings and at most half the remaining *candidates* will survive. So, the number of *candidates* surviving this stage is at most $(2 - \alpha^2)^{-1}$. In all subsequent stages, again only one *candidate* can complete the marking without encountering any markings and at most half the remaining *candidates* will survive. Hence, after

$$p > \lceil \log(2 - \alpha^2)^{-1} \rceil$$

additional stages for sure there will be only one *candidate* left. Thus, the protocol correctly terminates.

To determine the total number of messages, consider that in stage i before wrap-around, each *candidate* causes at most $4d_i$ "Marking" messages to mark its boundary and another $4d_i$ "SeenbyLarger" messages, for a total of $8d_i = 8\alpha^i$ messages; as the number of *candidates* is at most as expressed by equation 3.33, the total number of messages in this pre-wrap-around stage will be at most

$$O(n\alpha^2 /(2 - \alpha^2)(\alpha - 1)).$$

In each phase after wrap-around, there is only a constant number of *candidates*, each sending $O(\sqrt{n})$ messages. As the number of such phases is constant, the total number of messages sent after wrap-around is $O(\sqrt{n})$.

Choosing $\alpha \approx 1.1795$ yields the desired bound

$$\mathbf{M}[MarkBorder] = \Theta(n). \tag{3.34}$$

The preceding analysis ignores the fact that α^i is not an integer: The distance to travel must be rounded up and this has to be taken into account in the analysis.

However, the effect is not large and will just affect the low-order terms of the cost (Exercise 3.10.55).

The algorithm as given is not very time efficient. In fact, the ideal time can be as bad as $O(n)$ (Exercise 3.10.56). The protocol can be, however, modified so that without changing its message complexity, the algorithm requires no more than $O(\sqrt{n})$ time (Exercise 3.10.57).

The protocol we have described is tailored for square tori. If the torus is not square but rectangular with length l and width w ($l \leq w$), then the algorithm can be adapted to use $\Theta(n + l \log l/w)$ messages (Exercise 3.10.58).

Unoriented Torus   The algorithm we just described solved the problem of electing a leader in an oriented torus, for example, among the buildings in Manhattan (well known for its mesh-like design), by sending a messenger along east-west streets and north-south avenues, turning at the appropriate corner. Consider now the same problem when the streets have no signs and the entities have no compass.

Interestingly, the same strategy can be still used: A *candidate* needs to mark off a square; the orientation of the square is irrelevant. To be able to travel along a square, we just need to know how to

1. forward a message "in a straight line," and
2. make the "appropriate turn."

We will discuss how to achieve each, separately.

(1) *Forwarding in a Straight Line.* We first consider how to forward a message in the direction opposite to the one from which the message was received, without knowing the directions.

Consider an entity x, with its four incident links, and let a, b, c, and d be the arbitrary port numbers associated with them; (see Figure 3.38); to forward a message in a straight line, x needs to determine that a and d are opposite, and so are b and c. This can be easily accomplished by having each entity send its identity to each of its four neighbors, which will forward it to its three other neighbors; the entity will in turn acquire the identity and relative position of each entity at distance 2. As a result,

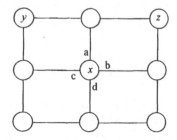

FIGURE 3.38: Even without a compass, x can determine which links are opposite.

x will know the two pairs of opposite port numbers. In the example of Figure 3.38, x will receive the message originating from z via both port a and port b; it, thus, knows that a is not opposite to b. It also receives the message from y via ports a and c; thus x knows also that a is not opposite to c. Then, x can conclude that a is opposite to d.

It will then locally relabel one pair of opposite ports as *east*, *west*, and the other *north*, *south*; it does not matter which pair is chosen first.

(2) *Making the Appropriate Turn.* As a result of the the previous operation, each entity x knows two *perpendicular* directions, but the naming (north, south) and (east, west) might not be consistent with the one done by other entities. This can create problems when wanting to make a consistent turn.

Consider a message, originating by x which is traveling "south" (according to x's view of the torus); to continue to travel "south" can be easily accomplished as each entity knows how to forward a message in a straight line. At some point, according to the protocol, the message must turn, say to "east" (always according to x's view of the torus), and continue in that direction.

To achieve the turn correctly, we add a simple information, called *handrail*, to a message. The *handrail* is the id of the neighbor in the direction the message must turn and the name of the direction. In the example of Figure 3.38, if x is sending a message *south* that must then turn *east*, the handrail in the message will be the id of its eastern neighbor q plus the direction "east." Because every entity knows the ids and the relative position of all the entities within distance 2, when y receives this message with the handrail from x, it can determine what x means by "east," and thus in which direction the message must turn (when the algorithm prescribes it).

Summarizing, even without a compass, we can execute the protocol *MarkBorder*, by adding the preprocessing phase and including the handrail information in the messages.

The cost of the preprocessing is relatively small: Each entity receives four messages for its immediate neighbors and 4×3 for entities at distances 2, for a total of $16n$ messages.

3.5 ELECTION IN CUBE NETWORKS

3.5.1 Oriented Hypercubes

The k-dimensional *hypercube* H_k, which we have introduced in Section 2.1.3, is a common interconnection network, consisting of $n = 2^k$ nodes, each with degree k; hence, in H_k there are $m = k2^{k-1} = O(n \log n)$ edges.

In an oriented hypercube H_k, the port numbers $1, 2, \ldots, k$ for the k edges incident on a node x are called *dimensions* and are assigned according to the "construction rules" specifying H_k (see Fig. 2.3).

We will solve the election problem in oriented hypercubes using the approach *electoral stages* that we have developed for ring networks. The metaphor we will use is that of a *fencing tournament*: in a stage of the tournament, each *candidate*, called *duelist*, will be assigned another duelist, and each pair will have a *match*; as a result of the match, one duelist will be promoted to the next stage, the other excluded from further competition. In each stage, only half of the duelists enter the next stage; at the end, there will be only one duelist that will become the *leader* and notify the others.

Deciding the outcome of a match is easy: The duelist with the smaller id will win; for reasons that will become evident later, we will have the defeated duelist remember the shortest path to the winning duelist.

The crucial and difficult parts are how pairs of opposite duelists are formed and how a duelist finds its competitor. To understand how this can be done efficiently, we need to understand some structural properties of oriented hypercubes.

A basic property of an oriented hypercube is that if we remove from H_k all the links with label greater than i (i.e., consider only the first i dimensions), we are left with 2^{k-i} disjoint oriented hypercubes of dimension i; denote the collection of these smaller cubes by $H_{k:i}$. For example, removing the links with label 3 and 4 from H_4 will result into four disjoint oriented hypercubes of dimension 2 (see Figure 3.39 (a and b)).

What we will do is to ensure that

(I) at the end of stage $i - 1$, there will be only one duelist left in each of the oriented hypercubes of dimension $i - 1$ of $H_{k:i-1}$.

So, for example, at the end of stage 2, we want to have only one duelist left in each of the four hypercubes of dimension 2 (see Figure 3.39(c)).

Another nice property of oriented hypercubes is that if we add to $H_{k:i-1}$ the links labeled i (and, thus, construct $H_{k:i}$) the elements of $H_{k:i-1}$ will be grouped into pairs. We can use this property to form the pairs of duelists in each stage of the tournament:

(II) A duelist x starting stage i will have as its opponent the duelist in the hypercube of dimension $i - 1$ connected to x by the link labeled i.

Thus, in stage i, a duelist x will send a Match message to (and receive a Match message from) the duelist y in hypercube (of dimension $i - 1$) that is on the other side of link i. The Match message from x will contain the id id(x) (as well as the path traveled so far) and will be sent across dimension i (i.e., the link with label i). The entity z on the other end of the link might, however, not be the duelist y and might not even know who (and where) y is (Figure 3.40).

We need the Match message from x to reach its opponent y. We can obtain this by having z broadcast the message in its $(i - 1)$-dimensional hypercube (e.g., using protocol *HyperFlood* presented in Section 2.1.3); in this way, we are sure that y will receive the message. Obviously, this approach is an expensive one (as determined in Exercise 3.10.59).

To solve this problem efficiently, we will use the following observation. If node z is not the duelist (i.e., $z \neq y$), node z was defeated in a previous stage, say $i_1 < i$; it knows the (shortest) path to the duelist z_{i_1}, which defeated it in that stage, and can thus forward the message to it. Now, if $z_{i_1} = y$, then we are done: The message from x has arrived and the match can take place. Otherwise, in a similar way, z_{i_1} was

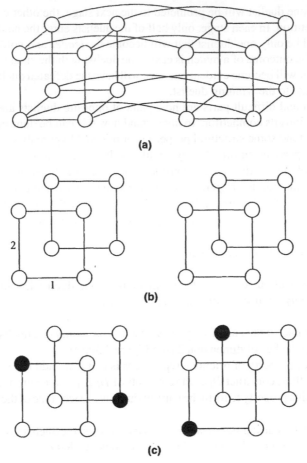

FIGURE 3.39: (a) The four-dimensional hypercube H_4, (b) the collection $H_{4:2}$ of two-dimensional hypercubes obtained by removing the links with labels greater than 2, and (c) duelists (in black) at the end of stage 2.

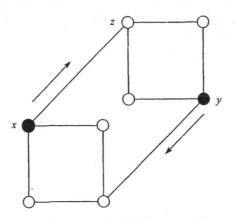

FIGURE 3.40: Each duelist (in black) sends a Match message that must reach its opponent.

defeated in some subsequent stage i_2, $i_1 < i_2 < i$; it, thus, knows the (shortest) path to the duelist z_{i_2}, which defeated it in that stage and can thus forward the message to it. In this way, the message from x will eventually reach y; the path information in the message is updated during its travel so that y will know the dimensions traversed by the message from x to y in chronological order. The Match message from y will reach x with similar information.

The match between x and y will take place both at x and y; only one of them, say x, will enter stage $i + 1$, while the other, y, is defeated.

From now on, if y receives a Match message, it will forward it to x; as mentioned before, we need this to be done on the shortest path. How can y (the defeated duelist) know the shortest path to x (the winner)?

The Match message y received from x contained the labels of *a walk* to it, not necessarily the shortest path. Fortunately, it is easy to determine the shortcuts in any path using the properties of the labeling. Consider a sequence α of labels (with or without repetitions); remove from the sequence any pair of identical labels and sort the remaining ones, obtaining a *compressed* sequence $\overline{\alpha}$. For example, if $\alpha = \langle 231345212 \rangle$, then $\overline{\alpha} = \langle 245 \rangle$.

The important property is that if we start from the same node x, the walk with labels α will lead to the same node y as the walk with labels $\overline{\alpha}$. The other important property is that $\overline{\alpha}$ actually corresponds to the shortest path between x and y. Thus, y needs only to compress the sequence contained in the Match message sent by x.

IMPORTANT. We can perform the compression *while* the message is traveling from x to y; in this way, the message will contain at most k labels.

Finally, we must consider the fact that owing to different transmission delays, it is likely that the computation in some parts of the hypercube is faster than in others. Thus, it may happen that a duelist x in stage i sends a Match message for its opponent, but the entities on the other side of dimension i are still in earlier stages.

So, it is possible that the message from x reaches a duelist y in an earlier stage $j < i$. What y should do with this message depends on future events that have nothing to do with the message: If y wins all matches in stages j, $j + 1, \ldots, i - 1$, then y is the opponent of x in stage i, and it is the destination of the message; on the contrary, if it loses one of them, it must forward the message to the winner of that match. In a sense, the message from x has arrived "too soon"; so, what y will do is to delay the processing of this message until the "right" time, that is, until it enters stage i or it becomes defeated. Summarizing,

1. A *duelist* in stage i will send a Match message on the edge with label i.
2. When a *defeated* node receives a Match message, it will forward it to the winner of the match in which it was defeated.
3. When a *duelist* y in stage i receives a Match message from a *duelist* x in stage i, if $\mathrm{id}(x) > \mathrm{id}(y)$, then y will enter stage $i + 1$, otherwise it will become *defeated* and compute the shortest path to x.

4. When a *duelist* y in stage *j* receives a Match message from a *duelist* x in stage *i* > *j*, y will enqueue the message and process it (as a newly arrived one) when it enters stage *i* or becomes *defeated*.

The protocol terminates when a duelist wins the *k*th stage. As we will see, when this happens, that duelist will be the only one left in the network.

The algorithm, protocol *HyperElect*, is shown in Figures 3.41 and 3.42. *Next-Duelist* denotes the (list of labels on the) path from a *defeated* node to the duelist that *defeated* it. The Match message contains (*Id**, *stage**, *source**, *dest**), where *Id** is the identity of the *duelist* x originating the message; *stage** is the stage of this match; *source** is (the list of labels on) the path from the duelist x to the entity currently processing the message; and *dest** is (the list of labels on) the path from the entity currently processing the message to a target entity (used to forward message by the shortest path between a defeated entity and its winner). Given a list of labels *list*, the protocol uses the following functions:

– *first(list)* returns the first element of the list;
– *list* ⊕ *i* (respectively, ⊖) updates the given path by adding (respectively, eliminating) a label *i* to the list and compressing it.

To store the delayed messages, we use a set *Delayed* that will be kept *sorted* by stage number; for convenience, we also use a set *delay* of the corresponding stage numbers.

Correctness and termination of the protocol derive from the following fact (Exercise 3.10.61):

Lemma 3.5.1   *Let* $id(x)$ *be the smallest id in one of the hypercubes of dimension i in* $H_{k:i}$. *Then x is a duelist at the beginning of stage* $i + 1$.

This means that when $i = k$, there will be only one duelist left at the end of that stage; it will then become *leader* and notify the others so to ensure proper termination.

To determine the cost of the protocol, we need to determine the number of messages sent in a stage *i*. For a *defeated* entity z, denote by $w(z)$ its opponent (i.e., the one that won the match). For simplicity of notation, let $w^j(z) = w(w^{j-1}(z))$ where $w^0(z) = z$.

Consider an arbitrary $H \in H_{k:i-1}$; let y be the only *duelist* in H in stage *i* and let z be the entity in H that receives first the Match message for y from its opponent. Entity z must send this message to y; it forwards the message (through the shortest path) to $w(z)$, which will forward it to $w(w(z)) = w^2(z)$, which will forward it to $w(w^2(z)) = w^3(z)$, and so on, until $w^t(z) = y$. There will be no more than *i* such "forward" points (i.e., $t \leq i$); as we are interested in the worst case, assume this to be the case. Thus, the total cost will be the sum of all the distances between successive forward points, plus one (from x to z). Denote by $d(j - 1, j)$ the distance between $w^{j-1}(z)$ and $w^j(z)$; clearly $d(j - 1, j) \leq j$ (Exercise 3.10.60); then the total number of messages required for the Match message from a duelist x in stage *i* to reach its

PROTOCOL HyperElect.

- States: $S = \{$ASLEEP, DUELLIST, DEFEATED, FOLLOWER, LEADER$\}$;
  $S_{\text{INIT}} = \{$ASLEEP$\}$; $S_{\text{TERM}} = \{$FOLLOWER, LEADER$\}$.
- Restrictions: **IR** $\cup Oriented\,Hypercube$.

ASLEEP
>
> *Spontaneously*
> **begin**
>> stage:= 1; delay:=0; value:= $id(x)$;
>> Source:= [stage];
>> Dest:= [];
>> **send**("Match", value, stage, Source, Dest) **to** 1;
>> **become** DUELLIST;
> **end**
>
> *Receiving*("Match", value*, stage*, Source*, Dest*)
> **begin**
>> stage:= 1; value:= $id(x)$;
>> Source:= [stage];
>> Dest:= [];
>> **send**("Match", value, stage, Source, Dest) **to** 1;
>> **become** DUELLIST;
>> **if**   stage* =stage **then**
>>> PROCESS_MESSAGE;
>> **else**
>>> DELAY_MESSAGE;
>> **endif**
> **end**

DUELLIST
>
> *Receiving*("Match", value*, stage*, Source*, Dest*)
> **begin**
>> **if**   stage* =stage **then**
>>> PROCESS_MESSAGE;
>> **else**
>>> DELAY_MESSAGE;
>> **endif**
> **end**

DEFEATED
>
> *Receiving*("Match", value*, stage*, Source*, Dest*)
> **begin**
>> **if**   Dest* = [] **then** Dest*:= NextDuelist; **endif**
>> $l:=first$(Dest*); Dest:=Dest* $\ominus l$; Source:= Source* $\oplus l$;
>> **send**("Match", value*, stage*, Source, Dest) **to** l;
> **end**
>
> *Receiving*("Notify")
> **begin**
>> **send** ("Notify") **to** $\{l \in N(x) : l > $ **sender**$\}$;
>> **become** FOLLOWER;
> **end**

FIGURE 3.41: Protocol *HyperElect.*

```
Procedure PROCESS_MESSAGE
begin
    if   value* > value then
        if   stage* =k then
            send ("Notify") to N(x);
            become LEADER;
        else
            stage:= stage+1; Source:=[stage] ; dest:= [];
            send("Match", value, stage, Source, Dest) to stage;
            CHECK;
        endif
    else
        NextDuelist := Source;
        CHECK_ALL;
        become DEFEATED;
    endif
end


Procedure DELAY_MESSAGE
begin
    Delayed ⇐ (value*, stage*, Source*, Dest*);
    delay ⇐ stage*;
end


Procedure CHECK
begin
    if   Delayed ≠ ∅ then
        next:=Min{delay};
        if   next = stage then
            (value*, stage*, Source*, Dest*) ⇐ Delayed;
            delay:= delay-{next};
            PROCESS_MESSAGE
        endif
    endif
end


Procedure CHECK_ALL
begin
    while   Delayed ≠ ∅ do
        (value*, stage*, Source*, Dest*) ⇐ Delayed;
        if   Dest* [] then Dest*:= NextDuelist; endif
        l:=first(Dest*) ; Dest:=Dest* ⊖l ; Source:= Source* ⊕l
        send("Match", value*, stage*, Source, Dest) to l;
    endwhile
end
```

FIGURE 3.42: Procedures used by Protocol *HyperElect.*

opposite y will be at most

$$L(i) = 1 + \sum_{j=1}^{i-1} d(j-1, j) = 1 + \sum_{j=1}^{i-1} j = 1 + \frac{i \cdot (i-1)}{2}.$$

Now we know how much does it cost for a Match message to reach its destination. What we need to determine is how many such messages are generated in each stage;

in other words, we want to know the number n_i of *duelists* in stage i (as each will generate one such message). By Lemma 3.5.1, we know that at the beginning of stage i, there is only one *duelist* in each of the hypercubes $H \in H_{k:i-1}$; as there are exactly $\frac{n}{2^{i-1}} = 2^{k-i+1}$ such cubes,

$$n_i = 2^{k-i+1}.$$

Thus, the total number of messages in stage i will be

$$n_i L(i) = 2^{k-i+1}\left(1 + \frac{i\cdot(i-1)}{2}\right)$$

and over all stages, the total will be

$$\sum_{i=1}^{k} 2^{k-i+1}\left(1 + \frac{i\cdot(i-1)}{2}\right) = 2^k\left(\sum_{i=1}^{k}\frac{i}{2^{i-1}} + \sum_{i=1}^{k}\frac{i^2}{2^i} + \sum_{i=1}^{k}\frac{i}{2^i}\right) = 6\,2^k - k^2 - 3k - 7.$$

As $2^k = n$, and adding the $(n-1)$ messages to broadcast the termination, we have

$$\mathbf{M}[HyperElect] \leq 7n - (\log n)^2 - 3\log n - 7. \tag{3.35}$$

That is, we can elect a leader in less than $7n$ messages! This result should be contrasted with the fact that in a ring we need $\Omega(n \log n)$ messages.

As for the time complexity, it is not difficult to verify that protocol *HyperFlood* requires at most $O(\log^3 N)$ ideal time (Exercise 3.10.62).

Practical Considerations The $O(n)$ message cost of protocol *HyperElect* is achieved by having the Match messages convey path information in addition to the usual id and stage number. In particular, the fields *Source* and *Dest* have been described as lists of labels; as we only send *compressed* paths, *Source* and *Dest* contain at most $\log n$ labels each. So it would appear that the protocol requires "long" messages. We will now see that in practice, each list only requires $\log n$ bits (i.e., the cost of a counter).

Examine a compressed sequence of edge labels $\overline{\alpha}$ in H_k (e.g., $\overline{\alpha} = \langle 1457 \rangle$ in H_8); as the sequence is compressed, there are no repetitions. The elements in the sequence are a subset of the integers between 1 and k; thus $\overline{\alpha}$ can be represented as a binary string $\langle b_1, b_2, \ldots, b_k \rangle$ where each bit $b_j = 1$ if and only if j is in $\overline{\alpha}$. Thus, the list $\overline{\alpha} = \langle 1457 \rangle$ in H_8 is uniquely represented as $\langle 10011010 \rangle$. Thus, each of *Source* and *Dest* will be just a $k = \log n$ bits variable.

This also implies that the cost in terms of bits of the protocol will be no more than

$$\mathbf{B}[HyperElect] \leq 7n(\log \mathbf{id} + 2\log n + \log\log n), \tag{3.36}$$

where the $\log\log n$ component is to account for the *stage* field.

3.5.2 Unoriented Hypercubes

Hypercubes with arbitrary labellings obviously do not have the properties of oriented hypercubes. It is still possible to take advantage of the highly regular structure of hypercubes to do better than in ring networks. In fact (Problem 3.10.8),

Lemma 3.5.2 $\mathcal{M}(\textbf{Elect}/\textbf{IR}; \textit{Hypercube}) \leq O(n \log \log n)$

To date, it is not known whether it is possible to elect a leader in an hypercube in just $O(n)$ messages even when it is not oriented (Problem 3.10.9).

3.6 ELECTION IN COMPLETE NETWORKS

We have seen how structural properties of the network can be effectively used to overcome the additional difficulty of operating in a fully symmetric graph. For example, in oriented hypercubes, we have been able to achieve $O(n)$ costs, that is, comparable to those obtainable in trees.

In contrast, a ring has very few links and no additional structural property capable of overcoming the disadvantages of symmetry. In particular, it is so sparse (i.e., $m = n$) that it has the worst diameter among regular graphs (to reach the furthermost node, a message must traverse $d = n/2$ links) and no short cuts. It is thus no surprising that election requires $\Omega(n \log n)$ messages.

The ring is the sparsest network and it is an extreme in the spectrum of regular networks. At the other end of the spectrum lies the complete graph K_n; in K_n, each node is connected directly to every other node. It is thus the densest network

$$m = \tfrac{1}{2} n(n - 1)$$

and the one with smallest diameter

$$d = 1.$$

Another interesting property is that K_n contains every other network G as a subgraph! Clearly, physical implementation of such a topology is very expensive.

Let us examine how to exploit such very powerful features to design an efficient election protocol.

3.6.1 Stages and Territory

To develop an efficient protocol for election in complete networks, we will use *electoral stages* as well as a new technique, *territory acquisition*.

In *territory acquisition*, each *candidate* tries to "capture" its neighbors (i.e., all other nodes) one at a time; it does so by sending a Capture message containing its id as well as the number of nodes captured so far (the *stage*). If the attempt is successful, the attacked neighbor becomes *captured*, and the *candidate* enters the next stage and continues; otherwise, the *candidate* becomes *passive*. The *candidate* that is successful in capturing all entities becomes the *leader*.

Summarizing, at any time an entity is *candidate*, *captured*, or *passive*. A *captured* entity remembers the id, the stage, and the link to its "owner" (i.e., the entity that captured it). Let us now describe an electoral stage.

1. A *candidate* entity x sends a Capture message to a neighbor y.
2. If y is *candidate*, the outcome of the attack depends on the stage and the id of the two entities:
   (a) If $stage(x) > stage(y)$, the attack is successful.
   (b) If $stage(x) = stage(y)$, the attack is successful if $id(x) < id(y)$; otherwise x becomes *passive*.
   (c) If $stage(x) < stage(y)$, x becomes *passive*.
3. If y is *passive*, the attack is successful.
4. If y is already *captured*, then x has to defeat y's owner z before capturing y. Specifically, a Warning message with x's id and stage is send by y to its owner z.
   (a) If z is a *candidate* in a higher stage, or in the same stage but with a smaller id than x, then the attack to y is *not* successful: z will notify y that, in turn, will notify x.
   (b) In all other cases (z is already *passive* or *captured*, z is a *candidate* in a smaller stage, or in the same stage but with a larger id than x), the attack to y is *successful*: z notifies x via y, and if *candidate* it becomes *passive*.
5. If the attack is successful, y is *captured* by x, x increments $stage(x)$ and proceeds with its conquest.

Notice that each attempt from a *candidate* costs exactly two messages (one for the Capture, one for the notification) if the neighbor is also a *candidate* or *passive*; instead, if the neighbor was already *captured*, two additional messages will be sent (from the neighbor to its owner, and back).

The strategy just outlined will indeed solve the election problem (Exercise 3.10.65). Even though each attempt costs only four (or fewer) messages, the overall cost can be prohibitive; this is because of the fact that the number n_i of candidates at level i can in general be very large (Exercise 3.10.66).

To control the number n_i, we need to ensure that a node is captured by at most one candidate in the same level. In other words, the territories of the candidates in stage i must be mutually disjoint. Fortunately, this can be easily achieved.

First of all, we provide some intelligence and decisional power to the *captured* nodes:

(I) If a *captured* node y receives a Capture message from a *candidate* x that is in a stage smaller than the one known to y, then y will immediately notify x that the attack is unsuccessful.

As a consequence, a *captured* node y will only issue a Warning for an attack at the highest level known to y. A more important change is the following:

(II) If a *captured* node y sends a Warning to its owner z about an attack from x, y will wait for the answer from z (i.e., locally enqueue any subsequent Capture message in same or higher stage) before issuing another Warning.

As a consequence, if the attack from x was successful (and the stage increased), y will send to the new owner x any subsequent Warning generated by processing the enqueued Capture messages. After this change, the territory of any two candidates in the same level are guaranteed to have no nodes in common (Exercise 3.10.64).

Protocol *CompleteElect* implementing the strategy we have just designed is shown in Figures 3.43, 3.44, and 3.45.

Let us analyze the cost of the protocol.

How many candidates there can be in stage i? As each of them has a territory of size i and these territories are disjoint, there cannot be more than $n_i \leq n/i$ such *candidates*. Each will originate an attack that will cost at most four messages; thus, in stage i, there will be at most $4n/i$ messages.

Let us now determine the number of stages needed for termination. Consider the following fact: if a *candidate* has conquered a territory of size $\frac{n}{2} + 1$, no other *candidate* can become *leader*. Hence, a *candidate* can become *leader* as soon as it reaches that stage (it will then broadcast a termination message to all nodes).

Thus the total number of messages, including the $n - 1$ for termination notification, will be

$$n + 1 + \sum_{i=1}^{n/2} 4n_i \ \leq \ n + 1 + 4n \sum_{i=1}^{n/2} \frac{1}{i} \ = \ 4n H_{n/2} + n + 1,$$

which gives the overall cost

$$\text{M}[CompleteElect] \leq 2.76 \, n \log n - 1.76n + 1. \tag{3.37}$$

Let us now consider the *time* cost of the protocol. It is not difficult to see that in the worst case, the ideal time of protocol *CompleteElect* is linear (Exercise 3.10.67):

$$\text{T}[CompleteElect] = O(n). \tag{3.38}$$

This must be contrasted with the $O(1)$ time cost of the simple strategy of each entity sending its id immediately to all its neighbors, thus receiving the id of everybody else, and determining the smallest id. Obviously, the price we would pay for a $O(1)$ time cost is $O(n^2)$ messages.

Appropriately combining the two strategies, we can actually construct protocols that offer optimal $O(n \log n)$ message costs with $O(n/\log n)$ time (Exercise 3.10.68).

The time can be further reduced at the expense of more messages. In fact, it is possible to design an election protocol that, for any $\log n \leq k \leq n$, uses $O(nk)$ messages and $O(n/k)$ time in the worst case (Exercise 3.10.69).

PROTOCOL CompleteElect.

- S = {ASLEEP, CANDIDATE,PASSIVE, CAPTURED, FOLLOWER, LEADER};
  S_{INIT} = {ASLEEP}; S_{TERM} = {FOLLOWER, LEADER}.
- Restrictions: **IR** $\cup CompleteGraph$.

ASLEEP
> *Spontaneously*
> **begin**
>> stage:= 1; value:= $id(x)$;
>> Others:= $N(x)$;
>> next ← Others;
>> send("Capture", stage, value) **to** next;
>> **become** CANDIDATE;
> **end**

> *Receiving*("Capture", stage*, value*)
> **begin**
>> send("Accept", stage*, value*) **to** sender;
>> stage:= 1;
>> owner:= **sender**;
>> ownerstage:= stage* +1;
>> **become** CAPTURED;
> **end**

CANDIDATE
> *Receiving*("Capture", stage*, value*)
> **begin**
>> **if** (stage* < stage) **or** ((stage* = stage) **and**
>> (value* > value)) **then**
>>> send("Reject", stage) **to** sender;
>> **else**
>>> send("Accept", stage*, value*) **to** sender;
>>> owner:= **sender**;
>>> ownerstage:= stage* +1;
>>> **become** CAPTURED;
>> **endif**
> **end**

> *Receiving*("Accept", stage, value)
> **begin**
>> stage:= stage+1;
>> **if** stage $\geq 1 + n/2$ **then**
>>> send("Terminate") **to** $N(x)$;
>>> **become** LEADER;
>> **else**
>>> next ← Others;
>>> send("Capture", stage, value) **to** next;
>> **endif**
> **end**

(CONTINUES ...)

FIGURE 3.43: Protocol *CompleteElect* (I).

3.6.2 Surprising Limitation

We have just developed an efficient protocol for election in complete networks. Its cost is $O(n \log n)$ messages. Observe that this is the same as we were able to do in *ring* networks (actually, the multiplicative constant here is *worse*).

```
CANDIDATE
      Receiving("Reject", stage*)
      begin
          become PASSIVE;
      end

      Receiving("Terminate")
      begin
          become FOLLOWER;
      end

      Receiving("Warning", stage*, value*)
      begin
          if  (stage* < stage) or ((stage* = stage) and
            (value* > value)) then
              send("No", stage) to sender;
          else
              send("Yes", stage*) to sender;
              become PASSIVE;
          endif
      end


PASSIVE
      Receiving("Capture", stage*, value*)
      begin
          if  (stage* < stage) or ((stage* = stage) and
            (value* > value)) then
              send("Reject", stage) to sender;
          else
              send("Accept", stage*, value*) to sender;
              ownerstage:= stage* +1;
              owner:= sender;
              become CAPTURED;
          endif
      end

      Receiving("Warning", stage*, value*)
      begin
          if  (stage* < stage) or ((stage* = stage) and
            (value* > value)) then
              send("No", stage) to sender;
          else
              send("Yes", stage*) to sender;
          endif
      end

      Receiving("Terminate")
      begin
          become FOLLOWER;
      end

(CONTINUES ...)
```

FIGURE 3.44: Protocol *CompleteElect* (II).

Unlike rings, in complete networks, each entity has a direct link to all other entities and there is a total of $O(n^2)$ links. By exploiting all this communication hardware, we should be able to do better than in rings, where there are only n links, and where entities can be $O(n)$ far apart.

CAPTURED

```
    Receiving("Capture", stage*, value*)
    begin
        if  stage* < ownerstage then
            send("Reject", ownerstage) to sender;
        else
            attack:= sender;
            send("Warning", value*, stage*) to owner;
            close N(x) - {owner};
        endif
    end

    Receiving("No", stage*)
    begin
        open N(x);
        send("Reject", stage*) to attack;
    end

    Receiving("Yes", stage*)
    begin
        ownerstage:= stage*+1;
        owner:= attack;
        open N(x);
        send("Accept", stage*, value*) to attack;
    end

    Receiving("Warning", stage*, value*)
    begin
        if  (stage* < ownerstage) then
            send("No", ownerstage) to sender;
        else
            send("Yes", stage*) to sender;
        endif
    end

    Receiving("Terminate")
    begin
        become FOLLOWER;
    end
```

FIGURE 3.45: Protocol *CompleteElect* (III).

The most surprising result about complete networks is that in spite of having available the largest possible amount of connection links and a direct connection between any two entities, for election they *do not fare better than ring networks*.

In fact, any election protocol will require in the worst case $\Omega(n \log n)$ messages, that is,

Property 3.6.1 $\mathcal{M}(\textbf{Elect/IR}; K) = \Omega(n \log n)$

To see why this is true, observe that any election protocol also solves the *wake-up* problem: To become *defeated* or *leader*, an entity must have been active (i.e., *awake*). This simple observation has dramatic consequences. In fact, any wake-up protocol requires at least $.5n \log n$ messages in the worst case (Property 2.2.5); thus, any Election protocol requires in the worst case the same number of messages.

This implies that as far as election is concerned, the very large expenses due to the physical construction of $m = (n^2 + n)/2$ links are not justifiable as the same performance and operational costs can be achieved with only $m = n$ links arranged in a ring.

3.6.3 Harvesting the Communication Power

The lower bound we have just seen carries a very strong and rather surprising message for network development: in so far election is concerned, complete networks are not worth the large communication hardware costs. The facts that Election is a basic problem and its solutions are routinely used by more complex protocols makes this message even stronger.

The message is surprising because the complete graph, as we mentioned, has the most communication links of any network and the shortest possible distance between any two entities.

To overcome the limit imposed by the lower bound and, thus, to harvest the communication power of complete graphs, we need the presence of some additional tools (i.e., properties, restrictions, etc.). The question becomes: which tool is powerful enough? As each property we assume restricts the applicability of the solution, our quest for a powerful tool should be focused on the least restrictive ones.

In this section, we will see how to answer this question. In the process, we will discover some intriguing relationships between port numbering and consistency and shed light on some properties of whose existence we already had an inkling in earlier section.

We will first examine a particular labeling of the ports that will allow us to make full use of the communication power of the complete graph.

The first step consists in viewing a complete graph K_n as a ring R_n, where any two nonneighboring nodes have been connected by an additional link, called *chord*. Assume that the label associated at x to link (x, y) is equal to the (clockwise) distance from x to y in the ring. Thus, each link in the ring is labeled 1 in the clockwise direction and $n - 1$ in the other. In general, if $\lambda_x(x, y) = i$, then $\lambda_y(y, x) = n - i$ (see Figure 3.46); this labeling is called *chordal*.

Let us see how election can be performed in a complete graph with such a labeling.

First of all, observe the following: As the links labeled 1 and $n - 1$ form a ring, the entities could ignore all the other links and execute on this subnet an election protocol for rings, for example, *Stages*. This approach will yield a solution requiring $2n \log n$ messages in the worst case, thus already improving on *CompleteElect*. But we can do better than that.

Consider a *candidate* entity x executing stage i: It will send an election message each in both directions, which will travel along the ring until they reach another *candidate*, say y and z (see Figure 3.47). This operation will require the transmission of $d(x, y) + d(x, z)$ messages. Similarly, x will receive the Election messages from both y and z, and decide whether it survives this stage or not, on the basis of the received ids.

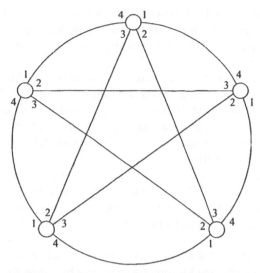

FIGURE 3.46: A complete graph with chordal labeling. The links labeled 1 and 4 form a ring.

Now, in a complete graph, there exists a direct link between x and y, as well as between x and z; thus, a message from one to the other could be conveyed with only one transmission. Unfortunately, x does not know which of its $n - 1$ links connect it to y or to z; y and z are in a similar situation. In the example of Figure 3.47, x does not know that y is the node at distance 5 along the ring (in the clockwise direction), and thus the port connecting x to it is the one with label 5. If it did, those four defeated nodes in between them could be bypassed. Similarly, x does not know that z is at distance -3 (i.e., at distance 3 in the counterclockwise direction) and thus reachable through port $n - 3$. However, this information can be acquired.

Assume that the Election message contains also a counter, initialized to one, which is increased by one unit by each node forwarding it. Then, a candidate receiving the Election message knows exactly which port label connects it to the originator of that message. In our example, the election message from y will have a counter equal to 5 and will arrive from link 1 (i.e., counterclockwise), while the message from z will

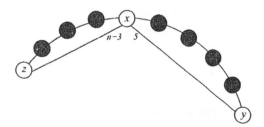

FIGURE 3.47: If x knew $d(x, y)$ and $d(x, z)$, it could reach y and z directly.

have a counter equal to 3 and will arrive from link $n-1$ (i.e., clockwise). From this information, x can determine that y can be reached directly through port 5 and z is reachable through link $n-3$. Similarly, y (respective z) will know that the direct link to x is the one labeled $n-5$ (respective 3).

This means that in the next stage, these chords can be used instead of the corresponding segments of the ring, thus saving message transmissions. The net effect will be that in stage $i+1$, the candidates will use the (smaller) ring composed only of the chords determined in the previous stage, that is, messages will be sent only on the links connecting the candidates of stage i, thus, completely bypassing all entities defeated in stage $i-1$ or earlier.

Assume in our example that x enters stage $i+1$ (and thus both y and z are defeated); it will prepare an election message for the candidates in both directions, say u and v, and will send it directly to y and to z. As before, x does not know where u and v are (i.e., which of its links connect it to them) but, as before, it can determine it.

The only difference is that the counter must be initialized to the *weight* of the chord: Thus, the counter of the Election message sent by x directly to y is equal to 5, and the one to z is equal to 3. Similarly, when an entity forwards the Election message through a link, it will add to the counter the weight of that link.

Summarizing, in each stage, the candidates will execute the protocol in a smaller ring. Let $R(i)$ be the ring used in stage i; initially $R(1) = R_n$. Using the ring protocol *Stages* in each stage, the number of messages we will be transmitting will be exactly $2(n(1) + n(2) + \ldots + n(k))$, where $n(i)$ is the size of $R(i)$ and $k \leq \log n$ is the number of stages; an additional $n-1$ messages will be used for the leader to notify the termination.

Observe that all the rings $R(2), \ldots, R(k)$ do not have links in common (Exercise 3.10.70). This means that if we consider the graph G composed of all these rings, then the number of links $m(G)$ of G is exactly $m(G) = n(2) + \ldots + n(k)$. Thus, to determine the cost of the protocol, we need to find out the value of $m(G)$.

This can be determined in many ways. In particular, it follows from a very interesting property of those rings. In fact, each $R(i)$ is "contained" in the interior of $R(i+1)$: All the links of $R(i)$ are chords of $R(i+1)$, and these chords do not cross. This means that the graph G formed by all these rings is *planar*; that is, can be drawn in the plane without any edge crossing. A well known fact of planar graphs is that they are sparse, that is, they contain very few links: not more than $3(n-2)$ (if you did not know it, now you do). This means that our graph G has $m(G) \leq 3n-6$. As our protocol, which we shall call *Kelect-Stages*, uses $2(n(1) + m(G)) + n$ messages in the worst case, and $n(1) = n$, we have

$$\mathbf{M}[\textit{Kelect–Stages}] < 8n - 12.$$

A less interesting but more accurate measurement of the message costs follows from observing that the nodes in each ring $R(i)$ are precisely the entities that were candidates in stage $i-1$; thus, $n(i) = n_{i-1}$. Recalling that $n_i \leq \frac{1}{2}n_{i-1}$, and as $n_1 = n$, we have $n(1) + n(2) + \ldots + n(k) \leq n + \sum_{i=1}^{k-1} n_i < 3n$, which will give

$$\mathbf{M}[\textit{Kelect–Stages}] < 7n \qquad\qquad (3.39)$$

Notice that if we were to use *Alternate* instead of *Stages* as ring protocol (as we can), we would use fewer messages (Exercise 3.10.72).

In any case, the conclusion is that the chordal labeling allows us to finally harvest the communication power of complete graphs and do better than in ring networks.

3.7 ELECTION IN CHORDAL RINGS (⋆)

We have seen how election requires $\Omega(n \log n)$ messages in rings and can be done with just $O(n)$ messages in complete networks provided with chordal labeling. Interestingly, oriented rings and complete networks with chordal labeling are part of the same family of networks, known as *loop networks* or *chordal rings*.

3.7.1 Chordal Rings

A chordal ring $C_n \langle d_1, d_2, \ldots, d_k \rangle$ of size n and k-chord structure $\langle d_1, d_2, \ldots, d_k \rangle$, with $d_1 = 1$, is a ring R_n of n nodes $\{p_0, p_1, \ldots, p_{n-1}\}$, where each node is also directly connected to the nodes at distance d_i and $N - d_i$ by additional links called *chords*. The link connecting two nodes is labeled by the distance that separates these two nodes on the ring, that is, following the order of the nodes on the ring: Node p_i is connected to the node $p_{i+d_j} \bmod n$ through its link labeled d_j (as shown in Figure 3.48). In particular, if the link between p and q is labeled d at p, this link is labeled $n - d$ at q.

Note that the oriented ring is the chordal ring $C_n \langle 1 \rangle$ where label 1 corresponds to "right," and $n - 1$ to "left." The complete graph with chordal labeling is the chordal

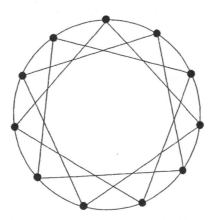

FIGURE 3.48: Chordal ring $C_{11} \langle 1, 3 \rangle$.

ring $C_n \langle 1, 2, 3, \cdots, \lfloor n/2 \rfloor \rangle$ In fact, rings and complete graphs are two extreme topologies among chordal rings.

Clearly, we can exploit the techniques we designed for complete graph with chordal labeling to develop an efficient election protocol for the entire class of chordal ring networks. The strategy is simple:

1. Execute an efficient ring election protocol (e.g., *Stages* or *Alternate*) on the outer ring. As we did in *Kelect*, the message sent in a stage will carry a counter, updated using the link labels, that will be used to compute the distance between two successive *candidates*.

2. Use the chords to bypass *defeated* nodes in the next stage.

Clearly, the more the distances can be "bypassed" by the chords, the more the messages we will be able to save. As an example, consider the chordal ring $C_n \langle 1, 2, 3, 4, ..., t \rangle$, where every entity is connected to its distance-t neighborhood in the ring. In this case (Exercise 3.10.76), a leader can be elected with a number of messages not more than

$$O \left(n + \frac{n}{t} \log \frac{n}{t} \right).$$

A special case of this class is the complete graph, where $t = \lfloor n/2 \rfloor$; in it we can bypass any distance in a single "hop" and, as we know, the cost becomes $O(n)$.

Interestingly, we can achieve the same $O(n)$ result with fewer chords. In fact, consider the chordal ring $C_n \langle 1, 2, 4, 8, ..., 2^{\lceil \log n/2 \rceil} \rangle$; it is called *double cube* and $k = \lceil \log n \rceil$. In a double cube, this strategy allows election with just $O(n)$ messages (Exercise 3.10.78), like if we were in a complete graph and had all the links.

At this point, an interesting and important question is what is the smallest set of links that must be added to the ring to achieve a linear election algorithm. The double cube indicates that $k = O(\log n)$ suffices. Surprisingly, this can be significantly further reduced (Problem 3.10.12); furthermore, in that case (Problem 3.10.13), the $O(n)$ cost can be obtained even if the links have arbitrary labels.

3.7.2 Lower Bounds

The class of chordal rings is quite large; it includes rings and complete graphs, and the cost of electing a leader varies greatly depending on the structure. For example, we have already seen that the complexity is $\Theta(n \log n)$ and $\Theta(n)$ in those two extreme chordal rings.

We can actually establish precisely the complexity of the election problem for the entire class of chordal rings $C_n^t = C_n \langle 1, 2, 3, 4..., t \rangle$. In fact, we have (Exercise 3.10.77)

$$\mathcal{M}(\mathbf{Elect}/IR; C_n^t) = \Omega \left(n + \frac{n}{t} \log \frac{n}{t} \right). \tag{3.40}$$

Notice that this class includes the two extremes. In view of the matching upper bound (Exercise 3.10.76), we have

Property 3.7.1 *The message complexity of* **Elect** *in* C_n^l *under* **IR** *is* $\Theta\left(n + \frac{n}{l}\log\frac{n}{l}\right)$.

3.8 UNIVERSAL ELECTION PROTOCOLS

We have so far studied in detail the election problem in *specific* topologies; that is, we have developed solution protocols for restricted classes of networks, exploiting in their design all the graph properties of those networks so as to minimize the costs and increase the efficiency of the protocols. In this process, we have learned some strategies and principles, which are, however, very general (e.g., the notion of *electoral stages*), as well as the use of known techniques (e.g., broadcasting) as modules of our solution.

We will now focus on the main issue, the design of *universal election protocols*, that is, protocols that run in every network, requiring neither a priori knowledge of the topology of the network nor that of its properties (not even its size). In terms of communication software, such protocols are obviously totally *portable*, and thus highly desirable.

We will describe two such protocols, radically different from each other. The first, *Mega-Merger*, which constructs a rooted spanning tree, is highly efficient (optimal in the worst case); the protocol is, however, rather complex in terms of both specifications and analysis, and its correctness is still without a simple formal proof. The second, *Yo-Yo*, is a minimum-finding protocol that is exceedingly simple to specify and to prove correct; its real cost is, however, not yet known.

3.8.1 Mega-Merger

In this section, we will discuss the design of an efficient algorithm for leader election, called *Mega-Merger*. This protocol is topology independent (i.e., universal) and constructs a (minimum cost) rooted spanning tree of the network.

Nodes are small villages each with a distinct *name*, and edges are roads each with a different *distance*. The goal is to have all villages merge into one large megacity. A city (even a small village will be considered such) always tries to merge with the closest neighboring city.

When merging, there are several important issues that must be resolved. First and foremost is the *naming* of the new city. The resolution of this issue depends on how far the involved cities have progressed in the merging process, that is, on the *level* they have reached and on whether the merger decision is shared by both cities.

The second issue to be resolved during a merging is the decision of which roads of the new city will be serviced by *public transports*. When a merger occurs, the roads of the new city serviced by public transports will be the roads of the two cities already serviced plus only the shortest road connecting them.

Let us clarify some of these concepts and notions, as well as the basic rules of the game.

1. A *city* is a rooted tree; the nodes are called *districts*, and the root is also known as *downtown*.
2. Each city has a *level* and a unique *name*; all districts eventually know the name and the level of their city.
3. Edges are *roads*, each with a distinct distance (from a totally ordered set). The city roads are only those serviced by public transport.
4. Initially, each node is a city with just one district, itself, and no roads. All cities are initially at the same level.

Note that as a consequence of rule (1), every district knows the direction (i.e., which of its links in the tree leads) to its downtown (Figure 3.49).

5. A city must merge with its closest neighboring city. To request the merging, a *Let-us-Merge* message is sent on the shortest road connecting it to that city.
6. The decision to request for a merger must originate from downtown and until the request is resolved, no other request can be issued from that city.

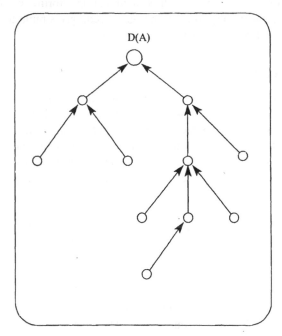

FIGURE 3.49: A city is a tree rooted in its downtown.

7. When a merger occurs, the roads of the new city serviced by public transports will be the roads of the two cities already serviced plus the shortest road connecting them.

Thus, to merge, the downtown of city A will first determine the shortest link, which we shall call the *merge link*, connecting it to a neighboring city; once this is done, a *Let-us-Merge* is sent through that link; the message will contain information identifying the city, its level, and the chosen merge link. Once the message reaches the other city, the actual merger can start to take place. Let us examine the components of this entire process in some details.

We will consider city A, denote by $D(A)$ its downtown, by level(A) its current level, and by $e(A) = (a, b)$ the *merge link* connecting A to its closest neighboring city; let B be such a city. Node b will be called the *entry point* of the request from A to B, and node a the *exit point*.

Once the *Let-us-Merge* message from a in A reaches the district b of B, three cases are possible.

If the two cities have the same level and each asks to merge with the other, we have what is called a *friendly merger*: The two cities merge into a new one; to avoid any conflict, the new city will have a new name and a new downtown, and its level is increased:

8. If level(A) = level(B) and the merge link chosen by A is the same as that chosen by B (i.e., $e(A) = e(B)$), then A and B perform a *friendly merger*.

If a city asks a merger with a city of *higher* level, it will just be *absorbed*, that is, it will acquire the name and the level of the other city:

9. If level(A) < level(B), A is *absorbed* in B.

In all other cases, the request for merging and, thus, the decision on the name are *postponed* :

10. If level(A) = level(B), but the merge link chosen by A is not the same as that chosen by B (i.e., $e(A) \neq e(B)$), then the merge process of A with B is *suspended* until the level of b's city becomes larger than that of A.

11. If level(A) > level(B), the merge process of A with B is *suspended*: x will locally enqueue the message until the level of b's city is at least as large as the one of A. (As we will see later, this case will never occur.)

Let us see these rules in more details.

Absorption   The absorption process is the conclusion of a merger request sent by A to a city with a higher level (rule 9). As a result, city A becomes part of city

B acquiring the name, the downtown, and the level of B. This means that during absorption,

(i) the logical orientation of the roads in A must be modified so that they are directed toward the new downtown (so rule (1) is satisfied);

(ii) all districts of A must be notified of the name and level of the city they just joined (so rule (2) is satisfied).

All these requirements can be easily and efficiently achieved. First of all, the entry point b will notify a (the exit point of A) that the outcome of the request is absorption, and it will include in the message all the relevant information about B (name and level). Once a receives this information, it will broadcast it in A; as a result, all districts of A will join the new city and know its name and its level.

To transform A so that it is rooted in the new downtown is fortunately simple. In fact, it is sufficient to logically direct toward B the link connecting a to b and to "flip" the logical direction only of the edges in the path from the exit point a to the old downtown of A (Exercise 3.10.79), as shown in Figure 3.50. This can be done as follows: Each of the districts of B on the path from a to D(A), when it receives the broadcast from a, will locally direct toward B two links: the one from which the broadcast message is received and the one toward its old downtown.

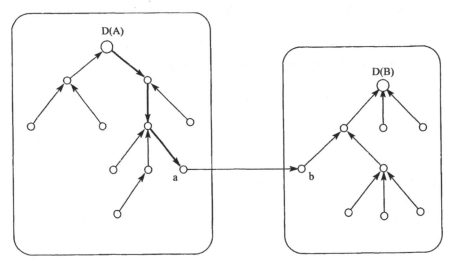

FIGURE 3.50: Absorption. To make the districts of A be rooted in $D(B)$, the logical direction of the links (in bold) from the downtown to the exit point of A has been "flipped."

Friendly Merger   If A and B are at the same level in the merging process (i.e., level(A) = level(B)) and want to merge with each other (i.e., $e(A) = e(B)$), we have a friendly merger. Notice that if this is the case, a must also receive a *Let-us-Merge* message from b.

The two cities now become one with a new downtown, a new name, and an increased level:

(i) The new downtown will be the one of a and b that has smaller id (recall that we are working under the **ID** restriction).

(ii) The name of the new city will be the name of the new downtown.

(iii) The level will be increased by one unit.

Both a and b will independently compute the new name, level, and downtown. Then each will broadcast this information to its old city; as a result, all districts of A and B will join the new city and know its name and its level.

Both A and B must be transformed so that they are rooted in the new downtown. As discussed in the case of absorption, it is sufficient to "flip" the logical direction only of the edges in the path from the a to the old downtown of A, and of those in the path from b to the old downtown of B (Figure 3.51).

Suspension In two cases (rules (10) and (11)), the merge request of A must be suspended: b will then locally enqueue the message until the level of its city is such that it can apply rule (8) or (9). Notice that in case of suspension, nobody from city A knows that their request has been suspended; because of rule (6), no other request can be launched from A.

Choosing the Merging Edge According to rule (6), the choice of the merging edge $e(A)$ in A is made by the downtown $D(A)$; according to rule (5), $e(A)$ must be the shortest road connecting A to a neighboring city. Thus, $D(A)$ needs to find the minimum length among all the edges incident on the nodes of the rooted tree A; this will be done by implementing rule (5) as follows:

(5.1) Each district a_i of A determines the length d_i of the shortest road connecting it to another city (if none goes to another city, then $d_i = \infty$).

(5.2) $D(A)$ computes the smallest of all the d_i.

Concentrate on part (5.1) and consider a district a_i; it must find among its incident edges the shortest one that leads to another city.

IMPORTANT. Obviously, a_i does not need to consider the *internal roads* (i.e., those that connect it to other districts of A). Unfortunately, if a link is *unused*, that is, no message has been sent or received through it, it is impossible for a_i to know if this road is internal or leads to a neighboring city (Figure 3.52). In other words, a_i must also try the internal unused roads.

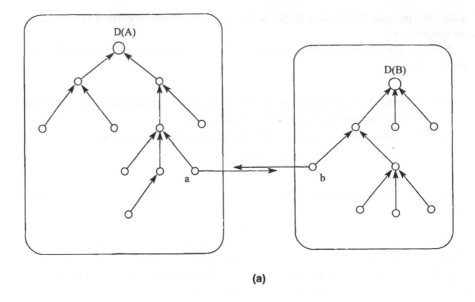

(a)

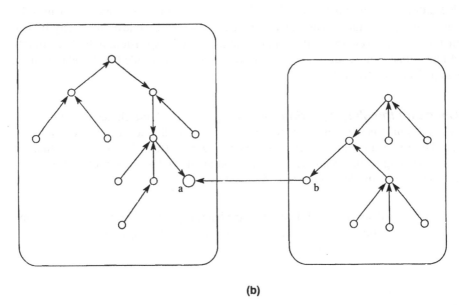

(b)

FIGURE 3.51: Friendly merger. (a) The two cities have the same level and choose the same merge link. (b) The new downtown is the exit node (*a* or *b*) with smallest id.

Thus, a_i will determine the shortest unused edge e, prepare a *Outside?* message, send it on e, and wait for a reply. Consider now the district c on the other side of e, which receives this message; c knows the name(C) and the level(C) of its city (which could, however, be changing).

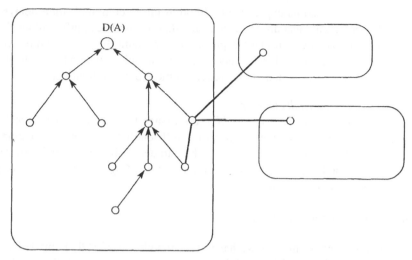

FIGURE 3.52: Some unused links might lead back to the city.

If name(A) = name(C) (recall that the message contains the name of A), c will reply *Internal* to a_i, the road e will be marked as internal (and no longer used in the protocol) by both districts, and a_i will restart its process to find the shortest local unused edge.

If name(A) ≠ name(C), it does not necessarily mean that the road is not internal. In fact, it is possible that while c is processing this message, its city C is being absorbed by A. Observe that in this case, level(C) must be *smaller* than level(A) (because by rule (8) only a city with smaller level will be absorbed). This means that if name(A) ≠ name(C) but level(C) ≥ level(A), then C is not being absorbed by A, and C is for sure a different city; thus, c will reply *External* to a_i, which will have, thus, determined what it was looking for: d_i = length(e).

The only case left is when name(A) ≠ name(C) and level(C) < level(A), the case in which c cannot give a sure answer. So, it will not: c will postpone the reply until the level of its city becomes greater than or equal to that of A. Note that this means that the computation in A is suspended until c is ready.

NOTE. As a consequence of this last case, rule (11) will never be applied (Exercise 3.10.80).

In conclusion to determine if a link is internal should be simple, but, due to concurrency, the process is neither trivial nor obvious.

Concentrate on part (5.2). This is easy to accomplish; it is just a minimum finding in a rooted tree, for which we can use the techniques discussed in Section 2.6.7. Specifically, the entire process is composed of a *broadcast* of a message informing all districts in the city of the current name and level (i) of the city, followed by a *covergecast*.

Issues and Details We have just seen in details the process of determining the merge link as well as the rules governing a merger. Because of the asynchronous nature of the system and its unpredictable (though finite) communication delays, it will probably be the case that different cities and districts will be at different levels at the same time. In fact, our rules take explicitly into account the interaction between neighboring cities at different levels. There are a few situations where the application of the rules will not be evident and thus require a more detailed treatment.

(I) *Discovering a friendly merger*

We have seen that when the *Let-us-Merge* message from A to B arrives at b, if level$(A) =$ level(B), the outcome will be different (friendly merger or postponement) depending on whether $e(A) = e(B)$ or not. Thus, to decide if it is a friendly merger, b needs to know both $e(A)$ and $e(B)$. When the *Let-us-Merge* message sent from a arrives to b, it knows $e(A) = (a, b)$.

Question. How does b know $e(B)$?

The answer is interesting. As we have seen, the choice of $e(B)$ is made by the downtown $D(B)$, which will forward the merger request message of B towards the exit point.

If $e(A) = e(B)$, b is the exit point and, thus, it will *eventually* receive the message to be sent to a; then (and only then) b will know the answer to the question, and that it is dealing with a friendly merger.

If $e(A) \neq e(B)$, b is not the exit point. Note that, unless b is on the way from downtown $D(B)$ to the exit point, b will *not* even know what $e(B)$ is.

Thus, what really happens when the *Let-us-Merge* message from A arrives at b, is the following. If b has received already a *Let-us-Merge* message from its downtown to be sent to a, then b knows that is a friendly merger; also a will know when it receives the request from b.

(Note for hackers: thus, in this case, no reply to the request is really necessary.)

Otherwise b does not know; thus it waits: if it is a friendly merger, sooner or later the message from its downtown will arrive and b will know; if B is requesting another city, eventually the level of b's city will increase becoming greater than level(A) (which, as A is still waiting for the reply, cannot increase), and thus result in A being absorbed.

(II) *Overlapping discovery of an internal link*

In the merge-link calculation, when the *Outside?* message from a in A is sent to neighbor b in B, if name$(A) =$ name(B) then the link (a, b) is internal and should be removed from consideration by both a and b. As b knows (it just found out receiving the message) but a possibly does not, b will send to a the reply *Internal*. However, if b also had sent to a an *Outside?* message, when a receives that message, it will find out that (a, b) is internal, and the *Internal* reply would be redundant. In other words, if a and b from the same city independently send to each other an *Outside?* message, there is no need for either of them to reply *Internal* to the other.

(III) *Interaction between absorption and link calculation*

A situation that requires attention is due to the interaction between merge-link calculation and absorption. Consider the *Let-us-Merge* message sent by a on merge link $e(A) = (a, b)$ to b, and let level$(A) = j < i =$ level(B); thus, A will have to be absorbed in B.

Suppose that, when b receives the message, it is computing the merge link for its city B; as its level is i, we will call it the i-level merge link. What b will do in this case, is to first proceed with the absorption of A (so to involve it in the i-level merge-link computation), and then to continue its own computation of the merge link. More precisely, b will start the broadcast in A of the name and level of B asking the districts there to participate in the computation of the i-level merge link for B, and then resume its computation.

Suppose instead that b has already finished computing the i-level merge link for its city B; in this case, b will broadcast in A the name and level of B (so to absorb A), but without requesting them to participate in the computation of the i-level merge link for B (it is too late).

(IV) *Overlap between notification and i-level merge-link calculation*

As mentioned, the i-level merge-link calculation is started by a broadcast informing all districts in the city of the current name and level (i) of the city. Let us call "start-next" the function provided by these messages.

Notice that broadcasts are already used following the discovery of a friendly merger or an absorption. Consider the case of a friendly merger. When the two exit points know that it is a friendly merger, the notification they broadcast will inform all districts in the merged city of the new level, new name, and to start computing the next merge link. In other words, the notification is exactly the "start next" broadcast.

In the case of an absorption, as we just discussed, a "start-next" broadcast is needed only if it is not too late for the new districts to participate in the current calculation of the merge link. If it is not too late, the notification message contains the request to participate in the next merge-link calculation; thus, it is just the propagation of the current "start-next" broadcast in this new part of the city.

In other words, the "notification" broadcasts act as "start-next" broadcasts, if needed.

3.8.2 Analysis of Mega-Merger

A city only carries out one merger request at a time, but it can be asked concurrently by several cities, which in turn can be asked by several others. Some of these requests will be postponed (because the level is not right, or the entry node does not (yet) know what the answer is, etc.) Due to communication delays, some districts will be taking decisions on the basis of the information (level and name of its city) that is obsolete. It is not difficult to imagine very intricate and complex scenarios that can easily occur.

How do we know that, in spite of concurrency and postponements and communication delays, everything will eventually work out? How can we be assured that some decisions will not be postponed forever, that is, there will not be *deadlock*? What guarantees that, in the end, the protocol terminates and a single leader will be elected? In other words, how do we know that the protocol is correct?

Because of its complexity and the variety of scenarios that can be created, there is no satisfactory complete proof of the correctness of the *Mega-Merger* protocol. We will discuss here a partial proof that will be sufficient for our learning purposes. We will then analyze the cost of the Protocol. Finally, we will discuss the assumption of having distinct lengths associated to the links, examine some interesting connected properties, and then remove the assumption.

Progress and Deadlock   We will first discuss the progress of the computation and the absence of deadlock. To do so, let us pinpoint the cases when the activity of a city C is halted by a district d of another city D. This can occur only when computing the merge edge, or when requesting a merger on the merge edge $e(C)$; more precisely, there are three cases:

(i) When computing the merge edge, a district c of C sends the *Outside?* message to d and D has a smaller level than C.

(ii) A district c of C sends the *Let-us-Merge* message on the merge edge $e(C) = (c, d)$; D and C have the same level but it is not a friendly merger.

(iii) A district c of C sends the *Let-us-Merge* message on the merge edge $e(C) = (c, d)$; D and C have the same level and it is a friendly merger, but d does not know yet.

In cases (i) and (ii), the activities of C are suspended and will be resolved (if the protocol is correct) only in the "future," that is, after D changes level. Case (iii) is different in that it will be resolved within the "present" (i.e., in this level); we will call this case a *delay* rather than a *suspension*.

Observe that if there is no suspension, there is no problem.

Property 3.8.1   *If a city at level l will not be suspended, its level will eventually increase (unless it is the megacity).*

To see why this is true, consider the operations performed by a city C at a level l: Compute the merge edge and send a merge request on the merge edge. If it is not suspended, its merge request arrives at a city D with either a larger level (in which case, C is absorbed and its level becomes level(D)) or the same level and same merge edge (the case in which the two cities have a friendly merger and their level increases).

So, only suspensions can create problems, but not necessarily so.

Property 3.8.2   *Let city C at level l be suspended by a district d in city D. If the level of the city of D becomes greater than l, C will no longer be suspended and its level will increase.*

This is because once the level of D becomes greater than the level of C, d can answer the *Outside?* message in case (i), as well as the *Let-us-Merge* message in case (ii).

Thus, the only real problem is the presence of a city suspended by another whose level will not grow. We are now going to see that this cannot occur.

Consider the *smallest* level l of any city at time t, and concentrate on the cities C operating at that level at that time.

Property 3.8.3   *No city in C will be suspended by a city at higher level.*

This is because for a suspension to exist, the level of D can *not* be greater than the level of C (see the cases above).

Thus, if a city $C \in C$ is suspended, it is for some other city $C' \in C$. If C' is not suspended at level l, its level will increase; when that happens, C will no longer be suspended. In other words, there would be no problems as long as there are no cycles of suspensions within C, that is, as long as there is no cycle $C_0, C_1, \ldots, C_{k-1}$ of cities of C where C_i is suspended by C_{i+1} (and the operation on the indices are modulo k). The crucial property is the following:

Property 3.8.4   *There will be no cycles of suspensions within C.*

The proof of this property is based heavily on the fact that each edge has a unique length (we have assumed that.) and that the merge edge $e(C)$ chosen by C is the shortest of all the unused links incident on C. Remember this fact and let us proceed with the proof.

By contradiction, assume that the property is false. That is, assume there is a cycle $C_0, C_1, \ldots, C_{k-1}$ of cities of C where C_i is suspended by C_{i+1} (the operation on the indices are modulo k). First of all observe that as all these cities are at the same level, the reason they are suspended can only be that each is involved in an "unfriendly" merger, that is, case (ii). Let us examine the situation more closely: Each C_i has chosen a merge edge $e(C_i)$ connecting it to C_{i+1}; thus, C_i is suspending C_{i-1} and is suspended by C_{i+1}. Clearly, both $e(C_{i-1})$ and $e(C_i)$ are incident on C_i. By definition of merging edge (recall what we said at the beginning of the proof), $e(C_i)$ is shorter than $e(C_{i-1})$ (otherwise C_i would have chosen it instead); in other words, the length d_i of the road $e(C_i)$ is smaller than the length d_{i11} of $e(C_{i+1})$. This means that $d_0 > d_1 > \ldots > d_{k-1}$, but as it is a circle of suspensions, C_{k-1} is suspended by C_0, that is, $d_{k-1} > d_0$. We have reached a contradiction, which implies that our assumption that the property does not hold is actually false; thus, the property is true.

As a consequence of the property, all cities in C will eventually increase their level: first, the ones involved in a friendly merger, next those that had chosen them for a merger (and thus absorbed by them), then those suspended by the latter, and so on.

This implies that *at no time there will be deadlock* and *there is always progress*: Use the properties to show that the ones with smallest level will increase their value; when this happens, again the ones with smallest level will increase it, and so on. That is,

Property 3.8.5   *Protocol* Mega-Merger *is deadlock free and ensures progress.*

Termination   We have just seen that there will be no deadlock and that progress is guaranteed. This means that the cities will keep on merging and eventually the megacity will be formed. The problem is how to detect that this has happened. Recall that no node has knowledge of the network, not even of its size (it is not part of the standard set of assumptions for election); how does an entity finds out that all the nodes are now part of the same city? Clearly, it is sufficient for just one entity to determine termination (as it can then broadcast it to all the others).

Fortunately, *termination detection* is simple to achieve; as one might have suspected, it is the downtown of the megacity that will determine that the process is terminated.

Consider the downtown $D(A)$ of city A, and the operations it performs: It coordinates the computation of the merge link and then originates a merge request to be sent on that link. Now, the merge link is the shortest road going to *another* city. If A is already the megacity, there are no other cities; hence all the unused links are internal. This means that when computing the merge link, every district will explore every unused link left and discover that each one of them is internal; it will thus choose ∞ as its length (meaning that it does not have any outgoing links). This means that the minimum-finding process will return ∞ as the smallest length. When this happens, $D(A)$ understands that the mega-merger is completed, and can notify all others. (Notification is not really necessary: Exercise 3.10.81.)

As the megacity is a rooted tree with the downtown as its root, $D(A)$ becomes the *leader*; in other words,

Property 3.8.6 *Protocol* Mega-Merger *correctly elects a leader.*

Cost In spite of the complexity of protocol *Mega-Merger*, the analysis of its cost is not overly difficult. We will first determine how many levels there can be and then calculate the total number of messages transmitted by entities at a given level.

The Number of Levels A district acquires a larger level because its city has been either absorbed or involved in a friendly merger. Notice that when there is absorption, only the districts in one of the two cities increase their level, and thus the max level in the system will not be increased. The max level can only increase after a friendly merger.

How high can the max level be ? We can find out by linking the minimum number of districts in a city to the level of the city.

Property 3.8.7 *A city of level i has at least 2^i districts.*

This can be proved easily by induction. It is trivially true at the beginning (i.e., $i = 0$). Let it be true for $0 \leq i \leq k - 1$. A level k city can only be created by a friendly merger of two level $k - 1$ cities; hence, by inductive hypothesis, such a city will have at least $2 \, 2^{k-1} = 2^k$ districts; thus the property is true also for $i = k$.

As a consequence,

Property 3.8.8 *No city will reach a level greater than $\log n$.*

The Number of Messages per Level   Consider a level i; some districts will reach this level from level $i - 1$ or even lower; others might never reach it (e.g., because of absorption, they move from a level lower than i directly to one larger than i). Consider only those districts that do reach level i and let us count how many messages they transmit in this level. In other words, as each message contains the level, we need to determine how many messages are sent in which the level is i.

We do know that every district (except the downtown) of a city of level i receives a broadcast message informing it that its current level is i, and to start computing the i-level merge-link (this last part may not be included). Hence at most every district will receive such a message, accounting for a total of n messages.

If the received broadcast also requests to compute the i-level edge-merge link, a district must find its shortest outgoing link, by using *Outside?* messages.

IMPORTANT. For the moment, we will not consider the *Outside?* messages sent to internal roads (i.e., where the reply is *Internal*); they will be counted separately later.

In this case, the district will send at most one *Outside?* message that causes a reply *External*. The district will then participate in the convergecast, sending one message toward the downtown. Hence, all these activities will account for a total of at most $3n$ messages.

Once the i-level merge-links have been determined, the *Let-us-Merge* messages are originated and sent to and across the merge-links. Regardless of the final outcome of the request, the forwarding of the i-level *Let-us-Merge* message from the downtown $D(A)$ to the new city through the merge edge $e(A) = (a, b)$ will cause at most $n(A)$ transmissions in a city A with $n(A)$ districts ($n(A) - 1$ internal and one on the merge edge). This means that these activities will cost in total at most

$$\sum_{A \in \text{City}(i)} n(A) \le n$$

messages where City(i) is the set of the cities reaching level i.

This means that excluding the number of level i messages *Outside?* whose reply is *Internal*, the total number of messages sent in level i is

Property 3.8.9 $Cost(i) \le 5n$

The Number of Useless Messages   In the calculation so far we have excluded the *Outside?* messages whose reply was *Internal*. These messages are in a sense "useless" as they do not bring about a merger; but they are also unavoidable. Let us measure their number. On any such road there will be two messages, either the *Outside?* message and the *Internal* reply, or two *Outside?* messages. So, we only need to determine the number of such roads. These roads are not part of the city (i.e., not serviced by public transport). As the final city is a tree, the total number of the publicly serviced roads is exactly $n - 1$. Thus, the total number of the other roads is exactly $m - (n - 1)$. This means that the total number of useless messages will be

Property 3.8.10 $Useless = 2(m - n + 1)$

The Total Combining Properties 3.8.8, 3.8.9, and 3.8.10, we obtain the total number of messages exchanged in total by protocol *Mega-Merger* during all its levels of execution.

To these, we need to add the $n - 1$ messages because of the downtown of the megacity broadcasting termination (eventhough these could be saved: Exercise 3.10.81), for a total of

$$\mathrm{M}[Mega-Merger] \leq 2m + 5n \log n + n + 1. \tag{3.41}$$

Road Lengths and Minimum-Cost Spanning Trees

In all the previous discussions we have made some nonstandard assumptions about the edges. We have in fact assumed that each link has a value, which we called length, and that those values are unique.

The existence of link values is not uncommon. In fact, dealing with networks, usually there is a value associated with a link denoting, for example, the cost of using that link, the transmission delays incurred when sending a message through it, and so forth.

In these situations, when constructing a spanning tree (e.g., to use for broadcasting), the prime concern is how to construct the one of *minimum cost*, that is, where the sum of the values of its link is as small as possible. For example, if the value of the link is the cost of using it, a minimum-cost spanning tree is one where broadcasting would be the cheapest (regardless of who is the originator of the broadcast). Not surprisingly, the problem of constructing a minimum-cost spanning tree is important and heavily investigated.

We have seen that protocol *Mega-Merger* constructs a rooted spanning tree of the network. What we are going to see now is that this tree is actually the unique minimum-cost spanning tree of the network. We are also going to see how the nonstandard assumptions that we have made about the existence of unique lengths can be easily removed.

Minimum-Cost Spanning Trees

In general, a network can have several minimum-cost spanning trees. For example, if all links have the same value (or have no value), then every spanning tree is minimal. By contrast,

Property 3.8.11 *If the link values are distinct, a network has a unique minimum-cost spanning tree.*

Assuming that there are distinct values associated to the links, protocol *Mega-Merger* constructs a rooted spanning tree of the network. What we are going to see now is that this tree is actually the unique minimum-cost spanning tree of the network.

To see why this is the case, we must observe a basic property of the minimum-cost spanning tree T. A *fragment* of T is a subtree of T.

Property 3.8.12 *Let A be a fragment of T, and let e be the link of minimum value among those connecting A to other fragments; let B be the fragment connected by A. Then the tree composed by merging A and B through e is also a fragment of T.*

This is exactly what the *Mega-Merger* protocol does: It constructs the minimum-cost spanning tree T (the megacity) by merging fragments (cities) through the appropriate edges (merge link). Initially, each node is a city and, by definition, a single node is a fragment. In general, each city A is a fragment of T; its merge link is chosen as the shortest (i.e., minimum value) link connecting A to any neighboring city (i.e., fragment); hence, by Property 3.8.12, the result of the merger is also a fragment.

Notice that the correctness of the process depends crucially on Property 3.8.11, and thus on the distinctness of the link values.

Creating Unique Lengths We will now remove the assumptions that there are values associated to the links and these values are unique.

If there are no values (the more general setting), then a unique value can be easily given to each link using the fact that the nodes have unique ids: To link $e = (a, b)$ associate the sorted pair $d(e) = \langle \text{Min}\{\text{id}(a), \text{id}(b)\}, \text{Max}\{\text{id}(a), \text{id}(b)\}\rangle$ and use the lexicographic ordering to determine which edge has smaller length. So, for example, the link between nodes with ids 17 and 5 will have length $\langle 5, 17 \rangle$, which is smaller than $\langle 6, 5 \rangle$ but greater than $\langle 4, 32 \rangle$. To do this requires, however, that each node knows the id of all its neighbors. This information can be acquired in a preprocessing phase, in which every node sends to its neighbors, its id (and will receive theirs from them); the cost will be two additional messages on each link. Thus, even if there are no values associated to the links, it is possible to use protocol *Mega-Merger*. The price we have to pay is $2m$ additional messages.

If there are values but they are not (known to be) unique, they can be made so, again using the fact that the nodes have unique ids. To link $e = (a, b)$ with value $v(e)$ associate the sorted triple $d(e) = \langle v(e), \text{Min}\{\text{id}(a), \text{id}(b)\}, \text{Max}\{\text{id}(a), \text{id}(b)\}\rangle$. Thus, links with the same values will now be associated to different lengths. So, for example, the link between nodes with ids 17 and 5 and value 7 will have length $\langle 7, 5, 17 \rangle$, which is smaller than $\langle 7, 6, 5 \rangle$ but greater than $\langle 7, 4, 32 \rangle$. Also, in this case, each node needs to know the id of all its neighbors. The same preprocessing phase will achieve the goal with only $2m$ additional messages.

Summary Protocol *Mega-Merger* is a universal protocol that constructs a (minimum-cost) spanning tree and returns it rooted in a node, thus electing a leader. If there are no initial distinct values on the links, a preprocessing phase needs to be added, in which each entity exchanges its unique id with its neighbors; then the actual execution of the protocol can start. The total cost of the protocol (with or without preprocessing phase) is $O(m + n \log n)$, which, we will see, is worst case optimal.

The main drawback of *Mega-Merger* is its design complexity, which makes any actual implementation difficult to verify.

3.8.3 YO-YO

We will now examine another universal protocol for leader election. Unlike the previous one, it has simple specifications, and its correctness is simple to establish. This protocol, called *YO-YO*, is a minimum-finding algorithm and consists of two parts: a preprocessing phase and a sequence of iterations. Let us examine them in detail.

Setup In the preprocessing phase, called *Setup*, every entity x exchanges its id with its neighbors. As a result, it will receive the id of all its neighbors. Then, x will logically orient each incident link (x, y) in the direction of the entity (x or y), with the largest id. So, if $id(x) = 5$ and its neighbor y has $id(y) = 7$, x will orient (x, y) toward y; notice that y will also do the same. In fact, the orientation of each link will be consistent at both end nodes.

Consider now the directed graph $\vec{G}$ so obtained. There is a very simple but important property:

Property 3.8.13 $\vec{G}$ *is acyclic.*

To see why this is true, consider by contradiction the existence of a directed cycle $x_0, x_1, \ldots, x_k$; this means that $id(x_0) < id(x_1) < \ldots < id(x_{k-1})$ but, as it is a cycle, $id(x_{k-1}) < id(x_0)$, which is impossible.

This means that $\vec{G}$ is a *directed acyclic graph* (*DAG*). In a DAG, there are three types of nodes:

- *source* is a node where all the links are out-edges; thus, a source in $\vec{G}$ is a node with an id smaller than that of all its neighbors, that is, it is a *local minimum*;
- *sink* is a node where all the links are in-edges; thus, a sink in $\vec{G}$ is a node whose id is larger than that of all its neighbors, that is, it is a *local maximum*;
- *internal node* is a node, which is neither a source nor a sink.

As a result of the setup, each node will know whether it is a source, a sink, or an internal node. We will also use the terminology of "down" referring to the direction toward the sinks, and "up" referring to the direction toward the sources (see Figure 3.53).

Once this preprocessing is completed, the second part of the algorithm start. As *YO-YOs* is a minimum-finding protocol, only the local minima (i.e., the sources) will be the *candidates* (Figure 3.54).

Iteration The core of the protocol is a sequence of iterations. Each iteration acts as an electoral stage in which some of the candidates are removed from consideration. Each iteration is composed of two parts, or *phases*, called *YO-* and *-YO*.

YO- This phase is started by the sources. Its purpose is to propagate to each sink the smallest among the values of the sources connected[3] to that sink (see Figure 3.54(a)).

1. A source sends its value down to all its out-neighbors.
2. An internal node waits until it receives a value from all its in-neighbors. It then computes the minimum of all received values and sends it down to its out-neighbors.
3. A sink waits until it receives a value from all its in-neighbors. It then computes the minimum of all received values and starts the second part of the iteration.

---

[3] In the sense that there is a directed path from the source to that sink.

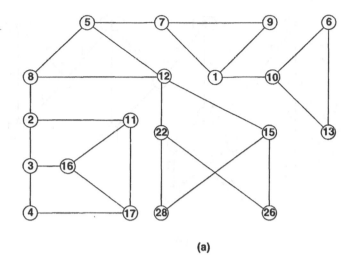

(a)

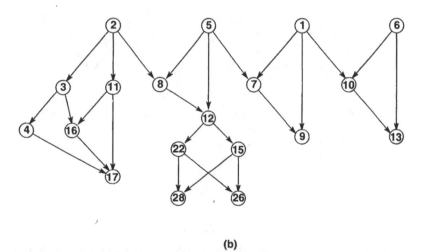

(b)

FIGURE 3.53: In the Setup phase, (a) the entities know their neighbors' ids and (b) orient each incident link toward the smaller id, creating a DAG.

-YO   This phase is started by the sinks. Its purpose is to eliminate some candidates, transforming some sources into sinks or internal nodes. This is done by having the sinks inform their connected sources of whether or not the id they sent is the smallest seen so far (see Figure 3.54(b)).

4. A sink sends *YES* to all in-neighbors from which the smallest value has been received. It sends *NO* to all the others.
5. An internal node waits until it receives a vote from all its out-neighbors. If all votes are *YES*, it sends *YES* to all in-neighbors from which the smallest value

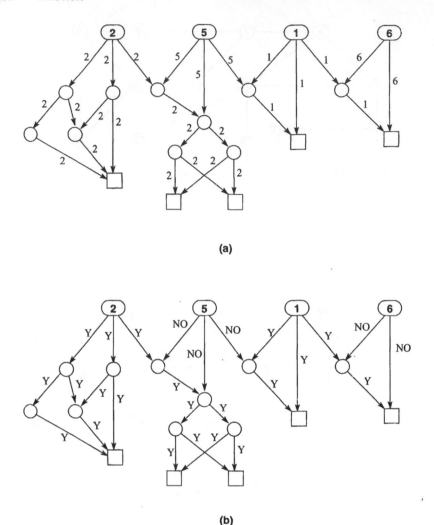

(a)

(b)

FIGURE 3.54: In the Iteration stage, only the *candidates* are sources. (a) In the YO- phase, the ids are filtered down to the sinks. (b) In the -YO phase, the votes percolate up to the sources.

has been received and *NO* to all the others. If at least a vote was *NO*, it sends *NO* to all its in-neighbors.

6. A source waits until it receives a vote from all its out-neighbors. If all votes are *YES*, it survives this iteration and starts the next one. If at least a vote was *NO*, it is no longer a candidate.

Before the next iteration can be started, the directions on the links in the DAG must be modified so that only the sources that are still candidate (i.e., those that received only *YES*) will still be sources; clearly, the modification must be done

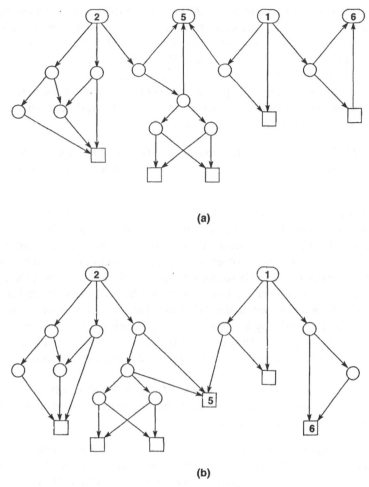

(a)

(b)

FIGURE 3.55: (a) In the -YO phase, we flip the logical direction of the links on which a NO is sent, (b) creating a new DAG, where only the surviving *candidates* will be sources.

without creating cycles. In other words, we must transform the DAG into a new one, whose only sources are the undefeated ones in this iteration. This modification is fortunately simple to achieve. We need only to "flip" the direction of each link where a *NO* vote is sent (see Figure 3.55(a)). Thus, we have two meta-rules for the -*YO* part:

7. When a node x sends *NO* to an in-neighbor y, it will reverse the (logical) direction of that link (thus, y becomes now an out-neighbor of x).

8. When a node y receives *NO* from an out-neighbor x, it will reverse the (logical) direction of that link (thus, x becomes now an in-neighbor of y).

As a result, any source that receives a *NO* will cease to be a source; it can actually become a sink. Some sinks may cease to be such and become internal nodes, and some internal nodes might become sinks. However, no sink or internal node will ever become a source (Exercise 3.10.83). A new DAG is, thus, created, where the sources are only those that received all *YES* in this iteration (see Figure 3.55(b)).

Once a node has completed its part in the -*YO* phase, it will know whether it is a source, a sink, or an internal node in the new DAG. The next iteration could start now, initiated by the sources of the new DAG.

Property 3.8.14 *Applying an iteration to a DAG with more than one source will result into a DAG with fewer sources. The source with smallest value will still be a source.*

In each iteration, some sources (at least one) will be no longer sources; in contrast to this, the source with the smallest value will be eventually the only one left under consideration. In other words, eventually the DAG will have a single source (the overall minimum, say c), and all other nodes are either sinks or internal nodes. How can c determine that it is the only source left, and thus it should become the leader?

If we were to perform an iteration now, only c's value will be sent in the *YO*- phase, and only *YES* votes will be sent in the -*YO* phase. The source c will receive only *YES* votes; but c has received only *YES* votes in every iteration it has performed (that is why it survived as a source). How can c distinguish that this time is different, that the process should end? Clearly, we need some additional mechanisms during the iterations.

We are going to add some meta-rules, called *Pruning*, which will allow to reduce the number of messages sent during the iterations, as well as to ensure that termination is detected when only one source is left.

Pruning The purpose of pruning is to remove from the computation, nodes and links that are "useless," do not have any impact on the result of the iteration; in other words, if they were not there, still the same result would be obtained: The same sources would stay sources, and the others defeated. Once a link or a node is declared "useless," during the next iterations it will be considered *nonexistent* and, thus, not used.

Pruning is achieved through two meta-rules.

The first meta-rule is a structural one. To explain it, recall that the function of the sinks is to reduce the number of sources by voting on the received values. Consider now a sink that is a leaf (i.e., it has only one in-neighbor); such a node will receive only one value; thus it can only vote *YES*. In other words, a sink leaf can only agree with the choice (i.e., the decision) made by its parent (i.e., its only neighbor). Thus, a sink leaf is "useless."

9. If a sink is a leaf (i.e., it has only one in-neighbor), then it is useless; it then asks its parent to be pruned. If a node is asked to prune an out-neighbor, it will do so by declaring useless (i.e., removing from consideration in the next iterations) the connecting link.

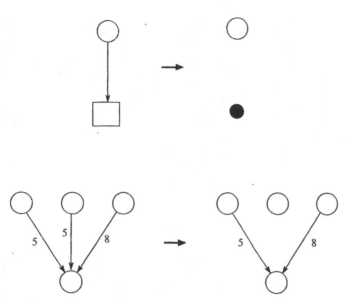

FIGURE 3.56: Rules of pruning.

Notice that after pruning a link, a node might become a sink; if it is also a leaf, then it becomes useless.

The other meta-rule is geared toward reducing the communication of redundant information. During YO- phase, a (internal or sink) node might receive the value of the same source from more than one in-neighbor; this information is clearly redundant as, to do its job (choose the minimum received value), it is enough for the node to receive just one copy of that value. Let x receive the value of source s from in-neighbors $x_1, \ldots, x_k, k > 1$. This means that in the DAG, there are directed paths from s to (at least) k distinct in-neighbors of x. This also means that if the link between x and one of them, say x_1, did not exist, the value from s would still arrive to x from those other neighbors, $x_2, \ldots, x_k$. In fact, if we had removed the links between x and all those in-neighbors *except one*, x would still have received the value of s from that neighbor. In other words, the links between x and $x_1, \ldots, x_k$ are redundant: It is sufficient to keep one; all others are useless and can be pruned. Notice that the choice regarding the link that should be kept is irrelevant.

10. If in the YO- phase, a node receives the same value from more than one in-neighbor, it will ask all of them *except one* to prune the link connecting them and it will declare those links useless. If a node receives such a request, it will declare useless (i.e., remove from consideration in the next iterations) the connecting link.

Notice that after pruning a link because of rule (10), a sink might become a leaf and thus useless (by rule (9)) (see Figure 3.57).

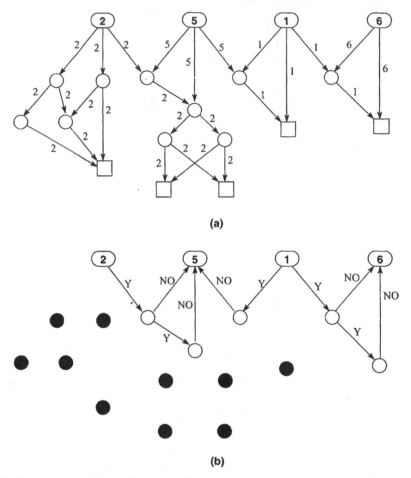

(a)

(b)

FIGURE 3.57: The effects of pruning in the first iteration: Some nodes (in black) and links are removed from consideration.

The pruning rules require communication: In rule (7), a sink leaf needs to ask its only neighbor to declare the link between them useless; in rule (8), a node receiving redundant information needs to ask some of its neighbors to prune the connecting link. We will have this communication take place during the *-YO* phase: The message containing the vote will also include the request, if any, to declare that link useless. In other words,

pruning is performed when voting.

Let us return now on our concern on how to detect termination. As we will see, the pruning operations, integrated in the *-YO* phase, will do the trick. To understand how and why, consider the effect of performing a full iteration (with pruning) on a DAG with only one source.

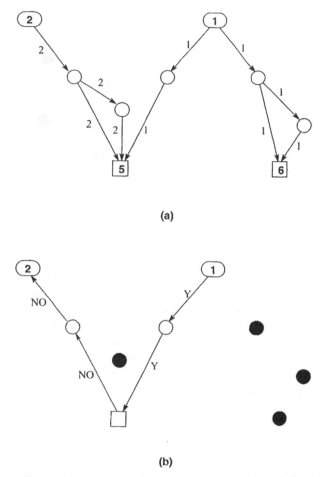

(a)

(b)

FIGURE 3.58: The effects of pruning in the second iteration: Other nodes (in black) and links are removed from consideration.

Property 3.8.15 *If the DAG has a single source, then, after an iteration, the new DAG is composed of only one node, the source.*

In other words, when there is a single source c, all other nodes will be removed, and c will be the only useful node left. This situation will be discovered by c when, because of pruning, it will have no neighbors (Figure 3.59).

Costs The general formula expressing the costs of protocol *YO-YO* is easy to establish; however, the exact determination of the costs expressed by the formula is still an open research problem. Let us derive the general formula.

In the Setup phase, each node sends its value to all its neighbors; hence, on each link there will be two messages sent, for a total of $2m$ messages.

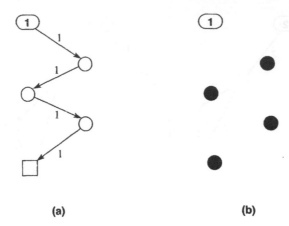

(a)   (b)

FIGURE 3.59: The effects of pruning in the third iteration: Termination is detected as the source has no more neighbors in the DAG.

Consider now an iteration. In the YO- stage, every useful node (except the sinks) sends a message to its out-neighbors; hence, on each link still under consideration, there will be exactly one message sent. Similarly, in the -YO stage, every useful node (except the sources) sends a message to its in-neighbors; hence, on each link there will be again only one message sent. Thus, in total in iteration i there will be exactly $2m_i$ messages, where m_i is the number of links in the DAG used at stage i.

The notification of termination from the leader can be performed by broadcasting on the constructed spanning tree with only $n-1$ messages.

Hence, the total cost will be

$$2 \sum_{i=0}^{k(G)} m_i + n - 1,$$

where $m_0 = m$ and $k(G)$ is the total number of iterations on network G.

We need now to establish the number of iterations $k(G)$. Let $D(1) = \vec{G}$ be the original DAG obtained from G as a result of setup. Let $G(1)$ be the undirected graph defined as follows: There is a node for each source in $D(1)$ and there is a link between two nodes if and only if the two corresponding sources have a sink in common[4]. Consider now the diameter $d(G(1))$ of this graph.

Property 3.8.16 *The number of iteration is at most* $\lceil \log \operatorname{diam}(G(1)) \rceil + 1$.

To see why this is the case, consider any two neighbors a and b in $G(1)$. As, by definition, the corresponding sources in $D(1)$ have a common sink, at least one of these two sources will be defeated (because the sink will vote YES to only one of them). This means that if we take any path in $G(1)$, at least half of the nodes on that path will correspond to sources that will cease to be such at the end of this iteration.

---

[4] In a DAG, two sources a and b are said to have a common sink c if c is reachable from both a and b.

Furthermore, if (the source corresponding to) a survives, it will now have a sink in common with each of the undefeated (sources corresponding to) neighbors of b. This means that if we consider the new DAG $D(2)$, the corresponding graph $G(2)$ is exactly the graph obtained by removing the nodes associated to the defeated sources, and linking together the nodes previously at length two. In other words, $d(G(2)) \leq \lceil d(G(1))/2 \rceil$.

Similar will be the relationship between the graphs $G(i-1)$ and $G(i)$ corresponding to the DAG $D(i-1)$ of iteration $i-1$ and to the resulting new DAG $D(i)$, respectively. In other words, $d(G(i)) \leq \lceil d(G(i-1))/2 \rceil$. Observe that $\mathrm{diam}(G(i)) = 1$ corresponds to a situation where all sources except one will be defeated in this iteration, and $d(G(i)) = 0$ corresponds to the situation where there is only one source left (which does not know it yet). As $d(G(i)) \leq 1$ after at most $\lceil \log \mathrm{diam}(G(1)) \rceil$ iterations, the property follows:

As the diameter of a graph cannot be greater than the number of its nodes, and as the nodes of $G(1)$ correspond to the sources of $\vec{G}$, we have that

$$ k(G) \leq \lceil \log s(\vec{G}) \rceil \leq \lceil \log n \rceil. $$

We can thus establish that *without pruning*, that is, with $m_i = m$, we have a $O(m \log n)$ total cost

$$ \mathbf{M}[Yo-Yo \; (\textit{without pruning})] \; \leq \; 2 \, m \; \log n + l.o.t. \tag{3.42} $$

The unsolved problem is the determination of the real cost of the algorithm, when the effects of pruning are taken into account.

3.8.4 Lower Bounds and Equivalences

We have seen a complex but rather efficient protocol, *MegaMerger*, for electing a leader in an arbitrary network. In fact, it uses $O(m + n \log n)$ messages in the worst case. This means that in a ring network it uses $O(n \log n)$ messages and it is thus optimal, without even knowing that the network is a ring.

The next question we should ask is how efficient a universal election protocol can be. In other words,

what is the complexity of the election problem?

The answer is not difficult to derive.

First of all observe that any election protocol requires to send a message on *every* link. To see why this is true, assume by contradiction that indeed there is a correct universal election protocol A that in every network G and in every execution under **IR** does not send a message on every link of G. Consider a network G and an execution of A in G; let z be the entity that becomes *leader* and let $e = (x, y) \in E$ be a link where no message is transmitted by A (Figure 3.60(a)).

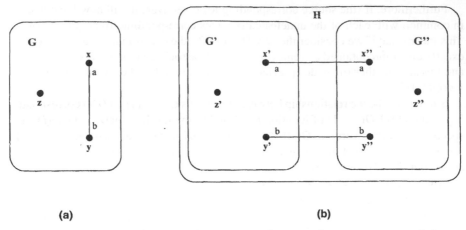

(a)   (b)

FIGURE 3.60: Every universal election protocol must send messages on every link.

We will now construct a new graph H as follows: We make two copies of G and remove from both of them the edge e; we then connect these two graphs G' and G'' by adding two new edges $e_1 = (x', x'')$ and $e_2 = (y', y'')$, where x' and x'' (respective y' and y'') are the copies of x (respective y) in G' and G'', respectively, and where the labels are: $\lambda_{x'}(e_1) = \lambda_{x''}(e_1) = \lambda_x(e)$ and $\lambda_{y'}(e_1) = \lambda_{y''}(e_2) = \lambda_y(e)$ (see Figure 3.60(b)).

Run exactly the same execution of A we did in G on the two components G' and G'' of H: As no message was sent along (x, y) in G, this is possible, but as no message was sent along (x, y) in the original execution, x' and x'' will never send messages to each other in the current execution; similarly, y' and y'' will never send messages to each other. This means that the entities of G' will never communicate with the entities of G'' during this execution; thus, they will not be aware of their existence and will operate solely within G'; similarly for the entities of G''.

This means that when the execution of A in G' terminates, entity z' will become *leader*; but similarly, entity z'' in G'' will become *leader* as well. In other words, two *leaders* will be elected, contradicting the correctness of protocol A. In other words,

$$\mathcal{M}(\textbf{Elect}/\textbf{IR}) \geq m.$$

This lower bound is powerful enough to provide us with interesting and useful information; for example, it states that $\Omega(n^2)$ messages are needed in a complete graph if you do not know that is a complete graph. By contrast, we know that there are networks where election requires way more than m messages; for example, in rings $m = n$ but we need $\Omega(n \log n)$ messages. As a universal election protocol must run in every network, including rings, we can say that in the worst case,

$$\mathcal{M}(\textbf{Elect}/\textbf{IR}) \geq \Omega(m + n \log n). \tag{3.43}$$

This means that protocol *MegaMerger* is the worst case *optimal* and we know the complexity of the election problem.

Property 3.8.17   *The message complexity of election under* **IR** *is* $\Theta(m + n \log n)$.

We are now going to see that constructing a spanning tree **SPT** and electing a leader **Elect** are *strictly equivalent*: Any solution to one of them can be easily modified so as to solve the other with the same message cost (in order of magnitude).

First of all, observe that , similarly to the Election problem, **SPT** also requires a message to be sent on every link (Exercise 3.10.85):

$$\mathcal{M}(\mathbf{SPT/IR}) \geq m. \tag{3.44}$$

We are now going to see how we can construct a spanning-tree construction algorithm from any existing election protocol. Let A be an election protocol; consider now the following protocol B:

1. Elect a *leader* using A.
2. The *leader* starts the execution of protocol *Shout*.

Recall that protocol *Shout* (seen in Section 2.5) will correctly construct a spanning tree if there is a unique initiator. As the *leader* elected in step (1) is unique, a spanning tree will be constructed in step (2). So, protocol B solves **SPT**. What is the cost ? As *Shout* uses exactly $2m$ messages, we have

$$M[B] = M[A] + 2m.$$

In other words, with at most $O(m)$ additional messages, any election protocol can be made to construct a spanning tree; as $\Omega(m)$ messages are needed anyway (Equation 3.44), this means that

$$\mathcal{M}(\mathbf{SPT/IR}) \leq \mathcal{M}(\mathbf{Elect/IR}). \tag{3.45}$$

Focus now on a spanning-tree construction algorithm C. Using C as the first step, it is easy to construct an election protocol D where (Exercise 3.10.86)

$$M[D] = M[C] + O(n).$$

In other words, the message complexity of **Elect** is no more than that of **Elect** plus at most another $O(n)$ messages; as election requires more than $O(n)$ messages anyway (Property 3.8.17), this means that

$$\mathcal{M}(\mathbf{Elect/IR}) \leq \mathcal{M}(\mathbf{SPT/IR}). \tag{3.46}$$

Combining Equations 3.45 and 3.46, we have not only that the problems are *computationally equivalent*

$$\textbf{Elect}(I\,R) \equiv \textbf{SPT}(I\,R) \tag{3.47}$$

but also that they have the same complexity:

$$\mathcal{M}(\textbf{Elect}/\textbf{IR}) = \mathcal{M}(\textbf{SPT}/\textbf{IR}). \tag{3.48}$$

Using similar arguments, it is possible to establish the computational and complexity equivalence of election with several other problems (e.g., see Exercise 3.10.87).

3.9 BIBLIOGRAPHICAL NOTES

Election in a ring network is one of the first problems studied in distributed computing from an algorithmic point of view. The first solution protocol, *All the Way*, is due to Gerard Le Lann [29] proposal for unidirectional rings. Also for unidirectional rings, protocol *AsFar* was developed by Ernie Chang and Rosemary Roberts [12]; it was later analyzed experimentally by Friedman Mattern [34] and analytically by Christian Lavault [31]. The probabilistic bidirectional version *ProbAsFar* was proposed and analyzed by Ephraim Korach, Doron Rotem, and Nicola Santoro [28]. Hans Bodlaender and Jan van Leeuwen later showed how to make it deterministic and provided further analysis [8]; the exact asymptotic average value has been derived by Christian Lavault [30].

The idea beyond the first $\Theta(n \log n)$ worst-case protocol, *Control*, is due to Dan Hirschberg and J.B. Sinclair [22]. Protocol *Stages* was designed by Randolph Franklin [17]; the more efficient *Stages with Feedback* was developed by Ephraim Korach, Doron Rotem, and Nicola Santoro [27].

The first $\Theta(n \log n)$ worst case protocol for unidirectional rings, *UniStages*, was designed by Danny Dolev, Maria Klawe, and Michael Rodeh [15]. The more efficient *MinMax* is due to Gary Peterson [39]. The even more efficient protocol *MinMax+* has been designed by Lisa Higham and Theresa Przytycka [21]. Bidirectional versions of *MinMax* with the same complexity as the original (Problem 3.10.4) have been independently designed by Shlomo Moran, Mordechai Shalom, and Shmuel Zaks [35], and by Jan van Leeuwen and Richard Tan [44].

The lower bound for unidirectional rings is due to Jan Pachl, Doron Rotem, and Ephraim Korach [36]. James Burns developed the first lower bound for bidirectional rings [9]. The lower bounds when n is known (Exercises 3.10.45 and 3.10.47), as well as others, are due to Hans Bodlaender [5–7].

The $O(n)$ election protocol for *tori* was designed by Gary Peterson [38] and later refined for unoriented tori by Bernard Mans [33].

The quest for a $O(n)$ election protocol for *hypercubes* with dimensional labelings was solved independently by Steven Robbins and Kay Robbins [40], Paola Flocchini and Bernard Mans [16], and Gerard Tel [43]. Stefan Dobrev [13] has designed a protocol that allows $O(n)$ election in hypercubes with *any* sense of direction, not just the dimensional labeling (Exercise 3.10.63). The protocol for *unoriented hypercubes* has been designed by Stefan Dobrev and Peter Ruzicka [14].

The first optimal $\Theta(n \log n)$ protocol for *complete networks* was developed by Pierre Humblet [23]; an optimal protocol that requires $O(n)$ messages on the average (Exercise 3.10.74) was developed by Mee Yee Chan and Francis Chin [10]. The lower bound is due to Ephraim Korach, Shlomo Moran, and Shmuel Zaks [26], who also designed another optimal protocol. The optimal protocol *CompleteElect*, reducing the $O(n \log n)$ time complexity to $O(n)$, was designed by Yeuda Afek and Eli Gafni [2]; the same bounds were independently achieved by Gary Peterson [38]. The time complexity has been later reduced to $O(\frac{n}{\log n})$ without increasing the message costs (Exercise 3.10.68) by Gurdip Singh [42].

The fact that a chordal labeling allows to fully exploit the communication power of the complete graph was observed by Michael Loui, Teresa Matsushita, and Douglas West, who developed the first $O(n)$ protocol for such a case [32]. Stefan Dobrev [13] has designed a protocol that allows $O(n)$ election in complete networks with *any* sense of direction, not just the chordal labeling (Exercise 3.10.75).

Election protocols for *chordal rings*, including the doublecube, were designed and analyzed by Hagit Attiya, Jan van Leeuwen, Nicola Santoro, and Shmuel Zaks [3]. The quest for the smallest cord structure has seen k being reduced from $O(\log n)$ first to $O(\log \log n)$ by T.Z. Kalamboukis and S.L. Mantzaris [24], then to $O(\log \log \log n)$ by Yi Pan [37], and finally to $O(1)$ (Problem 3.10.12) by Andreas Fabri and Gerard Tel [unpublished]. The observation that in such a chordal ring, election can be done in $O(n)$ messages even if the links are arbitrarily labeled (Problem 3.10.13) is due to Bernard Mans [33].

The first $O(m + n \log n)$ universal election protocol was designed by Robert Gallager [18]. Some of the ideas developed there were later used in *MegaMerger*, developed by Robert Gallager, Pierre Humblet, and Philip Spira, that actually constructs a min-cost spanning tree [19]. The $O(n \log n)$ time complexity of *MegaMerger* has been reduced first to $O(n \log^* n)$ by Mee Yee Chan and Francis Chin [11] and then to $O(n)$ (Problem 3.10.14) by Baruch Awerbuch [4] without increasing the message complexity. It has been further reduced to $\Theta(d)$ (Problem 3.10.15) by Hosame Abu-Amara and Arkady Kanevsky but at the expense of a $O(m \log d)$ message cost [1]; the same reduction has been obtained independently by Juan A. Garay, Shay Kutten, and David Peleg [20]. Protocol *YO-YO* was designed by Nicola Santoro ; the proof that it requires at most $O(\log n)$ stages is due to Gerard Tel.

The computational relationship between the traversal and the election problems has been discussed and analyzed by Ephraim Korach, Shay Kutten, and Shlomo Moran [25]. The $\Omega(m + n \log n)$ lower bound for universal election as well as some of the other computational equivalence relationships were first observed by Nicola Santoro [41].

3.10 EXERCISES, PROBLEMS, AND ANSWERS

3.10.1 Exercises

Exercise 3.10.1   Modify protocol *MinF-Tree* (presented in Section 2.6.2) so as to implement strategy *Elect Minimum Initiator* in a tree. Prove its correctness and analyze its costs. Show that, in the worst case, it uses $3n + k_* - 4 \leq 4n - 4$ messages.

Exercise 3.10.2   Design an efficient single-initiator protocol to find the minimum value in a ring. Prove its correctness and analyze its costs.

Exercise 3.10.3   Show that the time costs of protocol *All the Way* will be at most $2n - 1$. Determine also the minimum cost and the condition that will cause it.

Exercise 3.10.4   Modify protocol *All the Way* so to use strategy *Elect Minimum Initiator*.

Exercise 3.10.5   Modify protocol *AsFar* so to use strategy *Elect Minimum Initiator*. Determine the average number of messages assuming that any subset of k_* entities is equally likely to be the initiators.

Exercise 3.10.6   Expand the rules of protocol *Stages* described in Section 3.3.4, so as to enforce message ordering.

Exercise 3.10.7   Show that in protocol *Stages*, there will be at most one enqueued message per closed port.

Exercise 3.10.8   Prove that in protocol *Stages with Feedback*, the minimum distance between two candidates in stage i is $d(i) \geq 2^{i-1}$.

Exercise 3.10.9   Show an initial configuration for $n = 8$ in which protocol *Stages* will require the most messages. Describe how to construct the "worst configuration" for any n.

Exercise 3.10.10   Determine the ideal time complexity of protocol *Stages*.

Exercise 3.10.11   Modify protocol *Stages* using the *min-max* approach discussed in Section 3.3.7. Prove its correctness. Show that its message costs are unchanged.

Exercise 3.10.12   Write the rules of protocol *Stages** described in Section 3.3.4.

Exercise 3.10.13   Assume that in *Stages* candidate* x in stage i receives a message $M*$ with stage $j > i$. Prove that if x survives, then $id(x)$ is smaller not only of $id*$ but also of the ids in the messages "jumped over" by $M*$.

Exercise 3.10.14   Show that protocol *Stages** correctly terminates.

Exercise 3.10.15   Prove that the message and time costs of *Stages** are no worse that those of *Stages*. Produce an example in which the costs of *Stages** are actually *smaller*.

Exercise 3.10.16   Write the rules of protocol *Stages with Feedback* assuming *message ordering*.

Exercise 3.10.17   Derive the ideal time complexity of protocol *Stages with Feedback*.

Exercise 3.10.18   Write the rules of protocol *Stages with Feedback* enforcing *message ordering*.

Exercise 3.10.19   Prove that in protocol *Stages with Feedback*, the number of ring segments where no feedback will be transmitted in stage i is n_{i+1}.

Exercise 3.10.20   Prove that in protocol *Stages with Feedback*, the minimum distance between two candidates in stage i is $d(i) \geq 3^{i-1}$.

Exercise 3.10.21   Give a more accurate estimate of the message costs of protocol *Stages with Feedback*.

Exercise 3.10.22   Show an initial configuration for $n = 9$ in which protocol *Stages with Feedback* will require the most stages. Describe how to construct the "worst configuration" for any n.

Exercise 3.10.23   Modify protocol *Stages with Feedback* using the *min-max* approach discussed in Section 3.3.7. Prove its correctness. Show that its message costs are unchanged.

Exercise 3.10.24   Implement the *alternating step* strategy under the same restrictions and with the same cost of protocol *Alternate* but without closing any port.

Exercise 3.10.25   Determine initial configurations that will force protocol *Alternate* to use k steps when $n = F_k$.

Exercise 3.10.26   Show that the worst case number of steps of protocol *Alternate* is *achievable* for *every* $n > 4$.

Exercise 3.10.27   Determine the ideal time complexity of protocol *Alternate*.

Exercise 3.10.28   Modify protocol *Alternate* using the *min-max* approach discussed in Section 3.3.7. Prove its correctness. Show that its message costs are unchanged.

Exercise 3.10.29   Show the step-by-step execution of *Stages* and of *UniStages* in the ring of Figure 3.3. Indicate for each step, the values know at the candidates.

Exercise 3.10.30 Determine the ideal time complexity of protocol *UniStages*.

Exercise 3.10.31 Modify protocol *UniStages* using the *min-max* approach discussed in Section 3.3.7. Prove its correctness. Show that its message costs are unchanged.

Exercise 3.10.32 Design an exact simulation of *Stages with Feedback* for unidirectional rings. Analyze its costs.

Exercise 3.10.33 Show the step-by-step execution of *Alternate* and of *UniAlternate* in the ring of Figure 3.3. Indicate for each step, the values know at the candidates.

Exercise 3.10.34 Without changing its message cost, modify protocol *UniAlternate* so that it does not require Message Ordering.

Exercise 3.10.35 Prove that the ideal time complexity of protocol *UniAlternate* is $O(n)$.

Exercise 3.10.36 Modify protocol *UniAlternate* using the *min-max* approach discussed in Section 3.3.7. Prove its correctness. Show that its message costs are unchanged.

Exercise 3.10.37 Prove that in protocol *MinMax*, if a *candidate* x survives an even stage i, its predecessor $l(i, x)$ becomes *defeated*.

Exercise 3.10.38 Show that the worst case number of steps of protocol *MinMax* is *achievable*.

Exercise 3.10.39 Modify protocol *MinMax* so that it does not require Message Ordering. Implement your modification and throughly test your implementation.

Exercise 3.10.40 For protocol *MinMax*, consider the configuration depicted in Figure 3.32. Prove that once envelope $(11, 3)$ reaches the *defeated* node z, z can determine that 11 will survive this stage.

Exercise 3.10.41 Write the rules of Protocol *MinMax+* assuming message ordering.

Exercise 3.10.42 Write the rules of Protocol *MinMax+* without assuming message ordering.

Exercise 3.10.43 Prove Property 3.3.1.

Exercise 3.10.44 Prove that in protocol *MinMax+*, if an envelope with value v reaches an even stage $i + 1$, it saves at least F_i messages in stage i with respect to *MinMax (Hint: Use Property 3.3.1.)*.

Exercise 3.10.45 Prove that even if the entities know n, $\text{ave}_A(I \mid n \; known) \geq (\frac{1}{4} - \epsilon)$ $n \log n$ for any election protocol A for unidirectional rings.

Exercise 3.10.46 Prove that in bidirectional rings, $\text{ave}_A(I) \geq \frac{1}{2} n H_n$ for any election protocol A.

Exercise 3.10.47 Prove that even if the entities know n, $\text{ave}_A(I \mid n \; known) \geq \frac{1}{2} n \log n$ for any election protocol A for unidirectional rings.

Exercise 3.10.48 Determine the exact complexity of Wake-Up in a mesh of dimensions $a \times b$.

Exercise 3.10.49 Show how to broadcast from a corner of a mesh dimensions $a \times b$ with less than $2n$ messages.

Exercise 3.10.50 In Protocol *ElectMesh*, in the first stage of the election process, if an interior node receives an election message, it will reply to the sender "I am in the interior," so that no subsequent election messages are sent to it. Explain why it is possible to achieve the same goal *without* sending those replies.

Exercise 3.10.51 Consider the following simple modification to Protocol *ElectMesh*: When sending a wake-up message, a node includes the information of whether it is an internal, a border, or a corner node. Then, during the first stage of the election, a border node uses this information if possible to send the election message only along the outer ring (it might not be possible.). Show that the protocol so modified uses at most $4(a + b) + 5n + k_* - 32$ messages.

Exercise 3.10.52 Broadcasting in Oriented Mesh. Design a protocol that allows to broadcast in an oriented mesh using $n - 1$ messages regardless of the location of the initiator.

Exercise 3.10.53 Traversal in Oriented Mesh. Design a protocol that allows to traverse an oriented mesh using $n - 1$ messages regardless of the location of the initiator.

Exercise 3.10.54 Wake-Up in Oriented Mesh. Design a protocol that allows to wake-up all the entities in an oriented mesh using less than $2n$ messages regardless of the location and the number of the initiators.

Exercise 3.10.55 Show that the effect of rounding up α^i does not affect the order of magnitude of the cost of Protocol *MarkBorder* derived in Section 3.4.2 (*Hint: Show that it amounts to at most eight extra messages per* candidate *per stage with an insignificant change in the bound on the number of* candidates *in each stage*).

Exercise 3.10.56   Show that the ideal time of protocol *MarkBorder* can be as bad as $O(n)$.

Exercise 3.10.57   Improving Time in Tori (⋆⋆) Modify Protocol *MarkBorder* so that the time complexity is $O(\sqrt{n})$ without increasing the message complexity. Ensure that the modified protocol is correct.

Exercise 3.10.58   Election in Rectangular Torus (⋆) Modify Protocol *MarkBorder* so that it elects a leader in a rectangular torus of dimension $l \times w$ ($l \leq w$), using $\Theta(n + l \log l/w)$ messages.

Exercise 3.10.59   Determine the cost of electing a leader in an oriented hypercube if in protocol *HyperElect* the propagation of the Match messages is done by broadcasting in the appropriate subcube instead of "compressing the address."

Exercise 3.10.60   Prove that in protocol *HyperElect* the distance $d(j - 1, j)$ between $w^{j-1}(z)$ and $w^j(z)$ is at most j.

Exercise 3.10.61   Prove Lemma 3.5.1, that is, that during the execution of protocol *HyperElect*, the only duelists in stage i are the entities with the smallest id in one of the hypercubes of dimension $i - 1$ in $H_{k:i-1}$.

Exercise 3.10.62   Show that the time complexity of Protocol *HyperFlood* is $O(\log^3 N)$.

Exercise 3.10.63 (⋆⋆)   Prove that it is possible to elect a leader in a hypercube using $O(n)$ messages with *any* sense of direction *(Hint: Use long messages)*.

Exercise 3.10.64   Prove that in the strategy *CompleteElect* outlined in Section 3.6.1, the territories of any two candidates in the same stage have no nodes in common.

Exercise 3.10.65   Prove that the strategy *CompleteElect* outlined in Section 3.6.1 solves the election problem.

Exercise 3.10.66   Determine the cost of the strategy *CompleteElect* described in Section 3.6.1 in the worst case *(Hint: Consider how many candidates there can be at level i)*.

Exercise 3.10.67   Analyze the ideal time cost of protocol *CompleteElect* described in Section 3.6.1.

Exercise 3.10.68   Design an election protocol for complete graphs that, like *CompleteElect*, uses $O(n \log n)$ messages but uses only $O(n/ \log n)$ time in the worst case.

Exercise 3.10.69   Generalize the answer to Exercise 3.10.68. Design an election protocol for complete graphs that, for any $\log n \leq k \leq n$, uses $O(nk)$ messages and $O(n/k)$ time in the worst case.

Exercise 3.10.70   Prove that all the rings $R(2), \ldots, R(k)$ where messages are sent by protocol *Kelect* do not have links in common.

Exercise 3.10.71   Write the code for, implement, and test protocol *Kelect-Stages*.

Exercise 3.10.72 (⋆)   Consider using the ring protocol *Alternate* instead of *Stages* in *Kelect*. Determine what will be the cost in this case.

Exercise 3.10.73 (⋆⋆)   Determine the average message costs of protocol *Kelect-Stages*.

Exercise 3.10.74 (⋆)   Show how to elect a leader in a complete network with $O(n \log n)$ messages in the worst case but only $O(n)$ on the average.

Exercise 3.10.75 (⋆⋆)   Prove that it is possible to elect a leader in a complete graph using $O(n)$ messages with any sense of direction.

Exercise 3.10.76   Show how to elect a leader in the chordal ring $C_n \langle 1, 2, 3, 4 \ldots, t \rangle$ with $O\left(n + \frac{n}{t} \log \frac{n}{t}\right)$ messages.

Exercise 3.10.77   Prove that in chordal ring C_n' electing a leader requires at least $\Omega\left(n + \frac{n}{t} \log \frac{n}{t}\right)$ messages in the worst case *(Hint: Reduce the problem to that of electing a leader on a ring of size n/t).*

Exercise 3.10.78   Show how to elect a leader in the *double cube* $C_n \langle 1, 2, 4, 8 \ldots, 2^{\lceil \log n \rceil} \rangle$ with $O(n)$ messages.

Exercise 3.10.79   Consider a merger message from city A arriving at neighbouring city B along merge link (a, b) in protocol *Mega-Merger*. Prove that if we reverse the logical direction of the links on the path from $D(A)$ to the exit point a and direct toward B the merge link, the union of A and B will be rooted in the downtown of A.

Exercise 3.10.80   District b of B has just received a *Let-us-Merge* message from a along merge link (a, b). From the message, b finds out that $level(A) > level(B)$; thus, it postpones the request. In the meanwhile, the downtown $D(B)$ chooses (a, b) as its merge link. Explain why this situation will never occur.

Exercise 3.10.81   Find a way to avoid notification of termination by the downtown of the megacity in protocol *Mega-Merger* (Hint: Show that by the time the downtown understands that the mega-merger is completed, all other districts already know that their execution of the protocol is terminated).

Exercise 3.10.82 **Time Costs.** Show that protocol *Mega-Merger* uses at most $O(n \log n)$ ideal time units.

Exercise 3.10.83 Prove that in the *YO-YO* protocol, during an iteration, no sink or internal node will become a source.

Exercise 3.10.84 Modify the *YO-YO* protocol so that upon termination, a spanning tree rooted in the leader has been constructed. Achieve this goal *without* any additional messages.

Exercise 3.10.85 Prove that to solve **SPT** under **IR**, a message must be sent on every link.

Exercise 3.10.86 Show how to transform a spanning-tree construction algorithm C so as to elect a leader with at most $O(n)$ additional messages.

Exercise 3.10.87 Prove that under **IR**, the problem of finding the smallest of the entities' values is computationally equivalent to electing a leader and has the same message complexity.

3.10.2 Problems

Problem 3.10.1 **Josephus Problem.** Consider the following set of electoral rules. In stage i, a candidate x sends its id and receives the id from its two neighboring candidates, $r(i, x)$ and $l(i, x)$: x does not survive this stage if and only if its id is larger than both received ids. Analyze the corresponding protocol *Josephus*, determining in particular the number of stages and the total number of messages both in the worst and in the average case. Analyze and discuss its time complexity.

Problem 3.10.2 **Alternating Steps** ($\star$) Design a *conflict resolution* mechanism for the *alternating steps* strategy to cope lack of orientation in the ring. Analyze the complexity of the resulting protocol

Problem 3.10.3 **Better Stages** ($\star\star$) Construct a protocol based on electoral stages that guarantees $n_i \leq \frac{n_{i-1}}{b}$ with cn messages transmitted in each stage, where $\frac{c}{\log b} < 1.89$.

Problem 3.10.4 **Bidirectional** *MinMax* ($\star$) Design a bidirectional version of *Min-Max* with the same costs.

Problem 3.10.5 **Distances in** *MinMax+* ($\star\star$) In computing the cost of protocol *MinMax+* we have used $\text{dis}(i) = F_{i+2}$. Determine what will be the cost if we use $\text{dis}(i) = 2^i$ instead.

Problem 3.10.6   *MinMax+* **Variations** (★★) In protocol *MinMax+* we use "promotion by distance" only in the even stages and "promotion by witness" only in the odd stages. Determine what would happen if we use

1. only "promotion by distance" but in every stage;
2. only "promotion by witness" but in every stage;
3. "promotion by distance" in every stage and "promotion by witness" only in odd stages;
4. "promotion by witness" in every stage and "promotion by distance" only in even stages;
5. both "promotion by distance" and "promotion by witness" in *every* stage.

Problem 3.10.7   Bidirectional Oriented Rings. (★★★) Prove or disprove that there is an efficient protocol for bidirectional oriented rings that cannot be used nor simulated neither in unidirectional rings nor in general bidirectional ones with the same or better costs.

Problem 3.10.8   Unoriented Hypercubes. (★) Design a protocol that can elect a leader in a hypercube with arbitrary labelling using $O(n \log \log n)$ messages. Implement and test your protocol.

Problem 3.10.9   Linear Election in Hypercubes. (★★★) Prove or disprove that it is possible to elect a leader in an hypercube in $O(n)$ messages even when it is not oriented.

Problem 3.10.10   Oriented Cube-Connected Cycles (★) Design an election protocol for an oriented CCC using $O(n)$ messages. Implement and test your protocol.

Problem 3.10.11   Oriented Butterfly. Design an election protocol for an oriented *butterfly*. Determine its complexity. Implement and test your protocol.

Problem 3.10.12   Minimal Chordal Ring (★★) Find a chordal ring with $k = 2$ where it is possible to elect a leader with $O(n)$ messages.

Problem 3.10.13   Unlabelled Chordal Rings (★★) Show how to elect a leader in the chordal ring of Problem 3.10.12 with $O(n)$ messages even if the edges are arbitrarily labeled.

Problem 3.10.14   Improved Time (★) Show how to elect a leader using $O(m + n \log n)$ messages but only $O(n)$ ideal time units.

Problem 3.10.15   Optimal Time (★★) Show how to elect a leader in $O(d)$ time using at most $O(m \log d)$ messages.

3.10.3   Answers to Exercises

Answer to Exercise 3.10.21

The size of the areas where no feedback is sent in stage i can vary from one another, from stage to stage, and from execution to execution. We can still have an estimate of their size. In fact, the distance d_i between two candidates in stage i is $d(i) \geq 3^{i-1}$ (Exercise 3.10.20). Thus, the total number of message transmissions caused in stage i by the feedback will be at most $n - n_{i+1}3^{i-1}$, yielding a total of at most $3n - \sum_{i=1}^{\lceil \log_3 n \rceil} n_{i+1}3^{i-1}$ messages.

Answer to Exercise 3.10.44

Let $h_j(a)$ denote the *candidate* that originated message (a, j). Consider a message $(v, i + 1)$ and its originator $z = h_{i+1}(v)$; this message was sent after receiving (v, i) originated by $x = h_i(v)$.

Let $y = h_i(u)$ be the first *candidate* after x in the ring in stage i, and (u, i) the message it originated. As v survives this stage, which is odd (i.e., *min*), it must be that $v < u$.

Message (v, i) travels from x toward y; upon receiving (v, i), node z in this interval will generate $(v, i + 1)$. Now z cannot be after node $h_{i-1}(u)$ in the ring because by rule (IV) $w = h_{i-1}(u)$ would immediately generate $(v, i + 1)$ after receiving (v, i). In other words, either $z = w$ or z is before w. Thus we save at least $d(z, y) \geq d(w, y) = d(h_{i-1}(u), h_i(u)) \geq F_i$, where the last inequality is by Property 3.3.1.

Partial Answer to Exercise 3.10.66

Consider a *captured* node y that receives an attack after the other, say from a candidates x_1 in level i. According to the strategy, y will send a Warning to its owner z to inform it of this attack and wait for a reply; depending on the reply, it will notify x_1 of whether the attack was successful (the case in which y will be captured by x_1) or not. Assume now that while waiting, y receives an attack after the other, say from candidates $x_2, \ldots, x_k$ in that order, all in the same level i. According to the strategy, y will issue a Warning to its owner z for each of them. Observe now that if $id(z) > id(x_1) > \ldots > id(x_k)$, each of these attacks will be successful, and y will in turn be captured by all those candidates.

BIBLIOGRAPHY

[1] H. Abu-Amara and A. Kanevsky. On the complexities of leader election algorithms. In *5th IEEE International Conference on Computing and Information*, pages 202–206, Sudbury, May 1993.

[2] Y. Afek and E. Gafni. Time and message bounds for election in synchronous and asynchronous complete networks. *SIAM Journal on Computing*, 20(2):376–394, 1991.

[3] H. Attiya, J. van Leeuwen, N. Santoro, and Shmuel Zaks. Efficient elections in chordal ring networks. *Algorithmica*, 4:437–446, 1989.

[4] B. Awerbuch. Optimal distributed algorithms for minimum weight spanning tree, counting, leader election, and related problems. In *19th Annual ACM Symposium on Theory of Computing*, pages 230–240, New York City, May 1987.

[5] H.L. Bodlaender. A better lower bound for distributed leader finding in bidirectional, asynchronous rings of processors. *Information Processing Letters*, 27(6):287–290, 1988.

[6] H.L. Bodlaender. New lower bound techniques for distributed leader finding and other problems on rings of processors. *Theoretical Computer Science*, 81:237–256, 1991.

[7] H.L. Bodlaender. Some lower bound results for decentralized extrema-finding in rings of processors. *Journal on Computing and System Sciences*, 42(1):97–118, 1991.

[8] H.L. Bodlaender and J. van Leeuwen. New upperbounds for distributed extrema-finding in a ring of processors. In *Proc. 1st International Workshop on Distributed Algorithms (WDAG 1)*, pages 504–512, Ottawa, Aug 1985.

[9] J. Burns. A formal model for message passing systems. Technical Report UTR-91, Indiana University, 1981.

[10] M.Y. Chan and F.L.Y. Chin. Distributed election in complete networks. *Distributed Computing*, 3(1):19–22, 1988.

[11] M.Y. Chan and F.L.Y. Chin. Improving the time complexity of message-optimal distributed algorithms for minimum-weight spanning trees. *SIAM Journal on Computing*, 19(4):612–626, 1990.

[12] E.J.H. Chang and R. Roberts. An improved algorithm for decentralized extrema-finding in circular configurations of processes. *Communications of the ACM*, 22(5):281–283, May 1979.

[13] S. Dobrev. Leader election using any sense of direction. In *6th International Colloquium on Structural Information and Communication Complexity*, pages 93–104, Lacanau, July 1999.

[14] S. Dobrev and P. Ruzicka. Linear broadcasting and $O(n \log \log n)$ election in unoriented hypercubes. In *4th International Colloquium on Structural Information and Communication Complexity*, pages 53–68, Ascona, July 1997.

[15] D. Dolev, M. Klawe, and M. Rodeh. An $O(n \log n)$ unidirectional algorithm for extrema-finding in a circle. *Journal of Algorithms*, 3:245–260, 1982.

[16] P. Flocchini and B. Mans. Optimal elections in labeled hypercubes. *Journal of Parallel and Distributed Computing*, 33(1):76–83, 1996.

[17] W.R. Franklin. On an improved algorithm for decentralized extrema-finding in a circular configuration of processes. *Communications of the ACM*, 25(5):336–337, May 1982.

[18] R.G. Gallager. Finding a leader in a network with $O(e) + O(n \log n)$ messages. Technical Report Internal Memo, M.I.T., 1979.

[19] R.G. Gallager, P.A. Humblet, and P.M. Spira. A distributed algorithm for minimum spanning tree. *ACM Transactions on Programming Languages and Systems*, 5(1):66–77, 1983.

[20] J.A. Garay, S. Kutten, and D. Peleg. A sublinear time distributed algorithm for minimum-weight spanning trees. *SIAM Journal on Computing*, 27(1):302–316, February 1998.

[21] L. Higham and T. Przytycka. A simple, efficient algorithm for maximum finding on rings. *Information Processing Letters*, 58:319–324, 1996.

[22] D.S. Hirschberg and J.B. Sinclair. Decentralized extrema finding in circular configurations of processors. *Communications of the ACM*, 23:627–628, 1980.

[23] P.A. Humblet. Selecting a leader in a clique in $O(n \log n)$ messages. In *Proc. 23rd Conf. on Decision and Control*, pages 1139–1140, Las Vegas, Dec. 1984.

[24] T.Z. Kalamboukis and S.L. Mantzaris. Towards optimal distributed election on chordal rings. *Information Processing Letters*, 38(5):265–270, 1991.

[25] E. Korach, S. Kutten, and S. Moran. A modular technique for the design of efficient distributed leader finding algorithms. *ACM Transactions on Programming Languages and Systems*, 12(1):84–101, January 1990.

[26] E. Korach, S. Moran, and S. Zaks. Optimal lower bounds for some distributed algorithms for a complete network of processors. *Theoretical Computer Science*, 64:125–132, 1989.

[27] E. Korach, D. Rotem, and N. Santoro. Distributed election in a circle without a global sense of orientation. *International Journal of Computer Mathematics*, 16:115–124, 1984.

[28] E. Korach, D. Rotem, and N. Santoro. Analysis of a distributed algorithm for extrema finding in a ring. *Journal of Parallel and Distributed Computing*, 4:575–591, 1987.

[29] G. Le Lann. Distributed systems: Toward a formal approach. In *IFIP Conference on Information Processing*, pages 155–160, 1977.

[30] C. Lavault. Average number of messages for distributed leader-finding in rings of processors. *Information Processing Letters*, 30(4):167–176, 1989.

[31] C. Lavault. Exact average message complexity values for distributed election on bidirectional rings of processors. *Theoretical Computer Science*, 73(1):61–79, 1990.

[32] M.C. Loui, T.A. Matsushita, and D.B. West. Election in complete networks with a sense of direction. *Information Processing Letters*, 22:185–187, 1986. see also Information Processing Letters, vol.28:327, 1988.

[33] B. Mans. Optimal distributed algorithms in unlabeled tori and chordal rings. *Journal of Parallel and Distributed Computing*, 46(1):80–90, 1997.

[34] F. Mattern. Message complexity of simple ring-based election algorithms-an empirical analysis. In *9th IEEE International Conference on Distributed Computing Systems*, pages 94–100, 1989.

[35] S. Moran, M. Shalom, and S. Zaks. An $1.44...n \log n$ algorithm for distributed leader finding in bidirectional rings of processors. Technical Report RC 11933, IBM Research Division, 1986.

[36] J. Pachl, D. Rotem, and E. Korach. Lower bounds for distributed maximum finding algorithms. *Journal of the ACM*, 31:905–917, 1984.

[37] Y. Pan. An improved election algorithm in chordal ring networks. *International Journal of Computer Mathematics*, 40(3-4):191–200, 1991.

[38] G.L. Peterson. Improved algorithms for elections in meshes and complete networks. Technical report, Georgia Institute of Techchnology, December 1986.

[39] G.L. Peterson. An $O(n \log n)$ unidirectional algorithm for the circular extrema problem. *A.C.M. Transactions on Programming Languages and Systems*, 4(4):758–762, oct 1982.

[40] S. Robbins and K.A. Robbins. Choosing a leader on a hypercube. In N. Rishe, S. Najathe, and D. Tal, editors, *PARBASE-90, International Conference on Databases, Parallel Aarchitectures and their Applications*, pages 469–471, Miami Beach, 1990.

[41] N. Santoro. On the message complexity of distributed problems. *Journal of Computing and Information Sciences*, 13:131–147, 1984.

[42] G. Singh. Leader election in complete networks. *SIAM Journal on Computing*, 26(3):772–785, 1997.

[43] G. Tel. Linear election in oriented hypercubes. *Parallel Processing Letters*, 5:357–366, 1995.

[44] J. van Leeuwen and R.B. Tan. An improved upperbound for distributed election in bidirectional rings of processors. *Distributed Computing*, 2(3):149–160, 1987.

CHAPTER 4

Message Routing and Shortest Paths

4.1 INTRODUCTION

Communication is at the base of computing in a distributed environment, but the task to achieve it efficiently is neither simple nor trivial.

Consider an entity x that wants to communicate some information to another entity y; for example, x has a message that it wants to be delivered to y. In general, x does not know where y is or how to reach it (i.e., which paths lead to it); actually, it might not even know if y is a neighbor or not.

Still, the communication is always possible if the network $\vec{G}$ is strongly connected. In fact, it is sufficient for x to *broadcast* the information: every entity, including y will receive it. This simple solution, called *broadcast routing*, is obviously not efficient; on the contrary, it is impractical, expensive in terms of cost, and not very secure (too many other nodes receive the message), even if it is performed only on a spanning-tree of the network.

A more efficient approach is to choose a single path in $\vec{G}$ from x to y: The message sent by x will travel along this path only, relayed by the entities in the path, until it reaches its destination y. The process of determining a path between a *source* x and a *destination* y is known as *routing*.

If there is more than one path from x to y, we would obviously like to choose the "best" one, that is, the least expensive one. The cost $\theta(a, b) \geq 0$ of a link (a, b), traditionally called *length*, is a value that depends on the system (reflecting, e.g., time delay, transmission cost, link reliability, etc.), and the cost of a path is the sum of the costs of the links composing it. The path of minimum cost is called *shortest path*; clearly, the objective is to use this path for sending the message. The process of determining the most economic path between a source and a destination is known as *shortest-path routing*.

The (shortest-path) routing problem is commonly solved by storing at each entity x the information that will allow to address a message to its destination through a (shortest) path. This information is called *routing table*.

In this chapter we will discuss several aspects of the routing problem. First of all, we will consider the construction of the routing tables. We will then address

Design and Analysis of Distributed Algorithms, by Nicola Santoro
Copyright © 2007 John Wiley & Sons, Inc.

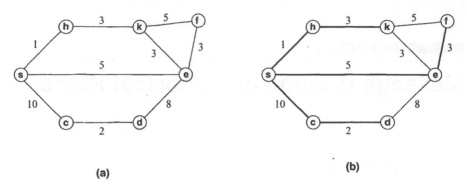

(a)

(b)

FIGURE 4.1: Determining the shortest paths from *s* to the other entities.

the problem of maintaining the information of the tables up to date, should changes occur in the system. Finally, we will discuss how to represent routing information in a compact way, suitable for systems where space is a problem. In the following, and unless otherwise specified, we will assume the set of restrictions **IR**: *Bidirectional Links* (BL), *Connectivity* (CN), *Total Reliability* (TR), and *Initial Distinct Values* (ID).

4.2 SHORTEST PATH ROUTING

The *routing table* of an entity contains information on how to reach any possible destination. In this section we examine how this information can be acquired, and the table constructed. As we will see, this problem is related to the construction of particular spanning-trees of the network. In the following, and unless otherwise specified, we will focus on shortest-path routing.

Different types of routing tables can be defined, depending on the amount of information contained in them. We will consider for now the *full* routing table: For each destination, there is stored a shortest path to reach it; if there are more than one shortest path, only the lexicographically smallest[1] will be stored. For example, in the network of Figure 4.1, the routing table *RT*(*s*) for *s* is shown in Table 4.1.

We will see different approaches to construct routing tables, some depending on the amount of local storage an entity has available.

4.2.1 Gossiping the Network Maps

A first obvious solution would be to construct at every entity the entire *map* of the network with all the costs; then, each entity can locally and directly compute its shortest-path routing table. This solution obviously requires that the local memory available to an entity is large enough to store the entire map of the network.

---

[1] The lexicographic order will be over the strings of the names of the nodes in the paths.

TABLE 4.1: Full Routing Table for Node s

Routing Destination	Shortest Path	Cost
h	(s, h)	1
k	$(s, h)(h, k)$	4
c	(s, c)	10
d	$(s, c)(c, d)$	12
e	(s, e)	5
f	$(s, e)(e, f)$	8

The map of the network can be viewed as an $n \times n$ array MAP(G), one row and one column per entity, where for any two entities x and y, the entry MAP$[x, y]$ contains information on whether link (x, y) exists, and if so on its cost. In a sense, each entity x knows initially only its own row MAP$[x, \star]$. To know the entire map, every entity needs to know the initial information of all the other entities.

This is a particular instance of a general problem called *input collection* or *gossip*: every entity has a (possibly different) piece of information; the goal is to reach a final configuration where every entity has all the pieces of information. The solution of the gossiping problem using normal messages is simple:

every entity broadcasts its initial information.

Since it relies solely on broadcast, this operation is more efficiently performed in a tree. Thus, the protocol will be as follows:

Map_Gossip:

1. An arbitrary spanning tree of the network is created, if not already available; this tree will be used for all communication.
2. Each entity acquires full information about its neighborhood (e.g., names of the neighbors, cost of the incident links, etc.), if not already available.
3. Each entity broadcasts its neighborhood information along the tree.

At the end of the execution, each entity has a complete map of the network with all the link costs; it can then locally construct its shortest-path routing table.

The construction of the initial spanning-tree can be done using $O(m + n \log n)$ messages, for example using protocol *MegaMerger*. The acquisition of neighborhood information requires a single exchange of messages between neighbors, requiring in total just $2m$ messages. Each entity x then broadcasts on the tree deg(x) items of information. Hence the total number of messages will be at most

$$\sum_x \deg(x)(n - 1) = 2m(n - 1).$$

Thus, we have

$$\mathbf{M}[\textit{Map\_Gossip}] = 2\,m\,n + \textit{l.o.t.} \tag{4.1}$$

This means that, in *sparse* networks, all the routing tables can be constructed with at most $O(n^2)$ normal messages. Such is the case of meshes, tori, butterflies, and so forth.

In systems that allow *very long messages*, not surprisingly the gossip problem, and thus the routing table construction problem, can be solved with substantially fewer messages (Exercises 4.6.3 and 4.6.4).

The time costs of gossiping on a tree depend on many factors, including the diameter of the tree and the number of initial items an entity initially has (Exercise 4.6.2).

4.2.2 Iterative Construction of Routing Tables

The solution we have just seen requires that each entity has locally available enough storage to store the entire map of the network. If this is not the case, the problem of constructing the routing tables is more difficult to resolve.

Several traditional *sequential* methods are based on an *iterative* approach. Initially, each entity x knows only its neighboring information: for each neighbor y, the entity knows the cost $\theta(x, y)$ of reaching it using the direct link (x, y). On the basis of this initial information, x can construct an *approximation* of its routing table. This imperfect table is usually called *distance vector*, and in it the cost for those destinations x knows nothing about will be set to ∞. For example, the initial distance vector for node s in the network of Figure 4.1 is shown in Table 4.2.

This approximation of the routing table will be refined, and eventually corrected, through a sequence of iterations. In each iteration, every entity communicates its current distance vector with all its neighbors. On the basis of the received information, each entity updates its current information, replacing paths in its own routing table if the neighbors have found better routes.

How can an entity x determine if a route is better ? The answer is very simple: when, in an iteration, x is told by a neighbor y that there exists a path π_2 from y to z with cost g_2, x checks in its current table the path π_1 to z and its cost g_1, as well as the cost $\theta(x, y)$. If $\theta(x, y) + g_2 < g_1$, then going directly to y and then using π_2 to reach z is less expensive than going to z through the path π_1 currently in the table. Among several better choices, obviously x will select the best one.

TABLE 4.2: Initial Approximation of RT(s)

Routing Destination	Shortest Path	Cost
h	(s, h)	1
k	?	∞
c	(s, c)	10
d	?	∞
e	(s, e)	5
f	?	∞

TABLE 4.3: Initial Distance Vectors

	s	h	k	c	d	e	f
s	-	1	∞	10	∞	5	∞
h	1	-	3	∞	∞	∞	∞
k	∞	3	-	∞	∞	3	5
c	10	∞	∞	-	2	∞	∞
d	∞	∞	∞	2	-	8	∞
e	5	∞	3	∞	8	-	3
f	∞	∞	5	∞	∞	3	-

Specifically, let $V_y^i[z]$ denote the cost of the "best" path from y to z known to y in iteration i; this information is contained in the distance vector sent by y to all its neighbors at the beginning of iteration $i + 1$. After sending its own distance vector and upon receiving the distance vectors of all its neighbors, entity x computes

$$w[z] = \text{Min}_{y \in N(x)}(\theta(x, y) + V_y^i[z])$$

for each destination z. If $w[z] < V_x^i[z]$, then the new cost and the corresponding path to z is chosen, replacing the current selection.

Why should interaction just with the neighbors be sufficient follows from the fact that the cost $\gamma_a(b)$ of the shortest path from a to b has the following defining property:

Property 4.2.1 $\gamma_a(b) = \begin{cases} 0 & \text{if } a = b \\ \text{Min}_{w \in N(a)} \{\theta(a, w) + \gamma_w(b)\} & \text{otherwise.} \end{cases}$

The Protocol *Iterated_Construction* based on this strategy converges to the correct information and will do so after at most $n - 1$ iterations (Exercise 4.6.8). For example, in the graph of Figure 4.1, the process converges to the correct routing tables after only two iterations; see Tables 4.3–4.5 : for each entity, only the cost information for every destination is displayed.

The main advantage of this process is that the amount of *storage* required at an entity is proportional to the size of the routing table and *not* to the map of the entire system.

TABLE 4.4: Distance Vectors After First Iteration

	s	h	k	c	d	e	f
s	-	1	4	10	12	5	8
h	1	-	3	11	∞	6	8
k	4	3	-	∞	11	3	5
c	10	11	∞	-	2	10	∞
d	12	∞	11	2	-	8	11
e	5	6	3	10	8	-	3
f	8	8	5	∞	11	3	-

TABLE 4.5: Distance Vectors After Second Iteration

	s	h	k	c	d	e	f
s	-	1	4	10	12	5	8
h	1	-	3	11	13	6	8
k	4	3	-	13	11	3	5
c	10	11	13	-	2	10	13
d	12	13	11	2	-	8	11
e	5	6	3	10	8	-	3
f	8	8	5	13	11	3	-

Let us analyze the message and time costs of the associated protocol.

In each iteration, an entity sends its distance vector containing costs and path information; actually, it is not necessary to send the entire path but only the first hop in it (see discussion in Section 4.4). In other words, in each iteration, an entity x needs to send n items of information to its $\deg(x)$ neighbors. Thus, in total, an iteration requires $2nm$ messages. As this process terminates after at most $n - 1$ iterations, we have

$$\mathbf{M}[\textit{Iterated\_Construction}] = 2\,(n - 1)\,n\,m. \qquad (4.2)$$

That is, this approach is more expensive than the one based on constructing all the maps; it does, however, require less local storage.

As for the time complexity, let $\tau(n)$ denote the amount of ideal time required to transmit n items of information to the same neighbor; then

$$\mathbf{T}[\textit{Iterated\_Construction}] = (n - 1)\,\tau(n). \qquad (4.3)$$

Clearly, if the system allows *very long messages*, the protocol can be executed with fewer messages. In particular, if messages containing $O(n)$ items of information (instead of $O(1)$) are possible, then in each iteration an entity can transmit its entire distance vector to a neighbor with just *one* message and $\tau(n) = 1$. The entire process can thus be accomplished with $O(n, m)$ messages and the time complexity would then be just $n - 1$.

4.2.3 Constructing Shortest-Path Spanning Tree

The first solution we have seen, protocol *Map_Gossip*, requires that each entity has locally available enough storage to store the entire map of the network. The second solution, protocol *Iterative_Construction*, avoids this problem, but it does so at the expense of a substantially increased amount of messages.

Our goal is to design a protocol that, without increasing the local storage requirements, constructs the routing tables with a smaller amount of communication. Fortunately, there is an important property that will help us in achieving this goal.

Consider the paths contained in the full routing table RT(s) of an entity s, for example, the ones in Table 4.1.These paths define a subgraph of the network (as not every link is included). This subgraph is special: It is connected, contains all the nodes, and does not have cycles (see Figure 4.1 where the subgraph links are in bold); in other words,

it is a spanning tree!

It is called the *shortest path spanning tree rooted in* s(PT(s)),   sometimes also known as the *sink tree* of s.

This fact is important because it tells us that, to construct the routing table RT(s) of s, we just need to construct the shortest path spanning tree PT(s).

Protocol Design   To construct the shortest path spanning tree PT(s), we can adapt a classical *serial* strategy for constructing PT(s) starting from the source s:

Serial Strategy

- We are given a connected fragment T of PT(s), containing s (initially, T will be composed of just s).
- Consider now all the links going outside of T (i.e., to nodes not yet in T). To each such link (x, y) associate the value $v(x, y) = \gamma_s(x) + \theta(x, y)$, that is, $v(x, y)$ is the cost of reaching y from the source s by first going to x (through a shortest path) and then using the link (x, y) to reach y.
- Add to T the link (a, b) for which $v(a, b)$ is minimum; in case of a tie, choose the one leading to the node with the lexicographically smallest name.

The reason this strategy works is because of the following property:

Property 4.2.2   *Let T and (a, b) be as defined in the serial strategy. Then $T \cup (a, b)$ is a connected fragment T of* PT(s).

That is, the new tree, obtained by adding the chosen (a, b) to T, is also a connected fragment of PT(s), containing s, and it is clearly larger than T. In other words, using this strategy, the shortest path spanning-tree PT(s) will be constructed, starting from s, by adding the appropriate links, one at the time.

The algorithm based on this strategy will be a sequence of *iterations* started from the root. In each iteration, the outgoing link (a, b) with minimum cost $v(a, b)$ is chosen; the link (a, b) and the node b are added to the fragment, and a new iteration is started. The process terminates when the fragment includes all the nodes.

Our goal is now to implement this algorithm efficiently in a *distributed* way.

First of all, let us consider what a node y in the fragment T knows. Definitely y knows which of its links are part of the current fragment; it also knows the length $\gamma_s(y)$ of the shortest path from the source s to it.

IMPORTANT. Let us assume for the moment that y also knows which of its links are *outgoing* (i.e., lead to nodes outside of the current fragment) and which are *internal*.

In this case, to find the outgoing link (a, b) with minimum cost $v(a, b)$ is rather simple, and the entire iteration is composed of four easy steps:

Iteration

1. The root s broadcasts in T the start of the new iteration.
2. Upon receiving the start, each entity x in the current fragment T computes locally $v(x, y) = \gamma_s(x) + \theta(x, y)$ for each of its outgoing incident links (x, y); it then selects among them the link $e = (x, y')$ for which $v(x, y')$ is minimized.
3. The overall minimum $v(a, b)$ among all the locally selected $v(e)$'s is computed at s, using a minimum-finding for (rooted) trees (e.g., see Section 2.6.7), and the corresponding link (a, b) is chosen as the one to be added to the fragment.
4. The root s notifies b of the selection; the link (a, b) is added to the spanning-tree; b computes $\gamma_s(b)$, and s is notified of the end of the iteration.

Each iteration can be performed efficiently, in $O(n)$ messages, as each operation (broadcast, min-finding, notifications) is performed on a tree of at most n nodes.

There are a couple of problems that need to be addressed. A small problem is how can b compute $\gamma_s(b)$. This value is actually determined at s by the algorithm in this iteration; hence, s can communicate it to b when notifying it of its selection.

A more difficult problem regards the knowledge of which links are *outgoing* (i.e., they lead to nodes outside of the current fragment); we have assumed that an entity in T has such a knowledge about its links. But how can such a knowledge be ensured?

As described, during an iteration, messages are sent only on the links of T and on the link selected in that iteration. This means that the outgoing links are all *unexplored* (i.e., no message has been sent or received on them). As we do not know which are outgoing, an entity could perform the computation of step 2 for each of its *unexplored* incident links and select the minimum among those. Consider for example the graph of Figure 4.2(a) and assume that we have already constructed the fragment shown in Figure 4.2(b). There are four unexplored links incident to the fragment (shown as leading to square boxes), each with its value (shown in the corresponding square box); the link (s, e) among them has minimum value and is chosen; it is outgoing and it is added to the segment. The new segment is shown in Figure 4.2(c) together with the unexplored links incident on it.

However, not all unexplored links are outgoing: An unexplored link might be *internal* (i.e., leading to a node already in the fragment), and selecting such a link would be an error. For example, in Figure 4.2(c), the unexplored link (e, k) has value $v(e, k) = 7$, which is minimum among the unexplored edges incident on the fragment, and hence would be chosen; however, node e is already in the fragment.

We could allow for errors: We choose among the unexplored links and, if the link (in our example: (e, k)) selected by the root s in step 3 turns out to be internal

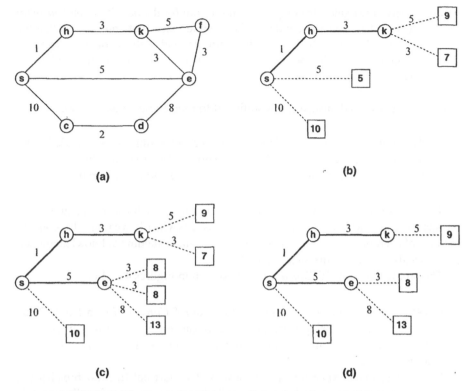

FIGURE 4.2: Determining the next link to be added to the fragment.

(*k* would find out in step 4 when the notification arrives), we eliminate that link from consideration and select another one. The drawback of this approach is its overall cost. In fact, since initially all links are unexplored, we might have to perform the entire selection process for every link. This means that the cost will be $O(nm)$, which in the worst case is $O(n^3)$: a high price to construct a single routing table.

A more efficient approach is to add a mechanism so that no error will occur. Fortunately, this can be achieved simply and efficiently as follows.

When a node *b* becomes part of the tree, it sends a message to all its neighbors notifying them that it is now part of the tree. Upon receiving such a message, a neighbor *c* knows that this link must no longer be used when performing shortest path calculations for the tree. As a side effect, in our example, when the link (s, e) is chosen in Figure 4.2(b), node *e* already knows that the link (e, k) leads to a node already in the fragment; thus such a link is not considered, as shown in Figure 4.2(d).

RECALL. We have used a similar strategy with the protocol for depth-first traversal, to decrease its time complexity.

IMPORTANT. It is necessary for *b* to ensure that all its neighbors have received its message before a new iteration is started. Otherwise, due to time delays, a neighbor *c* might receive the request to compute the minimum for the next iteration *before* the message from *b* has even arrived; thus, it is possible that *c* (not knowing yet that *b* is part of the tree) chooses its link to *b* as its minimum, and such a choice is selected as the overall minimum by the root *s*. In other words, it is still possible that an internal link is selected during an iteration.

Summarizing, to avoid mistakes, it is sufficient to modify rule 4 as follows:

4.′ The root *s* sends an *Expand* message to *b* and the link (*a*, *b*) is added to the spanning tree; *b* computes $\gamma_s(b)$, sends a notification to its neighbors, waits for their acknowledgment, and then notifies *s* of the end of the iteration.

This ensures that there will be only $n - 1$ iterations, each adding a new node to the spanning tree, with a total cost of $O(n^2)$ messages. Clearly we must also consider the cost of each node notifying its neighbors (and them sending acknowledgments), but this adds only $O(m)$ messages in total.

The protocol, called *PT_Construction*, is shown in Figures 4.3–4.6.

Analysis   Let us now analyze the cost of protocol *PT_Construction* in details. There are two basic activities being performed: the expansion of the current fragment of the tree and the announcement (with acknowledgments) of the addition of the new node to the fragment.

Let us consider the expansion first. It consists of a "start-up" (the root broadcasting the *Start_Iteration* message), a "convergecast" (the minimum value is collected at the root using the *MinValue* messages), two "notifications" (the root notifies the new node using the *Expansion* message, and the new node notifies the root using the *Iteration_Completed* message). Each of these operations is performed on the current fragment, which is a tree, rooted in the source. In particular, the start-up and the convergecast operations each cost only one message on every link; in the notifications, messages are sent only on the links in path from the source to the new node, and there will be only one message in each direction. Thus, in total, on each link of the tree constructed so far, there will be at most four messages due to the expansion; two messages will also be sent on the new link added in this expansion. Thus, in the expansion at iteration *i*, at most $4(n_i - 1) + 2$ messages will be sent, where n_i is the size of the current tree. As the tree is expanded by one node at the time, $n_i = i$. In fact, initially there is only the source; then the fragment is composed of the source and a neighbor, and so on. Thus, the total number of messages due to the expansion is

$$\sum_{i=1}^{n-1}(4(n_i - 1) + 2) = \sum_{i=1}^{n-1}(4i - 2) = 2n(n - 1) - 2(n - 1) = 2n^2 - 4n + 2.$$

The cost due to announcements and acknowledgments is simple to calculate: Each node will send a *Notify* message to all its neighbors when it becomes part of the tree

PROTOCOL PT_Construction.

- States: $\mathcal{S} = \{$ INITIATOR, IDLE, AWAKE, ACTIVE, WAITING_FOR_ACK, COMPUTING, DONE $\}$;
  $\mathcal{S}_{INIT} = \{$ INITIATOR,IDLE $\}$; $\mathcal{S}_{TERM} = \{$ DONE $\}$.
- Restrictions: **IR** ; UI.

INITIATOR
```
        Spontaneously
        begin
              source:= true;
              my_distance:= 0;
              ackcount:= |N(x)|;
              send(Notify) to N(x);
        end

        Receiving(Ack)
        begin
              ackcount:= ackcount - 1;
              if ackcount = 0 then
                 iteration:= 1;
                 v(x, y):= MIN{v(x, z) : z ∈ N(x)};
                 path_length:= v(x, y);
                 Children:={y};
                 send(Expand, iteration, path_length) to y;
                 Unvisited:= N(x) - {y};
                 become ACTIVE;
              endif
        end
```

IDLE
```
        Receiving(Notify)
        begin
              Unvisited:= N(x) - {sender};
              send(Ack) to sender;
              become AWAKE;
        end
```

AWAKE
```
        Receiving(Expand, iteration*, path_value*)
        begin
              my_distance:= path_value* ;
              parent:= sender;
              Children:= ∅;
              if |N(x)| > 1 then
                 send(Notify) to N(x) - {sender};
                 ackcounter:= |N(x)| - 1;
                 become WAITING_FOR_ACK;
              else
                 send(IterationCompleted) to parent;
                 become ACTIVE;
              endif
        end
```

FIGURE 4.3: Protocol *PT-Construction* (I)

```
AWAKE
          Receiving (Notify)
          begin
                Unvisited:= Unvisited-{sender};
                send(Ack) to sender;
          end

WAITING_FOR_ACK
                Receiving (Ack)
                begin
                      ackcount:= ackcount - 1;
                      if ackcount = 0 then
                        send(IterationCompleted) to parent;
                        become ACTIVE;
                      endif
                end


ACTIVE
                Receiving (Iteration_Completed)
                begin
                      if not(source) then
                        send(Iteration_Completed) to parent;
                      else
                        iteration:= iteration + 1;
                        send(Start_Iteration, iteration) to children;
                        Compute_Local_Minimum;
                        childcount:= 0;
                        become COMPUTING;
                      endif
                end

                Receiving(Start_Iteration, iteration*)
                begin
                      iteration:= iteration*;
                      Compute_Local_Minimum;
                      if children = Ø then
                        send(MinValue, minpath) to parent;
                      else
                        send(Start_Iteration, iteration) to children;
                        childcount:=0;
                        become COMPUTING;
                      endif
                end
```

FIGURE 4.4: Protocol *PT-Construction* (II)

and receives an *Ack* from each of them. Thus, the total number of messages due to the notifications is

$$2 \sum_{x \in V} |N(x)| = 2 \sum_{x \in V} \deg(x) = 4m.$$

To complete the analysis, we need to consider the final broadcast of the *Termination* message, which is performed on the constructed tree; this will add $n - 1$ messages to the total, yielding the following:

$$\mathbf{M}[PT\_Construction] \leq 2n^2 + 4m - 3n + 1 \tag{4.4}$$

ACTIVE

```
        Receiving (Expand, iteration*, path_value*)
        begin
            send (Expand, iteration*, path_value*) to exit;
            if exit = mychoice then
                Children := Children ∪ {mychoice};
                Unvisited := Unvisited − {mychoice};
            endif
        end


        Receiving (Notify)
        begin
            Unvisited:= Unvisited −{sender};
            send (Ack) to sender;
        end


        Receiving (Terminate)
        begin
            send (Terminate) to children;
            become DONE;
        end
```

COMPUTING

```
        Receiving (MinValue, path_value*)
        begin
            if path_value < minpath then
                minpath:= path_value*;
                exit:= sender;
            endif
            childcount :=childcount + 1;
            if childcount = |Children| then
                if not(source) then
                    send (MinValue, minpath) to parent;
                    become ACTIVE;
                else
                    Check_for_Termination;
                endif
            endif
        end
```

FIGURE 4.5: Protocol *PT_Construction* (III)

By adding a little bookkeeping, the protocol can be used to construct the routing table RT(s) of the source (Exercise 4.6.13). Hence, we have a protocol that constructs the routing table of a node using $O(n^2)$ messages.

We will see later how more efficient solutions can be derived for the special case when all the links have the same cost (or, alternatively, there is no cost on the links).

Note that we have made no assumptions other than that the costs are non-negative; in particular, we did *not* assume first in first out (FIFO) channels (i.e., message ordering).

4.2.4 Constructing All-Pairs Shortest Paths

Protocol *PT_Construction* allows us to construct the shortest-path tree of a node, and thus to construct the routing table of that entity. To solve the original problem of constructing all the routing table, also known as *all-pairs shortest-paths construction*,

```
Procedure Check_for_Termination
begin
    if minpath= inf then
        send (Terminate) to Children;
        become DONE;
    else
        send (Expand, iteration, minpath) to exit;
        become ACTIVE;
    endif
end


Procedure Compute_Local_Minimum
begin
    if Unvisited = Ø then
        minpath:= inf;
    else
        link_length:= v(x, y) = MIN{v(x, z) : z ∈ Unvisited};
        minpath:= my_distance + link_length;
        mychoice:= exit:= y;
    endif
end
```

FIGURE 4.6: Procedures used by protocol *PT_Construction*

this process must be repeated for all nodes. The complexity of resulting protocol *PT_All* follows immediately from equation 4.4:

$$\mathbf{M}[PT\_All] \leq 2n^3 - 3n^2 + 4(m-1)n \tag{4.5}$$

The costs of protocols *Map_Gossip*, *Iterative_Construction*, and *PT_All* are shown in Figure 4.7. Definitively better than protocol *Iterative_Construction*, protocol *PT_All* matches the worst case cost of *Map_Gossip* without requiring large amounts of local storage. Hence, it is an efficient solution.

It is clear that some information computed when constructing $PT(x)$ can be reused in the construction of $PT(y)$. For example, the shortest path from x to y is just the reverse of the one from y to x (under the bidirectional links assumption we are using); hence, we just need to determine one of them. Even stronger is the so-called *optimality principle*:

Property 4.2.3 *If a node x is in the shortest path π from a to b, then π is also a fragment of* $PT(x)$

Hence, once a shortest path π has been computed for the shortest path tree of an entity, this path can be added to the shortest path tree of all the entities in the path. So, in the example of Figure 4.1, the path $(s, e)(e, f)$ in $PT(s)$ will also be a part of

Algorithm	Cost	restrictions
Map_Gossip	$O(n\,m)$	$\Omega(m)$ local storage
Iterative_Construction	$O(n^2\,m)$	
PT_All	$O(n^3)$	
SparserGossip	$O(n^2 \log n)$	

FIGURE 4.7: Constructing *all* shortest path routing tables.

PT(e) and PT(f). However, to date, it is not clear how this fact can be used to derive a more efficient protocol for constructing all the routing tables.

Constructing a Sparser Subgraph   Interestingly, the number of messages can be brought down from $O(n^3)$ to $O(n^2 \log n)$ not by cleverly exploiting information but rather by cleverly constructing a spanning subgraph of the network, called *sparser* and then simulating the execution of *Map_Gossip* on it. To understand this subgraph, we need some terminology.

Given a subset $V' \subseteq V$ of the nodes, we call the *eccentricity* of $x \in V'$ in V' its largest distance from the other nodes of V', that is, $r(x, V') = \max_{y \in V'}\{d_G(x, y)\}$; then $r(V') = \max_{x \in V'}\{r(x, V')\}$ is called the *radius* of V'. The *density* of $x \in V'$ in V' instead is the number of its neighbors that are in V', that is, den$(x, V') = |N(x) \cup V'|$; the density of V' is the sum of the densities of all its nodes: den$(V') = \sum_{x \in V'}$ den(x, V').

Given a collection A of subsets of the nodes, the radius $r(A)$ of A will be just the largest among the radii of those subsets; the density den(A) will be just the sum of the densities of those subsets. A (a, b)-*sparser* is just a partition of the set V of nodes into subsets such that its radius is $r(S) = a$ and its density is den$(S) = b$.

The basic idea is to first of all

1. construct a sparser $V' = \langle V'_1, \ldots, V'_k \rangle$;
2. elect a leader x_i in each of its sets V'_i;
3. establish a path connecting the two leaders of each pair of neighboring subsets.

Then the execution of the protocol in G is simulated in the sparser. What this means is that

4. each leader executes the algorithm for each node in its subset;
5. whenever in the algorithm a message is sent from a node in V'_i to a node in V'_j, the message is sent by x_i to x_j.

An interesting consequence of (5) above is that the cost of a node u sending a message to all its neighbors, when simulated in the sparser, will depend on the number of subsets in which u has neighbors as well as on the distance between the corresponding leaders.

This means that for the simulation to be efficient, the radius should be small, $r(V') = O(\log n)$, and the density at most linear. den$(S) = O(n)$. Fortunately we have (Exercise 4.6.15):

Property 4.2.4   *Any connected graph G of n nodes has a* (log n. n)-*sparser.*

The existence of this good sparser is not enough; we must be able to construct it with a reasonable amount of messages. Fortunately, this is also possible (Exercise

4.6.16). When constructing it, there are several important details that must be taken care; in particular, the paths between the centers must be uniquely determined.

Once all of this is done, we must then define the set of rules (Exercise 4.6.17) to simulate protocol *MapGossip*. At this point, the resulting protocol, called *SparserGossip*, yields the desired performance

$$\mathbf{M}[SparserGossip] = O(n^2 \log n). \tag{4.6}$$

Using Long Messages   In systems that allow *very long messages*, not surprisingly the problem can be solved with fewer messages. For example, if messages can contain $O(n)$ items of information (instead of $O(1)$), *all* the shortest path trees can be constructed with just $O(n^2)$ messages (Exercise 4.6.18). If messages can contain $O(n^2)$ items, then *any graph problem* including the construction of all shortest path trees can be solved using $O(n)$ messages once a leader has been elected (requiring at least $O(m + n \log n)$ normal messages). A summary of all these results is shown in Figure 4.7.

4.2.5 Min-Hop Routing

Consider the case when all links have the same cost (or alternatively, there are no costs associated to the links), that is, $\theta(a, b) = \theta$ for all $(a, b) \in E$.

This case is special in several respects. In particular, observe that the shortest path from a to b will have cost $\gamma_a(b) = \theta \, d_G(a, b)$, where $d_G(a, b)$ is the distance (in number of hops) of a from b in G; in other words, the cost of a path will depend solely on the number of hops (i.e., the number of links) in that path. Hence, the shortest path between two nodes will be the one with minimum hops. For these reasons, routing in this situation is called *min-hop routing*.

An interesting consequence is that the shortest path spanning tree of a node coincides with its *breadth-first spanning tree*. In other words, a breadth-first spanning tree rooted in a node is the shortest path spanning tree of that node when all links have the same cost.

Protocol *PT_Construction* works for any choice of the costs, provided they are non-negative; so it constructs a breadth-first spanning tree if all the costs are the same. However, we can take advantage of the fact that all links have the same costs to obtain a more efficient protocol. Let us see how.

Breadth-First Spanning-Tree Construction   Without any loss of generality, let us assume that $\theta = 1$; thus, $\gamma_s(a) = d_G(s, a)$.

We can use the same strategy of protocol *PT_Construction* of starting from s and successively expanding the fragment; only, instead of choosing one link (and thus one node) at the time, we can choose several simultaneously: In the first step, s chooses all the nodes at distance 1 (its neighbors); in the second step, s chooses simultaneously all the nodes at distance 2; in general, in step i, s chooses simultaneously all the nodes at distance i; notice that before step i, none of the nodes at distance i was a part of the fragment. Clearly, the problem is to determine, in step i, which nodes are at distance i from s.

Observe this very interesting property: All the neighbors of s are at distance 1 from s; all their neighbors (not at distance 1 from s) are at distance 2 from s; in general,

Property 4.2.5 *If a node is at distance i from s, then its neighbors are at distance either $i - 1$ or i or $i + 1$ from s.*

This means that once the nodes at distance i from s have been chosen (and become part of the fragment), we need to consider only their neighbors to determine which nodes are at distance $i + 1$.

So the protocol, which we shall call BF, is rather simple. Initially, the root s sends a "start iteration 1" message to each neighbor indicating the first iteration of the algorithm and considers them its children. Each recipient marks its distance as 1, marks the sender as its *parent*, and sends an acknowledgment back to the parent. The tree is now composed of the root s and its neighbors, which are all at distance 1 from s.

In general, after iteration i all the nodes at distance up to i are part of the tree. Furthermore, each node at distance i knows which of its neighbors are at distance $i - 1$ (Exercise 4.6.19).

In iteration $i + 1$, the root *broadcasts* on the current tree a "start iteration $i + 1$" message. Once this message reaches a node x at distance i, it sends a "explore $i + 1$" message to its neighbors that are *not* at distance $i - 1$ (recall, x knows which they are) and waits for a reply from each of them. These neighbors are either at distance i like x itself, or at $i + 1$; those at distance i are already in the tree and so do not need to be included. Those at distance $i + 1$ must be attached to the tree; however, each must be attached only once (otherwise we create a cycle and do not form a tree; see Figure 4.8).

When a neighbor y receives the "Explore" message, the content of its reply will depend on whether or not y is already part of the tree. If y is not part of the tree, it now knows that it is at distance $i + 1$ from s; it then marks the sender as its *parent*, sends a positive acknowledgment to it, and becomes part of the tree. If y is part of the tree (even if it just happened in this iteration), it will reply with a negative acknowledgment.

When x receives the reply from y, if the reply is positive, it will mark y as a *child*, otherwise, it will mark y as already in the tree. Once all the replies have been received, it participates in a *convergecast* notifying the root that the iteration has been completed.

Cost Let us now examine the cost of protocol *BF*. Denote by n_i the number of nodes at distance at most i from s. In each iteration, there are three operations involving communication: (1) the broadcast of "Start"on the tree constructed so far; (2) the sending of "Explore" messages sent by the nodes at distance i, and the corresponding replies; and (3) the convergecast to notify the root of the termination of the iteration.

Consider first the cost of operation (2), that is, the cost of the "Explore" messages and the corresponding replies. Consider a node x at distance i. As already mentioned, its neighbors are at distance either $i - 1$ or i or $i + 1$. The neighbors at distance $i - 1$

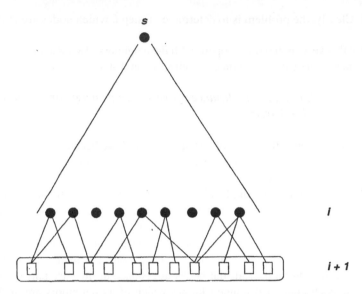

FIGURE 4.8: Protocol *BF* expands an entire level in each iteration.

sent an "Explore" message to x in stage $i - 1$, so x sent a reply to each of them. In stage i x sent an "Explore" message to all its other neighbors. Hence, in total, x sent just one message (either "Explore" or reply) to each of its neighbors. This means that in total, the number of "Explore" and "Reply" messages is

$$\sum_{x \in V} \| N(x) \| = 2m.$$

We will consider now the overall cost of operations (1) and (3). In iteration $i + 1$, both broadcast and convergecast are performed on the tree constructed in iteration i, thus costing $n_i - 1$ messages each, for a total of $2n_i - 2$ messages. Therefore, the total cost will be

$$\sum_{1 \le i < r(s)} 2(n_i - 1),$$

where $r(s)$ denotes the eccentricity of s (i.e., the hight of the breadth-first spanning tree of s).

Summarizing

$$M[BF] \le 2m + \sum_{1 \le i < r(s)} 2(n_i - 1) \le 2m + 2(n-1)\,d(G), \qquad (4.7)$$

where $d(G)$ is the diameter of the graph. We know that $n_i < n_{i+1}$ and that $n_{r(s)} = n$ in any network G and for any root s, but the actual values depend on the nature of G

and on the position of s. For example, in the *complete graph*, $r(s) = 1$ for any s, so the entire construction is completed in the first iteration; however, $m = n(n-1)/2$; hence the cost will be

$$n(n-1) + 2(n-1) = n^2 + n - 2.$$

On the contrary, if G is a *line* and s is an endpoint of the line, $r(s) = n - 1$ and in each iteration we only add one node (i.e., $n_i = i$); thus $\sum_{1 \leq i < r(s)} 2(n_i - 1) = n^2 - 4n + 3$; however, $m = n - 1$; hence the cost will be

$$2(n-1) + n^2 - 4n + 3 = n^2 - 2n + 1.$$

As for the time complexity, in iteration i, the "Start" messages travel from the root s to the nodes at distance $i - 1$, hence arriving there after $i - 1$ time units; therefore, the nodes at distance i will receive the "Explore i" message after i time units. At that time, they will start the convergecast to notify the root of the termination of the iteration; this process requires exactly i time units. In other words, iteration i will cost exactly $2i$ time units. Summarizing,

$$\mathbf{T}[BF] = 2 \sum_{1 \leq i \leq r(s)} i = r(s)(r(s) + 1) \leq d(G)^2 + d(G). \tag{4.8}$$

Multiple Layers: An Improved Protocol   To improve the costs, we must understand the structure of protocol *BF*. We know that the execution of protocol *BF* is a sequence of iterations, started by the root.

Each iteration $i + 1$ of protocol *BF* can be thought of as composed of three different phases:

1. *Initialization*: the root node broadcasts the "start iteration $i + 1$" along the already constructed tree, which will reach the leaves (i.e., the nodes at distance i from the root).
2. *Expansion*: in this phase, which is started by the leaves, new nodes (i.e., all those of level $i + 1$) are added to the tree forming a larger fragment.
3. *Termination*: the root is notified of the end of this iteration using a convergecast on the new tree.

Initialization and termination are bookkeeping operations that allow the root to somehow synchronize the execution of the algorithm, iteration by iteration. For this reason, the two of them, together, are also called *synchronization*. Each synchronization costs $O(n)$ messages (as it is done on a tree). Hence, this activity alone costs

$$O(nL)$$

messages where L is the number of iterations.

In the original protocol *BF*, we expand the tree one level at the time; hence $L = d(G)$ and the total cost for synchronization alone is $O(n \, d(G))$ messages (see

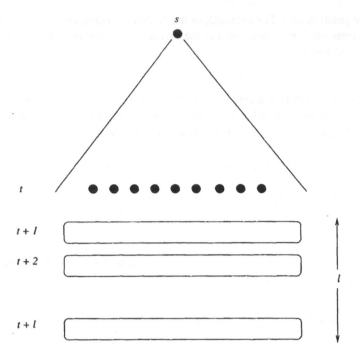

FIGURE 4.9: Protocol *BF_Levels* expands *l* levels in each iteration.

expression 4.7). This means that to reduce the cost of synchronization, we need to decrease the number of iterations. To do so, we need each iteration to grow the current tree by more than a single level, that is, we need each expansion phase to add several levels to the current fragment.

Let us see how to expand the current tree by $l \geq 1$ levels, in a single iteration, efficiently (see Figure 4.9). Assume that initially each node $x \neq r$ has a variable $level_x = \infty$, while $level_r = 0$.

Let t be the current level of the leaves; each leaf will start the exploration by sending *Explore*$(t + 1, l)$ to its still unexplored neighbors. In general, the expansion messages will be of the form *Explore*(*level, counter*), where *level* is the next level to be assigned and *counter* denotes how many more levels should be expanded by the node receiving the message.

When a node x not yet in the tree receives its first expansion message, say *Explore*(j, k) from neighbor y, it will *accept* the message, consider the sender y as its parent in the tree and set its own level to be j. It then considers the number k of levels still to be expanded. If $k = 0$, x sends immediately a *Positive*(j) reply to its parent y. Instead, if $k > 0$, x will send *Explore*$(j + 1, k - 1)$ to all its other neighbors and wait for their reply: Those that reply *Positive*$(j + 1)$ are considered its children, those that reply *Negative*$(j + 1)$ are considered not-children; if/when all have sent a reply with level $j + 1$, x sends a *Positive*(j) reply to its parent y.

Note that this first "Explore" message will not necessarily determine x's parent or level in the final tree; in fact, it is possible that x will receive later an $Explore(j', k')$ message with a smaller level $j' < j$ from a neighbor z. (Note: it might even be possible that $y = z$.) What we will do in this case is to have x "trow away" the work already done and "start from scratch" with the new information: x will accept the message, consider z its parent, set its level to j', send $Explore(j' + 1, k' - 1)$ to all its other neighbors (assuming $k' > 0$), and wait for their reply. Note that x might have to "trow away" work already done more than once during an iteration. How many times ? It is not difficult to figure out that it can happen at most $t - j + 1$ times, where j is the first level it receives in this iteration (Exercise 4.6.22).

We still have to specify under what conditions will a node x send a negative reply to a received message $Explore(j, k)$; the rule is simple: x will reply $Negative(j)$ if no shorter path is found from the root s to x, that is, if $j \geq level_x$.

A more detailed description of the expansion phase of the protocol, which we will call *BF_Levels*, is shown in Figure 4.10, describing the behavior of a node x not part of the current fragment. As mentioned, the expansion phase is started by the leaves of the current fragment, which we will call *sources* of this phase, upon receiving the *start iteration* message from the root. Each source will then send $Explore(t + 1, l)$ to their unexplored neighbors, where t is the level of the leaves and l (a design parameter) is the number of levels that will be added to the current fragment in this iteration. The *terminating phase* also is started by the sources (i.e., the leaves of the already existing fragment), upon receiving a reply to all their expansion messages.

When x receives $Explore(j, k)$ from its neighbor y:

1. If $j < level_x$, a shorter path from the root s to x has been found.
    (a) If x already has a parent, then x disregards all previous information (including the identity of its parent).
    (b) x considers y to be its parent, and sets $level_x = j$.
    (c) If $k > 0$, x sends $Explore(j + 1, k - 1)$ to all its neighbors except its parent. If $k = 0$, then a positive reply $Positive(j)$ is sent to the parent y.
2. Let $j > level_x$. In this case, this is not a shorter path to x; x replies with a negative acknowledgment $Negative(j)$.

When x receives a reply from its neighbor z:

1. If the level of the reply is $(level_x + 1)$ then:
    (a) if the reply is $Negative(level_x + 1)$, then x considers z a *non-child*.
    (b) if the reply is $Positive(level_x + 1)$ then x considers z a *child*.
    (c) If, with this message, x has now received a reply with level $(level_x + 1)$ from all its neighbors except its parent, then it sends $Positive(level_x)$ to its parent.
2. If the level of the reply is not $(level_x + 1)$ then the message is discarded.

FIGURE 4.10: Exploration phase of *BF_Levels*: x is not part of the current fragment

Correctness During the extension phase all the nodes at distance at most $t + l$ from the root are indeed reached, as can be easily verified (Exercise 4.6.23). Thus, to prove the correctness of the protocol, we need just to prove that those nodes will be attached to the existing fragment at the proper level.

We will prove this by induction on the levels. First of all, all the nodes at level $t + 1$ are neighbors of the sources and thus each will receive at least one *Explore*$(t + 1, l)$ message; when this happens, regardless of whatever has happened before, each will set its level to $t + 1$; as this is the smallest level that they can ever receive, their level will not change during the rest of the iteration.

Let it be true for the nodes up to level $t + k$, $1 \leq k \leq l - 1$; we will show that it also holds for the nodes in level $t + k + 1$. Let π be the path of length $t + k + 1$ from s to x and let u be the neighbor of x in this path; by definition, u is at level $t + k$ and, by inductive hypothesis, it has correctly set $(level_u) = t + k$. When this happened, u sent a message *Explore*$(t + k + 1, l - k - 1)$ to all its neighbors, except its parent. As x is clearly not u's parent, it will eventually receive this message; when this happens, x will correctly set $(level_x) = t + k + 1$. So we must show that the expansion phase will not terminate before x receives this message. Focus again on node u; it will not send a positive acknowledgment to its parent (and thus the phase can not terminate) until it receives a reply from all its other neighbors, including x. As, to reply, x must first receive the message, x will correctly set its level during the phase.

Cost To determine the cost of protocol *BF_Levels*, we need to analyze the cost of the synchronization and of the expansion phases.

The cost of a synchronization, as we discussed earlier, is at most $2(n - 1)$ messages, as both the initialization broadcast and the termination convergecast are performed on the currently available tree. Hence, the total cost of all synchronization activities depends on the number of *iterations*. This quantity is easily determined. As there are *radius*$(r) < d(G)$ levels, and we add l levels in every iteration, except in the last where we add the rest, the number of iterations is at most $\lceil d(G)/l \rceil$. This means that the total amount of messages due to synchronization is at most

$$2(n - 1) \left\lceil \frac{d(G)}{l} \right\rceil \leq 2 \frac{(n - 1)^2}{l}. \tag{4.9}$$

Let us now analyze the cost of the expansion phase in iteration i, $1 \leq i \leq \lceil d(G)/l \rceil$. Observe that in this phase, only the nodes in the levels $L(i) = \{(i - 1)l + 1, (i - 1)l + 2, \ldots, il - 1, il\}$ as well as the sources (i.e., the nodes at level $(i - 1)l$) will be involved, and messages will only be sent on the m_i links between them. The messages sent during this phase will be just *Explore*$(t + 1, l)$, *Explore*$(t + 2, l - 1)$, *Explore*$(t + 3, l - 2)$, $\ldots$, *Explore*$(t + l, 0)$, and the corresponding replies will be *Positive*(j) or *Negative*(j), $t + 1 \leq j \leq t + l$.

A node in one of the levels in $L(i)$ sends to its neighbors at most one of each of those *Explore* messages; hence there will be on each of edge at most $2l$ *Explore* messages (l in each direction), for a total of $2lm_i$. As for each *Explore* there is at most one reply, the total number of messages sent in this phase will be no more than $4lm_i$.

This fact, observing that the set of links involved in each iteration are disjoint, yields less than

$$\sum_{i=1}^{\lceil d(G)/l \rceil} 4\, l\, m_i = 4\, l\, m \tag{4.10}$$

messages for all the explorations of all iterations. Combining equations (4.9) and (4.10), we obtain

$$\mathrm{M}[BF\_Levels] \leq \frac{2(n-1)d(G)}{l} + 4\, l\, m. \tag{4.11}$$

If we choose $l = O(n/\sqrt{m})$, expression (4.11) becomes

$$\mathrm{M}[BF\_Levels] = O(n\,\sqrt{m}).$$

This formula is quite interesting. In fact, it depends not only on n but also on the *square root* of the number m of links.

If the network is *sparse* (i.e., it has $O(n)$ links), then the protocol uses only

$$O(n^{1.5})$$

messages; note that this occurs in any *planar* network.

The worst case will be with very *dense* networks (i.e., $m = O(n^2)$). However, in this case the protocol will use at most

$$O(n^2)$$

messages, which is no more than protocol BF.

In other words, protocol BF_Levels will have the same cost as protocol BF only for very dense networks and will be much better in all other systems; in particular, whenever $m = o(n^2)$, it uses a subquadratic number of messages.

Let us consider now the *ideal time* costs of the protocol. Iteration i consists of reaching levels $L(i)$ and returning to the root; hence the ideal time will be exactly $2il$ if $1 \leq i < \lceil d(G)/l \rceil$, and time $2d(G)$ in the last iteration. Thus, without considering the roundup, in total we have

$$\mathrm{T}[BF\_Levels] = \sum_{i=1}^{d(G)/l} 2\, l\, i = \frac{d(G)^2}{l} + d(G). \tag{4.12}$$

The choice $l = O(n/\sqrt{m})$ we considered when counting the messages will give

$$\mathrm{T}[BF\_Levels] = O(d(G)^2 \sqrt{m}/n),$$

TABLE 4.6: Summary: Costs of Constructing a Breadth-first Tree

Network	Algorithm	Messages	Time
General	BF	$O(m + nd)$	$O(d^2)$
General	BF_Levels	$O(n\sqrt{m})$	$O(d^2\sqrt{m}/n + d)$
Planar	BF_Levels	$O(n^{1.5})$	$O(d^2/\sqrt{n} + d)$

which, again, is the same ideal time as protocol BF only for very dense networks, and less in all other systems.

Reducing Time with More Messages (⋆)   If time is of paramount importance, better results can be obtained at the cost of more messages. For example, if in protocol *BF_Levels* we were to choose $l = d(G)$, we would obtain an *optimal time costs*.

$$T[BF\_Levels] = 2d(G).$$

IMPORTANT. We measure ideal time considering a synchronous execution where the communication delays are just one unit of time. In such an execution, when $l = d(G)$, the number of messages will be exactly $2m + n - 1$ (Exercise 4.6.25). In other words, in this synchronous execution, the protocol has *optimal message costs*. However, this is *not* the message complexity of the protocol, just the cost of that particular execution. To measure the message complexity we must consider all possible executions. Remember that to measure ideal time we consider only synchronous executions, while to measure message costs we must look at all possible executions, both synchronous and asynchronous (and choose the worst one).

The cost in messages choosing $l = d(G)$ is given by expression (4.11) that becomes

$$O(m\ d(G)).$$

This quantity is reasonable only for networks of small degree. By the way, a priori knowledge of $d(G)$ is not necessary to obtain these bounds (either time or messages; Exercise 4.6.24).

If we are willing to settle for a low but *suboptimal* time, it is possible to achieve it with a better message complexity. Let us see how.

In protocol *BF_Levels* the network (and thus the tree) is viewed as divided into "strips," each containing l levels of the tree. See Figure 4.11.

The way the protocol works right now, in the expansion phase, each source (i.e., each leaf of the existing tree) constructs its own bf-tree over the nodes in the next l levels. These bf-trees have differential growth rates, some growing quickly, some slowly. Thus, it is possible for a quickly growing bf-tree to have processed many more levels than a slower bf-tree. Whenever there are conflicts due to transmission delays (e.g., the arrival of a message with a better level) or concurrency (e.g., the arrival of another message with the same level), these conflicts are resolved, either

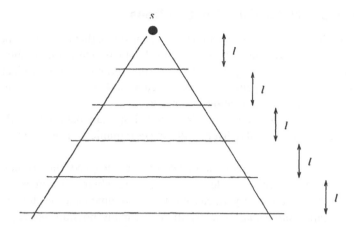

FIGURE 4.11: We need more efficient expansion of *l* levels in each iteration.

by "trowing away" everything already done and joining the new tree or sending a negative reply. It is the amount of work performed to take care of these conflicts that drives the costs of the protocol up. For example, when a node joins a bf-tree and has a (new) parent, it must send out messages to all its other neighbors; thus, if a node has a high degree and frequently changes trees, these adjacent edge messages dominate the communication complexity. Clearly, the problem is how to perform these operations efficiently.

Conflicts and overlap occurring during the constructions of those different bf-trees in the *l* levels can be reduced by organizing the sources into *clusters* and coordinating the actions of the sources that are in the same cluster, as well as coordinating the different clusters.

This in turn requires that the sources in the same cluster must be connected so as to minimize the communication costs among them. The connection through a tree is the obvious option and is called a *cover tree*. To avoid conflicts, we want that for different clusters the corresponding cover trees have no edges in common. So we will have a *forest* of cover trees, which we will call the *cover* of all the sources. To coordinate the different clusters in the cover, we must be able to reach all sources; this, however, can already be done using the current fragment (recall, the sources are the leaves of the fragment).

The message costs of the expansion phase will grow with the number of different clusters competing for the same node (the so-called *load factor*); on the contrary, the time costs will grow with the depth of the cover trees (the so-called *depth factor*). Notice that it is possible to obtain tradeoffs between the load factor and the depth factor by varying the size of the cover (i.e., the number of trees in the forest), for example, increasing the size of the forest reduces the depth factor while increasing the load factor.

We are thus faced with the problem of constructing clusters with small amount of competition and shallow cover trees. Achieving this goal yields a *time* cost of $O(d^{1+\epsilon})$ and a *message* cost of $O(m^{1+\epsilon})$ for any fixed $\epsilon > 0$. See Exercise 4.6.26.

4.2.6 Suboptimal Solutions: Routing Trees

Up to now, we have considered only *shortest-path routing*, that is, we have been looking at systems that *always* route a message to its destination through the shortest path.
We will call such mechanisms *optimal*. To construct optimal routing mechanisms, we
had to construct n shortest path trees, one for each node in the network, a task that
we have seen is quite communication expensive.

In some cases, the *shortest path* requirement is important but not crucial; actually,
in many systems, guarantee of delivery with few communication activities is the only
requirement.

If the shortest path requirement is relaxed or even dropped, the problem of constructing a routing mechanism (tables and forwarding scheme) becomes simpler and
can be achieved quite efficiently. Because they do not guarantee shortest paths, such
solutions are called *suboptimal*. Clearly there are many possibilities depending on
what (suboptimal) requirements the routing mechanism must satisfy.

A particular class of solutions is the one using a *single spanning tree* of the network
for all the routing, which we shall call *routing tree*. The advantages of such an approach
are obvious: We need to construct just one tree. Delivery is guaranteed and no more
that $diam(T)$ messages will be used on the tree T. Depending on which tree is used,
we have different solutions. Let us examine a few.

- *Center-Based Routing.* As the maximum number of messages used to deliver a
  message is at most $diam(T)$, a natural choice for a routing tree is the spanning tree
  with a small diameter. One such a tree is shortest path tree rooted in a center of
  the network. In fact, let c a center of G (i.e., a node where the *maximum* distance
  is minimized) and let $PT(c)$ be the shortest path tree of c. Then (Exercise 4.6.27),

$$diam(G) \leq diam(\mathrm{PT}(c)) \leq 2\mathrm{diam}(G).$$

  To construct such a tree, we need first of all to determine a center c and then
  construct $PT(c)$, for example, using protocol *PT_Construction*.

- *Median-Based Routing.* Once we choose a tree T, an edge $e = (x, y)$ of T linking
  the subtree $T[x - y]$ to the subtree $T[y - x]$ will be used every time a node
  in $T[x - y]$ wants to send a message to a node in $T[y - x]$, and viceversa
  (see Figure 4.12), where each use costs $\theta(e)$. Thus, assuming that overall every
  node generates the same amount of messages for every other node and all nodes
  overall generate the same amount of messages, the cost of using T for routing
  all this traffic is

$$Traffic(T) = \sum_{(x,y)\in T} |T[x - y]|\, |T[y - x]|\, \theta(x, y).$$

  It is not difficult to see that such a measure is exactly the sum of all distances
  between nodes (Exercise 4.6.28). Hence, the best tree T to use is one that

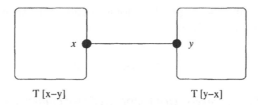

FIGURE 4.12: The message traffic between the two subtrees passes through edge $e = (x, y)$.

minimizes the sum of all distances between nodes. Unfortunately, to construct the minimum-sum-distance spanning tree of a network is not simple. In fact, the problem is NP-hard. Fortunately, it is not difficult to construct a near-optimal solution. In fact, let z be a *median* of the network (i.e., a node for which the *sum* of distances $SumDist(z) = \sum_{v \in V} d_G(x, z)$ to all other nodes is minimized) and let $PT(z)$ be the shortest path tree of z. If $T \star$ is the spanning tree that minimizes traffic, then (Exercise 4.6.29)

$$Traffic(PT(z)) \leq 2 \ Traffic(T\star).$$

Thus, to construct such a tree, we need first of all to determine a median z and then construct $PT(z)$, for example, using protocol *PT_Construction*.

- *Minimum-Cost Spanning-Tree Routing.* A natural choice for routing tree is a minimum-cost spanning tree (MST) of the network. The construction of such a tree can be done, for example, using protocol *MegaMerger* discussed in Chapter 3.

All the solutions above have different advantages; for example, the center-based one offers the best worst-case cost, while the median-based one has the best average cost. Depending on the nature of the systems and of the applications, each might be preferable to the others.

There are also other measures that can be used to evaluate a routing tree. For example, a common measure is the so-called *stretch factor* $\sigma_G(T)$ of a spanning tree T of G defined as

$$\sigma_G(T) = \text{Max}_{x,y \in V} \frac{d_T(x, y)}{d_G(x, y)}. \tag{4.13}$$

In other words, if a spanning tree T has a *stretch factor* α, then for each pair of nodes x and y, the cost of the path from x to y in T is at most α times the cost of the shortest path between x and y in G. A design goal could thus be to determine spanning trees with small stretch factors (see Exercises 4.6.30 and 4.6.31). These ratios are sometimes difficult to calculate.

Alternate, easier to compute, measures are obtained by taking into account only pairs of *neighbors* (instead of pairs of arbitrary nodes). One such measure is the so-called *dilation*, that is the length of the longest path in the spanning tree T corresponding to an edge of G, defined as

$$dilation_G(T) = \text{Max}_{(x,y)\in E} \; d_T(x, y).$$ (4.14)

We also can define the *edge-stretch* factor $\epsilon_G(T)$ (or *dilation factor*) of a spanning tree T of G as

$$\epsilon_G(T) = \text{Max}_{(x,y)\in E} \; \frac{d_T(x, y)}{\theta(x, y)}.$$ (4.15)

As an example, consider the spanning tree PT(c) used in the center-based solution; if all the link costs are the same, we have that for every two nodes x and y

$$1 \le d_G(x, y) \le d_{PT(c)}(x, y) \le d_{PT(c)} = d_G.$$

This means that in PT(c) (unweighted) stretch factor $\sigma_G(T)$, dilation $dilation_G(T)$, and edge-stretch factor $\epsilon_G(T)$ are all bounded by the same quantity, the diameter d_G of G.

For a given spanning tree T, the stretch factor and the dilation factor measure the *worst ratio* between the distance in T and in G for the same pair of nodes and the same edge, respectively. Another important cost measure is the *average stretch* factor describing the average ratio:

$$\overline{\sigma}_G(T) = \text{Average}_{x,y\in V} \; \frac{d_T(x, y)}{d_G(x, y)}$$ (4.16)

and the *average edge-stretch* factor (or average dilation factor) $\overline{\epsilon}_G(T)$ of a spanning tree T of G as

$$\overline{\epsilon}_G(T) = \text{Average}_{(x,y)\in E} \; \frac{d_T(x, y)}{\theta(x, y)}.$$ (4.17)

Construction of spanning trees with low average edge-stretch can be done effectively (Exercises 4.6.35 and 4.6.36).

Summarizing, the main disadvantage of using a *routing tree* for all routing tasks is the fact that the routing path offered by such mechanisms is not optimal. If this is not a problem, these solutions are clearly a useful and viable alternative to shortest path routing.

The choice of which spanning tree, among the many, should be used depends on the nature of the system and of the application. Natural choices include the ones described above, as well as those minimizing some of the cost measures we have introduced (see Exercises 4.6.31, 4.6.32, 4.6.33).

4.3   COPING WITH CHANGES

In some systems, it might be possible that the cost associated to the links change over time; think, for example, of having a tariff (i.e., cost) for using a link during weekdays different from the one charged in the weekend. If such a change occurs, the shortest path between several pairs of node might change, rendering the information stored in the tables obsolete and possibly incorrect. Thus, the routing tables need to be adjusted.

In this section, we will consider the problem of dealing with such events. We will assume that when the cost of a link (x, y) changes, both x and y are aware of the change and of the new cost of the link. In other words, we will replace the *Total Reliability* restriction with *Total Component Reliability* (thus, the only changes are in the costs) in addition to the *Cost Change Detection* restriction.

Note that costs that change in time can also describe the occurrence of some link failures in the system: The *crash failure* of an edge can be described by having its cost becoming exceedingly large. Hence, in the following, we will talk of link crash failures and of cost changes as the same types of events.

4.3.1   Adaptive Routing

In these *dynamical* networks where cost changes in time, the construction of the routing tables is only the first step for ensuring (shortest path) routing: There must be a mechanism to deal with the changes in the network status, adjusting the routing tables accordingly.

Map Update   A simple, albeit expensive solution is the *Map_Update* protocol.

It requires first of all that each table contains the *complete map* of the entire network; the next "hop" for a message to reach its destination is computed on the basis of this map. The construction of the maps can be done, for example, using protocol *Map_Gossip* discussed in Section 4.2.1. Clearly, any change will render the map inaccurate. Thus, integral part of this protocol is the update mechanism:

Maintenance

- as soon as an entity x detects a local change (either in the cost or in the status of an incident link), x will update its map accordingly and inform all its neighbors of the change through an "update" message;
- as soon as an entity y receives an "update" from a neighbor, it will update its map accordingly and inform all its neighbors of the change through an "update" message.

NOTE.   In several existing systems, an even more expensive *periodic* maintenance mechanism is used: Step 1 of the maintenance mechanism is replaced by having each node, periodically and even if there are no detected changes, send its entire map to all its neighbors. This is, for example, the case with the second Internet routing protocol:

The complete map is being sent to all neighbors every 10–60 s (10 s if there is a cost change; 60 s otherwise).

The great advantage of this approach is that it is fully adaptive and can cope with any amount and type of changes. The clear disadvantage is the amount of information required locally and the volume of transmitted information.

Vector Update   To alleviate some of the disadvantages of the *Map_Update* protocol, an alternative solution consists in using protocol *Iterative_Construction*, that we designed to construct the routing tables, to keep them up-to-date should faults or changes occur. Every entity will just keep its routing table.

Note that a single change might make all the routing tables incorrect. To complicate things, changes are detected only locally, where they occur, and without a full map it might be impossible to detect if it has any impact on a remote site; furthermore, if more several changes occur concurrently, their cumulative effect is unpredictable: A change might "undo" the damage inflicted to the routing tables by another change.

Whenever an entity x detects a local change (either in the cost or in the status of an incident link), the update mechanism is invoked, which will trigger an execution of possibly several iterations of protocol *Iterative_Construction*.

In regard to the update mechanism, we have two possible choices:

- recompute the routing tables: everybody starts a new *execution* of the algorithm, trowing away the current tables, or
- update current information: everybody starts a new *iteration* of the algorithm with x using the new data, continuing until the tables converge.

The first choice is very costly because, as we know, the construction of the routing tables is an expensive process. For these reasons, one might want to recompute only what and when is; hence the second choice is preferred.

The second choice was used as the original Internet routing protocol; unfortunately, it has some problems.

A well known problem is the so-called *count-to-infinity* problem. Consider the simple network shown in Figure 4.13. Initially all links have cost 1. Then the cost of link (z, w) becomes a *large* integer $K \gg 1$. Both nodes z and w will then start an iteration that will be performed by all entities. During this iteration, z is told by y that there is a path from y to w of cost 2; hence, at the end of the iteration, z sets its distance to w to 3. In the next iteration, y sets its distance from w to 4 because the best path to w (according to the vectors it receives from x and z) is through x. In general, after the $(2i + 1)$th iteration, x and z will set their cost for reaching w to $2(i + 1) + 1$, while z will set it to $2(i + 1)$. This process will continue until z sets its cost for w

FIGURE 4.13: The count-to-infinity problem.

to the actual value K. As K can be arbitrarily large, the number of iterations can be arbitrarily large.

Solving this problem is not easy. See Exercises 4.6.38 and 4.6.39.

Oscillation   We have seen some approaches to maintain routing information in spite of failures and changes in the system.

A problem common to all the approaches is called *oscillation*. It occurs if the cost of a link is proportional to the amount of traffic on the link. Consider, for example, two disjoint paths π_1 and π_2 between x and y, where initially π_1 is the "best" path. Thus, the traffic is initially sent to π_1; this will have the effect of increasing its cost until π_2 becomes the best path. At this point the traffic will be diverted on π_2 increasing its cost, and so forth. This oscillation between the two paths will continue forever, requiring continuous execution of the update mechanism.

4.3.2 Fault-Tolerant Tables

To continue to deliver a message through a shortest path to its destination in presence of cost changes or link crash failures, an entity must have up-to-date information on the status of the system (e.g., which links are up, their current cost, etc.). As we have seen, maintaining the routing tables correct when the topology of the network or the edge values may change is a very costly operation. This is true even if faults are very limited.

Consider, for example, a system where at any time there is at most one link down (not necessarily the same one at all times), and no other changes will ever occur in the system; this situation is called *single link crash failure* (SLF).

Even in this restricted case, the *amount of information* that must be kept in addition to the shortest paths is formidable (practically the entire map). This is because the crash failure of a single edge can dramatically change *all* the shortest path information. As the tables must be able to cope with every possible choice of the failed link, even in such a limited case, the memory requirements soon become unfeasible.

Furthermore when a link fails, *every* node must be notified so that it can route messages along the new shortest paths; the subsequent recovery of that node also will require such a notification. Such a notification process needs to be repeated at each crash failure and recovery, for the entire lifetime of the system. Hence, the *amount of communication* is rather high and never ending as long as there are changes.

Summarizing, the service of delivering a message through a *shortest path* in presence of cost changes or link crash failures, called *shortest path rerouting* (SR), is expensive (sometimes to the point of being unfeasible) both in terms of storage and communication.

The natural question is whether there exists a less expensive alternative. Fortunately, the answer is positive. In fact, if we relax the *shortest path rerouting* requirement and settle for lower quality services, then the situation changes drastically; for example, as we will see, if the requirement is just message delivery (i.e., not necessarily through a shortest path), this service be achieved in our SLF system with very simple routing tables and *without any maintenance mechanism*.

In the rest of this section, we will concentrate on the *single-link crash failure* case.

Point-of-failure Rerouting To reduce the amount of communication and of storage, a simple and convenient alternative is to offer, after the crash failure of an arbitrary *single* link, a lower quality service called *point-of-failure rerouting* (PR):

Point-of-failure (Shortest path) Rerouting:

1. if the shortest path is not affected by the failed link, then the message will be delivered through that path;
2. otherwise, when the message reaches the node where the crash failure has occurred (the "point of failure"), the message will then be rerouted through a (shortest) path to its destination if no other failure occurs.

This type of service has clearly the advantage that there is no need to notify the entities of a link crash failure and its subsequent reactivation (if any): The message is forwarded as there are no crash failures and if, by chance, the next link it must take has failed, it will be just then provided with an alternative route. This means that once constructed with the appropriate information for rerouting,

the routing tables do not need to be maintained or updated.

For this reason, the routing tables supporting such a service are called *fault-tolerant* tables.

The amount of information that a fault-tolerant table must contain (in addition to the shortest paths) to provide such a service will depend on what type of information is being kept at the nodes to do the rerouting and on whether or not the rerouting is guaranteed to be through a shortest path.

A solution consists in every node x knowing two (or more) *edge-disjoint paths* for each destination: the shortest path, and a secondary one to be used only if the link to the next "hop" in the shortest path has failed. So the routing mechanism is simple: When a message for destination r arrives at x, x determines the neighbor y in the shortest path to r. If (x,y) is up, x will send the message to y, otherwise, it will determine the neighbor z in the secondary path to r and forward the message to z.

The storage requirements of this solution are minimal: For each destination, a node needs to store in its routing table only one link in addition to the one in the fault-free shortest path. As we already know how to determine the shortest path trees, the problem is reduced to the one of computing the secondary paths (see Exercise 4.6.37).

NOTE. The secondary paths of a node do not necessarily form a tree.

A major drawback of this solution is that rerouting is not through a shortest path: If the crash failure occurs, the system does not provide any service other than message delivery. Although acceptable in some contexts, this level of service might not be tolerable in general. Surprisingly, it is actually possible to offer *shortest path rerouting* storing at each node only one link for each destination in addition to the one in the fault-free shortest path.

We are now going to see how to design such a service.

Point-of-Failure Shortest Path Rerouting   Consider a message originated by x and whose destination is s; its routing in the system will be according to the information contained in the shortest path spanning tree $PT(s)$. The tree $PT(s)$ is rooted in s; so every node $x \neq s$ has a parent $p_s(x)$, and every edge in $PT(s)$ links a node to its parent.

When the link $e_s[x] = (p_s(x), x)$ fails, it disconnects the tree into two subtrees, one containing s and the other x; call them $T[s - x]$ and $T[x - s]$; see Figure 4.14.

When e_x fails, a new path from x to s must be found. It cannot be *any*: It must be the shortest path possible between x and s in the network without $e_s[x]$.

Consider a link $e = (u, v) \in G \setminus PT(s)$, not part of the tree, that can reconnect the two subtrees created by the crash failure of $e_s[x]$, that is, $u \in T[s - x]$ and $v \in T[x - s]$. We will call such a link a *swap edge* for $e_s[x]$.

Using e we can create a new path from x to s. The path will consist of three parts: the path from x to v in $T[x/e_x]$, the edge (u, v), and the path from u to s; see Figure 4.15. The cost of going from x to s using this path will then be

$$d_{PT(s)}(s, u) + \theta(u, v) + d_{PT(s)}(v, x) = d(s, u) + \theta(u, v) + d(v, x).$$

This is the cost of using e as a swap for $e_s[x]$. For each $e_s[x]$ there are several edges that can be used as swaps, each with a different cost. If we want to offer shortest path rerouting from x to s when $e_s[x]$ fails, we must use the *optimal swap*, that is the swap edge for $e_s[x]$ of minimum cost.

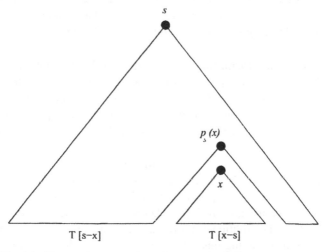

FIGURE 4.14: The crash failure of $e_s[x] = (p_s(x), x)$ disconnects the tree $PT(s)$.

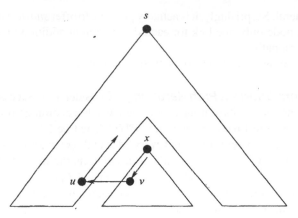

FIGURE 4.15: Point-of-failure rerouting using the swap edge $e = (u, v)$ of $e_s[x]$.

So the first task that must be solved is to how find the optimal swap for each edge $e_s[x]$ in PT(s). This computation can be done efficiently (Exercises 4.6.40 and 4.6.41); its result is that every node x knows the optimal swap edge for its incident link $e_s[x]$. To be used to construct the routing tables, this process must be repeated n times, one for each destination s (i.e., for each shortest path spanning tree PT(s)).

Once the information about the optimal swap edges has been determined, it needs to be integrated in the routing tables so as to provide point-of-failure shortest path rerouting.

The routing table of a node x must contain information about (1) the shortest paths as well as about (2) the alternative paths using the optimal swaps:

1. **Shortest path information.** First and foremost, the routing table of x contains for each destination s the link to the neighbor in the shortest path to s if there are no failures. Denote by $p_s(x)$ this neighbor. The choice of symbol is not accidental: This neighbor is the *parent* of x in PT(s) and the link is really $e_s[x] = (p_s(x), x)$.

2. **Alternative path information.** In the entry for the destination s, the routing table of x must also contain the information needed to reroute the message if $e_s[x] = (p_s(x), x)$ is down. Let us see what this information is.

   Let $e = (u, v)$ be the optimal swap edge that x has computed for $e_s[x]$; this means that the shortest path from x to s if $e_s[x]$ fails is by first going from x to v, then over the link (u, v), and finally from u to s. In other words, if $e_s[x]$ fails, x must reroute the message for s to v, that is, x must send it to its neighbor in the shortest path to v. The shortest paths to v are described by the tree PT(v); in fact, this neighbor is just $p_v(x)$ and the link over which the message to s must be sent when rerouting is precisely $e_v[x] = (p_v(x), x)$ (see Exercise 4.6.42).

   Concluding, the additional information x must keep in the entry for destination s are the rerouting link $e_v[x] = (p_v(x), x)$ and the closest node v on the optimal swap edge for $e_s[x]$; this information will be used only if $e_s[x]$ is down.

TABLE 4.7: Entry in the Routing Table of x; $e=(u,v)$ is the Optimal Swap Edge for $e_s[x]$

Final Destination	Normal Link	Rerouting Link	Swap Destination	Swap Link
s	$(p_s(x), x)$	$(p_v(x), x)$	v	(u,v)

Any message must thus contain, in addition to the *final destination* (node s in our example), also a field indicating the *swap destination* (node v in our example), the *swap link* (link (u, v) in our example), and a bit to explain which of the two must be considered (see Table 4.7). The *routing mechanism* is rather simple. Consider a message originating from r for node s.

PSR Routing Mechanism

1. Initially, r sets the final destination to s, the swap destination and the swap link to empty, and the bit to 0; it then sends the message toward the final destination using the normal link indicated in its routing table.
2. If a node x receives the message with final destination s and bit set to 0, then
   (a) if $x = s$, the message has reached its destination: s processes the message;
   (b) if $e_s[x] = (p_s(x), x)$ is up, x forwards the unchanged message on that link;
   (c) if $e_s[x] = (p_s(x), x)$ is down, then x
      i. copies to the swap destination and swap link fields of the message the swap destination and swap link entries for s in its routing table;
      ii. sets the bit to 1;
      iii. sends the message on the rerouting link indicated in its table.
3. If a node x receives the message with final destination s and bit set to 1, and swap destination set to v, then
   (a) if $x = v$, then
      i. it sets the bit to 0;
      ii. it sends the message on the swap link;
   (b) otherwise, it forwards the unchanged message on the link $e_v[x] = (p_v(x), x)$.

4.3.3   On Correctness and Guarantees

Adaptive Routing   In all *adaptive routing* approaches, maintenance of the tables is carried out by broadcasting information about the status of the network; this can

Destination	Mode	SwapDest	SwapLink	Content
s	1	v	(u, v)	INFO

FIGURE 4.16: Message rerouted by x using the swap edge $e = (u, v)$ of $e_s[x]$.

be done periodically or just when changes do occur. In all cases, news of changes detected by a node will eventually reach any node (still connected to it). However, because of time delays, while an update is being disseminated, nodes still unaware will be routing messages on the basis of incorrect information. In other words, as long as there are changes occurring in the system (and for some time afterwards), the information in the tables is unreliable and might be incorrect. In particular, it is likely that routing will *not* be done through a shortest path; it is actually possible that messages might not be delivered as long as there are changes. This sad status of affairs is not due to the individual solutions but solely due to the fact that time delays are unpredictable. As a result,

> *it is impossible to make any guarantee on correctness and in particular on shortest path delivery for adaptive routing mechanisms.*

This situation occurs even if the changes at any time are few and their nature limited, as the SLF. It would appear that we should be able to operate correctly in such a system; unfortunately this is not true:

> *It is impossible to provide shortest path routing even in the single-link crash failure case.*

This is because the crash failure of a single edge can dramatically change *all* the shortest path information; thus, when the link fails, every node must be notified so that it can route messages along the new shortest paths; the subsequent recovery of that node will also require such a notification. Such a notification process needs to be repeated at each crash failure and recovery, and again the unpredictable time delays will make it impossible to guarantee correctness of the information available at the entities, and thus of the routing decision they make on the basis of that information.

Question. What, if anything, can be guaranteed?

The only think that we can say is that, *if* the changes stop (or there are no changes for a long period of time), then the updates to the routing information converge to the correct state, and routing will proceed according to the existing shortest paths. In other words, if the "noise" caused by changes stops, eventually the entities get the correct result.

Fault-Tolerant Tables   In the *fault-tolerant tables* approach, no maintenance of the routing tables is needed once they have been constructed. Therefore, there are no broadcasts or notifications of changes that, because of delays, might affect the correctness of the routing.

However, also, fault-tolerant tables suffer because of the unpredictability of time delays. For example, even with the *single-link crash failure*, point-of-failure shortest-path rerouting can not be guaranteed to be correct: While the message for s is being rerouted from x toward the swap edge $e_s[x]$, the link $e_s[x]$ might recover (i.e., come up again) and another link on the may go down. Thus, the message will again be rerouted and might continue to do so if a "bad" sequence of recovery failure occurs.

In other words, not only the message will not reach s through a shortest path from the first point-of-failure, but it will not reach s at all as long as there is a change. It might be argued that such a sequence of events is highly unlikely, but it is possible. Thus, again,

Question. What, if anything, can be guaranteed?

As in the case of adaptive routing, the only guarantee is that *if* the changes stop (or there are no changes for a long period of time), then messages will be (during that time) correctly delivered through point-of-failure shortest paths.

4.4   ROUTING IN STATIC SYSTEMS: COMPACT TABLES

There are systems that are static in nature; for example, if *Total Reliability* holds, no changes will occur in the network topology. We will consider *static* also any system where the routing table, once constructed, cannot be modified (e.g., because they are hardcoded/hardwired). Such is, for example, any system etched on a chip; should faults occur, the entire chip will be replaced.

In these systems, an additional concern in the design of shortest path routing tables is their *size*, that is, an additional design goal is to construct table that are as small as possible.

4.4.1   The Size of Routing Tables

The full routing table can be quite large. In fact, for each of its $n - 1$ destinations, it contains the specification (and the cost) of the shortest path to that destination. This means that each entry possibly contains $O(n \log w)$ bits, where $w \geq n$ is the range of the entities' names, for a total table size of $O(n^2 \log w)$ bits. Assuming the best possible case, that is, $w = n$, the number of bits required to store all the n full routing tables is

$$S_{\text{FULL}} = O(n^3 \log n).$$

For large n, this is a formidable amount of space just to store the routing tables.

Observe that for any destination, the first entry in the shortest path will always be a link to a neighbor. Thus, it is possible to simplify the routing table by specifying for each destination y only the neighbor of x on the shortest path to it. Such a table is called *short*. For example, the short routing table for s in the network of Figure 4.1 is shown in Table 4.8.

In its short representation, each entry of the table of an entity x will contain $\log w$ bits to represent the destination's name and another $\log w$ bits to represent the neighbor's name. In other words, the table contains $2(n - 1) \log w$ bits. Assuming the best possible case, that is, $w = n$, the number of bits required to store *all* the routing tables is

$$2n(n - 1) \log n.$$

TABLE 4.8: Short Representation of RT(*s*)

Destination	Neighbor
h	*h*
k	*h*
c	*c*
d	*c*
e	*e*
f	*e*

This amount of space can be further reduced if, instead of the neighbors' names we use the local port numbers leading to them. In this case, the size will be $(n - 1)$ $(\log w + \log p_x)$ bits, where $p_x \geq \deg(x)$ is the range of the local port numbers of x. Assuming the best possible case, that is, $w = n$ and $p_x = \deg(x)$ for all x, this implies that the number of bits required to store all the routing tables is *at least*

$$S_{\text{SHORT}} = \sum_x (n - 1) \log \deg(x) = (n - 1) \log \Pi_x \deg(x),$$

which can be still rather large.

Notice that the same information can be represented by listing for each port the destinations reached via shortest path through that port; for example, see Table 4.9. This alternative representation of RT(x) uses only $\deg(x) + (n - 1) \log(n)$ bits for a total of

$$S_{\text{ALT}} = \sum_x (\deg(x) + (n - 1) \log n) = 2m + n(n - 1) \log n. \tag{4.18}$$

It appears that there is not much more that can be done to reduce the size of the table. This is, however, not the case if we, as designers of the system, had the power to choose the *names* of the nodes and of the links.

4.4.2 Interval Routing

The question we are going to ask is whether it is possible to drastically reduce this amount of storage if we know the network topology and we have the power of choosing the names of the nodes and the port labels.

An Example: Ring Networks   Consider for example a *ring* network, and assume for the moment that all links have the same cost.

TABLE 4.9: Alternative Short Representation of RT(*s*)

Port	Destinations
$port_s(h)$	h, k
$port_s(c)$	c, d
$port_s(e)$	e, f

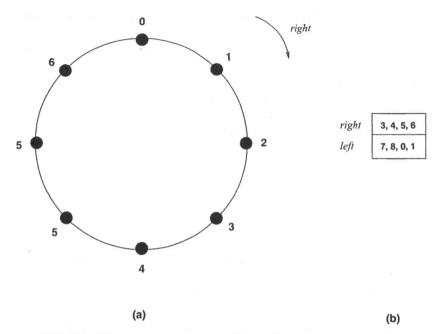

FIGURE 4.17: (a) assigning names and labels; (b) Routing table of node 2.

Suppose that we assign as names to the nodes consecutive integers, starting from 0 and continuing clockwise, and we label the ports *right* or *left* depending on whether or not they are in the clockwise direction. See Figure 4.17(a).

Concentrate on node 0. This node, like all the others, has only two links. Thus, whenever 0 has to route a message for $z > 0$, it must just decide whether to send it to *right* or to *left*. Observe that the choice will be *right* for $1 \leq z \leq \lfloor n/2 \rfloor$ and *left* for $\lfloor n/2 \rfloor + 1 \leq z \leq n - 1$. In other words, the destinations are consecutive integers (modulo n). This is true not just for node 0: If x has to route a message for $z \neq x$, the choice will be *right* if z is in the interval $\langle x + 1, x + 2, \ldots x + \lfloor n/2 \rfloor \rangle$ and *left* if z is in the interval $\langle x + \lfloor n/2 \rfloor + 1, \ldots, x - 1 \rangle$, where the operations are *modulo n*. See Figure 4.17(b).

In other words, in all these routing tables, the set of destinations associated to a port is an *interval* of consecutive integers, and, in each table, the intervals are *disjoint*. This is very important for our purpose of reducing the space.

In fact, an interval has a very short *representation*: It is sufficient to store the two *end* values, that is, just $2 \log n$ bits. We can actually do it with just $\log n$ bits; see Exercise 4.6.43. As a table consists just of two intervals, we have routing tables of $4 \log n$ bits each, for a grand total of just

$$4n \log n.$$

This amount should be contrasted with the one of Expression 4.18 that, in the case of rings, becomes $n^2 \log n + l.o.t..$. In other words, we are able to go from quadratic to just linear space requirements. Note that it is true even if the costs of the links are not all the same; see Exercise 4.6.44.

The phenomenon we have just described is not isolated, as we will discuss next.

Routing With Intervals   Consider the names of the nodes in a network G. Without any loss of generality, we can always assume that the names are consecutive positive integers, starting from 0, that is, the set of names is $Z_n = \{0, 1, \ldots, n-1\}$.

Given two integers $j, k \in Z_n$, we denote by (j, k) the sequence

$$(j, k) = \langle j, j+1, j+2, \ldots, k \rangle \text{ if } j < k$$
$$(j, k) = \langle j, j+1, j+2, \ldots, n-1, 0, 1, \ldots, k \rangle \text{ if } j \geq k.$$

Such a sequence (j, k) is called a circular *interval* of Z_n; the empty interval $\emptyset$ is also an interval of Z_n.

Suppose that we are able to assign names to the nodes so that the shortest path routing tables for G have the following two properties. At every node x,

1. **interval:** for each link incident to x, the (names of the) destinations associated to that link form a circular interval of Z_n;
2. **disjointness:** each destination is associated to only one link incident to x.

If this is the case, then we can have for G a very *compact representation* of the routing tables, like in the example of the ring network. In fact, for each link the set of destinations is an interval of consecutive integers, and, like in the ring, the intervals associated to the links of a given nodes are all disjoint.

In other words, each table consists of a set of intervals (some of them may be empty), one for each incident link. From the storage point of view, this is very good news because we can represent such intervals by just their *start* values (or, alternatively, by their end values).

In other words, the routing table of x will consist of just one entry for each of its links. This means that the amount of storage for its table is only $\deg(x) \log n$ bits. In turn, this means that the number of bits used in total to represent all the routing tables will be just

$$S_{\text{INTERVAL}} = \sum_x \deg(x) \log n = 2m \log n. \tag{4.19}$$

How will the *routing mechanism* then work with such tables? Suppose x has a message whose destination is y. Then x checks in its table which interval y is part of (as the intervals are disjoint, y will belong to exactly one) and sends the message to the corresponding link.

Because of its nature, this approach is called *interval routing*. If it can be done, as we have just seen, it allows for efficient shortest-path routing with a minimal amount of storage requirements.

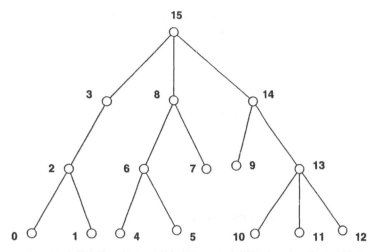

FIGURE 4.18: Naming for interval routing in trees

It, however, requires that we, as designers, find an appropriate way to assign names to nodes so that the interval and disjointness properties hold. Given a network G, it is not so obvious how to do it or whether it can be done at all.

Tree Networks   First of all we will consider *tree* networks. As we will see, in a tree it is always possible to achieve our goal and can actually be done in several different ways.

Given a tree T, we first of all choose a node s as the source, transforming T into the tree $T(s)$ rooted in s; in this tree, each node x has a parent and some children (possibly none). We then assign as names to the nodes consecutive integers, starting from 0, according to the *post-order traversal* of $T(s)$, for example, using procedure

$Post\_Order\_Naming(x, k)$
begin
    Unnamed_Children(x) := Children(x);
    while Unnamed_Children$(x) \neq \emptyset$ **do**
        $y \leftarrow$ Unnamed_Children(x);
        $Post\_Order\_Naming(y, k)$
    endwhile
    myname := k;
    $k := k + 1$;
end

started by calling $Post\_Order\ Naming(s, 0)$. This assignment of names has several properties. For example, any node has a larger name than all its descendents. More importantly, it has the *interval* and *disjointness* properties (Exercise 4.6.48). Informally, the interval property follows is because when executing $Post\_Order\_Naming$ with input (x, k), x and its descendents will be given as names consecutive integers starting from k. See for example Figure 4.19.

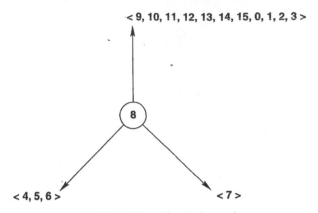

FIGURE 4.19: Disjoint intervals

Special Networks   Most regular network topologies we have considered in the past can be assigned names so that *interval routing* is possible. This is for example the case of the $p \times q$ *mesh* and *torus, hypercube, butterfly*, and *cube-connected-cycles*; see Exercises 4.6.51 and 4.6.52. For these networks the construction is rather simple.

Using a more complex construction, names can be assigned so that interval routing can be done also in any *outerplanar* graph (Exercise 4.6.53); recall that a graph is outerplanar if it can be drawn in the plane with all the nodes lying on a ring and all edges lying in the interior of the ring without crossings.

Question.   Can interval routing be done in every network?

The answer is unfortunately *No*. In fact there exist rather simple networks, the so-called *globe* outerplanar graph (one is shown in Figure 4.20), for which interval routing is *impossible* (Exercise 4.6.55).

Multi-Intervals   As we have seen, interval routing is a powerful technique but the classes of networks in which it is possible are rather limited.

To overcome somehow this limitation without increasing excessively the size of the routing table an approach is to associate to each link a small number of intervals. An interval-routing scheme that uses up to k intervals per edge is called a k-intervals routing scheme.

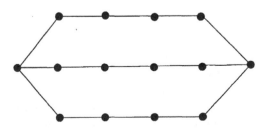

FIGURE 4.20: A *globe* graph: interval routing is not possible.

Clearly, with enough intervals we can find a scheme for every connected graph. The question is whether this can be achieved with a small k. The answer again is *No*.

In fact, there are graphs where $O(n)$ intervals are needed in each edge (Exercise 4.6.56).

Suboptimal Interval Routing   A reason why it is impossible to do interval routing in all graphs is that we require the tables to provide *shortest path*. The situation changes if we relax this requirement.

If we ask the tables to provide us just with *a path* to destination, not necessarily the shortest one, then we can use the approach already discussed in Section 4.2.6: We construct a single spanning tree T of the network G and use only the edges of T for routing.

Once we have the tree T, we then assign the names to the nodes using the naming algorithm for trees that provides interval routing. In this way, we obtain for G the very compact routing tables provided by interval routing. Clearly, the interval routing mechanism so constructed is optimal (i.e., shortest path) for the tree T but not necessarily so for the original network G. This means that *suboptimal interval routing* is always possible in any network.

Question. How much worse can a path provided by this approach be than the shortest one to the destination?

If we choose as tree T a breadth-first spanning tree rooted in a center of the graph G, then its diameter is at most twice the diameter of the original graph (the worst case is when G is a ring). This means that the longest route is never more than $2\ diam(G)$.

We can extend this approach by allowing the longest route to be within a factor $\beta \leq 2$ of the diameter of G and by using more than one interval. We have seen that it is possible to obtain $\beta = 2$ using a single interval per edge. The question then becomes whether using more intervals we can obtain a better scheme (i.e., a smaller β). The answer is again not very positive; for example, to have the longest route shorter than $\frac{3}{2}\ diam(G)$, then we need $O(\log n)$ labels (Exercise 4.6.58).

4.5 BIBLIOGRAPHICAL NOTES

The construction of routing table is a prerequisite for the functioning of many networks. One of the earliest protocols is due to William Tajibnapis [31]. The basic *MapGossip* for the construction of all routing tables is due to Eric Rosen [29]. Protocol *IteratedConstruction* is the distributed version of Bellman's sequential algorithm designed by Lestor Ford and D. Fulkerson [13]; from the start it has been the main routing algorithm in the Internet.

The same cost as *IteratedConstruction*, $O(n^2m)$, was incurred by several other protocols designed much later, including the ones of Philip Merlin and Adrian Segall [25] and by Jayadev Misra and Mani Chandy [22]. The improvement to $O(n^3)$ is due to Baruch Awerbuch, who designed a protocol to construct a single shortest path tree using $O(n^2)$ message [6]. The same bound is achieved by protocol *PT_Construction*, the efficient distributed implementation of Dijkstra's sequential algorithm designed by K. Ramarao and S. Venkatesan [28]. The even more efficient Protocol *SparserGossip* is due to Yeuda Afek and Moty Ricklin [1].

A protocol for systems allowing *long* messages was designed by Sam Toueg with cost $O(nm)$ [32]; the reduction to $O(n^2)$ is easy to achieve using protocol *MapGossip* by Eric Rosen [29] (Exercise 4.6.4), constructing, however, complete maps at each entity; the same cost but with less local storage (Exercise 4.6.18) has been obtained by S. Haldar [20].

The distributed construction of *min-hop* spanning trees has been extensively investigated. Protocol *BF* (known as the "Coordinated Minimum Hop Algorithm") is due to Bob Gallager [17]; a different protocol with the same cost was independently designed by To-Yat Cheung [8]. Also to Gallager [17] is due the idea of reducing time by partitioning the layers of the breadth-first tree into groups (Section 4.2.5) and a series of time-messages tradeoffs. Protocol *BF_Layers* has been designed by Greg Frederickson [15]. The problem of reducing time while maintaining a reasonable message complexity has been investigated by Baruch Awerbuch [3], Baruch Awerbuch and Bob Gallager [5], and Y. Zhu and To-Yat Cheung [35]. The near-optimal bounds (Exercise 4.6.26) have been obtained by Baruch Awerbuch [4].

The suboptimal solutions of center-based and median-based routing were first discussed in details by David Wall and Susanna Owicki [34]. The lower-bound on average edge-stretch and the construction of spanning trees with low average edge-stretch (Exercises 4.6.34, 4.6.35 and 4.6.36) are due to Noga Alon, Richard Karp, David Peleg, and Doug West [2].

The idea of point-of-failure rerouting was suggested independently by Enrico Nardelli, Guido Proietti, and Peter Widmayer[27] and by Hiro Ito, Kazuo Iwama, Yasuo Okabe, and Takuya Yoshihiro [21]. The distributed algorithm for computing the swap edges (Exercise 4.6.41) was designed by Paola Flocchini, Linda Pagli, Tony Mesa, Giuseppe Prencipe, and Nicola Santoro [12].

The idea of *compact routing* was introduced by Nicola Santoro and Ramez Kathib [30], who designed the interval routing for trees; this idea was then extended by Jan van Leeuwen and Richard Tan [24]. The interval routing for outerplanar graphs (Exercise 4.6.53) is due to Greg Frederickson and Ravi Janardan [16].

The more restrictive notion of *linear* interval routing (Exercise 4.6.54 and Problem 4.6.1) was introduced and studied by Erwin Bakker, Jan van Leeuwen, and Richard Tan [7]; the more general notion of *Boolean* routing was introduced by Michele Flammini, Giorgio Gambosi, and Sandro Salomone [11].

Several issues of compact routing have been investigated, among others, by Greg Frederickson and Ravi Janardan [16], Pierre Fraigniaud and Cyril Gavoille [14], and Cyril Gavoille and David Peleg [19]. Exercises 4.6.56, 4.6.57, and 4.6.58 are due to Cyril Gavoille and Eric Guevremont [18], Evangelos Kranakis and Danny Krizanc [23], and Savio Tse and Francis Lau [33], respectively.

Characterizations of networks supporting interval routing are due to Lata Narayanan and Sunil Shende [26], Tamar Eilam, Shlomo Moran, and Shmuel Zaks [9], and Michele Flammini, Giorgio Gambosi, Umberto Nanni, and Richard Tan [10].

4.6 EXERCISES, PROBLEMS, AND ANSWERS

4.6.1 Exercises

Exercise 4.6.1 Write the set of rules corresponding to Protocol *Map_Gossip* described in Section 4.2.1.

Exercise 4.6.2 (★★★) Consider a tree network where each entity has a single item of information. Determine the time costs of gossiping. What would the time costs be if each entity x initially has $deg(x)$ items?

Exercise 4.6.3 Consider a tree network where each entity has $f(n)$ items of information. Assume that messages can contain $g(n)$ items of information (instead of $O(1)$); with how many messages can gossiping be performed?

Exercise 4.6.4 Using your answer to question 4.6.3, with how many messages can all routing tables be constructed if $g(n) = O(n)$?

Exercise 4.6.5 Consider a tree network where each entity has $f(n)$ items of information. Assume that messages can contain $g(n)$ items of information (instead of $O(1)$); with how many messages can all items of information be collected at a *single* entity?

Exercise 4.6.6 Using your answer to question 4.6.5, with how many messages can all routing tables be constructed at that single entity if $g(n) = O(n)$?

Exercise 4.6.7 Write the set of rules corresponding to Protocol *Iterated_Construction* described in Section 4.2.2. Implement and properly test your implementation.

Exercise 4.6.8 Prove that Protocol *Iterated_Construction* converges to the correct routing tables and will do so after at most $n - 1$ iterations. *Hint: Use induction to prove that $V_x^i[z]$ is the cost of the shortest path from x to z using at most i hops.*

Exercise 4.6.9 We have assumed that the cost of a link is the same in both directions, that is, $\theta(x, y) = \theta(y, x)$. However, there are cases when $\theta(x, y)$ can be different from $\theta(y, x)$. What modifications have to be made so that protocol *Iterated_Construction* works correctly also in those cases?

Exercise 4.6.10 In protocol *PT_Construction*, no action is provided for an *idle* entity receiving an *Expand* message. Prove that such a message will never be received in such a state.

Exercise 4.6.11 In procedure *Compute_Local_Minimum* of protocol *PT_Construction*, an entity might set path_length to infinity. Show that if this happens, this entity will set path_length to infinity in all subsequent iterations.

Exercise 4.6.12 In protocol *PT_Construction*, each entity will eventually set path_length to infinity. Show that when this happens to a leaf of the constructed tree, that entity can be removed from further computations.

Exercise 4.6.13 Modify protocol *PT_Construction* so that it constructs the routing table RT(s) of the source s.

Exercise 4.6.14 We have assumed that the cost of a link is the same in both directions, that is, $\theta(x, y) = \theta(y, x)$. However, there are cases when $\theta(x, y)$ can be different from $\theta(y, x)$. What modifications have to be made so that protocol *PT_Construction* works correctly also in those cases?

Exercise 4.6.15 Prove that any G has a $(\log n, n)$ sparser.

Exercise 4.6.16 Show how to construct a $(\log n, n)$ sparser with $O(m + n \log n)$ messages.

Exercise 4.6.17 Show how to use a $(\log n, n)$ sparser to solve the all-pairs shortest paths problem in $O(n^2 \log n)$ messages.

Exercise 4.6.18 Assume that messages can contain $O(n)$ items of information (instead of $O(1)$). Show how to construct *all* the shortest path trees with just $O(n^2)$ messages.

Exercise 4.6.19 Prove that, after iteration $i - 1$ of protocol *BF_Construction*,
(a) all the nodes at distance up to $i - 1$ are part of the tree;
(c) each node at distance $i - 1$ knows which of its neighbors are at distance $i - 1$.

Exercise 4.6.20 Write the set of rules corresponding to protocol *BF* described in Section 4.2.2. Implement and properly test your implementation.

Exercise 4.6.21 Write the set of rules corresponding to protocol *BF_Levels*. Implement and properly test your implementation.

Exercise 4.6.22 Let *Explore*(j, k) be the first message x accepts in the expansion phase of protocol *BF_Levels*. Prove that the number of times x will change its level in this phase is at most $j - t + 1 < l$.

Exercise 4.6.23 Prove that in the *expansion* phase of an iteration of protocol *BF_Levels*, all nodes in levels $t + 1$ to $t + l$ are reached and attached to the existing fragment, where t is the level of the sources (i.e., the leaves in the current fragment).

Exercise 4.6.24 Consider protocol *BF_Levels* when $l = d(G)$. Show how to obtain the same message and time complexity without any a priori knowledge of $d(G)$.

Exercise 4.6.25 Prove that if we choose $l = d(G)$ in protocol *BF_Levels*, then in any synchronous execution the number of messages will be exactly $2m + n - 1$.

Exercise 4.6.26 ($\star\star$) Show how to construct a breadth-first spanning tree in time $O(d(G)^{1+\epsilon})$ using no more than $O(m^{1+\epsilon})$ messages, for any $\epsilon > 0$.

Exercise 4.6.27 Let c be a center of G and let SPT(c) be the shortest path tree of c. Prove that $diam(G) \leq 2\, diam(\text{SPT}(c))$.

Exercise 4.6.28 Let T be a spanning tree of G. Prove that $\sum_{(x,y)\in T} |T[x - y]|$ $|T[y - x]|w(x, y) = \sum_{u,v\in T} d_T(u,v)$.

Exercise 4.6.29 (median-based routing)
Let z be a *median* of G (i.e., a node for which the sum of distances to all other nodes is minimized) and let PT(z) be the shortest path tree of z. Prove that *Traffic*(PT(z)) ≤ 2 *Traffic*($T\star$), where $T\star$ is the spanning tree of G for which *Traffic* is minimized.

Exercise 4.6.30 Consider a ring network R_n with weighted edges. Prove or disprove that PT(c) = MSP(R_n), where c is a center of R_n and MSP(R_n) is the minimum-cost spanning tree of R_n.

Exercise 4.6.31 Consider a ring network R_n with weighted edges. Let c and z be a center and a median of R_n, respectively.

1. For each of the following spanning trees of R_n, compare the *stretch* factor and the *edge-stretch* factor: PT(c), PT(z), and the minimum-cost spanning tree MSP(R_n).
2. Determine bounds on the average *edge-stretch* factor of PT(c), PT(z), and MSP(R_n).

Exercise 4.6.32 ($\star$) Consider a $a \times a$ square mesh $M_{a,a}$ where all costs are the same.

1. Is it possible to construct two spanning trees T' and T'' such that $\sigma(T') < \sigma(T'')$ but $\epsilon(T') > \epsilon(T'')$? Explain.
2. Is it possible to construct two spanning trees T' and T'' such that $\overline{\sigma}(T') < \overline{\sigma}(T'')$ but $\overline{\epsilon}(T') > \overline{\epsilon}(T'')$? Explain.

Exercise 4.6.33 Consider a square mesh $M_{a,a}$ where all costs are the same. Construct two spanning trees T' and T'' such that $\sigma(T') < \sigma(T'')$ but $\overline{\epsilon}(T') > \overline{\epsilon}(T'')$.

Exercise 4.6.34 ($\star$) Show that there are graphs G with unweighted edges where $\overline{\epsilon}_G(T) = \Omega(\log n)$ for every spanning tree T of G.

Exercise 4.6.35 ($\star\star$) Design an efficient protocol for computing a spanning tree with low average edge-stretch of a network G with *unweighted* edges.

Exercise 4.6.36 ($\star\star$) Design an efficient protocol for computing a spanning tree with low average edge-stretch of a network G with *weighted* edges.

Exercise 4.6.37 ($\star$) Design a protocol for computing the secondary paths of a node x. You may assume that the shortest-path tree PT(x) has already been constructed and that each node knows its and its neighbors' distance from x. Your protocol should use no more messages than that required to construct PT(x).

Exercise 4.6.38 (split horizon) ($\star\star$) Consider the following technique, called *split horizon*, for solving the *count-to-infinity* problem discussed in Section 4.3.1: During an iteration, *a* node a does *not* send its cost for destination c to its neighbor b if b is the next node in the "best" path (so far) from a to c. In the example of Figure 4.13, in the first iteration y does not send its cost for w to z, and thus z will correctly set its cost for w to K. In the next two iterations y and x will correctly set their cost for w to $K + 1$ and $K + 2$, respectively. Prove or disprove that split horizon solves the count-to-infinity problem.

Exercise 4.6.39 (split horizon with poison reverse) ($\star\star$) Consider the following technique, called *split horizon with poison reverse*, for solving the *count-to-infinity* problem discussed in Section 4.3.1: During an iteration, *a* node a sends its cost for destination c set to ∞ to its neighbor b if b is on the "best" path (so far) from a to c. Prove or disprove that split horizon with poison reverse solves the count-to-infinity problem.

Exercise 4.6.40 ($\star$) Design an efficient protocol that, given a shortest-path spanning tree PT(s), determines an optimal swap for every edge in PT(s): At the end of the execution, every node x knows the optimal swap edge for its incident link $e_s[x]$. Your protocol should use no more than $O(nh(s))$ messages, where $h(s)$ is the height of PT(x).

Exercise 4.6.41 ($\star$) Show how to answer Exercise 4.6.40 using no more than $O(n^\star(s))$ messages, where $n^\star(s)$ is the number of edges in the transitive closure of PT(x).

Exercise 4.6.42 Let $e = (u,v)$ be the optimal swap edge that x has computed for $e_s[x]$. Prove that, if $e_s[x]$ fails, to achieve point-of-failure shortest path rerouting, x must send the message for s to the incident link $(p_v(x), x)$.

Exercise 4.6.43 Show how to represent the intervals of *a ring* with just $\log n$ bits per interval.

Exercise 4.6.44 Show how that the intervals of *a ring* can be represented with just $\log n$ bits per interval, even if the costs of the links are not all the same.

Exercise 4.6.45 Let G be a network and assume that we can assign names to the nodes so that in each routing table, the destinations for each link form an interval. Determine what conditions the intervals must satisfy so that they can be represented with just $\log n$ bits each.

Exercise 4.6.46 Redefine properties *interval* and *disjointness* in case the n integers used as names are not consecutive, that is, they are chosen from a larger set Z_w, $w > n$.

Exercise 4.6.47 Show an assignment of names in a tree that does *not* have the *interval* property. Does there exists an assignment of distinct names in a tree that has the *interval* property but not the *disjointness* one? Explain your answer.

Exercise 4.6.48 Prove that in a tree, the assignment of names by Post-Order traversal has both *interval* and *disjointness* properties.

Exercise 4.6.49 Prove that in a tree, also the assignment of names by *Pre-Order* traversal has both *interval* and *disjointness* properties.

Exercise 4.6.50 Determine whether interval routing is possible in the regular graph shown in Figure 4.21. If so, show the routing table; otherwise explain why.

Exercise 4.6.51 Design an optimal interval routing scheme for $p \times q$ *mesh* and *torus*. How many bits of storage will it require?

Exercise 4.6.52 Design an optimal interval routing scheme for d-dimensional (a) *hypercube*, (b) *butterfly*, and (c) *cube-connected cycles*. How many bits of total storage will each require?

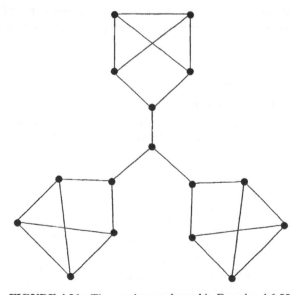

FIGURE 4.21: The regular graph used in Exercise 4.6.55.

Exercise 4.6.53 (★★) Show how to assign names to the nodes of an *outerplanar* graph so that interval routing is possible.

Exercise 4.6.54 (★★) If for every x all the intervals in its routing table are strictly increasing (i.e., there is no "wraparound" node "0), the interval routing is called *linear*. Prove that there are networks for which there exists interval routing but linear interval routing is impossible.

Exercise 4.6.55 Prove that in the globe graph of Figure 4.20, interval routing is not possible.

Exercise 4.6.56 (★★) Consider the approach of k-interval routing. Prove that there are graphs that require $k = O(n)$ intervals.

Exercise 4.6.57 (★★) Consider allowing each route to be within a factor α from optimal. Prove that if we want $\alpha = 2$, there are graphs that require $O(n^2)$ bits of storage at each node.

Exercise 4.6.58 (★★) Consider allowing the longest route to be within a factor β from the diameter diam(G) of the network, using at most k labels per edge. Prove that if we want $\beta < \frac{3}{2}$, then there are graphs that require $O(\log n)$ bits of storage at each node.

4.6.2 Problems

Problem 4.6.1   Linear Interval Routing. (★★) If for every x all the intervals in its routing table are strictly increasing (i.e., there is no "wraparound" node 0), the interval routing is called *linear*. Characterize the class of graphs for which there exists a linear interval routing.

4.6.3 Answers to Exercises

Partial Answer to Exercise 4.6.26.
Choose the size of the strip to be $k = \sqrt{d(G)}$. A *strip cover* is a collection of trees that span all the source nodes of a strip. In iteration i, first of all construct a "good" cover of strip i.

Answer to Exercise 4.6.29.
Observe that for any spanning tree T of G, $Traffic(T) = \sum_{u,v \in V} d_T(u,v)$ (Exercise 4.6.28). Let $SumDist(x) = \sum_{u \in V} d_G(u, x)$; clearly $Traffic(T\star) \geq \sum_{x \in V} SumDist(x)$. Let z be a *median* of G (i.e., a node for which $SumDist$ is minimized); then $SumDist(z) \leq \frac{1}{n} Traffic(T\star)$. Thus we have that $Traffic(\mathrm{PT}(z)) = \sum_{u,v \in V} d_{\mathrm{PT}(z)}(u, v) \leq \sum_{u,v \in V} (d_{\mathrm{PT}(z)}(u, z) + d_{\mathrm{PT}(z)}(z, v)) \leq (n - 1) \sum_{u \in V} (d_{\mathrm{PT}(z)}(u, z) + (n - 1) \sum_{v \in V} (d_{\mathrm{PT}(z)}(v, z) = 2(n - 1) SumDist(z) \leq 2Traffic(T\star)$.

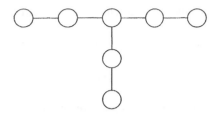

FIGURE 4.22: Graph with interval routing but where no linear interval routing exists.

Answer to Exercise 4.6.43.
In the table of node x, the interval associated to *right* always starts with $x + 1$ while the one associated to *left* always ends with $x - 1$. Hence, for each interval, it is sufficient to store only the other end value.

Partial Answer to Exercise 4.6.54.
Consider the graph shown in Figure 4.22.

BIBLIOGRAPHY

[1] Y. Afek and M. Ricklin. Sparser: a paradigm for running distributed algorithms. *Journal of Algorithms*. 14(2):316–28, March 1993.

[2] N. Alon, R.M. Karp, D. Peleg, and D. West. A graph-theoretic game and its application to the k-server problem. *SIAM Journal of Computing*, 24:78–100, 1995.

[3] B. Awerbuch. Reducing complexities of the distributed max-flow and breadth-first-search algorithms by means of network synchronization. *Networks*, 15:425–437, 1985.

[4] B. Awerbuch. Distributed shortest path algorithms. In *Proc. 21st Ann. ACM Symp. on Theory of Computing*, pages 490–500, 1989.

[5] B. Awerbuch and R.G. Gallager. A new distributed algorithm to find breadth first search trees. *IEEE Transactions on Information Theory*. 33:315–322, 1987.

[6] B. Awerbuch. Complexity of network synchronization. *Journal of the ACM*, 32(4): 804–823, October 1985.

[7] E.M. Bakker, Jan van Leeuwen, and Richard Tan. Linear interval routing. *Algorithms Review*, 2(2):45–61, 1991.

[8] T.-Y. Cheung. Graph traversal techniques and the maximum flow problem in distributed computation. *IEEE Transactions on Software Engineering*, 9:504–512, 1983.

[9] T. Eilam, S. Moran, and S. Zaks. The complexity of the characterization of networks supporting shortest-path interval routing. In *4th International Colloquium on Structural Information and Communication Complexity*, pages 99–11, Ascona, 1997.

[10] M. Flammini, G. Gambosi, U. Nanni, and R.B. Tan. Characterization results of all shortest paths interval routing schemes. *Networks*, 37(4):225–232, 2001.

[11] M. Flammini, G. Gambosi, and S. Salomone. Boolean routing. In *7th International Workshop on Distributed Algorithms*, pages 219–233, Lausanne, 1993.

[12] P. Flocchini, L. Pagli, T. Mesa, G. Prencipe, and N. Santoro. Point-of-failures shortest path rerouting: computing the optimal swaps distributively. *IEICE Transactions*, 2006.

[13] L. R. Ford and D. R. Fulkerson. *Flows in Networks*. Princeton University Press, 1962.

[14] P. Fraigniaud and C. Gavoille. Interval routing schemes. *Algorithmica*, 21(2):155–182, 1998.

[15] G.N. Frederickson. A distributed shortest path algorithm for a planar network. *Information and Computation*, 86(2):140–159, June 1990.

[16] G.N. Frederickson and R. Janardan. Designing networks with compact routing tables. *Algorithmica*, 3:171–190, June 1988.

[17] R.G. Gallager. Distributed minimum hop algorithms. Technical Report LIDS-P-1175, Laboratory for Information and Decision Systems, Massachusetts Institute of Technology, 1982.

[18] C. Gavoille and E. Guevremont. Worst case bounds for shortest path intervalrouting. *Journal of Algorithms*, 27:1–25, 1998.

[19] C. Gavoille and D. Peleg. The compactness of interval routing. *SIAM Journal on Discrete Mathematics*, 12(4):459–473, 1999.

[20] S. Haldar. An 'all pairs shortest paths' distributed algorithm using $2n^2$ messages. In *Proceedings of the 19th International Workshop on Graph-Theoretic Concepts in Computer Science (WG'93)*, Utrecht, Netherlands, June 1993.

[21] H. Ito, K. Iwama, Y. Okabe, and T. Yoshihiro. Single backup table schemes for shortest-path routing. *Theoretical Computer Science*, 333:347–353, 2004.

[22] J. Misra K.M. Chandi. Distributed computations on graphs: shortest path algorithms. *Communications of ACM*, 25(11):833–837, November 1982.

[23] Evangelos Kranakis and Danny Krizanc. Lower bounds for compact routing. In *13th Symposium on Theoretical Aspects of Computer Science*, pages 529–540, Grenoble, feb 1996.

[24] J. van Leeuwen and R.B. Tan. Interval routing. *The Computer Journal*, 30:298–307, 1987.

[25] P.M. Merlin and A. Segall. A failsafe distributed routing protocol. *IEEE Transactions on Communications*, 27(9):1280–1287, sept 1979.

[26] L. Narayanan and S. Shende. Characterization of networks supporting shortest-path interval labelling schemes. In *3rd International Colloquium on Structural Information and Communication Complexity*, pages 73–87, 1996.

[27] E. Nardelli, G. Proietti, and P. Widmayer. Swapping a failing edge of a single source shortest paths tree is good and fast. *Algoritmica*, 35:56–74, 2003.

[28] K.V.S. Ramarao and S. Venkatesan. On finding and updating shortest paths distributively. *Journal of Algorithms*, 13(2):235–257, 1992.

[29] E.C. Rosen. The updating protocol of Arpanet's new routing algorithm. *Computer Networks*, 4:11–19, 1980.

[30] N. Santoro and R. Khatib. Labeling and implicit routing in networks. *The Computer Journal*, 28:5–8, 1985.

[31] W.D. Tajibnapis. A correctness proof of a topology information maintenance protocol for a distributed computer network. *Communications of the ACM*, 20(7):477–485, 1977.

[32] S. Toueg. An all-pairs shortest-path distributed algorithm, 1980.

[33] S.S.H. Tse and F.C.M. Lau. On the space requirement of interval routing. *IEEE Transactions On Computers*, 48(7):752–757, July 1999.

[34] D.W. Wall and S. Owicki. Construction of centered shortest-path trees in networks. *Networks*, 13(2):207–332, 1983.

[35] Y. Zhu and T.-Y. Cheung. A new distributed breadth-first-search algorithm. *Information Processing Letters*, 25:329–333, 1987.

CHAPTER 5

Distributed Set Operations

5.1 INTRODUCTION

In a distributed computing environment, each entity has its own data stored in its local memory. Some data items held by one entity are sometimes related to items held by other entities, and we focus and operate on them. An example is the set of the ids of the entities. What we did in the past was to operate on this set, for example, by finding the smallest id or the largest one. Another example is the set of the single values held by each entity, and the operation was to find the overall rank of each of those values. In all these examples, the relevant data held by an entity consist of just a single data item.

In general, an entity x has a set of relevant data D_x. The union of all these local sets forms a *distributed set* of data

$$\mathcal{D} = \bigcup_x D_x \tag{5.1}$$

and the tuple

$$\langle D_{x_1}, D_{x_2}, \ldots, D_{x_n} \rangle$$

describes the *distribution* of $\mathcal{D}$ among the entities $x_1, x_2 \ldots, x_n$. Clearly there are many different distributions of the same distributed set.

There are two main types of operations that can be performed on a distributed set:

1. *queries* and
2. *updates*.

A *query* is a request for some information about the global data set $\mathcal{D}$, as well as about the individual sets D_x forming $\mathcal{D}$. A query can originate at any entity. If the entity where the query originates has locally the desired information, the query can be answered immediately; otherwise, the entity will have to communicate with other entities to obtain the desired information. As usual, we are concerned with the communication costs, rather than the local processing costs, when dealing with answering a query.

Design and Analysis of Distributed Algorithms, by Nicola Santoro
Copyright © 2007 John Wiley & Sons, Inc.

An *update* is a request to change the composition of the distributed set. There are two basic updates: the request to add a new element to the set, an operation called *insertion*; and the request to remove an element from the set, an operation called *deletion*. The third basic update is the request to change the value of an existing item of the set, an operation called *change*. Note that a change can be seen as a deletion of the item with the old value followed by an insertion of an item with the new value.

There are many distributions of the same set. In a distribution, the local sets are not necessarily distinct or disjoint. Two extreme cases serve to illustrate the spectrum of distributions and the impact that the structure of the distribution has when handling queries and performing updates. One extreme distribution is the *partition* where the local sets have no elements in common:

$$D_i \cup D_j = \emptyset, \quad i \neq j.$$

At the other end of the spectrum is the *multiple-copy* distribution where every entity has a copy of the entire data set.

$$\forall i \quad D_i = \mathcal{D}.$$

A multiple-copy distribution is excellent for queries but poor for updates. Queries are easy because all entities possess all the data; hence every answer can be derived locally, without any communication. However, an update will require modification of the data held at each and every entity; in the presence of concurrent updates, this process becomes exceedingly difficult.

The situation is reversed in the partition. As each data item is located in only one site, answering a query requires searching through all potential entities to find the one that has locally stored the required data. By contrast, to perform an update is easy because the change is performed in only the entity having the item, and there is no danger of concurrent updates on the same item.

In most cases, the data are *partially replicated*; that is, some data items are stored at more than one entities while others are to be found at only one entity. This means that, in general, we have to face and deal with the problems of both extremes, partition and multiple-copy distributions, without the advantages of either one.

In the following we will first focus on an important class of queries, called *order statistics*; the problem of answering such queries is traditionally called *selection*. As selection as well as most queries is more easily and efficiently solved if the distribution is sorted, we will also investigate the problem of *sorting* the distributed data. We will then concentrate on distributed *set operations*; that is, computing union, intersection, and differences of the local sets. The ability to perform such operations has a direct impact on the processing of complex queries usually performed in databases.

To focus on the problems, we will assume the standard set of restrictions **IR** (Connectivity, Total Reliability, Bidirectional Links, Distinct Identifiers). For simplicity, as local processing time does not interest us when we consider the cost of our protocols, we will assume that all of the data stored at an entity are sorted.

IMPORTANT. As we consider arbitrary distributions of the data set, it is possible that a data item a is in more than one local set. As we assume ID, we can use the ids of the entities to break ties and create a total order even among copies of the same value; so, for example, if a is in both D_x and D_y where $id(x) > id(y)$, then we can say that the copy of a in D_x is "greater" than the one in D_y. In this way, if so desired, the copies can also be considered distinct and included in the global data set $\mathcal{D}$ by the union operation (5.1).

5.2 DISTRIBUTED SELECTION

5.2.1 Order Statistics

Given a totally ordered data set $\mathcal{D}$ of size N distributed among the entities, the *distributed selection* problem is the general problem of locating $\mathcal{D}[K]$, the Kth smallest element of $\mathcal{D}$. Problems of this type are called *order statistics*, to distinguish them from the more conventional *cardinal statistics* (e.g., average, standard deviation, etc.). Unlike cardinal statistics, ordinal ones are more difficult to compute in a distributed environment.

We have already seen and examined the problem of computing $\mathcal{D}[1]$ (i.e., the minimum value), and $\mathcal{D}[N]$ (i.e., the maximum value). Other elements whose ranks are of particular importance are the *medians* of the data set. If N is odd, there is only one *median*, $\mathcal{D}[\lceil N/2 \rceil]$. If N is even, there are two medians: the *lower median* $\mathcal{D}[N/2]$ and the *upper median* $\mathcal{D}[N/2 + 1]$.

Unlike the case of $\mathcal{D}[1]$ and $\mathcal{D}[N]$, the problem of finding the median(s) and of K selection for an arbitrary value of K is not simple, and considerably more expensive to resolve. The complexity of the problem depends on many parameters including the number n of entities, the size $N = |\mathcal{D}|$ of the set, the number $n_x = |D_x|$ of elements stored at an entity x, the rank K of the element being sought, and the topology of the network.

Before proceeding to examine strategies for its solution, let us introduce a fundamental property and a basic observation that will be helpful in our designs.

Let $\vec{\mathcal{D}}[K]$ denote the Kth *largest* element of the data set. Then

Property 5.2.1 $\mathcal{D}[K] = \vec{\mathcal{D}}[N - K + 1]$

Thus looking for the Kth smallest is the same as looking for the $(N - K + 1)$th largest. Consider, for example, a set of 10 distinct elements; the 4th smallest is clearly the 7th largest; see Figure 5.1 where the elements $d_1, \ldots, d_{10}$ of the set are represented and sorted in an increasing order. This fact has many important consequences, as we will see later.

The other useful tool is based on the trivial observation.

Property 5.2.2 $D_x[K + 1] > \mathcal{D}[K] > \vec{D}_x[N - K + 2]$.

This means that, if an entity x has more than K items, it needs only to consider the smallest K items. Similarly, if x has more than $(N - K + 1)$ items, it needs only to consider the largest $(N - K + 1)$ items.

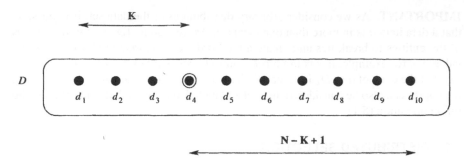

FIGURE 5.1: The Kth smallest is precisely the $(N - K + 1)$th largest.

Finally, we will assume that the selection process will be coordinated by a single entity and that all communication will take place on a spanning tree of the network. Although it does not matter for the correctness of our protocols which entity is selected as coordinator and which spanning tree is chosen for communication, for efficiency reasons it is convenient to choose as coordinator a *communication center s* of the network and to choose as a spanning-tree SP(s) the shortest path spanning tree for s. Recall (Section 2.6.6) that a communication center e is a node that minimizes the sum of the distances to all other nodes (i.e., $\sum_v d_G(v, s)$ is minimum). Also recall (Section 4.2.3) that, by definition of the shortest path spanning tree, PT(s) is such that $d_G(v, s) = d_{PT(s)}(v, s)$ for all entities v. In the following we will assume that s is used as coordinator, and for simplicity we will denote PT(s) simply as T.

5.2.2 Selection in a Small Data Set

We will first consider the selection problem when the data set is rather small; more precisely, we consider data sets where $N = O(n)$. A special instance of a small distributed set is when every D_x is a *singleton*: it contains just a single element d_x; this is, for example, the case when the only data available at a node is its *id*.

Input Collection   As the data set is small, the simple solution of collecting all the data at the coordinator and letting s solve locally the problem is actually not unfeasible from a complexity point of view.

The cost of collecting all the data items at s is clearly $\sum_v d_G(v, s)$. To this, we must add an initial broadcast to notify the entities to send their data to the coordinator, and (if needed) a final broadcast to notify them of the final result; as these are done on a tree, their cost will be $2(n - 1)$ messages. Hence the total cost of this protocol that we can call *Collect* is

$$\mathbf{M}[Collect] = \sum_v d_G(v, s) + 2(n - 1) \tag{5.2}$$

communication.

Notice that, depending on the network,

$$n - 1 \le \sum_v d_G(v, s) \le \left(\tfrac{n}{2} - 1\right)\tfrac{n}{2}$$

where the lower bound is achieved, for example, when G is a complete graph, and the upper is achieved, for example, when G is a ring. So $\mathbf{M}[Collect] = O(n^2)$ in the worst case.

This approach is somehow an overkill as the entire set is collected at s.

Truncated Ranking It might be possible to reduce the amount of messages by making it dependent on the value of K. In fact we can use the existing ranking protocol for trees (Exercise 2.9.4) and execute it on T until the Kth smallest item is found. The use of the ranking algorithm will then cost no more than

$$\sum_{Rank(v) \le K} 2d_G(v, s).$$

Note that, if $K > N - K + 1$ we can exploit Property 5.2.1 and use the ranking algorithm to assign ranks in decreasing order until the $(N - K + 1)$th *largest* element is ranked. In this case, the cost will then be no more than

$$\sum_{Rank(v) \ge K} d_G(v, e).$$

To this we must add the initial broadcast to set up the ranking and a final broadcast to notify the entities of the final result; as these are done on a tree, their cost will be $2(n - 1)$ messages. Hence, assuming $K \le N - K + 1$, the total cost of this protocol that we can call *Rank* is

$$\mathbf{M}[Rank] \le \sum_{Rank(v) \le K} 2d_G(v, s) + 2(n - 1). \tag{5.3}$$

Notice that, depending on the network,

$$2(K - 1) \le \sum_{Rank(v) \le k} 2d_G(v, e) \le \tfrac{K}{2}\left(n - \tfrac{K}{2} + 1\right)$$

where the lower bound is achieved, for example, when G is a complete graph, and the upperbound could be achieved, for example, when G is a ring. This means that, in any case,

$$\mathbf{M}[Rank] \le n\Delta$$

where $\Delta = \text{Min}\{K, N - K + 1\}$. In other words, if K (or $N - K + 1$) is small, *Rank* will be much more efficient than *Collect*. As K becomes larger, the cost increases until, when $K = N/2$, the two protocols have the same cost.

IMPORTANT. The protocols we have seen are generic, in that they apply to any topology. For particular networks, it is possible to take advantage of the properties of the topology so to obtain a more efficent selection protocol. This is the case of the *ring* (Exercise 5.6.1), the *mesh* (Exercise 5.6.2), and the *complete binary tree* (Exercise 5.6.3). The problem of designing a selection protocol that uses $o(n^2)$ messages in the worst case is still unsolved (Problem 5.6.1).

5.2.3 Simple Case: Selection Among Two Sites

In the previous section we have seen how to perform selection when the number of data items is small: $N = O(n)$. In general, this is not the case; in fact, not only N is much larger than n but it is order of magnitude so. So, in general, the techniques that we have seen so far are clearly not efficient. What we need is a different strategy to deal with the general case, in particular when $N >> n$.

In this section we will examine this problem in a simple setting when $n = 2$; that is, there are only two entities in the system, x and y. We will develop efficient solution strategies; some of the insights will be useful when faced with a more general case in later sections.

Median   Let us consider first the problem of determining the *lower median*, that is, $\mathcal{D}[\lceil N/2 \rceil]$. Recall that this is the unique element that has exactly $\lceil N/2 \rceil - 1$ elements smaller than itself and exactly $\lfloor N/2 \rfloor$ elements larger than itself.

A simple solution is the following. First of all, one of the entities (e.g., the one where the selection query originates, or the one with the smallest id) is elected, which will receive the entire set of the other entity. The elected entity, say x, will then locally determine the median of the set $D_x \cup D_y$ and communicate it, if necessary, to the other entity. Notice that as x has now locally available the entire data set, it can answer any selection query, not just for the lower median. The drawback of this solution is that the amount of communication is significant as an entire local set is transferred. We can obviously elect the entity with the larger set to minimize the amount of messages; still, $O(N)$ messages must be transferred in the worst case.

A more efficient technique is clearly needed. We can design such a technique on the basis of a simple observation: if we compare the medians of the two local sets, then we can immediately eliminate almost *half* of the elements from consideration.

Let us see why and how. Assume for simplicity that each local set contains $N/2 = 2^{p-1}$ elements; this means that both D_x and D_y have a lower median, $m_x = D_x[2^{p-2}]$ and $m_y = D_y[2^{p-2}]$ respectively. The lower median will have exactly $N/2 - 1 = 2^p - 1$ elements smaller than itself and exactly $N/2 = 2^p$ elements larger than itself. For example, consider the two sets of size $N/2 = 16$ shown in Figure 5.2(a) where each black circle indicates a data element, and in each set the elements are shown locally sorted in a left-to-right increasing order; then $m_x = D_x[8]$ and $m_y = D_y[8]$.

Assume that $m_x > m_y$; then each element in D_x larger than m_x must also be larger than m_y. This means that each of them is larger than at least 2^{p-2} elements in D_x and that of at least 2^{p-2} elements in D_y; that is, it has at least $2^{p-2} + 2^{p-2} = 2^{p-1} = N/2$ elements smaller than itself, and therefore it can *not* be the lower median. In other

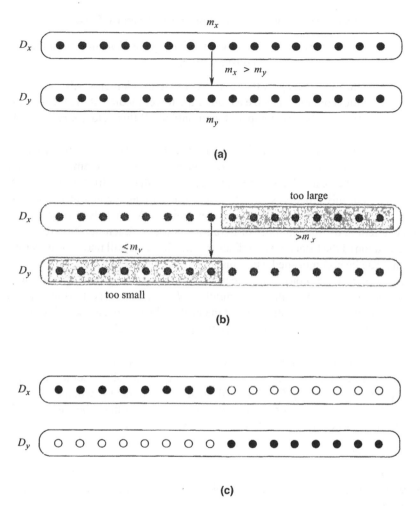

FIGURE 5.2: Half of the elements can be discarded after a single comparison of the two local medians.

words, any element larger than the largest of the median of the two sets can be discounted from consideration as it is larger than the overall median. See Figure 5.2(b).

Similarly, all the elements in D_y smaller than m_x can be discounted as well. In fact, each such element would be smaller that at least 2^{p-2} elements in its own set and at least $2^{p-2} + 1$ elements in the other set; that is, it has at least $2 2^{p-2} + 1 = 2^{p-1} + 1 = N/2 + 1$ elements larger than itself, and therefore it can *not* be the lower median. See Figure 5.2(b).

Thus, by locally calculating and then exchanging the median of each set, at least half of the elements of each set, and therefore half of the total number of elements, can be discounted; shown as white circle in Figure 5.2(c).

There is a very interesting and important property (Exercise 5.6.4):

the overall lower median is the lower median of the elements still under consideration.

This means that we can reapply the same process to the elements still under consideration: the entities communicate to each other the lower median of the local elements under consideration, these are compared, and half of all this data are removed from consideration.

In other words, we have just designed a protocol, that we shall call *Halving*, that is composed of a sequence of iterations; in each, half of the elements still under consideration are discarded and the sought global median is still the median of the considered data; this process is repeated until only a single element is left at each site and the median can be unambiguously determined. As we halve the problem size at every iteration, the total number of iterations is log N. Each iteration requires the communication of the local lower medians (of the elements still under consideration), a task that can be accomplished using just one message per iteration.

The working of the protocol has been described assuming that N is a power of two and that both sets have the same number $N/2$ of elements. Fortunately, these two assumptions are not essential. In fact the protocol *Halving* can be adjusted to two arbitrarily sized sets without changing its complexity: Exercise 5.6.5.

Arbitrary K We have just seen a simple and efficient protocol for finding the overall (lower) median $\mathcal{D}[\lceil N/2 \rceil]$ of a set $\mathcal{D}$ distributed over two sites. Let us consider the general problem of selecting $\mathcal{D}[K]$, the Kth smallest element of $\mathcal{D}$ when K is arbitrary, $1 \leq k \leq N$. Assume again, for simplicity, that the two sets have the same size $N/2$. We know already how to deal with the case of $K = \lceil N/2 \rceil$.

Case $K < \lceil N/2 \rceil$

Consider first the case when $K < \lceil N/2 \rceil$. This means that each of the two sites has locally *more* than K elements. An example with $N/2 = 12$ and $K = 4$ is shown in Figure 5.3.

Consider the set D_x. As we are looking for the Kth smallest data item overall, any data item greater than $D_x[K]$ cannot be $\mathcal{D}[K]$ (as it will be larger than at least K data items). This means that we can immediately discount all these items, keeping only K items still under consideration. For example, in Figure 5.3(a) we have $N/2 = 12$ items shown in a left-to-right increasing order; if $K = 4$, then all the items greater than $D_x[4]$ are too large to be $\mathcal{D}[4]$: Figure 5.3(b). Similarly, we can keep under consideration in D_y just $D_y[K]$ and the items that are smaller.

IMPORTANT. Notice that $\mathcal{D}[K]$ is also the Kth smallest item among those kept in consideration; this is because we have discounted only the elements *larger* than $\mathcal{D}[K]$.

What is the net result of this ? We are now left with two sets of items, each of size K; see Figure 5.3(c). Among those items, we are looking for the Kth smallest

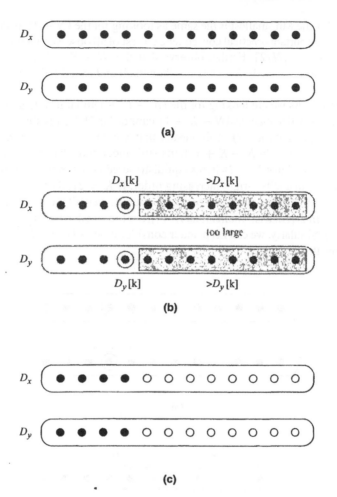

FIGURE 5.3: All the elements greater than the local Kth smallest element can be discarded.

element. In other words, once this operation has been performed, the problem we need to solve is to *determine the lower median of the elements under consideration.* We already know how to solve this problem efficiently.

In other words, if $K < N/2$ we can reduce the problem to that of finding the lower median. Notice that this is accomplished without any communication, once it is known that we are looking for $\mathcal{D}[K]$.

Case $K > \lceil N/2 \rceil$

Consider next the case when $K > \lceil N/2 \rceil$. This means that each of the two sites has locally *less* than K elements, thus we cannot use the approach we did for $K < \lceil N/2 \rceil$. Still, we can make a similar reduction also in this case. To see how and why, consider the following obvious but important property of *any* totally ordered set.

Looking for the Kth smallest is the same as looking for the $(N - K + 1)$th largest. This fact is an important practical consequence. First of all observe that if $K > \lceil N/2 \rceil$ then $N - K + 1 < \lceil N/2 \rceil$. Further observe that the $(N - K + 1)$th *largest* item is the only one that has exactly $N - k$ larger than itself and exactly $K - 1$ smaller than itself.

Consider D_x. As we are looking for the $(N - K + 1)$th largest data item overall, any data item smaller than $\vec{D}_x[N - K + 1]$ cannot be $\vec{\mathcal{D}}[K]$ (as there are at least $N - K + 1$ larger data items). This means that we can immediately discount all these items, keeping only $N - K + 1$ items still under consideration. For example, in Figure 5.4(a) we have $N = 24$ items equidistributed between the two sites, whose items are shown in a left-to-right increasing order. If $K = 21$, then $N - K + 1 = 4$; that is, we are looking for the 4th largest item overall; then all the items smaller than the 4th largest in D_x, that is, smaller than $D_x[4]$, are too small to be $\mathcal{D}[21] = \vec{\mathcal{D}}[4]$, see Figure 5.3(b). Similarly, we can keep under consideration in D_y just $\vec{D}_y[N - K + 1]$ and the items that are larger.

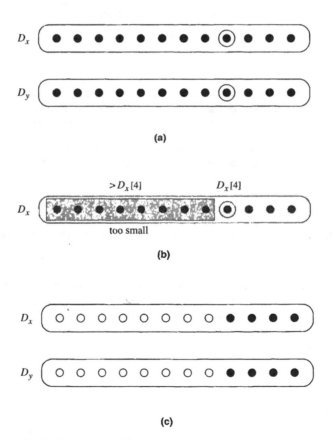

(a)

(b)

(c)

FIGURE 5.4: All the data item smaller than the local $(N{-}K{+}1)$th *largest* element can be discarded.

IMPORTANT. Notice that $\mathcal{D}[K]$ is the $(N - K + 1)$th largest item among those kept in consideration; this is because we have discounted only elements *smaller* than $\mathcal{D}[K]$.

What is the net result of this ? We are now left with two sets of items, each of size $N - K + 1$; see Figure 5.4(c). Among those items, we are looking for the $(N - K + 1)$th largest element. In other words, once this operation has been performed, the problem we need to solve is to *determine the upper median of the elements under consideration*. We already know how to solve this problem efficiently.

Summary   Regardless of the value of K we can always transform the K-selection problem into a median-finding problem. Notice that this is accomplished without any additional communication, once it is known that we are looking for $\mathcal{D}[K]$.

In the description we have assumed that both sites have the same number of element, $N/2$. If this is not the case, it is easy to verify (Exercise 5.6.6) that the same type of reduction can still take place.

Hacking   As we have seen, median finding is "the" core problem to solve. Our solution, *Halving*, is efficient. This protocol can be made more efficient by observing that we can discard (because it is too large to be the median) any element greater than m_x not only in D_x but also in D_y (if there is any); similarly, we can discard the elements smaller than m_y (because it is too small to be the median) not only from D_y but also from D_x (if there is any). In this way we can reduce the amount of elements still under consideration by more than half, thus possibly reducing the number of iterations.

CAUTION: The number of discarded items that are greater than the median might be larger than the number of discarded items that are smaller than the median (or vice versa). This means that the overall lower median we are looking for is no longer the median of the elements left under consideration.

In other words, after removing items from consideration, we might be left with a general selection problem. By now, we know how to reduce a selection problem to the median-finding one. The resulting protocol, that we shall call *GeneralHalving*, will use a few more messages, in each iteration but might yield a larger reduction (Exercise 5.6.7).

Generalization   This technique can be generalized to three sites; however, we are no longer able to reduce the number of items still under consideration to at most half at each iteration (Exercise 5.6.9). For larger $n > 3$ the technique we have designed for two sites is unfortunately no longer efficiently scalable. Fortunately, some lessons we have learned when dealing with the two sites are immediately and usefully applicable to any n, as we will discuss in the next section.

5.2.4   General Selection Strategy: RankSelect

In the previous section we have seen how to perform selection when the number of data items is small or there are only two sites. In general, this is not the case. For example, in most practical applications, the number of sites is 10–100, while the amount of data at each site is $\geq 10^6$. What we need is a different strategy to deal with the general case.

Let us think of the set $\mathcal{D}$ containing the N elements as a *search space* in which we need to find $d^* = \mathcal{D}[K]$, unknown to us, and the only thing we know about d^* is its rank $Rank[d^*, \mathcal{D}] = K$. An effective way to handle the problem of discovering d^* is to reduce as much as possible the search space, eliminating from consideration as many items as possible, until we find d^* or the search space is small enough (e.g., $O(n)$) for us to apply the techniques discussed in the previous section.

Suppose that we (somehow) know the rank $Rank[d, \mathcal{D}]$ of a data item d in $\mathcal{D}$. If $Rank[d, \mathcal{D}] = K$ then d is the element we were looking for. If $Rank[d, \mathcal{D}] < K$ then d is too small to be d^*, and *so are all the items smaller than d*. Similarly, if $Rank[d, \mathcal{D}] > K$, then d is too large to be d^*, and *so are all the items larger than d*.

This fact can be employed to design a simple and, as we will see, rather efficient selection strategy:

Strategy *RankSelect*:

1. Among the data items under consideration, (initially, they all are) choose one, say d.
2. Determine its overall rank $k' = Rank[d, \mathcal{D}]$.
3. If $k' = K$ then $d = d^*$ and we are done. Else, if $k' < K$, (respectively, $k' > K$) remove from consideration d all the data items *smaller* (respectively, *larger*) than d and restart the process.

Thus, according to this strategy, the selection process consists of a sequence of iterations, each reducing the search space, performed until d^* is found. Notice that we could stop the process as soon as just few data items (e.g., $O(n)$) are left for consideration, and then apply protocol *Rank*.

Most of the operations performed by this strategy are rather simple to implement. We can assume that a spanning tree of the network is available and will be used for all communication, and an entity is elected to coordinate the overall execution (becoming the root of the tree for this protocol). Any entity can act as a coordinator and any spanning-tree T of the network will do. However, for efficiency reasons, it is better to choose as a coordinator the communication center s of the network, and choose as a tree T the shortest path spanning-tree $PT(s)$ of s.

Let $d(i)$ be the item selected at the beginning of iteration i. Once $d(i)$ is chosen, the determination of its rank is a trivial broadcast (to let every entity know $d(i)$) started by the root s and a convergecast (to collect the partial rank information) ending at the root s. Recall Exercise 2.9.43.

Once $d(i)$ has determined the rank of $d(i)$, s will notify all other entities of the result: $d(i) = d^*, d(i) < d^*$, or $d(i) > d^*$; each entity will then act accordingly (terminating or removing some elements from consideration).

The only operation still to be discussed is how we choose $d(i)$. The choice of $d(i)$ is quite important because it affects the number of iterations and thus the overall complexity of the resulting protocol. Let us examine some of the possible choices and their impact.

Random Choice   We can choose $d(i)$ *uniformly at random*; that is, in such a way that each item of the search space has the same probability of being chosen.

How can s choose $d(i)$ uniformly at random ? In Section 2.6.7 and Exercise 2.9.52 we have discussed how to select, in a tree, uniformly at random an item from the initial distributed set. Clearly that protocol can be used to choose $d(i)$ in the first iteration of our algorithm. However, we cannot immediately use it in the subsequent iterations. In fact, after an iteration, some items are removed from consideration; that is, the search space is reduced. This means that, for the next iteration, we must ensure we select an item that is still in *new* search space. Fortunately, this can be achieved with simple readjustments to the protocol of Exercise 2.9.52, achieving the same cost in each iteration (Exercise 5.6.10). That is, each iteration costs at most $2(n-1) + d_T(s, x)$ messages and $2r(s) + d_T(s, x)$ ideal time units for the random selection plus an additional $2(n-1)$ messages and $2r(s)$ time units to determine the rank of the selected element.

Let us call the resulting protocol *RandomSelect*. To determine its global cost, we need to determine the number of iterations. In the worst case, in iteration i we remove from the search space only $d(i)$; so the number of iterations can be as bad as N, for a worst case cost of

$$M[RandomSelect] \leq (4(n-1) + r(s))\, N, \qquad (5.4)$$

$$T[RandomSelect] \leq 5\, r(s)\, N. \qquad (5.5)$$

However, *on the average*, the power of making a random choice is evident; in fact (Exercise 5.6.11):

Lemma 5.2.1   *The expected number of iterations performed by Protocol* Random-Select *until termination is at most*

$$1.387 \log N + O(1).$$

This means that, on the average

$$M_{\text{average}}[RandomSelect] = O(n \log N), \qquad (5.6)$$

$$T_{\text{average}}[RandomSelect] = O(n \log N). \qquad (5.7)$$

As mentioned earlier, we could stop the strategy *RankSelect*, and thus terminate protocol *RandomSelect*, as soon as $O(n)$ data items are left for consideration, and then apply protocol *Rank*. See Exercise 5.6.12.

Random Choice with Reduction We can improve the average message complexity by exploiting the properties discussed in Section 5.2.1. Let $\Delta(i) = \min\{K(i), N(i) - K(i) + 1\}$.

In fact, by Property 5.2.2, if at the beginning of iteration i, an entity has more than $K(i)$ elements under consideration, it needs to consider only the $K(i)$ smallest and immediately remove from consideration the others; similarly, if it has more than $N(i) - K(i) + 1$ items, it needs to consider only the $N(i) - K(i) + 1$ largest and immediately remove from consideration the others.

If every entity does this, the search space can be further reduced even before the random selection process takes place. In fact, the net effect of the application of this technique is that each entity will have at most $\Delta(i) = \min\{K(i), N(i) - K(i) + 1\}$ items still under consideration during iteration i. The root s can then perform random selection in this *reduced* space of size $n(i) \leq N(i)$. Notice that d^* will have a new rank $k(i) \leq K(i)$ in the new search space.

Specifically, our strategy will be to include, in the broadcast started by the root s at the beginning of iteration i, the values $N(i)$ and $K(i)$. Each entity, upon receiving this information, will locally perform the reduction (if any) of the local elements and then include in the convergecast the information about the size of the new search space. At the end of the convergecast, s knows both $n(i)$ and $k(i)$ as well as all the information necessary to perform the random selection in the reduced search space.

In other words, the total number of messages per iteration will be exactly the same as that of Protocol *RandomSelect*.

In the worst case this change does not make any difference. In fact, for the resulting protocol *RandomFlipSelect*, the number of iterations can still be as bad as N (Exercise 5.6.13), for a worst case cost of

$$M[RandomFlipSelect] \leq (2(n - 1) + r(s))\, N, \tag{5.8}$$

$$T[RandomFlipSelect] \leq 3\, r(s)\, N. \tag{5.9}$$

The change does however make a difference on the average cost. In fact, (Exercise 5.6.14)

Lemma 5.2.2   *The expected number of iterations performed by Protocol Random-FlipSelect until termination is less than*

$$\ln(\Delta) + \ln(n) + O(1)$$

where $\ln()$ denotes the natural logarithm (recall that $\ln() = .693 \log()$).

This means that, on the average

$$M_{\text{average}}[RandomFlipSelect] = O(n\,(\ln(\Delta) + \ln(n))) \tag{5.10}$$

$$T_{\text{average}}[RandomFlipSelect] = O(n\,(\ln(\Delta) + \ln(n))). \tag{5.11}$$

Also in this case, we could stop the strategy *RankSelect*, and thus terminate protocol *RandomSelect*, as soon as only $O(n)$ data items are left for consideration, and then apply protocol *Rank*. See Exercise 5.6.15.

Selection in a Random Distribution   So far, we have not made any assumption on the distribution of the data items among the entities. If we know something about how the data are distributed, we can clearly exploit this knowledge to design a more efficient protocol. In this section we consider a very simple and quite reasonable assumption about how the data are distributed.

Consider the set $\mathcal{D}$; it is distributed among the entities $x_1, \ldots, x_n$; let $n[x_j] = |D_{x_j}|$ be the number of items stored at x_j. The assumption we will make is that all the distributions of $\mathcal{D}$ that end up with $n[x_j]$ items at x_j, $1 \le j \le n$, are *equally likely*.

In this case we can refine the selection of $d(i)$. Let $z(i)$ be the entity where the number of elements still under consideration in iteration i is the largest; that is, $\forall x \ m(i) = |D_{z(i)}(i)| \ge |D_x(i)|$. (If there is more than one entity with the same number of items, choose an arbitrary one.) In our protocol, which we shall call *Random-RandomSelect*, we will choose $d(i)$ to be the $h(i)$th smallest item in the set $D_{z(i)}(i)$, where

$$h(i) = \left\lceil K(i)\left(\tfrac{m(i)+1}{N+1}\right) - \tfrac{1}{2} \right\rceil.$$

We will use this choice until there are less than n items under consideration.

At this point, in Protocol *RandomRandomSelect* we will use Protocol *RandomFlipSelect* to finish the job and determine d^*.

Notice that also in this protocol, each iteration can easily be implemented (Exercise 5.6.16) with at most $4(n - 1) + r(s)$ messages and $5r(s)$ ideal time units.

With the choice of $d(i)$ we have made, the average number of iterations, until there are less than n items left under consideration, is indeed small. In fact (Exercise 5.6.17),

Lemma 5.2.3   *Let the randomness assumption hold. Then the expected number of iterations performed by Protocol RandomRandomSelect until there are less than n items under consideration is at most*

$$\tfrac{4}{3} \lfloor \log \log \Delta + 1 \rfloor.$$

This means that, on the average

$$M_{\text{average}}[RandomRandomSelect] = O(n(\log \log \Delta + \log n)) \text{ and} \quad (5.12)$$

$$T_{\text{average}}[RandomRandomSelect] = O(n(\log \log \Delta + \log n)). \quad (5.13)$$

Filtering   The drawback of all previous protocols rests on their worst case costs: $O(nN)$ messages and $O(r(s)N)$ time; notice that this cost is more than that of *input collection*, that is, of mailing all the items to s. It can be shown that the probability of the occurrence of the worst case is so small that it can be neglected. However, there might be systems where such a cost is not affordable under any circumstances. For these systems, it is necessary to have a selection protocol that, even if less efficient on the average, can guarantee a reasonable cost even in the worst case.

The design of such a system is fortunately not so difficult; in fact it can be achieved with the strategy *RankSelect* with the appropriate choice of $d(i)$.

As before, let D_x^i denote the set of elements still under consideration at x in iteration i and $n_x^i = |D_x^i|$ denote its size. Consider the (lower) median $d_x^i = D_x^i[\lceil n_x^i/2 \rceil]$ of D_x^i, and let $M(i) = \{d_x^i\}$ be the set of these medians. With each element in $M(i)$ associate a *weight*; the weight associated with d_x^i is just the size of the corresponding set n_x^i.

Filter: Choose $d(i)$ to be the *weighted* (lower) median of $M(i)$.

With this choice, the number of iterations is rather small (Exercise 5.6.18):

Lemma 5.2.4   *The number of iterations performed by Protocol* Filter *until there are no more than n elements left under consideration is at most*

$$2.41 \log(N/n).$$

Once there are at most n elements left after consideration, the problem can be solved using one of the known techniques, for example, *Rank*, for small sets.

However, each iteration requires a complex operation; in fact we need to find the median of the set $M(i)$ in iteration i. As the set is small (it contains at most n elements), this can be done using, for example, Protocol *Rank*. In the worst case, it will require $O(n^2)$ messages in each iteration. This means that, in the worst case,

$$M[Filter] = O\left(n^2 \log \frac{N}{n}\right) \tag{5.14}$$

$$T[Filter] = O\left(n \log \frac{N}{n}\right). \tag{5.15}$$

5.2.5   Reducing the Worst Case: ReduceSelect

The worst case we have obtained by using the *Filter* choice in strategy *RankSelect* is reasonable but it can be reduced using a different strategy.

This strategy, and the resulting protocol that we shall call *ReduceSelect*, is obtained mainly by combining and integrating all the techniques we have developed so far for reducing the search space with new, original ones.

Reduction Tools   Let us summarize first of all the main basic tool we have used so far.

Reduction Tool 1: Local Contraction   If entity x has more than Δ items under consideration, it can immediately discard any item greater than the local Kth smallest element and any item smaller than the local $(N - K + 1)$th largest element.

This tool is based on Property 5.2.2. The requirement for the application of this tool is that each site must know K and N. The net effect of the application of this tool is that, afterwards, each site has at most Δ items under considerations that are stored locally. Recall that we have used this reduction tool already when dealing with the two sites case, as well as in Protocol *RandomFlipSelect*.

A different type of reduction is offered by the following tool.

Reduction Tool 2: Sites Reduction   If the number of entities n is greater than K (respectively, $N - K + 1$), then $n - N$ entities (respectively $n - N + K - 1$) and all their data items can be removed from consideration. This can be achieved as follows.

1. Consider the set $D_{\min} = \{D_x[1]\}$ (respectively $D_{\max} = \{D_x[|D_x|]\}$) of the smallest (respectively, the largest) item at each entity.
2. Find the Kth smallest (respectively, $(N - K + 1)$th largest) element, call it w, of this set. NOTE: This set has n elements; hence this operation can be performed using protocol *Rank*.
3. If $D_x[1] > w$ (respectively $D_x[|D_x|] < w$) then the entire set D_x can be removed from consideration.

This reduction technique immediately reduces the number of *sets* involved in the problem to at most Δ. For example, consider the case of searching for the 7th largest item when the N data items of $\mathcal{D}$ are distributed among $n = 10$ entities. Consider now the largest element stored at each entity (they form a set of 10 elements), and find the 7th largest of them. The 8th largest element of this set cannot possibly be the 7th largest item of the entire distributed set $\mathcal{D}$; as it is the largest item stored at the entity from which it originated, none of the other items stored at that entity can be the 7th largest element either; so we can remove from consideration the entire set stored at that entity. Similarly we can remove also the sets where the 9th and the 10th largest came from.

These two tools can obviously be used one after the other. The *combined* use of these two tools reduces the problem of selection in a search space of size N distributed among n sites to that of selection among Min $\{n, \Delta\}$ sites, each with at most Δ elements. This means that, after the execution of these two tools, the new search space contains at most Δ^2 data items.

Notice that once the tools have been applied, if the size of the search space and/or the rank of f^* in that space have changed, it is possible that the two tools can be successfully applied again.

For example, consider the case depicted in Table 5.1, where $N = 10,032$ is distributed among $n = 5$ entities, $x_1, \ldots x_5$, and where we are looking for the Kth smallest element in this set, where $K = 4096$. First observe that, when we apply the two Reduction Tools, only the first one (*Contraction*) will be successful. The effect will be to remove from consideration many elements from x_1, all larger than f^*. In other words, we have significantly reduced the search space without changing the rank of f^* in the search space. If we apply *again* the two Reduction Tools to the new

TABLE 5.1: Repeated use of the Reduction Tools

N : size of search space	K : rank of f^* in search space	x_1	x_2	x_3	x_4	x_5
10, 032	4, 096	10, 000	20	5	5	2
4, 126	4, 096	4, 096	20	5	5	2
65	33	33	20	5	5	2

configuration, again only the first one (*Contraction*) will be successful; however the second will further drastically reduce the size of the search space (the variable N) from 4126 to 65 and the rank of f^* in the new search space (the variable K) from 4096 to 33.

This fact means that we can iterate Local Contraction until there will no longer be any change in the search space and in the rank of f^* in the search space. This will occur when at each site x_i the number of items still under consideration n_i' is *not greater* than $\Delta' = \min\{K', N' - K' + 1\}$, where N' is the size of the search space and K' the rank of f^* in the search space. We will then use the Sites Reduction tool.

The reduction protocol *REDUCE* based on this repeated use of the two Reduction Tools is shown in Figure 5.5.

Lemma 5.2.5   *After the execution of Protocol* REDUCE, *the number of items left under consideration is at most*

$$\Delta \min\{n, \Delta\}.$$

The single execution of Sites Reduction requires selection in a small set discussed in Section 5.2.2.

Each execution of Local Contraction required by Protocol *REDUCE* requires a broadcast and a convergecast, and costs $2(n - 1)$ messages and $2r(s)$ time. To determine the total cost we need to find out the number of times Local Contraction is executed. Interestingly, this will occur a constant number of times, three times to be precise (Exercise 5.6.19).

REDUCE

```
begin
    N' = N;  K' = K;  Δ' = Δ;  n'ᵢ = nᵢ,  1 ≤ i ≤ n;
    while ∃xᵢ such that n'ᵢ > Δ' do
        perform Local Contraction;
        * update the values of N', K', Δ', n'ᵢ(1 ≤ i ≤ n)*
    endwhile
    if n > Δ' then
        perform Sites Reduction;
    endif
end
```

FIGURE 5.5: Protocol *REDUCE*.

Cutting Tools   The new tool we are going to develop is to be used whenever the number n of sets is at most Δ and each entity has at most Δ items; this is, for example, the result of applying Tools 1 and 2 described before. Thus, the search space contains at most Δ^2 items. For simplicity, and without loss of generality, let $K = \Delta$ (the case $N - K + 1 = \Delta$ is analogous).

To aid in the design, we can visualize the search space as an array D of size $n \times \Delta$, where the rows correspond to the sets of items, each set sorted in an increasing order, and the columns specify the rank of that element in the set. So, for example, $d_{i,j}$ is the jth smallest item in the set stored at entity x_i. Notice that there is no relationship among the elements of the same column; in other words, D is a matrix with sorted rows but unsorted columns.

Each column corresponds to a set of n elements distributed among the n entities. If an element is removed from consideration, it will be represented by $+\infty$ in the corresponding entry in the array.

Consider the set $C(2)$, that is, all the second-smallest items in each site. Focus on the kth smallest element $m(2)$ of this set, where

$$k = \lceil K/2 \rceil.$$

By definition, $m(2)$ has exactly $k - 1$ elements smaller than itself in $C(2)$; each of them, as well as $m(2)$, has another item smaller than itself in its own row (this is because they are second-smallest in their own set). This means that, as far as we know, $m(2)$ has *at least*

$$(k - 1) + k = 2k - 1 \geq K - 1$$

items smaller than itself in the global set D; this implies that any item *greater* than $m(2)$ *cannot be* the Kth smallest item we are looking for. In other words, if we find $m(2)$, then we can remove from consideration any item larger than $m(2)$.

Similarly, we can consider the set $C(2^i)$, where $2^i \leq K$, composed of the 2^ith smallest items in each set. Focus again on the kth smallest element $m(2^i)$ of $C(2^i)$, where

$$k = \lceil K/2^i \rceil.$$

By definition, $m(2^i)$ has exactly $k - 1$ elements smaller than itself in $C(2)$; each of them, as well as $m(2^i)$, has another $2^i - 1$ items smaller than itself in its own row (this is because they are the 2^ith smallest in their own set). This means that $m(2^i)$ has *at least*

$$(k - 1) + k\,(2^i - 1) \;=\; k\,2^i - 1 \geq \frac{K}{2^i}\,2^i - 1 = K - 1$$

items smaller than itself in the global set D; this implies that any item *greater* than $m(2^i)$ *cannot* be the Kth smallest item we are looking for. In other words, if we find $m(2^i)$, then we can remove from consideration any item larger than $m(2^i)$.

Thus, we have a generic Reduction Tool using columns whose index is a power of two.

CUT

```
begin
    k = ⌈K/2⌉;
    l := 2;
    while k ≥ log K and search space is not small do
        if in C(2ˡ) there are ≥ k items still under
        consideration then
            * use the CuttingTool : *
            find the kth smallest element m(l) of C(l);
            remove from consideration all the elements
            greater than m(l).
        endif
        k := k/2;
        l := 2l;
    endwhile
end
```

FIGURE 5.6: Protocol *CUT*.

Cutting Tool Let $l = 2^i \leq K$ and $k = \lfloor K/l \rfloor$. Find the kth smallest element $m(l)$ of $C(l)$, and remove from consideration all the elements greater than $m(l)$.

The *Cutting Tool* can be implemented using any protocol for selection in small sets (recall that each $C(l)$ has at most n elements), such as *Rank*; a single broadcast will notify all entities of the outcome and allow each to reduce its own set if needed.

On the basis of this tool we can construct a reduction protocol that sequentially uses the *Cutting Tool* first using $C(2)$, then $C(4)$, then $C(8)$, and so on. Clearly, if at any time the search space becomes small (i.e., $O(n)$), we terminate. This reduction algorithm, that we will call *CUT*, is shown in Figure 5.6.

Let us examine the reduction power of Procedure *CUT*. After executing the *Cutting Tool* on $C(2)$, only one column, $C(1)$, might remain unchanged; all others, including $C(2)$, will have *at least* half of the entries $+\infty$. In general, after the execution of *Cutting Tool* on $C(l = 2^i)$, only the $l - 1$ columns $C(1), C(2), \ldots, C(l-1)$ might remain unchanged; all others, including $C(l)$ will have *at least* $n - K/l$ of the entries $+\infty$ (Exercise 5.6.20). This can be used to show (Exercise 5.6.21) that

Lemma 5.2.6 *After the execution of Protocol* CUT, *the number of items left under consideration is at most*

$$\min\{n, \Delta\} \log \Delta.$$

Each of the $\lfloor \log \Delta \rfloor$ execution of the *Cutting Tool* performed by Protocol *CUT* requires a selection in a set of size at most $\min\{n, \Delta\}$. This can be performed using any of the protocols for selection in a small set, for example, Protocol *Rank*. In the worst case, it will require $O(n^2)$ messages in each iteration. This means that, in the worst case,

$$M[CUT] = O(n^2 \log \Delta), \tag{5.16}$$

$$T[CUT] = O(n \log \Delta). \tag{5.17}$$

ReduceSelect

begin
    REDUCE;
    if search space greater than $O(\Delta')$ **then** *CUT*
    if search space greater than $O(n)$ **then** *Filter*
    Rank;
end

FIGURE 5.7: Protocol *ReduceSelect*.

Putting It All Together We have examined a set of Reduction Tools. Summarizing, Protocol *REDUCE*, composed of the application of Reduction Tools 1 and 2, reduces the search space from N to at most Δ^2. Protocol *CUT*, composed of a sequence of applications of the Cutting Tool, reduces the search space from Δ^2 to at most $\min\{n, \Delta\} \log \Delta$.

Starting from these reductions, to form a full selection protocol, we will first reduce the search space from $\min\{n, \Delta\} \log \Delta$ to $O(n)$ (e.g. using Protocol *Filter*) and then use a protocol for small sets (e.g. *Rank*) to determine the sought item.

In other words, resulting algorithm, Protocol *ReduceSelect*, will be as shown in Figure 5.7, where Δ' is the new value of Δ after the execution of *REDUCE*.

Let us examine the cost of Protocol *ReduceSelect*. Protocol *REDUCE*, as we have seen, requires at most 3 iterations of Local Contractions, each using $2(n-1)$ messages and $2r(s)$ time, and one execution of Sites Reduction that consists in an execution of *Rank*. Protocol *CUT* is used with $N \leq \min\{n, \Delta\}\Delta$ and, as we have seen, thus, requires at most $\log \Delta$ iterations of the Cutting Tools, each consisting in an execution of *Rank*. Protocol *Filter*, as we have seen, is used with $N \leq \min\{n, \Delta\} \log \Delta$ and, as we have seen, thus, requires at most $\log \log \Delta$ iterations, each costing $2(n-1)$ messages and $2r(s)$ time plus an execution of *Rank*. Thus, in total, we have

$$M[ReduceSelect] = (\log \Delta + 4.5 \log \log \Delta + 2)M[Rank]$$

$$+ (6 + 4.5 \log \log \Delta)(n - 1), \tag{5.18}$$

$$T[ReduceSelect] = (\log \Delta + 4.5 \log \log \Delta + 2)T[Rank]$$

$$+ (6 + 4.5 \log \log \Delta)2r(s). \tag{5.19}$$

5.3 SORTING A DISTRIBUTED SET

5.3.1 Distributed Sorting

Sorting is perhaps the most well known and investigated algorithmic problem. In distributed computing systems, the setting where this problem takes place as well as its nature is very different from the serial as well as parallel ones. In particular, in our setting, sorting must take place in networks of computing entities where no central controller is present and no common clock is available. Not surprisingly, most

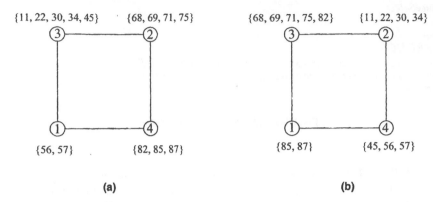

FIGURE 5.8: Distribution sorted according to (a) $\pi = \langle 3124 \rangle$ and (b) $\pi = \langle 2431 \rangle$.

of the best serial and parallel sorting algorithms do very poorly when applied to a distributed environment. In this section we will examine the problem, its nature, and its solutions.

Let us start with a clear specification of the task and its requirements. As before in this chapter, we have a *distribution* $\langle D_{x_1}, \ldots, D_{x_n} \rangle$ of a set $\mathcal{D}$ among the entities $x_1, \ldots, x_n$ of a system with communication topology G, where D_{x_i} is the set of items stored at x_i. Each entity x_i, because of the Distinct Identifiers assumption ID, has a unique identity id(i), from a totally ordered sets. For simplicity, in the following we will assume that the ids are the numbers $1, 2, \ldots, n$ and that id(i) = i, and we will denote D_{x_i} simply by D_i.

Let us now focus on the definition of a sorted distribution. A distribution is (quite reasonably) considered sorted if, whenever $i < j$, all the data items stored at x_i are smaller than the items stored at x_j; this condition is usually called *increasing* order. A distribution is also considered sorted if all the smallest items are in x_n, the next ones in x_{n-1}, and so on, with the largest ones in x_1; usually, we call this condition *decreasing* order. Let us be precise.

Let π be a permutation of the indices $\{1, \ldots, n\}$. A distribution $\langle D_1, \ldots, D_n \rangle$ is *sorted according to π* if and only if the following *Sorting Condition* holds:

$$\pi(i) < \pi(j) \implies \forall d' \in D_i, d'' \in D_j \quad d' < d''. \tag{5.20}$$

In other words, if the distribution is sorted according to π, then all the smallest items must be in $x_{\pi(1)}$, the next smallest ones in $x_{\pi(2)}$, and so on, with the largest ones in $x_{\pi(n)}$. So the requirement that the data are sorted according to the increasing order of the ids of the entities is given by the permutation $\pi = \langle 1\, 2\, \ldots n \rangle$. The requirement of being sorted in a decreasing order is given by the permutation $\pi = \langle n\, (n-1) \ldots 1 \rangle$. For example, in Figure 5.8(b), the set is sorted according to the permutation $\pi = \langle 2\, 4\, 3\, 1 \rangle$; in fact, all the smallest data items are stored at x_2, the next ones in x_4, the yet larger ones in x_3, and all the largest data items are stored at x_1. We are now ready to define the problem of sorting a distributed set.

Sorting Problem   Given a distribution $\langle D_1, \ldots, D_n \rangle$ of $\mathcal{D}$ and a permutation π, the distributed *sorting problem* is the one of moving data items among the entities so that, upon termination,

1. $\langle D'_1, \ldots, D'_n \rangle$ is a distribution of $\mathcal{D}$, where D'_i is the final set of data at x_i;
2. $\langle D'_1, \ldots, D'_n \rangle$ is sorted according to π.

Note that the definition does not say anything about the relationship between the sizes of the initial sets D_is and those of the final sets D'_is. Depending on which requirement we impose, we have different versions of the problem. There are three fundamental requirements:

invariant-sized sorting: $|D_i| = |D'_i|$, $1 \leq i \leq n$, that is, each entity ends up with the same number of items it started with.

equidistributed sorting: $|D_{\pi(i)}| = \lceil N/n \rceil$ for $1 \leq i < n$ and $|D_{\pi(n)}| = N - (n-1)\lceil N/n \rceil$, that is, every entity receives the same amount of data, except for $x_{\pi(n)}$ that might receive fewer items.

compacted sorting: $|D_{\pi(i)}| = \min\{w, \ N - (i-1)w\}$, where $w \geq \lceil N/n \rceil$ is the *storage capacity* of the entities, that is, each entity, starting from $x_{\pi(1)}$, receives as many unassigned items as it can store.

Notice that equidistributed sorting is a compacted sorting with $w = \lceil N/n \rceil$. For some of the algorithms we will discuss, it does not really matter which requirement is used; for some protocols, however, the choice of the requirement is important. In the following, unless otherwise specified, we will use the *invariant-sized* requirement.

From the definition, it follows that when sorting a distributed set the relevant factors are the permutation according to which we sort, the topology of the network in which we sort, the location of the entities in the network, as well as the storage requirements. In the following two sections, we will examine some special cases that will help us understand these factors, their interplay, and their impact.

5.3.2   Special Case: Sorting on a Ordered Line

Consider the case when we want to sort the data according to a permutation π, and the network G is a line where $x_{\pi(i)}$ is connected to $x_{\pi(i+1)}$, $1 \leq i < n$. This case is very special. In fact, the entities are located on the line in such a way that their indices are ordered according to the permutation π. (The data, however, is not sorted.) For this reason, G is also called an *ordered line*. As an example, see Figure 5.9, where $\pi = \langle 1, 2, \ldots, n \rangle$.

A simple sorting technique for an ordered line is *OddEven-LineSort*, based on the parallel algorithm *odd-even-transposition sort*, which is in turn based on the well known serial algorithm *Bubble Sort*. This technique is composed of a sequence of iterations, where initially $j = 0$.

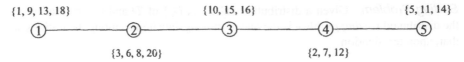

FIGURE 5.9: A distribution on a ordered line of size $n = 5$.

Technique *OddEven-LineSort*:

1. In iteration $2j + 1$ (an *odd* iteration), entity x_{2i+1} exchanges its data with neighbour $x_{2i+2}, 0 \le i \le \lfloor \frac{n}{2} \rfloor - 1$; as a result, x_{2i+1} retains the smallest items while x_{2i+2} retains the largest ones.

2. In iteration $2j$ (an *even* iteration), entity x_{2i} exchanges its data with neighbour $x_{2i+1}, 1 \le i \le \lfloor \frac{n}{2} \rfloor - 1$; as a result, x_{2i} retains the smallest items while x_{2i+1} retains the largest ones.

3. If no data items change of place at all during an iteration (other than the first), then the process stop.

A schematic representation of the operations performed by the technique *OddEven-LineSort* is by means of the "sorting diagram": a synchronous TED (time-event diagram) where the exchange of data between two neighboring entities is shown as a bold line connecting the time lines of the two entities. The sorting diagram for a line of $n = 5$ entities is shown in Figure 5.10. In the diagram are clearly visible the alternation of "odd" and "even" steps.

To obtain a fully specified protocol, we still need to explain two important operations: *termination* and *data exchange*.

Termination.   We have said that we terminate when no data items change of place at all during an iteration. This situation can be easily determined. In fact, at the end of an iteration, each entity x can set a Boolean variable *change* to *true* or *false* to indicate whether or not its data set has changed during that iteration. Then, we can check (by computing the **AND** of those variables) if no data items have changed place at all during that iteration; if this is the case for every entity, we terminate, else we start the next iteration.

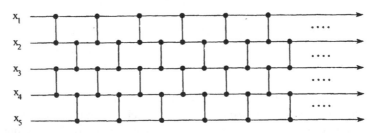

FIGURE 5.10: Diagram of operations of *OddEven-LineSort* in a line of size $n = 5$.

Data Exchange. At the basis of the technique there is the exchange of data between two neighbors, say x and y; at the end of this exchange, that we will call *merge*, x will have the smallest items and y the largest ones (or vice versa). This specification is, however, not quite precise. Assume that, before the merge, x has p items while y has q items, where possibly $p \neq q$; how much data should x and y retain after the merge? The answer depends, partially, on the storage requirements.

- If we are to perform a *invariant-sized* sorting, x should retain p items and y should retain q items.
- If we are to perform a *compacted* sorting, x should retain $min\{w, (p + q)\}$ items and y retain the others.
- If we are to perform a *equidistributed* sorting, x should retain $\min\{\lceil N/n \rceil, p + q\}$ items and y retain the others. Notice that, in this case each entity need to know both n and N.

The results of the execution of *OddEven-LineSort* with an *invariant-sized* in the sorted line of Figure 5.9 is shown in Table 5.2.

The correctness of the protocol, although intuitive, is not immediate (Exercises 5.6.23, 5.6.24, 5.6.25, and 5.6.26). In particular, the so-called "$0 - 1$ principle" (employed to prove the correctness of the similar parallel algorithm) can *not* be used directly in our case. This is due to the fact that the local data sets D_i may contain several items, and may have different sizes.

Cost The *time* cost is clearly determined by the number of iterations. In the worst case, the data items are initially sorted the "wrong" way; that is, the initial distribution is sorted according to permutation $\pi' = \langle \pi(n), \pi(n - 1), \ldots, \pi(1) \rangle$. Consider the largest item; it has to move from x_1 to x_n; as it can only move by one location per iteration, to complete its move it requires $n - 1$ iterations. Indeed this is the actual cost for some initial distributions (Exercise 5.6.27).

Property 5.3.1 OddEven-LineSort *sorts an equidistributed distribution in $n - 1$ iterations if the required sorting is (a) invariant-sized, or (b) equidistributed, or (c) compacted.*

TABLE 5.2: Execution of *OddEven-LineSort* on the System of Figure 5.9

iteration	x_1	x_2	x_3	x_4	x_5
1	$\{1,9,13,18\} \rightarrow$	$\leftarrow \{3,6,8,20\}$	$\{2,7,12\} \rightarrow$	$\leftarrow \{10,15,16\}$	$\{5,11,14\}$
2	$\{1,3,6,8\}$	$\{9,13,18,20\} \rightarrow$	$\leftarrow \{2,7,10\}$	$\{12,15,16\} \rightarrow$	$\leftarrow \{5,11,14\}$
3	$\{1,3,6,8\} \rightarrow$	$\leftarrow \{2,7,9,10\}$	$\{13,18,20\} \rightarrow$	$\leftarrow \{5,11,12\}$	$\{14,15,16\}$
4	$\{1,2,3,6\}$	$\{7,8,9,10\} \rightarrow$	$\leftarrow \{5,11,12\}$	$\{13,18,20\} \rightarrow$	$\leftarrow \{14,15,16\}$
5	$\{1,2,3,6\} \rightarrow$	$\leftarrow \{5,7,8,9\}$	$\{10,11,12\} \rightarrow$	$\leftarrow \{13,14,15\}$	$\{16,18,20\}$
6	$\{1,2,3,5\}$	$\{6,7,8,9\} \rightarrow$	$\leftarrow \{10,11,12\}$	$\{13,14,15\} \rightarrow$	$\leftarrow \{16,18,20\}$

Interestingly, the number of iterations can actually be much *more* than $n - 1$ if the initial distribution is not equidistributed.

Consider, for example, an *invariant-sized* sorting when the initial distribution is sorted according to permutation $\pi' = \langle \pi(n), \pi(n - 1), \ldots, \pi(1) \rangle$. Assume that x_1 and x_n have each kq items, while x_2 has only q items. All the items initially stored in x_1 must end up in x_n; however, in the first iteration only q items will move from x_1 to x_2; because of the "odd-even" alternation, the next q items will leave x_1 in the 3rd iteration, the next q in the 5th, and so on. Hence, the total number of iterations required for all data to move from x_1 to x_n is *at least* $n - 1 + 2(k - 1)$. This implies that, in the worst case, the time costs can be considerably high (Exercise 5.6.28):

Property 5.3.2 OddEven-LineSort *performs an invariant-sized sorting in at most* $N - 1$ *iterations. This number of iterations is achievable.*

Assuming (quite unrealistically) that the entire data set of an entity can be sent in one time unit to its neighbor, the time required by all the merge operations is exactly the same as the number of iterations. In contrast to this, to determine termination, we need to compute the **AND** of the Boolean variables *change* at each iteration. This operation can be done on a line in time $n - 1$ at each iteration. Thus, in the worst case,

$$\mathbf{T}[OddEven - LineSort_{\text{invariant}}] = O(nN). \tag{5.21}$$

Similarly, bad time costs can be derived for equidistributed sorting and compacted sorting.

Let us focus now on the number of *messages* for *invariant-sized* sorting. If we do not impose any size constraints on the initial distribution then, by Property 5.3.2, the number of iterations can be as bad as $N - 1$; as in each iteration we perform the computation of the function **AND**, and this requires $2(n - 1)$ messages, it follows that the protocol will use

$$2(n - 1)(N - 1)$$

messages just for computing the **AND**. To this cost we still need to add the number of messages used for the transfer of data items. Hence, without storage constraints on the initial distribution, the protocol has a very high cost due to the high number of iterations possible.

Let us consider now the case when the initial distribution is equidistributed. By property 5.3.1, the number of iterations is at most $n - 1$ (instead of $N - 1$). This means that the cost of computing the **AND** is $O(n^2)$ (instead of $O(Nn)$). Surprisingly, even in this case, the total number of messages can be very high.

Property 5.3.3 OddEven-LineSort *can use* $O(Nn)$ *messages to perform an invariant-sized sorting. This cost is achievable even if the data is initially equidistributed.*

To see why this is the case, consider an initial equidistribution sorted according to permutation $\pi' = \langle \pi(n), \pi(n-1), \ldots, \pi(1) \rangle$. In this case, every data item will change location in each iteration (Exercise 5.6.29), that is, $O(N)$ messages will be sent in each iteration. As there can be $n-1$ iterations with an initial equidistribution (by Property 5.3.1), we obtain the bound. Summarizing:

$$\mathbf{M}[OddEven - LineSort]_{\text{invariant}} = O(nN). \tag{5.22}$$

That is, using Protocol *OddEven-LineSort* can costs as much as broadcasting *all the data* to *every entity*. This results holds even if the data is initially equidistributed. Similar bad message costs can be derived for equidistributed sorting and compacted sorting.

Summarizing, Protocol *OddEven-LineSort* does not appear to be very efficient.

IMPORTANT. Each line network is ordered according to a permutation. However, this permutation might not be π, according to which we need to sort the data. What happens in this case?

The protocol *OddEven-LineSort* does *not* work if the entities are not positioned on the line according to π, that is, when the line is not ordered according to π. (Exercise 5.6.30). The question then becomes how to sort a set distributed on an unsorted line. We will leave this question open until later in this chapter.

5.3.3 Removing the Topological Constraints: Complete Graph

One of the problems we have faced in the the line graph is the constraint that the topology of the network imposes. Indeed, the line graph is one of the worst topologies for a tree, as its diameter is $n-1$. In this section we will do the opposite: We will consider the complete graph, where every entity is directly connected to every other entity; in this way, we will be able to remove the constraints imposed by the network topology. Without loss of generality (since we are in a complete network), we assume $\pi = \langle 1, 2, \ldots, n \rangle$.

As the complete graph contains every graph as a subgraph, we can choose to operate on whichever graph suites best our computational needs. Thus, for example, we can choose an ordered line and use protocol *OddEven-LineSort* we discussed before. However, as we have seen, this protocol is not very efficient.

If we are in a complete graph, we can adapt and use some of the well known techniques for serial sorting.

Let us focus on the classical *Merge-Sort* strategy. This strategy, in our distributed setting becomes as follows: (1) the distribution to be sorted is first divided in two partial distributions of equal size; (2) each of these two partial distribution is independently sorted recursively using MergeSort; and (3) then the two sorted partial distributions are merged to form a sorted distribution.

The problem with this strategy is that the last step, the merging step, is *not* an obvious one in a distributed setting; in fact, after the first iteration, the two sorted distributions to be merged are scattered among many entities. Hence the question: How do we efficiently "merge" two sorted distributions of several sets to form a sorted distribution?

There are many possible answers, each yielding a different merge-sort protocol. In the following we discuss a protocol for performing distributed merging by means of the odd-even strategy we discussed for the ordered line.

Let us first introduce some terminology. We are given a distribution $D = \langle D_1, \ldots, D_n \rangle$. Consider now a subset $\{D_{j_1}, \ldots, D_{j_q}\}$ of the data sets, where $j_i < j_{i+1}$ $(1 \leq i \leq q)$. The corresponding distribution $D' = \langle D_{j_1}, \ldots, D_{j_q} \rangle$ is called a *partial distribution* of D. We say that the partial distribution d' is sorted (according to $\pi = \langle 1, \ldots, n \rangle$) if all the items in D_{j_i} are smaller that the items in $D_{j_{i+1}}$, $1 \leq i < q$. Note that it might happen that D' is sorted while D is not.

Let us now describe how to *odd-even-merge* a sorted partial distribution $\langle A_1, \ldots, A_{\frac{p}{2}} \rangle$ with a sorted partial distribution $\langle A_{\frac{p}{2}+1}, \ldots, A_p \rangle$ to form a sorted distribution $\langle A_1, \ldots, A_p \rangle$, where we are assuming for simplicity that p is a power of 2.

OddEven-Merge *Technique*:

1. If $p = 2$, then there are two sets A_1 and A_2, held by entities y_1 and y_2, respectively. To odd-even-merge them, each of y_1 and y_2 sends its data to the other entity; y_1 retains the smallest while y_2 retains the largest items. We call this basic operation simply *merge*.

2. If $p > 2$, then the odd-even-merge is performed as following:

   (a) first recursively odd-even-merge the distribution $\langle A_1, A_3, A_5, \ldots, A_{\frac{p}{2}-1} \rangle$ with the distribution $\langle A_{\frac{p}{2}+1}, A_{\frac{p}{2}+3}, A_{\frac{p}{2}+5}, \ldots, A_{p-1} \rangle$;

   (b) then recursively odd-even-merge the distribution $\langle A_2, A_4, A_6, \ldots, A_{\frac{p}{2}} \rangle$ with the distribution $\langle A_{\frac{p}{2}+2}, A_{\frac{p}{2}+4}, A_{\frac{p}{2}+6}, \ldots, A_p \rangle$;

   (c) finally, merge A_{2i} with A_{2i+1} $(1 \leq i \leq \frac{p}{2} - 1)$

The technique *OddEven-Merge* can then be used to generate the *OddEven-MergeSort* technique for sorting a distribution $\langle D_1, \ldots, D_n \rangle$. As in the classical case, the technique is defined recursively as follows:

OddEven-MergeSort *Technique*:

1. recursively odd-even-merge-sort the distribution $\langle D_1, \ldots, D_{\frac{n}{2}} \rangle$,

2. recursively odd-even-merge-sort the distribution $\langle D_{\frac{n}{2}+1}, \ldots, D_n \rangle$

3. odd-even-merge $\langle D_1, \ldots, D_{\frac{n}{2}} \rangle$ with $\langle D_{\frac{n}{2}+1}, \ldots, D_n \rangle$

Using this technique, we obtain a protocol for sorting a distribution $\langle D_1, \ldots, D_n \rangle$; we shall call this protocol like the technique itself: Protocol *OddEven-MergeSort*.

To determine the communication costs of this protocol need to "unravel" the recursion.

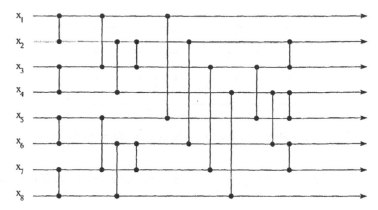

FIGURE 5.11: Diagram of operations of *OddEven-MergeSort* with $n = 8$.

When we do this, we realize that the protocol is a sequence of $1 + \log n$ iterations (Exercise 5.6.32). In each iteration (except the last) every entity is paired with another entity, and each pair will perform a simple merge of their local sets; half of the entities will perform this operation twice during an iteration. In the last iteration all entities, except x_1 and x_n, will be paired and perform a merge.

Example   Using the sorting diagram to describe these operations, the structure of an execution of Protocol *OddEven-MergeSort* when $n = 8$ is shown in Figure 5.11. Notice that there are 4 iterations; observe that, in iteration 2, merge will be performed between the pairs (x_1, x_3), (x_2, x_4), (x_5, x_7), (x_6, x_8); observe further that entities $x_2, x_3, x_6. x_7$ will each be involved in one more merge in this same iteration.

Summarizing, in each of the first $\log n$ iterations, each entity sends is data to one or two other entities. In other words the entire distributed set is transmitted in each iteration. Hence, the total number of messages used by Protocol *OddEven-MergeSort* is

$$\mathbf{M}[OddEven - MergeSort] = O(N \log n). \tag{5.23}$$

Note that this bound holds regardless of the storage requirement.

IMPORTANT. Does the protocol work ? Does it in fact sorts the data ? The answer to these questions is: *not always*. In fact, its correctness depends on several factors, including the storage requirements.

It is not difficult to prove that the protocol correctly sorts, regardless of the storage requirement, if the initial set is equidistributed (Exercise 5.6.33).

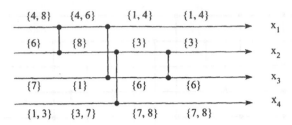

FIGURE 5.12: *OddEven-MergeSort* does not correctly perform an invariant sort for this distribution.

Property 5.3.4 OddEven-MergeSort *sorts any equidistributed set if the required sorting is (a) invariant-sized, (b) equidistributed, or (c) compacted.*

However, if the initial set is not equidistributed, the distribution obtained when the protocol terminates might *not* be sorted. To understand why, consider performing an invariant sorting in the system of $n = 4$ entities shown in Figure 5.12; items 1 and 3, initially at entity x_4, should end up in entity x_1, but item 3 is still at x_4 when the protocol terminates. The reason for this happening is the "bottleneck" created by the fact that only one item at a time can be moved to each of x_2 and x_3. Recall that the existence of bottlenecks was the reason for the high number of iterations of Protocol *OddEven-LineSort*. In this case, the problem makes the protocol incorrect. It is indeed possible to modify the protocol, adding enough appropriate iterations, so that the distribution will be correctly solved. The type and the number of the additional iterations needed to correct the protocol depends on many factors. In the example shown in Figure 5.12, a single iteration consisting of a simple merge between x_1 and x_2 would suffice. In general, the additional requirements depend on the specifics of the size of the initial sets; see, for example, Exercise 5.6.34.

5.3.4 Basic Limitations

In the previous sections we have seen different protocols, examined their behavior, and analyzed their costs. In this process we have seen that the amount of data items transmitted can be very large. For example, in *OddEven-LineSort* the number of messages is $O(Nn)$, the same as sending every item everywhere. Even not worrying about the limitations imposed by the topology of the network, protocol *OddEven-MergeSort* still uses $O(N \log n)$ messages when it works correctly. Before proceeding any further, we are going to ask the following question: How many messages need to be sent anyway? we would like the answer to be independent of the protocol but to take into account both the topology of the network and the storage requirements. The purpose of this section is to provide such an answer, to use it to assess the solutions seen so far, and to understand its implications. On the basis of this, we will be able to design an efficient sorting protocol.

Lower Bound There is a minimum necessary amount of data movements that must take place when sorting a distributed set. Let us determine exactly what costs must be incurred *regardless of the algorithm* we employ.

The basic observation we employ is that, once we are given a permutation π according to which we must sort the data, there are some inescapable costs. In fact, if entity x has some data that according to π must end up in y, then this data must move from x to y, regardless of the sorting algorithm we use. Let us state these concepts more precisely.

Given a network G, a distribution $\mathbf{D} = \langle D_1, \ldots, D_n \rangle$ of $\mathcal{D}$ on G, and a permutation π let $\mathbf{D}' = \langle D_1', \ldots, D_n' \rangle$ be the result of sorting $\mathbf{D}$ according to π. Then $|D_i \cap D_j'|$ items must travel from x_i to x_j; this means that the amount of data transmission for this transfer is *at least*

$$|D_i \cap D_j'|\, d_G(x_i . x_j).$$

How this amount translates into number of messages depends on the size of the messages. A message can only contain a (small) constant number of data items; to obtain a uniform measure, we consider just one data item per message. Then

Theorem 5.3.1   *The number of messages required to sort* $\mathbf{D}$ *according to* π *in* G *is at least*

$$\mathbf{C}(\mathbf{D}, G, \pi) = \sum_{i \neq j} |D_i \cap D_j'|\, d_G(x_i, x_j).$$

This expresses a lower bound on the amount of messages for distributed sorting; the actual value depends on the topology G and the storage requirements. The determination of this value in specific topologies for different storage requirements is the subject of Exercises 5.6.35–5.6.38.

Assessing Previous Solutions   Let us see what this bound means for situations we have already examined. In this bound, the topology of the network plays a role through the distances $d_G(x_i, x_j)$ between the entities that must transfer data, while the storage requirements play a role through the sizes $|D_i'|$ of the resulting sets.

First of all, note that, by definition, for all x_i, x_j, we have

$$d_G(x_i, x_j) \leq d(G);$$

furthermore,

$$\sum_{i \neq j} |D_i \cap D_j'| \leq N. \tag{5.24}$$

To derive lower bounds on the number of messages for a specific network G, we need to consider for that network the worst possible allocation of the data, that is, the one that maximizes $\mathbf{C}(\mathbf{D}, G, \pi)$.

Ordered Line.   *OddEven-LineSort*
Let us focus first on the *ordered line* network.

If the data is not initially equidistributed, it easy to show scenarios where $O(N)$ data must travel a $O(n)$ distance along the line. For example, consider the case when x_n initially contains the smallest $N - n + 1$ items while all other entities have just a single item each; for simplicity, assume $(N - n + 1)/n$ to be integer. Then for *equidistributed* sorting we have $|D_n \cap D'_j| = (N - n + 1)/n$ for $j < n$; this means that at least

$$\sum_{j<n} |D_n \cap D'_j| \, d_G(x_n, x_j) = \sum_{j<n} j \, (N - n + 1)/n = \Omega(nN)$$

messages are needed to send the data initially in x_n to their final destinations. The same example holds also in the case of *compact* sorting.

In the case of *invariant* sorting, surprisingly, the same lower bound exists even when the data is initially equidistributed; for simplicity, assume N/n to be integer and n to be even. In this case, in fact, the worst initial arrangement is when the data items are initially sorted according to the permutation $\langle \frac{n}{2} + 1, \frac{n}{2} + 2, \ldots, n - 1, n, 1, 2, \ldots, \frac{n}{2} - 1, \frac{n}{2} \rangle$, while we want to sort them according to $\pi = \langle 1, 2, \ldots, n \rangle$. In this case we have that all the items initially stored at x_i, $1 \le i \le n/2$, must end up in $x_{\frac{n}{2}+i}$, and vice versa, that is, $D'_i = D_{\frac{n}{2}+i}$. Furthermore, in the ordered line, $d(x_i, x_{\frac{n}{2}+i}) = \frac{n}{2}$, $1 \le i \le n/2$. This means that each item *must* travel distance $\frac{n}{2}$. That is the total amount of communication must be at least

$$\sum_{i \ne j} |D_i \cap D'_j| \, d_G(x_i, x_j) = \frac{n}{2}N = \Omega(nN).$$

Summarizing, in the ordered line, regardless of the storage requirements, $\Omega(nN)$ messages need to be sent in the worst case.

This fact has a surprising consequence. It implies that the complexity of the solution for the ordered line, protocol *OddEven-LineSort*, was not bad after all. On the contrary, protocol protocol *OddEven-LineSort* is worst-case *optimal*.

Complete Graph.   *OddEven-MergeSort*
Let us turn to the *complete graph*. In this graph $d_G(x_i, x_j) = 1$ for any two distinct entities x_i and x_j. Hence, the lower bound of Theorem 5.3.1 in the complete graph K becomes simply

$$\mathbf{C(D}, K, \pi) = \sum_{i \ne j} |D_i \cap D'_j|. \tag{5.25}$$

This means that, by relation 5.24, in the complete graph no more than N messages *need* to be sent in the worst case. At the same time, it is not difficult to find, for each type of storage requirement, a situation where this lower bound becomes $\Omega(N)$, even when the set is initially equidistributed (Exercise 5.6.35).

In other words, the number of messages that need to be sent in the worst case is *no more* and *no less* than $\Omega(N)$.

By Contrast, we have seen that protocol *OddEven-MergeSort* always uses $O(N \log N)$ messages; thus, there is a large gap between upper bound and lower bound. This indicates that protocol *OddEven-MergeSort*, even when correct, is far from optimal.

Summarizing, the expensive *OddEven-LineSort* is actually optimal for the ordered line, while *OddEven-MergeSort* is far from being optimal in the complete graph.

Implications for Solution Design   The bound of Theorem 5.3.1 expresses a cost that *every* sorting protocol must incur. Examining this bound, there are two considerations that we can make.

The first consideration is that, to design an efficient sorting protocol, we should not worry about this necessary cost (as there is nothing we can do about it), but rather focus on reducing the *additional* amount of communication. We must, however, understand that the necessary cost is that of the messages that move data items to their final destination (through the shortest path). These messages are needed anyway; any other message is an extra cost, and we should try to minimize these.

The second consideration is that, as the data items must be sent to their final destinations, we could use the additional cost just to find out what the destinations are. This simple observation leads to the following strategy for a sorting protocol, as described from the individual entity point of view:

Sorting Strategy

1. First find out where your data items should go.
2. Then send them there through the shortest-paths.

The second step is the necessary part and causes the cost stated by Theorem 5.3.1. The first step is the one causing extra cost. Thus, it is an operation we should perform efficiently.

Notice that there are many factors at play when determining where the final destination of a data item should be. In fact, it is not only due to the permutation π but also to factors such as which final storage requirement is imposed, for example, on whether the final distribution must be invariant-sized, or equidistributed, or compacted.

In the following section we will see how to efficiently determine the final destination of the data items.

5.3.5   Efficient Sorting: SelectSort

In this section our goal is to design an efficient sorting protocol using the strategy of first determining the final destination of each data item, and only then moving the items there. To achieve this goal, each entity x_i has to efficiently determine the sets

$$D_i \cap D'_{\pi(j)},$$

that is, which of its *own* data items must be sent to $x_{\pi(j)}$, $1 \le j \le n$. How can this be done ? The answer is remarkably simple.

First observe that the final destination of a data item (and thus the final distribution $\mathbf{D}'$) depends on the permutation π as well as on the final storage requirement. Different criteria determine different destinations for the same data item. For example, in the ordered line graph of Figure 5.9, the final destination of data item 16 is x_5 in an invariant-sized final distribution; x_4 in an equidistributed final distribution; and x_3 in an compacted final distribution with storage capacity $w = 5$.

Although the entities do not know beforehand the final distribution, once they know π and the storage requirement used, they can find out the number

$$k_j = |D'_{\pi(j)}|$$

of data items that must end up in each $x_{\pi(j)}$.

Assume for the moment that the k_js are known to the entities. Then, each x_i knows that $D'_{\pi(1)}$ at the end must contain the k_1 smallest data items; $D'_{\pi(2)}$ at the end must contain the next k_2 smallest, etc., and $D'_{\pi(n)}$ at the end must contain the k_n largest item. This fact has an immediate implication.

Let $b_1 = \mathcal{D}[k_1]$ be the k_1th smallest item overall. As $x_{\pi(1)}$ must contain in the end the k_1 smallest items, then all the items $d \le b_1$ must be sent to $x_{\pi(1)}$. Similarly, let $b_j = \mathcal{D}[\sum_{l \le j} k_l]$ be the $(k_1 + \ldots + k_j)$th smallest item overall; then all the items d with $b_{j-1} < d \le b_j$ must be sent to $x_{\pi(j)}$. In other words,

$$D_i \cap D'_{\pi(j)} = \{d \in D_i : b_{j-1} < d \le b_j\}.$$

Thus, to decide the final destination of its own data items, each x_i needs only to know the values of items $b_1, b_2, \ldots b_n$. To determine each of these values we just need to solve a distributed selection problem, whose solution protocols we have discussed earlier in this chapter.

This gives raise to a general sorting strategy, that we shall call *SelectSort*, whose high-level description is shown in Figure 5.13. This strategy is composed of $n - 1$ iterations. Iteration j, $1 \le j \le n - 1$ is started by $x_{\pi(j)}$ and it is used to determine at each entity x_i which of its own items must be eventually sent to $x_{\pi(j)}$ (i.e., to determine $D_i \cap D'_{\pi(i)}$). More precisely:

1. The iteration starts with $x_{\pi(j)}$ broadcasting the number k_j of items that, according to the storage requirements, it must end up with.

2. The rest of the iteration then consists of the distributed determination of the k_jth smallest item among the data items still under consideration (initially, all data items are under consideration).

3. The iterations terminates with the broadcast of the found item b_j: Upon receiving it, each entity y determines, among the local items still under consideration, those that are smaller or equal to b_1; x_i then assigns $x_{\pi(j)}$ to be the destination for those items, and removes them from consideration.

Strategy *SelectSort*

begin
    for $j = 1, \ldots, n - 1$ **do**
        Collectively determine $b_j = \mathbf{D}[k_j]$ using distributed
        selection;
        * Assign destination: *
        $D_{i,j} := \{d \in D_i : b_{j-1} < d \le b_j\}$;
    endfor
    $D_{i,n} := \{d \in D_i : b_{n-1} < d\}$;
    for $j = 1, \ldots, n - 1$ **do**
        * Send all data items to their final destination: *
        send $D_{i,j}$ **to** $x_{\pi(j)}$;
    endfor
end

FIGURE 5.13: Strategy *SelectSort*.

At the end of the $(n - 1)$th iteration, each entity x_i assigns $x_{\pi(n)}$ to be the destination for any local item still under consideration. At this point, the final destination of each data item has been determined; thus, they can be sent there.

To transform this technique into a protocol, we need to add a final step in which each entity sends the data to their discovered destinations. We also need to ensure that $x_{\pi(j)}$ knows k_j at the beginning of the jth iteration; fortunately, this condition is easy to achieve (Exercise 5.6.39). Finally, we must specify the protocol used for distributed selection in the iterations. If we choose protocol *ReduceSelect* we have discussed in Section 5.2.5, we will call the resulting sorting algorithm Protocol *SelectSort* (see Exercise 5.6.40).

IMPORTANT. Unlike the other two sorting protocols we have examined, Protocol *SelectSort* is *generic*, that is, it works in any network, regardless of its topology. Furthermore, unlike *OddEven-MergeSort*, it always correctly sorts the distribution.

To determine the cost of protocol *SelectSort*, first observe that both the initial and the final broadcast of each iteration can be integrated in the execution of *ReduceSelect* in that iteration; hence, the only *additional cost* of these protocols (i.e., the cost to find the final destination of each data item) is solely due to the $n - 1$ executions of *ReduceSelect*. Let us determine these additional cost.

Let $M[K, N]$ denote the number of messages used to determine the kth smallest out of a distributed set of N elements. As we have chosen protocol *ReduceSelect*, then (recall expression 5.18) we have

$$M[K, N] = \log(\min\{K, N - K + 1\})M[Rank] + l.o.t.$$

where $M[Rank]$ is the number of messages required to select in a small set. Let $K_i = \sum_{j \le i} k_j$. Then, the total *additional cost* of the resulting protocol

SelectSort is

$$\sum_{1 \le i \le n-1} M[k_i, N - K_{i-1}] = M[Rank] \sum_{1 \le i \le n-1} \log(\min\{k_i, N - K_i + 1\}) + l.o.t..$$

$$(5.26)$$

IMPORTANT. Notice that $M[Rank]$ is a function of n only, whose value depends on the topology of the network G, but does *not* depend on N. Hence the *additional cost* of the protocol *SelectSort* is always of the form $O(f_G(n) \log N)$. So as long as this quantity is of the same order (or smaller) than the necessary cost for G, protocol *SelectSort* is *optimal*.

For example, in the *complete graph* we have that $M[Rank] = O(n)$. Thus, Expression 5.26 becomes $O(n^2 \log N/n)$. Recall (Equation 5.25) that the necessary cost in a complete graph is at most N. Thus, protocol *SelectSort* is optimal, with total cost (necessary plus additional) of $O(N)$, whenever $N >> n$, for example, when $N \ge n^2 \log n$. In contrast, protocol *OddEven-MergeSort* has always worst-case cost of $O(N \log n)$, and it might even not sort.

The determination of the cost of protocol *SelectSort* in specific topologies for different storage requirements is the subject of Exercises 5.6.41–5.6.48.

5.3.6 Unrestricted Sorting

In the previous section we have examined the problem of sorting a distributed set according to a given permutation. This describes the common occurrence when there is some a priori ordering of the entities (e.g., of their ids), according to which the data must be sorted.

There are, however, occurrences where the interest is to sort the data with no a priori restriction on what ordering of the sites should be used. In other words, in these cases, the goal is to sort the data according to *a* permutation. This version of the problem is called *unrestricted sorting*.

Solving the unrestricted sorting problem means that we, as designers, have the choice of the permutation according to which we will sort the data. Let us examine the impact of this choice in some details.

We have seen that, for a given permutation π, once the storage requirement is fixed, there is an amount of message exchanges that must necessarily be performed to transfer the records to their destinations; this amount is expressed by Theorem 5.3.1.

Observe that this necessary cost is smaller for some permutations than for others. For example, assume that the data is initially equidistributed sorted according to $\pi_1 = \langle 1, 2, \ldots, n \rangle$, where n is even. Obviously, there is *no* cost for an equidistributed sorting of the set according to π_1, as the data is already in the proper place. By contrast, if we need to sort the distribution according to $\pi_2 = \langle n, n - 1, \ldots, 2, 1 \rangle$, then, even with the same storage requirement as before, the operation will be very costly: At least N messages must be sent, as every data item must necessarily move.

Thus, it is reasonable to ask that the entities choose the permutation $\bar{\pi}$, which *minimizes* the necessary cost for the given storage requirement. For this task, we express the storage requirements as a tuple $k = \langle k_1, k_2, \ldots, k_n \rangle$ where $k_j \leq w$ and $\sum_{1 \leq j \leq n} k_j = N$: The sites of the sorted distribution $\mathbf{D}'$ must be such that $|D'_{\bar{\pi}(j)}| = k_j$. Notice that this generalized storage requirement includes both the compacted (i.e., $k_j = w$) and equidistributed (i.e., $k_j = N/d$) ones, but not necessarily the identical requirement.

More precisely, the task we are facing, called *dynamic sorting*, is the following: given the distribution $\mathbf{D}$, a requirement tuple $k = \langle k_1, k_2, \ldots, k_n \rangle$, we need to determine the permutation $\bar{\pi}$ such that,

$$\forall \pi, \quad \sum_{i=1}^{n} \sum_{j=1}^{n} |D_i \cap D'_j(\bar{\pi})| \, d_G(x_i, x_j) \leq \sum_{i=1}^{n} \sum_{j=1}^{n} |D_i \cap D'_j(\pi)| \, d_G(x_i, x_j) \quad (5.27)$$

where $\mathbf{D}'(\pi) = \langle D'_1(\pi), D'_2(\pi), \ldots, D'_n(\pi) \rangle$ is the resulting distribution sorted according to π. To determine $\bar{\pi}$ we must solve an optimization problem. Most optimization problems, although solvable, are computationally expensive as they are in NP. Surprisingly, and fortunately, our problem is not. Notice that there might be more than one permutation achieving such a goal; in this case, we just choose one (e.g., the alphanumerically smallest).

To determine $\bar{\pi}$ we need to minimize the necessary cost over *all* possible permutations π. Fortunately, we can do it without having to determine each $\mathbf{D}'(\pi)$. In fact, regardless of which permutation we eventually determine to be $\bar{\pi}$, because of the storage requirements we know that

$$k_j = |D'_{\bar{\pi}(j)}|$$

data items must end up in $x_{\bar{\pi}(j)}$, $1 \leq j \leq n$. Hence, we can determine which items of x_i must be sent to $x_{\bar{\pi}(j)}$ even without knowing $\bar{\pi}$. In fact, let $b_j = \mathcal{D}[\sum_{1 \leq l \leq j} k_l]$ be the $(k_1 + \ldots + k_j)$th smallest item overall; then all the items d with $b_{j-1} < d \leq b_j$ must be sent to $x_{\bar{\pi}(j)}$. In other words,

$$D_{i,\bar{\pi}(j)} = D_i \cap D'_{\bar{\pi}(j)} = \{d \in D_i : b_{j-1} < d \leq b_j\}.$$

This means that we can use the same technique as before: the entities collectively determine the items $b_1, b_2, \ldots b_n$ employing a distributed selection protocol; then each entity x_i uses these values to determine which of its own data items must be sent to $x_{\bar{\pi}(j)}$. To be able to complete the task, we do need to know which entity is $x_{\bar{\pi}(j)}$, that is, we need to determine $\bar{\pi}$. To this end, observe that we can rewrite expression 5.27 as

$$\forall \pi, \quad \sum_{i=1}^{n} \sum_{j=1}^{n} |D_{i,\bar{\pi}(j)}| \, d_G(x_i, x_{\bar{\pi}(j)}) \leq \sum_{i=1}^{n} \sum_{j=1}^{n} |D_{i,\pi(j)}| \, d_G(x_i, x_{\pi(j)}). \quad (5.28)$$

Strategy *DynamicSelectSort*

```
begin
    for  j = 1,...,n − 1  do
        Collectively determine  bⱼ = D[kⱼ]
        using distributed selection;
        Dᵢ,ⱼ := {d ∈ Dᵢ : bⱼ₋₁ < d ≤ bⱼ};
        nᵢ(j) := |Dᵢ,ⱼ|;
    endfor
    Dᵢ,ₙ := {d ∈ Dᵢ : bₙ₋₁ < d};
    nᵢ(n) := |Dᵢ,ₙ|;
    if  xᵢ ≠ x̄  then
        send  ⟨nᵢ(1),...,nᵢ(n)⟩  to  x̄;
    else
        wait until receive information from all entities;
        determine  π̄  and notify all entities;
    endif
    send  Dᵢ(j)  to  x_{π(j)},  1 ≤ j ≤ n;
end
```

FIGURE 5.14: Strategy *DynamicSelectSort*.

Using this fact, $\bar{\pi}$ can be determined in low polynomial time once we know the sizes $|D_{i,\bar{\pi}(j)}|$ as well as the distances $d_G(x, y)$ between all pair of entities (Exercise 5.6.49).

Therefore, our overall solution strategy is the following: First each entity x_i determines the local sets $D_i(j)$ using distributed selection; then, using information about the sizes $|D_{i,j}|$ of those sets and the distances $d_G(x, y)$ between entities, a single entity $\bar{x}$ determines the permutation $\bar{\pi}$ that minimizes Expression 5.28; finally, once $\bar{\pi}$ is made known, each entity send the data to their final destination. A high level description is shown in Figure 5.14. Missing from this description is the collection at the coordinator $\bar{x}$ of the distance information; this can be achieved simply by having each entity x send to $\bar{x}$ the distances from its neighbors $N(x)$.

Once all details have been specified, the resulting Protocol *DynamicSelectSorting* will enable to sort a distribution according to the permutation, unknown a priori, that minimizes the necessary costs. See Exercise 5.6.50.

The *additional costs* of the protocol are not difficult to determine. In fact, Protocol *DynamicSelectSorting* is exactly the same as Protocol *SelectSort* with two additional operations: (1) the collection at $\bar{x}$ of the distance and size information, and (2) the notification by $\bar{x}$ of the permutation $\bar{\pi}$. The first operation requires $|N(x_i)| + n$ items of information to be sent by each entity x to $\bar{x}$: The $|N(x_i)|$ distances from its neighbors and the n sizes $|D_{i,\bar{\pi}(j)}|$. The second operation consists on sending $\bar{\pi}$ which is composed of n items of information. Hence, the cost incurred by Protocol *DynamicSelectSorting in addition to* that of Protocol *SelectSort* is:

$$\sum_{x} (|N(x)| + 2n) \, d_G(x, \bar{x}). \tag{5.29}$$

Notice that this cost does *not* depend on the size N of the distributed set, and it is less than the total *additional costs* of Protocol *SelectSort*. This means that, with twice the additional cost of Protocol *SelectSort*, we can sort *minimizing the necessary costs*.

So for example, if the data was already sorted according to some unknown permutation, Protocol *DynamicSelectSorting* will recognize it, determine the permutation, and no data items will be moved at all.

5.4 DISTRIBUTED SETS OPERATIONS

5.4.1 Operations on Distributed Sets

A key element in the functionality of distributed data is the ability to answer queries about the data as well as about the individual sets stored at the entities. Because the data is stored in many places, it is desirable to answer the query in such a way as to minimize the communication. We have already discussed answering simple queries such as *order statistics*.

In systems dealing mainly with distributed data, such as distributed database systems, distributed file systems, distributed objects systems, and so forth the queries are much more complex, and are typically expressed in terms of primitive operations. In particular, in relational databases, a query will be an expression of *join*, *project*, and *select* operations. These operations are actually operations on sets and can be re-expressed in terms of the traditional operators *intersection*, *union*, and *difference* between sets. So to answer a query of the form "Find all the computer science students as well as those social science students enrolled also in anthropology but not in sociology", we will need to compute an expressions of the form

$$A \cup ((B \cap C) - (B \cap D)) \tag{5.30}$$

where A, B, C, and D are the sets of the students in computer science, social sciences, anthropology, and sociology, respectively.

Clearly, if these sets are located at the entity x where the query originates, that entity can locally compute the results and generate the answer. However, if the entity x does *not* have all the necessary data, x will have to involve other entities causing communication. It is possible that each set is actually stored at a different entity, called the *owner* of that set, and none of them is at x.

Even assuming that x knows which entities are the owners of the sets involved, there are many different ways and approaches that can be used to perform the computation. For example, all those sets could be sent by the owners to x, which will then perform the operation locally and answer the query. With this approach, call it $A1$, the volume of data items that will be moved is

$$\text{Vol}(A1) = |A| + |B| + |C| + |D|.$$

The actual number of messages will depend on the size of these sets as well as on the distances between $x(A)$, $x(B)$, $x(C)$, $x(D)$, and x, where $x(\cdot)$ denotes the owner of the specified set. In some cases, for example in complete networks, the number of messages is given precisely by these sizes.

Another approach is to have $x(B)$ sending B to $x(C)$; $x(C)$ will then locally compute $B \cap C$ and send it to $x(D)$, which will locally compute $(B \cap C) - (B \cap D) = (B \cap C) - D$ and send it to $x(A)$ that will compute the final answer and send it to x. The amount of data moved with this approach, call it $A2$, is

$$\mathrm{Vol}(A2) = |B| + |B \cap C| + |(B \cap C) - D| + |A \cup ((B \cap C) - D)|.$$

Depending on the sizes of the sets resulting from the partial computations, $A1$ could be better than $A2$.

Other approaches can be devised, each with its own cost. For example, as $(B \cap C) - D = B \cap (C - D)$, we could have $x(C)$ send C to $x(D)$, which will use it to compute $C - D$ and send the result to $x(B)$; if we also have $x(A)$ send A to $x(B)$, $x(B)$ can compute Expression 5.30, and send the result to x. The volume of transmitted items with this approach, call it $A3$, will be

$$\mathrm{Vol}(A3) = |C| + |C - D| + |A| + |A \cup ((B \cap C) - D)|.$$

IMPORTANT. In each approach, or *strategy*, the original expression is broken down into subexpressions, each to be evaluated just at a single site. For example, in approach $A2$ expression 5.30 is decomposed into three sub-expressions: $E1 = (B \cap C)$ to be computed by $x(C)$, $E2 = E1 - D$ to be computed by $x(D)$, and $E3 = A \cup E3$ to be computed by $x(A)$. A strategy also specifies, for each entity involved in the computation, to what other sites it must send its own set or the results of local evaluations. For example, in approach $A2$, $x(B)$ must send B to $x(C)$; $x(C)$ must send $E1$ to $x(D)$; $x(D)$ must send $E2$ to $x(A)$; and $x(A)$ must send $E3$ to the originator of the query x.

As already mentioned, the amount of items transferred by a strategy depends on the size of the results of the subexpressions (e.g., $|B \cap C|$). Typically these sizes are not known a priori; hence, it is in general impossible to know beforehand which of these approaches is better from a communication point of view. In practice, *estimates* are used on those sizes to decide the best strategy to use. Indeed, a large body of studies exists on how to estimate the size of an intersection or a union or a difference of two or more sets. In particular, an entire research area, called *distributed query processing*, is devoted to the study of the problem of computing the "best" strategy, and related problems.

We can, however, express a *lower bound* on the number of data that must be moved. As the entity x where the query originates must provide the answer, then, assuming x has none of the sets involved in the query, it must receive the entire answer. That is

Theorem 5.4.1 *For every expression E, if the set of the entity x where the query originates is not involved in the expression, then for any strategy S*

$$\mathrm{Vol}(S) \geq |E|.$$

What we will examine in the rest of this section is how we can answer queries efficiently by cleverly organizing the local sets. In fact, we will see how the sets can be locally structured so that the computations of those subexpressions (and, thus, the answer to those queries) can be performed minimizing the volume of data to be moved. To perform the structuring, there is need of some information at each entity; if not available, it can be computed in a prestructuring phase.

5.4.2 Local Structure

We first of all see how we can structure at each entity x_i the local data D_i so to answer operations of intersections and differences with the minimum amount of communication. The method we use to structure a local set is called *Intersection Difference Partioning* (IDP).

The idea of this method is to store each set D_i as a collection Z_i of disjoint subsets such that operations of union, intersection, and difference among the data sets can be computed easily, and with the least amount of data transfers.

Let us see precisely how we construct the partition Z_i of the data set D_i. For simplicity, let us momentarily rename the other $n - 1$ sets D_j ($j \neq i$) as $S_1, S_2, \ldots, S_{n-1}$.

Let us start with the entire set

$$Z_{0,1}^i = D_i. \tag{5.31}$$

We first of all partition it into two subsets: $Z_{1,1}^i = D_i \cap S_1$ and $Z_{1,2}^i = D_i - S_1$. Then recursively, we partition $Z_{l,j}^i$ into two subsets:

$$Z_{l+1,2j-1}^i = Z_{l,j}^i \cap S_{l+1} \tag{5.32}$$

$$Z_{l+1,2j}^i = Z_{l,j}^i - S_{l+1}. \tag{5.33}$$

We continue this process until we obtain the sets $Z_{n-1,j}^i$'s; these sets form exactly the partition of D_i we need. For simplicity, we will denote $Z_{n-1,j}^i$ simply as Z_j^i; hence the final partition of D_i will be denote by

$$Z_i = \langle Z_1^i, Z_2^i, \ldots, Z_m^i \rangle \tag{5.34}$$

where $m = 2^{n-1}$.

Example   Consider the three sets $D_1 = \{a, b, e, f, g, m, n, q\}$, $D_2 = \{a, e, f, g, o, p, r, u, v\}$ and $D_3 = \{e, f, p, r, m, q, v\}$ stored at entities x_1, x_2, x_3, respectively. Let us focus on D_1; it is first subdivided into $Z_{1,1}^i = D_1 \cup D_2 = \{a, e, f, g\}$ and $Z_{1,2}^i = D_1 - D_2 = \{b, m, n, q\}$. These are then subdivided creating the final partition Z_1 composed of $Z_{2,1}^1 = \{e, f\}$, $Z_{2,2}^1 = \{a, g\}$, $Z_{2,3}^1 = \{m, q\}$, and $Z_{2,4}^1 = \{b, n\}$.

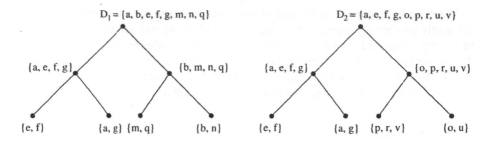

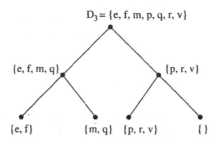

FIGURE 5.15: Trees created by DSP.

This recursive partitioning of the set D_i creates a binary tree T_i. The root (considered to be at level 0) corresponds to the entire sets D_i. Each node in the tree corresponds to a subset (one of the $Z^i_{l,j}$'s) of this set; note that this subset is possibly empty. For a node at level $l - 1$ corresponding to subset S, its left child corresponds to the subset $S \cap S_j$ while the right child corresponds to the subset $S - S_j$. The trees for the three sets of the example above are shown in Figure 5.15.

Notice that at each level of the tree (including the last level $l = n - 1$), the entire set is represented:

Property 5.4.1 $D_i = \bigcup_{(1 \leq j \leq 2^l)} Z^i_{l,j}$

In other words, $\langle Z^i_{l,1}, Z^i_{l,2}, \ldots, Z^i_{l,2^l} \rangle$ is a partition of D_i.

Further observe that each level $l \geq 1$ of the tree describes the relationship between elements of D_i and those in the set S_l. In particular, the sets corresponding to the *left* children of level l are precisely the elements in common between D_i and S_l:

Property 5.4.2 $\bigcup_{(1 \leq j \leq 2^{l-1})} Z^i_{l,2j-1} = D_i \cap S_l$

By contrast, the sets corresponding to the *right* children of level l are precisely the elements in D_i that are *not* part of S_j:

Property 5.4.3 $\bigcup_{(1 \leq j \leq 2^{l-1})} Z^i_{l,2j} = D_i - S_l$

This means that, if we were to store at x_i the entire tree T_i (i.e., all the sets $Z^i_{l,j}$'s), then x_i can immediately answer any query of the form $D_i - D_j$ and $D_i \cap D_j$ for any j. In other words, if each x_i has available its tree T_i then any query of the form $D_i - D_j$ and $D_i \cap D_j$ can be answered by x_i *without any communication*.

We are going to see now that it is possible to achieve the same goal storing at x_i only the last partition Z_i (i.e., the leaves of the tree).

Observe that each level l of the tree contains not only the entire set D_i but also information about the relationship between D_i and all the sets $S_1, S_2, \ldots, S_l$. In particular, the last level $l = n - 1$ (i.e., the final partition), contains information about the relationship between D_i and all the other sets. More precisely, the information contained in each node of the tree T_i is also contained in the final partition and can be reconstructed from there:

Property 5.4.4 $$Z^i_{l,j} = \bigcup_{(1 \le k \le 2^{n-1-l})} Z^i_{k + (j-1) \, 2^{n-1-l}}$$

Summarizing, each entity x_i structures its local set D_i as the collection $Z_i = \langle Z^i_1, Z^i_2, \ldots, Z^i_m \rangle$ of disjoint subsets created using the IDP method. This collection contain all the information contained in each node of the tree T_i.

IMPORTANT. Notice that when structuring D_i as the partition Z_i, the number of data items stored at x_i is still $|D_i|$, that is, *no* additional data items are stored anywhere.

5.4.3 Local Evaluation (⋆)

Locally Computable Expressions   If each x_i stores its set D_i as the partition Z_i, then each entity is immediately capable of computing the result of many expressions involving set operations.

For example, we know that the partition Z_i contains all the information contained in each node of the tree T_i (Property 5.4.4), thus, by Properties 5.4.2 and 5.4.3 it follows that x_i can answer *without any communication* any query of the form $D_i - D_j$ and $D_i \cap D_j$. In fact,

$$D_i \cap S_l = \bigcup_{(1 \le j \le 2^{l-1}, \; 1 \le k \le 2^{n-1-l})} Z^i_{k + (j-1) \, 2^{n-l}} \tag{5.35}$$

$$D_i - S_l = \bigcup_{(1 \le j \le 2^{l-1}, \; 1 \le k \le 2^{n-1-l})} Z^i_{k + (2j-1) \, 2^{n-l-1}}. \tag{5.36}$$

Actually, x_i has locally available the answer to *any* expression composed of differences and intersections, involving any number of sets, provided that D_i is the left operand in the differences involving D_i. So for example, the query $(D_1 - D_2) \cap (D_3 - (D_4 \cap D_5))$ can be answered immediately both at x_1 and x_3 (see Exercise 5.6.51). Also some queries involving unions as well as intersections and differences can be answered immediately and locally. For example, both $(D_1 - (D_2 \cap D_3))$ and $((D_1 - D_2) \cap (D_1 \cup D_3))$ can be answered by x_1.

Exactly what expressions can be answered by x_i? To answer this question, observe the following:

if expression E can be answered locally by x_i, then x_i can answer also $E \cap E'$ and $E - E'$, where E' is an arbitrary expression on the local sets;

if two expressions E_1 and E_2 can be answered locally by x_i, so can be the expressions $E_1 \cup E_2$.

Using these two facts and starting with D_i, we can characterize the set $E(x_i)$ of all the expressions that can be answered by x_i directly without communication.

Local Evaluation Strategy   Let us see now how can x_i determine the answer to a query in $E(x_i)$ from the information stored in the final partition $Z_i = \langle Z_1^i, Z_2^i, \ldots, Z_m^i \rangle$, where $m = 2^{n-1}$.

First of all, let us introduce some terminology. We will call *address* of Z_j^i the Boolean representation $b(j)$ of $j - 1$ using $n - 1$ bits, for example, in Figure 5.15, the subset $Z_{2,3}^1 = \{m, q\}$ has address $\langle 10 \rangle$, while $\langle 11 \rangle$ is the address of the subset $Z_{2,4}^1$.

An expression on k operands is *sequential* if it is of the form

$$((\ldots(((O_1 \; o_1 \; O_2) \; o_2 \; O_3) \; o_3 \; O_4)\ldots) \; o_{k-1} \; O_k)$$

where the O_j are the operands and o_j are the set operators. An example of a sequential expression is $(((A \cup B) - C) \cup B)$.

First consider the set $E^-(x_i) \subset E(x_i)$ of sequential expressions in $E(x_i)$ where

1. D_i is the first operand,
2. each of the other sets S_j appears at most once, and
3. the only operators are intersection and difference.

For example, the expression $(((D_i \cap S_3) - S_1) \cap S_2)$ is in $E^-(x_i)$. To answer queries in $E^-(x_i)$ there is a simple strategy that x_i can follow:

Strategy Bitmask

1. Create a bitmask of size $n - 1$.
2. For each set S_j
   (a) if S_j is the right operand of an intersection operator, then place 0 in the jth position of the bitmask;
   (b) if S_j is the right operand of a difference operator, then place a 1 in the jth position of the bitmask;
   (c) if S_j is not involved in the query at all, place the *wildcard* symbol $\star$ in the jth position of the bitmask.

3. Perform the union of all the subsets in the final partition whose address matches the pattern of the bitmask, where *wildcard* symbol $\star$ is matched both by 0 and 1.

Example   The bitmask associated to expression

$$(((D_i \cap S_3) - S_1) \cap S_4) \qquad (5.37)$$

when $n = 6$ will be $\langle \star\, 0\, 0\, \star\, 1 \rangle$. Entity x_i will then calculate the union of the sets in its final partition Z_i whose addresses match the bitmask; that is, the sets with address $\langle 00001 \rangle$, $\langle 00011 \rangle$, $\langle 10001 \rangle$, $\langle 10011 \rangle$. Thus, to answer query (5.37), x_i will just calculate

$$Z_2^i \cup Z_4^i \cup Z_{34}^i \cup Z_{36}^i. \qquad (5.38)$$

It is not difficult to verify that indeed by calculating (5.38) we obtain the answer to precisely query (5.38); in fact, the Evaluation Strategy Bitmask is correct (Exercise 5.6.53).

Summarizing, using strategy *Bitmask* entity x_i can directly evaluate any expression in $E^-(x_i)$; those are, however, only a small subset of all the expressions in $E(x_i)$.

Let us now examine how to extend to all queries in $E(x_i)$ the result we have just obtained. The key to the extension is the fact that any expression of $E(x)$ can be re-expressed as the union of sub-expressions in $E^-(x_i)$ (Exercise 5.6.54).

Property 5.4.5   *For every $Q \in E(x)$ there are $Q(1), \ldots, Q(k) \in E^-(x_i)$, $k \geq 1$, such that $Q = \bigcup_{1 \leq j \leq k} Q(j)$.*

For example, $(D_i - (S_2 \cup S_4))$ can be re-expressed as $(D_i - S_2) \cup (D_i - S_4)$. Similarly

$$((S_1 \cap S_2) \cup D_i) - (S_4 \cap S_5) = ((D_i \cup S_1) - S_4 - S_5) \cap ((D_i \cup S_2) - S_4 - S_5).$$

Thus, to answer a query in $E(x_i)$, entity x_i will first re-formulate it as union of expressions in $E^-(x_i)$, evaluate each of them using strategy *Bitmask* and then perform their union.

Strategy Local Evaluation

1. Re-formulate Q as union of expressions $Q(1), \ldots, Q(k)$ in $E^-(x_i)$.
2. Evaluate each $Q(j)$ using strategy *Bitmask*.
3. Perform the union of all the obtained results.

Notice that all this can be done by x_i locally, without any communication.

5.4.4   Global Evaluation

Let us now examine the problem of answering a query Q originating at an entity x once every local set D_i has been stored as the partition Z^i. If the query can be answered directly (i.e., $Q \in E(x)$), x will do so. Otherwise, the query will be decomposed into subqueries that can be locally evaluated at one or more entities, the results of these partial evaluations are then collected at x so that the original query can be answered. Our goal is to ensure that the volume of data items to be moved is minimized. To achieve this goal, we use the following property

Property 5.4.6   *For every expression Q there are $k \leq n$ subexpressions $Q(1)$, $Q(2)$, ..., $Q(k)$ such that*

1. $\forall Q(j) \, \exists y_j \, Q(j) \in E(y_j)$,
2. $Q(i) \cap Q(j) = \emptyset$ *for* $i \neq j$,
3. $Q = \bigcup_{1 \leq j \leq k} Q(j)$.

That is, *any* query Q can be re-expressed as the union of subqueries $Q(1), \ldots, Q(k)$, where each subquery can be answered directly by just one entity, once its local set has been stored using the partitioning method; furthermore, the answer to any two different subqueries is disjoint (Exercise 5.6.55). This gives raise to our strategy for evaluating an arbitrary query:

Strategy Global

1. x decomposes Q into $Q(1)$, $Q(2)$, ..., $Q(k)$ satisfying Property 5.4.6, and informs each y_j of $Q(j)$;
2. y_j locally and directly evaluates $Q(j)$ and sends the result to x; and
3. x computes the union of all the received items.

To understand the advantages of this strategy, let us examine again the implications of Property 5.4.6. As the results of any two subqueries are disjoint, while the union of all results of the subqueries is precisely what we are asking for, we have that:

Property 5.4.7   *Let $Q(1)$, $Q(2)$, ..., $Q(k)$ satisfy Property 5.4.6 for Q. Then*

$$|Q| = \sum_{1 \leq j \leq k} |Q(j)|.$$

This means that, for every query Q, in our Strategy *Global* the only data items that might be moved to x are those in the final answer, that is,

$$\text{Vol}[Global] \leq |Q|.$$

In other words, strategy *Global* is *optimal*. This optimality is with regards to the amount of data items that will be moved.

There are different possible decompositions of a query Q into subqueries satisfying Property 5.4.6. All of them are equally acceptable to our strategy, and they all provide optimal volume costs.

IMPORTANT. To calculate the cost in terms of *messages* we need to take into account also the distances between the nodes in the network. In this regard, some decompositions may be better than others. The problem of determining the decomposition that requires less messages is a difficult one, and no solution is known till date.

5.4.5 Operational Costs

An important consideration is that of the cost of setting up the final partitions at each entity. Once in this format, we have seen how complex queries can be handled with minimal communication. But to get it in this format requires communication; in fact each entity must somehow receive information from all the other entities about their sets. In a complete network this can require just a single transmission of each set to a predetermined coordinator that will then compute and send the appropriate partition to each entity; hence, the total cost will be $O(N)$ where N is the total amount of data. By contrast, in a line network the total cost can be as bad as $O(N^2)$, for example, if all sets have almost the same size. It is true that this cost is incurred only once, at set-up time. If the goal is only to answer a few queries, the cost of setup may exceed that of simply performing the queries without using the partitioned sets. But for persistent distributed data, upon which many queries may be placed, this is an efficient solution.

Another consideration is that of the addition or removal of data from the distributed sets. As each entity contains some knowledge about the contents of all other entities, any time an item is added to or removed from one of the sets, every entity must update its partition to reflect this fact. Fortunately, the cost of doing this does not exceed the cost of broadcasting the added (or removed) item to each entity. Clearly this format is more effective for slowly changing distributed data sets.

5.5 BIBLIOGRAPHICAL NOTES

The problems of distributed selection and distributed sorting were studied for a *small* set by Greg Frederickson in special networks (exercises 5.6.1–5.6.3) [4], and by Shmuel Zaks [23]. Always in a small set, the cost using bounded messages and, thus, the bit complexity has been studied by Mike Loui [8] in ring networks; by Ornan Gerstel, Yishay Mansour, and Shmuel Zaks in a star [5]; and in trees by Ornan Gerstel and Shmuel Zaks [6] , and by Alberto Negro, Nicola Santoro, and Jorge Urrutia [12]. Selection among *two sites* was first studied by Michael Rodeh [14]; his solution was later improved by S. Mantzaris [10], and by Francis Chin and Hing Ting [3].

Reducing the *expected* costs of distributed selection has been the goal of several investigations. Protocol *RandomSelect* was designed by Liuba Shrira, Nissim Francez, and Michael Rodeh [21]. Nicola Santoro, Jeffrey Sidney, and Stuart Sidney designed Protocol *RandomFlipSelect* [19]. Protocol *RandomRandomSelect* is due to Nicola Santoro, Michael Scheutzow, and Jeffrey Sidney [17].

General selection protocols, with emphasis on the *worst case*, were developed by Doron Rotem, Nicola Santoro, and Jeffrey Sidney [16], and by Nicola Santoro and Jeffrey Sidney [18]. The more efficient protocol *Filter* was developed by John Marberg and Eli Gafni [11]. The even more efficient protocol *ReduceSelect* was later designed by Nicola Santoro and Ed Suen [19].

The sorting protocols Odd-Even Mergesort algorithm, on which Protocols *OddEven-LineSort* and *OddEven-MergeSort* are based, was developed by Kenneth Batcher [1].

The first general distributed sorting algorithm is due to Lutz Wegner [22]. More recent but equally costly sorting protocols have been designed by To-Yat Cheung [2], and by Peter Hofstee, Alain Martin, and Jan van de Snepscheut [7]; experimental evaluations were performed by Wo-Shun Luk and Franky Ling [9]. The optimal *SelectSort* was designed by Doron Rotem, Nicola Santoro, Jeffrey B. Sidney [15], who also designed protocol *DynamicSelectSort*. Other protocols include those designed by Hanmao Shi and Jonathan Schaeffer [20].

There is an extensive amount of investigations on database queries, whose computation requires the use of distributed set operations like union, intersection and difference. The entire field of *distributed query processing* is dedicated to this topic, mostly focusing on the estimation of the size of the output of a set operation and thus of the entire query. The IDP structure for minimum-volume operations on distributed sets was designed and analyzed in this context by Ekow Otoo, Nicola Santoro, Doron Rotem [13].

5.6 EXERCISES, PROBLEMS, AND ANSWERS

5.6.1 Exercises

Exercise 5.6.1 ($\star$) Consider a *ring* network where each entity has just one item. Show how to perform selection using $O(n \log^3 n)$ messages.

Exercise 5.6.2 ($\star$) Consider a *mesh* network where each entity has just one item. Show how to perform selection using $O(n \log^{\frac{3}{2}} n)$ messages.

Exercise 5.6.3 ($\star$) Consider a network whose topology is a *complete binary tree* where each entity has just one item. Show how to perform selection using $O(n \log n)$ messages.

Exercise 5.6.4 Prove that after discarding the elements greater than m_x from D_x and discarding the elements greater than m_y from D_y, the overall lower median is the lower median of the elements still under considerations.

Exercise 5.6.5 Write protocol *Halving* so that it works with any two arbitrarily sized sets with the same complexity.

Exercise 5.6.6 Prove that the K-selection problem can be reduced to a median-finding problem regardless of K and of the size of the two sets.

Exercise 5.6.7 Modify protocol *Halving* as follows: In iteration i,

(a) discard from both D_x^i and D_y^i, all elements greater than $\max\{m_x^i, m_y^i\}$ and all those smaller than $\min\{m_x^i, m_y^i\}$, where D_x^i and D_y^i denote the set of elements of D_x and D_y still under consideration at the beginning of stage i, and m_x^i and m_y^i denote their lower medians;

(b) transform the problem again into a median finding one.

Write the corresponding algorithm, *GeneralHalving*, prove its correctness, and analyze its complexity.

Exercise 5.6.8 Implement protocol *GeneralHalving* of Exercise 5.6.7, throughly test it, and run extensive experiments. Compare the experimental results with the theoretical ones.

Exercise 5.6.9 (⋆⋆) Extend the technique of protocol *Halving* to work with three sets, D_x, D_y, and D_z. Write the corresponding protocol, prove its correctness, and analyze its complexity.

Exercise 5.6.10 Random Item Selection (⋆) Modify the protocol of Exercise 2.9.52 so that it can be used to select uniformly at random an element still under consideration in each iteration of Strategy *RankSelect*. Your protocol should use at most $2(n-1) + d_T(s, x)$ messages and $2r(s) + d_T(s, x)$ ideal time units in each iteration. Prove both correctness and complexity.

Exercise 5.6.11 (⋆) Prove that the expected number of iterations performed by Protocol *RandomSelect* until termination is at most $1.387 \log N + O(1)$.

Exercise 5.6.12 (⋆) Determine the number of iterations if we terminate protocol *RandomSelect*, as soon as the search space contains at most cn items, where c is a fixed constant. Determine the total cost of this truncated execution followed by an execution of protocol *Rank*.

Exercise 5.6.13 Prove that in the worst case, the number of iterations performed by Protocol *RandomFlipSelect* until termination is N.

Exercise 5.6.14 (⋆⋆) Prove that the expected number of iterations performed by Protocol *RandomFlip* until termination is less than $\ln(\Delta) + \ln(n) + O(1)$.

Exercise 5.6.15 (⋆) Determine the number of iterations if we terminate protocol *RandomFlipSelect*, as soon as the search space contains at most cn items, where c is a fixed constant. Determine the total cost of this truncated execution followed by an execution of protocol *Rank*.

Exercise 5.6.16 Write Protocol *RandomRandomSelect* ensuring that each iteration uses at most $4(n-1) + r(s)$ messages and $5r(s)$ ideal time units. Implement the protocol and throughly test your implementation.

Exercise 5.6.17 (⋆⋆) Prove that the expected number of iterations performed by Protocol *RandomRandomSelect* until there are less than n items left under consideration is at most $\frac{4}{3}\lfloor \log\log \Delta + 1\rfloor$.

Exercise 5.6.18 Prove that the number of iterations performed by Protocol *Filter* until there are no more than n elements left under consideration is at most $2.41\log(N/n)$.

Exercise 5.6.19 Prove that in the execution of Protocol *REDUCE*, Local Contraction is executed at the most three times.

Exercise 5.6.20 Prove that after the execution of *Cutting Tool* on $C(l = 2^i)$, only the $l - 1$ columns $C(1), C(2), \ldots, C(l-1)$ might remain unchanged; all others, including $C(l)$ will have *at least* $n - K/l$ of the entries $+\infty$.

Exercise 5.6.21 Prove that after the execution of Protocol *CUT* there will be at most $\min\{n, \Delta\}\log \Delta$ items left under consideration.

Exercise 5.6.22 Consider the system shown in Figure 5.9. How many items will x_5 have

(a) after a *compacted* sorting with $w = 5$?
(b) after an *equidistributed* sorting?

Justify your answer.

Exercise 5.6.23 Prove that *OddEven-LineSort* performs an invariant-sized sort of an equidistribution on an ordered line.

Exercise 5.6.24 (⋆) Prove that *OddEven-LineSort* performs an invariant-sized sort of any distribution on an ordered line.

Exercise 5.6.25 (⋆) Prove that *OddEven-LineSort* performs a compacted sort of any distribution on an ordered line.

Exercise 5.6.26   ($\star$) Prove that *OddEven-LineSort* performs an equidistributed sort of any distribution on an ordered line.

Exercise 5.6.27   Prove that *OddEven-LineSort* sorts an equidistributed distribution in $n - 1$ iterations regardless of whether the required sorting is invariant-sized, equidistributed, or compacted with all entities having the same capacity.

Exercise 5.6.28   Prove that there are some initial conditions under which protocol *OddEven-LineSort* uses $N - 1$ iterations to perform invariant-size sorting of N items distributed on a sorted line, regardless of the number n of entities.

Exercise 5.6.29   Consider an initial equidistribution sorted according to permutation $\pi' = \langle \pi(n), \pi(n - 1), \ldots, \pi(1) \rangle$. Prove that, executing protocol *OddEven-LineSort* in this case, every data item will change location in each iteration.

Exercise 5.6.30   Prove that when $n > 3$, if the line is not sorted according to π, then protocol *OddEven-LineSort* terminates but does *not* sort the data according to π.

Exercise 5.6.31   Write the set of rules of protocol *OddEven-MergeSort*. Implement the protocol and throughly test it.

Exercise 5.6.32   Prove that protocol *OddEven-MergeSort* is a sequence of $1 + \log n$ iterations and that in each iteration (except the last) every data item is sent once or twice to another entity.

Exercise 5.6.33   Prove that protocol *OddEven-MergeSort* correctly sorts, regardless of the storage requirement, if the initial set is equidistributed.

Exercise 5.6.34   Consider an initial distribution where x_1 and x_n have the same number $K = (N - n + 2)/2$ of data items, while all other entities have just a single data item. Augment protocol *OddEven-MergeSort* so as to perform an invariant sort when $\pi = \langle 1, 2, \ldots, n \rangle$. Show the corresponding sorting diagram. How many additional simple *merge* operations are needed? How many operations does your solution perform? Determine the time and message costs of your solution.

Exercise 5.6.35   For each of the three storage requirements (invariant, equidistributed, compacted) show a situation where $\Omega(N)$ messages need to be sent to sort in a complete network, even when the data are initially equidistributed.

Exercise 5.6.36   Determine for each of the three storage requirements (invariant, equidistributed, compacted) a lower bound, in terms of n and N on the amount of necessary messages for sorting in a *ring*. What would be the bound for initially equidistributed sets?

Exercise 5.6.37 ($\star$) Determine for each of the three storage requirements (invariant, equidistributed, compacted) a lower bound, in terms of n and N on the amount of necessary messages for sorting in a labeled *hypercube*. What would be the bound for initially equidistributed sets?

Exercise 5.6.38 ($\star$) Determine for each of the three storage requirements (invariant, equidistributed, compacted) a lower bound, in terms of n and N on the amount of necessary messages for sorting in an oriented *torus*. What would be the bound for initially equidistributed sets?

Exercise 5.6.39 Show how $x_{\pi(i)}$ can find out k_i at the beginning of the ith iteration of strategy *SelectSort*. Initially, each entity knows only its index in the permutation (i.e., $x_{\pi(i)}$ knows i) as well as the storage requirements.

Exercise 5.6.40 Write the set of rules of Protocol *SelectSort*. Implement and test the protocol. Compare the experimental costs with the theoretical bounds.

Exercise 5.6.41 Establish for each of the storage requirements the worst-case cost of protocol *SelectSort* to sort an equidistributed set in a *ordered line*. Determine under what conditions the protocol is optimal for this network. Compare this cost with the one of protocol *OddEven-LineSort*.

Exercise 5.6.42 Establish for each of the storage requirements the worst-case cost of protocol *SelectSort* to sort a distributed set in a *ordered line*. Determine under what conditions the protocol is optimal for this network. Compare this cost with the one of protocol *OddEven-LineSort*.

Exercise 5.6.43 Establish for each of the storage requirements the worst-case cost of protocol *SelectSort* to sort an equidistributed set in a *ring*. Determine under what conditions the protocol is optimal for this network *(Hint: Use result of Exercise 5.6.36)*.

Exercise 5.6.44 Establish for each of the storage requirements the worst-case cost of protocol *SelectSort* to sort a distributed set in a *ring*. Determine under what conditions the protocol is optimal for this network *(Hint: Use result of Exercise 5.6.36)*.

Exercise 5.6.45 Establish for each of the storage requirements the worst-case cost of protocol *SelectSort* to sort an equidistributed set in a labeled *hypercube* of dimension d. Determine under what conditions the protocol is optimal for this network *(Hint: Use result of Exercise 5.6.37)*.

Exercise 5.6.46 Establish for each of the storage requirements the worst-case cost of protocol *SelectSort* to sort a distributed set in a labeled *hypercube* of dimension d. Determine under what conditions the protocol is optimal for this network *(Hint: Use result of Exercise 5.6.37)*.

Exercise 5.6.47   Establish for each of the storage requirements the worst-case cost of protocol *SelectSort* to sort an equidistributed set in a oriented *torus* of dimension $p \times q$. Determine under what conditions the protocol is optimal for this network. *(Hint: Use result of Exercise 5.6.38)*.

Exercise 5.6.48   Establish for each of the storage requirements the worst-case cost of protocol *SelectSort* to sort a distributed set in a oriented *torus* of dimension $p \times q$. Determine under what conditions the protocol is optimal for this network *(Hint: Use result of Exercise 5.6.38)*.

Exercise 5.6.49   Show how in strategy DynamicSelectSort the coordinator $\bar{x}$ can determine $\bar{\pi}$ from the received information in $O(n^3)$ local processing activities.

Exercise 5.6.50   Write the set of rules of Protocol *DynamicSelectSorting*. Implement and test the protocol. Compare the experimental costs with the theoretical bounds.

Exercise 5.6.51   Prove that the query $(D_1 - D_2) \cap (D_3 - (D_4 \cap D_5))$ can be answered immediately at both x_1 and x_3 if each of the sets is stored by its entity using the DSP method.

Exercise 5.6.52   Show that expressions 5.38 and 5.38 are equal.

Exercise 5.6.53   Prove that using strategy *Bitmask*, entity x_i can directly evaluate any expression in $E^-(x_i)$.

Exercise 5.6.54 $(\star)$ Prove Property 5.4.5: Any expression of $E(x)$ can be re-expressed as the union of sub-expressions in $E^-(x_i)$.

Exercise 5.6.55 $(\star)$ Prove Property 5.4.6.

5.6.2   Problems

Problem 5.6.1 $(\star\star\star)$ Design a generic protocol to perform selection in a small set using $o(n^2)$ messages in the worst case.

5.6.3   Answers to Exercises

Partial Answer to Exercise 5.6.4.
Among the 2^{p-1} elements removed from consideration, exactly 2^{p-2} are greater than the median while exactly 2^{p-2} are smaller than the median.

Answer to Exercise 5.6.13.
Without loss of generality, let $K \leq N - K + 1$. Then, for the first $N - 2K + 2$ iterations, the adversary will choose $d(i)$ to be the *largest* item in the search space. In this way, only $d(i)$ will be removed from the search space in that iteration;

furthermore, we still have $K(i + 1) \le N(i + 1) - K(i + 1) + 1$ where $K(i)$ and $N(i)$ are the rank of d^* and the size of the search space at the beginning of iteration i. As in these iterations we are removing only elements larger than d^*, after the $N - 2K + 1$ iterations d^* is the median of the search space. At this point, the adversary will alternate selecting $d(i)$ to be the *smallest* item in the search space in one iteration and the *largest* item in the next one. In this way, only $d(i)$ will be removed and d^* continues to be the (lower) median of the search space. Hence, the additional number of iterations is exactly $2K - 2$, for a total of N iterations.

Partial Answer to Exercise 5.6.18.
Show that at least $1/4$ of the items are removed from consideration at each iteration.

Partial Answer to Exercise 5.6.19.
Let $K(j)$ and $N(j)$ be the rank of f^* in the search space and the size of the search space at the end of iteration j of the **while** loop in Protocol *REDUCE*. Call an iteration a *flip* if $\Delta(j) = N(j - 1) - \Delta(j - 1) + 1 < \Delta(j - 1)$. First of all observe that if the $(j + 1)$th iteration is not a flip, then it is the last iteration. Let the $(j + 1)$th iteration be a flip, and let $q(j + 1)$ be the number of entities whose local search space is reduced in this iteration; $q(j + 1)$ must be at least 1, otherwise the iteration would not be a flip. We will show that $q(j + 1) = 1$. By contradiction, if $q(j + 1) > 1$, there must be at least two entities x and y that will have their search space reduced in iteration $(j + 1)$. That is, $N(x, j) > \Delta(j)$ and $N(y, j) > \Delta(j)$ where $N(x, j)$ and $N(y, j)$ denote the number of items still under consideration at x and y, respectively, at the end of the jth iteration. Then $N(j) \ge N(x, j) + N(y, j) \ge 2\Delta(j)$. This means that $N(j) - \Delta(j) + 1 > \Delta(j)$, which implies that $\Delta(j + 1) = \min\{\Delta(j), N(j) - \Delta(j) + 1\} = \Delta(j)$, contradicting the fact that iteration $(j + 1)$ is a flip. Hence, $q = 1$, that is, if iteration $(j + 1)$ is a flip, only one entity will reduce its search space in that iteration. To complete the proof, we must prove that the jth and the $(j + 1)$th iterations cannot both be flips.

Answer to Exercise 5.6.22.
(a) none; (b) one.

Answer to Exercise 5.6.28.
Consider the initial condition where the initial distribution is sorted according to $\langle n, n - 1, \ldots, 1 \rangle$. Let x_1 and x_n each contain $(N - n + 2)/2$ items, while all other entities have only one item each. Then trivially, in the each odd iteration only one item can leave x_1. Hence, the last item to move from x_1 to x_n will do so in the $(N - n + 2)/2$th *odd* iteration, which is the $(N - n + 1)$th iteration overall; this item reaches x_n after an additional $n - 2$ iterations. Hence, the claimed $N - 1$ total number of iterations before termination.

Answer to Exercise 5.6.30.
Without loss of generality let $\pi = \langle 1, 2, \ldots, n \rangle$. If the line is not sorted according to π, then there is an entity x_i whose neighbors in the line, y and z, have indices

"greater" (respectively "smaller") than it, that is, $y = x_j$ and $z = x_k$ where both j and k are greater (respectively, smaller) than i. Without loss of generality let $j > k$ (respectively, $j < k$); that is, once sorted, the data stored in y must be greater (respectively smaller) than the data stored in z. Among the data initially stored at z, include the *largest* data item $\mathcal{D}[N]$ (respectively the *smallest* item $\mathcal{D}[1]$). For the data to be sorted, this item must move from $z = x_k$ to $y = x_j$, passing through x_i. However, as $k > i$ (respectively $k < i$), according to the protocol z will never send $\mathcal{D}[N]$ (respectively $\mathcal{D}[1]$) to x_i.

Answer to Exercise 5.6.39.

If the storage requirement is invariant sized, then $k_i = |D_{\pi(i)}|$, which is known to $x_{\pi(i)}$.

If the requirement is equidistributed, then the entities need to know $\lceil N/n \rceil$; both n and N, if not already known can be easily acquired (e.g., using *saturation* on a spanning-tree). Then, $k_i = \lceil N/n \rceil$ for $1 \le i \le n - 1$.

If the storage requirement is compacted with parameter w, then $k_i = w$ for $1 \le i \le \lceil N/w \rceil$, while $k_i = 0$ for $i > \lceil N/w \rceil$. Again, knowing N allows each entity to know what the size of its final set of data items.

Answer to Exercise 5.6.49.

Observe that if $\overline{\pi}(j) = k$, then to transfer to x_k all the data items that must end up there requires the transmission of $\beta_{j \to k} = \sum_{j=1}^{n} |D_{i,j}| \, d_G(x_i, x_k)$ messages. Define variables $z_{j,k}$ to be equal to 1 if $\overline{\pi}(j) = k$, 0 otherwise. Then minimization of e ex pression 5.28 reduces to finding a $0 - 1$ solution for the linear programming assignment problem:

$$\text{Minimize } g[Z] = \sum_{j=1}^{n} \sum_{k=1}^{n} \beta_{j \to k} z_{j,k}$$

$$\sum_{k=1}^{n} z_{j,k} = 1 \ (1 \le j \le n)$$

$$\sum_{j=1}^{n} z_{j,k} = 1 \ (1 \le k \le n)$$

$$z_{j,k} \ge 0 \ (1 \le j, k \le n).$$

A single entity can solve this problem in $O(n^3)$ local processing activities once the $\beta_{j \to k}$'s are available at that entity.

BIBLIOGRAPHY

[1] K.E. Batcher. Sorting networks and their applications. In *AFIPS Spring Joint Computer Conference*, pages 307–314, 1968.

[2] To-Yat Cheung. An algorithm with decentralized control for sorting files in a network. *Journal of Parallel and Distributed Computing*, 7(3):464–481, 1989.

[3] F. Chin and H.F. Ting. An improved algorithm for finding the median distributively. *Algorithmica*, 2:235–249, 1987.

[4] G.N. Frederickson. Distributed algorithms for selection in sets. *Journal of Computing and System Science*, 37(3):337–348, 1988.

[5] O. Gerstel, Y. Mansour, and S. Zaks. Bit complexity of order statistics on a distributed star network. *Information Processing Letters*, 30(3):127–132, 1989.

[6] O. Gerstel and S. Zaks. The bit complexity of distributed sorting. *Algorithmica*, 18: 405–416, 1997.

[7] H.P. Hofstee, A.J. Martin, and J.L.A. van de Snepscheut. Distributed sorting. *Science of Computer Programming*, 15(2–3):119–133, 1990.

[8] M.C. Loui. The complexity of sorting on distributed systems. *Information and Control*, 60:70–85, 1984.

[9] W.S. Luk and Franky Ling. An analytical/empirical study of distributed sorting on a local area network. *IEEE Transactions on Software Engineering*, 15(5):575–586, 1989.

[10] S.L. Mantzaris. An improved algorithm for finding the median distributively. *Algorithmica*, 10(6):501–504, 1993.

[11] J.M. Marberg and E. Gafni. Distributed sorting algorithms for multi-channel broadcast networks. *Theoretical Computer Science*, 52(3):193–203, 1987.

[12] A. Negro, N. Santoro, and J. Urrutia. Efficient distributed selection with bounded messages. *IEEE Transaction on Parallel and Distributed Systems*, 8:397–401, 1997.

[13] E.J. Otoo, N. Santoro, and D. Rotem. Improving semi-joint evaluation in distributed query processing. In *7th International Conference on Distributed Computing Systems.*, pages 554–561, sept 1987.

[14] M. Rodeh. Finding the median distributively. *Journal of Computing and Systems Science*, 24(2):162–167, 1982.

[15] D. Rotem, N. Santoro, and J. B. Sidney. Distributed sorting. *IEEE Transaction on Computers*, 34:372–376, 1985.

[16] D. Rotem, N. Santoro, and J.B. Sidney. Shout-echo selection in distributed files. *Networks*, 16:77–86, 1986.

[17] N. Santoro, M. Scheutzow, and J.B. Sidney. On the expected complexity of distributed selection. *Journal of Parallel and Distributed Computing*, 5:194–203, 1988.

[18] N. Santoro and J.B. Sidney. Order statistics on distributed sets. In *20th Allerton Conf. on Communication, Control and Computing*, pages 251–256, 1982.

[19] N. Santoro and E. Suen. Reduction techniques for selection in a distributed file. *IEEE Transactions on Computers*, 38(6):891–896, 1989.

[20] H. Shi and J. Schaeffer. Parallel sorting by regular sampling. *Journal of Parallel and Distributed Computing*, 14(4):361–372, 1992.

[21] L. Shrira, N. Francez, and M. Rodeh. Distributed k-selection: From a sequential to a distributed algorithm. In *2nd ACM Sympsium on Principles of Distributed Computing*, pages 143–153, 1983.

[22] L.M. Wegner. Sorting a distributed file in a network. *Computer Networks*, 8(5/6):451–462, December 1984.

[23] S. Zaks. Optimal distributed algorithms for sorting and ranking. *IEEE Transactions on Computers*, 34:376–380, 1985.

CHAPTER 6

Synchronous Computations

6.1 SYNCHRONOUS DISTRIBUTED COMPUTING

6.1.1 Fully Synchronous Systems

In the distributed computing environments we have considered so far, we have not made any assumption about *time*. In fact, from the model, we know only that in absence of failure, a message transmitted by an entity will eventually arrive to its neighbor: the *Finite Delays* axiom. Nothing else is specified, so we do not know for example *how much time* will a communication take. In our environment, each entity is endowed with a *local clock*; still no assumption is made on the functioning of these clocks, their rate, and how they relate to each other or to communication delays.

For these reasons, the distributed computing environments described by the basic model are commonly referred to as *fully asynchronous systems*. They represent one extreme in the spectrum of message-passing systems with respect to time.

As soon as we add temporal restrictions, making assumptions on the the local clocks and/or communication delays, we describe different systems within this spectrum.

At the other extreme are *fully synchronous systems*, distributed computing environments where there are strong assumptions both on the local clocks and on communication delays. These systems are defined by the following two restrictions about time: *Synchronized Clocks* and *Bounded Transmission Delays*.

Restriction 6.1.1 Synchronized Clocks
All local clocks are incremented by one unit simultaneously.

In other words, all local clocks 'tick' simultaneously. Notice that this assumption does not mean that the clocks have the same value, but just that their value is incremented at the same time. Further notice that the interval of time between consecutive increments in general need not be constant. For simplicity, in the following we will assume that this is the case and denote by δ the constant; see Figure 6.1.

Design and Analysis of Distributed Algorithms, by Nicola Santoro
Copyright © 2007 John Wiley & Sons, Inc.

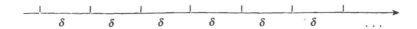

FIGURE 6.1: In a fully synchronous system, all clocks tick periodically and simultaneously, and there is a known upperbound Δ on communication delays.

By Convention,

1. entities will transmit messages (if needed) to their neighbors only at the strike of a clock tick;
2. at each clock tick, an entity will send at most one message to the same neighbor.

Restriction 6.1.2   Bounded Communication Delays
There exists a known upper bound on the communication delays experienced by a message in absence of failures.

In other words, there is a constant Δ such that in absence of failures, every message sent at time T will arrive and be processed by time $T + \Delta$. In terms of clock ticks, this means that in absence of failures, every message sent at local clock tick t will arrive and be processed by clock tick $t + \lceil \frac{\Delta}{\delta} \rceil$ (sender's time); see Figure 6.1.

Summarizing, a fully synchronous system is a distributed computing environment where both the above restrictions hold. Notice that knowledge of Δ can be replaced by knowledge of $\lceil \frac{\Delta}{\delta} \rceil$.

6.1.2 Clocks and Unit of Time

In a fully synchronous system, two consecutive clock ticks constitute a *unit of time*, and we measure the *time* costs of a computation in terms of the number of clock ticks elapsed from the time the first entity starts the computation to the time the last entity terminates its participation in the computation.

Notice that, in this "clock time," there is an underlying notion of "real time" (or physical time), one that exists outside the system (and independent of it), in terms of which we express the distance δ between clock ticks as well as the bound Δ on communication delays.

We can redefine the unit of time to be composed of $u > 1$ consecutive clock ticks. In other words, we can define *new* clock ticks, each comprising u old ones, and act accordingly. In particular, each entity will only send messages at the beginning of

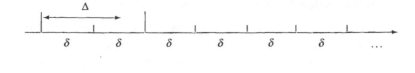

FIGURE 6.2: Redefine the *clock ticks* so that the delays are unitary.

a new time unit and does not send more than one message to the same neighbor in each new time unit. Clearly, the entities must agree on when the new time unit starts.

After the transformation, we can still measure time costs of a computation correctly: If the execution of a protocol lasts K new time units, its time cost is uK original clock ticks.

Observe that if we choose $u = \lceil \frac{\Delta}{\delta} \rceil$ (Figure 6.2), then with the new clocks communication delays become *unitary*: If an entity x sends a message at the (new) local clock tick t to a neighbor, in absence of failures, the message is received and processed there at the (new) clock tick $t + 1$ (sender's time). In other words,

> any fully synchronous system can be transformed so as to have unitary delays.

This means that we can assume, without loss of generality, that the following restriction holds:

Restriction 6.1.3   Unitary Communication Delays
In absence of failures, a transmitted message will arrive and be processed after at most one clock tick.

The main advantage of doing this redefinition of unit of time is that it greatly simplifies the design and analysis of protocols for fully synchronous systems. In fact, it is common to find fully synchronous systems defined directly as having unitary delays.

IMPORTANT. In the following, the pair of Restrictions 6.1.1 and 6.1.3, defining a fully synchronous system with unitary delay, will be denoted simply by **Synch**.

6.1.3 Communication Delays and Size of Messages

A fully synchronous system, by definition, guarantees that, in absence of failures, any allowed message will encounter bounded delays. More precisely, by definition, for any message M, the communication delay $\tau(M)$ encountered by M in absence of failures will always be

$$\tau(M) \leq \Delta. \tag{6.1}$$

Notice that this must hold regardless of the size (i.e., the number of bits) of M. Let us examine this fact carefully. By Restriction 6.1.2, Δ is bounded. For Δ to be bounded $\tau(M)$ must be bounded. This fact implies that the size of M must be bounded: To assume otherwise means that the system allows communication of unbounded messages in bounded time, an impossibility. This means,

Property 6.1.1   Bounded messages
In fully synchronous systems, messages have bounded length.

In other words, there exists a constant c (depending on the system) such that each message will contain at most c *bits*. Bounded messages are also called *packets* and the constant c is called *packet size*.

IMPORTANT. The packet size c is a system parameter. It could be related to other system parameters such as n (the network size) or m (the number of links). However, it can*not* depend on input values (unless they are also bounded).

The bounded messages property has important practical consequences. It implies that if the information an entity x must transmit does not fit in a packet, that information must be "split up" and transmitted using several packets. More precisely, the transmission of $w > c$ bits to a neighbor actually requires the transmission of $M[w]$ messages where

$$M[w] \geq \left\lceil \frac{w}{c} \right\rceil.$$

This fact affects not only the message costs but also the time costs. As at most one message can be sent to a neighbor at a given clock tick, the number of clock ticks required by the transmission of $w > c$ bits is

$$CT[w] \geq \left\lceil \frac{w}{c} \right\rceil.$$

6.1.4 On the Unique Nature of Synchronous Computations

Fully synchronous computing environments are dramatically different from the asynchronous ones we have considered so far. The difference is radical[1] and provides

---

[1] that is, it goes to the roots

the protocol designer working in a fully synchronous environment with computational means and tools that are both unique and very powerful. In the following we will briefly describe two situations providing an insight in the unique nature of synchronous computations.

Overcoming Lower Bounds: Different Speeds   As a first example of a synchronous algorithm, we will discuss a protocol for *leader election* in synchronous rings. We assume the standard restrictions for elections (**IR**), as well as **Synch**; the goal is to elect as leader the *candidate* with the smallest value. The protocol is essentially *AsFar* with an interesting new idea.

Recall that in *AsFar* each entity originates a message with its own id, forwards only messages with the smallest id seen so far, and trashes all the other incoming messages. The message with the smallest value will never be trashed; hence it will make a full tour of the ring and return to its originator; every other message will be trashed by the first entity with a smaller id it encounters. We have seen that this protocol has an optimal message complexity on the average but uses $O(n^2)$ messages in the worst case.

The interesting new idea is to have each message travel along the ring at a different *speed*, proportional to the id it contains, so that messages with smaller ids travel faster than those with larger values. In this way, a message with a small id can "catch up" with a slower message (containing a larger id); when this happens, the message with the larger id will be trashed. In other words, a message with a large id is trashed not only if it reaches an entity aware of a smaller id but also if it is reached by a message with a smaller id.

However, in a synchronous system, every message transmission will take at most one time unit; so, in a sense, all messages travel at the same speed. How can we implement variable speeds in a synchronous system? The answer is simple:

(a) When an entity x receives a message with a value **i** smaller than any seen so far by x, instead of immediately forwarding the message along the ring (as the protocol *AsFar* would require), x will hold this message for an amount of time (i.e., a number of clock ticks) $f(\mathbf{i})$ directly proportional to the value **i**.

(b) If a message with a smaller value arrives at x during this time, x will remove **i** from consideration and process the new value. Otherwise, after holding **i** for $f(\mathbf{i})$ clock ticks, x will forward it along the ring.

The effect is that a message with value **i** will be effectively traveling along the ring at speed $1 + f(\mathbf{i})$: If originally sent at time 0, it will be sent at time $1 + f(\mathbf{i})$ to the next entity, and again at time $2 + 2f(\mathbf{i})$, $3 + 3f(\mathbf{i})$, and so on, until it is trashed or completes the tour of the ring.

In this simple way, a we have implemented both *variable speeds* and the "catch-up" of slow messages by faster ones!

The correctness of this new protocol follows from the fact that again, the message with the smallest id will never be trashed and will thus return to its originator; every other message will be trashed either because of arriving to an entity that has seen a smaller id or because of being reached by a message with a smaller id.

To determine the cost of the protocol, called *Speed*, obviously we must take care of several implementation details (variables, bookkeeping, start, speed, etc.), but the basic mechanism is there. Let us assume for the moment that all entities are initially *candidates* and start at the same time.

For every choice of the monotonically increasing *speed* function f we will obtain a different cost. In particular, by choosing

$$f(\mathbf{i}) = 2^{\mathbf{i}},$$

we have a very interesting situation. In fact, by the time (the message with) the smallest id $\mathbf{i}_1$ has traveled all along the ring causing n transmissions, the second smallest $\mathbf{i}_2$ could have traveled at most halfway the ring causing $n/2$ transmissions, the third smallest could have traveled at most $n/4$, and in general the jth smallest could have traveled at most distance $\frac{n}{2^{j-1}}$. In other words, with this choice of speed function, the total number of transmissions until the entity with smallest value becomes *leader* is

$$\sum_{j=1}^{n} \frac{n}{2^{j-1}} < 2n.$$

As the protocol will just need an additional n messages for the final notification, we have

$$\mathbf{M}[Speed] = O(n). \tag{6.2}$$

This result is remarkable: This message complexity is *lower* than the $\Omega(n \log n)$ lowerbound for leader election in asynchronous rings ! It clearly shows a fundamental *complexity* difference between synchronous and asynchronous systems.

To achieve this result, we have used *time* directly as a computational tool: to implement the *variable speeds* of the messages and to select the appropriate waiting function f.

The result must be further qualified; in fact, it is correct assuming that the entity values are small enough to fit into a packet. In other words, it is correct but only if provided that the input values are bounded by 2^c; we will denote this additional restriction on the size of the input by *InputSize*(2^c).

To have a better understanding of the amount of transmissions, we can measure the number of bits:

$$\mathbf{B}[Speed] = O(n \log \mathbf{i}), \tag{6.3}$$

where $\mathbf{i}$ is the range of the input values.

We have assumed that all entities start at the same time. This assumption is not essential: It suffices that we first perform a *wake-up*, and elect a leader only among

PROTOCOL Speed

- States: $S = \{$ASLEEP, CANDIDATE, RELAYER, FOLLOWER, LEADER$\}$;
  $S_{\text{INIT}} = \{$ASLEEP$\}$;
  $S_{\text{TERM}} = \{$FOLLOWER, LEADER$\}$.
- Restrictions: **RI** ∪ **Synch** ∪ Ring ∪ InputSize(2^c).

```
ASLEEP
        Spontaneously
        begin
            min:= id(x);
            send("FindMin", min) to right;
            become CANDIDATE;
        end

        Receiving("FindMin", id*)
        begin
            min:= id*;
            send("FindMin", min) to other;
            become RELAYER;
        end


CANDIDATE
        Receiving("FindMin", id*)
        begin
            if id* < min then
               PROCESS-MESSAGE;
               become RELAYER
            else
               if id* = id(x) then
                  send(Notify) to other;
                  become LEADER
               endif;
            endif
        end

        When (c(x) = alarm)
        begin
            send("FindMin", min) to direction;
        end

        Receiving(Notify)
        begin
            send(Notify) to other;
            become FOLLOWER;
        end
```

FIGURE 6.3: Protocol *Speed.*

the spontaneous initiators (i.e., the others will not originate a message but will still actively participate in the trashing and waiting processes). The election messages themselves can act as "wake-up" messages, traveling at normal (i.e., unitary) speed until they reach the first spontaneous initiator, and only then traveling at the assigned speed. In this way, we still obtain a $O(n)$ message complexity (Exercise 6.6.3).

```
RELAYER
        Receiving("FindMin", id*)
        begin
            if id* < min then
                PROCESS-MESSAGE;
            endif
        end

        When (c(x) = alarm)
        begin
            send("FindMin", min) to direction;
        end

        Receiving(Notify)
        begin
            send(Notify) to other;
            become FOLLOWER;
        end

Procedure PROCESS-MESSAGE
begin
    min:= id*;
    direction:= sender;
    set alarm:= c(x) + f(id*);
end
```

FIGURE 6.4: Rule for *Relayer* and Procedure *Process-Message* used by protocol *Speed*.

The modified protocol *Speed* is shown in Figures 6.3 and 6.4; $c(x)$ denotes the local clock of the entity x executing the protocol, and *When* denotes the external event of the alarm clock ringing.

Beyond the Scenes   The results expressed by Equations 6.2 and 6.3 do not tell the whole story. If we calculate the *time* consumed by protocol *Speed* we find (Exercise 6.6.4) that

$$\mathbf{T}[Speed] = O(n2^{\mathbf{i}}).\qquad(6.4)$$

In other words,

the time is exponential.

It is actually worse than it sounds. In fact, it is exponential not in n (a system parameter) but in the range **i** of the *input values*.

Overcoming Transmission Costs: 2-bit Communication   We have seen how, in a synchronous environment, the lowerbounds established for asynchronous problems do not necessarily hold. This is because of the additional computational power of fully synchronous systems.

FIGURE 6.5: Entity x sends only two packets.

The most clear and (yet) surprising example of the difference between synchronous and asynchronous environments is the one we will discuss now.

Consider an entity x that wants to communicate to a neighbor y some information, unknown to y. Recall that in a fully synchronous system messages are bounded: If I want to transmit w bits, I will have to send $\lceil \frac{w}{c} \rceil$ packets and therefore at least $\lceil \frac{w}{c} \rceil$ time units or clock ticks. Still, x can communicate the information to y transmitting only two packets (!), regardless of the packet size (!!) and regardless of the information (!!!), provided it is finite.

Property 6.1.2   *In absence of failures, any finite sequence of bits can be communicated transmitting two messages, regardless of the message size.*

Let us see how this extraordinary result is possible. Let α be the sequence of bits that x wants to communicate to y; let 1α be the sequence α prefixed by the bit 1 (e.g., if $\alpha = 011$, then $1\alpha = 1011$. Let $I(1\alpha)$ denote the integer whose binary encoding is 1α; for example, $T(1011) = 11$. Consider now the following protocol:

PROTOCOL *TwoBits*.

1. Entity x (see Figure 6.5):
   (a) it sends to y a message "Start-Counting";
   (b) it waits for $I(1\alpha)$ clock ticks, and then
   (c) sends a message "Stop-Counting".
2. Entity y (Figure 6.6) :
   (a) upon receiving the "Start-Counting" message, it records the current value c_1 of the local clock;
   (b) upon receiving the "Start-Counting" message, it records the current value c_2 of the local clock. Clearly $c_2 - c_1 = I(1\alpha)$, from which α can be reconstructed.

As the message size is irrelevant and the string 1α is finite but arbitrary, the property states that in absence of failures,

any finite amount of information can be communicated by transmitting just 2 bits!

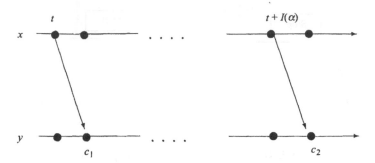

FIGURE 6.6: Entity y can reconstruct the information.

IMPORTANT. In synchronous computing there is a difference between *communication* and *transmission*. In fact, unlike asynchronous systems where transmission of messages is the only way in which neighboring entities can communicate, in synchronous systems *absence of transmission* can be used to communicate information, as we have just seen. In other words, in synchronous systems *silence is expressive*. This is the radical difference between synchronous and asynchronous computing environments. We will investigate how to exploit it in our designs.

Beyond the Scenes The property, as stated, is incomplete from a complexity point of view. In fact, in a synchronous system, time and transmission complexities are intrinsically related to a degree nonexistent in asynchronous systems. In the example above, the *constant* bit complexity is achieved at the cost of a time complexity that is *exponential* in the length of the sequence of bits to be communicated. In fact, x has to wait $I(1\alpha)$ time units, but

$$2^{|\alpha|} \leq I(1\alpha) \leq 2^{|\alpha|+1} - 1,$$

where $|\alpha|$ denotes the size (i.e., the number of bits) of α.

Once again, there is an exponential time cost to be paid for the the remarkable use of time.

6.1.5   The Cost of Synchronous Protocols

In a fully synchronous system, time and transmission complexities are intrinsically related to a degree nonexistent in asynchronous systems. As we have discussed in the subsection "Beyond the Scenes" of Section 6.1.4, to say "we can solve the election in a ring with $O(n)$ messages" or "we can communicate the Encyclopædia Britannica transmitting 2 bits" is correct but *incomplete*. We have been able to achieve those results because we have used time as a computational element; however, *time* must be charged, and the protocol must pay for it.

In other words, the cost of a fully synchronous protocol is *both* time *and* transmissions. More precisely, the *communication cost* of a fully synchronous protocol P is a couple $\langle \mathbf{P}, \mathbf{T} \rangle$, where $\mathbf{P}$ denotes the number of packets and $\mathbf{T}$ denotes the number of time units. We will more often use the number of bits $\mathbf{B}$ instead of $\mathbf{P}$; thus, our common measure will be the couple

$$\text{Cost}[P] = \langle \mathbf{B}[P], \ \mathbf{T}[P] \rangle.$$

So, for example, the complexity of Protocol *Speed* is

$$\text{Cost}[Speed(\mathbf{i})] = \langle O(n \log \mathbf{i}), \ O(n2^{\mathbf{i}}) \rangle$$

and that of Protocol *TwoBits* is

$$\mathcal{C}[TwoBits(\alpha)] = \langle 2, \ O(2^{|\alpha|}) \rangle.$$

Summarizing, the cost of a fully synchronous protocol is both *time and bits*. In general, we can trade off one for the other, transmitting more bits to use less time, or vice versa, depending on our design goals.

6.2 COMMUNICATORS, PIPELINE, AND TRANSFORMERS

In a system of communicating entities, the most basic and fundamental problem is obviously the process of an entity, *the sender* efficiently and accurately communicating information to another entity, the *receiver*. If these two entities are neighbors, this problem is called *Two-Party Communication* (**TPC**) problem. In an asynchronous system, this problem has only one solution: The sender puts the information into messages and transmits those messages.

In fully synchronous systems, as we have already observed, transmission of bits is not the only way of communicating information; for example, in a fault-free system, if no bit is received at local time $t + 1$, then none was transmitted at time t. Hence, absence of transmission, or *silence*, is detectable and can be used to convey information. In fact, there are many possible solutions to the *Two-Party Communication* problem, called *communicators*, each with different costs. We have already seen one, Protocol *TwoBits*.

In this section we will examine the design of efficient communicators. Owing to the basic nature of the process, the choice of a communicator will greatly affect the overall performance of the higher level protocols employed in the system.

We will then discuss the problem of communicating information at a distance, that is, when the *sender* and the *receiver* are not neighbors. We will see how this and related problems can be efficiently solved using a technique well known in very large scale integration (VLSI) and parallel systems: *pipeline*.

We will also examine the notion of asynchronous-to-synchronous *transformer*, a "compiler" that given in input an asynchronous protocol solving a problem $\mathcal{P}$

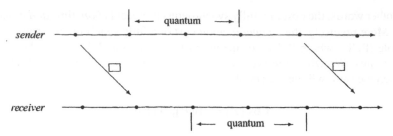

FIGURE 6.7: For the *sender*, a quantum is the number of clock ticks between two successive transmissions; for the *receiver*, it is the interval between two successive arrivals.

generates an efficient synchronous protocol solving $\mathcal{P}$. Such a transformer is a useful tool to solve problems for which an asynchronous solution is already known. Communicators are an essential component of a transformer; in fact, as we will see, different communicators result in different costs for the generated synchronous protocol. This is one more reason to focus on the design of efficient communicators.

In the following, we will assume that no failure will occur, that is, we operate under restriction *Total Reliability*.

6.2.1 Two-Party Communication

Consider the simple task of an entity, the *sender*, communicating information to a neighbor, the *receiver*.

At each time unit, the *sender* can either transmit a packet or remain silent; a packet transmitted by the sender at time t will be received and processed by the *receiver* at time $t + 1$ (sender's time). The interval of time between two successive transmissions by the *sender* is called a *quantum of silence* (or, simply, *quantum*); if there are no failures, the interval of time between the two arrivals will be the same for the *receiver* (see Figure 6.2.1). The quantum is zero if the packets are sent at two consecutive clock ticks.

Thus, to communicate information, the *sender* can use not only the transmission of several packets, but also the quanta of silence between successive transmissions. For example, in the *TwoBits* protocol, the *sender* was using the transmission of two packets as well as the quantum of silence between them. In general, the transmission of k packets $p_0, p_1, \ldots, p_{k-1}$ defines $k - 1$ quanta $\mathbf{q}_1, \mathbf{q}_2, \ldots, \mathbf{q}_{k-1}$, where $\mathbf{q}_i$ is the interval between the transmissions of p_{i-1} and p_i, $1 \leq i \leq k - 1$. The ordered sequence

$$\langle p_0 : \mathbf{q}_1 : p_1 : \ldots : \mathbf{q}_{k-1} : p_{k-1} \rangle$$

we will called *communication sequence*.

Clearly, there are many different ways in which we can design a protocol for the two entities to communicate using transmissions and silence, depending on the value of k we choose, the content of the packets, the size c of the packets, and so forth. Each design will yield a different cost.

The problem of performing this task is called the *Two-Party Communication* problem, and any solution protocol is called a *communicator*.

A communicator must specify the operations of the *sender* and of the *receiver*. In particular, a communicator is composed of

- an *encoding function*, specifying how to encode the information into the communication sequence of packets and silence;
- a *decoding function*, specifying how to reconstruct the information from the communication sequence of packets and silence.

Associated with any communicator are clearly two related cost measures: the total number of packets transmitted and the total number of clock ticks elapsed during the communication; as we will see, the study of the two-party communication problem in synchronous networks is really the study of the *trade-off* between time and transmissions.

IMPORTANT. To simplify the discussion, in the following, we will consider that a packet contains just a single bit, that is, $c = 1$. Everything we will say is easily extendable to the case $c > 1$.

2-bit Communicators We have already seen the most well known communicator, Protocol *TwoBits*. This protocol, also known as C_2, belongs to a class of communicators called *k-bit Communicators* where the number of transmitted packets is a constant k fixed a priori and known to both entities.

In C_2, to communicate a positive integer i, the *sender* transmits two packets, b_0 and b_1, waiting i time units between the two transmissions; the *receiver* computes the quantum of silence q_1 between the two transmissions and decodes it as the information. In other words, the *communication pattern* is

$$\langle b_0 \,:\, q_1 \,:\, b_1 \rangle.$$

The encoding function is

$$\text{encode}(i) = \langle b_0 \,:\, i \,:\, b_1 \rangle$$

and the decoding function is

$$\text{decode}(b_0 \,:\, q_1 \,:\, b_1) = q_1.$$

Thus, the total amount of time from the time the *sender* starts the first transmission to the time the *receiver* decodes the information is the quantum of silence plus the two time units used for transmitting the bits. Thus, the cost of the protocol is

$$\text{Cost}[\, C_2(i)] = \langle 2, i + 2 \rangle. \tag{6.5}$$

Hacking. We can improve the time complexity by exploiting the fact that the two transmitted bits b_0 and b_1 can be used to convey some information about **i**. In fact, it is possible to construct a communicator, called $\mathcal{R}_2$, that communicates **i** transmitting 2 bits and only $2 + \frac{1}{4}$ time units (Exercise 6.6.6). Clearly, a better time complexity will be obtained if packets contain more than a single bit; that is, $c > 1$ (Exercise 6.6.7).

3-bit Communicators

Let us examine what difference transmitting an extra packet has on the overall cost of communication. First of all, observe that with three packets b_0, b_1 and b_2, we have two quanta of silence: the interval of time q_1 between the transmission of b_0 and b_1 and the interval q_2 between the transmission of b_1 and b_2. In other words, the communication pattern is

$$\langle b_0 \; : \; \mathbf{q}_1 \; : \; b_1 \; : \; \mathbf{q}_2 \; : \; b_2 \rangle.$$

With this extra quantum to our disposal, consider the following strategy. If the *sender* could communicate $\sqrt{\mathbf{i}}$ using a single quantum, the receiver can reconstruct **i** by squaring the received quantum, and the entire process will cost still 2 bits (to delimit the quantum) but only $\sqrt{\mathbf{i}} + 2$ time ! The problem with this strategy is that $\sqrt{\mathbf{i}}$ might not be an integer, while a quantum must be an integer. The *sender* can obviously use a quantum $\mathbf{q}_1 = \lfloor \sqrt{\mathbf{i}} \rfloor$, which is an integer, and the *receiver* can compute $\mathbf{q}_1^2$, which, however, might be smaller than **i**. What the *sender* can do is to use the second quantum $\mathbf{q}_2$ to communicate how far $\mathbf{q}_1^2$ is from **i**, that is, $\mathbf{q}_2 = \mathbf{i} - \mathbf{q}_1^2$. In this way, the *receiver* is capable to reconstruct **i**: It simply computes $\mathbf{q}_1^2 + \mathbf{q}_2$.

In other words, the encoding function is

$$\text{encode}(\mathbf{i}) = \langle b_0 \; : \; \lfloor \sqrt{\mathbf{i}} \rfloor \; : \; b_1 \; : \; \mathbf{i} - \left(\lfloor \sqrt{\mathbf{i}} \rfloor \right)^2 \; : \; b_2 \rangle.$$

For example, $encode(8, 425) = \langle b_0 \; : 91 : \; b_1 \; : \quad 144 : \quad b_2 \rangle$. The decoding function is

$$\text{decode}(b_0 \; : \; \mathbf{q}_1 \; : \; b_1 : \; \mathbf{q}_2 : \; b_2) = \mathbf{q}_1^2 + \mathbf{q}_2.$$

The time required by this protocol is clearly $\mathbf{q}_1 + \mathbf{q}_2 + 3$; as $x - \lfloor \sqrt{x} \rfloor^2 \leq 2\lfloor \sqrt{x} \rfloor$, we have

$$\mathbf{q}_1 + \mathbf{q}_2 + 3 = \lfloor \sqrt{\mathbf{i}} \rfloor + \mathbf{i} - \lfloor \sqrt{\mathbf{i}} \rfloor^2 + 3 \; \leq \; 3\lfloor \sqrt{\mathbf{i}} \rfloor + 3.$$

In other words, this protocol, called $\mathcal{C}_3$, has *sublinear* time complexity. The resulting cost is

$$\mathcal{C}ost[\mathcal{C}_3(\mathbf{i})] = \langle 3 \, , \, 3\lfloor \sqrt{\mathbf{i}} \rfloor + 3 \rangle. \tag{6.6}$$

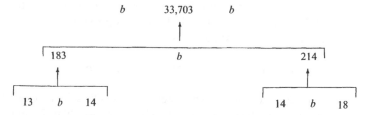

FIGURE 6.8: Constructing the encoding of 33,703 when $k = 5$.

Hacking. We can improve the time complexity by exploiting the fact that the transmitted packets can be used to convey some information about **i**. In fact, it is possible to construct a communicator, called $\mathcal{R}_3$, that communicates I transmitting 3 bits and only $\lfloor \sqrt{\mathbf{i}} \rfloor + 3$ time units (Exercise 6.6.8). Again, the more bits a packet contains, the better will be the time costs (Exercise 6.6.9).

($2^d + 1$)-bit Communicators   A solution protocol using $k = 2^d + 1$ bits can be easily obtained extending the idea employed for $k = 2^1 + 1 = 3$. The encoding of **i** can be defined recursively as follows:

encoding $(\mathbf{i}) = \langle b \; : \; E(I_1) \; : \; b \rangle$

$$
E(I_i) = \begin{cases} E(I_{2i}) \; : \; b \; : \; E(I_{2i+1}) & \text{if } 1 < i < k - 1 \\ \text{quantum of length } I_i & \text{if } k - 1 \leq i \leq 2k - 3, \end{cases}
$$

where

$I_1 = \mathbf{i}$, $I_{2i} = \lfloor \sqrt{I_i} \rfloor$, and $I_{2i+1} = I_i - I_{2i}^2$, and b is an arbitrary packet. So, for example, the encoding of $\mathbf{i} = 33,703$ when $k = 5$ is $\langle b\ 13\ b\ 14\ b\ 14\ b\ 18\ b \rangle$ (see Figure 6.8).

To obtain $\mathbf{i} = I_1$, the *receiver* will recursively compute

$$
I_i = I_{2i}^2 + I_{2i+1}.
$$

Exactly $k - 1$ quanta will be used, and k bits will be transmitted. The time costs will be $O(\mathbf{i}^{\frac{1}{k}})$ (Exercise 6.6.10).

Optimal ($k+1$)-bit Communicators ($\star$)   When designing efficient communicators, several questions arise naturally: How good are the communicators we have designed so far? In general, if we use $k + 1$ transmissions, what is the best time that can be achieved and which communicator will be able to achieve it?

In this section we will answer these questions. We will design a general class of solution protocols and analyze their cost; we will then establish lower bounds and show that the proposed protocols achieve these bounds and are therefore optimal.

Our goal is now to design protocols that can communicate *any* positive integer I transmitting $k + 1$ packets and using as little time as possible. Observe that with $k + 1$ packets the communication sequence is

$$\langle b_0 : \mathbf{q}_1 : b_1 : \mathbf{q}_2 : b_2 : \ldots : \mathbf{q}_k : b_k \rangle.$$

We will first of all make a distinction between protocols that do not care about the content of the transmitted protocols (like $\mathcal{C}_2$ and $\mathcal{C}_3$) and those (like $\mathcal{R}_2$ and $\mathcal{R}_3$) that use those packets to convey information about I.

The first class of protocols are able to tolerate the type of transmission failures called *corruptions*. In fact, they use packets only to delimit quanta; as it does not matter what the content of the packet is (but only that it is being transmitted), these protocols will work correctly even if the value of the bits in the packets is changed during transmission. We will call them as corruption-tolerant communicators.

The second class exploits the content of the packets to convey information about I; hence, if the value of just one of the bits is changed during transmission, the entire communication will become corrupted. In other words, these communicators need reliable transmission for their correctness.

Clearly, the bounds and the optimal solution protocols are different for the two classes.

We will consider the first class in details; the second types of communicators will be briefly sketched at the end. As before, we will consider for simplicity the case when a packet is composed of a single bit, that is $c = 1$; the results can be easily generalized to the case $c > 1$.

Corruption-Tolerant Communication   If transmissions are subject to corruptions, the value of the received packets cannot be relied upon, and so they are used only to delimit quanta. Hence, the only meaningful part of the communication sequence is the $k-$tuple of quanta

$$\langle \mathbf{q}_1, \mathbf{q}_2, \ldots, \mathbf{q}_k \rangle.$$

Thus, the (infinite) set $\mathcal{Q}_k$ of all possible k-tuples $\langle \mathbf{q}_1, \mathbf{q}_2, \ldots, \mathbf{q}_k \rangle$, where the $\mathbf{q}_i$ are nonnegative integers, describes all the possible communication sequences.

What we are going to do is to associate to each communication sequence $Q[I] \in \mathcal{Q}_k$ a different integer I. Then, if we want to communicate I, we will use the unique sequence of quanta described by $Q[I]$.

To achieve this goal we need a bijection between k-tuples and nonnegative integers. This is not difficult to do; it is sufficient to establish a *total order* among tuples as follows.

Given two k-tuples $Q = \langle q_1, q_2, \ldots, q_k \rangle$ and $Q' = \langle q'_1, q'_2, \ldots, q'_k \rangle$ of positive integers, we say that $Q < Q'$ if

1. $\sum_i q_i < \sum_i q'_i$ or
2. $\sum_i q_i = \sum_i q'_i$ and $q_j = q'_j$ for $1 \le j < l$, and $q_l < q'_l$ for some index l, $1 \le l \le k + 1$.

I	0	1	2	3	4	5	6	7	8	9	10
Q[I]	0,0,0	0,0,1	0,1,0	1,0,0	0,0,2	0,1,1	0,2,0	1,0,1	1,1,0	2,0,0	0,0,3

11	12	13	14	15	16	17	18	19	20	21	22
0,1,2	0,2,1	0,3,0	1,0,2	1,1,1	1,2,0	2,0,1	2,1,0	3,0,0	0,0,4	0,1,3	0,2,2

23	24	25	26	27	28	29	30	31	32	33	34
0,3,1	0,4,0	1,0,3	1,1,2	1,2,1	1,3,0	2,0,2	2,1,1	2,2,0	3,0,1	3,1,0	4,0,0

FIGURE 6.9: The first 35 elements of Q_3 according to the total order.

That is, in this total order, all the tuples where the sum of the quanta is t are smaller than those where the sum is $t + 1$; so, for example $\langle 2, 0, 0 \rangle$ is smaller than $\langle 1, 1, 1 \rangle$. If the sum of the quanta is the same, the tuples are lexicographically ordered; so, for example, $\langle 1, 0, 2 \rangle$ is smaller than $\langle 1, 1, 1 \rangle$. The ordered list of the first few elements of Q_3 is shown in Figure 6.9.

In this way, if we want to communicate integer I we will use the k-tuple Q whose rank (starting from 0) in this total order is I. So, for example, in Q_3, the triple $\langle 1, 0, 3 \rangle$ has rank 25, and the triple $\langle 0, 1, 4 \rangle$ corresponds to integer 36.

The solution protocol, which we will call $Order_k$, thus uses the following encoding and decoding schemes.

Protocol Order$_k$

Encoding Scheme: Given I, the Sender

(E1) finds $Q_k[I] = \langle a_1, a_2, \ldots, a_k \rangle$;
(E2) it sets encoding$(I) := \langle b_0 : a_1 : b_1 : \ldots, : a_k : b_k \rangle$, where the b_i are bits of arbitrary value.

Decoding Scheme: Given $(\langle b_0 : a_1 : b_1 : \ldots, : a_k : b_k \rangle)$, the *receiver*

(D1) extracts $Q = \langle a_1, a_2, \ldots, a_k \rangle$;
(D2) it finds I such that $Q_k[I] = Q$;
(D3) it sets decoding$(\langle b_0 : a_1 : b_1 : \ldots, : a_k : b_k \rangle) := I$.

The correctness of the protocol derives from the fact that the mapping we are using is a bijection. Let us examine the cost of protocol $Order_k$.

The number of bits is clearly $k + 1$.

$$\mathbf{B}[Order_k](I) = k + 1. \tag{6.7}$$

What is the time? The communication sequence $\langle b_0 : \mathbf{q}_1 : b_1 : \mathbf{q}_2 : b_2 : \ldots : \mathbf{q}_k : b_k \rangle$ costs $k + 1$ time units spent to transmit the bits $b_0, \ldots, b_k$, plus $\sum_{i=1}^{k} \mathbf{q}_i$ time

units of silence. Hence, to determine the time $T[Order_k](I)$ we need to know the sum of the quanta in $Q_k[I]$. Let $f(I, k)$ be the smallest integer t such that $I \leq \binom{t+k}{k}$.
Then (Exercise 6.6.12),

$$\mathbf{T}[Order_k](I) = f(I, k) + k + 1. \tag{6.8}$$

Optimality We are now going to show that protocol $Order_k$ is *optimal* in the worst case. We will do so by establishing a lower bound on the amount of time required to solve the two-party communication problem using exactly $k + 1$ bit transmissions. Observe that $k + 1$ time units will be required by any solution algorithm to transmit the $k + 1$ bits; hence, the concern is on the amount of *additional* time required by the protocol.

We will establish the lower bound assuming that the values I we want to transmit are from a *finite* set U of integers. This assumption makes the lower bound *stronger* because for infinite sets, the bounds can only be worse.

Without any loss of generality, we can assume that $U = Z_w = \{0, 1, \ldots, w - 1\}$, where $|U| = w$.

Let $c(w, k)$ denote the number of additional time units needed in the worst case to solve the two-party communication problem for Z_w with $k + 1$ bits that can be corrupted during the communication.

To derive a bound on $c(w, k)$, we will consider the dual problem of determining the size $\omega(t, k)$ of the largest set for which the two-party communication problem can always be solved using $k + 1$ corruptible transmissions and at most t additional time units. Notice that with $k + 1$ bit transmissions, it is only possible to distinguish k quanta; hence, the dual problem can be rephrased as follows:

Determine the largest positive integer $w = \omega(t, k)$ such that every $x \in Z_w$ can be communicated using k distinguished quanta whose total sum is at most t.

This problem has an exact solution (Exercise 6.6.14):

$$\omega(t, k) = \binom{t+k}{k}. \tag{6.9}$$

This means that if U has size $\omega(t, k)$, then t additional time units are *needed* (in the worst case) by any communicator that uses $k + 1$ unreliable bits to communicate values of U. If the size of U is not precisely $\omega(t, k)$, we can still determine a bound. Let $f(w, k)$ be the smallest integer t such that $\omega(t, k) \geq w$. Then

$$c(w, k) = f(w, k). \tag{6.10}$$

That is

Theorem 6.2.1 *Any corruption-tolerant solution protocol using $k + 1$ bits to communicate values from Z_w requires $f(w, k) + k + 1$ time units in the worst case.*

In conjunction with Equation 6.8, this means that

protocol $Order_k$ is a worst case optimal.

We can actually establish a lower bound on the average case as well (Exercise 6.6.15), and prove (Exercise 6.6.16) that

protocol $Order_k$ is average-case optimal

Corruption-Free Communication (⋆⋆) If bit transmissions are error free, the value of a received packet can be trusted. Hence it can be used to convey information about the value I the *sender* wants to communicate to the *receiver*. In this case, the entire communication sequence, bits and quanta, is meaningful.

What we do is something similar to what we just did in the case of corruptible bits. We establish a *total order* on the set W_k of the $2k + 1$ tuples $\langle b_0, q_1, b_1, q_2, b_2, \ldots, q_k, b_k \rangle$ corresponding to all the possible communication sequences. In this way, each tuple $2k + 1$-tuple $W[i] \in W_k$ has associated a distinct integer: its rank i. Then, if we want to communicate I, we will use the communication sequence described by $W[I]$.

In the total order we choose, all the tuples where the sum of the quanta is t are smaller than those where the sum is $t + 1$; so, for example, in W_2, $\langle 1, 2, 1, 0, 1 \rangle$ is smaller than $\langle 0, 0, 0, 3, 0 \rangle$. If the sum of the quanta is the same, tuples (bits and quanta) are lexicographically ordered; so, for example, in W_2, $\langle 1, 1, 1, 1, 1 \rangle$ is smaller than $\langle 1, 2, 0, 0, 0 \rangle$.

The resulting protocol is called $Order+_k$. Let us examine its costs. The number of bits is clearly $k + 1$. Let $g(I, k)$ be the smallest integer t such that $I \leq 2^{k+1} \binom{t + k}{k}$. Then (Exercise 6.6.13),

$$\mathbf{B}[Order+_k](I) = k + 1 \tag{6.11}$$

$$\mathbf{T}[Order+_k](I) = g(I, k) + k + 1. \tag{6.12}$$

Also, protocol $Order+_k$ is worst-case and average-case optimal (see exercises 6.6.17, 6.6.18, and 6.6.19).

Other Communicators The protocols $Order_k$ and $Order+_k$ belong to the class of $k + 1$-bit communicators where the number of transmitted bits is fixed a priori and known to both the entities. In this section, we consider *arbitrary communicators*, where the number of bits used in the transmission might not be not predetermined (e.g., it may change depending on the value I being transmitted).

352   SYNCHRONOUS COMPUTATIONS

With arbitrary communicators, the basic problem is obviously how the *receiver* can decide when a communication has ended. This can be achieved in many different ways, and several mechanisms are possible. Following are two classical ones:

Bit Pattern. The *sender* uses a special pattern of bits to notify the end of communication. For example, the *sender* sets all bits to 0, except the last, which is set to 1; the drawback with this approach is that the bits cannot be used to convey information about I.

Size Communication. As part of the communication, the *sender* communicates the total number of bits it will use. For example, the *sender* uses the first quantum to communicate the number of bits it will use in this communication; the drawback of this approach is that the first quantum cannot be used to convey information about I.

We now show that, however ingenious the employed mechanism be, the results are not much better than those obtained just using optimal $k + 1$-bit communicators. In fact, an arbitrary communicator can only improve the worst-case complexity by an *additive* constant.

This is true even if the *receiver* has access to an *oracle* revealing (at no cost) for each transmission the number of bits the *sender* will use in that transmission.

Consider first the case of corruptible transmissions. Let $\gamma(t, b)$ denote the size of the largest set for which an oracle-based communicator uses *at most* b corruptible bits and at most $t + b$ time units.

Theorem 6.2.2 $\gamma(t, b) < \omega(t + 1, b)$

Proof. As up to $k + 1$ corruptible bits can be transmitted, by Equation 6.9,

$$\gamma(t, b) = \sum_{j=1}^{k} \omega(t, j) = \sum_{j=1}^{k} \binom{t+j}{j} = \binom{t+k+1}{k} - 1 < \binom{t+1+k}{k}$$

$$= \omega(t + 1, b). \qquad \blacksquare$$

This implies that, in the worst case, communicator $Order_k$ requires at most one time unit more than any strategy of any type which uses the same maximum number of corruptible bits.

Consider now the case of incorruptible transmissions. Let $\alpha(t, b)$ denote the size of the largest set for which an oracle-based communicator uses *at most* b reliable bits and at most $t + b$ time units. To determine a bound on $\alpha(t, b)$, we will first consider the size $\beta(t, k)$ of the largest set for which a communicator *without an oracle* uses always *at most* b reliable bits and at most $t + b$ time units. We know (Exercises 6.6.17) that

Lemma 6.2.1 $\beta(t, k) = 2^{k+1} \binom{t+k}{k}.$

From this, we can now derive

Theorem 6.2.3 $\alpha(t, b) < \beta(t + 1, b).$

Proof. As up to $k + 1$ incorruptible bits can be transmitted, $\alpha(t, b) = \sum_{j=1}^{k} \beta(t, j)$.

By Lemma 6.2.1, $\sum_{j=1}^{k} \beta(t, j) = \sum_{j=1}^{k} 2^{j+1} \binom{t+j}{j} < 2^{k+1} \binom{t+1+k}{k}$

$= \beta(t + 1, k)$.   ∎

This implies that, in the worst case, communicator $Order_{+k}$ requires at most one time unit more than any strategy of any type which uses the same maximum number of incorruptible bits.

6.2.2 Pipeline

Communicating at a Distance   With *communicators* we have addressed the problem of communicating information between two neighboring entities. What happens if the two entities involved, the *sender* and the *receiver*, are not neighbors? Clearly the information from the sender x can still reach the receiver y, but other entities must be involved in this communication. Typically there will be a chain of entities, with the sender and the receiver at each end; this chain is, for example, the *shortest path* between them. Let $x_1, x_2, \ldots, x_{p-1}. x_p$ be the chain, where $x_1 = x$ and $x_p = y$; see Figure 6.10.

The simplest solution is that first x_1 communicates the information I to x_2, then x_2 to x_3, and so on until x_{p-1} has the information and communicates it to x_p. Using communicator C between each pair of neighbors, this solution will cost

$$(p - 1)\,\mathrm{Bit}(C, I)$$

bits and

$$(p - 1)\,\mathrm{Time}(C, I)$$

time, where $\mathrm{Bit}(C, I)$ and $\mathrm{Time}(C, I)$ are the bit and time costs, respectively of communicating information I using C. For example, using protocol *TwoBits*, x can communicate I to y with $2(p - 1)$ bits in time $I(p - 1)$. There are many variations of this solutions; for example, each pair of neighbors could use a different type of communicator.

There exists a way of drastically reducing the time *without* increasing the number of bits. This can be achieved using a well known technique called *pipeline*.

The idea behind pipeline is very simple. In the solution we just discussed, x_1 waits until it receives the information from x_0 and then communicates it to x_2. In pipeline, instead of waiting, x_1 will start immediately to communicate it to x_2. In fact, each x_j

FIGURE 6.10: Communicating information from x to y through a line.

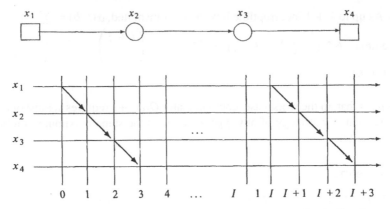

FIGURE 6.11: Time–Event diagram showing the communication of I in pipeline from x_1 to x_4.

will start communicating the information to x_{j+1} without waiting to receive it form x_{j-1}; the crucial point is that x_{j+1} starts exactly one time unit after x_{j-1}.

To understand how can an entity x_j communicate an information it does not yet have, consider x_2 and assume that the communicator being used is *TwoBits*. Let x_1 start at time t; then x_2 will receive the "Start-Counting" signal at time $t + 1$. Instead of just waiting to receive the "Stop-Counting" message from x_1, x_2 will also start immediately the communication: It sends a "Start-Counting" signal to x_3 and starts waiting the quantum of silence. It is true that x_2 does not know I, so it does not know how long it has to wait. However, at time $t + I$, entity x_1 will send the "Stop-Counting" signal that will arrive at x_2 one time unit later, at time $t + I + 1$. This is happening *exactly* I time units after x_2 sent the "Start-Counting" signal to x_3. Thus, if x_2 now forwards the "Stop-Counting" signal to x_3, it acts exactly like if it had the information I from the start!

The reasoning we just did to explain why pipeline works at x_2 applies to each of the x_j. So, the answer to the question above is that each entity x_j will know the information it must communicate exactly in time. An example is shown in Figure 6.11, where $p = 4$. The sender x_1 will start at time 0 and send the "Stop-Counting" signal at time I. Entities x_2, x_3 will receive and send the "Start-Counting" at time 1 and 2, respectively; they will receive and send the "Stop-Counting" at time $I + 1$ and $I + 2$, respectively.

Summarizing, the entities will start staggered by one time unit and will terminate staggered by one time unit. Each will be communicated the value I communicated by the sender.

Regardless of the communicator C employed (the same by all entities), the overall solution protocol *CommLine* is composed of two simple rules:

PROTOCOL *CommLine*

1. x_1 communicates the information to x_2.
2. Whenever x_j receives a signal from x_{j-1}, it forwards it to x_{j+1} $(1 < j < p)$.

How is local termination detected ? As each entity uses the same communicator C, each x_j will know when the communication from x_{j-1} has terminated $(1 < j \leq p)$.

Let us examine the cost of this protocol. Each communication is done using communicator C; hence the total number of *bits* is the same as in the nonpipelined case:

$$(p - 1)\,\text{Bits}(C, I). \tag{6.13}$$

However, the time is different as the $p - 1$ communications are done in pipeline and not sequentially. Recall that the entities in the line start a unit of time one after the other. Consider the last entity x_p. The communication of I from x_{p-1} requires $\text{Time}(C, I)$; however, x_{p-1} starts this communication only $p - 2$ time units after x_1 starts its communication to x_2. This means that the total time used for the communication is only

$$(p - 1) + \text{Time}(C, I). \tag{6.14}$$

That is, the term $p - 1$ is *added* to and not *multiplied* by $\text{Time}(C, I)$. In the example of Figure 6.11, where $p = 4$ and the communicator is *TwoBits*, the total number of bits is $6 = 2(p - 1)$. The receiver x_4 receives "Start-Counting" at time 3 and the "Stop-Counting" at time $i + 3$; hence the total time is $I + 3 = I + p - 1$;

Let us stress that we use the same number of bits as a nonpipelined (i.e., sequential) communication; the improvement is in the time costs.

Computing in Pipeline   Consider the same chain of entities $x_1, x_2, \ldots, x_{p-1}, x_p$ we have just examined. We have seen how information can be efficiently communicated from one end of the chain of entities to the other by *pipelining* the output of the *communicators* used by the entities. We will now see how we can use pipeline in something slightly more complex than plain communication.

Assume that each entity x_j has a value I_j, and we want to compute the *largest* of those values. Once again, we can solve this problem sequentially: First x_1 communicates I_1 to x_2; each x_j $(1 < j < p)$ waits until it receives from x_{j-1} the largest value so far, compares it with its own value I_j, and forwards the largest of the two to x_{j+1}. This approach will cost

$$(p - 1)\,\text{Bit}(C, I_{\max})$$

bits, where C is the communicator used by the entities and $I_{\max}$ is the largest value. The time will depend on where $I_{\max}$ is located; in the worst case, it is x_1 and the time will be

$$(p - 1)\,\text{Time}(C, I_{\max}).$$

Let us see how pipeline can be used in this case. Again, we will make all entities in the chain start staggered by one unit of time, and each entity will start waiting a quantum of time equal to its own value.

Let t the time when x_1 (and thus the entire process) starts; for simplicity, assume that they use protocol *TwoBits*. Concentrate on x_2. At time $t + 1$ it receives the "Start-Counting" signal from x_1 and sends it to x_3. Its goal is to communicate to x_3 the largest of I_1 and I_2; to do so, it must send the "Stop-Counting" signal to x_3 *exactly* at time $t' = t + 1 + Max\{I_1, I_2\}$. The question is how can x_2 know $Max\{I_1, I_2\}$ in time. The answer is fortunately simple.

The "Stop-Counting" message from x_1 arrives at x_2 at time $t + 1 + I_1$ (i.e., I_1 time units after the "Start-Counting" signal). There are three possible cases.

1. If $I_1 < I_2$, this message will arrive while x_2 is still counting its own value I_2; thus, x_2 will know that its value is the largest. In this case, it will just keep on waiting its value and send the "Stop-Counting" signal to x_3 at the correct time $t + 1 + I_2 = t + 1 + Max\{I_1, I_2\} = t'$.

2. If $I_1 = I_2$, this message will arrive exactly when x_2 finishes counting its own value I_2; thus, x_2 will know that the two values are identical. The "Stop-Counting" signal will be sent to x_3 immediately, that is, at the correct time $t + 1 + I_2 = t + 1 + Max\{I_1, I_2\} = t'$.

3. If $I_1 > I_2$, x_2 will finish waiting its value *before* this message arrives. In this case, x_2 will wait until it receives "Stop-Counting" signal from x_1, and then forward it. Thus, the "Stop-Counting" signal will be sent to x_3 at the correct time $t + 1 + I_1 = t + 1 + Max\{I_1, I_2\} = t'$.

That is, x_2 will always send $Max\{I_1, I_2\}$ in time to x_3.

The same reasoning we just used to understand how x_2 can know $Max\{I_1, I_2\}$ in time can be applied to verify that indeed each x_j can know $Max\{I_1, I_2, \ldots, I_{j-1}\}$ in time (Exercise 6.6.23). An example is shown in Figure 6.12.

We have described the solution using *TwoBits* as the communicator. Clearly any communicator C can be used, provided that its encoding is *monotonically increasing*,

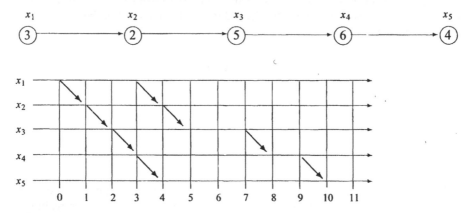

FIGURE 6.12: Time–Event diagram showing the computation of the largest value in pipeline.

that is, if $I > J$, then in C the communication sequence for I is lexicographically smaller than that for J. Note that protocols $Order_k$ and $Order+_k$ are *not* monotonically increasing; however, it is not difficult to redefine them so that they have such a property (Exercises 6.6.21 and 6.6.22).

The total number of bits will then be

$$(p - 1) \, \text{Bits}(C, I_{\max}), \tag{6.15}$$

the same as that without pipeline. The time instead is at most

$$(p - 1) + \text{Time}(C, I_{\max}). \tag{6.16}$$

Once again, the number of bits is the same as that without pipeline; the time costs are instead greatly reduced: The factor $(p - 1)$ is additive and not multiplicative.

Similar reductions in time can be obtained for other computations, such as computing the minimum value (Exercise 6.6.24), the sum of the values (Exercise 6.6.25), and so forth.

The approach we used for these computations in a chain can be generalized to arbitrary tree networks; see for example Problems 6.6.5 and 6.6.6.

6.2.3 Transformers

Asynchronous-to-Synchronous Transformation   The task of designing a fully synchronous solution for a problem can be easily accomplished if there is already a known asynchronous solution A for that problem. In fact, since A makes no assumptions on time, it will run under every timing condition, including the fully synchronous ones. Its cost in such a setting would be the number of messages $M(A)$ and the "ideal" time $T(A)$. Note that this presupposes that the size $m(A)$ of the messages used by A is not greater than the packet size c (otherwise, the message must be broken into several packets, with a corresponding increasing message and time complexity).

We can actually exploit the availability of an asynchronous solution protocol A in a more clever way and with a more efficient performance than just running A in the fully synchronous system. In fact, it is possible to transform *any* asynchronous protocol A into an efficient synchronous one S, and this transformation can be done *automatically*. This is achieved by an *asynchronous-to-synchronous transformer* (or just *transformer*), a "compiler" that, given in input an asynchronous protocol solving a problem $\mathcal{P}$, generates an efficient synchronous protocol solving $\mathcal{P}$.

The essential component of a transformer is the *communicator*. Let C be a universal communicator (i.e., a communicator that works for all positive integers). An asynchronous-to-synchronous transformer $\tau[C]$ is obtained as follows.

Transformer $\tau[C]$ Given any asynchronous protocol A, replace the asynchronous transmission-reception of each message in A by the communication, using C, of the information contained in that message.

In other words, we replace each "**send** *message*" instruction in algorithm A by an instruction "**communicate** *content of message*," where the communication is performed using the communicator C. It is not difficult to verify that if A solves problem $\mathcal{P}$ for a class $\mathcal{G}$ of system topologies (i.e., graphs), then $\tau[C](A) = S$ is a fully synchronous protocol that solves $\mathcal{P}$ for the graphs in $\mathcal{G}$. Note that in a practical implementation, we must take care of several details (e.g., overlapping arrival of messages) that we are not discussing here.

Let us calculate now the cost of the obtained protocol $S = \tau[C](A)$ in a graph $G \in \mathcal{G}$; let $M(A)$, $T_{\text{casual}}(A)$, and $m(A)$ denote the *message* complexity, the *causal time* complexity, and the *size* of the largest message, respectively, of A in G. Recall that the causal time complexity is the length of the longest chain of causally related message transmissions over all possible executions. For some protocols, it might be difficult to determine the causal time; however, we know that $T_{\text{casual}}(A) \leq M(A)$; hence we always have an upperbound.

In the transformation, the transmission (and corresponding reception) of I in A is replaced by the communication of I using communicator C; this communication requires Time(C, I) time and Packets(C, I) packets.

As at most $T_{\text{casual}}(A)$ messages must be sent sequentially (i.e., one after the other) and $I \leq 2^{m(A)}$, the total number of clock ticks required by S will be

$$\text{Time}(S) \leq T_{\text{casual}}(A) \times \text{Time}(C, 2^{m(A)}). \qquad (6.17)$$

As the information of each of the $M(A)$ messages must be communicated, and the messages have size at most $m(A)$, the total number of packets $\mathbf{P}(S)$ transmitted by the synchronous protocol S is just

$$\mathbf{P}(S) \leq M(A) \times \text{Packets}(C, m(A)). \qquad (6.18)$$

In other words,

Lemma 6.2.2   Transformation Lemma *For every universal communicator C there exists an asynchronous-to-synchronous transformer $\tau[C]$. Furthermore, for every asynchronous protocol A, the packet-time cost of $\tau[C](A)$ is at most*

$$\text{Cost}[\ \tau[C](A)\ ] \leq \langle M(A)\,\text{Packets}(C, m(A))\,,\ T_{\text{casual}}(A)\,\text{Time}(C, 2^{m(A)})\rangle.$$

This simple transformation mechanism might appear to yield inefficient solutions for the synchronous case. To dispel this false appearance, we will consider an interesting application.

Application: Election in a Synchronous Ring

Consider the problem of electing a leader in a synchronous ring. We assume the standard restrictions for elections (**IR**), as well as **Synch**. We have seen several efficient election algorithms for asynchronous ring networks in previous chapters. Let us choose one and examine the effects of the transformer.

Consider protocol *Stages*. Recall that this protocol uses $M(Stages) = 2n \log n + O(n)$; each message contains a value; hence, $m(Stages) = \log \mathbf{i}$, where $\mathbf{i}$ is the range of the input values; regarding the causal time, as $T_{casual}(A) \leq M(A)$ for every protocol A, we have $T_{casual}(Stages) \leq 2n \log n + O(n)$.

To apply the Transformation Lemma, we need to choose a universal communicator. Let us choose a not very efficient one: *TwoBits*; recall that the cost of communicating integer I is 2 bits and $I + 2$ time units. Let us now apply the transformation lemma. We then have a new election protocol $SynchStages= \tau[TwoBits](Stages)$ for synchronous ring; as

$$\text{Time}(TwoBits, 2^{m(Stages)}) = 2^{\log \mathbf{i}} + 2 = \mathbf{i} + 2,$$

by Lemma 6.2.2, we have

$$\mathbf{T}(SynchStages) \; \leq 2n \log(n) \, (\mathbf{i} + 2) + l.o.t \tag{6.19}$$

and

$$\mathbf{B}(SynchStages) \; = 2M(Stages) \leq 2n \log(n) + O(n). \tag{6.20}$$

This result must be compared with the bounds of the election algorithm *Speed* specifically designed for synchronous systems (see Figure 6.13): The transformation lemma yields bounds that are *order of magnitude better* than those previously obtained by specifically designed algorithm.

Once we have obtained a solution protocol using a transformer, both the bits and the time complexity of this solution depend on the communicator employed by the transformer. Sometimes, the time complexity can be further reduced without increasing the number of bits by using *pipeline*. For example, during every stage of protocol *Stages* and thus of protocol *SynchStages*, the information from each *candidate* must reach the neighboring *candidate* on each side. This operation, as we have already seen, can be efficiently done in pipeline, yielding a reduction in time costs (Exercise 6.6.26).

Design Implications   The transformation lemma gives a basis of comparison for designing efficient synchronous solutions to problems for which there already exist asynchronous solutions. To improve on the bounds obtained by the use of the transformation lemma, it is necessary to more explicitly and cleverly exploit the availability of "time" as a computational tool. Some techniques that achieve this goal for some specific problems are described in the next sections.

Protocol	Bits	Time
Speed	$O(n \log \mathbf{i})$	$O(2^{\mathbf{i}} n)$
SynchStages	$O(n \log n)$	$O(\mathbf{i} \, n \log n)$

FIGURE 6.13: The transformer yields a more efficient ring election protocol

When designing a protocol, our aim must be to avoid the transmission of unbounded messages; in particular, if the input values are drawn from some unbounded universe (e.g., positive integers) and the goal of the computation is the evaluation of a function of the input values, then the messages cannot contain such values. For example, the "trick" on which the transformation lemma is based is an instance of a simple and direct way of exploiting time by *counting* it; in this case, the actual value is communicated but not transmitted.

6.3 MIN-FINDING AND ELECTION: WAITING AND GUESSING

Our main goal as protocol designers is to exploit the fact that in synchronous systems, time is an explicit computational tool, so as to develop efficient solutions for the assigned task or problem. Let us consider again two problems that we have extensively studied for asynchronous networks: *minimum-finding* and *election*. We assume the standard restrictions for minimum-finding (**R**), as well as *Synch*; in the case of election, we obviously assume Initial Distinct Values (ID) also.

We have already seen a solution protocol, *Speed*, designed for synchronous *ring* networks; we have observed how its low message costs came at the expense of a time complexity that is exponential in the range of the input values.

The Transformation Lemma provides a tool that automatically produces a synchronous solution when an asynchronous one is already available. We have seen how the use of a transform leads to an *election* protocol for rings, *SynchStages*, with reduced bits and time costs. By integrating pipeline, we can obtain further improvements.

The cost of minimum-finding and election can be significantly reduced by using other types of "temporal" tools and techniques. In this section, we will describe two basic techniques that make an explicit use of time, *waiting* and *guessing*. We will describe and use them to efficiently solve **MinFinding** and **Election** in rings and other networks.

6.3.1 Waiting

Waiting is a technique that uses time not to transmit a value (as in the communicators), but to ensure that a desired condition is verified.

Waiting in Rings   Consider a ring network where each entity x has as initial value a positive integer $id(x)$. Let us assume, for the moment, that the ring is unidirectional and that all entities start at the same time (i.e., simultaneous initiation). Let us further assume that the ring size n is known.

The way of finding the minimum value using *waiting* is surprisingly simple. What an entity x will initially do is *nothing*, but just wait. More precisely,

Waiting

1. The entity x *waits* for a certain amount of time $f(id(x), n)$.
2. If nothing happens during this time, the entity determines "I am the smallest" and sends a "Stop" message.

3. If, instead, while waiting the entity receives a "Stop" message, it determines "I am not the smallest" and forwards the message.

With the appropriate choice of the *waiting function* f, this surprisingly simple protocol works correctly!

To make the process work correctly, the entities with the smallest value must finish waiting before anybody else does (in this way, each of them will correctly determine "I am the minimum"). In other words, the waiting function f must be monotonically decreasing: if $id(x) < id(y)$ then

$$f(id(x), n) < f(id(y, n)).$$

This is, however, not sufficient. In fact, it is also necessary that every entity whose value is *not* the smallest receives a "Stop" message while still waiting (in this way, each of them will correctly determine "I am *not* the minimum"). To achieve this, it is necessary that if x originates a "Stop" message, this message would reach every entity y with $id(x) < id(y)$ while y is still waiting, that is, if $id(x) < id(y)$, then

$$f(id(x), n) + d(x, y) < f(id(y), n), \tag{6.21}$$

where $d(x, y)$ denotes the distance of y from x in the ring. This must hold regardless of the distance $d(x, y)$ and regardless of how small $id(y)$ is (provided $id(y) > id(x)$). As $d(x, y) \leq n - 1$ for every two entities in the ring, and the smallest value larger than $id(x)$ is clearly $id(x) + 1$, any function f satisfying the following inequality

$$\begin{cases} f(0) & = 0 \\ f(v, n) + n - 1 < f(v + 1, n) \end{cases} \tag{6.22}$$

will make protocol *Wait* function correctly. Such is, for example, the waiting function

$$f(i, n) = i \, n. \tag{6.23}$$

As an example, consider the ring topology shown in Figure 6.14(a) where $n = 6$. The entities with the smallest value, 3, will finish waiting before all others: After $6 \times 3 = 18$ units of time they send a message along the ring. These messages travel along the ring encountering the other entities while they are still waiting, as shown in Figure 6.14(b).

IMPORTANT. Protocol *Wait* solves the minimum-finding problem, not the election: Unless we assume initial distinct values, more than one entity might have the same smallest value, and they will all correctly determine that they are the minimum.

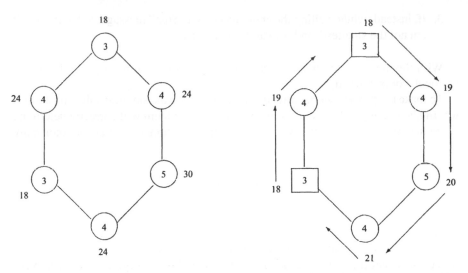

FIGURE 6.14: (a) The time when an entity x would finish waiting; (b) the messages send by the entities with value 3 at time $6 \times 3 = 18$ reach the other entities while they are still waiting.

As an example of execution of waiting under the (ID) restriction, consider the ring topology shown in Figure 6.15 where $n = 6$, and the values outside the nodes indicate how long each entity would wait. The unique entity with the smallest value, 3, will be elected after $6 \times 3 = 18$ units of time. Its "Stop" message travels along the ring encountering the other entities while they are still waiting.

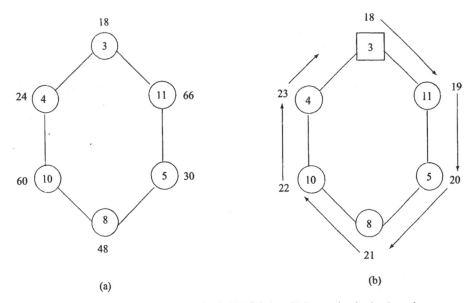

FIGURE 6.15: Execution with Initial Distinct Values: a leader is elected.

Protocol	Bits	Time	Notes
Speed	$O(n \log i)$	$O(2^i n)$	
SynchStages	$O(n \log n)$	$O(i \, n \log n)$	
Wait	$O(n)$	$O(i \, n)$	n known

FIGURE 6.16: Waiting yields a more efficient ring election protocol

What is the *cost* of such a protocol?

Only an entity that becomes *minimum* originates a message; this message will only travel along the ring (forwarded by the other entities that become *large*) until the next *minimum* entity. Hence the total number of messages is just n; as these messages are signals that do not contain any value, we have that Wait uses only $O(n)$ bits. This is the least amount of transmissions possible ever.

Let us consider the time. It will take $f(i_{min}, n) = i_{min}n$ time units for the entities with the smallest value to decide that they are the minima; at most, $n - 1$ additional time units are needed to notify all others. Hence, the time is $O(i, n)$, where i is the range of the input values. Compared with the other protocols we have seen for election in the ring, *Speed* and *SynchStages*, the bit complexity is even better (see Figure 6.16).

Without Simultaneous Initiation We have derived this surprising result assuming that the entities start simultaneously. If the entities can start at any time, it is possible that an entity with a large value starts so much before the others that it will finish waiting before the others and incorrectly determine that it is the minimum.

This problem can be taken care of by making sure that although the entities do not start at the same time, they will start not too far away (in time) from each other. To achieve this, it is sufficient to perform a *wake-up*: When an entity spontaneously wants to start the protocol, it will first of all send a "Start" message to its neighbor and then start waiting. An inactive entity will become active upon receiving the "Start" message, forward it, and start its waiting process.

Let $t(x)$ denote the time when entity x becomes awake and starts its waiting process; then, for any two entities x and y,

$$\forall x, y \quad t(y) - t(x) \leq d(x, y); \tag{6.24}$$

in particular, no two entities will start more than $n - 1$ clock ticks off from each other.

The waiting function f must now take into account this fact. As before, it is necessary that if $\text{id}(x) < \text{id}(y)$, then x must finish waiting before y *and* its message should reach y while still waiting; but now this must happen *regardless* of at what time $t(x)$ entity x starts and at what time $t(y)$ entity y starts; that is, if $\text{id}(x) < \text{id}(y)$,

$$t(x) + f(\text{id}(x), n) + d(x, y) < t(y) + f(\text{id}(y), n). \tag{6.25}$$

As $d(x, y) < n$ for every two entities in the ring, by Equation 6.24, and by setting $f(0) = 0$, it is easy to verify that any function f satisfying the inequality

$$\begin{cases} f(0) & = 0 \\ f(v, n) + 2n - 1 < f(v + 1, n) \end{cases} \tag{6.26}$$

will make protocol *Wait* function correctly even if the entities do not start simultaneously. Such is, for example, the waiting function

$$f(v, n) = 2\, n\, v. \tag{6.27}$$

The cost of the protocol is slightly bigger, but the order of magnitude is the same. In fact, in terms of bits we are performing also a *wake-up* that, in a unidirectional ring, costs n bits. As for the time, the new waiting function is just twice as the old one; hence, the time costs are at most doubled. In other words, the costs are still those indicated in Figure 6.16.

In Bidirectional Rings We have considered unidirectional rings. If the ring is *bidirectional*, the protocol requires marginal modifications, as shown in Figure 6.17. The same costs as the unidirectional case can be achieved with the same waiting functions.

On the Waiting Function We have assumed that the ring size n is known to the entities; it is indeed used in the requirements for waiting functions (Expressions 6.22 and 6.26).

An interesting feature (Exercise 6.6.31) is that those requirements would work even if a quantity $\bar{n}$ is used instead of n, provided $\bar{n} \geq n$. Hence, it is sufficient that the entities know (the same) upperbound $\bar{n}$ on the network size.

If the entities have all available a value $\bar{n}$ that is, however, *smaller* than n, its use in a waiting function instead of n would in general lead to incorrect results. There is, however, a range of values for $\bar{n}$ that would still guarantee the desired result (Exercise 6.6.32).

A final interesting observation is the following. Consider the general case when the entities have available neither n nor a common value $\bar{n}$, that is, each entity only knows its initial value $\text{id}(x)$. In this case, if each entity uses in the waiting function its value $\text{id}(x)$ instead of n, the function would work in some cases, for example, when all initial values $\text{id}(x)$ are not smaller than n. See Exercise 6.6.33.

Universal Waiting Protocol The waiting technique we have designed for rings is actually much more general and can be applied in *any* connected network G, regardless of its topology. It is thus a *universal* protocol.

The overall structure is as follows:

1. First a *reset* is performed with message "Start."
2. As soon as an entity x is active, it starts *waiting* $f(\text{id}(x), n)$ time units.

PROTOCOL Wait

- States: $S = \{$ASLEEP, CANDIDATE, LARGE, MINIMUM$\}$;
  $S_{INIT} = \{$ASLEEP$\}$;
  $S_{TERM} = \{$LARGE, SMALL$\}$.
- Restrictions: **R** ∪ **Synch** ∪ Ring ∪ Known(n).

ASLEEP

> *Spontaneously*
> **begin**
>   set alarm:= $c(x) + f(id(x), \text{n})$;
>   send("Start") **to** *right*;
>   direction := right;
>   **become** CANDIDATE;
> **end**
>
> *Receiving*("Start")
> **begin**
>   set alarm:= $c(x) + f(id(x), \text{n})$;
>   send("Start") **to other**;
>   direction := **other**;
>   **become** CANDIDATE;
> **end**

CANDIDATE

> *When* ($c(x) =$ alarm)
> **begin**
>   send("Over") **to** direction;
>   **become** MINIMUM;
> **end**
>
> *Receiving*("Over")
> **begin**
>   send("Over") **to other**;
>   **become** LARGE;
> **end**

FIGURE 6.17: Protocol *Wait*.

3. If, nothing happens while x is *waiting*, x determines that "I am the minimum" and initiates a *reset* with message "Stop."

4. If, instead, a "Stop" message arrives while x is waiting, then it stops its *waiting*, determines that "I am *not* the minimum" and participates in the *reset* with message "Stop."

Again, regardless of the initiation times, it is necessary that the entities with the smallest value finish waiting before the entities with larger value *and* that all those other entities receive a "Stop" message while still waiting. That is, if $id(x) < id(y)$, then

$$t(x) + f(\text{id}(x)) + d_G(x, y) < t(y) + f(\text{id}(y)),$$

where $d_G(x, y)$ denotes the distance between x and y in G, and $t(x)$ and $t(y)$ are the times when x and y start waiting.

Clearly, for all x, y,

$$|t(x) - t(y)| \leq d_G(x, y);$$

hence, setting $f(0) = 0$, we have that any function satisfying

$$\begin{cases} f(0) & = 0 \\ f(v) + 2d_G < f(v + 1) \end{cases} \tag{6.28}$$

makes the protocol correct, where d_G is the diameter of G. This means that, for example, the function

$$f(v) = 2\,v\,(d_G + 1) \tag{6.29}$$

would work. As $n - 1 \geq d_G$ for every G, this also means that the function

$$f(v) = 2\,v\,n$$

we had determined for rings actually works in every network; it might not be the most efficient though (Exercises 6.6.29 and 6.6.30).

Applications of Waiting   We will now consider two rather different applications of protocol *Wait*. The first is to compute two basic Boolean functions, *AND* and *OR*; the second is to reduce the time costs of protocol *Speed* that we discussed earlier in this chapter. In both cases we will consider unidirectional ring for the discussion; the results, however, trivially generalize to all other networks.

In discussing these applications, we will discover some interesting properties of the waiting function.

Computing AND and OR   Consider the situation where every entity x has a Boolean value $b(x) \in \{0, 1\}$, and we need to compute the *AND* of all those values. Assume as before that the size n of the ring is known. The *AND* of all the values will be 1 if and only if $\forall x \; b(x) = 1$, that is, *all* the values are 1; otherwise the result is 0.

Thus, to compute *AND* it suffices to know if there is at least one entity x with value $b(x) = 0$. In other words, we just need to know whether *the smallest value is* 0 or 1.

With protocol *Waiting* we can determine the smallest value. Once this is done, the entities with such a value know the result. If the result of *AND* is 1, *all* the entities have value 1 and are in state *minimum*, and thus know the result. If the result of *AND* is 0, the entities with value 0 are in state *minimum* (and thus know the result), while the others are in state *large* (and thus know the result).

Notice that if an entity x has value $b(x) = 0$, using the waiting function of expression 6.27, its waiting time will be $f(b(x)) = 2\,b(x)\,n = 0$. That is, if an entity has value 0, it does not wait at all. To determine the cost of the overall protocol is quite simple (Exercise 6.6.35).

In a similar way we can use protocol *Waiting* to compute the OR of the input values (Exercise 6.6.36).

Reducing Time Costs of Speed The first synchronous election protocol we have seen for ring networks is *Speed*, discussed in Section 6.1.4. (NOTE: to solve the election problem it assumes initial distinct values.) On the basis of the idea of messages traveling along the ring at different speeds, this protocol has unfortunately a terrifying time complexity: exponential in the (a priori unbounded) smallest input value $i_{\min}$ (see Figure 6.16). Protocol *Waiting* has a much better complexity, but it requires knowledge of (an upperbound on) n; on the contrary, protocol *Speed* requires no such knowledge.

It is possible to reduce the time costs of *Speed* substantially by adding *Waiting* as a preliminary phase.

As each entity x knows only its value id(x), it will first of all execute *Waiting* using $2id(x)^2$ as the waiting function.

Depending on the relationship between the values and n, the *Waiting* protocol might work (Exercise 6.6.33), determining the unique minimum (and hence electing a leader). If it does not work (a situation that can be easily detected; see Exercise 6.6.34), the entities will then use *Speed* to elect a leader.

The overall cost of this combine protocol *Wait + Speed* clearly depends on whether the initial *Waiting* succeeds in electing a leader or not.

If *Waiting* succeeds, we will not execute *Speed* and the cost will just be $O(i_{\min}^2)$ time and $O(n)$ bits.

If *Waiting* does not succeed, we must also run *Speed* that costs $O(n)$ messages but $O(n2^{i_{\min}})$ time. So the total cost will be $O(n)$ messages and $O(i_{\min}^2 + n2^{i_{\min}}) = O(n2^{i_{\min}})$ time. However, if *Waiting* does not succeed, it is guaranteed that the smallest initial value is at most n, that is $i_{\min} < n$ (see again Exercise 6.6.33). This means that the overall time cost will be only $O(n2^n)$.

In other words, whether the initial *Waiting* succeeds or not, protocol *Wait+Speed* will use $O(n)$ messages. As for the time, it will cost either $O(i_{\min}^2)$ or $O(n2^n)$, depending on whether the waiting succeeds or not. Summarizing, using *Waiting* we can reduce the time complexity of *Speed* from $O(n2^i)$ to

$$O(\operatorname{Max}\{i^2,\ n2^n\})$$

adding at most $O(n)$ bits.

Application: Randomized Election   If the assumption on the uniqueness of
the identities does not hold, the election problem cannot be solved obviously by any
minimum-finding process, including *Wait*. Furthermore, we have already seen that
if the nodes have no identities (or, analogously, all have the same identity), then
no deterministic solution exists for the election problem, duly renamed *symmetry
breaking* problem, regardless of whether the network is synchronous or not. This
impossibility result applies to *deterministic* protocols, that is, protocols where every
action is composed only of deterministic operations.

A different class of protocols are those where an entity can perform operations
whose result is *random*, for example, tossing a dice, and where the nature of the action depends on outcome of this random event. For example, an entity can toss a coin
and, depending on whether the result is "head" or "tail," perform a different operation.
These types of protocols will be called *randomized*; unlike their deterministic coun-
terparts, randomized protocols give no guarantees, either on the correctness of their
result or on the termination of their execution. So, for example, some randomized
protocols always terminate but the solution is correct only with a given probability;
this type of protocols is called *Monte Carlo*. Other protocols will have the correct
solution if they terminate, but they terminate only with a given probability; this type
of protocols are called *Las Vegas*.

We will see how protocol *Wait* can be used to generate a surprisingly simple and
extremely efficient *Las Vegas* protocol for symmetry breaking. Again we assume that
n is known. We will restrict the description to unidirectional rings; the results can,
however, be generalized to several other topologies (Exercises 6.6.37-6.6.39).

1. The algorithm is composed of a sequence of rounds.
2. In each round, every entity randomly selects an integer between 0 and b as its
   identity, where $b \leq n$.
3. If the minimum of the chosen values is unique, that entity will become *leader*;
   otherwise, a new round is started.

To make the algorithm work, we need to design a mechanism to find the minimum
and detect if it is unique. But this is exactly what protocol *Wait* does. In fact, protocol
Wait not only finds the minimum value but also allows an entity x with such a value
to detect if it is the only one. In fact,

- If x is the only minimum, its message will come back *exactly* after n time units;
  in this case, x will become *leader* and send a *Terminate* message to notify all
  other entities.
- If there are more than one minimum, x will receive a message *before* n time
  units; it will then send a "Restart" message and start the next round.

In other words, each round is an execution of protocol *Wait*; thus, it costs $O(n)$
bits, including the "Restart" (or "Termination") messages. The time used by protocol
Wait is $O(ni)$. In our case the values are integers between 0 and b, that is, $i \leq b$. Thus,
each round will cost at most $O(nb)$ time.

We have different options with regard to the value b and how the random choice of the identities is made. For example, we can set $b = n$ and choose each value with same probability (Exercise 6.6.40); notice, however, that the larger the b is, the larger the time costs of each round will be. We will use instead $b = 1$ (i.e., each entity randomly chooses either 0 or 1) and employ a *biased coin*. Specifically, in our protocol, which we will call *Symmetry*, we will employ the following criteria:

Random Selection Criteria In each round, every entity selects 0 with probability $\frac{1}{n}$, and 1 with probability $\frac{n-1}{n}$.

Up to now, except for the random selection criteria, there has been little difference between *Symmetry* and the deterministic protocols we have seen so far. This is going to change soon.

Let us compute the *number of rounds* required by the protocol until termination. The surprising thing is that this protocol might *never terminate*, and thus the number of rounds is potentially *infinite*.

In fact, with a protocol of type *Las Vegas*, we know that *if* it terminates, it solves the problem, but it might not terminate. This is not a good news for those looking for protocols with a guaranteed performance. The advantage of this protocol is instead in the low *expected* number of rounds before termination.

Let us compute this quantity. Using the random selection criteria described above, the protocol terminates as soon as exactly one entity chooses 0. For this to happen, one entity x must choose 0 (this happens with probability $\frac{1}{n}$), while the other $n - 1$ entities must choose 1 (this happen with probability $(\frac{n-1}{n})^{n-1}$). As there are $\binom{n}{1} = n$ choices for x, the probability of exactly one entity chooses 0 is

$$\binom{n}{1} \frac{1}{n} (\tfrac{n-1}{n})^{n-1} = (\tfrac{n-1}{n})^{n-1}.$$

For n large enough, this quantity is easily bounded; in fact

$$\lim_{n \to \infty} \left(\frac{n-1}{n} \right)^{n-1} = \frac{1}{e}, \tag{6.30}$$

where $e \approx 2.7 \ldots$ is the basis of the natural logarithm. This means that with probability 1, protocol *Symmetry* will terminate after e rounds. In other words,

with probability 1, protocol Symmetry *will elect a leader with $O(n)$ bits in $O(n)$ time.*

Obviously, there is no guarantee that a leader will be elected with this cost or will be elected at all, but with high probability it will and at that cost. This shows the unique nature of randomized protocols.

6.3.2 Guessing

Guessing is a technique that allows some entities to determine a value not by transmitting it but by guessing it. Again we will consider the *minimum finding* and *election* problems in *ring* networks. Let us assume, for the moment, that the ring is unidirectional and that all entities start at the same time (i.e., simultaneous initiation). Let us further assume that the ring size n is known.

Minimum-Finding as a Guessing Game   At the base of the *guessing* technique there is a basic utility protocol *Decide*(p), where p is a parameter available to all entities. Informally, protocol *Decide(p)* is as follows:

Decide (p): Every entity x compares its value id(x) with the protocol parameter p. If id(x) $\leq p$, x sends a message; otherwise, it will forward any received message.

There are only two possible situations and outcomes:

$S1$: All local values are greater than p; in this case, no messages will be transmitted: There will be "silence" in the system.

$S2$: At least one entity x has id(x) $\leq p$; in this case, every entity will send and receive a message: There will be "noise" in the system.

The goal of protocol *Decide* is to make all entities know in which of the two situations we are. Let us examine how an entity y can determine whether we are in situation $S1$ or $S2$. If id(y) $\leq p$, then y knows immediately that we are in situation $S2$. However, if id(y) $> p$, then y does not know whether all the entities have values greater than p (situation $S1$) or some entities have a value smaller than or equal to p (situation $S2$). It does know that if we are in situation $S2$, it will eventually receive a message; by contrast, if we are in situation $S1$, *no* message will ever arrive.

Clearly, to decide, y must wait; also clearly, it cannot wait forever. How long should y wait? The answer is simple: If a message was sent by an entity, say x, a message will arrive at y within at most $d(x, y) < n$ time units from the time it was sent. Hence, if y does not receive any message in the first n time units since the start, then none is coming and we are in situation $S1$. For this reason, n time units after the entities (simultaneously) start the execution of protocol *Decide*(p), all the entities can decide which situation ($S1$ or $S2$) has occurred. The full protocol is shown in Figure 6.18.

IMPORTANT. Consider the execution of *Decide*(p).

– If situation $S1$ occurs, it means that *all* the values, including $i_{min} = $ Min$\{$id(x)$\}$, are greater than p, that is, $p < i_{min}$. We will say that p is an *underestimate* on i_{min}.

– If situation $S2$ occurs, it means that there are some values that are not greater than i_{min}; thus, $p \geq i_{min}$. We will say that p is an *overestimate* on i_{min}.

SUBPROTOCOL Decide(p)

- Input: positive integer p;
- States: $S = \{$START, DECIDED, UNDECIDED$\}$:
  $S_{INIT} = \{$START$\}$;
  $S_{TERM} = \{$DECIDED$\}$.
- Restrictions: $\mathbf{R} \cup \mathbf{Synch} \cup$ Ring $\cup$ Known$(n) \cup$ Simultaneous Start.

```
START
      Spontaneously
      begin
          set alarm:= c(x)+n;
          if id(x) ≤ v then
             decision:= high;
             send("High") to rigth;
             become DECIDED;
          else
             become UNDECIDED;
          endif
      end


UNDECIDED
      Receiving("High")
      begin
          decision:= high;
          send("High") to other;
          become DECIDED;
      end

      When (c(x) = alarm)
      begin
          decision:= low;
          become DECIDED;
      end
```

FIGURE 6.18: SubProtocol *Decide(p)*.

These observations are summarized in Figure 6.19.

NOTE. The condition $p = i_{min}$ is also considered an overestimate.

Using this fact, we can reformulate the minimum-finding problem in terms of a *guessing game*:

- Each entity is a *player*. The minimum value i_{min} is a number, previously chosen and unknown to the player, that must be guessed.
- The player can ask question of type "Is the number greater than p?"

Situation	Condition	Name	Time	Bits
S1	$p < i_{min}$	"underestimate"	n	0
S2	$p \geq i_{min}$	"overestimate"	n	n

FIGURE 6.19: Results and costs of executing protocol *Decide*.

- Each question corresponds to a simultaneous execution of *Decide(p)*. Situations $S1$ and $S2$ correspond to a "YES" and a "NO" answer to the question, respectively.

A *guessing* protocol will just specify which questions should be asked to discover i_{min}. Initially, all entities choose the same initial guess p_1 and simultaneously perform *Decide(p_1)*. After n time units, all entities will be aware of whether or not i_{min} is greater than p_1 (situation $S1$ and situation $S2$, respectively). On the basis of the outcome, a new guess p_2 will be chosen by all entities that will then simultaneously perform *Decide(p_2)*. In general, on the basis of the outcome of the execution of *Decide(p_i)*, all entities will choose a new guess p_{i+1}. The process is repeated until the minimum value i_{min} is unambiguously determined.

Depending on which strategy is employed for choosing p_{i+1} given the outcome of *Decide(p_i)*, different minimum-finding algorithms will result from this technique.

Before examining how to best play (and win) the game, let us discuss the *costs* of asking a question, that is, of executing protocol *Decide*.

Observe that the number of *bits* transmitted when executing *Decide* depends on the situation, $S1$ or $S2$, we are in. In fact in situation $S1$, no messages will be transmitted at all. By contrast, in situation $S2$, there will be exactly n messages; as the content of these messages is not important, they can just be single bits. Summarizing, If our guess is an overestimate, we will pay n bits; if it is an underestimate, it will cost nothing.

As for the *time* costs, each execution of *Decide* will cost n time units regardless of whether it is an underestimate or overestimate.

This means that we pay n time units for *each* question; however, we pay n bits only if our guess is an overestimate. See Figure 6.19.

Our goal must, thus, be to discover the number, asking few questions (to minimize time) of which as few as possible are overestimates (to minimize transmission costs). As we will see, we will unfortunately have to trade off one cost for the other.

We will first consider a simplified version of the game, in which we know an upperbound M on the number to be guessed, that is, we know that $i_{min} \in [1, M]$ (see Figure 6.20). We will then see how to easily and efficiently establish such a bound.

Playing the Game   We will now investigate how to design a successful strategy for the guessing game. The number i_{min} to be guessed is known to be in the interval $[1, M]$ (see Figure 6.20).

Let us denote by q the number of questions and by $k \leq q$ the number of overestimates used to solve the game; this will correspond to a minimum-finding protocol that uses qn time and kn bits. As each overestimate costs us n bits, to design an overall

FIGURE 6.20: Guessing in an interval.

FIGURE 6.21: Linear search is the only possibility when $k = 1$.

strategy that uses only $O(n)$ bits *in total* (like we did with protocol *Waiting*), we must use only a *constant* (i.e., $O(1)$) number of overestimates; clearly, we want to use as few questions as possible.

Let us first solve the problem with $k = 1$, that is, we want to find the minimum with *only one* overestimate. As the number (i.e., when $p = i_{min}$) is already an overestimate when we find it, $k = 1$ means that we can *never* use as a guess a value greater than i_{min}.

For this setting, there is only one possible solution strategy, *linear search*: The guesses will be $p_1 = 1, p_2 = 2, p_3 = 3, \cdots$ All these guesses will be underestimates; when we hit $p_{i_{min}}$, there will be our first and only overestimate. See Figure 6.21. The number of questions will be exactly i_{min}; that is, in the worst case, the cost will be

$$k = 1 \; ; \; q = M.$$

Let us now allow one more overestimate, that is, $k = 2$. Several strategies are now possible. A solution is to partition the interval into $\lceil \sqrt{M} \rceil$ consecutive pieces of size $\lceil \sqrt{M} \rceil$. (If M is not a perfect square, the last interval will be smaller than the others.) See figure 6.22.

We will first search sequentially among the points $a_1 = \lceil \sqrt{M} \rceil - 1, a_2 = 2\lceil \sqrt{M} \rceil - 2, \cdots$, until we hit an overestimate. At this point we know the interval where i_{min} is.

The second overestimate is then spent to find i_{min} inside that interval using sequential search (as in the case $k = 1$). In the worst case, we have to search all the a_j and all of the last interval, that is, in the worst case the cost will be

$$k = 2 \; ; \; q = 2\sqrt{M}.$$

Notice that by allowing a single additional overestimate (i.e., using an additional n bits) we have been able to reduce the time costs from linear to sublinear. In other words, the trade-off between bits and time is not linear.

It is easy to generalize this approach (Exercise 6.6.43) so as to find i_{min} with a worst-case cost of

$$k \; ; \; q = k \, M^{1/k}.$$

FIGURE 6.22: Dividing the interval when $k = 2$.

IMPORTANT. Notice that the cost is a trade-off between questions and overestimates: The more overestimates we allow, the fewer questions we need to ask. Furthermore, the trade-off is nonlinear: The reduction in number of questions achieved by adding a single overestimate is rather dramatic.

As every overestimate costs n bits, the total number of bits is $O(n\ k)$. The total amount of time consumed with this approach is at most $O(n\ k\ M^{1/k})$.

The Optimal Solution We have just seen a solution strategy for our guessing game when the value to be guessed is in a known interval. How good is this strategy?

In the case $k = 1$, there is only one possible solution strategy. However, for $k > 1$ several strategies and solutions are possible. Thus, as usual, to answer the above question we will establish a lower bound. Surprisingly, in this process, we will also find the (one and only) optimal solution strategy.

To establish a lower bound (and find out if a solution is good) we need to answer the following question:

Q1: What is the smallest number of questions q needed to *always* win the game in an interval of size M using no more than k overestimates?

Instead of answering this question directly, we will "flip its arguments" and formulate another question:

Q2: With q questions of which at most k are overestimates, what is the largest M so that we can *always* win the game in an interval of that size ?

We will answer this one. The answer will obviously depend on both q and k, that is, M will be some function $h(q, k)$. Let us determine this function.

Some things we already know. For example, if we allow only one overestimate (i.e., $k = 1$), the only solution strategy is linear search, that is,

$$h(q, 1) = q. \tag{6.31}$$

On the contrary, if we allow every question to be an overestimate (i.e., $k = q$), then we can always win in a much larger interval, in fact (Exercise 6.6.44),

$$h(q, q) = 2^q - 1. \tag{6.32}$$

Before we proceed, let us summarize the problem we are facing:

1. We have at our disposal q questions of which only k can be overestimates.
2. We must always win.
3. We want to know the size $h(q, k)$ of the largest interval in which this is possible.

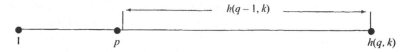

FIGURE 6.23: If the initial guess p is an underestimate, the largest interval has size $p + h(q - 1, k)$.

Whatever the strategy be, it must start with a question. Let p be this first guess. There are two possibilities; this is either an underestimate or an overestimate.

If p is an underestimate (i.e., $i_{\min} > p$), we are left with $q - 1$ questions, but we still have k overestimates at our disposal. Now, the largest interval in which we can always win with $q - 1$ questions of which k can be overestimates is $h(q - 1, k)$. This means that if p is the first question (Figure 6.23), the largest interval has size

$$h(q, k) = p + h(q - 1, k).$$

On the basis of this, it would seem that to make the interval as large as possible, we should choose our first guess p to be as large as possible. However, we must take into account the possibility that our first guess turns out to be an overestimate.

If p is an overestimate, we have spent both one question and one overestimate; furthermore, we know that the number is in the interval $[1, p]$. This means that the initial guess p we make must guarantee that we *always* win in the interval $[1, p]$ with $q - 1$ questions and $k - 1$ overestimates. Thus, the largest p can be

$$p = h(q - 1, k - 1).$$

This means that

$$h(q, k) = h(q - 1, k) + h(q - 1, k - 1), \tag{6.33}$$

where the boundary conditions are those of expressions 6.31 and 6.32; see Figure 6.24. Solving this recurrence relation (Exercise 6.6.45), we obtain the unique solution

$$h(q, k) = \sum_{j=0,k-1} \binom{q}{j}. \tag{6.34}$$

FIGURE 6.24: The initial guess p could be an overestimate; this cannot be larger than $h(q - 1, k)$.

We have found the answer to question **Q2**. If we now "flip the answer," we can answer also question **Q1** and determine a lower bound on q given M and k.

In fact, if $M = h(q, k)$, then the minimum number of questions to always win in $[1, M]$ with at most k overestimates (our original problem) is precisely q. In general, the answer is the smallest q such that $M \le h(q, k)$.

IMPORTANT. In the process of finding a lower bound, we have actually found the (one and only) *optimal* solution strategy to guess in the interval $[1, M]$ with at most k overestimates.

Let us examine this strategy.

Optimal Search Strategy   To optimally search in $[1, M]$ with at most k overestimates:

1. use as a guess $p = h(q - 1, k - 1)$, where $q \ge k$ is the smallest integer such that $M \le h(q, k)$;
2. if p is an underestimate, then optimally search in $[p + 1, M]$ with k overestimates;
3. if it is an overestimate, then optimally search in $[1, p]$ with $k - 1$ overestimates.

This strategy is guaranteed to use the fewest questions.

Unbounded Interval   We have found the optimal solution strategy using at most k overestimates but assuming that the interval in which i_{min} lies is known. If this is not the case, we can always first of all establish an upperbound on i_{min}, thus determining an interval and then search in that interval.

To bound the value i_{min}, again we use guesses, $g(1), g(2), g(3), \ldots$, where $g :$ $N \to Z$ is a monotonically increasing function. The first time we hit an overestimate, say with $g(t)$, we know that $g(t - 1) < i_{min} \le g(t)$ and hence the interval to search is $[g(t - 1) + 1, g(t)]$. See Figure 6.25. This process requires exactly t questions and one overestimate.

We are now left to guess i_{min} in an interval of size $M = \Delta(t) = g(t) - g(t - 1) + 1$ with $k - 1$ overestimates. (Recall, we just spent one to determine the interval.) Using the optimal solution strategy, this can be done with $h(\Delta(t), k - 1)$ questions. The entire process will thus require at most

$$t + h(\Delta(t), k - 1)$$

questions of which at most k are overestimates.

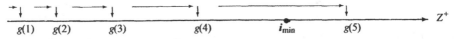

FIGURE 6.25: In an unbounded interval, we first establish an upper bound on i_{min}.

Protocol	Bits	Time	Notes
Speed	$O(n \log i)$	$O(2^i n)$	
SynchStages	$O(n \log n)$	$O(i\, n \log n)$	
Wait	$O(n)$	$O(i\, n)$	n known
Guess	$O(kn)$	$O(i^{1/k} kn)$	n known

FIGURE 6.26: Using $k = O(1)$, Guessing is more efficient than other election protocols.

Depending on which function g we use, we obtain different costs. For example, choosing $g(j) = 2^j$ (i.e., doubling our guess at every step), $t = \lceil \log i_{\min} \rceil$ and $\Delta(t) < i_{\min}$. This means that the number of questions used by the entire process is at most

$$\lceil \log i_{\min} \rceil + h(i_{\min}, k - 1).$$

Better performances are possible using different functions g; for example (Exercise 6.6.46), with k overestimates, it is possible to reduce the total number of questions to

$$2\, h(i_{\min},\ k) - 1.$$

Recall that each question costs n time units and if it is an overestimate it also costs n bits. Thus, the complexity of the resulting minimum-finding protocol *Guess* becomes $O(kn)$ bits and $O(kn\, i^k)$. This means that for any fixed k, the guessing approach yields an election protocol that is far more efficient than the ones we have considered so far, as shown in Figure 6.26.

Removing the Assumptions

Knowledge of n   We have assumed that n is known. This knowledge is used only in procedure *Decide*, employed as a timeout for those entities that do not know if a message will arrive. Clearly the procedure will work even if a quantity $\bar{n} \geq n$ is used instead of n, provided. Hence, it is sufficient that the entities know (the same) upperbound $\bar{n}$ on the network size.

Network Topology   We have described our protocol assuming that the network is a ring. However, the optimal search strategy for the guessing game is independent of the network topology. To be implemented, it requires subprotocol *Decide(p)* that has been described only for rings. This protocol can be made *universal*, and can thus work in every network, by simple modifications. In fact (Exercise 6.6.47), it suffices:

1. to transform it into a *reset* with message "High" started by those entities with $\mathrm{id}(x) \leq p$; and
2. to use as the timeout an upperbound $\bar{d}$ on the diameter d of the network.

Notice that each question will now cost $\bar{d}$ time units. The number w of bits transmitted if the guess is an overestimate depends on the situation; it is, however, always bounded as follows:

$$m \leq w \leq 2m.$$

Simultaneous Start   We have assumed that all entities start the first execution of *Decide* simultaneously. This assumption can actually be removed by simply using a wake-up procedure at the very beginning (so to bound the delays between initiation times) and using a longer delay between successive guesses (Exercise 6.6.48).

6.3.3 Double Wait: Integrating Waiting and Guessing

We have seen two basic techniques, *Waiting* and *Guessing*. Their use has led to bit-optimal and time-efficient solutions for the minimum-finding and election problems; we have described them for ring networks, but we have seen that they are indeed universal. Their only drawback is that they require knowledge of n (or of some upperbound on the diameter d). In contrast, both *Speed* and *SynchStages* did not require such an a priori knowledge.

If this knowledge is not available, it can, however, be acquired somehow during the computation. We are going to see now how this can be done using *both* waiting and guessing. We will focus solely on the *election* problem; thus, we will be operating under restrictions of initial distinct values. Once again, we will restrict the description to unidirectional ring networks. We also assume that all entities start within $n - 1$ time units from each other (e.g., they first execute a wake-up).

What we are going to do is to still use the *waiting* technique to find the smallest value; as we do not know n (nor an upperbound on it), we are going to use the *guessing* strategy to discover an upperbound on n. Let us discuss it in some details.

Overall Strategy   Each entity is going to execute protocol *Wait* using a guess $g(1)$ on n. We know that if $g(1) \geq n$, then protocol *Wait* works (Exercise 6.6.31), that is, the entity with smallest value finishes waiting before all other entities, it becomes *small*, it sends a message, and its message reaches all other entities while they are still waiting.

The problem occurs if $g(1) < n$; in fact, in this case, it is possible that two or more entities with different ids will stop waiting, become *small*, and send a message. If we are able to detect if $g(1) < n$, we can then restart with a different, larger guess $g(2) > g(1)$. In general, if $g(j - 1)$ fails (i.e., $g(j - 1) < n$), we can restart with a larger guess $g(j) > g(j - 1)$; this process will terminate as soon as $g(j) \geq n$.

Consider now an entity x that in step j finishes waiting, becomes *small*, and sends a message. If $g(j) \geq n$, no other entity sends any message, so, after n time units, x receives its own message. By contrast, if $g(j) < n$, several entities might become *small* and originate messages, each traveling along the ring until it reaches a *small* entity; hence x would receive the message transmitted by some other entity. Summarizing, in the first case, x receives its own message; in the second case, the message was originated by somebody else.

Without knowing n, how can x *know whether the received message is its own?*

Clearly, if each message contains the id of its originator, the problem is trivially solved. However, the number of bits transmitted by just having such a message traveling along the ring will be $O(n \log i)$, resulting in an unbounded quantity (see Figure 6.26).

The answer is provided by understanding how transmission delays work in a synchronous ring.

Consider the delay $n_x(j)$ from the time x transmits its message to the time a message arrives at x. If x receives its own message, then $n_x(j) = n$. By contrast, if x receives the message of somebody else, this will happen *before* n time units. That is, $n_x(j) < n$.

So what x needs to do is to verify whether or not $n_x(j) = n$. This can be done by employing the *waiting* technique again, using $n_x(j)$ for n in the waiting function. If indeed $n_x(j) = n$, x will again finish waiting without receiving any message and send a new message, and this message will travel along the ring after exactly $n_x(j) = n$ time units. If instead $n_x(j) < n$, as we will see, x will notice that something is wrong (i.e., it will receive a message while waiting, it will receive a message before $n_x(j)$ time units, or it will receive no message $n_x(j)$ time units after it sent one, etc.); in this case, it will start the $(j + 1)$th iteration.

Informally the strategy, called *DoubleWait*, is as follows:

Strategy *DoubleWait*:

1. Each entity will execute a first *Wait* using the current guess $g(j)$ on the unknown n. Consider an entity x that finishes waiting without receiving any message. It will send a message "Wait1," become *testing*, and wait for a message to arrive keeping track of the time. Let $n_x(j)$ be the delay from when x sent its "Wait1" message to when x received one. If the guess was correct (i.e., $g(j) \geq n > g(j - 1)$), then this message would be the one it sent and $n_x(j) = n$.

2. If x notices something wrong (e.g., $n_x(j) \leq g(j - 1)$, or $n_x(j) > g(j)$, etc.), it will send a "Restart" message to make everybody restart with a new guess $g(j + 1)$.

3. If x does not notice anything wrong, x will *assume* that indeed $t_x(j) = n$ and will start a *second Wait* (with a different waiting function) to verify the guess. If the guess is correct, x is the only entity doing so; it should thus finish waiting without receiving any message. Furthermore, the message "Wait2" it sends now should arrive exactly after $n_x(j)$ time units.

4. If x now notices something wrong (i.e., a message arrives while waiting; a message does not arrive exactly after $n_x(j)$ time units), it will send a "Restart" message to make everybody start with a new guess $g(j + 1)$.

5. Otherwise, x considers the guess verified, becomes the *leader*, and sends a "Terminate" message.

6. An entity receiving a "Wait1' message while doing the first *Waiting* will forward received messages and wait for either a "Restart" or "Terminate." In the first case it restarts with a new guess; in the second case, it becomes *defeated*.

What we have to show now is that with the appropriate choice of waiting functions, it is *impossible* for an entity x to be fooled. That is, if x does not notice anything wrong in the first and in the second waiting and becomes *leader*, then indeed the message x receives is its own and nobody else will become *leader*.

Choosing the Waiting Functions   What we have to do now is to choose the two waiting functions f and h so that it is impossible for an entity x to be *fooled*. In other words, it is impossible that the "Wait1" and "Wait2" messages x receives have actually been sent by somebody else, say y and z, and that by pure coincidence both these messages arrived $n_x(j)$ time units after x sent its corresponding messages.

IMPORTANT. These functions must satisfy the properties of waiting functions, that is, if $g(j) \geq n$, then for all u and v with $\text{id}(u) < \text{id}(v)$,

$$f(\text{id}(u), j) + 2(n - 1) < f(\text{id}(v), j)$$

$$h(\text{id}(u), j) + 2(n - 1) < h(\text{id}(v), j).$$

NOTE. We can assume that the entities start the current stage using guess $g(j)$ within $n - 1$ time units from each other; this is enforced in the first stage by the initial wake-up, and in the successive stages by the "Reset" messages.

To determine the waiting functions f and h we need, let us consider the situation in more details, and let us concentrate on x and see under what conditions it would be fooled. Denote by $t(x, j)$ the delay between the time the first entity starts the jth iteration and the time x starts it.

Entity x starts at time $t(x, j)$, waits $f(\text{id}(x), j)$ time, and then sends its "Wait1" message; it receives one at time

$$t(x, j) + f(\text{id}(x), j) + n_x(j).$$

Notice that to "fool" x, this "Wait1" message must have been sent by some other entity, y. This means that y must also have waited without receiving any message; thus it sent its message at time $t(y, j) + f(\text{id}(y), j)$. This message arrives at x at time

$$t(y, j) + f(\text{id}(y), j) + d(y, x),$$

where, as usual, $d(y, x)$ is the distance from y to x. Hence, for x to be "fooled," it must be

$$t(x, j) + f(\text{id}(x), j) + n_x(j) = t(y, j) + f(\text{id}(y), j) + d(y, x). \qquad (6.35)$$

Concentrate again on entity x. After it receives the "Wait1" message, x waits again for an additional $h(\text{id}(x), j)$ time units, and then it sends its "Wait2" message; it receives one after $n_x(j)$ time units, that is, at time

$$t(x, j) + f(\text{id}(x), j) + n_x(j) + h(v, j) + n_x(j)$$
$$= t(x, j) + f(\text{id}(x), j) + h(\text{id}(x), j) + 2t_x(j).$$

At this point it becomes *leader* and sends a "Terminate" message.

If x has been fooled the first time, then also message "Wait2" was sent by some other entity z. It is not difficult to verify that if x has been fooled, then there is only one fooling entity, that is, $y = z$ (Exercise 6.6.49). To have sent a "Wait2" message, y must have not noticed anything wrong (otherwise it would have set a "Reset" instead). This means that similarly to x, y received a "Wait1" message $n_y(j)$ time units after it sent one, that is, at time $t(y, j) + f(\text{id}(y), j) + n_y(j)$. It waited for another $h(y, j)$ time units and then sent the "Wait2" message; this message thus arrived at x at time

$$t(y, j) + f(\text{id}(y), j) + n_y(j) + h(y, j) + d(y, x).$$

So, if x has been fooled, it must by accident happen that

$$t(x, j) + f(\text{id}(x), j) + h(\text{id}(x), j) + 2t_x(j)$$
$$= t(y, j) + f(\text{id}(y), j) + n_y(j) + h(\text{id}(y), j) + d(y, x). \qquad (6.36)$$

Subtracting Equation 6.35 from Equation 6.36, we have

$$h(\text{id}(x), j) + n_x(j) = h(\text{id}(y), j) + n_y(j). \qquad (6.37)$$

Summarizing, x will be fooled *if and only if* the condition of Equation 6.37 occurs. Notice that this condition does *not* depend on the first waiting function f but only on the second one h. What we have to do is to choose a waiting function h that makes the condition of Equation 6.37 impossible. For example, the function

$$h(\text{id}(x), j) = 2\, g(j)\, \text{id}(x) + g(j) - n_x(j)$$

is a correct waiting function and will cause Equation 6.37 to become

$$\text{id}(x) = \text{id}(y). \qquad (6.38)$$

As the identities are distinct (because of ID restriction), this means that $x = y$, that is, the messages x receives are its own. In other words, with this waiting function, nobody will be fooled.

Summarizing, regardless of the waiting function f and of the monotonically increasing guessing function g, with the appropriate choice of the second waiting function h, protocol *DoubleWait* correctly elects a leader. (Exercises 6.6.50, 6.6.51, and 6.6.52.)

The Cost of DoubleWait   Now that we have established the correctness of the protocol, let us examine its costs.

The protocol consists of a sequence of iterations. In iteration j, a guess $g(j)$ is made on the unknown ring size n. The terminating condition is simply $g(j) \geq n$; in this case, the entity with the smallest value becomes leader; in all other cases, a new iteration is started.

The *number of iterations* $\mathbf{j}$ required by the protocol is easily determined. As the protocol terminates as soon as $g(j) \geq n$,

$$\mathbf{j} = \lceil g^{-1}(n) \rceil, \tag{6.39}$$

where g^{-1} is the inverse of g, that is, $\mathbf{j}$ is the smallest positive integer j such that $g(j) \geq n$.

In an iteration, the guess $g(j)$ is employed in the execution of a first waiting, using waiting function $f(x, j)$. As a result, either a new iteration is started or a second waiting, using function $h(x, j)$, is executed; as a result of this other waiting, either the algorithm terminates or a new iteration is started, depending on whether or not $g(j) \geq n$.

The overall cost of the protocol depends on the two waiting functions, f and h, as well as on the monotonically increasing function $g : N \to Z$ specifying the guesses.

To determine the cost, we will first examine the number of bits and then determine the time. As we will see, we will have available many choices and, again, we will be facing a trade-off between time and bits.

Bits   Each iteration consists of at most two executions of the waiting technique (with different waiting functions). Each iteration, except the last, will be aborted and a "Restart" message will signal the start of the next iteration.

In other words, each iteration $j \leq \mathbf{j}$ is started by a "Restart" (in the very first one it acts as the wake-up); this costs exactly n signals. As part of the first waiting, "Wait1" messages will be sent, for a total of n signals. In the worst case there will also be a second waiting with "Wait2" message, causing no more than n signals. Hence, each iteration except the last will cost at most $3n$ signals. The last iteration has also a "Terminate" message costing exactly n signals.

Hence, the total number of bits transmitted by *DoubleWait* will be at most

$$\mathbf{B}[DoubleWait] = 3\,c\,n\,\mathbf{j} + c\,n = 3\,c\,n\,\lceil g^{-1}(n) \rceil + c\,n,$$

where $c = O(1)$ is the number of bits necessary to distinguish between the "Restart," "Wait1," "Wait2," and "Terminate" messages.

Time Consider now the time costs of *DoubleWait*. Obviously, the time complexity of an iteration is directly affected by the values of the waiting functions f and h, which are in turn affected by the value $g(j)$ they must necessarily use in their definition. The overall time complexity is also affected by the number of iterations $\mathbf{j} = \lceil g^{-1}(n) \rceil$ that depends on the choice of the function g.

Let us first of all choose the waiting functions f and h. The ones we select are

$$f(\text{id}(x), j) = 2\, g(j)\, \text{id}(x), \tag{6.40}$$

which is the standard waiting function when the entities do not start at the same time and where $g(j)$ is used instead of n; and

$$h(\text{id}(x), j) = 2\, g(j)\, \text{id}(x) + g(j) - n_x(j), \tag{6.41}$$

which is the one that, we have already seen, makes "fooling" impossible. With these choices made, we can determine the amount of time the protocol uses until termination. In fact, it is immediate to verify (Exercise 6.6.53) that the number of time units till termination is *less* than

$$\mathbf{T}[DoubleWait] = 2(n-1) + (4\, i_{\min} + 2) \sum_{j=1}^{\mathbf{j}} g(j).$$

Again, this quantity depends solely on the choice of the guessing function g.

Trade-offs: Choosing The Guessing Function The results we have obtained for the number of bits and the amount of time are expressed in terms of the guessing function g. This is the only parameter we have not yet chosen. Before we proceed, let us examine what is the impact of such a choice.

The protocol terminates as soon as $g(j) \geq n$, that is, after $\mathbf{j} = \lceil g^{-1}(n) \rceil$ iterations. If we have a fast-growing function g, this will happen rather quickly, requiring few iterations. For example, if we choose $g(j) = 2\, g(j-1)$ (i.e., we double every time), then $\mathbf{j} = \lceil \log n \rceil$; we could choose something faster, say $g(j) = g(j-1)^2$ (i.e., we square every time) obtaining $\mathbf{j} = \lceil \log \log n \rceil$, or $g(j) = 2^{g(j-1)}$ (i.e., we exponentiate every time) obtaining $\mathbf{j} = \lceil \log^{\star} n \rceil$, where $\log^{\star}$ denotes the number of times you must take a log before the value becomes 1. So it would seem that to reduce the bit complexity, we need f to grow as fast as possible.

By contrast, the value $g(j)$ is a factor in the time complexity. In particular, the larger is $g(j)$, the more we have to wait. To understand how *bad* this impact can be, consider just the very last iteration $\mathbf{j}$ and assume that we just missed n, that is $g(\mathbf{j}-1) = n-1$. In this last iteration we wait for roughly $4\, \text{id}(x)\, g(\mathbf{j}) = 4\, \text{id}(x)\, g(\lceil g^{-1}(n) \rceil)$ time units.

$g(j)$	Bits	Time
$g(j) = 2g(j-1)$	$O(n \log n)$	$O(n \, i)$
$g(j) = g(j-1)^2$	$O(n \log \log n)$	$O(n^2 \, i)$
$g(j) = 2^{g(j-1)}$	$O(n \log^* n)$	$O(2^n \, i)$

FIGURE 6.27: Some of the trade-offs offered by the choice of g in *DoubleWait*.

This does not *appear* to be too bad; after all, $g(g^{-1}(n)) = n$. How much bigger than n can $g(\lceil g^{-1}(n) \rceil)$ be ? It depends on how fast g grows. If we choose $g(j) = 2 \, g(j-1)$, then $g(\lceil g^{-1}(n) \rceil) = 2 \, (n-1)$. However, if we choose $g(j) = g(j-1)^2$, then we have $g(\lceil g^{-1}(n) \rceil) = (n-1)^2$, and the choice $g(j) = 2^{g(j-1)}$ would give us $g(\lceil g^{-1}(n) \rceil) = 2^{(n-1)}$. Thus clearly, from the time-complexity point of view, we want a function g that does not grow very fast at all.

To help us in the decisional process, let us restrict to a class of functions. A function g is called *superincreasing* if for all $j > 1$

$$g(j) \geq \sum_{s=1}^{j-1} g(s). \qquad (6.42)$$

If we restrict ourselves to superincreasing functions, then the bit and time costs of *DoubleWait* become (Exercise 6.6.54)

$$\mathbf{B}[DoubleWait] \leq 3 \, c \, n \, \lceil g^{-1}(n) \rceil + c \, n \qquad (6.43)$$

$$\mathbf{T}[DoubleWait] \leq 2(n-1) + (8 \, i_{min} + 2) \, g(\lceil g^{-1}(n) \rceil). \qquad (6.44)$$

These bounds show the existence and the nature of the trade-off between time and bits. Some interesting choices are shown in Figure 6.27.

Examining the trade-off, we discover two important features of protocol *Double-Wait*:

1. the bit complexity is always *independent* of the entities values and, thus, bounded;
2. the time complexity is always *linear* in the smallest entity value.

Comparing the cost of *Double Wait* with the cost of the other ring election protocols that do not require knowledge of (an upperbound on) n, it is clear that *DoubleWait* outperforms *Speed* that has an unbounded bit complexity and a time complexity exponential in the input values. As for *SynchStages*, notice that by choosing $g(j) = 2g(j-1)$, *DoubleWait* has the same bit costs but a better time complexity (see Figure 6.28); with a different choice of g, it is possible to have the same time of *SynchStages* but with a smaller bit complexity (Exercise 6.6.55).

Protocol	Bits	Time	Notes
Speed	$O(n \log i)$	$O(n\, 2^i)$	
SynchStages	$O(n \log n)$	$O(n \log n\, i)$	
DoubleWait	$O(n \lceil g^{-1}(n) \rceil)$	$O(g(\lceil g^{-1}(n)\rceil)\, i)$	
Wait	$O(n)$	$O(n\, i)$	n known
Guess	$O(kn)$	$O(k\, n\, i^{1/k})$	n known
Symmetry	$O(n)$	$O(n)$	n known; randomized

FIGURE 6.28: Summary of Election techniques for synchronous rings.

Notice that the bit complexity can be *asymptotically* reduced to $O(n)$, matching the one obtained by the protocols, *Wait* and *Guess* that assume knowledge of an upperbound on n; clearly this is achieved at the expense of an exorbitant time complexity.

An exact $O(n)$ bit complexity with a reasonable time can, however, be achieved without knowing n using *DoubleWait* in conjunction with other techniques (Problem 6.6.9).

6.4 SYNCHRONIZATION PROBLEMS: RESET, UNISON, AND FIRING SQUAD

A fully synchronous system is by definition highly synchronized, so it might appear strange to talk about the need for *synchronization* in the system and the computational problems related to it. Regardless of the oddity, the need and the problems exist and are quite important.

There is first of all a synchronization problem related to the local clocks themselves. We know that in a synchronous environment all local clocks tick at the same time; however, they might not sign the same value. A synchronous system is said to be *in unison* if indeed all the clock values are the same. Notice that once a system is in unison, it will remain so unless the values of some clocks are locally altered. The *unison* problem is how to achieve such a state, possibly with several independent initiators.

Then there two synchronization problems related to the computational states of the entities. The first of them we have already seen, the *wake-up* or *reset* problem: All entities must enter a special state (e.g., *awake*); the process can be started by any number of entities independently. Notice that in this specification there is no mention of *when* an individual entity must enter such a state; in fact, in the solutions we have seen, entities become awake at different times.

Also, in the *firing squad* problem all entities must enter a special state (usually called *firing*), but they must do so *at the same time* and *for the first time*.

Firing squad synchronization is obviously stronger than reset. It is also stronger than unison: With unison, all entities arrive at a point where they are operating with the same clock value, and thus, in a sense, they *are* in the same "state" at the same time; however, the entities do not necessarily know when.

We are going to consider all three problems and examine their nature and interplay in some details. All of them will be considered under the standard set of restriction **R** plus obviously **Synch**.

6.4.1 Reset/Wake-Up

In *reset*, all entities must enter the same state within finite time. One important application of reset is when a distributed protocol is only initiated by a subset of the entities in the system, and we need all entities in the system to eventually begin executing the protocol. When reset is applied at the first step of a protocol, it is called *wake-up*. The *wake-up* or *reset* problem is a fundamental problem and we have extensively examined in asynchronous systems.

In fully synchronous systems it is sometimes also called *weak unison*; its solution is usually a preliminary step in larger computations (e.g, *Wait, Guess, DoubleWait*), and it is mostly used to keep the initiation times of the main computation bounded. For example, in protocol *Wait* applied to a network G (not necessarily a ring) of known diameter d, the initial wake-up ensures that all entities become awake within d time units from the start.

For computations that use *wake-up* as a tool, their cost obviously depends on the cost of the wake-up. Consider for example electing a leader in a *complete graph K_n* using the *waiting* technique. Not counting the wake-up, the election will cost only $n - 1$ bits, and it can be done in $4i_{min} + 1$ time units (see Equation 6.29); recall that in a complete graph, $d = 1$. Also, the wake-up can be done fast, in 1 time unit, but this can cost $O(n^2)$ bits. In other words, the dominant bit cost in the entire election protocol is the one of the wake-up, and it is unbearably high. Sometimes it is desirable to obtain wake-up protocols that are slower but use fewer transmissions.

In the rest of this section we will concentrate on the problem of wake-up in a *complete network*. The difficulty of waking up in *asynchronous* complete networks, which we discussed in Section 2.2, does not disappear in *synchronous* complete networks. In fact, in complete networks where the port numbers are arbitrary, $\Omega(n^2)$ signals must be sent in the worst case.

Theorem 6.4.1 *In a synchronous complete network with arbitrary labeling, wake-up requires $\Omega(n^2)$ messages in the worst case.*

To see why this is true, consider any wake-up protocol W that works for any complete networks regardless of the labeling. By contradiction, let W use $o(n^2)$ signals in *every* complete network of size n.

We will first consider a complete network K_n^1 with chordal labeling: A Hamiltonian cycle is identified, and a link (x, y) is labeled with the distance from x to y according to that cycle. The links incident on x will, thus, be labeled $1, 2, \ldots, n - 1$. On this network, we will consider the following execution:

- E_1: Every entity starts the wake-up simultaneously.

Concentrate on an entity x; let $L(x)$ be the set of port numbers on which a message was sent or received by x during this execution. Observe that because all entities start at the same time and because of the symmetry of the labeling, $L(x) = L(y)$ for all entities x and y. In fact, if x sends a signal via port number j, so will everybody else, and all of them will receive it from port number $n - j$. As protocol W is correct, within a finite number t of time time units, all the entities terminate. As, by assumption, every execution uses only $o(n^2)$ signals, $|L(x)| = l = o(n)$.

We construct now a complete network K_n^2 with a different labeling. In this network, we select $l + 1$ entities $x_0, x_1, \ldots, x_l$, and label the links between them with a "almost chordal" labeling using the labels in $L(x)$. All others links in the network are labeled arbitrarily without violating local orientation (this can always be done: Exercises 6.6.57 and 6.6.58). In this network consider the following execution:

- E_2: Only the selected entities will start and will do so simultaneously.

In this execution only few ($|L(x)| + 1 = o(n)$) entities start. From the point of view of these initiators, everything in this execution happens exactly as if they were in the other execution in the other network: Messages will be sent and received exactly from the same ports in the same steps in both executions. In particular, none of them will send a signal outside its "little clique." Hence, none of the other nodes will receive any signal; as those entities did not wake up spontaneously, this means that none of them will wake up at all. In particular, none of them will send any signal to the initiators; hence no initiator will receive a signal from outside the "little clique." Therefore, the initiators will act as if they are in K_n^1 and the execution is E_1; thus, at time t the initiators will all terminate the execution of the protocol. However, the majority of the nodes is not awake, nor will it ever become awake, contradicting the correctness of the protocol.

In other words, there is no correct wake-up protocol for the complete networks that will always require less than $O(n^2)$ transmissions.

Summarizing, regardless of the protocol and the techniques (e.g., communicator, pipeline, waiting, guessing, etc.), and regardless of the fact that we can use time as a computational tool, wake-up will cost $\Omega(n^2)$ signals in the worst case.

6.4.2 Unison

A synchronous system is said to be *in unison* if all the clock values are the same. The *unison* problem is how to achieve such a state, possibly with several independent initiators. Notice that once a system is in unison, it will remain so unless the values of some clocks are locally altered.

Let us examine a very simple protocol for achieving *unison*. Each entity will execute a sequence of stages, each taking one unit of time, starting either spontaneously or upon receiving a message from another entity.

Protocol *MaxWave*:

1. An initiator x starts by sending to all its neighbors the value of its local clock c_x.

2. A noninitiator y starts upon receiving messages from neighbors: It increases those values by one time unit, computes the largest among these values and its own clock value, resets its clock to such a maximum, and sends it to all its neighbors.

3. In stage $j > 1$, an entity (initiator or not) checks the clock values it receives from its neighbors and increases each one of them by one time unit; it then compares these values with each other as well as with its own. If the value of the local clock is maximum, no message is sent; else, the local clock is set to the largest of all values, and this value is sent to all the neighbors (that sent a smaller value).

Consider the largest value t_{max} among the local clocks when the protocol starts. It is not difficult to see that this value (increased by one unit at each instant of time) reaches every entity, and every entity will set its local clock to such a time value (Exercise 6.6.59). In other words, with this simple protocol, that we shall call *MaxWave*, the entities are guaranteed to operate in unison within finite time.

Let us discuss how long this process takes. Unison happens as soon as every entity whose initial clock value was smaller than t_{max} receives t_{max} (properly incremented). In the worst case, only one entity z has t_{max} at the beginning, and this entity is the last one to start. This value (properly incremented) has to reach every other entity in the network; this propagation will require at most a number of time units equal to the diameter d of the network; as z will start at most d time units after the first entity, this means that

the system operates in unison after at most 2d time units from the start.

How can an entity detect termination ? How does it know whether the system is now operating in unison ? Necessarily, an entity must know d (or an upperbound on d, e.g., n) to be able to know when the protocol is over.

The amount $2d$ is from the (global) time t the first entities started the execution of the protocol. An entity x starts participating at some (global) time $t(x) \geq t$. Thus, assuming that (an upperbound on) d is known a priori to all entities, at time $t(x) + 2d$ entity x knows for sure that the system is operating in unison. (this time can actually be reduced; see Exercise 6.6.60). In other words, entities may terminate at different times; their termination will, however, be within at most d time units from each other.

What is the number of messages that will be transmitted? A very rough overestimate is easily obtained by assuming that each entity x transmits to all its $|N(x)|$ neighbors in each of the $2d$ time units; this gives

$$2d \sum_x |N(x)| = 4\,d\,m.$$

This is a gross overestimate. In fact, once an entity receives the max time, it will transmit only in this step and no more. So the entities with the largest value will transmit to their neighbors only once; their neighbors will transmit only twice; in general, the entities at distance j from the entities with the largest value will transmit only $j + 1$ time. We also know that an entity does not send the max time to those neighbors from which it received it. The actual cost depends on the topology of the network and the actual initiation times. For some networks, the cost is not difficult to determine (Exercises 6.6.61 and 6.6.62).

Assuming that we are operating not on an arbitrary graph but on a *tree* (e.g., a previously constructed spanning tree of the network), we immediately have $m = n - 1$; we can make accurate measurements (Exercise 6.6.63).

In all this discussion, we have made an *implicit assumption* that the clock values we are sending are *bounded* and fit inside a message. However, time and thus the clock values are *unbounded*. In fact, clock values increase at each time unit; in our protocol, the transmitted values were increased at each time unit and the largest was propagated. Therefore, the solution we have described is *not feasible*.

To ensure that the values are bounded, we concentrate on the definition of the problem: Our goal is to achieve *unison*, that is, we want all local clocks to sign the same value. Notice that the definition does not care for what that value is, but only for that it is the same for all entities. Armed with this understanding, we make a very simple modification to the *MaxWave* protocol:

When an entity starts MaxWave, *it first resets its local clock to* 0.

In this way, the maximum value transmitted is at most $2d$ (Exercise 6.6.64), which is bounded.

6.4.3   Firing Squad

Firing squad synchronization is a problem stricter than unison. It requires that all entities enter a predefined special state, *firing*, for the first time simultaneously. More precisely, all the entities are initially in *active* state, and each *active* entity can at any time spontaneously become *excited*. The goal is to coordinate the entities so that, within finite time from the time the first entity becomes *excited*, all entities become *firing* simultaneously and for the first time.

In its original form, the problem was described for synchronous cellular automata (i.e., computational entities with $O(1)$ memory) placed in a line of unknown length n, and where the leftmost entity in the line is the sole initiator, known as the "general". Note that as cellular automata only have a constant memory size, they cannot represent (nor count up to) nonconstant values such as n or d.

We are interested in solving this problem in our setting, where the entities have at least $O(\log n)$ bits of local memory, and thus they can count up to n. Again we are looking for a protocol that can work in any network; observe that the entities need to know or to compute (an upperbound on) d to terminate.

If the network is a *tree*, or we have available a *spanning tree* of the network, then a simple efficient solution exists, on the basis of *saturation* (Exercise 6.6.68). This protocol uses at most $3n - 2$ signals and $n - 2$ messages each containing a value of at most d, for a total of $O(n \log n)$ bits; the time is at most $3d - 3$. The bit complexity can be reduced to $O(n)$ still using only $O(n)$ time (Exercise 6.6.69). That is, firing squad can be solved in networks with an available spanning tree in optimal time and bits.

What happens if there is no spanning tree available? Even worse, what happens if no spanning tree is constructible (e.g., in anonymous network)? The problem can still be solved. To do so, let us explore the relationship between *firing squad* and *unison*. First observe that as all entities become *firing* simultaneously, if each entity resets its local clock when it becomes *firing*, all local clocks will have the same value 0 at the same time. In other words,

> *any solution to the firing squad problem will also solve the unison problem.*

The converse is not necessarily true. In unison, all the local clocks will at some point sign the same value; however, the entities might not know exactly when this happens. They might become aware (i.e., terminate) at different times; but for firing squad synchronization we need that they make a decision *simultaneously*, that is, with no difference in time.

Surprisingly, protocol *MaxWave* actually solves the *firing squad* problem in networks where no spanning tree is available. To see why this is true, consider the modification we made to ensure that the transmitted values are bounded: When an entity starts the protocol, it *first* resets its local clock to 0.

Let t be the global time when the protocol starts, that is, t is the time when the first entities rest their clock to 0. We will call such entities "initiators." Two simple observations (Exercises 6.6.70 and 6.6.71):

Property 6.4.1

1. *If a message originated by an initiator reaches entity y at time $t + w$, then the value of that message (incremented by 1) is exactly w.*
2. *Regardless of whether y has already independently started or starts now, the current value of its local clock will be smaller than w; thus, y will set its clock in unison with the clocks of the initiators.*

Summarizing, every noninitiator receives a message from the initiators, and as soon as an entity receives a message originated by the initiators (i.e., carrying the max reset time), it will become in unison with the initiators. Thus, an entity x is in unison with the initiators at time $t + d(x, I)$, where $d(x, I)$ denotes the distance between x and the closest initiator. As $d(x, I) \leq d$, this means that

> *all clocks will be in unison after at most d time units from the start.*

Once the clocks are in unison, unless someone resets them, they keep on being in unison. As nobody is resetting the clocks again, this means that all entities will be in unison at time $t + d$. The value of the clocks at that time is exactly d.

This means that when the reset local clock signs time d, the entity knows that indeed the entire system is in unison; if the entity enters state *firing* at this time, it is guaranteed that all other entities will do the same simultaneously, and for the first time, solving the firing squad problem.

Summarizing, protocol *MaxWave* solves the firing squad problem in d time units:

$$\mathbf{T}[MaxWave] = d, \qquad (6.45)$$

and this is worst-case optimal. The number of messages is less than $2\,d\,m$ and each contains at most $\log d$ bit, that is,

$$\mathbf{B}[MaxWave] < 2\,m\,d\,\log d. \qquad (6.46)$$

The bit complexity can be reduced at the expense of time, by using *communicators* to communicate the content of the messages (Exercises 6.6.66 and 6.6.67).

6.5 BIBLIOGRAPHICAL NOTES

Some of the work on synchronous computing was done very early on in the context of *Cellular Automata* and *Systolic Arrays*; in particular, *pipeline* is a common computational tool in VLSI systems (which include systolic arrays).

In the framework of distributed computing, the first important result on (fault-free) synchronous computations is protocol *Speed* designed by Greg Frederickson and Nancy Lynch [9], and independently by Paul Vitanyi [26] (whose version of the protocol actually works with a weaker form of full synchrony, called Archimedean Time Assumption or ATA).

This result has alerted algorithmic researchers to the existence of the field. Some of the first improvements were due to Eli Gafni [11] and Alberto Marchetti-Spaccamela [17], who reduced the time but still kept the unbounded bit complexity. Subsequent improvements to bounded bit complexity and to reduced time costs were obtained by using (and combining) communicators, waiting and guessing.

Communicators have been used for a while. The so-called "one-bit" protocol (e.g., see Problem 6.6.1) was originally proposed and used by Hagit Attiya, Marc Snir, and Manfred Warmuth [3] and later rediscovered by Amotz Bar-Noi, Joseph Naor, and Moni Naor [4]. The size communicator is due to Bernd Schmeltz [24]. C_2 is "folk" knowledge, while C_3 is due to Paul Vitanyi [unpublished]. The optimal k-communicators have been designed by Una-May O'Reilly and Nicola Santoro [20].

The first combined use of communicators and pipeline is due to B. Schmeltz [24]. The computations in trees using pipeline are due to Paola Flocchini [8]. The asynchronous-to-synchronous *transform* is due to Una-May O'Reilly and Nicola Santoro [19].

The *waiting* technique was independently discovered by Eli Gafni [11], who used it to reduce the time costs of *Speed*, and by Nicola Santoro and Doron Rotem [23], who designed protocol *Wait*. Protocol *Guess* has been designed by Jan van Leeuwen, Nicola Santoro, Jorge Urrutia, and Shmuel Zaks [16]. *Double Waiting* is due to Mark Overmars and Nicola Santoro [21].

The first *bit-optimal* election protocol for rings is due to Hans Bodlaender and Gerard Tel [5]; it does, however, require exponential time. The time has been subsequently drastically reduced (Problem 6.6.9) without increasing the bit complexity by Mark Overmars and Nicola Santoro [21].

The problem of *symmetry breaking* was first studied for rings by Alon Itai and Michael Rodeh [14] and for other networks by Doron Rotem and Nicola Santoro [23]. The simpler and more efficient protocol *Symmetry* has been designed by Greg Frederickson and Nicola Santoro [10]. These results have been extended to environments with ATA-synchrony by Paul Spirakis and Basil Tampakas [25]. The *maximum-finding* protocol for rings of Problem 6.6.7 has been designed by Paola Alimonti, Paola Flocchini, and Nicola Santoro [1].

The trade-offs for *wake-up* in complete graphs with chordal labeling are due to Amos Israeli, Evangelos Kranakis, Danny Krizanc, and Nicola Santoro [13]. The *unison* problem has been first studied (in a slightly different context) by Shimon Even and Sergio Rajsbaum [6, 7], and in the context of self-stabilization by Mohamed Gouda and Ted Herman [12]. Bounding the message size was studied by Anish Arora, Shlomi Dolev, and Mohamed Gouda [2], always in the context of self-stabilization.

The *firing squad* problem was originally proposed for Cellular Automata by J. Myhill and reported by E. Moore [18]. In our context, the problem was first studied for synchronous trees by Raul Ramirez and Nicola Santoro [22]; the optimal solution has been designed by Ephraim Korach, Doron Rotem, and Nicola Santoro [15]. The universal protocol *MaxWave* is a simple extension of existing unison solutions.

6.6 EXERCISES, PROBLEMS, AND ANSWERS

6.6.1 Exercises

Exercise 6.6.1 Determine the number of messages of protocol *Speed* if the waiting function is $f(v) = c^v$, for an integer $c > 2$.

Exercise 6.6.2 Determine the number of messages of protocol *Speed* if the waiting function is $f(v) = v^c$, for an integer $c > 1$.

Exercise 6.6.3 Modify protocol *Speed* so that even if the entities do not start simultaneously, a leader is elected with $O(n)$ messages.

Exercise 6.6.4 Prove that Protocol *Speed* requires $2^i n$ time units.

Exercise 6.6.5 Modify protocol C_2 so that it communicates any integer i, *positive or negative*, transmitting 2 bits and $O(|i|)$ time units.

Exercise 6.6.6 Construct a protocol R_2 that communicates any positive integer I transmitting 2 bits and only $2 + \frac{I}{4}$ time units.

Exercise 6.6.7   Consider protocol *TwoBits* when each packet contains $c > 1$ bits. Use the content of the packets to convey information about the value i to be communicated. Determine the time costs that can be achieved.

Exercise 6.6.8   Construct a protocol R_3 that communicates any positive integer I transmitting 3 bits and only $\lfloor \sqrt[3]{I} \rfloor + 3$ time units.

Exercise 6.6.9   Consider a system where packets contain $c > 1$ bits. Modify protocol R_3 using the content of the packets so as to reduce the time costs. Determine the amount of savings that can be achieved.

Exercise 6.6.10   Prove that the communicator described in Section 6.2.1 uses at most $O(i^{\frac{1}{k}})$ time units.

Exercise 6.6.11   Use the content of the transmitted bits so as to reduce the time costs of the communicator described in Section 6.2.1. Show how a time cost of at most $(k - 1)(I/4)^{\frac{1}{k-1}} + k$ clock ticks can be achieved.

Exercise 6.6.12   Prove that communicator $Order_k$ uses $f(I, k) + k + 1$ time to communicate I, where $f(I, k)$ is the smallest integer t such that $I \leq \binom{t + k}{k}$.

Exercise 6.6.13   Prove that communicator $Order_{k+}$ uses $g(I, k) + k + 1$ time to communicate I, where $g(I, k)$ is the smallest integer t such that $I \leq 2^{k+1} \binom{t + k}{k}$.

Exercise 6.6.14   Prove that $\omega(t, k) = \binom{t + q}{q}$.

Exercise 6.6.15   Prove that any protocol using $k + 1$ corruptible bits to communicate values from U requires

$$\left(f(|U|, k)^2 \left(|U| - \sum_{0 \leq i < t} i \binom{i + k - 1}{k - 1} \right) + \sum_{0 \leq i < f(|U|, k)} i \binom{i + k - 1}{k} \right) |U|^{-1}$$

additional time *on the average*.

Exercise 6.6.16   Prove that protocol $Order_k$ is average-case optimal.

Exercise 6.6.17   Let $\beta(t, k)$ denote the size of the largest set for which the two-party communication problem can always be solved transmitting $k + 1$ reliable bits and at most t additional time units. Prove that $\beta(t, k) = 2^{k+1} \binom{t + k}{k}$.

Exercise 6.6.18   Let $r(w, k)$ denote the number of additional time units needed in the worst case to solve the two-party communication problem for Z_w with $k + 1$ bits, in absence of corruptions. Let $\beta(t, k)$ be as in Exercise 6.6.17, and let $g(w, k)$ be the smallest integer t such that $\beta(t, k) \geq x$. Prove that $r(w, k) = g(w, k)$.

Exercise 6.6.19   Let $\beta(t, k)$ be as in Exercise 6.6.17, and let $g(w, k)$ be the smallest integer t such that $\beta(t, k) \geq x$. Prove that $r(w, k) = g(w, k)$. Prove that any solution protocol using $k + 1$ reliable bits to communicate values from U requires

$$\frac{\Sigma_i \binom{i + k - 1}{k - 1}}{2^{k+1} \binom{g(|U|, k) + k}{k}} \text{ time on the average.}$$

Exercise 6.6.20   Prove that protocol Order$+_k$ is average-case optimal.

Exercise 6.6.21   ($\star$) A communicator is *monotonically increasing* if, whenever $I > J$, the communication sequence for I is lexicographically smaller than that for J. Communicators Order$_k$ are optimal and corruption tolerant; however, they are *not* monotonically increasing for $k > 2$; thus, they cannot be used in pipeline for computing the minimum. Determine a class *MonotoneOrder$_k$* of optimal corruption-tolerant communicators that *are* monotonically increasing.

Exercise 6.6.22   Communicators Order$+_k$ are optimal but *not* monotonically increasing for $k > 2$; thus, they can not be used in pipeline for computing the minimum. Determine a class *MonotoneOrder$+_k$* of optimal communicators that *are* monotonically increasing.

Exercise 6.6.23   Write a protocol for finding the largest value in a chain using the *2-bit communicator* and pipeline. Prove its correctness.

Exercise 6.6.24   Minimum-Finding in Pipeline. Write a protocol for finding the *smallest* value in a chain using the *2-bit communicator* and pipeline. Prove its correctness. Determine its costs.

Exercise 6.6.25   Sum-Finding in Pipeline. Write a protocol for finding the *sum* of all the values in a chain using the *2-bit communicator* and pipeline. Prove its correctness. Determine its costs.

Exercise 6.6.26   Protocol *SynchStages* is the transformation of *Stages* using communicator *TwoBits*. Add *pipeline* to this protocol to convey information from a *candidate* to a neighboring one. Prove its correctness. Analyze its costs; in particular, determine the reduction in time with respect to the nonpipelined version.

Exercise 6.6.27   Modify protocol *Wait* so that it finds the minimum value only among the initiators.

Exercise 6.6.28 Determine the *smallest* waiting function that allows protocol *Wait* to work correctly without simultaneous initiation: (a) in a unidirectional ring; (b) in a bidirectional ring.

Exercise 6.6.29 Determine the *smallest* waiting function that allows protocol *Wait* to work correctly with simultaneous initiation: (1) in a $a \times b$ mesh; (2) in a $a \times b$ torus; (3) in a k-dimensional hypercube; (4) in a complete network.

Exercise 6.6.30 Determine the *smallest* waiting function that allows protocol *Wait* to work correctly *without* simultaneous initiation: (1) in a $a \times b$ mesh; (2) in a $a \times b$ torus; (3) in a k-dimensional hypercube.

Exercise 6.6.31 Prove that protocol *Wait* would work even if a quantity $\bar{n} \geq n$ is used instead of n.

Exercise 6.6.32 Determine under what conditions protocol *Wait* would work if a quantity $n > \bar{n}$ is used instead of n in the waiting function.

Exercise 6.6.33 Assuming distinct initial values, characterize what would happen to protocol *Wait* in a ring network if each entity x uses $2\mathrm{id}(x)^2$ as its waiting function. In particular, determine under what conditions the protocol would certainly work.

Exercise 6.6.34 Under the conditions of Exercise 6.6.33, show how all the entities can efficiently detect whether the protocol does not work.

Exercise 6.6.35 Determine the cost of computing the *AND* of all input values in a synchronous ring of known size n using protocol *Waiting*.

Exercise 6.6.36 Describe how to efficiently use protocol *Wait* to compute the *OR* of the input values in a synchronous ring of known size n. Determine its cost.

Exercise 6.6.37 Modify protocol *Symmetry* so that it works efficiently in a bidirectional square *torus* of known dimension. Determine its exact costs.

Exercise 6.6.38 Modify protocol *Symmetry* so that it works efficiently in a unidirectional square *torus* of known dimension. Determine its costs.

Exercise 6.6.39 Prove that with simultaneous initiation, protocol *Symmetry* can be modified so as to work correctly in every network of known girth. (*Hint:* Use the girth instead of n in the waiting function.)

Exercise 6.6.40 Determine the complexity of protocol *Symmetry* if we use in random selection criteria $b = n$ and choose each value with the same probability $\frac{1}{n}$.

Exercise 6.6.41 Modify protocol *Decide* so as to compute the OR of the input values in a synchronous ring of known size n. Prove its correctness and determine its cost.

Exercise 6.6.42 Write protocol *Guess* and implement it; throughly test your implementation.

Exercise 6.6.43 Show how to find i_{min} with k overestimates using $q = k \, M^{1/k}$ questions.

Exercise 6.6.44 Show how we can always win the guessing game in an interval of size $2^q - 1$ with q question if they are all allowed to be overestimates.

Exercise 6.6.45 Show how to obtain a unique solution to the recurrence relation of expression 6.33.

Exercise 6.6.46 Determine a function g to bound i_{min} so that the total time for finding with k overestimates is at most $2 \, h(i_{min}, \, k) - 1$.

Exercise 6.6.47 Modify subprotocol *Decide(p)* so that it will work in every network, regardless of its topology. Assume that an upperbound on the diameter of the network is known a priori. Prove its correctness.

Exercise 6.6.48 Modify subprotocol *Decide(p)* so that protocol *Guess* works correctly even if the entities do not start simultaneously.

Exercise 6.6.49 Prove that, in *DoubleWait*, if x is being "fooled," then both the "Wait1" and the "Wait2" message it receives are sent by the same entity.

Exercise 6.6.50 Let the entities start the jth iteration of *DoubleWait* within $n - 1$ time units from each other. Prove that the entity with the smallest value becomes *leader* and all other will become *defeated* in that iteration.

Exercise 6.6.51 Let the entities start the jth iteration of *DoubleWait* within $n - 1$ time units from each other. Prove that if an entity x becomes *leader* in this iteration, then $g(j) \geq n > g(j - 1)$.

Exercise 6.6.52 Let the entities start the jth iteration of *DoubleWait* within $n - 1$ time units from each other. Prove that if $g(j) < n$, then all entities start the $(j + 1)$th iteration within $n - 1$ time units from each other.

Exercise 6.6.53 Prove that the time used by protocol *DoubleWait*, with the choices of f and h specified by Expressions 6.40 and 6.41, is at most $2(n - 1) + (4 i_{min} + 2) \sum_{j=1}^{j} g(j)$.

Exercise 6.6.54   Consider protocol *DoubleWait*, where f and h are as in Expressions 6.40 and 6.41, and g is superincreasing. Prove that the time is at most $2(n-1) + (8 i_{min} + 2) g(\lceil g^{-1}(n) \rceil)$.

Exercise 6.6.55   Consider protocol *DoubleWait*, where f and h are as in Expressions 6.40 and 6.41. Determine the number of bits if the time is $O(n \log n \, i)$.

Exercise 6.6.56   (**) Determine whether or not there is a choice of g that makes *DoubleWait* more efficient than *SynchStages* in both time and bits.

Exercise 6.6.57   Let $L = (a_1, b_1), \ldots, (a_k, b_k)$ be the k pairs of distinct labels $a_i, b_i \in \{1, \ldots, n\}$. Consider now a complete network of n nodes; in this network, select $2k + 1$ nodes $x_0, x_1, , \ldots, x_{2k}$. Show that it is always possible

1. to label the links between these nodes only with pairs from L (e.g., the link (x_0, x_1) will be labeled a_3 at x_0 and b_3 at x_1), and
2. to label all others links in the network with labels in $\{1, \ldots, n\}$ without violating local orientation anywhere.

Exercise 6.6.58   Consider exactly the same question as in Exercise 6.6.57, where, however, n is even and exactly one pair in L, say (a_1, b_1) is composed of identical labels, i.e., $a_1 = b_1$.

Exercise 6.6.59   Prove that in protocol *MaxWave*, the largest of the local clock values (when the execution starts) will reach (properly increased) every entity, and each entity will set its local clock to such a (properly increased) time value.

Exercise 6.6.60   Consider protocol *MaxWave* when the entities do not start necessarily at the same time, and let d be known. Let t be the (global) time the first entities start the execution of the protocol and let $t(x) \geq t$ be the global time when x starts. Modify the protocol so that (eventhough x does not know t) at time $t + 2d$ it knows for sure that the system is operating in unison.

Exercise 6.6.61   Determine the message cost of protocol *MaxWave*

a. in a unidirectional ring,
b. in a bidirectional ring.

You may assume that n is known.

Exercise 6.6.62   Determine the message cost of protocol *MaxWave* in a k-dimensional hypercube.

Exercise 6.6.63   Determine the worst-case and average-case message costs of protocol *MaxWave* in a tree network.

Exercise 6.6.64 Let, in protocol*MaxWave*, each entity reset its local clock to 0 when it starts the protocol. Prove that in this way, the maximum value transmitted is at most $2d$.

Exercise 6.6.65 Consider the unison protocol *MinWave* where instead of setting the clocks to and propagating the largest value, we set the clock to and propagate the *smallest* value. Prove correctness, termination, and costs of protocol*MinWave*.

Exercise 6.6.66 Determine the bit and time costs of protocol *MaxWave* if the content of a message is communicated using the *2-bit communicator*.

Exercise 6.6.67 Determine the bit and time costs of protocol *MaxWave* if the content of a message is communicated using a *k-bit communicator*.

Exercise 6.6.68 Show how to solve the firing squad problem on a tree using at most $4n - 4$ messages, each containing a value of at most d, and in time at most $3d - 3$.

Exercise 6.6.69 ($\star$) Show how to solve the firing squad problem on a tree using only $O(n)$ *bits* in $O(d)$ time.

Exercise 6.6.70 In protocol *MaxWave*, let a message originated by an initiator reach another entity y at time $t + w$. Prove that the value of that message (incremented by 1) is exactly w.

Exercise 6.6.71 In protocol *MaxWave*, let a message originated by an initiator reach another entity y at time $t + w$. Prove that regardless of whether y has already independently started or starts now, the current value of its reset local clock will be *smaller* than w; thus, y will set its clock in unison with the clocks of the initiators.

6.6.2 Problems

Problem 6.6.1 (OneBit Protocol) Determine under what conditions information can be communicated using only 1 bit and describe the corresponding *OneBit* protocol.

Problem 6.6.2 (BitPattern Communicator) Consider the class of communicators that use a bit set to 1 to denote termination. Determine the minimum cost that can be achieved and design the corresponding protocol.

Problem 6.6.3 (2-BitPattern Communicator) ($\star$) Consider the class of communicators that use two successive transmissions of 1 to denote termination. Determine the minimum cost that can be achieved and design the corresponding protocol.

Problem 6.6.4 (Size Communicator) Consider the class of communicators that use the first quantum to communicate the total number of bits that will be transmitted.

Determine the minimum cost that can be achieved and design the corresponding protocol.

Problem 6.6.5 (Pipeline in Trees: Max) Write the protocol for finding the *maximum* of all the values in a tree using the *2-bit communicator* and pipeline. Prove its correctness. Determine its costs.

Problem 6.6.6 (Pipeline in Trees: Min) Write the protocol for finding the *minimum* of all the values in a tree using the *2-bit communicator* and pipeline. Prove its correctness. Determine its costs.

Problem 6.6.7 (Maximum Finding I)   (★★) Consider a ring of known size n. Each entity has a positive integer value; they all start at the same time, but their values are not necessarily distinct. The *maximum-finding* problem is the one of having all the entities with the largest value become *maximum* and all the other *small*. Design a protocol to solve the maximum-finding problem in time linear in i_{max} using at most $O(n \log n)$ bits.

Problem 6.6.8 (Maximum Finding II)   (★★★) Determine whether the *maximum-finding* problem in a ring of known size can be solved in time linear in i_{max} with $O(n)$ bits.

Problem 6.6.9 (Bit-Optimal Election I)   (★★) Show how to elect a leader in a ring with only $O(n)$ bits without knowing n. Possibly the time should be polynomial in i or exponential in n. *(Hint: Use a single iteration of* DoubleWait *as a preprocessing phase.)*

Problem 6.6.10 (Bit-Optimal Election II)   (★★★) Determine whether or not it is possible to elect a leader without knowing n with $\Theta(n)$ bits in time *sublinear* in i, that is, to match the complexity achievable when n is known.

Problem 6.6.11 (Unison without knowing d)   (★★) Consider the unison problem when there is no known upperbound on the diameter d of the network. Prove or disprove that in this case the unison problem *cannot* be solved with explicit termination.

Problem 6.6.12   (Firing in a Line of CA with 6 States)   (★★) Finite cellular automata (CA) can only have a constant memory size, which means they cannot store a counter. The goal is thus to solve the firing squad problem with the least amount of time and to do so with the least amount of memory. The measure we use for the memory is the max number of different values that can to be stored in the memory, and it is called the *number of states* of the automaton. Consider a line of CA with only one initiator (located at the end of the line). Develop a solution that uses only six states.

Problem 6.6.13 (Firing in a Line of CA with 5 States)   (★★★) Consider a line of CA with only one initiator (located at the end of the line). Develop a solution using only five states or prove it can not be done.

6.6.3 Answers to Exercises

Answer to Exercise 6.6.4

Consider the entity x that will become *leader*. It did spontaneously initiate the protocol; its message traveled along the ring at the speed of $f(i_x) + 1 = 2^{i_x} + 1$, where i_x is the input value of x; hence, its message returned after $(n-1)(2^{i_x} + 1)$ time units; another n time units are required for the notification message.

Answer to Exercise 6.6.6

Let

$$b_0 = \begin{cases} 0 \text{ if } I \text{ even} \\ 1 \text{ if } I \text{ odd} \end{cases}.$$

If we were to encode I in the sequence $\langle b_1 \mid \lfloor \frac{I}{2} \rfloor \mid b_0 \rangle$, the *receiver* can reconstruct I using as a decoding function $decode(b_0 \mid q_1 \mid b_1) = 2q_1 + b_0$, where b_0 is used as an integer value. In this way, we have effectively cut the quantum of time in half: The waiting time becomes $2 + \frac{I}{2}$. It can be actually further reduced. Let

$$b_1 = \begin{cases} 0 \text{ if } \lfloor \frac{I}{2} \rfloor \text{ even} \\ 1 \text{ if } \lfloor \frac{I}{2} \rfloor \text{ odd} \end{cases}.$$

If we were to encode I in the sequence $\langle b_1 \mid \lfloor \frac{\lfloor \frac{I}{2} \rfloor}{2} \rfloor \mid b_0 \rangle$, the *receiver* can reconstruct I using as a decoding function $decode(b_0 \mid q_1 \mid b_1) = 2(2q_1 + b_1) + b_0$, where both b_0 and b_1 are treated as integer values. The waiting time then becomes $2 + \frac{I}{4}$.

Answer to Exercise 6.6.6

Consider the following communicator $\mathcal{R}_3$: The first bit, b_0, is used to indicate whether $y = \lfloor \sqrt{I} \rfloor$ is odd; the second bit, b_2, is used to indicate whether $z = I - \lfloor \sqrt{I} \rfloor^2$ is odd; the third bit, b_3, is used to indicate whether $w = \lfloor \frac{z}{2} \rfloor$ is odd. The two quanta waited are $q_1 = \lfloor \frac{y}{2} \rfloor$ and $q_2 = \lfloor \frac{w}{2} \rfloor$. To obtain I the receiver simply computes $(2q_1 + b_0)^2 + (4q_2 + 2b_1 + b_2)$, where the bits are treated as integer values. For example, if $I = 7387$, we have $y = 85$, $z = 162$, and $w = 81$; thus, the two quanta are $q_1 = 42$ and $q_2 = 40$, while the bits are $b_0 = 1$, $b_1 = 0$, and $b_2 = 1$. The quantity $(2q_0 + b_0)^2 + (4q_1 + 2b_1 + b_2)$ computed by the receiver is indeed I. Notice that $q_0 = \lfloor \frac{y}{2} \rfloor = \left\lfloor \frac{\lfloor \sqrt{I} \rfloor}{2} \right\rfloor$ and, as $z \leq 2\lfloor \sqrt{I} \rfloor$, $q_1 = \lfloor \frac{w}{2} \rfloor = \left\lfloor \frac{\lfloor \frac{z}{2} \rfloor}{2} \right\rfloor \leq \frac{\lfloor \sqrt{I} \rfloor}{2}$; thus, this protocol has time-bits complexity at most $\langle 3, \lfloor \sqrt{I} \rfloor + 3 \rangle$.

The protocol is correct (Exercise 6.6.11). Exactly $k - 1$ quanta will be used, and k bits will be transmitted. It is easy to verify that $I_{2i+1} \leq \lfloor \sqrt{I_i} \rfloor$; since $I_{2i} = \lfloor \sqrt{I_i} \rfloor$

by definition, it as follows that each quantum is at most $\left(\frac{x}{4}\right)^{\frac{1}{k-1}}$. Hence, the time complexity is at most

$$(k-1)(I/4)^{\frac{1}{k-1}} + k.$$

Partial Answer to Exercise 6.6.11

The encoding of I can be defined recursively as follows:

$$E(I) = \langle b_0 \mid E(I_1) \mid b_{k-1}\rangle,$$

where

$$E(I_i) = \begin{cases} E(I_{2i}) \mid b_i \mid E(I_{2i+1}) & \text{if } 1 < i < k-1 \\ \text{quantum of length } I_i & \text{if } k-1 \le i \le 2k-3 \end{cases}$$

$$I_1 = \left\lfloor \frac{\left\lfloor \frac{I}{2} \right\rfloor}{2} \right\rfloor, I_{2i} = \lfloor \sqrt{I_i} \rfloor, I_{2i+1} = \left\lfloor \frac{I_i - I_{2i}^2}{2} \right\rfloor, \text{ and}$$

$$b_i = I_{2i+1} \bmod 2, b_{k-1} = \left\lfloor \frac{I}{2} \right\rfloor \bmod 2.$$

To obtain I, the *receiver* will recursively compute $I_i = I_{2i}^2 + (2I_{2i+1} + b_i)$ until I_1 is determined; then, $I = 4I_1 + 2b_{k-1} + b_1$.

Answer to Exercise 6.6.14

We want to prove that $\omega(t, k) = \binom{t+q}{q}$. Let $w = \omega(t, k)$; by definition, it must be possible to communicate any element in $Z_w = \{0, 1, \dots, w\}$ using $q = k-1$ distinguished quanta requiring at most time t. In other words, $\omega(t, q+1)$ is equal to the number of distinct q-tuples $\langle t_1, t_2, \dots, t_q \rangle$ of positive integers such that $\sum_{1 \le i \le k} t_i \le t$. Given a positive integer x, let $T_k[x]$ denote the number of compositions of x of size q, that is,

$$T_q[x] = |\{\langle x_1, x_2, \dots, x_q \rangle : \sum x_j = x, x_j \in Z^+\}|.$$

As $T_q[x] = \binom{x+q-1}{q-1}$, it follows that

$$\omega(t, q+1) = \sum_i T_q[i] = \sum_i \binom{i+q-1}{q-1} = \binom{t+q}{q},$$

which proves that $\omega(t, k) = \binom{t+q}{q}$.

Answer to Exercise 6.6.15

Let $f(|U|, q) = t$. First of all we prove that for any solution protocol P for $C_{q+1}(U)$, there exists a partition of U into $t + 1$ disjoint subsets $U_0, U_1, \ldots, U_t$, such that

1. $|U_i| = \dbinom{i + q - 1}{q - 1}$, $0 \leq i < t$, $|U_t| \leq \dbinom{t + q - 1}{q - 1}$,

2. the time $P(x)$ required by P to communicate $x \in U_i$ is $P(x) \geq i$.

As $f(|U|, q) = t$, by Equation 6.9, U is the largest set for which the two-party communication problem can always be solved using $b = q + 1$ transmissions and at most t additional time units. Given a protocol P for $C_{q+1}(U)$, order the elements $x \in U$ according to the time $P(x)$ required by P to communicate them; let $\ddot{U}$ be the corresponding ordered set. Define $\ddot{U}_i$ to be the subset composed of the elements of $\ddot{U}$ whose ranking, with respect to the ordering defined above, is in the range $\sum_{0 \leq j < i} \dbinom{j + q - 1}{q - 1}$, $\sum_{0 \leq j \leq i} \dbinom{j + q - 1}{q - 1}$. As $f(|U|, q) = t$, it follows that $|\ddot{U}_i| = \dbinom{i + q - 1}{q - 1}$ for $0 \leq i < t$ and $|\ddot{U}_t| \leq \dbinom{t + q - 1}{q - 1}$, which proves part 1.

We will now show that for every $x \in \ddot{U}_i$, $P(x) \geq i$. By contradiction, let this not be the case. Let $j \leq t$ be the smallest index for which there exists an $x \in \ddot{U}_i$ such that $P(x) < j$. This implies that there exists a $j\prime < t$ such that $|\{x \in U : P(x) = j\prime\}| > \dbinom{j\prime + q - 1}{k - 1}$. In other words, in protocol P, the number of elements that are uniquely identified using q quanta for a total of $j\prime$ time is greater than the number $T_q[j\prime] = \dbinom{j\prime + q - 1}{q - 1}$ compositions of $j\prime$ of size k: a clear contradiction. Hence, for every $x \in \ddot{U}_i$, $P(x) \geq i$, proving part 2. At this point, the rest of the proof easily follows.

Answer to Exercise 6.6.17

The number of distinct assignment of values to $q + 1$ distinguished bits is 2^{q+1}. The number of distinct q-tuples $\langle t_1, t_2, t_q \rangle$ of positive integers such that $\sum_j t_j \leq t$ is $\omega(t, k)$ (from 6.9). Therefore, $\beta(t, k) = 2^{q+1} \omega(t, k) = 2^{q+1} \dbinom{t + q}{q}$.

Partial answer to Exercise 6.6.19

First prove the following: Let $\mu(|U|, q) = t$; for any solution protocol P using k reliable bits to communicate values from U, there exists a partition of U into $t + 1$

disjoint subsets $U_0, U_1, \ldots, U_t$, such that

1. $|U_i| = 2^{q+1} \begin{pmatrix} i+q-1 \\ q-1 \end{pmatrix}, 0 \le i < t$, and $|U_t| = 2^{q+1} \begin{pmatrix} t+q-1 \\ q-1 \end{pmatrix}$,

2. the time $P(x)$ required by P to communicate $x \in U_i$ is $P(x) \ge i$.

Then the rest of the proof easily follows.

Answer to Exercise 6.6.44
Hint: Use *binary search.*

Answer to Exercise 6.6.49
Let x be fooled and incorrectly become *leader* at the end of the jth iteration. According to the algorithm the only way that x has for becoming *leader* is the following:

1. At time $t(x, j)$, x starts waiting for $f(x, j)$. Note that during this time x must not receive any message to become a leader later.
2. At time $t(x, j) + f(x, j)$, x sends a "Wait1" message and becomes checking.
3. At time $t(x, j) + f(x, j) + n_x(j)$, it receives a Wait1 message and starts the second waiting. Note that during this time, x must not receive any message in order to become a leader later.
4. At time $t(x, j) + f(x, j) + n_x(j) + h(x, j)$, it sends a "Wait2" message and becomes checking-again.
5. At time $t(x, j) + f(x, j) + g(x, j) + 2n_x(j)$, it receives a "Wait2" message and becomes *leader.*

Let $y \neq x$ and $z \neq x$ be the entities that originated the "Wait1" and "Wait2" messages, respectively, received by x. Notice that to originate these messages, y and z can not be *passive* (they might become so later, though).

The "Wait1" message is sent by y only after it successfully finished the waiting $f(y, j)$ time units. That is, the "Wait1" message will be sent by y at time $t(y, j) + f(y, j)$. This message requires $d(y, x)$ unit times to reach x. Therefore, $t(x, j) + f(x, j) + m(x, j) = t(y, j) + f(y, j) + d(y, x)$.

The "Wait2" message will arrive at x at time $t(x, j) + f(x, j) + 2m(x, j) + g(x, j)$.

By contradiction, let $z \neq y$. Consider first the case when y is located in the path from z to x. In this case, the "Wait2" message originated by z will reach y before x. If y is still waiting to receive a "Wait1" message, the reception of this not forward the "Wait2" message and "Wait2" message will alert it to something wrong; it will not forward the "Wait2" message to x and send a "Restart" instead, and thus, x will not become *leader.* Therefore, z is located on the path from y to

x. In this case, the "Wait1" message originated by y reaches z before arriving to x. As we have assumed that this message will arrive to x, it means that z must have forwarded it; the only way it could have done so is by becoming *passive*, but in this case z will not originate a *Wait2* message, contradicting the assumption we have made.

Answer to Exercise 6.6.50
Let x be the entity with the smallest *id*, and denote this value by i.

Entity x will start at time $t(x, j)$ and would stop waiting at time $t(x, j) + f(x, j)$. As the entities start the iteration within time units from each other, for every other entity j $t(x, j) - t(y, j) \le n - 1$; as $d(x, y) \le n - 1$, this means that

$$t(x, j) + f(x, j) + d(x, y) \le f(x, j) + 2(n - 1).$$

Recall that f is a waiting function; this means that as x has the smallest identity and $g(j) \ge n$, $f(x, j) + 2(n - 1) < f(y, j)$ for every other entity y. Thus,

$$t(x, j) + f(x, j) + d(x, y) < f(y, j).$$

That is, x will finish waiting before anybody else; its message will travel along the ring transforming into *passive* all other entities and will reach x after $n_x = n$ time units. Thus, x will be the only entity starting the second waiting, and its "Wait2" message will reach x again after $n_x = n$ time units. Hence, x will validate its guess, become *leader*, and notify all other entities of termination.

Answer to Exercise 6.6.52
We know (Exercises 6.6.50 and 6.6.51) that if $n \notin \partial(j - 1)$, then no entity becomes a leader in the $(j - 1)$th iteration. According to the leader election algorithm, if an entity becomes neither leader nor passive during the $(j - 1)$ iteration, it becomes active and unconditionally sends an R message for the jth iteration. At this point the jth iteration starts with bounded delays.

The proof of this Lemma is based on the proof that is impossible for all the entities in the $(j - 1)$th iteration become passive and, therefore, no leader is elected and there is no active entities that can send the R message.

First, let x be the entity with the smallest i_x, called i. And let all the entities become passive in the $(j - 1)$th iteration. Note that according to the algorithm the only way for an entity to become passive is receiving a C message when is in the waiting state, that is, during $f(x, j - 1)$ the entity x must receive a C message in order to become passive. Let y denote the entity that originates the C message. The C message will be arriving to x in exactly $t(y, j - 1) + f(y, j - 1) + d(y, x)$ time units. Thus, in order that x becomes passive, it follows that

$$t(x, j - 1) + f(x, j - 1) > t(y, j - 1) + f(y, j - 1) + d(y, x)$$

$$t(x, j - 1) + i(b_{j-1} + 1) > t(y, j - 1) + i_y(b_{j-1} + 1) + d(y, x).$$

As i is the smallest value, $i < i_y$ and, therefore, $i(b_{j-1} + 1) < i_y(b_{j-1} + 1)$. Then to hold (3), it must be

$$t(x, j - 1) > t(y, j - 1) + d(y, x),$$

contradicting the fact that all the entities start the $(j - 1)$th iteration with bounded delay. Therefore, it is impossible that all the entities become passive in any iteration. In conclusion, if $n \notin \partial(j - 1)$ an R message is sent by an active entity and the next iteration start with bounded delays proving in this way the Lemma 3.

Answer to Exercise 6.6.53

Let x be the entity with the smallest value, and let $\mathbf{i}$ be that value. Entity x starts executing the protocol at most $n - 1$ time units after the other entities. It starts the $(j + 1)$th iteration less than $f(x, j) + 2n_x(j) + h(x, j)$ time units after x started the jth iteration. As

$$f(x, j) + g(x, j) + 2n_x(j) = 2g(j)\mathbf{i} + 2g(j)\mathbf{i} + g(j) - n_x(j) + 2n_x(j)$$
$$= (4\mathbf{i} + 1)g(j) + n_x(j),$$

the total time required until x becomes *leader* is at most

$$n - 1 + \sum_{j=1}^{j} ((4\mathbf{i} + 1)g(j) + n_x(j)).$$

As there are also the $n - 1$ time units before the "Terminate" message notifies all entities, the total time for the algorithm is at most

$$2(n - 1) + \sum_{j=1}^{j} ((4\mathbf{i} + 1)g(j) + n_x(j)).$$

Notice that if $g(j) < n_x(j)$, then x would detect the anomaly and send a "Restart"; thus, we can assume that in the expression above the actual time spent is $Min\{g(j), n_x(j)\}$. Then the above expression becomes: $2(n - 1) + (4\mathbf{i} + 2) \sum_{j=1}^{j} g(j)$.

Answer to Exercise 6.6.54

The last iteration is $\mathbf{j} = \lceil g^{-1}(n) \rceil$; as g is superincreasing, $g(\mathbf{j}) \geq \sum_{i=1}^{j-1} g(j)$. The algorithm terminates in less than $2(n - 1) + (4\, i_{min} + 2) \sum_{j=1}^{j} g(j)$ time units. Now, $(4i_{min} + 2) \sum_{j=1}^{j} g(j) \leq 2(n - 1) + (4i_{min} + 2)2g(\mathbf{j})$.

Answer to Exercise 6.6.60

Sketch: Use a counter, initially set to 0; in each step, set it to the largest of the received counters increased by one and add it to any message sent in that step. When the counter is equal to $2d$, stop.

Answer to Exercise 6.6.68

Use *saturation*: Each of the two *saturated* nodes computes its eccentricity; the largest of the two is communicated to their subtrees, starting a "countdown." When the furthermost entity receives the message, their value becomes simultaneously 0 and they all enter state *firing* at the same time. This protocol uses at most $3n - 2$ signals for the wake-up and saturation and an additional $n - 2$ messages for the countdown, each containing a value of at most d. The time is at most $2d$ for wake-up and saturation; at most, additional d time units are needed for the countdown.

BIBLIOGRAPHY

[1] P. Alimonti, P. Flocchini, and N. Santoro. Finding the extrema of a distributed multiset of values. *Journal of Parallel and Distributed Computing*, 37:123–133, 1996.

[2] A. Arora, S. Dolev, and M. Gouda. Maintaining digital clocks in step. *Parallel Processing Letters*, 1(1):11–18, 1991.

[3] H. Attiya, M. Snir, and M.K. Warmuth. Computing on an anonymous ring. *Journal of the ACM*, 35(4):845–875, 1988.

[4] A. Bar-Noi, J. Naor, and M. Naor. One bit algorithms. *Distributed Computing*, 4(1):3–8, 1990.

[5] H.L. Bodlaender and G. Tel. Bit optimal election in synchronous rings. *Information Processing Letters*, 36(1):53–56, 1990.

[6] S. Even and S. Rajsbaum. The use of a synchronizer yields maximum computation rate in distributed networks. In *22nd ACM Symposium on Theory of Computing*, pages 95–105, 1990.

[7] S. Even and S. Rajsbaum. Unison, canon and sluggish clocks in networks controlled by a synchronizer. *Mathematical System Theory*, 28:421–435, 1995.

[8] P. Flocchini. *Informazione Strutturata e Calcolo Distribuito*. PhD thesis, University of Milan, Milano, Italy, 1995.

[9] G.N. Frederickson and N.A. Lynch. Electing a leader in a synchronous ring. *Journal of the ACM*, 34(1):95–115, 1987.

[10] G.N. Frederickson and N. Santoro. Breaking symmetry in synchronous networks. In T. Papatheodorou F. Makedon K. Mehlhorn and P. Spirakis, editors, *VLSI Algorithms and Architectures*, volume 227 of *LNCS*, pages 26–33, Loutraki, July 1986.

[11] E. Gafni. Improvements in the time complexity of two message-optimal election algorithms. In *4th ACM Symposium on Principles of Distributed Computing*, pages 175–185, Minaki, Aug. 1985.

[12] M. Gouda and T. Herman. Stabilizing unison. *Information Processing Letters*, 35(4):171–175, 1990.

[13] A. Israeli, E. Kranakis, D. Krizanc, and N. Santoro. Time-message trade-offs for the weak unison problem. *Nordic Journal of Computing*, 4(4):317–329, Winter 1997.

[14] A. Itai and M. Rodeh. Symmetry breaking in distributed networks. *Information and Computation*, 88(1):60–87, Sept. 1990.

[15] E. Korach, D. Rotem, and N. Santoro. Distributed algorithms for finding centers and medians in networks. *ACM Transactions on Programming Languages and Systems*, 6(3):380–401, July 1984.

[16] J. van Leeuwen, N. Santoro, J. Urrutia, and S. Zaks. Guessing games and distributed computations in synchronous networks. In *14th International Colloquium on Automata, Languages and Programming*, pages 347–356, Karlsruhe, 13–17 July 1987.

[17] A. Marchetti-Spaccamela. New protocols for the election of a leader in a ring. *Theoretical Computer Science*, 54(1):53–64, 1987.

[18] E.F. Moore. The firing squad synchronization problem. In *Sequential Machines: Selected Papers*, pages 213–214. Addison-Wesley, 1964.

[19] U.-M. O'Reilly and N. Santoro. Asynchronous to synchronous transformations. In *4th International Conference on Principles of Distributed Systems*, pages 265–282, Paris, 2000.

[20] U.-M. O'Reilly and N. Santoro. Tight bounds for synchronous communication of information using bits and silence. *Discrete Applied Mathematics*, 129:195–209, 2003.

[21] M.H. Overmars and N. Santoro. Improved bounds for electing a leader in a synchronous ring. *Algorithmica*, 18(2):246–262, June 1997.

[22] R.J. Ramirez and N. Santoro. Distributed control of updates in multiplecopy databases: a time optimal algorithm. In *4th Berkeley Conference on Distributed Data Management and Computer Networks*, pages 191–207, Berkeley, August 1979.

[23] N. Santoro and D. Rotem. On the complexity of distributed elections in synchronous graphs. In *11th International Workshop on Graph-Theoretical Concepts in Computer Science*, pages 337–346, 1985.

[24] B. Schmeltz. Optimal tradeoff between time and bit complexity in synchronous rings. In *7th Symposium on Theoretical Computer Science*, pages 275–284, 1990.

[25] P.G. Spirakis and B. Tampakas. Efficient distributed algorithms by using the archimedean time assumption. *Informatique Theorique et Applications*, 23(1):113–128, 1989.

[26] P. Vitanyi. Distributed elections in an archimedean ring of processors. In *16th ACM Symposium on Theory of Computing*, pages 542–547, 1984.

CHAPTER 7

Computing in Presence of Faults

7.1 INTRODUCTION

In all previous chapters, with few exceptions, we have assumed total reliability, that is, the system is failure free. Unfortunately, total reliability is practically nonexistent in real systems. In this chapter we will examine how to compute, if possible, when failures can and do occur.

7.1.1 Faults and Failures

We speak of a *failure* (or *fault*) whenever something happens in the systems that deviates from the expected correct behavior. In distributed environments, failures and their causes can be very different in nature. In fact, a malfunction could be caused by a design error, a manufacturing error, a programming error, physical damage, deterioration in the course of time, harsh environmental conditions, unexpected inputs, operator error, cosmic radiations, and so forth. Not all faults lead (immediately) to computational errors (i.e., to incorrect results of the protocol), but some do. So the goal is to achieve *fault-tolerant* computations, that is, our aim is to design protocols that will proceed correctly in spite of the failures. The unpredictability of the occurrence and nature of a fault and the possibility of multiple faults render the design of fault-tolerant distributed algorithms very difficult and complex, if at all possible. In particular, the more components (i.e., entities, links) are present in the system, the greater is the chance of one or more of them being/becoming faulty.

Depending on their cause, faults can be grouped into three general classes:

- *execution* failures, that is, faults occurring during the execution of the protocol by an entity; examples of protocol failures are computational errors occurring when performing an action, as well as execution of the incorrect rule.
- *transmission* failures, due to the incorrect functioning of the transmission subsystem; examples of transmission faults are the loss or corruption of a transmitted message as well as the delivery of a message to the wrong neighbor.

- *component* failures, such as the deactivation of a communication link between two neighbors, the shutdown of a processor (and thus of the corresponding entity), and so forth.

Note that the same fault can occur because of different causes, and hence classified differently. Consider, for example, a message that an entity x is supposed to send (according to the protocol) to a neighbor y but never arrives. This fault could have been caused by x failing to execute the "send" operation in the protocol: an execution error; by the loss of the message by the transmission subsystem: a transmission error; or by the link (x, y) going down: a component failure.

Depending on their duration, faults are classified as transient or permanent.

- A *transient* fault occurs and then disappears of its own accord, usually within a short period of time. A bird flying through the beam of a microwave transmitter may cause lost bits on some network. A transient fault happens once in a while; it may or may not reoccur. If it continues to reoccur (not necessarily at regular intervals), the fault is said to be *intermittent*. A loose contact on a connector will often cause an intermittent fault. Intermittent faults are difficult to diagnose.
- A *permanent* failure is one that continues to exist until the fault is repaired. Burnout chips, software bugs, and disk head crashes often cause permanent faults.

Depending on their geographical "spread", faults are classified as localized or ubiquitous.

- *Localized* faults occur always in the same region of the system, that is, only a fixed (although a priori unknown) set of entities/links will exhibit a faulty behavior.
- *Ubiquitous* faults will occur anywhere in the system, that is, all entities/links will exhibit at some point or another a faulty behavior.

Note that usually transient failures are ubiquitous, while intermittent and permanent failures tend to be localized.

Clearly no protocol can be resilient to an arbitrary number of faults. In particular, if the entire system collapses, no protocol can be correct. Hence, the goal is to design protocols that are able to withstand up to a certain amount of faults of a given type.

Another fact to consider is that not all faults are equally *dangerous*. The danger of a fault lies not necessarily in the severity of the fault itself but rather in the consequences that its occurrence might have on the correct functioning of the system. In particular, danger for the system is intrinsically related to the notion of detectability. In general, if a fault is easily detected, a remedial action can be taken to limit or circumvent the damage; if a fault is hard or impossible to detect, the effects of the initial fault may spread throughout the network creating possibly irreversible damage. For example, the permanent fault of a link going down forever is obviously more severe than if that link failure is just transient. In contrast, the permanent failure of the link might be more easily detectable, and thus can be taken care of, than the occasional mulfanctioning of the link. In this example, the less severe fault (the transient one) is potentially more dangerous for the system.

With this in mind, when we talk about fault-tolerant protocols and fault-resilient computations, we must always qualify the statements and clearly specify the type and number of faults that can be tolerated. To do so, we must first understand what are the limits to the fault tolerance of a distributed computing environment, expressed in terms of the nature and number of faults that make a nontrivial computation (im)possible.

7.1.2 Modeling Faults

Given the properties of the system and the types of faults assumed to occur, one would like to know the maximum number of faults that can be tolerated. This number is called the *resiliency*. To establish the resiliency, we need to be more precise on the types of faults that can occur. In particular, we need to develop a *model* to describe the failures in the system.

Faults, as mentioned before, can be due to execution errors, transmission errors, or component failures; the same fault could be caused by any of those three causes and hence could be in any of these three categories. There are several failure models, each differing on what is the factor "blamed" for a failure.

IMPORTANT. Each failure model offers a way of describing (some of the) faults that can occur in the system. *A model is not reality, only an attempt to describe it.*

Component Failure Models   The more common and most well known models employed to discuss and study fault tolerance are the *component failures* models.

In all the *component failure* models, the blame for any fault occurring in the system must be put on a component, that is, only components can fail, and if something goes wrong, it is because one of the involved components is faulty. Depending on which components are blamed, there are three types of component failure models: entity, link, and hybrid failure models.

- In the *entity failure* (EF) model, only nodes can fail. For example, if a node crashes, for whatever reason, that node will be declared *faulty*. In this model, a link going down will be modeled by declaring one of the two incident nodes to be *faulty* and to lose all the message to and from its neighbor. Similarly, the corruption of a message during transmission must be blamed on one of the two incident nodes that will be declared to be *faulty*.
- In the *link failure* (LF) model, only links can fail. For example, the loss of a message over a link will lead to that link being declared *faulty*. In this model, the crash of a node is modeled by the crash of all its incident links. The event of an entity computing some incorrect information (because of a execution error) and sending it to a neighbor, will be modeled by blaming the link connecting the entity to the neighbor; in particular, the link will be declared to be responsible for corrupting the content of the message.

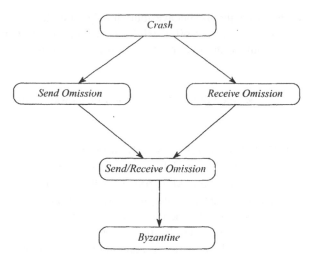

FIGURE 7.1: Hierarchy of faults in the EF model.

- In the *hybrid failure* (HF) model, both links and nodes can be faulty. Although more realistic, this model is little known and seldom used.

NOTE. In all three component failure models, the status *faulty* is permanent and is not changed, even though the faulty behavior attributed to that component may be never repeated. In other words, once a component is marked with being *faulty*, that mark is never removed; so, for example, in the link failure model, if a message is lost on a link, that link will be considered faulty forever, even if no other message will ever be lost there.

Let us concentrate first on the *entities failure* model. That is, we focus on systems where (only) entities can fail. Within this environment, the nature of the failures of the entities can vary. With respect to the danger they may pose to the system, a hierarchy of failures can be identified.

1. With *crash* faults, a faulty entity works correctly according to the protocol, then suddenly just stops any activity (processing, sending, and receiving messages). These are also called *fail-stop* faults. Such a hard fault is actually the most benign from the overall system point of view.

2. With *send/receive omission* faults, a faulty entity occasionally loses some received messages or does not send some of the prepared messages. This type of faults may be caused by buffer overflows. Notice that crash faults are just a particular case of this type of failure: A crash is a send/receive omission in which all messages sent to and and from that entity are lost. From the point of view of detectability, these faults are much more difficult than the previous one.

3. With *Byzantine* faults, a faulty entity is not bound by the protocol and can perform any action: It can omit to send or receive any message, send incorrect

information to its neighbors, behave maliciously so as to make the protocol fail. Undetected software bugs often exhibit Byzantine[1] faults. Clearly, dealing with Byzantine faults is going to be much more difficult than dealing with the previous ones.

A similiar hierarchy between faults exists in the link as well as in hybrid failures models.

Communication Failures Model   A totally different model is the *communication failure* or *dynamic fault* (DF) model; in this model, the blame for any fault is put on the communication subsystem. More precisely, the communication system can lose, corrupt, and deliver to the incorrect neighbor. As in this model, only the communication system can be faulty, a component fault such as the crash failure of a node, is modeled by the communication system losing all the messages sent to and from that node. Notice that in this model, no mark (permanent or otherwise) is assigned to any component.

In the *communication failure* model, the communication subsystem can cause only three types of faults:

1. An *omission*: A message sent by an entity is never delivered.
2. An *addition*: A message is delivered to an entity, although none was sent.
3. A *corruption*: A message is sent but one with different content is received.

While the nature of omissions and corruptions is quite obvious, that of additions is less so. Indeed, it describes a variety of situations. The most obvious one is when sudden noise in the transmission channel is mistaken for transmission of information by the neighbor at the other end of the link. The more important occurrence of additions in sytems is rather subtle, as an addition models the reception of a "nonauthorized message" (i.e., a message not transmitted by any authorized user). In this sense, additions model messages surreptitiously inserted in the system by some outside, and possibly malicious, entity. Spam being sent from an unsuspecting site clearly fits the description of an addition. Summarizing, additions do occur and can be very dangerous.

These three types of faults are quite incomparable with each other in terms of danger. The hierarchy comes into place when two or all of these basic fault types can simultaneously occur in the system. The presence of all three types of faults creates what is called a *Byzantine* faulty behavior. The situation is depicted in Figure 7.2.

Clearly, no protocol can tolerate any number of faults of any type. If the entire system collapses, no computation is possible. Thus, when we talk about fault-tolerant protocols and fault-resilient computations, we must always qualify the statements and clearly specify the type and number of faults that can be tolerated.

---

[1] The term "Byzantine" refers to the Byzantine Empire (330–1453 AD), the long-lived eastern component of the Roman Empire whose capital city was Byzantium (now Istanbul), in which endless conspiracies, intrigue, and untruthfulness were alleged to be common among the ruling class.

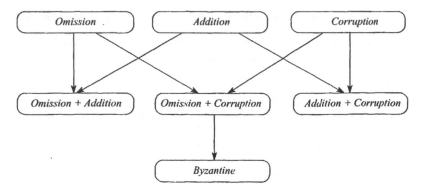

FIGURE 7.2: Hierarchy of combinations of fault types in the *DF* model.

7.1.3 Topological Factors

Our goal is to design protocols that can withstand as many and as dangerous faults as possible and still exhibit a reasonable cost. What we will be able to do depends not only on our ability as designers but also on the inherent limits that the environment imposes. In particular, the impact of a fault, and thus our capacity to deal with it and design fault-tolerant protocols, depends not only on the type and number of faults but also on the communication topology of the system, that is, on the graph G.

This is because all nontrivial computations are *global*, that is, they require the participation of possibly all entities. For this reason, *Connectivity* is a restriction required for all nontrivial computations. Even when initially existent, in the lifetime of the system, owing to faults, connectivity may cease to hold, rendering correctness impossible. Hence, the capacity of the topological structure of the network to remain connected in spite of faults is crucial.

There are two parameters that directly link topology to reliability and fault tolerance:

- *edge connectivity* $c_{edge}(G)$ is the minimum number of edges whose removal destroys the (strong) connectivity of G;
- *node connectivity* $c_{node}(G)$ is the minimum number of nodes whose removal destroys the (strong) connectivity of G.

NOTE. In the case of a complete graph, the node connectivity is always defined as $n - 1$.

Clearly, the higher the connectivity, the higher the resilience of the system to component failures. In particular,

Property 7.1.1 *If $c_{edge}(G) = k$, then for any pair x and y of nodes there are k edge-disjoint paths connecting x to y.*

Network G	Node Connectivity $c_{node}(G)$	Edge Connectivity $c_{edge}(G)$	Max Degree $\deg(G)$
Tree T	1	1	$\leq n-1$
Ring R	2	2	2
Torus Tr	4	4	4
Hypercube H	$\log n$	$\log n$	$\log n$
Complete K	$n-1$	$n-1$	$n-1$

FIGURE 7.3: Connectivity of some networks.

Property 7.1.2 *If $c_{node}(G) = k$, then for any pair x and y of nodes there are k node-disjoint paths connecting x to y.*

Let us consider some examples of connectivity. A tree T has the lowest connectivity of all undirected graphs: $c_{edge}(T) = c_{node}(T) = 1$, so any failure of a link or a node disconnects the network. A ring R faces little better as $c_{edge}(R) = c_{node}(R) = 2$. Higher connectivity can be found in denser graphs. For example, in a hypercube H, both connectivity parameters are $\log n$. Clearly the highest connectivity is to be found in the complete network K. For a summary, see Figure 7.3.

Note that in all connected networks G the node connectivity is not greater than the edge connectivity (Exercise 7.10.1) and neither can be better than the maximum degree:

Property 7.1.3 $\forall G, \quad c_{node}(G) \leq c_{edge}(G) \leq \deg(G)$

As an example of the impact of *edge connectivity* on the existence of fault-tolerant solutions, consider the *broadcast* problem **Bcast**.

Lemma 7.1.1 *If k arbitrary links can crash, it is impossible to broadcast unless the network is $(k+1)$-edge-connected.*

Proof. If G is only k-edge-connected, then there are k edges whose removal disconnects G. The failure of those links will make some nodes unreachable from the initiator of the broadcast and, thus, they will never receive the information. By contrast, if G is $(k+1)$-edge-connected, then even after k links go down, by Property 7.1.1, there is still a path from the initiator to all other nodes. Hence flooding will correctly work. ∎

As an example of the impact of *node-connectivity* on the existence of fault-tolerant solutions, consider the problem of an initiator that wants to broadcast some information, but some of the entities may be down. In this case, we just want the nonfaulty entities to receive the information. Then (Exercise 7.10.2),

Lemma 7.1.2 *If k arbitrary nodes can crash, it is impossible to broadcast to the nonfaulty nodes unless the network is $(k+1)$-node-connected.*

7.1.4 Fault Tolerance, Agreement, and Common Knowledge

In most distributed computations there is a need to have the entities to make a local but coordinated decision. This coordinated decision is called an *agreement*.

For example, in the *election* problem, every entity must decide whether it is the leader or not. The decision is local but must satisfy some global constraint (only one entity must become leader); in other words, the entities must agree on which one is the leader. For any problem requiring an agreement, the sets of constraints defining the agreement are different. For example, in *minimum finding*, the constraint is that all and only the entities with the smallest input value must become minimum. For example, in *ranking* when every entity has an initial data item, the constraint is that the value decided by each entity is precisely the rank of its data item in the overall distributed set.

When there are no faults, reaching these agreements is possible (as we have seen in the other chapters) and often straightforward. Unfortunately, the picture changes dramatically in presence of faults. Interestingly, the impact that faults have on problems requiring agreement for their solution has common traits, in spite of the differences of the agreement constraints. That is, some of the impact is the same for all these problems.

For these reasons, we consider an abstract agreement problem where this common impact of faults on agreements is more evident.

In the *p-Agreement Problem* (**Agree(p)**), each entity x has an input value $v(x)$ from some known set (usually $\{0, 1\}$) and must terminally decide upon a value $d(x)$ from that set within a finite amount of time. Here, "terminally" means that once made, the decision cannot be modified. The problem is to ensure that at least p entities decide on the same value. Additional constraints, called *nontriviality* (or sometimes *validity* constraints), usually exist on the value to be chosen; in particular, if all values are initially the same, the decision must be on that value. This nontriviality constraint rules out default-type solutions (e.g., "always choose 0").

Depending on the value of p, we have different types of agreement problems. Of particular interest is the case of $p = \lceil \frac{n}{2} \rceil + 1$ that is called *strong majority*.

When $p = n$, we have the well known *Unanimity* or *Consensus Problem* (**Consensus**) in which all entities must decide on the same value, that is,

$$\forall x, y \in \mathcal{E}. \, d(x) = d(y). \tag{7.1}$$

The consensus problem occurs in many different applications. For example, consider an aircraft where several sensors are used to decide if the moment has come to drop a cargo; it is possible that some sensors detect "yes" while others "not yet." On the basis of these values, a decision must be made on whether or not the cargo is to be dropped now. A solution strategy for our example is to drop the cargo only if all sensors agree; another is to decide for a drop as soon as at least one of the sensors indicates so. Observe that the first solution corresponds to computing the **AND** of the sensors' values; in the consensus problem this solution corresponds to each entity x setting $d(x) = \text{AND}(\{v(y) : y \in \mathcal{E}\})$. The second solution consists of determining the

OR of those values, that is, $d(x) = \text{OR}(\{v(y) : y \in \mathcal{E}\})$. Notice that in both strategies, if the initial values are identical, each entity chooses that value. Another example is in distributed database systems, where each site (the entity) of the distributed database must decide whether to accept or drop a transaction; in this case, all sites will agree to accept the transaction only if no site rejects the transaction. The same solutions strategy apply also in this case.

Summarizing, if there are no faults, consensus can be easily achieved (e.g., by computing the **AND** or the **OR** of the values). Lower forms of agreement, that is, when $p < n$, are even easier to resolve.

In presence of faults, the situation changes drastically and even the problem must be restated. In fact, if an entity is faulty, it might be unable to participate in the computation; even worse, its faulty behavior might be an active impediment for the computation. In other words, as faulty entities cannot be required to behave correctly, the agreement constraint can hold only for the nonfaulty entities. So, for example, a consensus problem we are interested in is *Entity-Fault-Tolerant Consensus* (**EFT-Consensus**).

Each nonfaulty entity x has an input value $v(x)$ and must terminally decide upon a value $d(x)$ within a finite amount of time. The constraints are

1. *agreement*: all *nonfaulty* entities decide on the same value;
2. *nontriviality*: if all values of the nonfaulty elements are initially the same, the decision must be on that value.

Similarly, we can define lower forms (i.e., when $p < n$) of agreement in presence of entity failures (**EFT-Agree(p)**).

For simplicity (and without any loss of generality), we can consider the Boolean case, that is when the values are all in $\{0, 1\}$. Possible solutions to this problem are, for example, computing **AND** or the **OR** of the input values of the nonfaulty entities, or the value of an elected leader. In other words, consensus (fault tolerant or not) can be solved by solving any of a variety of other problems (e.g., function evaluation, leader election, etc.). For this reason, the consensus problem is *elementary*: If it cannot be solved, then none of those other problems can be solved either.

Reaching agreement, and consensus in particular, is strictly connected with the problem of reaching *common knowledge*. Recall (from Section 1.8.1) that common knowledge is the highest form of knowledge achievable in a distributed computing environment. Its connection to consensus is immediate. In fact, any solution protocol P to the (fault-tolerant) consensus problem has the following property: As it leads all (nonfaulty) entities to decide on the same value, say d, then within finite time the value d becomes common knowledge among all the nonfaulty entities. By contrast, any (fault-tolerant) protocol Q that creates common knowledge among all the nonfaulty entities can be used to make them decide on a same value and thus achieve consensus.

IMPORTANT. This implies that common knowledge is as *elementary* as consensus: If one cannot be achieved, neither can be other.

7.2 THE CRUSHING IMPACT OF FAILURES

In this section we will examine the impact that faults have in distributed computing environments. As we will see, the consequences are devastating even when faults are limited in quantity and danger. We will establish these results assuming that the entities have distinct values (i.e., under restriction **ID**); this makes the bad news even worse.

7.2.1 Node Failures: Single-Fault Disaster

In this section we examine *node failures*. We consider the possibility that entities may fail during the computation and we ask under what conditions the nonfaulty entities may still carry out the task. Clearly, if all entities fail, no computation is possible; also, we have seen that some faults are more dangerous than others. We are interested in computations that can be performed, *provided* that at most a certain number f of entities fail, and those failures are of a certain type τ (i.e., danger).

We will focus on achieving fault-tolerant *consensus* (problem **EFT-Consensus** described in Section 7.1.4), that is, we want all nonfailed entities to agree on the same value. As we have seen, this is an elementary problem.

A first and immediate limitation to the possibility of achieving consensus in presence of node failures is given by the *topology* of the network itself. In fact, by Lemma 7.1.2, we know that if the graph is *not* $(k + 1)$-node-connected, a broadcast to nonfaulty entities is impossible if k entities can crash. This means that

Lemma 7.2.1 *If $k \geq 1$ arbitrary entities can possibly crash, fault-tolerant consensus can not be achieved if the network is not $(k + 1)$-node-connected.*

This means, for example, that in a tree, if a node goes down, consensus among the others cannot be achieved.

Summarizing, we are interested in achieving consensus, *provided* that at most a given number f of entities fail, those failures are of at most a certain type τ of danger, and the node-connectivity of the network c_{node} is high enough. In other words, the problem is characterized by those three paramenters, and we will denote it by *EFT-Consensus(f, τ, c_{node})*.

We will start with the simplest case:

- $f = 1$, that is, at most one entity fails;
- $\tau = crash$, that is, if an entity fails, it will be in the most benign way;
- $c_{node} = n - 1$, that is, the topology is not a problem as we are in the complete graph.

In other words, we are in a complete network (every entity is connected to every other entity); at most one entity will crash, leaving all the other entities connected to each other. What we want is that these other entities agree on the same value, that is, we want to solve problem *EFT-Consensus(1, $crash$, $n - 1$)*. Unfortunately,

Theorem 7.2.1   (Single-Fault Disaster)   *EFT-Consensus* $(1, crash, n - 1)$ *is unsolvable.*

In other words, fault-tolerant consensus cannot be achieved even under the best of conditions. This really means that it is impossible to design fault-tolerant solutions for practically all important problems, as each could be used to achieve fault-tolerant consensus.

Before proceeding further with the consequences of this result, also called *FLP Theorem* (after the initials of those who first proved it), let us see why it is true.

What we are going to do is to show that no protocol can solve this problem, that is, no protocol always correctly terminate within finite time if an entity can crash. We will prove it by contradiction. We assume that a correct solution protocol P indeed exists and then show that there is an execution of this protocol in which the entities fail to achieve consensus in finite time (even if no one fails at all).

The proof is neither simple nor complex. It does require some precise terminology and uses some constructs that will be very useful in other situations also. We will need not only to describe the problem but also to define precisely the entire environment, including executions, events, among others. Some of this notation has already been introduced in Section 1.6.

Terminology   Let us start with the *problem*. Each entity x has an *input register* I_x, a write-once *output register* O_x, as well as unlimited internal storage. Initially, the input register of an entity is a value in $\{0, 1\}$, and all the output registers are set to the same value $b \notin \{0, 1\}$; once a value $d_x \in \{0, 1\}$ is written in O_x, the content of that register is no longer modifiable. The goal is to have all nonfailed entities set, in finite time, their output registers to the same value $d \in \{0, 1\}$, subject to the nontriviality condition (i.e., if all input values are the same, then d must be that value).

Let us consider next the *status* of the system and the *events* being generated during an execution of the solution protocol P.

An entity reacts to external events by executing the actions prescribed by the protocol P. Some actions can generate events that will occur later. Namely, when an entity x sends a message, it creates the future event of the arrival of that message; similarly, when an entity sets the alarm clock, it creates the future event of that alarm ringing. (Although an entity can reset its clock as part of its processing, we can assume, without loss of generality, that each alarm will always be allowed to ring at the time it was originally set for.)

In other words, as described in Chapter 1, at any time t during the execution of a protocol, there is a set *Future(t)* of the events that have been generated so far but have not happened yet. Recall that initially, *Future(0)* contains only the set of the spontaneous events. To simplify the discussion, we assume that all entities are initiators (i.e., the set *Future(0)* contains an impulse for each entity), and we will treat both spontaneous events and the ringing of the alarm clocks as the same type of events and call them *timeouts*. We represent by (x, M) the event of x receiving message M, and by $(x, \emptyset)$ the event of a timeout occurring at x.

As we want to describe what happens to the computation if an entity fails by crashing, we add special system events called *crashes*, one per entity, to the initial set of events *Future(0)*, and denote by $(x, crash)$ the crash of entity x. As we are interested only in executions where there is at most one crash, if event $(x, crash)$ occurs at time t, then all other crash events will be removed from *Future(t)*. Furthermore, if x crashes, all the messages sent to x but not arrived yet will no longer be processed; Similarly, any timeout set by x but not occurred yet, will no longer occur. In other words, if event $(x, crash)$ occurs at time t, all events (arrivals and timeouts) involving x will be removed from all *Future(t')* with $t' \geq t$.

Recall from Section 1.6 that the *internal state* of an entity is the value of all its registers and internal storage. Also recall that the *configuration* $C(t)$ of the system at time t is a snapshot of the system at time t; it contains the internal state of each entity and the set *Future(t)* of the future events that have been generated so far. A configuration is *nonfaulty* if no crash event has occured so far, *faulty* otherwise. Particular configurations are the *initial configuration*, when all processes are at their initial state and *Future* is composed of all and only the spontaneous and crash events; by definition, all initial configurations are nonfaulty.

When an arrival or a timeout event ϵ occurs at x, x will act according to the protocol P: It will perform some local processing (thus changing its internal state); it might send some messages and set up its alarm clock; in other words, there will be a change in the configuration of the system (because event ϵ has been removed from *Future*, the internal state of x has changed, and some new events have been possibly added to *Future*). Clearly the configuration changes also if the event ϵ is a crash; notice that this event can occur only if no crash has occured before. Regardless of the nature of event ϵ, we will denote the new configuration as $\epsilon(C)$ where C was the configuration when the event occurred; we will say that ϵ is *applicable* to C and that the configuration $\epsilon(C)$ is reachable from C.

We can extend this notation and say that a sequence of events $\psi = \epsilon_1 \epsilon_2 \ldots \epsilon_k$ is applicable to configuration C if ϵ_k is applicable to C, and ϵ_{k-1} is applicable to $\epsilon_k(C)$, and ϵ_{k-2} is applicable to $\epsilon_{k-1}(\epsilon_k(C))$, ..., and ϵ_1 is applicable to $\epsilon_2(\ldots(\epsilon_k(C))\ldots)$; we will say that the resulting configuration $C' = \epsilon_1(\epsilon_2(\ldots(\epsilon_k(C))\ldots)) = \psi(C)$ is *reachable* from C.

If an entity x sets the output register O_x to either 0 or 1, we say that x has decided on that value, and that state is called a *decision state*. The output register value cannot be changed after the entity has reached a decision state, that is, once x has made a decision, that decision cannot be altered. A configuration where all nonfailed entities have decided on the same value is called a *decision configuration*; depending on the value, we will distinguish between a 0-decision and a 1-decision configuration.

Notice that once an entity makes a decision it cannot change it; hence, all configurations reachable by a 0-decision configuration are also 0-decision (similarly in the case of 1-decision).

Consider a configuration C and the set $\mathcal{C}(C)$ of all configurations reachable from C. If *all* decision configurations in this set are 0-decision (respective 1-decision), we say that C ia 0-*valent* (respective 1-*valent*); in other words, in a v-valent configuration, whatever happens, the decision is going to be on v. If, instead, there are both 0-decision

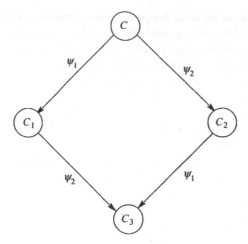

FIGURE 7.4: Commutativity of disjoint sequences of events.

and 1-decision configurations in $\mathcal{C}(C)$, then we say that C is *bivalent*; in other words, in a bivalent configurations, which value is going to be chosen depends on the future events.

An important property of sequences of events is the following. Suppose that from some configuration C, the sequences of events ψ_1 and ψ_2 lead to configurations C_1 and C_2, respectively. If the entities affected by the events in ψ_1 are all different from those affected by the events in ψ_2, then ψ_2 can be applied to C_1 and ψ_1 to C_2, and both lead to the same configuration C_3 (see Figure 7.4). More precisely,

Lemma 7.2.2   *Let ψ_1 and ψ_2 be sequences of events applicable to C such that*

1. *the sets of entities affected by the events in ψ_1 and ψ_2, respectively, are disjoint; and*

2. *at most one of ψ_1 and ψ_2 includes a crash event.*

Then, both $\psi_1\psi_2$ and $\psi_2\psi_1$ are applicable to C. Furthermore, $\psi_1(\psi_2(C)) = \psi_2(\psi_2(C))$.

If a configuration is reachable from some initial configuration, it will be called *accessible*; we are interested only in accessible configurations. Consider an accessible configuration C; a sequence of events applicable to C is *deciding* if it generates a decision configuration; it is *admissible* if all messages sent to nonfaulty entities are eventually received. Clearly, we are interested only in admissible sequences.

Proof of Impossibility   Let us now proceed with the proof of Theorem 7.2.1.

By contradiction, assume that there is a protocol P that correctly solves the problem EFT-Consensus(1, *crash*, $n - 1$), that is, in every execution of P in a complete graph with at most one crash, within finite time all nonfailed entities decide on the same value (subject to the nontriviality condition). In other words, if we consider all the possible executions of P, *every admissible sequence of events is deciding*.

The proof involves three steps. We first prove that among the initial configurations, there is at least one that is *bivalent* (i.e., where, depending on the future events, both a 0 and a 1 decision are possible). We then prove that starting from a bivalent configuration, it is always possible to reach another bivalent configuration. Finally, using these two results, we show how to construct an infinite admissible sequence that is not deciding, contradicting the fact that all admissible sequence of events in the execution of P are deciding.

Lemma 7.2.3   *There is a bivalent initial configuration.*

Proof. By contradiction, let all initial configurations be univalent, that is, either 0- or 1-valent. Because of the nontriviality condition, we know that there is at least one 0-valent initial configuration (the one where all input values are 0) and one 1-valent initial configuration (the one where all input values are 0). Let us call two initial configurations *adjacent* if they differ only in the initial value of a single entity.

For any two initial configurations C and C', it is always possible to find a chain of initial configurations, each adjacent to the next, starting with C and ending with C'. Hence, in this sequence there exists a 0-valent initial configuration C^0 adjacent to a 1-valent initial configuration C^1. Let x be the entity in whose initial value they differ. Now consider an admissible deciding sequence ψ for C^0 in which the first event is $(crash, x)$. Then, ψ can be applied also to C^1, and the corresponding configurations at each step of the sequence are identical except for the internal state of entity x. As the sequence is deciding, eventually the same decision configuration is reached. If it is 1-decision, then C^0 is bivalent; otherwise, C^1 is bivalent. In either case, the assumed nonexistence of a bivalent initial configuration is contradicted. ■

Lemma 7.2.4   *Let C be a nonfaulty bivalent configuration, and let $\epsilon = (x, m)$ be a noncrash event that is applicable to C. Let $\mathcal{A}$ be the set of nonfaulty configurations reachable from C without applying ϵ, and let $\mathcal{B} = \epsilon(\mathcal{A}) = \{\epsilon(A) \mid A \in \mathcal{A} \text{ and } \epsilon \text{ is applicable to } A\}$ (See Figure 7.5). Then, $\mathcal{B}$ contains a nonfaulty bivalent configuration.*

Proof. First of all, observe that as ϵ is applicable to C, by definition of $\mathcal{A}$ and because of the unpredictability of communication delays, ϵ is applicable to every $A \in \mathcal{A}$.

Let us now start the proof. By contradiction, assume that every configuration $B \in \mathcal{B}$ is univalent. In this case, $\mathcal{B}$ contains both 0-valent and 1-valent configurations (Exercise 7.10.4).

Call two configurations *neighbors* if one is reachable from the other after a single event, and *x-adjacent* if they differ only in the internal state of entity x. By an easy induction (Exercise 7.10.5), there exist two x-adjacent (for some entity x) neighbors $A^0, A^1 \in \mathcal{A}$ such that $D_0 = \epsilon(A^0)$ is 0-valent and $D_1 = \epsilon(A^1)$ is 1-valent. Without loss of generality, let $A^1 = \epsilon'(A^0)$ where $\epsilon' = (y, m')$.

Case I. If $x \neq y$, then $D_1 = \epsilon'(D_0)$ by Lemma 7.2.2. This is impossible as any successor of a 0-valent configuration is also 0-valent (see Figure 7.6).

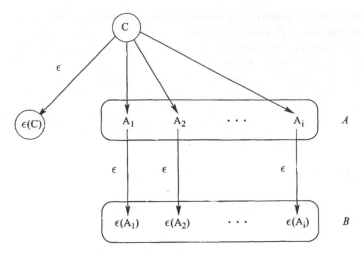

FIGURE 7.5: The situation of Lemma 7.2.4.

Case II. If $x = y$, then consider the two configurations $E_0 = c_x(D_0)$ and $E_1 = c_x(D_1)$, where $c_x = (x, crash)$; as both ϵ and ϵ' are noncrash events involving x, and the occurrence of c_x removes from *Future* all the future events involving x, it follows that E_0 and E_1 are x-*adjacent*. Therefore, if we apply to both the same sequence of events not involving x, they will remain x-*adjacent*. As P is correct, there must be a finite sequence ψ of (noncrash) events not involving x that, starting from E_0, reaches a decision configuration; as E_0 is 0-valent, $\psi(E_0)$ is 0-decision (see Figure 7.7). As the events in ψ are noncrash and do not involve x, they are applicable also to E_1 and $\psi(E_0)$ and $\psi(E_1)$ are x-adjacent. This means that all entities other than x have the same state in $\psi(E_0)$ and in $\psi(E_1)$; hence, also $\psi(E_1)$ is 0-decision. As E_1 is 1-valent,

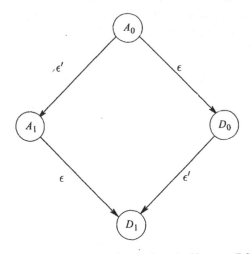

FIGURE 7.6: The situation in Case 1 of Lemma 7.2.4.

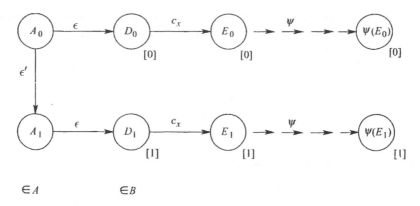

FIGURE 7.7: The situation in Case 2 of Lemma 7.2.4. The valency of the configuration, if known, is in square brackets.

$\psi(E_1)$ is also 1-valent, a contradiction. So B contains a bivalent configuration; as, by definition, B is only composed of nonfaulty configurations, the lemma follows. ∎

Any deciding sequence ψ of events from a bivalent initial configuration goes to a univalent configuration, so there must be some single event in that sequence that generates a univalent configuration from a bivalent one; it is such an event that determines the eventual decision value. We now show that using Lemmas 7.2.4 and 7.2.3 as tools, it is always possible to find a fault-free execution that avoids such events, creating a fault-free admissible but nondeciding sequence.

We ensure that the sequence is admissible and nondeciding in the following way.

1. We maintain a queue Q of entities, initially in an arbitrary order.
2. We remove from the set of initial events all the crash events, that is, we consider only fault-free executions.
3. We maintain the future events sorted (in increasing order) according to the time they were originated.
4. We construct the sequence in stages as follows:
   (a) The execution begins in a bivalent initial configuration C_b whose existence is assured by Lemma 7.2.3.
   (b) Starting stage i from a bivalent configuration C, say at time t, consider the first entity x in the queue that has an event in *Future(t)*. Let ϵ be the first event for x in *Future(t)*.
   (c) By Lemma 7.2.4, there is a bivalent configuration C' reachable from C by a sequence of events, say ψ, in which ϵ is the last event applied. The sequence for stage i is precisely this sequence of events ψ.
   (d) We execute the constructed sequence of events, ending in a bivalent configuration.
   (e) We move x and all preceeding entities to the back of the queue and start the next stage.

In any infinite sequence of such stages every entity comes to the front of the queue infinitely many times and receives every message sent to it. The sequence of events so constructed is therefore admissible. As each stage starts and ends in a bivalent configuration, a decision is never reached. The sequence of events so constructed is therefore nondeciding.

Summarizing, we have shown that there is an execution in which protocol P never reaches a decision, even if no entity crashes. It follows that P is not a correct solution to our consensus problem.

7.2.2 Consequences of the Single-Fault Disaster

The Single-Failure Disaster result of Theorem 7.2.1 dashes any hope for the design of fault-tolerant distributed solution protocols for nontrivial problems and tasks. Because the consensus problem is an elementary one, the solution of almost every nontrivial distributed problem can be used to solve it, but as consensus cannot be solved even if just a single entity may crash, also all those other problems cannot be solved if there is the possibility of failures.

The negative impact of this fact must not be underestimated; its main consequence is that

> *it is impossible to design fault-tolerant communication software.*

This means that to have fault tolerance, the distributed computing environment must have additional properties. In other words, while in general not possible (because of Theorem 7.2.1), some degree of fault tolerance might be achieved in more restricted environments.

To understand which properties (and thus restrictions) would suffice we need to examine the proof of Theorem 7.2.1 and to understand what are the particular conditions inside a general distributed computing environment that make it work. Then, if we disable one of these conditions (by adding the appropriate restriction), we might be able to design a fault-tolerant solution.

The reason why Theorem 7.2.1 holds is that, as communication delays are finite but unpredictable, it is impossible to distinguish between a link experiencing very long communication delays and a failed link. In our case, the crash failure of an entity is equivalent to the simultaneous failure of all its links. So, if entity x is waiting for a reply from y and it has not received one so far, it cannot decide whether y has crashed or not. It is this "ambiguity" that leads, in the proof, to the construction of an admissible but nondeciding infinite sequence of events.

This means that to disable that proof we need to ensure that this fact (i.e., this "ambiguity") cannot occur. Let us see how this can be achieved.

First of all observe that if communication delays[2] were bounded and clock synchronized, then no ambiguity would occur: As any message would take at most Δ time, if entity x sends a message to y and does not receive the expected reply from y within 2Δ time, it can correctly decide that y has crashed. This means that, in

---

[2] Recall that communication delays include both transmission and processing delays.

synchronous systems, the proof of Theorem 7.2.1 does not hold; in other words, the restrictions *Bounded Delays* and *Synchronized Clocks* together disable that proof.

Next observe that the reason why in a synchronous environment the ambiguity is removed is because the entities can use *timeouts* to reliably detect if a crash failure has occurred. Indeed, the availability of any *reliable fault detector* would remove any ambiguity and thus disable that proof of Theorem 7.2.1. In other words, either restriction *Link-Failure Detection* or restriction *Node-Failure Detection* would disable that proof even if communication delays are unbounded.

Observing the proof, another point we can make is that it assumes that all initial bivalent configuration are nonfaulty, that is, the fault has not occurred yet. This is necessary in order to give the "adversary" the power to make an entity crash when most appropriate for the proof. (Simple exercise question : Where in the proof does the adversary exercise this power?) If the crash has occurred *before* the start of the execution, the adversary loses this power. It is actually sufficient that the faulty entity crashes before it sends any message, and the proof does no longer hold. This means that it might still be possible to tolerate some crashes if they have already occurred, that is, they occur before the faulty entities send messages. In other words, the restriction *Partial Reliability* stating that no faults will occur *during* the execution of the protocol would disable the proof, even if communication delays are unbounded and there are no reliable fault detectors.

Notice that disabling the proof we used for Theorem 7.2.1 does not imply that the Theorem does not hold; indeed a different proof could still work. Fortunately, in those restricted environments we have just indicated that the entire Theorem 7.2.1 is no longer valid, as we will see later.

Finally, observe that the unsolvability stated by Theorem 7.2.1 means that there is no *deterministic* solution protocol. It does not, however, rule out *randomized* solutions, that is, protocols that use randomization (e.g., flip of a coin) inside the actions. The main drawback of randomized protocols is that they do not offer any certainty: Either termination is not guaranteed (except with high probability) or correctness is not guaranteed (except with high probability).

Summarizing, the Single-Failure Disaster result imposes a dramatic limitation on the design of fault-tolerant protocols. The only way around (possibly) is by substantially restricting the environment: investing in the software and hardware necessary to make the system *fully synchronous*; constructing *reliable fault detectors* (unfortunately, none exists so far except in fully synchronous systems); or, in the case of crash faults only, ensuring somehow that all the faults occur before we start, that is, *partial reliability*. Alternatively, we can give up certainty on the outcome and use *randomization*.

7.3 LOCALIZED ENTITY FAILURES: USING SYNCHRONY

In fully synchronous environment, the proof of the Single-Failure Disaster theorem does not hold. Indeed, as we will see, synchronicity allows a high degree of fault tolerance.

Recall from Chapter 6 that a fully synchronous system is defined by two restrictions: *Bounded Delays* and *Synchronized Clocks*. We can actually replace the first restriction with the *Unitary Delays* one, without any loss of generality. These restrictions together are denoted by **Synch**.

We consider again the fault-tolerant consensus problem *EFT-Consensus* (introduced in Section 7.1.4) in the *complete graph* in case of component failures, and more specifically we concentrate on *entity failures*, that is, the faults are localized (i.e., restricted) to a set of entities (eventhough we do not know beforehand which they are). The problem asks for all the nonfaulty entities, each starting with an initial value $v(x)$, to terminally decide on the same value in finite time, subject to the nontriviality condition: If all initial values are the same, the decision must be on that value.

We will see that if the environment is fully synchronous, under some additional restrictions, the problem can be solved even when almost one third of the entities are Byzantine. In the case of crash failures, we can actually solve the problem tolerating any number of failures.

7.3.1 Synchronous Consensus with Crash Failures

In a synchronous system in which the faults are just *crashes* of entities, under some restrictions, consensus (among the nonfailed entities) can be reached regardless of the number f of entities that may crash. The restrictions considered here are

Additional Assumptions

1. *Connectivity, Bidirectional Links*;
2. *Synch*;
3. the network is a complete graph;
4. all entities start simultaneously;
5. the only type of failure is entity crash.

Note that an entity can crash while performing an action, that is, it may crash after sending some but not all the messages requested by the action.

Solution Protocols   In this environment there are several protocols that achieve consensus tolerating up to $f \leq n - 1$ crashes. Almost all of them adopt the same simple mechanism, *Tell All*(T), where T is an input parameter. The basic idea behind the mechanism is to collect at each nonfaulty entity enough information so that all nonfaulty entities are able to make the same decision by a given time.

Mechanism   *Tell All* (T)

- At each time step $t \leq T$, every nonfailed entity x sends to all its neighbors a message containing a "report" on everything it knows and waits for a similar message from each of them.

TellAll-Crash.

```
begin
    for   t = 0, ..., f  do
        compute rep(x, t);
        send rep(x, t) to N(x);
    endfor
    Oₓ := rep(x, f + 1);
end
```

FIGURE 7.8: Protocol *TellAll-Crash.*

- If x has not received a message from neighbor y by time $t + 1$, it knows that y has crashed; if it receives a message from y, it will know a "report" on what y knew at time t (note that in case of Byzantine faults, this "report" could be false).

For the appropriate choice of T and with the appropriate information sent in the "report," this mechanism enables the nonfaulty entities to reach consensus. The actual value of T and the nature of the report depend on the types and number of faults the protocol is supposed to tolerate.

Let us now see a fairly simple consensus protocol, called *TellAll-Crash* and on the basis of this mechanism, that tolerates up to $f \leq n - 1$ crashes. The algorithm is just mechanism *Tell All* where $T = f$ and the "report" consists of the **AND** function of all the values seen so far. More precisely,

$$
\mathrm{rep}(x, t) = \begin{cases} v(x) & \text{if } t = 0 \\ \mathbf{AND}(\mathrm{rep}(x, t - 1), M(x_1, t), \ldots, M(x_{n-1}, t)) & \text{otherwise} \end{cases} , \quad (7.2)
$$

where $x_1, \ldots, x_{n-1}$ are the neighbors of x and $M(x_i, t)$ denotes the message received by x from x_i at time t if any, otherwise $M(x_i, t) = 1$. The protocol is shown in Figure 7.8.

To see how and why protocol *TellAll-Crash* works, let us make some observations. Let F be the set of enties that crashed before or during the execution of the protocol, and S the others. Clearly, $|F| \leq f$ and $|F| + |S| = n$.

Property 7.3.1   *If all entities start with initial value* 1, *all entities in S will decide on* 1.

Property 7.3.2   *If an entity $x \in S$ has or receives a* 0 *at time $t \leq f$, then all entities in S will receive a* 0 *at time $t + 1$.*

Property 7.3.3   *If an entity $x \in S$ has or receives a* 0 *during the execution of the protocol, it will decide on* 0.

These three facts imply that all nonfailed entities will decide on 0 if at least one of them has initial value 0 and will decide on 1 if all entities have initially 1.

The only case left to consider is when all entities in S have initially 1 but some entities in F have initially 0. If any of the latter does not crash in the first step, by time $t = 1$ all entities in S will receive 0 and thus decide on 0 at time $f + 1$. This means that the nonfailed entities at time $t = f + 1$ will all decide on 0 *unless*

1. up to time f they have seen and received only 1; and
2. at time $f + 1$ some (but not all) of them receive 0.

In fact, in such a case, as the execution terminates at time $f + 1$, there is no time for the nonfailed entities that have seen 0 to tell the others.

Can this situation occur in reality ?

For this situation to occur, the 0 must have been sent at time f by some entity y_f; note that this entity must be in F and crash in this step, sending the 0 only to some of its neighbors (otherwise all entities in S and not just some would have received 0 at time $f + 1$). Also, y_f must have initially had 1 and received 0 only at time f (otherwise it would have sent it before and as it had not crashed yet, everybody would have received it). Let y_{f-1} be one of the entities that sent the 0 received by y_f at time f; note that this entity must be in F and crashed in that step, sending the 0 only to y_f and other entities not in S (otherwise all entities in S would receive 0 by time $f + 1$). Also, y_{f-1} must have initially had 1 and received 0 only at time $f - 1$ (otherwise it would have sent 0 before and as it had not crashed yet, everybody would have received it).

Using the same type of reasoning, for the situation to occur, there must be a sequence of entities $y_f, y_{f-1}, y_{f-2}, \ldots$ where entity y_{f-j} $(j \le f - 1)$ sent 0 to y_{f-j+1} and crashed at time $f - j$ before transmitting 0 to entities in S (otherwise all entities in S would receive 0 by time $f - j + 1$); furthermore, y_{f-j} initially had 1 and received only 1 until time $f - j$ (otherwise it would have sent 0 before and as it had not crashed yet, everybody would have received it). There must also be an entity y_0 that initially had 0, sent it to y_1 at time $t = 0$, and crashed before any other transmission. However, this implies that at least $f + 1$ entities crashed during the execution $(y_0, \ldots, y_f)$, which is absurd as by definition at most f entities crash.

Summarizing, this situation cannot occur. Hence,

Theorem 7.3.1 *Protocol* TellAll-Crash *solves* EFT-Consensus $(f, crash, n - 1)$ *in a fully synchronous complete network with simultaneous start for all $f \le n - 1$.*

Let us now look at the cost of protocol *TellAll-Crash*. It comprises $f + 1$ rounds in which each nonfailed entity sends a single bit to all its neighbors. Hence,

$$\mathbf{B}(TellAll - Crash) \le n(n - 1)(f + 1) \tag{7.3}$$

$$\mathbf{T}(TellAll - Crash) = f + 1. \tag{7.4}$$

Hacking   The bit complexity can be reduced somehow. Let us understand why and how.

First observe that the reason the nonfailed entities transmit in each round of protocol *TellAll-Crash* is only to propagate the 0 value one of them might have seen (and of which the other entities migh not yet be aware). In fact, if none of the entities sees a 0, they will only see and transmit 1 and decide on 1. In a sense, 1 is the default value and it will be decided upon *unless* a nonfailed entity sees a 0. This means that as long as an entity sees just 1, it is not going to change the default situation. Observe next that once an entity x sends 0 in a round t, there is no need for x to send it in the next rounds: If x does not crash in round t, the 0 will reach all nonfailed entities; if x crashes, it cannot send it anyway. Summarizing, *sending* 1 *is useless, and so is sending* 0 *for more than one round.*

On the basis of this fact, we can modify the protocol so that a nonfailed entity sends a message to its neighbor only the *first* time it sees 0. Interestingly, Facts 7.3.1–7.3.3 still hold for the new protocol, called *TellZero-Crash*, as shown in Figure 7.9. In fact, the proof of Theorem 7.3.1, with almost no modifications, can be used to show that

Theorem 7.3.2   *Protocol* TellZero-Crash *solves* EFT-Consensus $(f, crash, n-1)$ *in a fully synchronous complete network with simultaneous start for all* $f \le n - 1$.

Protocol *TellZero-Crash* still comprises $f + 1$ rounds. However, an entity transmits only the first time, if any, it sees 0. This means that

$$\mathbf{B}(TellZero - Crash) \le n(n-1) \tag{7.5}$$

$$\mathbf{T}(TellZero - Crash) = f + 1. \tag{7.6}$$

Notes and Remarks   These bounds have been established assuming that both the initial and the decision values are in $\{0, 1\}$. If this is not the case, we can still solve the problem with simple modifications to the original protocols. See Exercises 7.10.8 –7.10.10.

These bounds are established assuming that all entities start simultaneously. If this is not the case, we can still solve the problem by first performing a wake-up (with possibility of crashes). See Exercises 7.10.6 and 7.10.7.

TellZero-Crash

```
begin
    if  I_x = 0 then send 0 to N(x);
    for  t = 1,...,f  do
        compute  rep(x,t);
        if  (rep(x,t) = 0  and rep(x, t - 1) = 1) then send 0 to N(x);
    endfor
    O_x := rep(x, f + 1);
end
```

FIGURE 7.9: Protocol *TellZero-Crash.*

These bounds are established assuming that the network is a complete graph. If this is not the case, and the network is a graph G, the problem can still be solved, provided

$$f < c_{\text{node}}(G), \tag{7.7}$$

with exactly the same protocols. See Exercises 7.10.11 and 7.10.12.

7.3.2 Synchronous Consensus with Byzantine Failures

A Byzantine entity can send what it wants at any time it wants to any neighbor it wants. We should assume that the Byzantine entities are actually malicious, that is, they can send false information, tell lies, and generally act so as to make our protocol fail. The presence of Byzantine entities clearly makes the task of achieving a consensus among the nonfaulty entities quite difficult. Still, the fact that the system is *synchronous* makes this task possible in spite of a large number of faults. In fact, as we will see, in a synchronous complete graph, fault-tolerant consensus is possible even with $(\frac{n}{3} - 1)$ Byzantine entities.

This and related results are established under the following set **BA** of restrictions :

Additional Assumptions (BA)

1. *Connectivity, Bidirectional Links*;
2. *Synch*;
3. each entity has a unique id;
4. the network is a complete graph;
5. all entities start; simultaneously;
6. each entity knows the ids of its neighbors.

Achieving Byzantine Consensus   In this section, we present a fairly simple algorithm for Boolean consensus, that is, when initial and decision values are in $\{0, 1\}$; we will see later how to transform it into an algorithm for a general value consensus with the same cost.

We will use the same idea of protocol *TellZero-Crash* we described in the previous section when dealing with crash failures: We will use information messages only to propagate the value 0, if any; after an appropriate amount of steps, each nonfaulty entity will decide on 0 if one of the received values was 0.

Protocol *TellZero-Crash* was simply a "wake-up" process with the value 0 being the "wake-up message": Initially "awake" if the initial value is 0, an "awake" entity would send immediately and only once the "wake-up message" 0 to all its neighbors. As we are assuming that entities have distinct ids, we can differenciate 0s sent by different senders; furthermore, as we assume simultaneous start, we can also put the time step inside the message. This means that our wake-up messages are of the form $\langle 0, \text{id}(s), t \rangle$, where s is the sender, $\text{id}(s)$ its unique id, and t the time step when the message is sent.

Let us see what can go wrong if we were to use the same technique in a Byzantine setting.

- A Byzantine entity z can lie and forge messages; thus, z could send $\langle 0, \text{id}(x), t \rangle$ to y, with $x \neq z$. (It can also lie about the time t, but as the system is synchronous that would expose z as a faulty entity.)
- A Byzantine entity z can send different information to different neighbors; so, at the same time step t, it can send $\langle 0, \text{id}(z), t \rangle$ to x and nothing at all to y. As a consequence, some nonfaulty entities may decide 0 while others 1, violating consensus.

The first problem is not really severe; in fact, as each entity knows the identity of its neighbors (restrictions **BA**), when x receives a message it can detect whether the id inside is the correct one and trash the message if it is forged.

The second problem is, however, severe; as a consequence, a nonfaulty x can *not* simply accept any wake-up message it receives.

To see how to deal with this problem, note that what matters is not if a wake-up message was originated by a Byzantine entity, but rather if the same message was received by all nonfaulty entities. In fact, *if all nonfaulty entities accept the same information, then* (regardless of its origin) *they will take the same decision.*

Therefore, what we need is a mechanism, to be used by the protocol, that allows x to decide whether all the other nonfaulty entities also received this wake-up message; only then, x will accept the wake-up message, even if originated by a Byzantine entity. In other words, this mechanism must ensure that if the originator is nonfaulty, then the wake-up is accepted; if the originator is faulty, then it is accepted only if all nonfaulty entities received it.

The mechanism that we will call *RegisteredMail* and describe below dictates what actions must be taken when a nonfaulty entity wants to send a wake-up message, and when a nonfaulty entity receives this message.

Mechanism *RegisteredMail*:

1. To *send* a registered wake-up $\langle 0, \text{id}(x), t \rangle$ at time t, a nonfaulty entity x transmits a message $\langle \text{"init"}, 0, \text{id}(x), t \rangle$ to all entities at time t.

2. If a nonfaulty entity y receives $\langle \text{"init"}, 0, \text{id}(x), t \rangle$ from x at time $t+1$, it transmits $\langle \text{"echo"}, 0, \text{id}(x), t \rangle$ to all entities at time $t+1$.

3. If a nonfaulty entity y receives $\langle \text{"init"}, 0, \text{id}(x), t \rangle$ at time t', it ignores the message if $t' \neq t+1$ or the message is not from x or it already received a $\langle \text{"init"}, 0, \text{id}(x), t'' \rangle$ with $t'' \neq t$.

4. If a nonfaulty entity y by time $t' \geq t+2$ has received $\langle \text{"echo"}, 0, \text{id}(x), t \rangle$ from at least $f+1$ different entities, then y transmits $\langle \text{"echo"}, 0, \text{id}(x), t \rangle$ (if it has not already done so) at time t' to all entities.

5. If a nonfaulty entity y by time $t' \geq t+1$ has received $\langle \text{"echo"}, 0, \text{id}(x), t \rangle$ messages from at least $n-f$ different entities, then y *accepts* the registered wake-up $\langle 0, \text{id}(x), t \rangle$ (if it has not already done so) at time t'.

Let us now verify that *RegisteredMail* is exactly the mechanism we are looking for.

Theorem 7.3.3 *Let $n > 3f$; then Mechanism* RegisteredMail *satisfies the following conditions with respect to registered wake-up* $\langle 0, id(x), t \rangle$:

1. *if x is nonfaulty and sends the registered wake-up* $\langle 0, id(x), t \rangle$, *then the wake-up is accepted by all nonfaulty entities by time $t + 2$;*
2. *if the wake-up* $\langle 0, id(x), t \rangle$ *is accepted by any nonfaulty entity at time $t' > t$, then it is accepted by all nonfaulty entities by time $t' + 1$;*
3. *if x is nonfaulty and does not send the registered wake-up* $\langle 0, id(x), t \rangle$, *then the wake-up is not accepted by the nonfaulty entities.*

Proof. (1) Suppose that a nonfaulty entity x starts *RegisteredMail* at time t: It sends $\langle$"*init*", $0, id(x), t\rangle$ to all entities at time t; all the $n - f$ nonfaulty entities receive it and send $\langle$"*echo*", $0, id(x), t\rangle$ at time $t + 1$. Thus, by time $t + 2$, each nonfaulty entity receives $\langle$"*echo*", $0, id(x), t\rangle$ from at least $n - f$ entities and accepts the wake-up message $\langle 0, id(x), t \rangle$.

(2) Suppose that a registered wake-up $\langle 0, id(x), t \rangle$ is accepted by a nonfaulty entity y at time $t' > t$. Then y must have received at least $n - f$ $\langle$"*echo*", $0, id(x), t\rangle$ messages by time t'. These messages were sent at time $t' - 1$ or before. Among the $n - f$ senders of these messages, at least $(n - f) - f \geq f + 1$ are nonfaulty. As nonfaulty entities send the same message to all entities, every nonfaulty entity must have received at least $f + 1$ $\langle$"*echo*", $0, id(x), t\rangle$ messages by time t'. This means that all the nonfaulty entities have sent $\langle$"*echo*", $0, id(x), t\rangle$ by time t'; as a consequence, every nonfaulty entity receives at least $n - f$ $\langle$"*echo*", $0, id(x), t\rangle$ messages by time $t' + 1$. Therefore, the registered wake-up $\langle 0, id(x), t \rangle$ is accepted by all nonfaulty entities by time $t' + 1$.

(3) If a nonfaulty entity x does *not* start *RegisteredMail* at time t, then it sends no $\langle$"*init*", $0, id(x), t\rangle$ messages; thus, any message $\langle$"*init*", $0, id(x), t\rangle$ sent in the system is a forgery, that is, sent by a faulty entity. Therefore, if a nonfaulty entity y receives $\langle$"*init*", $0, id(x), t\rangle$ at time $t + 1$, because of restrictions **BA**, it can detect that the sender is not x and will not consider the message at all. In other words, the nonfaulty entities do not transmit $\langle$"*echo*", $0, id(x), t\rangle$ messages. As a consequence, the only $\langle$"*echo*", $0, id(x), t\rangle$ messages a nonfaulty entity receives are sent by faulty ones; as there are only f faulty entities and $n - f > f$, by Rule 3 of *RegisteredMail*, a nonfaulty entity never accepts the registered wake-up $\langle 0, id(x), t \rangle$. ∎

Now we describe a simple binary Byzantine agreement algorithm, called *TellZero-Byz*, that uses *RegisteredMail* for sending and accepting wake-up messages.

The algorithm operates in $f + 2$ stages, $0, \ldots, f + 1$, where stage i is composed of two time steps, $2i$ and $2i + 1$. In the first stage, at time 0, every nonfaulty entity with initial value 0 starts *RegisteredMail* to send a registered wake-up of a stage.

IMPORTANT. For simplicity, in the description of the protocol and in its analysis, when an entity sends a message, we will assume that it will send it also to itself (i.e., it will receive it in the next time unit).

Protocol *TellZero-Byz*:

1. At time 0, every nonfaulty entity x with $I_x = 0$ (i.e., whose initial value is 0) starts *RegisteredMail* to send $\langle 0, \mathrm{id}(x), 0 \rangle$.

2. At time $2i$ (i.e., in the first step of stage i), $1 \le i \le f + 1$, a nonfaulty entity x starts *RegisteredMail* to send $\langle 0, \mathrm{id}(x) \rangle, 2i \rangle$ if and only if x has accepted wake-up messages from at least $f + i - 1$ different entities by time $2i$, and x has not yet originated a wake-up message.

3. At time $2(f + 2)$ (i.e., in the first step of stage $f + 2$), a nonfaulty entity x decides on 0 if and only if *by that time* x has accepted wake-up messages from at least $2f + 1$ different entities. Otherwise, x decides 1.

Observe that the mechanism *RegisteredMail* is started only at *even* time steps. Let us now analyze the correctness and complexity of the protocol.

Theorem 7.3.4 *Protocol* TellZero-Byz *solves* EFT-Consensus $(f, Byzantine, n - 1)$ with *Boolean initial values in a synchronous complete network under restrictions* **BA** *for all* $f \le \frac{n}{3} - 1$.

Proof. By construction, the protocol terminates after $2(f + 2)$ time units. To prove the theorem we need to show that both nontriviality and agreement conditions hold.

Let us first consider *nontriviality*. If all nonfaulty entities have initial value 0, they all start *RegisteredMail* at time 0, and, by Theorem 7.3.3(1), they all accept these messages by time 2. In other words, each nonfaulty entity accepts wake-up messages from at least $n - f \ge 2f + 1$ different entities by time 2. Thus, according to the Protocol, they will all decide 0 when the protocol terminates.

If all nonfaulty entities have initial value 1, they do not send a registered wake-up. Actually, in this case, each nonfaulty entity never starts *RegisteredMail* at any time. In fact, to start *RegisteredMail* at time $t' > 0$, a nonfaulty entity needs to have accepted at least $f + 1$ wake-ups, but only the f faulty entities may possibly have sent one. Thus, according to the protocol, the nonfaulty entities will all decide 1 when the protocol terminates.

Let us now consider *agreement*. We need to show that, if a nonfaulty entity x decides 0, then all the other nonfaulty entities also decide 0. Let x decide 0; this means that by time $t = 2(f + 2)$, x must have accepted wake-up messages from at least $2f + 1$ different entities, some faulty and some not. Let R be the set of nonfaulty entities among these; then $|R| \ge (2f + 1) - f = f + 1$.

If all the entities in R have initial values 0, then each starts *RegisteredMail* at time 0 to send its wake-up message; thus, by Theorem 7.3.3(1), all nonfaulty entities accepted these messages by time 2. In other words, at time 2, each nonfaulty entity has accepted messages from $|R| \ge f + 1$ different entities; by rule 2 of *TellZero-Byz*, each nonfaulty entity y (that has not yet sent its own wakeup message) will now start *RegisteredMail* to send its wake-up message $\langle 0, y, 2\rangle$. By Theorem 7.3.3(1), all nonfaulty entities will accept these messages by time 4. Thus, they will all decide 0 when the protocol terminates, at time $2(f+2) \geq 4$.

Summarizing, if all the entities in R have initial values 0, by time 4 every nonfaulty entity x accepts wake-up messages from at least $n - f \geq 2f + 1$ different entities. Thus, they will all decide 0 when the protocol terminates at time $2(f+2) \geq 4$.

Consider now the case when one of the entities in R, say y, has initial value 1, and thus does not start *RegisteredMail* at time 0. As its message was accepted by x, y must have started *RegisteredMail* at some time $2i$, where $1 \leq i \leq f + 1$. Notice that by rule 2 of *TellZero-Byz*, to have started *RegisteredMail* at time $2i$, y must have accepted by that time at least $f + i - 1$ different wake-up messages (none of them originated by itself). Further observe that, by Theorem 7.3.3(2), these $f + i - 1$ wake-up messages are accepted by all nonfaulty entities by time $2i + 1$. Finally observe that the wake-up message originated by y at time $2i$, by Theorem 7.3.3(1), is accepted by all nonfaulty entities by time $2i + 2$. Summarizing, each nonfaulty entity accepts at least $(f + i - 1) + 1 = f + i$ wake-up messages by time $2i + 2$.

This means that if $i \leq f$, all nonfaulty entities that have not started *RegisteredMail* already will do so by time $2i + 2$. Thus, by time $2i + 4 \leq 2f + 4 = 2(f+2)$ every nonfaulty entity has accepted at least $n - f \geq 2f + 1$ different wake-up messages; therefore, it will decide 0 when the protocol terminates.

By contrast, if $i = f + 1$, then every nonfaulty entity has accepted $f + i \geq 2f + 1$ different wake-up messages by time $2(f+1) + 2 = 2(f+2)$, and, thus, they will all decide 0 when the protocol terminates at that time. ∎

Let us now examine the complexity of Protocol *TellZero-Byz*.

The protocol terminates after $2(f+2)$ time units. During this time, a nonfaulty entity x will start the execution of *RegisteredMail* at most once. Each of these executions uses $n - 1$ "init" messages and at most $n(n - 1)$ "echo" messages; hence, the overall total of messages generated by the nonfaulty entities is at most

$$(n - f)(n - 1)(n + 1).$$

A faulty entity z can send messages to all its neighbors at each time unit, for a total of $2(f + 2)(n - 1)$. Of these messages, the ones sent at even time units can be used by z to start the execution of *RegisteredMail* so as to generate more message transmissions. However, by rule 3 of *RegisteredMail*, only one attempt would be taken into account by a nonfaulty entity; hence, the number of additional messages caused by z is at most $n(n - 1)$. This means that, in total, the number of messages sent or generated by the faulty entities is at most

$$f(2(f + 2)(n - 1) + n(n - 1)).$$

Summarizing, as each message contains the entity's id, we have

$$\mathbf{B}(\textit{TellZero} - \textit{Byz}) \le (2f^2 + 4f + n + n^2 - fn + n - f)(n-1)$$

$$= O(n^3 \log i) \tag{7.8}$$

$$\mathbf{T}(\textit{TellZero} - \textit{Byz}) = 2(f+2), \tag{7.9}$$

where i denotes the range of the ids of the entities.

7.3.3 Limit to Number of Byzantine Entities for Agreement

We have seen that if the system is fully synchronous, then under restrictions **BA**, consensus is possible even if almost one third of the entities are faulty and their failure is Byzantine. In this section we are going to see that indeed $\frac{n}{3} - 1$ is the limit to the number of Byzantine entities the system can tolerate even under **BA**.

We will first consider the case $n = 3$ and show that it is not possible to tolerate a single faulty entity.

Theorem 7.3.5 *If $n = 3$, EFT-Consensus $(1, Byzantine, n-1)$ is unsolvable even if the system is fully synchronous and restrictions* **BA** *hold.*

Proof. When $n = 3$, the system is a synchronous ring R of three entities $\langle a, b, c \rangle$ (see Figure 7.10(a)). We show that it is impossible to tolerate a single Byzantine entity. By contradiction, let P be a solution protocol.

We will first of all construct a different network, a ring $\overline{R}$ of 6 nodes, $\langle a_1, b_1, c_1, a_2, b_2, c_2 \rangle$; see Figure 7.10(b), where

- $\text{id}(a_1) = \text{id}(a_2) = \text{id}(a)$; $\text{id}(b_1) = \text{id}(b_2) = \text{id}(b)$; and $\text{id}(c_1) = \text{id}(c_2) = \text{id}(c)$.
- $I_{a_1} = I_{b_1} = I_{c_1} = 0$; $I_{a_2} = I_{b_2} = I_{c_2} = 1$.

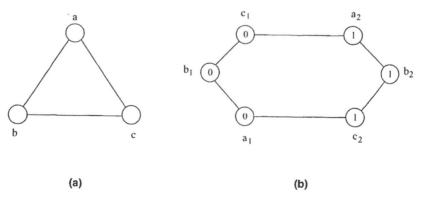

(a)   (b)

FIGURE 7.10: Two networks used in the proof of Theorem 7.3.5.

The entities in $\overline{R}$ do not know that the network they are in is not R. On the contrary, they all think to be in R; both a_1 and a_2 think to be a; similarly, b_1 and b_2 think to be b, and c_1 and c_2 think to be c.

We now let all these entities simultaneously start executing protocol P, without any faults. Call this execution α; we denote by $\alpha(x, y)$ the behavior of x toward its neighbor y in this execution, and by $\alpha(x)$ the behavior of x (with respect to itself and to its neighbors) in this execution. So, for example, $\alpha(c_1, a_2)$ denotes the behavior of c_1 towards a_2 in α.

We now consider the original ring R and focus on three different executions of protocol P; in each of these executions, two entities are nonfaulty and the third one is Byzantine. The behavior of the nonfaulty entities is fully determined by the protocol. For the Byzantine entity we chose a special (but possible) behavior, which is connected to the execution α in $\overline{R}$.

Execution E_1: In this execution, entities a and b are nonfaulty and have initial value 0, while c is faulty. In this execution, c behaves toward a as c_2 behaves toward a_1 in $\overline{R}$, and toward b as c_1 behaves toward b_1. See Figure 7.11. In other words $E_1(c, a) = \alpha(c_2, a_1)$ and $E_1(c, b) = \alpha(c_1, b_1)$. Notice that, the behavior of a (respective b) in this execution is identical to the one of a_1 (respective b_1) in α. That is, $E_1(a) = \alpha(a_1)$ and $E_1(b) = \alpha(b_1)$.

As we are assuming that P is correct, then in E_1, within finite time, a and b decide; as both have initial value 0, their decision will be 0. This means that a_1 and b_1 will also decide 0 in execution α.

Execution E_2: In this execution, entities b and c are nonfaulty and have initial value 1, while a is faulty. In this execution, a behaves toward b as a_2 behaves toward b_2 in $\overline{R}$, and toward c as a_1 behaves toward c_2, In other words $E_2(a, b) = \alpha(a_2, b_2)$ and $E_2(a, c) = \alpha(a_1, c_2)$ (see Figure 7.11). Notice that, the behavior of b (respectively c) in this execution is identical to the one of b_2 (respectively c_2) in α. That is, $E_2(b) = \alpha(b_2)$ and $E_2(c) = \alpha(c_2)$.

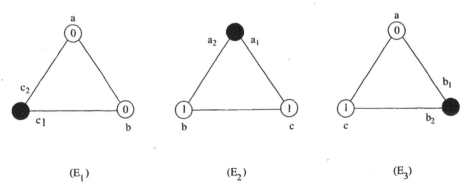

FIGURE 7.11: Executions E_1, E_2, and E_3 in the proof of Theorem 7.3.6.

As we are assuming that P is correct, then in E_2, within finite time, b and c decide; as both have initial value 1, their decision will be 1. This means that b_2 and c_2 will also decide 1 in execution α.

Execution E_3: In this execution, entities a and c are nonfaulty, with initial value 0 and 1, respectively; b is faulty. In this execution, b behaves toward a as b_1 behaves toward a_1 in $\overline{R}$, and toward c as b_2 behaves toward c_2, In other words $E_3(b, a) = \alpha(b_1, a_1)$ and $E_3(b, c) = \alpha(b_2, c_2)$ (see Figure 7.11). Notice that, the behavior of a (respective c) in this execution is identical to the one of a_1 (respective c_2) in α. That is, $E_3(a) = \alpha(a_1)$ and $E_3(c) = \alpha(c_2)$.

As we are assuming that P is correct, then in E_3, within finite time, b and c decide on the same value; as both have different initial values their decision will be either 1 or 0.

If a and c decide 1 in E_4, then a_1 and c_2 decide 1 in execution α, but we have just seen (from the discussion on Execution E_1) that a_1 decides 0 in execution α: a contradiction.

If a and c decide 0 in E_4, then a_1 and c_2 decide 0 in execution α, but we have just seen (from the discussion on Execution E_2) that c_2 decides 1 in execution α: a contradiction. ∎

Using this result, we can show that $\frac{n}{3} - 1$ is the limit for any n.

Theorem 7.3.6 *If $f \geq \frac{n}{3}$, EFT-Consensus (f, Byzantine, $n - 1$) is unsolvable even if the system is fully synchronous and restrictions* **BA** *hold.*

Proof. Consider a synchronous complete network K_n of $n > 3$ entities under restrictions **BA**. Assume by contradiction that there is a solution protocol P for this system when $f \geq \frac{n}{3}$.

Consider the synchronous ring R of three entities $\langle a, b, c \rangle$ under restrictions **BA** (see Figure 7.10(a)).

We will now construct, starting from P, an agreement protocol for R with one Byzantine faults as follows:

1. We first divide the entities of K_n into three sets, A, B, and C, of size at least 1 and at most f each;
2. we then set the initial values of the entities in A to I_a, those in B to I_b, and those in C to I_c;
3. entities a, b, and c now simulate the execution of P in K_n as follows:
   (a) entity a simulates all the entities in A, b simulates those in B, and c those in C;
   (b) messages within the same set are simulated, and messages between different sets are sent explicitly.

This protocol, $Sim(P)$, actually is a solution protocol for R. In fact, the Byzantine failure of an entity in R corresponds to the Byzantine failure of the assigned simulated set of entities of K_n; as each set contains at most f entities, protocol P will be able to tolerate such failures. In other words, if P is correct in K_n, $Sim(P)$ works correctly in the presence of a single Byzantine entity in R; however, by Theorem 7.3.5, this is impossible. Therefore, no such a P exists. ∎

7.3.4 From Boolean to General Byzantine Agreement

We have seen how to reach Boolean agreement in fully synchronous complete graphs. In this section, we are going to examine the cases when the input values are not Boolean.

We will see that it is possible to transform any solution protocol for the Boolean case into the one that works for an arbitrary, but a priori known, set of initial values IV.

We will call the resulting algorithm $FromBoolean(\cdot)$ where the input parameter is the Boolean Byzantine consensus protocol to be transformed. The transformation is achieved by adding four simple steps to the Boolean protocol, three before the start of its execution, the fourth upon its termination.

Let us now describe the algorithm. Given the set IV of values, let $\bar{v} \in$ IV be a distinguished element, which will be our *default* value; let $\iota, \emptyset \notin$ IV be two other distinguished values with $\iota \neq \emptyset$. In the protocol, each entity x uses four local variables $a \cdot x, b \cdot x, c \cdot x$, and $d \cdot x$. As before, we assume that when an entity sends a message to all other entities, it sends it also to itself (and it will receive it by the next time step). Let BP be the Boolean Byzantine consensus protocol employed by our algorithm.

Algorithm *FromBoolean(BP)*:

1. At time 0, each nonfaulty entity x sets $a \cdot x = I_x$ and $b \cdot x = c \cdot x = d \cdot x = \iota$ and sends $\langle\text{"first"}, a \cdot x\rangle$ to all entities.

2. At time 1, each nonfaulty entity x:

   (a) sets $b \cdot x := v$ if it has received $n - f$ or more copies of the same message $\langle\text{"first"}, v\rangle$, $v \in IV$; otherwise it sets $b.x = \emptyset$,

   (b) sends $\langle\text{"second"}, b \cdot x\rangle$ to all entities.

3. At time 2, each nonfaulty entity x:

   (a) sets $c \cdot x$ to the value, different from ι, that occurs most often among the received "second" messages, with ties broken arbitrarily; if all received "second" messages contain ι, no change is made to $c \cdot x$ (i.e., $c \cdot x = \emptyset$);

   (b) sets $d \cdot x = 1$ if it has received $n - f$ or more copies of the same message $\langle\text{"second"}, v\rangle$ with $v \in$ IV; otherwise it will set $d \cdot x = 0$. **Note:** The value of $d \cdot x$ is Boolean;

   (c) starts the execution of the Boolean Byzantine consensus protocol BP using the Boolean value $d \cdot x$ as its initial value.

4. When the execution of BP terminates, each nonfaulty entity x:

   (a) decides $c \cdot x$ if the Boolean decision is 1 and $c \cdot x \neq \emptyset$;

   (b) otherwise decides the default value $\bar{v}$.

An interesting property of the protocol is that in the "second" message all the nonfaulty entities send the same value (if any) from I.

Lemma 7.3.1 *Let x be a nonfaulty entity. If $b \cdot x \in IV$, then for any nonfaulty entity y, $b \cdot x = b \cdot y$.*

Proof. By contradiction, assume that nonfaulty entities x and y send $\langle$*"second"*, $b \cdot x\rangle$ and $\langle$*"second"*, $b \cdot y\rangle$, respectively, where $b \cdot x, b \cdot y \in \text{IV}$ but $b \cdot x \neq b \cdot y$.

Entity x sent $\langle$*"second"*, $b \cdot y\rangle$ because (according to the algorithm) it received at least $n - f$ "first" messages containing $b \cdot x$; of these, at least $(n - f) - f = n - 2f \geq f + 1$ were sent by nonfaulty entities. As each nonfaulty entity sends the same message to all entities, then also y receives at least $f + 1$ messages containing $b \cdot x$.

Observe that y sent $\langle$*"second"*, $b \cdot y\rangle$ because (according to the algorithm) it received at least $n - f$ "first" messages containing $b \cdot y$. This means that at time 2, entity y received in total at least $f + 1 + n - f > n$ "first" messages, which is impossible. ∎

Let us now examine the correctness of protocol *FromBoolean* when used in conjunction with a Boolean Byzantine consensus protocol BP (e.g., *TellZero-Byz*).

Theorem 7.3.7 *Protocol* FromBoolean(BP) *solves* EFT-Consensus (*f, Byzantine, $n-1$*) *in a synchronous complete network under restrictions* **BA** *for all $f \leq \frac{n}{3} - 1$.*

Proof. Let us first consider *nontriviality*. If all nonfaulty entities have the same initial value v, each of them will send $\langle$*"first"*, $v\rangle$ and receive at least $n - f$ such messages. Hence, they will set all their $b \cdot$ variable to v, send $\langle$ *"second"*, $v\rangle$, and receive at least $n - f$ such messages. As a consequence, each nonfaulty entity x will set $c \cdot x = v$ and $d \cdot x = 1$. As all nonfaulty entities have the the same initial Boolean value 1, in the execution of protocol BP, they will all choose 1. Hence, they will all decide v.

Consider now *agreement*. First observe that if in the execution of protocol BP the decision is 0, then all nonfaulty entities decide $\bar{v}$ by default, and agreement holds.

Let us then consider the case when in the execution of protocol BP the decision is 1. To be so, at least a nonfaulty entity x must have had $d \cdot x = 1$. This means that x has received at least $n - f$ "second" messages with the same value, say v; of these, at least $(n - f) - f = n - 2f \geq f + 1$ are sent by nonfaulty entities. This implies that any nonfaulty entity y receives at least $n - 2f$ $\langle$*"second"*, $v\rangle$ messages. Observe that by Lemma 7.3.1, only faulty entities will send a "second" message with a value $w \in I$ with $w \neq v$. In other words, each nonfaulty entity y receives at least $f + 1$ "second" messages with value v and at most f "second" messages with values other than v; therefore, y sets $c \cdot y = v$ before starting the Boolean protocol BP and, as the Boolean decision value is 1, upon termination y decides v. ∎

Let us now the cost of protocol *FromBoolean(BP)*. In particular, let us examine the cost that *FromBoolean* adds to BP.

As BP is started at time 2, and the final decision in *FromBoolean* is taken immediately upon termination of BP, the total time overhead is two additional time steps.

In each of these additional steps, every entity sends a message to all other entities. Hence, the total message overhead is $2n(n-1)$. Observe, however, that these messages contain values in IV and not in $\{0, 1\}$.

Summarizing, let **v** denote the range of the values; then

$$\mathbf{B}(FromBoolean(BP)) \leq 2n(n-1)\log \mathbf{v} + \mathbf{B}(BP) \tag{7.10}$$

$$\mathbf{T}(FromBoolean(BP)) = 2 + \mathbf{T}(BP). \tag{7.11}$$

For example, if we use the Boolean protocol *TellZero-Byz*, we will have

$$\mathbf{B}(FromBoolean(TellZero\text{-}Byz)) = O(n^2 \log \mathbf{v} + n^3 \log \mathbf{i}) \tag{7.12}$$

$$\mathbf{T}(FromBoolean(TellZero\text{-}Byz)) = 2f + 6, \tag{7.13}$$

where i denotes the range of the ids of the entities.

7.3.5 Byzantine Agreement in Arbitrary Graphs

Until now, when discussing localized Byzantine entity failures, we have been working under the restriction that the network topology is that of a complete graph K_n. In this section we are going to examine what happens if we remove this assumption from the list of additional restrictions BA, that is, we consider the problem of reaching consensus in a generic network G localized Byzantine entity failures. The new set of assumptions is the same as before except that knowledge of being in a complete graph is replaced with complete topological knowledge of the graph.

Additional Assumptions (GA)

1. *Connectivity, Bidirectional Links*;
2. *Synch*;
3. each entity has a unique id;
4. all entities have complete knowledge of the topology of the graph and of the identities of the entities;
5. all entities start simultaneously.

As the complete graph contains any graph G of n nodes as a subgraph, the limitation $f < \frac{n}{3}$ on the total number of failures tolerable in K_n (recall Theorem 7.3.6) obviously holds also for G. In other words, we cannot expect to do better (i.e., tolerate more faults) in G than in the complete graph. On the contrary, the reduced communication capabilities existing in G will create more limitations on the number of faults that can be tolerated in the complete graph.

We know that there is a link between the connectivity of the network and its fault tolerance. As Byzantine failures include crashes as special cases, the limitation $f < c_{node}(G)$ on the total number of crash failures tolerable in G (recall Equation 7.7) obviously holds in our case. Indeed, in the case of Byzantine failures the limitation becomes more severe (Exercise 7.10.17):

Theorem 7.3.8 *If* $f \geq \frac{c_{node}(G)}{2}$, *then* EFT-Consensus $(f, Byzantine, c_{node}(G))$ *is unsolvable even if G is fully synchronous and restrictions* **GA** *hold.*

Summarizing, by Theorems 7.3.6 and 7.3.8, the total number f of Byzantine faults in G can not be more than

$$ f \leq Min \left\{ \frac{n}{3}, \frac{c_{node}(G)}{2} \right\} - 1. \tag{7.14} $$

In other words, fewer than one third of the entities must be faulty, and the graph must be more than $2f$-node-connected. The interesting thing is that we can actually design a consensus protocol that tolerates those many faults in such networks. Let us see how.

By Property 7.1.2, we know that if G is $2f + 1$-node-connected, then between any two pair of nodes x and y there are at least $2f + 1$ node-disjoint paths. This fact can be used to establish reliable two-party communication mechanism as follows.

Mechanism *Two-Parties ByzComm*

- Each pair of nonfaulty entities x and y select $2f + 1$ node-disjoint paths connecting them (they can do so because by Restrictions **GA**, they both have complete topological knowledge); then, whenever x wants to communicate a message to y, it will send the message along all (and only) those paths.

- As at most f entities are faulty, at most f of those paths are dangerous and messages along them can be corrupted; in contrast, $f + 1$ are not faulty and the message is delivered correctly. In other words, a majority of the copies of the message from x to y will be correct. Thus, y can determine the correct message from x.

Observe that using Mechanism *Two-Parties ByzComm* any pair of nonfaulty entities x and y can simulate the existence of a direct communication link (x, y) between them (as if they were in a complete network). In other words, we can use any solution protocol P for a complete network K_n (e.g., *TellZero-Byz*) and execute it in G: Whenever an entity x is requested by P to send a message to y in K_n, x will use Mechanism *Two-Parties ByzComm* to achieve the same goal in G.

In the simulation, we need to redefine the unit of time; this is because, while in K_n the transmission of a message from x to y requires one time unit, in G the time involved is the length of the longest of the node-disjoint paths used by *Two-Parties ByzComm* to communicate messages from x to y. As the maximum distance between any two nodes is diam(G), we will make a time unit of protocol P correspond to diam(G) time units in the simulation of P in G (we can do that because the network is synchronous and by Restrictions **GA**, all nonfaulty entities start at the same time). The resulting protocol, that we will call *ByzComm(P)*, thus achieves the desired goal:

Theorem 7.3.9   *Protocol* ByzComm(P) *solves* EFT-Consensus ($f, Byzantine$, $2f + 1$) *in a synchronous* ($2f + 1$)-*node-connected network G under restrictions* **GA** *for all* $f \leq \frac{n}{3} - 1$.

The cost of *ByzComm(P)* depends obviously on the cost of protocol P and on the topology of G. Each time unit of P costs diam(G) $\leq n - 1$ time units in *ByzComm(P)*, where diam(G) as usual denotes the diameter of G.

Each message sent in P now requires the transmission of the same message over the $2f + 1$ predetermined paths, each of the length at most diam(G) $\leq n - 1$, for a total cost of at most ($2f + 1$)diam(G) messages. Additionally consider that the f faulty entities can send messages to all their neighbors at each time instant; this adds at most $f$deg(G) messages per time unit, where deg(G) as usual denotes the degree (i.e. the maximum number of neighbors of a node) of G. Observe that each message needs to specify both the sender x and the destination y and requires $2 \log n$ bits. Summarizing,

$$\mathbf{B}(ByzComm(P)) = O(f \ n \ \mathbf{B}(P) + fn^2 \log n \ \mathbf{T}(P)) \qquad (7.15)$$

$$\mathbf{T}(ByzComm(P)) \leq \text{diam}(G)\mathbf{T}(P). \qquad (7.16)$$

For example, in the case of Boolean consensus, if we use *TellZero-Byz*, we will have

$$\mathbf{B}(ByzComm(TellZero - Byz)) = O(f \ n^4 \ \log n) \qquad (7.17)$$

$$\mathbf{T}(ByzComm(TellZero - Byz)) = O(f \ n). \qquad (7.18)$$

Let us see what are the practical implications of Theorems 7.3.8 and 7.3.9. These two theorems together state that the presence of $f < \frac{n}{3}$ Byzantine entities can be tolerated *if and only if* the network is at least ($2f + 1$)-node connected, that is, if and only if $f \leq \frac{1}{2}(c_{node}(G) - 1)$. What does this mean for fault-tolerant computing in common interconnection networks in presence of Byzantine entity faults ? The answers are not very comforting.

For example, in a *ring* network R, as $c_{node}(R) = 2$, *not even a single Byzantine entity can be tolerated*, regardless of the size of the ring!

In a *torus Tr* we have $c_{node}(Tr) = 4$; hence *at most a single Byzantine entity can be tolerated*.

Network G	Node Connectivity $c_{node}(G)$	Byzantine Entities f
Ring R	2	0
Torus Tr	4	1
Hypercube H	$\log n$	$\frac{1}{2}\log\frac{n}{2}$
CubeConnectedCycle CCC	3	1

FIGURE 7.12: Number f of Byzantine entities tolerated in common networks.

Slightly better is fared in denser networks, such as the *hypercube H*; in fact, as $c_{node}(H) = \log n$, up to $\frac{1}{2}\log\frac{n}{2}$ Byzantine entities can be tolerated. These observations are summarized in Figure 7.12.

Theorem 7.3.10 *In a completely synchonous system, any deterministic f-resilient algorithm for Byzantine agreement requires $f + 1$ rounds of communication.*

7.4 LOCALIZED ENTITY FAILURES: USING RANDOMIZATION

7.4.1 Random Actions and Coin Flips

In a general asynchronous system, as we know, it is not possible to deal with even a single crash failure in the system even if the network is fully connected. This fact, the Single-Failure Disaster, holds for protocols where the operations performed by the entities in their actions are all *deterministic*.

By contrast, if we empower and allow the entities to perform *random* operations during their actions, then the proof of the Single-Failure Disaster theorem no longer holds.

Hence, a way to construct fault-tolerant protocols is to provide randomness to the entities. This can be achieved by providing the entities with the ability to flip coins during their actions; entities can then use the outcome to guide their operations.

For example, an entity in a ring network may flip a two-headed coin to decide to which neighbor it will send a prepared message: To the "left" if the outcome is "head," and to the "right" if the outcome is "tail." In this way, the choice of the neighbor is not specified by the algorithm (i.e., it is not deterministic), but it is rather the result of a "random" event (i.e., it is randomized).

Summarizing, coin flips return "random" values according to some specified probability distribution, and they may be used by the entities to determine their next move.

IMPORTANT. There are some important consequences about using randomization in protocols.

1. As the outcome of a coin flip is not known a priori, the number of possible executions depends not only on time delays but also on the outcome of the coin flips (which might be different in two different executions). This means that we must define a probability distribution on executions, assigning to executions probabilities according to the outcomes of the coin flips that generate them.

2. It might be possible to have executions that terminate with an incorrect result. The existence of incorrect executions might still be acceptable and permitted, provided they all occur with very low probability.

3. It might be possible to have executions that never terminate. The existence of nonterminating executions might still be acceptable and permitted, provided they all occur with very low probability.

Indeed, randomized protocols fit into three categories: *Monte Carlo*, *Las Vegas*, and *Hybrid* protocols.

- *Monte Carlo* protocols are distributed algorithms such that
  - they always terminate;
  - upon termination, the problem is solved correctly *with high probability*.
- *Las Vegas* protocols are distributed procedures such that
  - they terminate *with high probability*;
  - upon termination, the problem is always solved correctly.
- *Hybrid* protocols are distributed procedures such that
  - they terminate *with high probability*;
  - upon termination, the problem is solved correctly *with high probability*.

In other words, with randomization we must give up either the guarantee on correctness (in the Monte Carlo case) or the guarantee on termination (in the Las Vegas), or on both (if we so design). Indeed,

with randomization we give up certainty.

Thus randomization might be appropriate for situations and applications where the concern is on overall system performance rather than that of a single execution. By contrast, it might be unacceptable in critical systems and applications (e.g., nuclear power plant control, cardiovascular monitoring system, etc.) where correctness is of outmost importance.

In the rest of this chapter, we will see how to employ randomization to achieve some level of fault tolerance. Clearly our achievement can only be *with high probability*, with no other guarantee.

7.4.2 Randomized Asynchronous Consensus: Crash Failures

In this section we are going to consider an asynchronous complete graph where entities can crash. As we know, no deterministic solution protocol exists even if only one entity may crash.

For this setting, we are going to design a *Las Vegas* protocol that terminates with high probability and such that upon termination, consensus is achieved by the non-faulty entities in spite of up to $f < n/2$ crash failures. This result will be derived under the following set of restrictions:

Additional Assumptions (RA)

1. *Connectivity, Bidirectional Links*;
2. each entity has a unique id;
3. the network is a complete graph;
4. each entity has access to a fair coin;
5. the only type of failures is entity crash;
6. *Message Ordering* (i.e., FIFO links).

A Las Vegas Solution: Rand-Omit   The randomized protocol we will design will be a (possibly endless) sequence of asynchronous rounds. With high probability, $n - f$ entities will decide on the same value in some round; when this occurs the protocol will terminate.

In each round, every entity will broadcast a value, starting with its input value. Each entity keeps track of its own round r; during this round, the entity processes only the received messages with round number r; messages with round number $r' < r$ are discarded, and those with round number $r'' > r$ are saved and processed at the appropriate round (as if they had arrived just then).

Each round is composed of two stages, a *voting* stage and a *ratification* stage.

In the *voting* stage each entity transmits its current preference pref to all entities by sending a message of the form $\langle VOTE, r, \text{pref} \rangle$ and then waits to receive $n - f$ such messages; initially, the preference of an entity is its input value. As we will see, if any entity receives more than $n/2$ votes for a single value, all nonfaulty entities will decide on this value in the second stage.

In the *ratification* stage, any entity that has observed a majority of votes for value v sends a message $\langle RATIFY, r, v \rangle$ to all entities. An entity that has *not* observed a majority for either value sends instead a message $\langle RATIFY, r, ? \rangle$. As in the first stage, each entity waits to receive at least $n - f$ ratification messages. Any nonfaulty entity that receives even a single $\langle RATIFY, r, v \rangle$ message in round r changes its preference for round $r + 1$ to v. If, in addition, it receives more than f such messages, it immediately *decides* on v (if a decision has not been already made). If, by contrast, it receives only $\langle RATIFY, r, ? \rangle$ messages, it flips a fair coin (i.e., at random with uniform probability) to choose the new preference to be 0 or 1 for the next round.

The process then continues with the entity starting the next round $r + 1$.

Although the protocol goes on forever, the decision value of an entity is unique: Once a decision is made it cannot be changed. As described, each entity continues to run the protocol even after the decision is made; however, the protocol can be modified so that each entity terminates its execution at most one round after first setting its output value (Exercise 7.10.18). In the following, we assume that this is the case.

IMPORTANT. For simplicity, in the description of the protocol and in its analysis, when an entity sends a message, we will assume that it will send it also to itself.

Algorithm *Rand-Omit*

```
begin
      pref = Iₓ;  r := 1;  decide = FALSE;
      repeat
      STAGE 1
            send ⟨VOTE, r, pref⟩ to all;
            receive n − f messages ⟨VOTE, r, ∗⟩.
            if   all these messages contain the same value v then
                  found := v;
            else
                  found :=?
            endif
      STAGE 2
            send ⟨RATIFY, r, found⟩ to all.
            receive n − f messages ⟨RATIFY, r, ∗⟩.
            if   one or more contain a value w ≠? then
                  pref := w;
                  if ( (all contain the same value w ≠?) and not(decide) ) then
                        Oₓ := w;    /* i.e., decide on that value */
                        decide := TRUE;
                  endif
            else
                  pref := CoinFlip()
            endif
            r:= r+1;
      endrepeat
end
```

FIGURE 7.13: Algorithm *Rand-Omit.*

Let us now examine the correctness of the decision process if/when the protocol terminates.

Let $\text{pref}_x(r)$ denote the value variable pref of entity x at the beginning of round r, and let $\text{found}_x(r)$ denote the value of variable *found* in that round.

Lemma 7.4.1   (Nontriviality) *If, at the beginning of stage r, $\text{pref}_x(r) = v$ for every correct entity x, then all correct entities decide on v in that round.*

Proof. Let all correct entities have the same preference at the beginning of round r. Then each correct entity x broadcasts $\langle VOTE, r, v \rangle$; as at most f entities are faulty, every correct entity receives at least $n - f$ messages $\langle VOTE, r, v \rangle$. Hence, every correct entity sets broadcasts $\langle RATIFY, r, v \rangle$. Again, every correct entity receives at least $n - f$ messages $\langle RATIFY, r, v \rangle$ and decides on v. ∎

We will make use of a simple but important observation.

Property 7.4.1   *In every round r, either*

1. $\text{found}_x(r) \in \{1, ?\}$ for all correct x, or
2. $\text{found}_x(r) \in \{0, ?\}$ for all correct x.

Proof. Suppose to the contrary that, at some round r, there are two correct entities x and y such that $found_x(r) = 0$ and $found_y(r) = 1$. From the rule of Stage 1, it follows that x received $\langle VOTE, r, 0 \rangle$ from $n - f > \frac{n}{2}$ distinct entities and y received $\langle VOTE, r, 0 \rangle$ from $n - f \rangle \frac{n}{2}$ distinct entities. This means that the number of distinct entities in the system is at least $n \geq 2(n - f)$, but this implies $2f > n$: a contradiction. ■

This means that it is impossible that two entities decide at the same round on two different values.

We are now going to prove that all nonfaulty entities, if they decide, will decide on the same value.

Lemma 7.4.2 (**Agreement**) *Let r be the first round in which nonfaulty entities make a decision, and let x be such an entity. If x decides on v at round r, then every nonfaulty entity decides v by round $r + 1$.*

Proof. Suppose without loss of generality that at round r entity x decides on 0. First observe that, because of Property 7.4.1, any other entity y that decides at round r must also decide on 0. As x decides on 0, it must have received $\langle RATIFY, r, 0 \rangle$ from $n - f$ distinct entities. This means that every other correct entity receives $\langle RATIFY, r, 0 \rangle$ from at least $n - 2f \geq 1$ entities at round r. Hence, every noncrashed entity (including x) will set its new preference for round $r + 1$ to 0. Therefore at the beginning of Stage 1 of round $r + 1$, every nonfailed entity sends $\langle VOTE, r+1, 0 \rangle$ to all. This means that every nonfailed entity will receive at least $n - f$ such messages and will decide on 0 if it has not already done so. ■

It then remains to prove that the protocol terminates with high probability.

First of all observe that in a round r the preferences are not necessarily chosen at random; in fact, some entity x may set $pref(x)$ to a nonrandom value (because, in Stage 2 it received a message $\langle RATIFY, r, w \rangle$ with $w \neq ?$). However, by Property 7.4.1, all nonrandom preferences of correct entities are identical.

This means that in every round r there is a positive probability that the preferences (random or not) of all correct entities are identical, an event that we will call a *success*. When this happens, by Lemma 7.4.1, every correct entity will decide on the same value within that round.

As entities flip coins independently, the probability that a success happens within the first k rounds is (Exercise 7.10.19)

Lemma 7.4.3 $Pr[\text{success within k rounds}] \geq 1 - (1 - 2^{-(n-f)})^k$.

The good news is that this probability goes to 1 as k goes to infinity. Hence,

Lemma 7.4.4 (**Probabilistic Termination**) *Protocol* Rand-Omit *terminates with probability* 1.

The bad news is that it takes exponentially many rounds for the probability to become close to 1. Indeed, if we run the protocol for $k = c \, 2^{n-f}$ rounds, where c is a chosen constant, then

$$Pr[success\ within\ k\ rounds] \geq 1 - \frac{1}{e^c}. \tag{7.19}$$

In this case, this probability goes very quickly to 1 as c grows.

NOTE. If the number f is rather small, a *success* will be achieved in a constant number of rounds. In fact (Exercise 7.10.20),

Lemma 7.4.5 *Let* $f = O(\sqrt{n})$; *then the expected number of rounds to achieve a success is* $O(1)$.

NOTE. To terminate, it is not necessary that *all* correct entities start the same round with the same preference. It is sufficent that a large enough majority of them will do so; in fact, $\lfloor n/2 \rfloor + f + 1$ suffices (Exercise 7.10.21).

Hacking: Reducing the Number of Rounds We can use randomization further so as to reduce the expected number of rounds from exponential to sublinear when the number of faults is nearly one third.

We will do so in an efficient simulation of protocol *Rand-Omit*.

We will first translate our system of n entities, of which $f < \frac{n}{3}$ are faulty, into a system of $k > n$ entities, of which up to $r\,k$ are faulty, $1 > r > 0$. The translation is accomplished by creating k *committees*, each composed of s entities, where the values of parameters k and s will be discussed later; note that an entity may belong to several committees. This assignment of entities to committees creates a new "virtual" system composed of k entities: the committees. We then simulate the execution of protocol *Rand-Omit* in the new system of size k: Each committee will simulate a single entity running the protocol in this new system. We will call the resulting protocol *Committee*.

To correctly simulate the execution in the virtual system, the entities in a given committee must be able to agree on the messages received and messages to be sent by the committee. Call a committee *faulty* if one third or more of its members are faulty, *nonfaulty* otherwise. Then a nonfaulty committee must also be able to flip a reasonably unbiased coin *global* to that committee and independent of the coins of other nonfaulty committees.

All these factors can indeed be taken into account, and the correctness of the resulting Protocol *Committee* can be ensured (Problem 7.10.2).

We must still choose the values of parameters k and s; this will be done so as to minimize the costs of Protocol *Committee*.

We know that in a system of k entities, if the number of faulty entities is $f = O(\sqrt{k})$, then the expected number of rounds before termination of Protocol *Rand-Omit* is constant (Lemma 7.4.5). In this case, the expected number $\bar{k}$ of rounds of protocol *Committee* for the simulation is linear in the number $\bar{r}$ of rounds it takes a committee to simulate a single round of protocol *Rand-Omit*.

The quantity $\bar{r}$ is actually dominated by the cost of flipping a coin in each committee, which is dominated in turn by the maximum number $\bar{f}$ of faulty entities within a nonfaulty committee (Exercise 7.10.22). Thus, to minimize the cost of *Committee*, we need to choose a value of k that yields an appropriate value of $\bar{f}$. To do so, we use the following property (Exercise 7.10.23):

Lemma 7.4.6 *For any $1 > r > 0$ and $c > 0$, there exists an assignment of n entities to $k = O(n^2)$ committees such that for all choices of $f < n/(3+c)$ faulty entities, at most $O(r\,k)$ committees are faulty, and each committee has size $s = O(\log n)$.*

Using this property, if we choose $k = O(n^2)$, we have,

$$ f < n/(3+c) = O(n) = O(\sqrt{k}). $$

A first consequence is that protocol *Rand-Omit* will have a constant expected number of rounds in the simulated system of size k. The other consequence is that for $f = O(n)$, the number $\bar{f}$ of faulty entities in nonfaulty committees is $O(s)$; this means that each simulated round needs only $O(\log n)$ rounds in the real system.

Summarizing, the total number of expected rounds of protocol *Committee* will be $O(\log n)$.

7.4.3 Concluding Remarks

If all entities had access to a global source of random bits (unbiased and visible to all entities), then Byzantine Agreement could be achieved in *constant* expected time (Exercise 7.10.24). Unfortunately, such a source does not exist.

To implement something with similar properties is indeed possible by imposing additional assumptions, such as the existence of both digital signatures and a trusted dealer, or private channels and a trusted dealer (Problems 7.10.3 and 7.10.4).

In the case of *synchronous* systems, in addition to these general results, it is also possible to implement a global source of random bits by using digital signatures and secrete sharing (Problem 7.10.5).

7.5 LOCALIZED ENTITY FAILURES: USING FAULT DETECTION

The proof of the Single-Failure Disaster result is based on the fact that in an asynchronous system it is impossible to distinguish a slow entity from a failed one. This means that the availability of any *reliable fault detector* would remove any such ambiguity and thus disable that proof. So, for example, the presence of restriction *Link-Failure Detection* and/or restriction *Node-Failure Detection* would disable the proof of Theorem 7.2.1 even if communication delays are unbounded.

The problem is how to *construct* reliable fault detectors. We have seen how in fully synchronous systems the Single-Failure Disaster result does not hold. One reason is that if messages are never lost, synchrony yields a perfect failure detector for crash failures: As the absence of an anticipated message can be detected, a missing message indicates a faulty sender. To date, the only reliable fault detectors are those obtained in fully synchronous systems, and in a fully synchronous system we already have seen how to deal with failures. The real problem is that in systems that are not synchronous there are only *unreliable* fault detectors.

At this point, we have several intriguing and important questions. In particular, without synchrony,

- do we really need a completely reliable crash detector to achieve consensus?
- what is the "weakest" (i.e., the least reliable) detector we can usefully employ?

In this section we will discuss some of these questions and the connected problems. In our discussion and solutions, we will use an additional set of assumptions:

Additional Assumptions (FDA)

1. *Connectivity, Bidirectional Links*;
2. the network is a complete graph;
3. entities have unique ids;
4. entities can fail only by crashing;
5. each entity knows the ids of its neighbors.

7.5.1   Failure Detectors and Their Properties

A distributed *detector* of entity failures is a set of n failure-detection *modules*, one per entity, providing to each entity (possibly incorrect) information about the failures that occur in an execution. In particular, each module keeps a list of entities it suspects to be faulty. It can be consulted during any action of the protocol; upon consultation, the module returns a list of entities that the module currently suspects to have crashed.

As the failure modules can make mistakes, each module may be continually adding and removing entities from its list. For example, an entity may use its local clock to implement a failure module based on timeouts (even if the system is asynchronous). If x times out entity y because, for example, y failed to respond in a timely fashion to a message sent by x, it may be the case that y has not failed (e.g., the message is just slow). If x were to receive later a message from y, then x would know it had suspected y in error and would remove y from its list of suspects.

Furthermore, the failure-detection modules of two different entities need not agree on the list of entities that are suspected to have crashed.

Failure detectors are defined in terms of the properties they satisfy, rather than in terms of the actual implementation. In particular, two properties are considered: *completeness* (i.e., the assurance that faulty entities are indeed reported) and *accuracy* (i.e., the assurance that correct entities are not reported as faulty).

To see that both properties are necessary, note that the trivial failure detector *Paranoid*, in which each entity permanently suspects every other entity, will satisfy any completeness property: All faulty entities are indeed reported; however, *Paranoid* provides no real information about the actual failures. Similarly, the trivial failure detector *Naive*, in which each entity never suspects any other entity, will satisfy any accuracy property: No correct entity will ever be incorrectly reported as faulty; however, *Naive* too provides no real information about the failures. Thus, neither accuracy nor completeness suffices by itself.

Let us examine these two properties in more detail.

Completeness

We have two natural forms of this property:

1. *strong completeness*: eventually every entity that crashes is permanently suspected by every correct entity;
2. *weak completeness*: eventually every entity that crashes is permanently suspected by some correct entity (each failed entity may be suspected by a different correct entity).

Accuracy

The natural accuracy properties are

1. *perpetual strong accuracy*: no entity is suspected before it crashes;
2. *perpetual weak accuracy*: some correct entity is never suspected (by anyone);
3. *eventual strong accuracy*: there is a time after which correct entities are not suspected by any correct entity;
4. *eventual weak accuracy*: there is a time after which some correct entity is never suspected by any correct entity.

Perpetual strong accuracy is difficult (if not impossible) to achieve in many practical systems. Actually, perpetual weak accuracy is not very weak, because it guarantees that at least one correct entity is never suspected. Suppose that, as is frequently the case in real systems, the failure detector is implemented by a "heart beat" protocol in which entities repeatedly broadcast "I am alive" messages. Then even weak accuracy cannot be achieved (for example, it might be foiled if the network traffic is high and messages are delayed for too long). Thus in general (regardless of how the failure detector is implemented) even weak accuracy may be too strong a requirement for any failure detector to achieve. Fortunately, it is not necessary that the system *always* behave but only that it behave *eventually*, and even then only long enough for the entities to reach agreement, hence, the eventual accuracy properties.

A failure detector is said to be *perfect* if it satisfies strong completeness and perpetual strong accuracy: Every faulty entity is detected by every correct entity, and no correct entity is ever suspected faulty.

Note that in any fully synchronous system there is a perfect failure detector enjoying simultaneously the strong completeness and strong accuracy properties. In particular, in a fully synchronous system, every entity can broadcast "I am alive" at every time unit. If at some time unit entity x does not receive an "I am alive" message from entity y, then x knows y has failed.

Far from perfect are those failure detectors that satisfy only weak completeness and eventual weak accuracy. Still, any such detector is powerful enough for our purposes. In fact (Exercise 7.10.25),

Theorem 7.5.1 *Any failure detector that satisfies only weak completeness and eventual weak accuracy is sufficient for reaching consensus if at most $f < \frac{n}{2}$ entities can crash.*

We denote by Ω any failure detector that satisfies only weak completeness and eventual weak accuracy.

7.5.2 The Weakest Failure Detector

We will now answer the question of what is the "weakest" detector we need to achieve consensus in spite of crash failures. The answer is proved by designing an algorithm that allows to reduce a failure detector to another.

Before we proceed, we need to introduce some terminology.

A *failure pattern* F is a function describing the set of entities that have crashed through time: $F(t)$ is the set of entities that have crashed through time t, and clearly for all t, $F(t) \subseteq F(t+1)$. Let $crashed(F) = \cup_t F(t)$ denote the set of entities that crash under the failure pattern F, while $correct(F) = \mathcal{E} - crashed(F)$ denotes the set of entities that do not crash under F. We consider only failure patterns F such that at least one entity is correct, that is, $correct(F) \neq \emptyset$.

Typically, for any system and for any failure pattern F occurring in this system, there may be many executions with the same failure pattern. Let $D(F)$ denote the set of all failure detector histories that can occur in executions with failure pattern F and failure detector D; given a particular execution r and a variable v, let v^r denote the history of that variable during that execution.

We now define what it means for an algorithm T to transform a failure detector D into another failure detector D'; such an algorithm is called a *reduction* algorithm. First of all, algorithm T must use D to maintain a variable $output(x)$ at every entity x; this variable, which is part of the local state of x, emulates the output of D' at x.

Algorithm T transforms D into D' *if and only if* for every execution ϵ of T using D, $output^\epsilon = \{output(x)^\epsilon\} \in D'(F)$, that is, for every execution ϵ, the histories of the variables $output(x)$ in execution r can actually occur in some executions with detector D' and pattern F. Note that T need not emulate *all* the failure detector histories of D'; it suffices that all the failure detector histories it emulates be histories of D'.

If there is an algorithm T that transforms D into D', we write $D \geq D'$ and say that D *is reducible to* D'; we also say that D *is weaker than* D'. The intuition is that as T is able to use D to emulate D', D must provide at least as much information about entity failures as D' does.

If a reduction algorithm T is available that transforms D into D', then generally speaking, any problem that can be solved using failure detector D' can be solved using D instead. Suppose an algorithm A using failure detector D' solves our problem, but only D is available. The availability of T allows us to still execute A to solve the problem. This is achieved as follows:

1. Concurrently with A, entities run T to transform D into D'.
2. Modify algorithm A at entity x as follows: Whenever A requires that x query its failure detector module, x reads the current value of $output(x)$ (which is concurrently maintained by T) instead.

We now describe a reduction algorithm $REDUCE$ that transforms any given failure detector D that satisfies *weak completeness* into a failure detector D' that satisfies *strong completeness*. Furthermore, if D satisfies an accuracy property, then W does so as well.

Informally, $REDUCE$ works as follows. Every entity x periodically sends $\langle x, suspects(x) \rangle$ to every entity, where $suspects(x)$ denotes the set of entities that x suspects according to its local failure detector module $V[x]$. When x receives a message of the form $\langle y, suspects(y) \rangle$, it adds $suspects(y)$ to $output(x)$ and removes y from $output(x)$ (recall that $output(x)$ is the variable emulating the output of the failure detector module D).

More precisely, every entity x in $REDUCE$ executes the following:

- Initially:
  $output(x) \leftarrow \emptyset$
- Repeatedly:
  /* x queries its local failure detector module D_x */
  $suspects(x) \leftarrow D_x$;
  send $\langle x, suspects(x) \rangle$ **to** $N(x)$;
- Receiving $\langle y, suspects(y) \rangle$ from y :
  /* $output(x)$ emulates D'_x */
  $output(x) := output(x) \cup suspects(y) - \{y\}$;

Let ϵ be an arbitrary execution of $REDUCE$ using failure detector D. In the following, the execution ϵ and its failure pattern F are fixed. Thus, when we say that an entity crashes, we mean that it crashes in F. Similarly, when we say that an entity is correct, we mean that it is correct in ϵ. Let $H \in D(F)$ denote a history of failure detector D for pattern F.

We can show that $REDUCE$ satisfies the following property:

Lemma 7.5.1   (Transforming weak completeness into strong completeness)
Let z be any entity that crashes; if eventually some correct entity permanently suspects y in H, then eventually all correct entities permanently suspect y in $output^\epsilon$.

Proof. Let y be any entity that crashes. Suppose that there is a time t after which some correct entity x permanently suspects y in H. We must show that there is a time after which every correct entity suspects y in $output^\epsilon$. As y crashes, there is a time t' after which no entity receives a message from y. Consider the execution by entity x after time $t'' = \max(t, t')$. Entity x sends a message of the type $\langle (x, suspects(x) \rangle$ with $y \in suspects(x)$ to all entities. Eventually, every correct entity receives $\langle x, suspects(x) \rangle$ and adds y to its $output$. As no correct entity receives any messages from y after time t' and $t'' \geq t'$, no correct entity removes y from its $output$ after time t''. Thus, there is a time after which every correct entity permanently suspects y in $output^\epsilon$. ∎

Similarly, we can show (Exercises 7.10.26 and 7.10.27) that *REDUCE* satisfies the following two other properties:

Lemma 7.5.2   (Preserving perpetual accuracy)
Let y be any entity; if no entity suspects y in H before time t, then no entity suspects y in $output^\epsilon$ before time t.

Lemma 7.5.3   (Preserving eventual accuracy)
Let y be any correct entity; if there is a time after which no correct entity suspects y in H, then there is a time after which no correct entity suspects y in $output^\epsilon$.

From Lemmas 7.5.1, 7.5.2, and 7.5.3, it follows that *REDUCE* transforms any failure detector D that satisfies *weak completeness* into a failure detector D' that satisfies *strong completeness*, and if D satisfies an accuracy property, then D' does so as well. In other words,

Theorem 7.5.2   REDUCE *strengthens completeness while preserving accuracy.*

As a consequence, Ω is reducible to any failure detector that can be used to achieve consensus in an asynchronous system. In other words,

Theorem 7.5.3 Ω *is the weakest failure detector that can possibly be used to achieve consensus in presence of crash failures.*

7.6 LOCALIZED ENTITY FAILURES: PREEXECUTION FAILURES

7.6.1 Partial Reliability

We have seen that even in a complete graph, it is impossible to achieve consensus among the nonfaulty entities if just one entity may crash. The proof of the *Single Failure Disaster* relies heavily on the fact that the "adversary" can choose which entity fails as well as the moment when the failure occurs. In fact, if all the failure occur *before* the execution of the algorithm, the proof does not hold. Indeed, it might be *possible* to achieve complex tasks requiring consensus in spite of multiple failures, provided they have *all* occurred before the task starts.

NOTE. The condition that all faults, if any, occur before the computation takes place is expressed by the restriction *Partial Reliability* that states, "No faults will occur during the computation." Recall that the standard set of restrictions included instead *Total Reliability* that states, "No faults have occurred nor will occur."

7.6.2 Example: Election in Complete Network

Consider as an example the *Election* problem in the complete graph where some entities might have crashed. Under *Partial Reliability*, it is indeed possible to perform the election without synchrony, without randomization, and without fault detection even if $f \leq \lceil \frac{n}{2} \rceil - 1$ entities have crashed.

We will construct the algorithm by adapting the protocol *CompleteElect* we have designed for complete networks under *Total Reliability* in Section 3.6.

The changes we will make are essentially two:

1. In the original protocol, a *candidate* entity x starts by sending a "Capture" message to a single neighbor and waits for its reply. In our setting, this entity could have crashed, so x would never receive the reply. To overcome this, as at most f entities have crashed, at the beginning x will send the "Capture" message to $f + 1$ entities, to ensure that at least one of them is alive. As soon as x receives an "Accept" from one of them, it enters the next stage and sends its message to another entity. In other words, at any stage (except the last), a *candidate* entity will have $f + 1$ pending requests.

2. In the original protocol, a *candidate* entity x has only one pending "Capture" message and waits for its reply; if the reply is "Reject," x becomes *passive*. In our setting, x has $f + 1$ pending "Capture" messages and is waiting for a reply from each one of them (we know that at least one will arrive because at most f entities are faulty). So it may happen that while waiting for the reply from y, x receives several "Accept" messages whose effect is to increase the stage number of x. This means that if y sends a "Reject" to x, it is based on the old stage number of x. In particular, if the stage of y (enclosed in the received "Reject" message) is smaller than the current one of x or they are the same but the id of x is smaller than that of y (also enclosed in the received "Reject" message), x must reject the "Reject" command. What we will do instead is to have x settle its score with y once and for all. This *settlement* is achieved as follows: x will send a new "Capture" message to y with its new stage number and close all its other ports waiting for the reply from y. (That will arrive because we know that y is alive.) Note that the effect of closing the other ports is that the stage number and the status of x will not change before the reply from y arrives. When the reply arrives, x will either increase its stage (if it is "Accept") or become *passive* (if it is "Reject") before reopening all the ports.

    Note that the total number of pending "Capture" messages for x will still be $f + 1$: The previous one to y (no longer pending) is now replaced by the new one to y.

Few other details have to be taken care of when completing the description of the adapted protocol that we shall call *FT-CompleteElect* (Exercise 7.10.28).

In proving the *correctness* of the protocol, we must consider the effects of the changes we have made on the original protocol. Consider in particular the settlement process (change 2): x resends to y a "Capture" message with the new stage number and closes all its other ports; if only $\bar{x}$ is performing a settlement, this operation will not cause problems because y is alive and will respond. However, several entities may be doing settlements (closing all their ports but one and waiting for a reply from that one); so, for example, y might have closed the link to x waiting for a reply from another alive entity z. To ensure correctness, we must prove that x will indeed receive a reply from y. In other words, settlements must not create deadlocks, neither by themselves nor in combination with the closing of links when sending "Warning" messages. Fortunately, this is the case (Exercise 7.10.29). Thus every request ("Capture" or "Warning") sent to a nonfaulty entity receives a reply; in particular, after a settlement (e.g. between x and y) at most one of them is still *candidate* and if so it has increased its stage.

If an entity x has an owner, then both x and its owner are nonfaulty. A nonfaulty entity always replies to a "Warning" message; thus, when x sends a "Warning" to its owner and closes all its ports except the one to the owner, it will receive a reply from y and will thus reopen all its ports.

The rest of the correctness follows from some simple lemmas, whose proof is left as an exercise (Exercises 7.10.30 - 7.10.32):

Lemma 7.6.1   *Every entity eventually reaches stage greater than $\frac{n}{2}$, or it ceases to be a* candidate.

Lemma 7.6.2   *Assume an entity x ceases to be* candidate *as a result of a message originated by* candidate *y. Then, at any time after the time this message is processed by x, either the stage of y is greater than the stage of x or x and y are in the same stage, but $id(x) < id(y)$.*

Lemma 7.6.3   *At least one entity always remains a* candidate.

Lemma 7.6.4   *Let x be a* candidate *and s be its final size. The total number of times a "Capture" message was sent by x is at most $2s + f$.*

Proof.   When x initiates the algorithm, it sends $f + 1$ "Capture" messages. Every other "Capture" message it sends follows the reception of either an "Accept" or a "Reject" message. The number of "Accept" messages it receives as a *candidate* is $s - 1$. The number of "Reject" messages it receives as a *candidate* is at most s.   ∎

Let us now turn to the costs of Protocol *FT-CompleteElect*. First of all observe that (Exercise 7.10.33)

Lemma 7.6.5   *For every $l \geq 2$, if there are $l - 1$ candidates whose final size is not smaller than that of a* candidate *x, then the stage of x is at most ln.*

Now the number of messages can be easily determined. Let k denote the number of spontaneous initiators. The number of messages used for the leader announcement is $n - 1$. The total number of the other messages sent during an execution is bounded by four times the number of "Capture" messages sent by a *candidate*. In fact, exactly like in the original protocol *FT-CompleteElect*, a "Capture" message from x to y, in addition to the reply (either "Accept" or "Reject") from y, will cause at most two additional messages: a "Warning" from y to its owner z and the corresponding reply ("Yes" or "No").

Let s be the final size of a *candidate* x that initiated the algorithm. By Lemma 7.6.4, the number of times this *candidate* has sent a "Capture" message does not exceed $2s + f$. Entities that did not wake up spontaneously never become *candidates*. Thus by Lemma 7.6.4 the total number of messages is bounded by

$$n - 1 + 4 \sum_{1 \le j \le k} (2 \tfrac{n}{j} + f).$$

which gives us

$$\mathbf{M}[FT - CompleteElect] = O(n \log k + kf). \tag{7.20}$$

This cost is actually *optimal*. Let us see why. Examining this bound we notice that there are two components: $O(n \log k)$ and $O(kf)$. We do know that $\Omega(n \log k)$ messages are needed for election in complete networks even in the absence of failures; thus, the first component of the upperbound is indeed necessary. For the second component, consider first the case of a single initiator, that is, $k = 1$; this entity must send at least $f + 1$ messages, otherwise there is no guarantee that the algorithm will make any progress. Consider now the general case of $k \ge 1$ entities; as none of them knows k, each must act taking into account the possibility of being the only one; in other words, the adversary can slow down messages so that each of them will send at least $f + 1$ messages, for a total of at least $\Omega(kf)$. Hence, also the second component is necessary. In other words, the complete lowerbound

$$\Omega(n \log k + kf)$$

matches the upperbound (7.20), and hence protocol *FT-CompleteElect* is worst-case optimal.

7.7 LOCALIZED LINK FAILURES

We have seen the devastating impact of node failures in the general asynchronous environments. In this section, we study the impact of *link failures* by means of a tale.

We then see an example of how to design an application protocol that can tolerate link failures.

7.7.1 A Tale of Two Synchronous Generals

Imagine a military campaign a long time ago (before the radio communication was discovered). Two allied armies, each with its own general, are positioned on two opposite hilltops overlooking a valley from which a large enemy army will approach. Together, the allied forces can overwhelm the enemy if they attack at the appropriate time; by contrast, attacking at the inappropriate time or separately would clearly lead to a massacre of the attackers. Having decided beforehand not to be massacred, neither general will command his army to attack, unless sure that the allied army will also attack.

General A can see from his hilltop the enemy army. After many observations and calculations, A determines that dawn is the only time when a simultaneous attack by the allies will be successful. General A must now communicate this information to general B who, from the other hilltop, is unable to perform such calculations. In order not to alert the enemy, fires or torches cannot be used; so to communicate, a messenger must be employed. So general A deploys a messenger to deliver the message "Let us attack at dawn" to general B. Notice that as A does not want to be massacred, he will not attack unless he knows that general B has received this message and will attack at dawn.

To go from one hill to the other, the messenger has to traverse the valley and it takes no more than 1 hour. The problem is that there are enemy scouts patrolling the valley, and obviously there is the risk that the messenger is caught during the trip. See Figure 7.14. In spite of the danger, the messenger safely performs the trip and delivers the message to general B. Knowing that A will not attack unless he gets confirmation, B sends the messenger back with the message "Message received; let us attack at dawn."

Is this transmission of messages enough for the two generals to attack at dawn? The answer is *No*. In fact, if the messenger gets caught now, A will never get the message, and, not knowing whether or not B has received the first message, he will not risk being massacred by attacking alone.

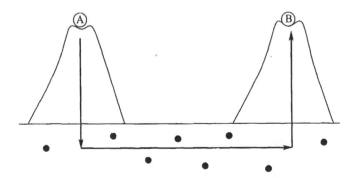

FIGURE 7.14: The path (in bold) between the two hilltops is unsafe because of the presence of enemy scouts (black circles) in the valley.

Fortunately, the messenger safely performs the trip back and delivers the message to general A. Will now the two generals attack at dawn? The answer again is *No*.

In fact, B does not know whether or not his confirmation message has reached A; he, however, knows that, if it did not, A will not attack; therefore, B, not wanting to risk a massacre, will not attack. Thus A must tell B that indeed the confirmation has arrived, sending again the messenger with the message "Confirmed. Let us attack at dawn."

The lucky messenger gets through again, delivering the message to B. But again, B reflects that A does not know that this message has arrived and therefore he would not attack.

Interestingly, continuing to send messages back and forth is not going to lead the two generals to attack at dawn, ever, even if the messenger is never intercepted by the enemy. In fact, the *Two Generals* problem of ensuring that both A and B attack at dawn is unsolvable:

Theorem 7.7.1   *The Two Generals problem has no solution even if the system is fully synchronous.*

Proof.   To see why this is true, let us be a bit more precise about the formulation of the problem. General A has an *input register* I_A initialized with a value in $\{0, 1\}$, and a write-once *output register* O_A initially set to $b \notin \{0, 1\}$; once a value $d_A \in \{0, 1\}$ is written in O_A, the content of that register is no longer modifiable. It is the same for general B. The goal is to have both generals set, in finite time, their output registers to the input value of A.

First of all observe that, in any execution of any solution protocol in which the two generals decide to attack (i.e., in which $I_A = 1$), at least one message must be delivered. Otherwise, B cannot distinguish this scenario from an execution in which A decides not to attack (i.e., in which $I_A = 0$), but no messages are delivered because the link is down.

Incidentally, this means that the link *must deliver at least a message before it fails* for the problem to be solvable. Let us assume that this is the case; we will see that, even so, the problem is unsolvable.

Suppose, by contradiction, that there exists a solution protocol. Among the executions of P that lead to the two general attacking, consider the execution E of minimal length (number of messages delivered), say k; from what said before, $k \geq 1$.

Without loss of generality, assume that the last (i.e., the kth) message delivered in E is from A to B (see Figure 7.15(a)). Let t be a time, after the message is received, when both generals decide to attack, that is, at time t, $O_A = O_B = 1$.

We will now show that the two generals could have made their decision earlier. Consider now the execution E' that is exactly the same as E except that this last message is lost because the link went down (see Figure 7.15(b)).

General A cannot distinguish between E and E'; as A will attack (i.e., set $O_A = 1$) in E, he will also attack in E', that is, at time t we have $O_A = 1$ also in E'. As the protocol is correct, if a general attacks, so will the other; thus B, within finite time, must decide to attack (i.e., set $O_B = 1$) also in E'.

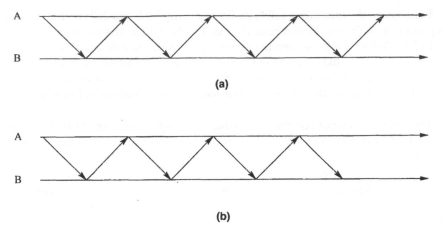

FIGURE 7.15: (a) Execution E: The two generals decide to attack. (b) Execution E': They must decide to attack also in this case.

In E' the number of messages that are delivered is $k - 1$. First consider the case $k - 1)0$; then in E' we send one less message than in E, contradicting the assumption that E is of minimal length. Consider now the case $k - 1 = 0$; then in E' no messages are delivered, contradicting the fact that at least one message must be delivered for an attack decision to be made. ∎

The problem here is that, to attack together, the two generals need to reach *common knowledge* ("the attack is at dawn"); in contrast, if the communication is not guaranteed, the generals cannot establish common knowledge because of asynchrony.

Note that what is important is not the fact that the link fails (i.e., the messager is cought) but the *possibility* that it may fail. In fact, in our tale, it does not fail.

An important consequence is that *even in a synchronous system, two neighbors cannot achieve common knowledge if the link between them may go down and no other link can be used to communicate between them.* This means that

Theorem 7.7.2 *If a single link can possibly fail, common knowledge cannot be achieved if the network is not 2-edge-connected, even if it is fully synchronous.*

In fact, if G is not 2-edge-connected, there is a *bridge*, that is, a link e whose removal will disconnect the network. Envision the two subgraphs connected by e as the two generals A and B in the tale, and e as the unsafe path between the two hilltops (see Figure 7.16). It follows by Theorem 7.7.1 that the entities in the two subgraphs cannot achieve common knowledge.

IMPORTANT. Let us stress that what makes the achievement of common knowledge (and, thus, the design of a fault-tolerant solution protocol) *impossible* is not the fact that faults occur but rather the fact that it is *possible* that they occur.

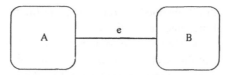

FIGURE 7.16: If the network is not 2-edge-connected, a possibly faulty bridge e makes common knowledge unattainable.

An immediate consequence of Theorem 7.7.2 is that if more than two links can possibly fail, then the connectivity requirements of the network must be clearly higher:

Lemma 7.7.1 *If any $F \geq 1$ links can possibly fail, common knowledge cannot be achieved if the network is not $(F + 1)$-edge-connected even if it is fully synchronous.*

Note the similiarity between the statements of Lemmas 7.7.1 and 7.1.1. This similiarity is not accidental. In fact, when dealing with link failures,

> *if we cannot broadcast, we cannot achieve common knowledge!*

Summarizing, the possibility that any F links fail makes it impossible to achieve common knowledge (and, thus, to solve consensus or any problem that requires a nontrivial agreement) in networks whose edge connectivity is less than $F + 1$.

7.7.2 Computing with Faulty Links

We have seen that if the number F of faulty links is equal to or greater than the edge connectivity of the network, it is impossible to compute. By contrast, with fewer faulty links, it is possible to achieve a reasonable level of fault tolerance.

Let us consider the case when the edge connectivity is $k + 1$ or higher; in this case, it is indeed possible to achieve consensus and to perform most computations when k links can fail, even if the failures are send/receive omissions and the system is asynchronous. The reason why this is possible is that in any network G, with fewer than $c_{\text{edge}}(G)$ faulty links, it is always possible to broadcast. For example, protocol *Flood* easily accomplishes this.

Indeed, protocol *Flood* allows to broadcast with send/receive omissions even if the number of faulty links is *greater* than $c_{\text{edge}}(G)$, as long as the failures do not disconnect the network. Furthermore, *Flood* is *independent* of F, unlike most fault-tolerant protocols where, for example, the number of iterations depends on F.

Once we can broadcast in spite of link failures, we can compute simple functions (e.g., AND, OR, Min, Max) and, thus, achieve consensus. If restriction *Initial Distinct Values* (ID) holds, we can perform Election: Every (initiator) entity will broadcast its value; the entity with the smallest value will become the leader. The overall cost will obviously depend on the cost of the broadcast protocol used.

For example, broadcasting with protocol *Flood*, the number of messages will be no more than that in a faulty-free execution: less than $2m(G)$. The time will be at most the diameter of the graph G' obtained by removing the faulty links from G. Thus, both time and number of messages are optimal.

In special graphs, it is clearly possible to achieve better bounds both for broadcasting and for election. In this section, we will examine this issue for the class of networks where the $O(n \, m(G))$ message cost would be the largest. In fact, we will consider a complete network and examine how to design efficient protocols that can withstand link failures even without any synchrony.

Broadcasting in a Complete Network with Faulty Links   In complete graphs, *broadcasting* in absence of failures is *trivial*: Sending the message to all the entity's neighbors is enough; the cost is a mere $n - 1$ messages.

Consider now broadcasting when out of the $n(n - 1)/2$ links, $F < n - 1$ are faulty. Their faulty behavior consists in occasionally losing messages sent over them (i.e. *send-receive omissions*), and their location is obviously not known. The use of protocol *Flood* would accomplish the task; the message cost is, however, rather high: $(n - 1)^2$ messages.

Let us see how broadcasting can be more efficiently achieved if $F < n - 1$ is known. Let x be the wanting to broadcast some information I. Consider the following broadcast protocol:

Protocol *TwoSteps*:

    1. x sends the message $\langle Info, I \rangle$ to $F + 1$ neighbors;

    2. an entity y receiving $\langle Info, I \rangle$ from x, sends $\langle Echo, I \rangle$ to all its neighbors.

Let us verify that the protocol correctly performs a broadcast if $F \langle n - 1$.

Consider an entity $y \neq x$ that did not receive the *Info* message because the link (x, y) is faulty. Let $p(x) \leq k$ be the total number of faulty links incident on x (including (x, y)). In the first step, at least $n - 1 - p(x)$ neighbors will receive the *Info* message; all of these will send an *Echo* message to everybody else, including y. This means that at least $n - 1 - p(x)$ *Echo* messages are sent to y; of those links at most $F - p(x)$ are faulty. But as $n - 1 > F$ we have that $n - 1 - p(x) > F - p(x)$, that is, at least one of those *Echo* messages will reach y (see Figure 7.17).

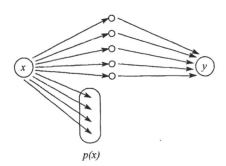

$p(x)$

FIGURE 7.17: Every entity y will receive the information broadcasted by x using protocol *TwoSteps*.

As for the cost of protocol *TwoSteps*, in the first step there are $F + 1$ messages; in the second step, at most $F + 1$ entities will each send $n - 2$ messages for a total of $(F + 1)(n - 2)$ messages. Summarizing,

$$\mathbf{M}[TwoSteps] = (F + 1)(n - 1). \tag{7.21}$$

This means that for any $F < n - 2$, this protocol will transmit fewer messages than *Flood*. The drawback is that the upperbound F on the number of faults must be known.

Election in a Complete Network with Faulty Links   Let us consider now the task of electing a leader in presence of faulty links. Clearly we need to assume that each entity has a unique identifier. Let us assume that all entities are initiators (if they are not, the first received message will act as an initiation impulse).

That the election task can be always accomplished if $F < n - 1$ is shown by the following simple strategy:

Strategy *FT-BcastElect*:

1. Each entity x broadcasts (using a F-tolerant protocol) its value $\mathrm{id}(x)$.
2. Once x has received the values of all other entities, x becomes leader if and only if its value is the smallest.

The overall cost of this strategy depends on the broadcast protocol employed. If protocol *TwoSteps* is used, the election will cost $n(F + 1)(n - 1)$ messages (that now must include the originator's id).

Hacking   In the case of fewer faults, $F \leq \frac{n-6}{2}$, we can actually design a more efficient election protocol, that we will call simply *FT-LinkElect*. This protocol is very similar to protocol *FT-CompleteElect* and, like it, it is based on the election protocol *CompleteElect* for nonfaulty complete graphs.

The protocol proceeds as a sequence of $\frac{n+2}{2F} + 1$ electoral stages and uses a parameter r, which will be discussed later. Before the algorithm starts, $stage(x) = 0$. When the algorithm starts, $stage(x)$ is set to 1 and every entity is in the *active* state.

(*Stage* of) Protocol *FT-LinkElect*:

Each stage is logically composed of four steps. Let x be active in stage i.

First Step: Entity x starts the stage by choosing pF still unselected neighbors and sending the message $\langle Capture, i, \mathrm{id}(x) \rangle$ to all of them; if $i = 1$ (i.e., in the first stage), then $p = r$, otherwise (i.e., in all other stages) $p = r - 1$.

Second Step: In the second step, the "Capture" messages sent by x will start to arrive. Upon receiving $\langle Capture, i, \mathrm{id}(x) \rangle$ from x, entity y, in $stage(v) = j$, compares $(i, d(x))$ with $(j, \mathrm{id}(y))$:

- if $i \langle j$ or $(i = j$ and $\mathrm{id}(x) \rangle \mathrm{id}(y))$, then y sends the message $\langle Reject, i, \mathrm{id}(x) \rangle$ to x;

- otherwise; y changes its stage to i;
    - if y it has no owner, it sets *owner* $:= x$, sends the message $\langle Accept \rangle$ to x, and becomes *passive*;
    - if y has a owner w, then y sends the message $\langle Warning, i, \text{id}(x) \rangle$ to w.

Third Step: In the third step, the "Warning" messages (if any) originated by the reception of the "Capture" messages from x will arrive, and replies will be generated and possibly arrive. Notice that this step might not take place at all, for example, if no "Warning" messages are sent or are sent on faulty links.

Upon receiving the message $\langle Warning, i, \text{id}(x) \rangle$ from y, entity w does as follows:

- if $i \langle stage(w)$ or $(i = stage(w)$ and $\text{id}(x) > \text{id}(w))$, then w sends the message $(No, i, \text{id}(x))$ to y; if y receives this message, it sends the message $\langle Reject, i, \text{id}(x) \rangle$ to x;
- otherwise, w sends the message $\langle Yes, i, \text{id}(x) \rangle$ to y and if it has no owner at that time, it sets *owner* $:= w$ and becomes *passive*; if y receives this $\langle Yes, i, \text{id}(x) \rangle$ message from w, y sets *owner* $:= x$ and sends the message $\langle Accept \rangle$ to x.

Fourth Step: In the fourth step, the replies (either "Accept" or "Reject") to the "Capture" messages arrive to x.

Upon receiving the message $\langle Reject, i, \text{id}(x) \rangle$ from y, entity x does as follows:

- if x has become *passive* (between the time it sends the first message to y and the time it receives the message from y), then x discards the message;
- if x is still *active*, x compares its own current $stage(x)$ with i :
    - if $i = stage(x)$, then it sets *owner* $:= x$ and becomes *passive*;
    - if $i < stage(x)$, the message is *out of date*; then x discards it and sends the message $\langle Capture, stage(x), \text{id}(x) \rangle$ to y.

Upon receiving the message $\langle Accept, i, \text{id}(x) \rangle$ from y, entity x does as follows:

- if x has become *passive* (between the time it sends the first message to y and the time it receives the message from y), then x discards the message;
- if x is still *active* and, including this message, it has received $(r-1)F$ "Accept" messages from stage i, it does the following:
    - if $i = \frac{n+2}{2F}$, then x becomes *leader* and starts protocol *TwoSteps* to broadcast termination of the election process;
    - otherwise, it starts stage $i + 1$.

Protocol *FT-LinkElect* indeed correctly elects a leader (Exercises 7.10.36–7.10.38 and Problem 7.10.6).

Let us examine the message *costs* of the protocol.

A $\langle Capture, i, \text{id}(x) \rangle$ message sent from x to y will generate a response, "Accept" or "Reject," from y to x; it can also cause a "Warning" sent from y to w (in the case where w is the owner of y) that, in turn, will cause a response, "Yes" or "No," from w to u.

In other words, the transmission of each "Capture" message will cause at most three other message transmissions. In the first stage, each entity sends rF "Capture" messages, so the total number of messages in this stage is at most $4nrF$. In stage $i > 1$, an active node sends $(r - 1)F$ "Capture" messages for a total of at most $4n_i rF$ messages, where n_i is the number of entities starting stage i; it is not difficult to verify that

$$n_i \leq n/(i - 1)(r - 1)F.$$

There are exactly $t = (n + 2)/2(r - 1)F$ stages. Then, the total number of messages during stages 2, 3, ..., t is

$$\sum_{2 \leq i \leq t} \frac{4rkn}{(i-1)(r-1)F}.$$

In the final stage, the leader sends $F + 1$ messages and each of the receivers generates in turn $n - 2$ messages. So the total number of messages of this stage is $(F + 1)(n - 1)$.

So the total number of messages is

$$4nrF + \sum_{2 \leq i \leq t} \frac{4rFn}{(i-1)(r-1)F} + (F + 1)(n - 1) = O\left(nrF + \frac{nr}{r-1} \log\left(\frac{n}{(r-1)F}\right) \right).$$

Let us now examine the time costs. We have seen that a *Capture* message generates at most four messages. Hence, each of the $(n + 2)/(r - 1)F$ stages of the leader election process takes at most four time units. We have to add two time units for the last stage of the algorithm. Then, the time needed for the execution of the algorithm is

$$\text{Time} = \frac{4(n+2)}{(r-1)F} + 2 = O\left(\frac{n}{(r-1)F}\right).$$

The parameter r yields a trade-off between time and messages: Increasing the value of r would decrease the time while increasing the number of messages. The best message complexity is achieved whenever $r = O(1)$. For example, with $r = 2$ we have

$$\mathbf{M}[FT - LinkElect] = O\left(nF + n \log\left(\frac{n}{F}\right) \right) \tag{7.22}$$

$$\mathbf{T}[FT - LinkElect] = O\left(\frac{n}{F} \right). \tag{7.23}$$

7.7.3 Concluding Remarks

We have seen that, although quite negative and restrictive, the result of Lemma 7.7.1 per se is not terribly discouraging: Even if several link may fail, it is possible to achieve a reasonable level of fault tolerance by sufficiently increasing the connectivity of the network. In other words, the price for having link fault tolerance are increased hardware costs.

In the case of complete networks with links that can fail with send/receive omissions, we have seen that it is always possible to elect a leader if $F \leq n - 2$; the cost is, however, quite high. We have also seen how to reduce the cost substantially if $F \leq \frac{n-6}{2}$. An interesting open problem is whether it is possible to design an equally efficient protocol tolerating the maximum amount of faults, that is, $F \leq n - 2$; see Problems 7.10.7 and 7.10.8.

Always in complete networks, it is actually possible to tolerate a much larger number of faults, indeed up to $\frac{n^2-2n}{2}$ send/receive omissions faulty links, *provided* that no more than $\frac{n}{2}$ incident links are faulty at each entity; furthermore, consensus under these conditions can be achieved quite efficiently (see Problem 7.10.10).

We have restricted our discussion to *send/receive omissions*; the situation clearly changes and the results do not hold if a faulty link can also *corrupt* the transmitted message.

7.7.4 Considerations on Localized Entity Failures

We have examined in details when and how, in synchronous system, we can cope with the presence of faulty entities. The bounds that we have seen are *tight*: We have designed protocols allowing consensus to be reached among the nonfaulty entities if the number of faulty entities did not exececd the bound; the presence of one more faulty entity would make the consensus task unreachable.

All our bounds have been established in terms of the number f of faulty entities present in the system; obviously we do not know beforehand who these entities are. It is only during the execution that their identity might become known.

We can consider this situation like that of an external observer that has available f *faulty* stickers to pin, one per faulty entity. When can the external observer declare an entity to be faulty and thus pin one of the stickers to it ? As long as the entity behaves correctly (i.e., according to the protocol), it cannot be clearly declared faulty. In contrast to this, as soon as it behaves incorrectly, it will be declared to be faulty by the observer, and the number of available stickers decreases by one. Note that not all f stickers will necessarily be assigned in every execution. For example, a Byzantine entity can behave correctly and never be identified by the observer.

IMPORTANT. In the setting we have established our bounds, *stickers are permanent*: once an entity is declared faulty, its sticker is never removed.

The consequence of this fact is that the results we have established apply only to systems where the faults are *localized and permanent*, that is, they are restricted to a *fixed* set of f entities.

Further note that an occasional transient failure of an entity (e.g., losing a single message just once) is treated by the external observer in the same way as a permanent failure of an entity: In both cases, the observer will pin a permanent *faulty* sticker to the entity. This leads to undesirable conclusions: In situations where every entity will occasionally lose a message (a situation that clearly occurs in real systems), the entire system will be declared unusable for any computation, even if the system is synchronous.

7.8 UBIQUITOUS FAULTS

In the previous section we have examined in details when and how, in synchronous system, we can cope with localized and permanent entity and link faults.

In general, the majority of failures have mostly a *transient* and *ubiquitous* nature; that is, faults can occur anywhere in the system and, following a failure, normal functioning can resume after a finite (although unpredictable) time. In particular, failures will occur on any communication link; almost every entity will experience at one time or another send or receive failure, and so forth.

In this section we will examine how we can deal with these communication failures, also called *dynamic faults* or *mobile faults*. For the designer of a protocol, these types of faults are much more difficult to handle than the ones that occur always in the same places. In the latter case, once a fault is detected, we know that we cannot trust that link; with mobile faults, detection will not help us with the future events.

It is, therefore, not surprising that the number of dynamic faults that can be tolerated at each time unit is by far less than that of the localized and permanent faults we can deal with. What is surprising is perhaps the fact that something *can* be done at all.

7.8.1 Communication Faults and Agreement

In a synchronous network, as we have already observed in Chapter 6, *silences are expressive*: We can have communication between entities even if no message is sent.

Let us more formally define what we mean by *communication* in the context of the agreement problem, and what is a faulty communication.

Given an entity x and a neighbor y in G, at each time unit t, a *communication* from x to y is a pair $\langle \alpha, \beta \rangle$ where α denotes what is sent by x to y at time t, and β denotes what is received by y from x at time $t + 1$. We denote by $\alpha = \emptyset$ the fact that at time t, x did not send any message to y; by $\beta = \emptyset$, we denote the fact that at time $t + 1$, y did not receive any message from x.

A communication $\langle \alpha, \beta \rangle$ from x to y at time t is *faulty* if $\alpha \neq \beta$, nonfaulty otherwise. We will distinguish between three types of faulty communication $\langle \alpha, \beta \rangle$:

1. $(\alpha \neq \emptyset = \beta)$ **omission**: the message sent by x to y at time t is not delivered to y by time $t + 1$;
2. $(\alpha = \emptyset \neq \beta)$ **addition**: a message from x is delivered to y at time $t + 1$, but x has sent no message to y at time t;

3. ($\emptyset \neq \alpha \neq \beta \neq \emptyset$) **corruption**: a message is sent by x to y at time t, but one with different content is received by y at time $t + 1$.

While the nature of omissions and corruptions is quite obvious, that of additions may appear strange and rather artificial at first. Instead, it describes a variety of situations. The most obvious one is when sudden noise in the transmission channel is mistaken for a message. However, the more important occurrence of additions in sytems is rather subtle: When we say that the received message "was not transmitted," what we really mean is that it "was not transmitted by any authorized user." Indeed, additions can be seen as messages surreptitiously inserted in the system by some outside, and possibly malicious, entity. Spam being sent from an unsuspecting site clearly fits the description of an addition. Summarizing, additions do occur and can be very dangerous.

These three types of faults are quite incomparable with each other in terms of danger. The hierarchy of faults comes into place when two or all of these basic fault types can occur in the system (see Figure 7.2). The presence of all three types of faults creates what is called a Byzantine faulty behavior.

Notice that most localized and permanent failures can be easily modeled by communication faults; for instance, omission of all messages sent by and to an entity can be used to describe the crash failure of that entity. Analogously, with enough dynamic communication faults of the appropriate type, it is easy to describe faults such as send and receive failures, Byzantine link failures, and so forth. In fact, with at most $2(n - 1)$ dynamic communication faults per time unit, we can simulate the interaction of one faulty entity with its neighbors, regardless of its fault type (Exercise 7.10.39).

As in the previous section, we will concentrate on the *Agreement Problem* **Agree(p)**.

The goal will be to determine if and how a certain level of agreement (i.e., value of p) can be reached in spite of a certain number F of dynamic faults of a given type τ occurring *at each time unit*; note that, as the faults are mobile, the set of faulty communications may change at each time unit.

Depending on the value of parameter p, we have different types of agreement problems. Of particular interest are *unanimity* (i.e., $p = n$) and *strong majority* (i.e., $k = \lceil \frac{n}{2} \rceil + 1$).

Note that any Boolean agreement requiring *less* than a strong majority (i.e., $p \leq \lceil n/2 \rceil$) can be trivially reached without any communication, for example, each entity chooses its input value. We are interested only in *nontrivial* agreements (i.e., $p > \lceil n/2 \rceil$).

7.8.2 Limits to Number of Ubiquitous Faults for Majority

The fact that dynamic faults are not localized but ubiquitous makes the problem of designing fault-tolerant software much more difficult. The difficulty is further increased by the fact that dynamic faults may be transient and not permanent (hence harder to detect).

Let us examine how much more difficult it is to reach a nontrivial (i.e., $p > \lceil\frac{n}{2}\rceil$) agreement in presence of dynamic communication faults.

Consider a complete network. From the results we have established in the case of entity failures, we know that if only one entity crashes, the other $n - 1$ can agree on the same value (Theorem 7.3.1). Observe that with $2(n - 1)$ *omissions* per clock cycle, we can simulate the crash failure of a single entity: All messages sent to and from that entity are omitted at each time unit. This means that if $2(n - 1)$ omissions per clock cycle are localized to a single entity all the time, then agreement among $n - 1$ entities is possible. What happens if those $2(n - 1)$ omissions per clock cycle are *mobile* (i.e., not localized to the same entity all the time)?

Even in this case, at most a single entity will be isolated from the rest at any one time; thus, one might still reasonably expect that an agreement among $n - 1$ entities can be reached even if the faults are dynamic. Not only this expectation is false, but actually it is impossible to reach even strong majority (i.e., an agreement among $\lceil n/2 \rceil + 1$ entities).

This results in an instance of a more general result that we will be going to derive and examine in this section. As a consequence, in a network $G = (V, E)$ with maximum node degree $\deg(G)$,

1. with $\deg(G)$ omissions per clock cycle, strong majority cannot be reached;
2. if the failures are any mixture of corruptions and additions, the same bound $\deg(G)$ holds for the impossibility of strong majority;
3. In the case of arbitrary faults (omissions, additions, and corruptions: the Byzantine case), strong majority cannot be reached if just $\lceil \deg(G)/2 \rceil$ transmissions may be faulty.

Impossibility of Strong Majority The basic result yielding the desired impossibility results for even strong majority is obtained using a "bivalency" technique similar to the one emplyed to prove the Single-Fault Disaster. However, the environment here is drastically different from the one considered there. In particular, we are now in a *synchronous* environment with all its consequences; in particular, delays are unitary; therefore, we cannot employ (to achieve our impossibility result) arbitrarily long delays. Furthermore, omissions are detectable! In other words, we cannot use the same arguments, the resources at our disposal are more limited, and the task of proving impossibility is more difficult.

With this in mind, let us refresh some of the terminology and definitions we need.

Let us start with the *problem*. Each entity x has an *input register* I_x, a write-once *output register* O_x, and unlimited internal storage. Initially, the input register of an entity is a value in $\{0, 1\}$, and all the output registers are set to the same value $b \notin \{0, 1\}$; once a value $d_x \in \{0, 1\}$ is written in O_x, the content of that register is no longer modifiable. The goal is to have at least $p > \lceil n/2 \rceil$ entities set, in finite time, their output registers to the same value $d \in \{0, 1\}$, subject to the nontriviality condition (i.e., if all input values are the same, then d must be that value).

The values of the registers and of the global clock, together with the program counters and the internal storage, comprise the *internal state* of an entity. The states in which the output register has value $v \in \{0, 1\}$ are distinguished as being *v-decision-states*.

A *configuration* of the system consists of the internal state of all entities at a given time. An *initial* configuration is one in which all entities are in an initial state at time $t = 0$. A configuration C has *decision value* v if at least p entities are in a v-decision state, $v \in \{0, 1\}$; note that as $p > \lceil n/2 \rceil$, a configuration can have at most one decision value.

At any time t, the system is in some configuration C, and every entity can send a message to any of its neighbors. What these messages will contain depends on the protocol and on C. We describe the messages by means of a *message array* $\Lambda(C)$ composed of n^2 entries defined as follows: If x_i and x_j are neighbors, then the entry $\Lambda(C)[i, j]$ contains the (possibly empty) message sent by x_i to x_j; if x_i and x_j are *not* neighbors, then we denote this fact by $\Lambda(C)[i, j] = *$, where $*$ is a distinguished symbol.

In the actual communication, some of these messages will not be delivered or their content will be corrupted, or a message will arrive when none has been sent.

We will describe what happens by means of another $n \times n$ array called *transmission matrix* τ for $\Lambda(C)$ and defined as follows: If x_i and x_j are neighbors, then the entry $\tau[i, j]$ of the matrix contains the communication pair (α, β), where $\alpha = \Lambda(C)[i, j]$ is what x_i sent and β is what x_j actually receives; if x_i and x_j are *not* neighbors, then we denote this fact by $\tau[i, j] = (*, *)$. Where no ambiguity arises, we will omit the indication C from $\Lambda(C)$.

Clearly, because of the different number and types of faults and different ways in which faults can occur, many transmission matrices are possible for the same Λ. We will denote by $\mathcal{T}(\Lambda)$ the set of all possible transmission matrices τ for Λ.

Once the transmission specified by τ has occurred, the clock is incremented by one unit to $t + 1$; depending on its internal state, on the current clock value, and on the received messages; each entity x_i prepares a new message for each neighbor x_j and enters a new internal state. The entire the system enters a new configuration $\tau\{C\}$. We will call τ an *event* and the passage from one configuration to the next a *step*.

Let $R^1(C) = R(C) = \{\tau\{C\} : \tau \in \mathcal{T}(\Lambda(C))\}$ be the set of all possible configurations resulting from C in one step, sometimes called *succeeding* configurations of C. Generalizing, let $R^k(C)$ be the set of all possible configurations resulting from C in $k > 0$ steps and $R^*(C) = \{C' : \exists t > 0, \ C' \in R^t(C)\}$ be the set of configurations reachable from C. A configuration that is reachable from some initial configuration is said to be *accessible*.

Let $v \in \{0, 1\}$. A configuration C is *v-valent* if there exists a $t \geq 0$ such that all $C' \in R^t(C)$ have decision value v, that is, a v-valent configuration will always result in at least K entities deciding on v. A configuration C is *bivalent* if there exist in $R^*(C)$ both a 0-valent and a 1-valent configuration.

If two configurations C' and C'' differ only in the internal state of entity x_j, we say that they are *j-adjacent*, and we call them *adjacent* if they are j-adjacent for some j.

We will be interested in sets of events (i.e., transmission matrices) that preserve adjacency of configurations. We call a set S of events j-*adjacency preserving* if for any two j-adjacent configurations C' and C'' there exist in S two events τ' and τ'' for $\lambda(C')$ and $\lambda(C'')$, respectively such that $\tau'(C')$ and $\tau''(C'')$ are j-adjacent. We call S *adjacency preserving* if it is j-adjacency preserving for *all* j.

A set S of events is *continuous* if for any configuration C and for any $\tau', \tau'' \in S$ for $\Lambda(C)$, there exists a finite sequence $\tau_0, \ldots, \tau_m$ of events in S for $\lambda(C)$ such that $\tau_0 = \tau'$, $\tau_m = \tau''$, and $\tau_i(C)$ and $\tau_{i+1}(C)$ are adjacent, $0 \le i < m$.

We are interested in sets of events with at most F faults that contain an event for all possible message matrices. A set S of events is F-*admissible*, $0 \le F \le 2|E|$ if for each message matrix Λ, there is an event $\tau \in S$ for Λ that contains at most F faulty transmissions; furthermore, there is an event in S that contains exactly F faulty transmissions.

As we will see, any set of F-admissible events that is both continuous and j-adjacency preserving for some j will make any strong majority protocol fail.

To prove our impossibility result, we are going to use two properties that follow immediately from the definitions of state and of event.

First of all, if an entity is in the same state in two different configurations A and B, then it will send the same messages in both configurations. That is, let $s_i(C)$ denote the internal state of x_i in C; then

Property 7.8.1 *For two configurations A and B, let $\Lambda(A)$ and $\Lambda(B)$ be the corresponding message matrices. If $s_j(A) = s_j(B)$ for some entity x_j, then $\langle \Lambda(A)[j, 1], \ldots, \Lambda(A)[j, n] \rangle = \langle \Lambda(B)[j, 1], \ldots, \Lambda(B)[j, n] \rangle$.*

Next, if an entity is in the same state in two different configurations A and B, and it receives the same messages in both configurations, then it will enter the same state in both resulting configurations. That is,

Property 7.8.2 *Let A and B be two configurations such that $s_j(A) = s_j(B)$ for some entity x_j, and let τ' and τ'' be events for $\Lambda(A)$ and $\Lambda(B)$, respectively. Let $\tau'[i, j] = (\alpha'_{i.j}, \beta'_{i.j})$ and $\tau''[i, j] = (\alpha''_{i.j}, \beta''_{i.j})$. If $\beta'_{i.j} = \beta''_{i.j}$ for all i, then $s_j(\tau'\{A\}) = s_j(\tau''\{B\})$.*

Given a set S of events and an agreement protocol P, let $\mathcal{P}(P, S)$ denote the set of all initial configurations and those that can be generated in all executions of P when the events are those in S.

Theorem 7.8.1 *Let S be continuous, j-adjacency preserving and F-admissible, $F > 0$. Let P be a $(\lfloor (n - 1)/2 \rfloor + 2)$–agreement protocol. If $\mathcal{P}(P, S)$ contains two accessible l-adjacent configurations, a 0-valent and a 1-valent one, then P is not correct in spite of F communication faults in S.*

Proof. Assume to the contrary that P is a $(\lfloor (n - 1)/2 \rfloor + 2)$–agreement protocol that is correct in spite of $F > 0$ communication faults when the only possible events are those in S.

Now let A and B be j-adjacent accessible configurations that are 0-valent and 1-valent, respectively.

As S is j-adjacency preserving, there exist in S two events, π_1 for $\Lambda(A)$ and ρ_1 for $\Lambda(B)$, such that the resulting configurations $\pi_1\{A\}$ and $\rho_1\{B\}$ are j-adjacent. For the same reason, there exist in S two events, π_2 and ρ_2, such that the resulting configurations $\pi_2\{\pi_1\{A\}\}$ and $\rho_2\{\rho_1\{B\}\}$ are j-adjacent. Continuing to reason in this way, we have that there are in S two events, π_t and ρ_t, such that the resulting configurations $\pi'(A) = \pi_t\{\pi_{t-1}\{\ldots \pi_2\{\pi_1\{A\}\}\ldots\}\}$ and $\rho'(A) = \rho_t\{\rho_{t-1}\{\ldots \rho_2\{\rho_1\{A\}\}\ldots\}\}$ are j-adjacent.

As P is correct, there exists a $t \geq 1$ such that $\pi'(A)$ and $\rho'(B)$ have a decision value. As A is 0-valent, at least $\lceil\frac{n}{2}\rceil + 1$ entities have decision value 0 in $\pi'(A)$; similarly, as B is 1-valent, at least $\lceil\frac{n}{2}\rceil + 1$ entities have decision value 1 in $\pi'(B)$. This means that there exists at least one entity x_i, $i \neq j$, that has decision value 0 in $\pi'(A)$ and 1 in $\rho'(B)$; hence, $s_i(\pi'(A)) \neq s_i(\rho'(B))$.

However, as $\pi'(A)$ and $\rho'(B)$ are j-adjacent, they only differ in the state of one entity, x_j: a contradiction. As a consequence, P is not correct. ∎

We can now prove the main negative result.

Theorem 7.8.2   Impossibility of Strong Majority
Let S be adjacency-preserving, continuous and F-admissible. Then no k-agreement protocol is correct in spite of F communication faults in S for $K > \lceil n/2 \rceil$.

Proof. Assume P is a correct ($\lceil n/2\rceil+1$)-agreement protocol in spite of F communication faults when the message system returns only events in S. In a typical bivalency approach, the proof involves two steps: First, it is argued that there is some initial configuration in which the decision is not already predetermined; second, it is shown that it is possible to forever postpone entering a configuration with a decision value.

Lemma 7.8.1 $\mathcal{P}(P, S)$ *has an initial bivalent configuration.*

Proof. By contradiction, let every initial configuration in $\mathcal{P}(P, S)$ be v-valent for $= v \in \{0, 1\}$ and let P be correct. As, by definition, there is at least a 0-valent initial configuration A and a 1-valent initial configuration B; then there must be a 0-valent initial configuration and a 1-valent initial configuration that are adjacent. In fact, let $A_0 = A$, and let A_h denote the configuration obtained by changing into 1 a single 0 input value of A_{h-1}, $1 \leq h \leq z(A)$, where $z(A)$ is the number of 0s in A; similarly define B_h, $0 \leq h \leq z(B)$ where $z(B)$ is the number of 0s in B. By construction, $A_{z(A)} = B_{z(B)}$. Consider the sequence

$$A = A_0, \; A_1, \; \ldots, \; A_{z(A)} = B_{z(B)}, \; \ldots B_1, \; B_0 = B.$$

In it, each configuration is adjacent to the following one; as it starts with a 0-valent and ends with a 1-valent configuration, it contains a 0-valent configuration adjacent to a 1-valent one. By Theorem 7.8.1 it follows that P is not correct: a contradiction. Hence, in $\mathcal{P}(P, S)$ there must be an initial bivalent configuration. ∎

Lemma 7.8.2 *Every bivalent configuration in $\mathcal{P}(P, S)$ has a succeeding bivalent configuration.*

Proof. Let C be a bivalent configuration in $\mathcal{P}(P, S)$. If C has no succeeding bivalent configuration, then C has at least one 0-valent and at least one 1-valent succeeding configuration, say A and B. Let $\tau', \tau'' \in S$ such that $\tau'(C) = A$ and $\tau''(C) = B$. As S is continuous, there exists a sequence $\tau_0, \ldots, \tau_m$ of events in S for $\lambda(C)$ such that $\tau_0 = \tau', \tau_m = \tau''$, and $\tau_i(C)$ and $\tau_{i+1}(C)$ are adjacent, $0 \le i < m$. Consider now the corresponding sequence of configurations:

$$A = \tau'(C) = \tau_0(C), \ \tau_1(C). \ \tau_2(C), \ \ldots, \ \tau_m(C) = \tau''(C) = B.$$

As this sequence starts with a 0-valent and ends with a 1-valent configuration, it contains a 0-valent configuration adjacent to a 1-valent one. By Theorem 7.8.1, P is not correct: a contradiction. Hence, every bivalent configuration in $\mathcal{P}(P, S)$ has a succeeding bivalent configuration. ∎

From Lemmas 7.8.1 and 7.8.2, it follows that there exists an infinite sequence of accessible bivalent configurations, each derivable in one step from the preceding one. This contradicts the assumption that for each initial configuration C there exists a $t \ge 0$ such that every $C' \in R^t(C)$ has a decision value; thus, P is not correct. This concludes the proof of Theorem 7.8.2. ∎

Consequences   The Impossibility of Strong Majority result provides a powerful tool for proving impossibility results for nontrivial agreement: If it can be shown that a set S of events is adjacency preserving, continuous, and F-admissible, then no nontrivial agreement is possible for the types and numbers of faults implied by S.

Obviously, not every set S of events is adjacency preserving; unfortunately, all the ones we are interested in are so. A summary is shown in Figure 7.18.

Omission Faults   We can use the Impossibility of Strong Majority result to prove that no *strong majority* protocol is correct in spite of $\deg(G)$ communication faults, even when the faults are only *omissions*.

Let **Omit** be the set of all events containing at most $\deg(G)$ omission faults. Thus, by definition, **Omit** is $\deg(G)$-admissible.

To verify that **Omit** is continuous, consider a configuration C and any two events $\tau', \tau'' \in \mathbf{O}$ for $\Lambda(C)$. Let $m'_1, m'_2, \ldots, m'_{f'}$ be the f' faulty communications in τ', and let $m''_1, m''_2, \ldots, m''_{f''}$ be the f'' faulty communications in τ''. As $\mathbf{O}$ is $\deg(G)$-admissible, $f' \le \deg(G)$ and $f'' \le \deg(G)$. Let $\tau'_0 = \tau'$, and let τ'_h denote the event obtained by replacing the faulty communication m'_h in τ'_{h-1} with a nonfaulty one (with the same message sent in both), $1 \le h \le f'$; Similarly define $\tau''_h, 0 \le h \le f''$.

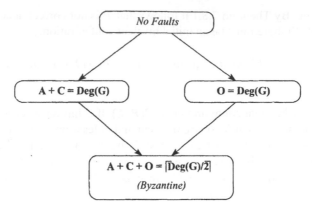

FIGURE 7.18: Impossibility. Minimum number of faults per clock cycle that may render **strong majority** impossible.

By construction, $\tau'_{f'} = \tau''_{f''}$. Consider the sequence

$$\tau'_0, \tau'_1, \ldots, \tau'_{f'} = \tau''_{f''}, \ldots, \tau''_1, \tau''_0.$$

In this sequence, each event is adjacent to the following one; furthermore, as by construction each event contains at most $\deg(G)$ omissions, it is in **Omit**. Thus, **Omit** is continuous.

We can now show that **Omit** is adjacency preserving. Given a message matrix Λ; let $\psi_{\Lambda,l}$ denote the event for Λ where all and only the messages sent by x_l are lost. Then, for each Λ and l, $\psi_{\Lambda,l} \in$ **Omit**. Let configurations A and B be l-adjacent. Consider the events $\psi_{\Lambda(A),l}$ and $\psi_{\Lambda(B),l}$ for A and B, respectively, and the resulting configurations A' and B'. By Properties 7.8.1 and 7.8.2, it follows that also A' and B' are l-adjacent. Hence **Omit** is adjacency preserving.

Summarizing,

Lemma 7.8.3 **Omit** *is $\deg(G)$-admissible, continuous, and adjacency preserving.*

Then, by Theorem 7.8.1, it follows that

Theorem 7.8.3 *No p-agreement protocol P is correct in spite of $\deg(G)$ omission faults in* **Omit** *for $p > \lceil n/2 \rceil$.*

Addition and Corruption Faults Using a similar approach, we can show that when the faults are additions and corruptions no strong majority protocol is correct in spite of $\deg(G)$ communication faults.

Let **AddCorr** denote the set of all events containing at most $\deg(G)$ addition and corruption faults. Thus, by definition, **AddCorr** is $\deg(G)$-admissible. It is not difficult to verify that **AddCorr** is continuous (Exercise 7.10.40).

We can prove that **AddCorr** is adjacency preserving as follows. For any two h-adjacent configurations A and B, consider the events π_h and ρ_h for $\Lambda(A) = \{\alpha_{ij}\}$ and $\Lambda(B) = \{\gamma_{ij}\}$, respectively where for all $(x_i, x_j) \in E$,

$$\pi_h[i, j] = \begin{cases} (\alpha_{ij}, \gamma_{ij}) & \text{if } i = h \text{ and } \alpha_{ij} = \Omega \\ (\alpha_{ij}, \alpha_{ij}) & \text{otherwise} \end{cases}$$

and

$$\rho_h[i, j] = \begin{cases} (\gamma_{ij}, \alpha_{ij}) & \text{if } i = h \text{ and } \alpha_{ij} \neq \Omega \\ (\gamma_{ij}, \gamma_{ij}) & \text{otherwise.} \end{cases}$$

It is not difficult to verify that $\pi_h, \rho_h \in$ **AddCorr** and the configurations $\pi_h(C')$ and $\rho_h(C'')$ are h-adjacent. Hence **AddCorr** is adjacency preserving.

Summarizing,

Lemma 7.8.4 **AddCorr** *is deg (G)-admissible, continuous, and adjacency preserving.*

Then, by Theorem 7.8.1, it follows that

Theorem 7.8.4 *No p-agreement protocol P is correct in spite of deg(G) communication faults in* **AddCorr** *for* $p > \lceil n/2 \rceil$.

Byzantine Faults   We now show that no strong majority protocol is correct in spite of $\lceil \deg(G)/2 \rceil$ arbitrary communication faults.

Let **Byz** be the set of all events containing at most $\lceil \deg(G)/2 \rceil$ communication faults, where the faults may be omissions, corruptions, and additions. By definition, **Byz** is $\lceil \deg(G)/2 \rceil$-admissible. Actually (see Exercises 7.10.41 and 7.10.42),

Lemma 7.8.5 **Byz** *is* $\lceil deg(G)/2 \rceil$-*admissible, continuous, and adjacency preserving.*

Then, by Theorem 7.8.1, it follows that

Theorem 7.8.5 *No p-agreement protocol P is correct in spite of* $\lceil deg(G)/2 \rceil$ *communication faults in* **Byz** *for* $p > \lceil n/2 \rceil$.

and dynamic result all if, at each

7.8.3 Unanimity in Spite of Ubiquitous Faults

In this section we examine the possibility of achieving *unanimity* among the entities, agreement in spite of dynamic faults. We will examine the problem under the following restrictions:

Additional Assumptions (MA)

1. *Connectivity, Bidirectional Links*;
2. *Synch*;
3. all entities start simultaneously;
4. each entity has a map of the network.

Surprisingly, unanimity can be achieved in several cases; the exact conditions depend not only on the type and number of faults but also on the edge connectivity $c_{edge}(G)$ of G.

In all cases, we will reach *unanimity*, in spite of F communication faults per clock cycle, by computing the **OR** of the input values and deciding on that value. This is achieved by first constructing (if not already available) a mechanism for correctly broadcasting the value of a bit within a fixed amount of time T in spite of F communication faults per clock cycle. This reliable broadcast, once constructed, is then used to correctly compute the logical **OR** of the input values: All entities with input value 1 will reliably broadcast their value; if at least one of the input values is 1 (thus, the result of **OR** is 1), then everybody will be communicated this fact within time T; on the contrary, if all input values are 0 (thus, the result of **OR** is 0), there will be no broadcasts and everybody will be aware of this fact within time T.

The variable T will be called *timeout*. The actual reliable broadcast mechanism will differ depending on the nature of the faults.

Single Type Faults: Omissions Consider the case when the communication errors are just *omissions*. That is, in addition to **MA** we have the restriction *Omission* that the only faults are omissions.

First observe that, because of Lemma 7.1.1, broadcast is impossible if $F \geq c_{edge}(G)$. This means that we might be able to tolerate at most $c_{edge}(G) - 1$ omissions for time unit.

Let $F \leq c_{edge}(G) - 1$. When broadcasting in this situation, it is rather easy to circumvent the loss of messages. In fact, it suffices for all entities involved, starting from the initiator of the broadcast, to send the same message to the same neighbors for several consecutive time steps. More precisely, consider the following algorithm:

Algorithm Bcast-Omit

1. To broadcast in G, node x sends its message at time 0 and continues transmitting it to all its neighbors until time $T(G) - 1$ (the actual value of the timeout $T(G)$ will be determined later);
2. a node y receiving the message at time $t < T(G)$ will transmit the message to all its other neighbors until time $T(G) - 1$.

Let us verify that if $F < c_{\text{edge}}(G)$, there are values of the timeout $T(G)$ for which the protocol performs the broadcast.

As G has edge connectivity $c_{\text{edge}}(G)$, by Property 7.1.1, there are at least $c_{\text{edge}}(G)$ edge-disjoint paths between x and y; furthermore, each of these paths has length at most $n - 1$. According to the protocol, x sends a message along all these $c_{\text{edge}}(G)$ paths. At any time instant, there are $F < c_{\text{edge}}(G)$ omissions; this means that at least one of these paths is free of faults. That is, at any time unit, the message from x will move one step further toward y along one of them. Since these paths have length at most $n - 1$, after at most $c_{\text{edge}}(G)(n - 2) + 1 = c_{\text{edge}}(G) n - 2 c_{\text{edge}}(G) + 1$ time units the message from x would reach y. This means that with

$$T(G) \geq c_{\text{edge}}(G) n - 2 c_{\text{edge}}(G) + 1,$$

it is possible to broadcast in spite of $F < c$ omissions per time units. This value for the timeout is rather high and depending on the graph G can be substantially reduced.

Let us denote by $T^*(G)$ the *minimum* timeout value ensuring algorithm *Bcast-Omit* to correctly perform the broadcast in G.

Using algorithm *Bcast-Omit* to compute the **OR** we have the following:

Theorem 7.8.6 *Unanimity can be reached in spite of $F = c_{edge}(G) - 1$ faults per clock cycle in time $T^*(G)$ |em transmitting at most $2 m(G) T^*(G)$ bits.*

What is the actual value of $T^*(G)$ for a given G? We have just seen that

$$T^*(G) \leq c_{\text{edge}}(G) n - 2c_{\text{edge}}(G) + 1. \tag{7.24}$$

A different available bound (Problem 7.10.1) is

$$T^*(G) = O(\text{diam}(G)^{c_{edge}(G)}). \tag{7.25}$$

They are both estimates on how much time it takes for the broadcast to complete. Which estimate is better (i.e., smaller) depends on the graph G.

For example, in a *hypercube* H, $c_{\text{edge}}(H) = \text{diam}(H) = \log n$; hence, if we use Equation 7.24 we have $O(n \log n)$ while with Equation 7.25 we would have a time $O(n^{\log\log n})$.

Actually, in a hypercube, both estimates are far from accurate. It is easy to verify (Exercise 7.10.43) that $T^*(H) \leq \log^2 n$. It is not so simple (Exercise 7.10.44) to show that the timeout is actually

$$T^*(H) \leq \log n + 2. \tag{7.26}$$

In other words, with only two time units more than that in the fault-free case, broadcast can tolerate up to $\log n - 1$ message losses per time unit.

Let us now focus on the bit costs of the protocol *Consensus-Omit* obtained by computing the **OR** of the input values by means of algorithm *Bcast-Omit*. We have seen that

$$\mathbf{B}(Bcast\text{-}Omit) \leq 2\, m(G)\, T^*(G).$$

With very little hacking, it is possible to remove the factor 2. In fact, if an entity x receives 1 from a neighbor y to which it has sent 1 (for one or more time units), then x knows that y has seen a 1; thus, x can stop sending messages to y. In this way, if two neighbors send messages to each other at the same time, then no more messages will be sent between them from now on. In other words, on a link at each time unit there is only one message, except at most once when there are two. Summarizing,

$$\mathbf{B}(Bcast - Omit) \leq m(G)\, T^*(G) + m(G). \tag{7.27}$$

Single Type Faults: Additions   Let us consider a system where the faults are additions, that is, messages are received although none was transmitted by any authorized user. To deal with additions in a fully synchronous system is possible but expensive. Indeed, if each entity transmits to its neighbors at each clock cycle, it leaves no room for additions. Thus, the entities can correctly compute the **OR** using a simple diffusion mechanism in which each entity transmits for the first $T(G) - 1$ time units: Initially, an entity sends its value; if at any time it is aware of the existence of a 1 in the system, it will only send 1 from that moment onward. The corresponding protocol is shown in Figure 7.19. The process clearly can terminate after $T(G) = diam(G)$ clock cycles. Hence,

Theorem 7.8.7   *Let the system faults be* additions. *Unanimity can be reached regardless of the number of faults in time* $T = diam(G)$ *transmitting* $2m(G)\, diam(G)$ *bits.*

Observe that, although expensive, it is no more so that what we have been able to achieve with just omissions.

Further observe that if a spanning tree S of G is available, it can be used for the entire computation. In this case, the number of bits is $2(n - 1)\, diam(S)$ while time is $diam(S)$.

Single Type Faults: Corruptions   Surprisingly, if the faults are just *corruptions*, unanimity can be reached *regardless of the number of faults*.

To understand this result, first consider, that as the only faults are corruptions, there are no omissions; thus, any message transmitted will arrive, although its content may be corrupted. Furthermore, there are no additions; thus, only the messages that are transmitted by some entity will arrive. This means that if an entity starts a broadcast protocol, every node will receive a message (although not necessarily the correct one).

PROTOCOL Consensus-Add

- States: $S = \{$ASLEEP, ZERO, ONE, DONE$\}$;
  $S_{INIT} = \{$ASLEEP$\}$;
  $S_{TERM} = \{$DONE$\}$.
- Restrictions: Simultaneous Start $\cup$ **Synch**.

ASLEEP
> *Spontaneously*
> **begin**
> > **setalarm** $c(x) = T(G)$;
> > **if** $I_x = 1$ **then**
> > > **become** *ONE;*
> >
> > **else** (i.e., $I_x = 0$)
> > > **become** *ZERO*
> >
> > **endif**
> > **send** $I_x = 1$ **to** $N(x)$;
>
> **end**

ZERO
> *Receiving* (value)
> **begin**
> > **if** *value* $= 1$ **then become** *ONE;*
> > **send** value **to** $N(x)$;
>
> **end**

> *When* $(c(x) =$ alarm)
> **begin**
> > $D_x = 0$;
> > **become** *DONE;*
>
> **end**

ONE
> *Receiving* (value)
> **begin**
> > **send** 1 **to** $N(x)$;
>
> **end**
> *When* $(c(x) =$ alarm)
> **begin**
> > $D_x = 1$;
> > **become** *DONE;*
>
> **end**

FIGURE 7.19: Protocol *Consensus-Add.*

We can use this fact in computing the **OR**. All entities with an input value 1 become
initiators of *WFlood*, in which all nodes participate. Regardless of its content, a message will always and only communicate the existence of an initial value 1; an entity
receiving a message thus knows that the correct value is 1 regardless of the content of
the message. If there is an initial value 1, as there are no omissions, all entities will receive a message within time $T(G) = \text{diam}(G)$. If all initial values are 0, no broadcast
is started and, as there are no additions, no messages are received; thus, all entities
will detect this situation because they will not receive any message by time $T(G)$.

The resulting protocol, *Consensus-Corrupt*, shown in Figure 7.20, yields the
following:

PROTOCOL Consensus-Corrupt

- States: $S = \{$ASLEEP, ZERO, ONE, DONE$\}$;
  $S_{\text{INIT}} = \{$ASLEEP$\}$;
  $S_{\text{TERM}} = \{$DONE$\}$.
- Restrictions: Simultaneous Start $\cup$ **Synch**.

ASLEEP
> *Spontaneously*
> **begin**
> > setalarm $c(x) = T(G)$;
> > **if** $I_x = 1$ **then**
> > > send Message **to** $N(x)$;
> > > **become** *ONE*;
> >
> > **else** (i.e., $I_x = 0$)
> > > **become** *ZERO*
> >
> > **endif**
>
> **end**

ZERO
> *Receiving* (Message)
> **begin**
> > send Message **to** $N(x) - \{sender\}$;
> > **become** *ONE*;
>
> **end**

> *When* $(c(x) = $ alarm)
> **begin**
> > $D_x = 0$;
> > **become** *DONE*;
>
> **end**

ONE
> *When* $(c(x) = $ alarm)
> **begin**
> > $D_x = 1$;
> > **become** *DONE*;
>
> **end**

FIGURE 7.20: Protocol *Consensus-Corrupt*.

Theorem 7.8.8 *Let the system faults be* corruptions. *Unanimity can be reached regardless of the number of faults in time* $T = diam(G)$ *transmitting at most* $2\, m(G)$ *bits.*

Composite Faults: Omissions and Corruptions If the system suffers from *omissions and corruptions*, the situation is fortunately no worse than that of systems with only omissions.

As there are no additions, no unintended message is generated. Indeed, in the computation of the **OR** , the only intended messages are those originated by entities with initial value 1 and only those messages (possibly corrupted) will be transmitted along the network. An entity receiving a message, thus, knows that the correct value is 1, regardless of the content of the message. If we use *Bcast-Omit*, we are guaranteed that everybody will receive a message (regardless of its content) within $T = T^*(G)$ clock cycles in spite of $c_{edge}(G) - 1$ or fewer omissions, if and only if at least one is originated (i.e., if there is at least an entity with initial value 1). Hence

Theorem 7.8.9 *Unanimity can be reached in spite of $F = c_{edge}(G) - 1$ faults per clock cycle if the system faults are* omissions and corruptions. *The time to agreement is $T = T^*(G)$ and the number of bits is at most $2\, m(G)T^*$.*

Observe that, although expensive, it is no more so that what we have been able to achieve with just omissions.

As in the case of only *omissions*, the factor 2 can be removed by the bit costs without any increase in time.

Composite Faults: Omissions and Additions Consider now the case of systems with *omissions and additions*.

To counter the negative effect of additions, each entity transmits to all their neighbors in every clock cycle. Initially, an entity sends its value; if at any time it is aware of the existence of a 1 in the system, it will only send 1 from that moment onward. As there are no corruptions, the content of a message can be trusted.

Clearly, with such a strategy, no additions can ever take place. Thus, the only negative effects are due to omissions; however, if $F \leq c_{edge}(G) - 1$, omissions cannot stop the nodes from receiving a 1 within $T = T^*(G)$ clock cycles if at least an entity has such an initial value. Hence

Theorem 7.8.10 *Unanimity can be reached in spite of $F = c_{edge}(G) - 1$ faults per clock cycle if the system faults are* omissions and additions. *The time to agreement is $T = T^*(G)$ and the number of bits is at most $2\, m(G)\, (T^*(G) - 1)$.*

Composite Faults: Additions and Corruptions Consider the environment when faults can be both *additions and corruptions*. In this environment messages are not lost but none can be trusted; in fact the content could be incorrect (i.e., a corruption) or it could be a fake (i.e., an addition).

This makes the computation of **OR** quite difficult. If we only transmit when we have 1 (as we did with only *corruptions*), how can we trust that a received message was really transmitted and not caused by an addition? If we always transmit the **OR** of what we have and receive (as we did with only *additions*), how can we trust that a received 1 was not really a 0 transformed by a corruption?

For this environment, indeed we need a more complex mechanism employing several techniques, as well as an additional restriction:

Additional restriction: The network G is known to the entities.

The first technique we use is that of *time splicing*:

Technique *Time Splice*:

1. We distinguish between *even* and *odd* clock ticks; an even clock tick and its successive odd click constitute a *communication cycle*.
2. To broadcast 0 (respective 1), x will send a message to all its neighbors only on *even* (respective *odd*) clock ticks.
3. When receiving a message at an *even* (respective *odd*) clock tick, entity y will forward it only on *even* (respective *odd*) clock ticks.

In this way, entities are going to propagate 1 only at odd ticks and 0 at even ticks.

This technique, however, does not solve the problem created by additions; in fact, the arrival of a fake message created by an addition at an odd clock tick can generate an unwanted propagation of 1 in the systems through the odd clock ticks.

To cope with the presence of additions, we use another technique based on the edge-connectivity of the network. Consider an entity x and a neighbor y. Let SP(x, y) be the set of the $c_{edge}(G)$ shortest disjoint paths from x to y, including the direct link (x, y); see Figure 7.21. To communicate a message from x to y, we use a technique in which the message is sent by x simultaneously on all the paths in SP(x, y). This technique, called *Reliable Neighbor Transmission*, is as follows:

Technique *Reliable Neighbor Transmission*:

1. For each pair of neighboring entities x, y and paths SP(x, y), every entity determines in which of these paths it resides.
2. To communicate a message M to neighbor y, y will send along each of the $c_{edge}(G)$ paths in SP(x, y) a message, containing M and the information about

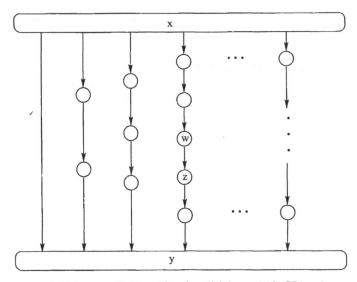

FIGURE 7.21: The $c_{edge}(G)$ edge-disjoint paths in SP(x, y).

the path, for t consecutive communication cycles (the value of t will be discussed later).

3. An entity z on one of those paths, upon receiving in communication cycle k a message for y with the correct path information, will forward it only along that path for $t - k$ communication cycles. A message with incorrect path information will be discarded.

Note that incorrect path information (owing to corruptions and/or additions) in a message for y received by z is *detectable* and so is incorrect timing as a result of the following:

- Because of local orientation, z knows the neighbor w from which it receives the message;
- z can determine if w is really its predecessor in the claimed path to y;
- z knows at what time such a message should arrive if really originated by x.

Let us now combine these two techniques together. To compute the **OR**, all entities broadcast their input value using the *Time Slice* technique: The broadcast of 1s will take place at odd clock ticks, that of 0s at even ones. However, every step of the broadcast, in which every involved entity sends the bit to its neighbors, is done using the *Reliable Neighbor Transmission* technique. This means that each step of the broadcast now takes t communication cycles.

Let us call *OR-AddCorrupt* the resulting protocol.

As there are no omissions, any transmitted message is possibly corrupted, but, it arrives; the clock cycle in which it arrives at y will indicate the correct value of the bit (even cycles for 0, odd for 1). Therefore, if x transmits a bit, y will eventually receive one and be able to decide the correct bit value. This is, however, not sufficient. We need now to choose the appropriate value of t so that y will not mistakenly interpret the arrival of bits due to additions and can decide if it was really originated by x.

The obvious property of *Reliable Neighbor Transmission* is that

Lemma 7.8.6 *In t communication cycles, at most $F\,t$ copies of incorrect messages arrive at y.*

The other property of *Reliable Neighbor Transmission* is less obvious. Observe that when x sends 1 to neighbor y using *Reliable Neighbor Transmission*, y will receive many copies of this "correct" (i.e., corrected using the properties of time slicing) bit. Let $l(x, y)$ be the maximum length of the paths in SP(x, y); and let $l = \max\{l(x, y) : (x, y) \in E\}$ be the largest of such lengths over all pairs of neighbors. Then (Exercise 7.10.50),

Lemma 7.8.7 *y will receive at least $(l - 1) + c_{edge}(G)(t - (l - 1))$ copies (possibly corrupted) of the bit from x within $t > l$ communication cycles.*

Entity y can determine the original bit sent by x provided that the number $(l-1) + c(G)(t-(l-1))$ of corrected copies received is greater than the number $(c(G)-1)t$ of incorrect ones. To achieve this, it is sufficient to request $t > (c(G)-1)(l-1)$. Hence, by Lemmas 7.8.6 and 7.8.7 we have

Lemma 7.8.8   *After $t > (c(G)-1)(l-1)$ communication cycles, y can determine* $b_{x,y}$.

Consider that broadcast requires $diam(G)$ steps, each requiring t communication cycles, each composed of two clock ticks. Hence

Lemma 7.8.9   *Using algorithm* OR-AddCorrupt, *it is possible to compute the* **OR** *of the input value in spite of $c_{edge}(G)-1$ additions and corruptions in time at most in $2 diam(G) (c_{edge}(G)-1)(l-1)$.*

Hence, unanimity can be guaranteed if at most $c_{edge}(G)-1$ additions and corruptions occur in the system:

Theorem 7.8.11   *Let the system faults be additions and corruptions. Unanimity can be reached in spite of $F = c_{edge}(G)-1$ faults per clock cycle; the time is $T \le 2\ diam(G)\ (c_{edge}(G)-1)\ (l-1)$ and the number of bits is at most $4m(G)(c_{edge}(G)-1)(l-1)$ bits.*

Byzantine Faults: Additions, Omissions, and Corruptions

In case of *Byzantine* faults, anything can happen: omissions, additions, and corruptions. Not surprisingly, the number of such faults that we are able to tolerate is quite small.

Still, using a simpler mechanism than that for *additions and corruptions*, we are able to achieve consensus, albeit tolerating fewer faults.

Indeed, to broadcast, we use precisely the technique *Reliable Neighbor Transmission* described in the previous section; we do *not*, however, use time slicing: This time, a communication cycle lasts only one clock cycle, that is, any received message is forwarded along the path immediately.

The decision process (i.e., how y, out of the possibly conflicting received messages, determines the correct content of the bit) is according to the simple rule:

Acceptance Rule

y selects as correct the bit value received most often during the t time units.

To see why the technique *Reliable Neighbor Transmission* with this *Acceptance Rule* will work, let us first pretend that no faults occur. If this is the case, then in each of the first $(l-1)$ clock cycles, a message from x will reach y through the direct link between x and y. In each later clock cycle out of the t cycles, a message from x to y will reach y on each of the at least $c_{edge}(G)$ paths. This amounts to a total of at least $(l-1) + c_{edge}(G)(t-(l-1))$ messages arriving at y if no fault occurs.

But, as we know, there can be up to $t(\lceil c_{\text{edge}}(G)/2 \rceil - 1)$ faults in these t cycles. This leaves us with a number of correct messages, that is, at least the difference between both quantities. If the number of correct messages is larger than the number of faulty ones, the *Acceptance Rule* will decide correctly. Therefore, we need that

$$(l - 1) + c_{\text{edge}}(G)(t - (l - 1)) > 2t(\lceil c_{\text{edge}}(G)/2 \rceil - 1).$$

This is satisfied for $t > (c_{\text{edge}}(G) - 1)(l - 1)$. We, therefore, get,

Lemma 7.8.10 *Broadcasting using* Reliable Neighbor Transmission *tolerates* $\lceil c_{edge}(G)/2 \rceil - 1$ *Byzantine communication faults per clock cycle and uses* $(c_{edge}(G) - 1)(l - 1) + 1$ *clock cycles.*

Hence, reliable broadcast can occur in spite of $\lceil c_{\text{edge}}/2 \rceil - 1$ Byzantine faults. Consider that in this case, broadcast requires $diam(G)$ clock ticks. Hence,

Theorem 7.8.12 *Let the system faults be* arbitrary. *Unanimity can be reached in spite of* $F = \lceil c_{edge}/2 \rceil - 1$ *faults per clock cycle; the time is at most* $T \leq diam(G)$ $(c_{edge} - 1)(l - 1)$.

7.8.4 Tightness

For all systems, except those where faults are just corruptions or just additions (and in which unanimity is possible regardless of faults), the bounds we have established are similar except that the possibility ones are expressed in terms of the *edge connectivity* $c_{\text{edge}}(G)$ of the graph, while the impossibility ones are in terms of the *degree* $\deg(G)$ of the graph. A summary of the possibility results is shown in Figure 7.22.

This means that in the case of *d-connected graphs*, the impossibility bounds are indeed tight:

1. With the number of faults (or more) specified by the impossibility bound, even strong majority is impossible;
2. with one less fault than specified by the impossibility bound, even unanimity can be reached, and
3. any agreement among less than a strong majority of the entities can be reached without any communication.

This large class of networks includes hypercubes, toruses, rings, complete graphs, and so forth. In these networks, the obtained results draw a precise "impossibility map" for the agreement problem in presence of dynamic communication faults, thus, clarifying the difference between the dynamic and the static cases.

For those graphs where $c_{\text{edge}}(G) < \deg(G)$, there is a gap between possibility and impossibility. Closing this gap is clearly a goal of future research.

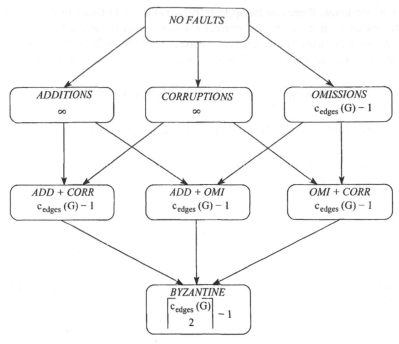

FIGURE 7.22: Maximum number of faults per clock cycle in spite of which *unanimity* is possible.

7.9 BIBLIOGRAPHICAL NOTES

Most of the work on computing with failures has been performed assuming *localized entity faults*, that is, in the entity failure model.

The *Single-Fault Disaster* theorem, suspected by many, was finally proved by Michael Fisher, Nancy Lynch, and Michael Paterson [22].

The fact that in a *complete network*, $f \geq \frac{n}{3}$ Byzantine entities render consensus impossible was proved by Robert Pease, Marshall Shostak, and Leslie Lamport [38]. The simpler proof used in this book is by Michael Fisher, Nancy Lynch, and Michael Merrit [21]. The first consensus protocol tolerating $f < \frac{n}{3}$ Byzantine entities was designed by Robert Pease, Marshall Shostak, and Leslie Lamport [38]; it, however, requires an exponential number of messages. The first polynomial solution is due to Danny Dolev and Ray Strong [17]. Mechanism *RegisteredMail* has been designed by T. Srikanth and Sam Toueg [48]; protocol *TellZero-Byz* is due to Danny Dolev, Michael Fisher, Rob Fowler, Nancy Lynch, and Ray Strong [16]; protocol *From-Boolean* that transform Boolean consensus protocols into ones where the values are not restricted was designed by Russel Turpin and Brian Coan [49]. The first polynomial protocol terminating in $f + 1$ rounds *and* tolerating $f < \frac{n}{3}$ Byzantine entities (Exercise 7.10.16) is due to Juan Garay and Yoram Moses [25].

The lower bound $f + 1$ on time (Exercise 7.10.15) was established by Michael Fisher and Nancy Lynch [20] for Byzantine faults; a simpler proof, using a bivalency argument, has been developed by Marco Aguilera and Sam Toueg [2]. The fact that the same $f + 1$ lower bound holds even for crash failures was proven by Danny Dolev and Ray Strong [17].

Consensus with Byzantine entities in particular classes of graphs was investigated by Cinthia Dwork, David Peleg, Nick Pippenger, and Eli Upfal [18], and by Pitior Berman and Juan Garay [4]. The problem in *general graphs* was studied by Danny Dolev [15], who proved that for $f \geq \frac{c_{node}(G)}{2}$ the problem is unsolvable (Exercise 7.10.17) and designed protocol *ByzComm* achieving consensus for smaller values of f.

The first *randomized* consensus protocol for localized entity failures, *Rand-Omit*, has been designed by Michael Ben-Or [3]. Protocol *Committee* that reduces the expected number of stages is due to Gabriel Bracha [5]. The fact that the existence of a global source of random bits (unbiased and visible to all entities) yields a constant expected time Byzantine Agreement (Exercise 7.10.24) is due to Michael Rabin [40], who also showed how to implement such a source using digital signatures and a trusted dealer (Problem 7.10.3); Problem 7.10.4 is due to Ran Canetti and Tal Rabin [6], and the solution to Problem 7.10.5 is due to Pesech Feldman and Silvio Micali [19].

The study of (unreliable) *failure detectors* for localized entity failures was initiated by Tushar Chandra and Sam Toueg [8], to whom Exercise 7.10.25 is due; the proof that Ω is the weakest failure detector is due to Tushar Chandra, Vassos Hadzilacos, and Sam Toueg [7].

The positive effect of *partial reliability* on consensus in an asynchronous complete network with crash failures was proven by Michael Fisher, Nancy Lynch, and Michael Paterson [22]. Protocol *FT-CompleteElect* that efficiently elects a leader under the same restriction was designed by Alon Itai, Shay Kutten, Yaron Wolfstahl, and Shmuel Zaks [30]. An election protocol that, under the same conditions, tolerates also link crashes has been designed by N. Nishikawa, T. Masuzawa, and N. Tokura [37].

There is clearly need to provide the entity failure model with a unique framework for proving results both in the asynchronous and in the synchronous case. Steps in this direction have been taken by Yoram Moses and Sergio Rajsbaum [36], by Maurice Herlihy, Sergio Rajsbaum, and Mark Tuttle [29], and Eli Gafni [24].

In the study of *localized link failures*, the *Two Generals* problem has been introduced by Jim Gray [26], who proved its impossibility; its reinterpretation in terms of common knowledge is due to Joseph Halpern and Yoram Moses [28].

The election problem with send/receive-omissions faulty links has been studied for *complete networks* by Hosame Abu-Amara [1], who developed protocol *FT-LinkElect*, later improved by J. Lohre and Hasame Abu-Amara [33]; Exercise 7.10.10 is due to G. Singh [47]. The case of *ring networks* was studied by Liuba Shrira and Oded Goldreich [46].

Election protocols in presence of Byzantine links were developed for complete networks by Hasan M. Sayeed, M. Abu-Amara, and Hasame Abu-Amara [44].

The presence of *localized* failures of both links and entities (the hybrid component failure model) has been investigated by Kenneth Perry and Sam Toueg [39], Vassos Hadzilacos [27], N. Nishikawa, T. Masuzawa, and N. Tokura [37], Flaviu Cristian,

Houtan Aghili, Ray Strong, and Danny Dolev [10], and more recently by Ulrich Schmid and Bettina Weiss [45].

The study of *ubiquitous* faults has been introduced by Nicola Santoro and Peter Widmayer who proposed the communication failure model. They established the impossibility results for strong majority and the possibility bounds for unanimity in *complete graphs* [41]; they later extended these results to *general graphs* [43].

Most of the research on ubiquitous faults has focused on reliable broadcast in the case of *omission* failures. The problem has been investigated in *complete graphs* by Nicola Santoro and Peter Widmayer [42], Zsuzsanna Liptak and Arfst Nickelsen [32], and Stefan Dobrev [12]. The bound on the broadcast time in *general graphs* (Problem 7.10.1) is due to Bogdan Chlebus, Krzysztof Diks, and Andrzej Pelc [9]; other results are due to Rastislav Kralovic, Richard Kralovic, Peter Ruzicka [31]. In hypercubes, the obvious $\log^2 n$ upperbound to broadcast time has been decreased by Pierre Fraigniaud and Claudine Peyrat [23], then by Gianluca De Marco and Ugo Vaccaro [35], and finally (Exercise 7.10.44) to $\log n + 2$ by Stefan S. Dobrev and Imrich Vrto, [13]. The case of *tori* (Exercise 7.10.47) has been investigated by Gianluca De Marco and Adele Rescigno [34], and by Stefan Dobrev and Imrich Vrto [14]. The more general problem of evaluating Boolean functions in presence of ubiquitous faults has been studied by Nicola Santoro and Peter Widmayer [42] only for *complete networks*; improved bounds for some functions have been obtained by Stefan Dobrev [11].

7.10 EXERCISES, PROBLEMS, AND ANSWERS

7.10.1 Exercises

Exercise 7.10.1 Prove that for all connected networks G different from the complete graph, the node connectivity is not larger than the edge connectivity

Exercise 7.10.2 Prove that, if k arbitrary nodes can crash, it is impossible to broadcast to the nonfaulty nodes unless the network is $(k + 1)$-node-connected.

Exercise 7.10.3 Prove that if we know how to broadcast in spite of k link faults, then we know how to reach consensus in spite of those same faults.

Exercise 7.10.4 Let C be a nonfaulty bivalent configuration, let $\epsilon = (x, m)$ be a noncrash event that is applicable to C; let $\mathcal{A}$ be the set of nonfaulty configurations reachable from C *without* applying ϵ, and let $\mathcal{B}\{\epsilon(A) \mid A \in \mathcal{A}\}$. Prove that if $\mathcal{B}$ does not contain any bivalent configuration, then it contains both 0-valent and 1-valent configurations.

Exercise 7.10.5 Let $\mathcal{A}$ be as in Lemma 7.2.4. Prove that there exist two x-adjacent (for some entity x) neighbors $A_0, A_1 \in \mathcal{A}$ such that $D_0 = \epsilon(A_0)$ is 0-valent, and $D_1 = \epsilon(A_1)$ is 1-valent.

Exercise 7.10.6 Modify Protocol *TellAll-Crash* so as to work without assuming that all entities start simultaneously. Determine its costs.

Exercise 7.10.7 Modify Protocol *TellZero-Crash* so to work without assuming that all entities start simultaneously. Show that $n(n-1)$ additional bits are sufficient. Analyze its time complexity.

Exercise 7.10.8 Modify Protocol *TellAll-Crash* so to work when the initial values are from a totally ordered set V of at the least two elements, and the decision must be on one of those values. Determine its costs.

Exercise 7.10.9 Modify Protocol *TellAll-Crash* so as to work when the initial values are from a totally ordered set V of at the least two elements, and the decision must be on one of the values initially held by an entity. Determine its costs.

Exercise 7.10.10 Modify Protocol *TellZero-Crash* so as to work when the initial values are from a totally ordered set V of at the least two elements, and the decision must be on one of those values. Determine its costs.

Exercise 7.10.11 Show that Protocol *TellAll-Crash* generates a consensus among the nonfailed entities of a graph G, provided $f < c_{node}(G)$. Determine its costs.

Exercise 7.10.12 Show that Protocol *TellZero-Crash* generates a consensus among the nonfailed entities of a graph G, provided $f < c_{node}(G)$. Determine its costs.

Exercise 7.10.13 Modify Protocol *TellZero-Crash* so that it generates a consensus among the nonfailed entities of a graph G, whenever $f < c_{node}(G)$, even if the entities do not start simultaneously and both the initial and decision values are from a totally ordered set V with more than two elements. Determine its costs.

Exercise 7.10.14 Prove that any consensus protocol tolerating f crash entity failures requires at least $f + 1$ rounds.

Exercise 7.10.15 Prove that any consensus protocol tolerating f Byzantine entities requires at least $f + 1$ rounds.

Exercise 7.10.16 Design a consensus protocol, tolerating $f < \frac{n}{3}$ Byzantine entities, that exchanges a polynomial number of messages and terminates in $f + 1$ rounds.

Exercise 7.10.17 Prove that if there are $f \geq \frac{c_{node}(G)}{2}$ Byzantine entities in G, then consensus among the nonfaulty entities cannot be achieved even if G is fully synchronous and restrictions **GA** hold.

Exercise 7.10.18 Modify protocol *Rand-Omit* so that each entity terminates its execution at most one round after first setting its output value. Ensure that your modification leaves unchanged all the properties of the protocol.

Exercise 7.10.19 Prove that with protocol *Rand-Omit*, the probability that a *success* occurs within the first k rounds is

$$Pr[success\ within\ k\ rounds\ ] \geq 1 - (1 - 2^{-\lfloor n/2 \rfloor + f + 1})^k.$$

Exercise 7.10.20 (⋆⋆) Prove that with protocol *Rand-Omit*, when $f = O(\sqrt{n})$, the expected number of rounds to achieve a *success* is only $O(1)$.

Exercise 7.10.21 Prove that if $\lfloor n/2 \rfloor + f + 1$ correct entities start the same round with the same preference, then all correct entities decide on that value within one round. Determine the expected number of rounds to termination.

Exercise 7.10.22 Prove that, in protocol *Committees*, the number $\bar{r}$ of rounds it takes a committees to simulate a single round of protocol *Rand-Omit* is dominated by the cost of flipping a coin in each committee, which is dominated in turn by the maximum number $\bar{f}$ of faulty entities within a nonfaulty committee.

Exercise 7.10.23 (⋆) Prove that, in protocol *Committees*, for any $1 > r > 0$ and $c > 0$, there exists an assignment of n entities to $k = O(n^2)$ committees such that for all choices of $f < n/(3 + c)$ faulty entities, at most $O(r\ k)$ committees are faulty, and each committee has size $s = O(\log n)$.

Exercise 7.10.24 Prove that if all entities had access to a global source of random bits (unbiased and visible to all entities), then Byzantine Agreement can be achieved in constant expected time.

Exercise 7.10.25 (⋆⋆) Prove that any failure detector that satisfies only weak completeness and eventual weak accuracy is sufficient for reaching consensus if at most $f < \frac{n}{2}$ entities can crash.

Exercise 7.10.26 Consider the reduction algorithm *Reduce* described in Section 7.5.2. Prove that *Reduce* satisfies the following property: Let y be any entity; if no entity suspects y in Hv before time t, then no entity suspects y in $output^r$ before time t.

Exercise 7.10.27 Consider the reduction algorithm *Reduce* described in Section 7.5.2. Prove that *Reduce* satisfies the following property: Let y be any correct entity; if there is a time after which no correct entity suspects y in Hv, then there is a time after which no correct entity suspects y in $output^r$.

Exercise 7.10.28 Write the complete set of rules of protocol *FT-CompleteElect*.

Exercise 7.10.29 Prove that the closing of the ports in protocol *FT-CompleteElect* will never create a deadlock.

Exercise 7.10.30   Prove that in protocol *FT-CompleteElect* every entity eventually reaches stage greater than $\frac{n}{2}$ or it ceases to be a *candidate*.

Exercise 7.10.31   Assume that, in protocol *FT-CompleteElect*, an entity x ceases to be *candidate* as a result of a message originated by *candidate* y. Prove that, at any time after the time this message is processed by x, either the stage of y is greater than the stage of x or x and y are in the same stage but $id(x) < id(y)$.

Exercise 7.10.32   Prove that in protocol *FT-CompleteElect* at least one entity always remains a *candidate*.

Exercise 7.10.33   Prove that in protocol *FT-CompleteElect*, for every $l \geq 2$, if there are $l - 1$ *candidates* whose final size is not smaller than that of a *candidate* x, then the stage of x is ar most ln.

Exercise 7.10.34   Let G be a complete networks where $k < n - 1$ links may occasionally lose messages. Consider the following 2-steps process started by an entity x: first x sends a message $M1$ to all its neighbors; then each node receiving the message from x will send a message $M2$ to all its other neighbors. Prove that every entity will receive either $M1$ or $M2$.

Exercise 7.10.35   Prove that Protocol *2-Steps* works even if $\frac{n}{2} - 1$ links are faulty at *every* entity.

Exercise 7.10.36   Prove that in protocol *FT-LinkElect* all the nodes in *Suppressor-Link(x)* are distinct.

Exercise 7.10.37   Consider protocol *FT-LinkElect*. Suppose that x precedes w in *Suppressor(v)*. Suppose that x eliminates y at time $t_1 \leq t$ and that y receives the fatal message $(Capture, i, id(w))$ from w at some time t_2. Prove that then, $t_1 < t_2$.

Exercise 7.10.38   Consider protocol *FT-LinkElect*. Suppose that x sends $K \geq k$ Capture messages in the execution. Prove that if no leader is elected, then x receives at least $K - k$ replies for these messages.

Exercise 7.10.39   Consider systems with dynamic communication faults. Show how to simulate the behavior of a faulty entity regardless of its fault type, using at most $2(n - 1)$ dynamic communication faults per time unit.

Exercise 7.10.40   Let **AddCorr** denote the set of all events containing at most $\deg(G)$ addition and corruption faults. Prove that **AddCorr** is continuous.

Exercise 7.10.41   Let **Byz** be the set of all events containing at most $\lceil \deg(G)/2 \rceil$ communication faults, where the faults may be omissions, corruptions, and additions. Prove that **Byz** is continuous.

Exercise 7.10.42   Let **Byz** be the set of all events containing at most $\lceil \deg(G)/2 \rceil$ communication faults, where the faults may be omissions, corruptions, and additions. Prove that **Byz** is adjacency preserving.

Exercise 7.10.43   Show that in a hypercube with n nodes with $F \leq \log n$ omissions per time step, algorithm *Bcast-Omit* can correctly terminate after $\log^2 n$ time units.

Exercise 7.10.44 (⋆⋆)   Prove that in a hypercube with n nodes with $F \leq \log n$ omissions per time step, algorithm *Bcast-Omit* can correctly terminate after $\log n + 2$ time units.

Exercise 7.10.45   Determine the value of $T^*(G)$ when G is a complete graph.

Exercise 7.10.46   Determine the value of $T^*(G)$ when G is a complete graph and k entities start the broadcast.

Exercise 7.10.47 (⋆⋆)   Determine the value of $T^*(G)$ when G is a torus.

Exercise 7.10.48   Write the code for the protocol *Consensus-OmitCorrupt*, informally described in Section 7.8.3, that allows to achieve consensus in spite of $F < c_{\text{edge}}(G)$ *omissions and/or corruptions* per time step. Implement and throughly test the protocol. Analyze experimentally its costs for a variety of networks.

Exercise 7.10.49   Write the code for the protocol *Consensus-OmitAdd*, informally described in Section 7.8.3 that allows to achieve consensus in spite of $F < c_{\text{edge}}(G)$ *omissions and/or additions* per time step. Implement and throughly test the protocol. Analyze experimentally its costs for a variety of networks.

Exercise 7.10.50   Prove that with mechanism *Reliable Bit Transmission*, in *absence of faults*, p_j will receive at least $(l - 1) + c(t - (l - 1))$ copies of the message from p_i within t communication cycles.

7.10.2   Problems

Problem 7.10.1   Prove that in any connected graph G we have $T^*(G) = O(\text{diam}(G)^{c_{\text{edge}}(G)})$.

Problem 7.10.2   Complete the description of protocol *Committee* and prove its correctness.

Problem 7.10.3   Consider a set of asynchronous entities connected in a complete graph. Show how the existence of both digital signatures and a trusted dealer can be used to implement a global source of random bits unbiased and visible to all entities.

Problem 7.10.4   Consider a set of asynchronous entities connected in a complete graph. Show how the existence of both private channels and a trusted dealer can be used to implement a global source of random bits unbiased and visible to all entities.

Problem 7.10.5   Consider a set of *synchronous* entities connected in a complete graph. Show how the existence of both digital signatures and secrete sharing can be used to implement a global source of random bits unbiased and visible to all entities.

Problem 7.10.6   Prove that protocol *FT-LinkElect* correctly elects a leader provided $k \leq \frac{n-6}{2}$. (Hint: Use the results of Exercises 7.10.36, 7.10.37, and 7.10.38).

Problem 7.10.7 (★★)   Consider a complete networks where $F < n - 1$ links can fail with send/receive omissions. Design an election protocol that uses $o(n^2 F)$ messages.

Problem 7.10.8 (★★★)   Consider a complete networks where $F < n - 1$ links can fail with send/receive omissions. Determine whether it is possible to elect a leader using $O(nF)$ messages.

Problem 7.10.9   Consider a complete graph where $f < \frac{n}{2}$ entities might have crashed but no more failures will occur. Consider the *Election* problem and assume that all identities are known to all (nonfaulty) entities. Show how the election can be performed using $O(kf)$ messages, where k is the number of initiators.

Problem 7.10.10 (★★)   Consider a complete graph where at *each* entity at most $f < \frac{n}{2}$ incident links may crash. Design a protocol to achieve unanimity using $O(n^2)$ messages.

7.10.3 Answers to Exercises

Answer to Exercise 7.10.1
Let $c_{edge}(G) = k$, and let $e_1, e_2, \ldots, e_k$ be k edges whose collective removal disconnects G. Let $x_1, x_2, \ldots, x_k$ be k nodes of G such that e_i is incident to x_i. The removal of $x_1, x_2, \ldots, x_k$ will also remove $e_1, e_2, \ldots, e_k$ disconnecting the network; hence, $c_{edge}(G) \leq k$.

Answer to Exercise 7.10.2
If G is only k-node-connected, then there are k nodes $x_1, x_2, \ldots, x_k$ whose removal disconnects G. Consider now a node x different from those nodes and make that node the initiator of the broadcast. The failure of all the x_i will disconnect G making some nonfaulty nodes unreachable from x; thus, they will never receive the information. By contrast, if G is $(k + 1)$-node-connected, then even after k nodes go down, by Property 7.1.2, there still is a path from the initiator to all remaining nodes. Hence, flooding will work correctly.

Answer to Exercise 7.10.4

As C is bivalent, there exist a 0-valent configuration E_0 and a 1-valent configuration E_1 reachable from C. Let $i \in \{0, 1\}$. First observe that if $E_i \in \mathcal{A}$ then $\epsilon(E_i) \in \mathcal{B}$; thus, $\mathcal{B}$ contains a i-valent configuration. If instead $E_i \notin \mathcal{A}$, then the event ϵ was used in reaching E_i; by definition, the configuration F_i resulting from the use of ϵ is in $\mathcal{B}$ and is, thus, univalent; as E_i can be reached from F_i, F_i must be i-valent; thus, $\mathcal{B}$ contains a i-valent configuration. As the reasoning holds for both $i = 0$ and $i = 1$, the claim is proved: $\mathcal{B}$ contains both 0-valent and 1-valent configurations.

Answer to Exercise 7.10.9

Hint: Use *Min* instead of **AND** in rep(x, t) and choose the default value appropriately.

Answer to Exercise 7.10.40

Consider a configuration C and any two events $\tau', \tau'' \in \textbf{AC}$ for $\Lambda(C)$. Let $m'_1, m'_2, \ldots, m'_{f'}$ be the f' faulty communications in τ', and let $m''_1, m''_2, \ldots, m''_{f''}$ be the f'' faulty communications in τ''. As **AC** is deg(G)-admissible, then $f' \leq \deg(G)$ and $f'' \leq \deg(G)$. Let $\tau'_0 = \tau'$, and let τ'_h denote the event obtained by replacing the faulty communication m'_h in τ'_{h-1} with a nonfaulty one (with the same message sent in both), $1 \leq h \leq f'$; similarly, define $\tau''_h, 0 \leq h \leq f''$. By construction, $\tau'_{f'} = \tau''_{f''}$. Consider the sequence $\tau'_0, \tau'_1, \ldots, \tau'_{f'} = \tau''_{f''}, \ldots, \tau''_1, \tau''_0$. In this sequence, each event is adjacent to the following one; furthermore, as by construction each event contains at most deg(G) additions and/or corruptions, it is in **AC**. Thus, **AC** is continuous.

Answer to Exercise 7.10.42

Given any two h-adjacent configurations A and B, consider the events π_h and ρ_h for $\Lambda(A) = \{\alpha_{ij}\}$ and $\Lambda(B) = \{\gamma_{ij}\}$, respectively, where for all $(x_i, x_j) \in E$

$$\pi_h[i, j] = \begin{cases} (\alpha_{ij}, \gamma_{ij}) & \text{if } i = h \text{ and } j \in \{j_{\lceil d(h)/2 \rceil + 1}, \ldots, j_{d(h)}\} \\ (\alpha_{ij}, \alpha_{ij}) & \text{otherwise} \end{cases}$$

and

$$\rho_h[i, j] = \begin{cases} (\gamma_{ij}, \alpha_{ij}) & \text{if } i = h \text{ and } j \in \{j_1, \ldots, j_{\lceil d(h)/2 \rceil}\}, \\ (\gamma_{ij}, \gamma_{ij}) & \text{otherwise} \end{cases}$$

where $d(h)$ denotes the degree of x_h and $\{j_1, j_2, \ldots, j_{d(h)}\}$ are the indices of the neighbors of x_h. Obviously the configurations $\pi_h(A)$ and $\rho_h(B)$ are h-adjacent; furthermore, as $d(h) \leq \deg(G)$ and both π_h and ρ_h contain at most $\lceil d(h)/2 \rceil$ faults, $\pi_h, \rho_h \in \textbf{Byz}$. Hence **Byz** is adjacency preserving.

Answer to Exercise 7.10.43

In a hypercube H, between any two nodes x and y there are $\log n$ edge-disjoint paths, each of length at most $\log n$. According to the protocol, x sends a message to all neighbors, thus, along all these $\log n$ paths. At any time instant, there are

$F < \log n$ omissions; this means that at least one of these paths is free of faults. That is, at any time unit, the message from x will move one step further toward y along one of them. As these paths have length at most $\log n$, after at most $\log n(\log n - 1) + 1 = \log^2 n - \log n + 1$ time units the message from x would reach y. As x and y are arbitrary, the claim follows.

Answer to Exercise 7.10.50

Let $b_{x,y} = 1$ (respectively, $b_{x,y} = 0$). For the first $l - 1$ odd (respectively, even) clock ticks y will receive the corrected copy of $b_{x,y}$ through link (x, y). During this time, the corrected copy of $b_{x,y}$ will travel down each of the other $c(G) - 1$ disjoint paths in SP(x, y), one link forward at each odd (respectively, even) clock tick. As the paths in SP(x, y) have length at most l, from the lth communication cycle onward, y will receive the corrected copy of $b_{x,y}$ from all the $c(G)$ disjoint paths in SP(x, y) at each odd (respectively even) clock tick. Thus, after $t > l$ communication cycles, y will receive at least $l - 1 + c(G)(t - (l - 1))$ corrected copies of $b_{x,y}$.

Answer to Exercise 7.10.19

As the coins are flipped independently, the probability of a *success* is

$$2^{-(\lfloor n/2 \rfloor + f + 1)}.$$

That means that for any round r, the probability of an *insuccess* is

$$Pr[insuccess] \leq 1 - 2^{-(\lfloor n/2 \rfloor + f + 1)}.$$

As the coin flips are independent, the probability of having an insuccess for k consecutive rounds is then,

$$Pr[insuccess\ for\ first\ k\ rounds] \leq (1 - 2^{-(\lfloor n/2 \rfloor + f + 1)})^k.$$

from which we have

$$Pr[success\ within\ k\ rounds] \geq 1 - (1 - 2^{-\lfloor n/2 \rfloor + f + 1})^k.$$

Answer to Exercise 7.10.26

Let y be any entity. Suppose that there is a time t before which no entity suspects y in H. No entity x sends a message of the type $\langle x, suspects(x) \rangle$ with $y \in suspects(x)$ before time t. Thus, no entity x adds y to $output(x)$ before time t.

Answer to Exercise 7.10.27

Let y be any correct entity. Suppose that there is a time t after which no correct entity suspects y in H. Thus, all entities that suspect y after time t eventually crash. Thus, there is a time t' after which no correct entity receives a message of the type $\langle z, suspects(z) \rangle$ with $y \in suspects(z)$. Let x be any correct entity. We must show that there is a time after which x does not suspect y in $output^r$. Consider the execution

Reduce by entity y after time t'. Entity y sends a message $M = \langle y, suspects(y) \rangle$ to x. When x receives M, it removes y from $output(x)$. As x does not receive any messages of the type $\langle z, suspects(z) \rangle$ with $y \in suspects(z)$ after time t', x does not add y to $output(x)$ after time t'. Thus, there is a time after which x does not suspect y in $output^r$.

Answer to Exercise 7.10.30

Assume, to the contrary, that entity x remains a *candidate* and its stage is forever smaller than or equal to $\frac{n}{2}$. Consider the time x reaches its final stage s, by receiving an "Accept" message. If one of the pending "Capture" messages of x now starts a settlement, then this settlement will eventually end, and either A will cease to be a *candidate* or its size will increase: a contradiction. Therefore, x is not involved in a settlement and all the edges over which it has received answers lead to entities in its domain. As x is always in its own domain, and its stage is $s \leq \frac{n}{2}$, it follows that the number of these edges is at most $\frac{n}{2} - 1$. There are at most $f < \frac{n}{2}$ other edges over which x has sent "Capture" messages without yet receiving a reply. Thus, the total number of edges over which x has sent its "Capture" messages is less than $n - 1$. Hence, it has at least one edge over which it has not yet sent a "Capture" message; when the reply is received, a "Capture" message is sent over such an edge. Within finite time, x must receive either a leader announcement message or a reply to one of its $f + 1$ "Capture" messages. If x receives either a leader announcement message or a "Reject" message that does not cause a settlement, then x ceases to be a *candidate*, a contradiction. If an "Accept" message is received, then the stage of x is incremented: a contradiction. If x receives a "Reject" message that generates a settlement, then either x will cease to be a *candidate* or its size will increase: a contradiction.

Answer to Exercise 7.10.32

Assume, to the contrary, that all entities cease to be *candidate* and consider their final stages. Let x be the entity in the largest stage (if more than one, let it be the one among them with the smallest id). Let y be the entity that originated the message that caused x to cease to be a *candidate*. By Lemma 7.6.2, after x receives that message, either the stage of y will be greater than that of x or they are the same but $id(x) < id(y)$, contradicting the definition of x.

Answer to Exercise 7.10.33

If an entity y captured by z is subsequently captured by x, then z ceases to be a *candidate* and from that time its stage is not greater than that of x (see Lemma 7.6.2). Thus domains of equal sizes (even viewed at different times) are disjoint.

BIBLIOGRAPHY

[1] H.H. Abu-Amara. Fault-tolerant distributed algorithm for election in complete networks. *IEEE Transactions on Computers*, 37(4):449–453, April 1988.

[2] M.K. Aguilera and S. Toueg. A simple bivalency proof that t-resilient consensus requires t+1 rounds. *Information Processing Letters*, 71:155–158, 1999.

[3] M. Ben-Or. Another advantage of free choice: Completely asynchronous agreement protocols. In *2nd ACM Symposium on Principles of Distributed Computing*, pages 27–30, 1983.

[4] P. Berman and J.A. Garay. Fast consensus in networks of bounded degree. *Distributed Computing*, 7(2):67–73, 1993.

[5] G. Bracha. An $O(logn)$ expected rounds randomized Byzantine generals protocol. In *17th ACM Symposium on the Theory of Computing*, pages 316–326, 1985.

[6] R. Canetti and T. Rabin. Fast asynchronous Byzantine agreement with optimal resilience. In *25th ACM Symposium on the Theory of Computing*, pages 42–51, 1993.

[7] T. Chandra, V. Hadzilacos, and S. Toueg. The weakest failure detector for solving consensus. *Journal of ACM*, 43(4):685–722, 1996.

[8] T. Chandra and S. Toueg. Unreliable failure detectors for deliable distributed systems. *Journal of ACM*, 43(2):225–267, 1996.

[9] B.S. Chlebus, K. Diks, and A. Pelc. Broadcasting in synchronous networks with dynamic faults. *Networks*, 27:309–318, 1996.

[10] F. Cristian, H. Aghili, R. Strong, and D. Dolev. Atomic broadcast: From simple message diffusion to Byzantine agreement. *Information and Computation*, 11:158–179, 1995.

[11] S. Dobrev. Computing input multiplicity in anonymous synchronous networks with dynamic faults. In *26th International Workshop on Graph-Theoretic Concepts in Computer Science*, pages 139–148, 1990.

[12] S. Dobrev. Communication-efficient broadcasting in complete networks with dynamic faults. In *9th Colloquium on Structural Information and Communication complexity*, pages 101–113, 2002.

[13] S. Dobrev and I. Vrto. Optimal broadcasting in hypercubes with dynamic faults. *Information Processing Letters*, 71:81–85. 1999.

[14] S. Dobrev and I. Vrto. Optimal broadcasting in even tori with dynamic faults. *Parallel Processing Letters*, 12:17–22, 2002.

[15] D. Dolev. The Byzantine generals strike again. *Journal of Algorithms*, 3(1):14–30, 1982.

[16] D. Dolev, M. L. Fischer, R. Fowler, N. A. Lynch, and H. R. Strong. Efficient Byzantine agreement without authentication. *Information and Control*, 52(3):256–274, 1982.

[17] D. Dolev and H. R. Strong. Polynomial algorithms for multiple processor agreement. In *14th ACM Symposium on Theory of Computing*, pages 401–407, Berlin, 1982.

[18] C. Dwork, D. Peleg, N. Pippenger, and E. Upfal. Fault tolerance in networks of bounded degree. *SIAM Journal on Computing*, 17(5):975–988, 1988.

[19] P. Feldman and S. Micali. An optimal probabilistic protocol for synchronous Byzantine agreement. *SIAM Journal on Computing*, 26(4):873–933, 1997.

[20] M. Fisher and N.A. Lynch. A lower bound for the time to assure interactive consistency. *Information Processing Letters*, 14(4):183–186, 1982.

[21] M. Fisher, N.A. Lynch, and M. Merritt. Easy impossibility proofs for distributed consensus. *Distributed Computing*, 1(1):26–39, 1986.

[22] M.J. Fisher, N.A. Lynch, and M.S. Paterson. Impossibility of distributed consensus with one faulty process. *Journal of the ACM*, 32(2):374–382, April 1985.

[23] P. Fraigniaud and C. Peyrat. Broadcasting in a hypercube when some calls fail. *Information Processing Letters*, 27(1):115–119, April 1991.

[24] E. Gafni. Round-by-round fault detectors:unifying synchrony and asynchrony. In *17th ACM Symposium on Principles of Distributed Computing*, pages 143–152, 1998.

[25] J.A. Garay and Y. Moses. Fully polynomial Byzantine agreement for $n > 3t$ processors in $t + 1$ rounds. *SIAM Journal on Computing*, 27(1):247–290, 1998.

[26] J. Gray. Notes on data base operating systems. In R.M. Graham, R. Bayer and G. Seegmuller, editors, *Operating Systems: An Advanced Course*, volume 60 of *LNCS*, Berlin, 1978. Springer.

[27] V. Hadzilacos. Connectivity requirements for Byzantine agreement under restricted types of failures. *Distributed Computing*, 2:95–103, 1987.

[28] J.Y. Halpern and Y. Moses. Knowledge and common knowledge in a distributed environment. *Journal of the ACM*, 37(3):549–587, July 1990.

[29] M. Herlihy, S. Rajsbaum, and M.R. Tuttle. Unifying synchronous and asynchronous message-passing models. In *17th ACM Symposium on Principles of Distributed Computing*, pages 133–142, 1998.

[30] A. Itai, S. Kutten, Y. Wolfstahl, and S. Zaks. Optimal distributed t-resilient election in complete networks. *IEEE Transactions on Software Engineering*, 16(1):415–420, April 1990.

[31] R. Kralovic, R. Kralovic, and P. Ruzicka. Broadcasting with many faulty links. In *10th International Colloquium on Structural Information Complexity*, pages 211–222, Umeå, June 2003.

[32] Z. Liptak and A. Nickelelsen. Broadcasting in complete networks with dynamic edge faults. In *4th International Conference on Principles of Distributed Systems*, pages 123–142, Paris, 2000.

[33] J. Lohre and H. Abu-Amara. Election in asynchronous complete networks with intermittent failures. *IEEE Transactions on Computers*, 43:778–787, 1994.

[34] G. De Marco and A. Rescigno. Tighter bounds on broadcasting in torus networks in presence of dynamic faults. *Parallel Processing Letters*, 10:39–49, 2000.

[35] G. De Marco and U. Vaccaro. Broadcasting in hypercubes and star graphs with dynamic faults. *Information Processing Letters*, 66:309–318, 1998.

[36] Y. Moses and S. Rajsbaum. A layered analysis of consensus. *SIAM Journal on Computing*, 31(4):989–1021, 2002.

[37] N. Nishikawa, T. Masuzawa, and N. Tokura. Fault-tolerant distributed algorithm in complete networks with link and processor failures. *IEICE Transactions on Information and Systems*, J74D-I(1):12–22, Jan 1991.

[38] M. Pease, R. Shostak, and L. Lamport. Reaching agreement in the presence of faults. *Journal of the ACM*, 27:228–234, April 1980.

[39] K.J. Perry and S. Toueg. Distributed agreement in the presence of processor and communication faults. *IEEE Transactions on Software Engineering*, SE-12:477–482, March 1986.

[40] M.O. Rabin. Randomized Byzantine generals. In *24th Annual IEEE Symp. on Foundations of Computer Science*, pages 403–409, 1983.

[41] N. Santoro and P. Widmayer. Time is not a healer. In *6th Annual Symposium on Theoretical Aspects of Computer Science*, pages 304–313, February 1989.

[42] N. Santoro and P. Widmayer. Distributed function evaluation in the presence of transmission faults. In *International Symposium on Algorithms*, pages 358–367, February 1990.

[43] N. Santoro and P. Widmayer. Majority and unanimity in synchronous networks with ubiquitous dynamic faults. In *12th Colloquium on Structural Information and Communication Complexity*, volume 3499 of *LNCS*, pages 262–276. Springer, 2005.

[44] H.Md. Sayeed, M. Abu-Amara, and H. Abu-Amara. Optimal asynchronous agreement and leader election algorithm for complete networks with Byzantine faulty links. *Distributed Computing*, 9:147–156, 1995.

[45] U. Schmid and B. Weiss. Formally verified Byzantine agreement in presence of link faults. In *22nd International Conference on Distributed Computing Systems*, pages 608–616, 2002.

[46] L. Shrira and O. Goldreich. Electing a leader in a ring with link failures. *Acta Informatica*, 24:79–91, 1987.

[47] G. Singh. Leader election in presence of link failures. *IEEE Transactions on Parallel and Distributed Systems*, 7(3):231–236, 1996.

[48] T. K. Srikanth and Sam Toueg. Simulating authenticated broadcasts to derive simple fault-tolerant algorithms. *Distributed Computing*, 2(2):80–94, 1987.

[49] R. Turpin and B.A. Coan. Extending binary Byzantine agreement to multivalued Byzantine agreement. *Information Processing Letters*, 18(2):73–76, 1984.

CHAPTER 8

Detecting Stable Properties

8.1 INTRODUCTION

The types of problems we are going to discuss in this chapter arise in very different contexts and situations, and sometimes they appear to have little (if any at all) in common. These problems arise, for example, in the context of *global termination*: detecting whether a computation (e.g., the execution of a protocol) has globally terminated; *garbage collection*: deciding whether some distributed objects (e.g., data items) are no longer needed within the system; *deadlock*: deciding whether a circular wait has been created within the system preventing any further progress.

All these problems do, however, share a very important trait:

1. We need to decide whether a certain *property* holds (e.g., a data object is garbage, an entity is deadlocked, all entities have terminated their execution).
2. The property is *stable*: If no external event occurs in the system, the property will continue to hold.

In the following we will examine two of these problems in detail, designing efficient solutions for them. We will then attack the task of designing a generic solution to the problem of detecting whether a stable property holds, regardless of the specific nature of the property.

8.2 DEADLOCK DETECTION

8.2.1 Deadlock

A *deadlock*, also known as *circular wait* or *deadly embrace*, describes a situation where a set of entities, unable to generate anything while waiting, is blocked forever, each waiting for some events that only other entities of the set can generate.

Deadlock is a dreaded occurrence in computer systems, leading to paralysis of all the entity involved, degraded performance, and possibly collapse of the entire system's activities. It is a dangerous subtle system failure occurring without any component suffering any fault. The most common places where deadlock may occur are within entities in an operating system and within transactions in a distributed database. Indeed, whenever some entities must suspend their activities until some event occurs, there is potential for deadlock, unless avoidance mechanisms are in place.

The fact that during a computation some entities are blocked waiting for some event to occur is dangerous but does not necessarily lead to deadlock. For example, in the generic election protocol *MegaMerger*, any entity sending an *Outside?* message to another city with lower level number was blocked, waiting for the level of that city to increase. Our protocol was designed (using distinctness of the edge costs) in such a way that, as we proved, no deadlock would occur. In other words, our protocol was designed with built-in *deadlock avoidance*. Unfortunately, in many applications, deadlock avoidance mechanisms are not feasible because of the costs associated with them: increased overhead, slowdown of the system, decreased performance, and so forth. In fact, in most situations, there is no built-in mechanism to ensure that entities do not become deadlocked; thus, deadlocks may and do occur. It is, therefore, necessary to have mechanisms to *detect* if a deadlock has been formed, and if so, to *resolve* somehow the impasse. While the resolution phase will clearly depend on the particular application and situation, the detection task is the same and we will focus on how to efficiently perform it.

The *deadlock detection* problem is the one of determining if there is a deadlock in the system. The solution protocol is started by any entity suspecting that it might be involved in a deadlock; it must terminate within finite time. There are actually three versions of this problem:

- *personal detection*: Within finite time, each initiator must determine whether or not it is involved in a deadlock.
- *component detection*: Within finite time, each initiator must determine whether or not it is involved in a deadlock. If a deadlock is found, then all entities involved must know.
- *system detection*: If a deadlock occurs in the system, then within finite time at least one entity finds it.

Our focus in this chapter will be on the first two types; the third will be discussed in the context of *continuous computations*. We will consider the problem under the standard assumptions: Connectivity, Bidirectional Links, Complete Reliability, as well as Unique Identifiers. We will also assume *Message Ordering*, that is, the links are first in first out (FIFO).

8.2.2 Detecting Deadlock: Wait-For Graph

Let us first of all describe the deadlock condition problem more precisely.

A set $S = \{s_1, ..., s_k\} \subseteq \mathcal{E}$ of $k > 1$ entities is *deadlocked* when the following two conditions simultaneously hold:

1. Each entity $s_i \in S$ is waiting for an event (called *permission*) that must be generated from another entity in the set;
2. no entity $s_i \in S$ can generate a permission while it is waiting.

If these two conditions hold, the entities in the set will be waiting forever, regardless of the nature of the permission and of why they are waiting for the "permission"; for example, it could be because s_i needs a resource held by s_j in order to complete its computation.

A useful way to understand the situations in which deadlock may occur is to describe the status of the entities during a computation, with respect to their waiting for some events, by means of a directed graph $\vec{W}$, called *wait-for graph*.

Each node in the wait-for graph represents an entity; if entity x is blocked waiting for events that can only be generated by entities $y_1, y_2, ..., y_k$, there will be directed edges $(x, y_1), (x, y_2), ..., (x, y_k)$ in $\vec{W}$. In other words, the out-neighbors in $\vec{W}$ of an entity x are all the entities whose permission x is waiting for, and the in-neighbors of x are those entities waiting for permission from x. In the following, we assume that $\vec{W} \subseteq \vec{G}$.

IMPORTANT. In some systems, an entity x might be waiting for permission from an entity y that is not a neighbor in the network. This means that there might be edges (x,y) in $\vec{W}$ that are not in $\vec{G}$. In this case, we assume that there is an underlining routing mechanism ensuring communication between any two entities; the costs of the protocols will have to be revised to take this into account.

By definition, we have the following simple properties:

Property 8.2.1   *All entities in a strongly connected component of $\vec{W}$ are deadlocked.*

Corollary 8.2.1   *If there is a directed cycle in $\vec{W}$, every entity in that cycle is deadlocked.*

Property 8.2.2   *Let $\vec{C}$ be a strongly connected component of $\vec{W}$. If there is a directed path in $\vec{W}$ from x to $\vec{C}$, then x is deadlocked.*

In other words, not only the entities in a strongly connected component (e.g., a cycle) but also those that can reach such a component are deadlocked.

By contrast, in absence of deadlock, $\vec{W}(t)$ is composed solely of directed acyclic graphs:

Property 8.2.3   *If each connected component of $\vec{W}$ is a directed acyclic graph, then there is no deadlock.*

In other words, in absence of deadlock, $\vec{W}(t)$ contains no cycles. This means that to determine if there is deadlock in the system is equivalent to determine if there is a cycle in the wait-for graph. For this reason, deadlock detection is sometimes referred to as the *cycle detection* problem.

However, this is not enough for personal and component detection. In this case, in fact we need to determine if an initiator is involved in a deadlock; this means (by Properties 8.2.1, 8.2.2, and 8.2.3) that we must determine whether or not that entity is part of or can reach a strongly connected component of the wait-for graph. Summarizing,

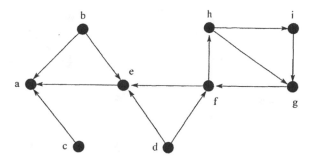

FIGURE 8.1: A single-component wait-for graph.

Theorem 8.2.1 *An entity x is deadlocked if and only if there is a directed path from x to a strongly connected component of $\vec{W}$.*

Consider for example the wait-for graph $\vec{W}$ shown in Figure 8.1 consisting of a single connected component. In $\vec{W}$ there is a strongly connected component, $\{f, g, h, i\}$, and only d can reach it. By Theorem 8.2.1, entities d, f, g, h, and i are deadlocked, while a, b, c, and e are not.

Notice that an entity can be involved in several deadlock cycles at once and can be linked to more than one strongly connected component.

8.2.3 Single-Request Systems

Let us consider the situation when each blocked entity waits for only one event to occur. That is, in $\vec{W}$, each entity has at most one out-neighbor. This situation occurs for example in systems where an entity is allowed to make only one request at a time and cannot proceed until the current request is granted; this situation is commonly called the *single-request model*.

First of all observe that, as each entity has at most one out-going link then the wait-for graph $\vec{W}$ has a very simple and interesting structure:

Property 8.2.4 *In the single-request model, each connected component of $\vec{W}$ is either a rooted tree or a crown.*

A *crown* is a directed graph formed by a single directed cycle where each entity in the cycle is the root of a (possibly empty) rooted tree; the cycle is called the *core* of the crown. In the wait-for graph shown in Figure 8.2, there are three components, two of which are rooted trees, and one is a crown.

Next observe that

Property 8.2.5 *In the single-request model,*

(a) *all entities of a crown are deadlocked;*

(b) *if there is no deadlock, then $\vec{W}$ contains no crowns.*

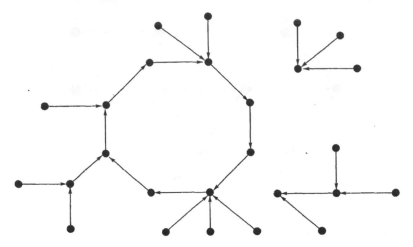

FIGURE 8.2: A wait-for graph composed of a crown and two rooted trees.

In other words, in absence of deadlock, $\vec{W}$ is a forest of rooted trees. This means that by Properties 8.2.4 and 8.2.5,

Theorem 8.2.2 *In the single-request model, an entity x is deadlocked if and only if it is part of a crown in $\vec{W}$.*

Thus, to determine if it is involved in a deadlock, an initiator x_0 must just determine whether it is in a crown or in a tree.

Let us see how this can be accomplished. A simple trivial solution is to collect all the information about the wait-for graph (i.e., which entities an entity is waiting for) at a single location (e.g., the initiator x_0) and check if there is a cycle or not. Although simple, this solution is clearly inefficient. Let us consider the following alternate strategy, where *DFlood* is flooding in directed graphs:

SimpleCheck

1. Let x_0 broadcast, using *DFlood*, in $\vec{W}$ a message "Are we in a deadlock ?"

2. If x_0 is not involved in a deadlock, the connected component of $\vec{W}$ to which it belongs is a rooted tree; thus, x_0's message will travel until it reaches the root, say r; at this point r can send a message "No deadlock in this component" back to x_0 (traversing those links in the opposite direction (recall, the links are bidirectional)).

3. Suppose now that x_0 is deadlocked. This means that the connected component of $\vec{W}$ to which it belongs is a crown. As a consequence, the message originated from x_0 will first of all reach the core and it will then travel along the cycle; this means that within finite time an entity r in the cycle will receive this message again. It will then discover that indeed the entire component is deadlocked. Note

that the entity r making this discovery is x_0 itself if x_0 is part of the core, or else it is the first node in the core closest to x_0 in $\vec{W}$. At this point, depending on the type of termination condition, r will either notify x_0 ("personal detection") or broadcast using *Flood* in $\vec{W}$ ("collective detection").

Let us examine the cost of this strategy. If the connected component $\vec{W}(x_0)$ of the wait-for graph to which x_0 belongs is a tree, then the total number of messages for x_0 to know that it is not currently deadlocked is $2\,d(x_0, r)$, where r is the root. If $\vec{W}(x_0)$ is a crown, then $d(x_0, r) + c(x_0)$ messages are needed to detect that there is a deadlock, where r is the entity in the core closest to x_0 and $c(x_0)$ is the size of the core (i.e., the length of the cycle); note that at this point only r knows that the deadlock exists. Depending on the termination condition, it can then start a broadcast (if a notification is needed) or a deadlock resolution protocol. Thus, in the first case an additional $O(|N(x_0)|)$ messages will be sent in the worst case, where $N(x_0)$ is the set of entities in $\vec{W}(x_0)$. We will call *SimpleCheck* the protocol implementing this strategy (Problem 8.6.1).

In the case of *multiple* initiators, as, we are assuming that the entities have unique identities, we can use the ids to distinguish among the messages sent by different initiators; thus, we can concurrently and independently have each of them run *SimpleCheck*. However, we can reduce the total number of messages. We can, for example, let only the initiator with the smallest id proceed in each component (unless a deadlock is already detected). The resulting protocol *SimpleCheck+* is shown in Figures 8.3 and 8.4, where in $N(x)$ and out $N(x)$ denote the in- and out-neighbors of x in $\vec{W}$, respectively.

The total cost can still be high. Let k denote the number of initiators in the same component. In the worst case, each of the k initial messages will travel to the core and go around the ring (although only one will be able to complete the tour of the core) costing possibly $O(n)$ transmissions, for a total of $O(kn)$ messages.

A better strategy would be to integrate into the protocol a leader-election process in each component among the initiators in that component (Problem 8.6.2).

8.2.4 Multiple-Requests Systems

In the previous section we considered the case when each entity waits for (at most) one permission at a time. What happens if we remove this restriction? In general, an entity can wait for permission from several other entities and cannot proceed until *all* of them have been granted; this situation is sometimes called the *AND-request* model. The situation in the AND-request model is much more complex than the one of the single-request model because an entity can be involved in several deadlock cycles at once and can be linked to more than one strongly connected component.

The problem is the one of determining if an initiator entity x_0 is involved in one or more deadlocks, and, if so (in the case of component detection), of notifying all other entities involved in the same deadlocks.

Simple Solution: GeneralSimpleCheck A simple but inefficient solution is a generalization of *SimpleCheck*; it consists of the initiator x_0 flooding the system

PROTOCOL SimpleCheck.

- States: $S =$ {INITIATOR, IDLE, ACTIVE, DEAD};
  $S_{INIT} =$ {INITIATOR, IDLE};
  $S_{TERM} =$ {IDLE,DEAD}.
- Restrictions: **RI**, Message Ordering.

```
IDLE
      Spontaneously
      begin
            if outN(x) ≠ Ø then /* I am waiting */
            send("Check", id) to outN(x);
                  checker-links:= Ø;
                  checker-id:= id;
            become ACTIVE;
      end

      Receiving("Check", value)
      begin
            if outN(x) = Ø then /* I am a root */
                  send("NoDeadlock", value) to sender;
            else
                  checker-links:={sender};
                  checker-id:= value;
                  send("Check", value) to outN(x);
                  become ACTIVE;
            endif
      end

      Receiving("Deadlock", value)
      begin
            send("Deadlock", value) to inN(x);
            become DEAD;
      end
```

FIGURE 8.3: Protocol *SimpleCheck+*(I).

(by broadcasting its "Check" message using *D-Flood* in $\vec{W}$) and of the entities letting redundant messages circulate through the system: If there is no deadlock, the messages will reach the sinks and will backtrack reaching the initiator; If there is a deadlock, at least an entity will detect that it is in a cycle. Let us describe this approach in some details.

In absence of deadlock: Consider first the case when the initiator x_0 is *not* involved in a deadlock; by Property 8.2.3, this means that the component of $\vec{W}$ in which x_0 resides is a DAG, say D. Recall that in a DAG there are three types of nodes: *source* (only out-neighbors), *sink* (only in-neighbors), and *internal* (both in- and out-neighbors). Clearly, sinks are unblocked.

Every internal node y receiving this message records the sender and the information in the message, adds to the message information its id, forwards it to all its out-neighbors, and waits for a reply from *all* of them. This message will eventually reach every sink of D; when a sink receives such a message, because it is unblocked, it will reply "No deadlock I can see."

If all received replies are "No deadlock I can see," the internal node y will send such a reply to the sender of the "Check" message originated by x_0. Thus, within

```
ACTIVE
      Receiving("Check", value)
      begin
          if value = checker-id then
              /* I have already received this message */
              send("Deadlock", value) to outN(x)∪inN(x);
              become DEAD;
          else
              checker-links:= checker-links ∪{sender};
              if value < checker-id then
                  checker-id:= value;
                  send("Check", value) to outN(x);
              endif
      end

      Receiving("Deadlock", value)
      begin
          send("Deadlock", value) to outN(x)∪inN(x) − {sender};
          become DEAD;
      end

      Receiving("NoDeadlock", value)
      begin
          send("NoDeadlock", value) to checker-links;
          become IDLE;
      end
```

FIGURE 8.4: Protocol *SimpleCheck+*(II).

finite time x_0 will receive such replies from all its out-neighbors and will correctly know that it is not involved in a deadlock.

In presence of deadlock: Let us now consider the case when the initiator x_0 is involved in a deadlock. This means (Theorem 8.2.1) that x_0 is either in a strongly connected component of $\vec{W}$ or linked to (at least one) such a component.

In this case, the "Check" message broadcasted by x_0 in $\vec{W}$ will reach all the strongly connected components to which x_0 is linked and will flood all of them.

Any time an *internal* node (i.e. a node that has both in- and out-neighbors) y receives the "Check" message, it first checks if it is included in the list of already visited nodes by this message; should this be the case, the existence of a deadlock involving the initiator x_0 as well as y is detected. Otherwise, y records the sender, adds to the message information its id, forwards it to all its out-neighbors, and waits for a reply from *all* of them. As before, if all received replies are "No deadlock I can see," y will send such a reply to all the senders of the"Check" message originated by x_0.

This means that, within finite time, in each one of them at least one entity will receive the message containing its own id in the list of already visited.

It is not difficult to prove that this approach, and the resulting protocol *GeneralSimpleCheck*, will solve the personal and component deadlock detection problem (Exercise 8.6.1). The cost is, however, prohibitive: The number of exchange messages could be exponential (Exercise 8.6.2).

Efficient Solution: LockGrant Let us examine how to use some of the same ideas but with a different approach to determine efficiently if the initiator x_0 is deadlocked.

Consider the component of x_0. In this component, any entity that is not waiting is obviously not deadlocked. By definition, these entities are *sinks* (i.e., do not have any out-neighbors); each of these entities actually knows that it is not deadlocked. Consider now an entity that is waiting, but the permissions it needs must all be granted by sinks: This entity is not deadlocked either. In fact, any entity waiting only for permissions from nondeadlocked entities is itself not deadlocked.

This observation gives us a strategy to determine all those entities that are *not* deadlocked:

Strategy *Grant*:

1. the initiator wakes up all the entities in the component;
2. starting from the sinks, an entity that knows it is not deadlocked will notify all the entities waiting for a permission from it (i.e., its in-neighbors);
3. if an entity is notified that all the entities from which it is waiting for a permission (i.e., its out-neighbors) are not deadlocked, it knows that it is not deadlocked.

It is not difficult to see that if there are no deadlocks in the component all entities will find out within finite time. The problem is whether there are cycles. In fact, in this case, an entity that is deadlocked will *not* receive a notification from all its out-neighbors. Owing to the fact that communication delays are unpredictable, an entity waiting for a notification does not know whether the notification is encountering a delay or no notification has been sent at all. What we need is a mechanism to ensure that the initiator x_0 detects termination and whether or not it is in a deadlock.

We will first of all construct a spanning tree, rooted in x_0, of the connected component of x_0 in the wait-for graph; we will do this while performing the wake-up and we will use the tree to allow x_0 to determine when the computation is over. These tasks are easily accomplished by using *Shout* on the wait-for graph. (Recall that the links are really bidirectional: The orientation is only logical.) However, a node will wait to send its reply to its parent until it has received a reply from all its other (in- and out-) neighbors.

The *Grant* strategy is embedded in the delayed *Shout*. When a *sink* y receives a "Shout" message for the first time, in addition to forwarding the "Shout," y will announce the fact that it is not deadlocked by sending a "Grant" message to all its in-neighbors. To deal efficiently with termination, the sink y will send a reply to its parent only after it has received not only a reply from all its other neighbors but also an acknowledgment for all its own "Grant" messages (note that it will always happen).

To know that it is deadlock free, a *nonsink* entity z must receive a "Grant" message from all its out-neighbors; until that happens (note that it might never happen), z will send an acknowledgment to any received "Grant" message. If it happens, that is, z receives "Grant" messages from all its out-neighbors, z realizes it is not deadlocked; thus, it will send a "Grant" message to all its in-neighbors. To deal efficiently with termination, z will acknowledge the last "Grant" message it received not immediately but only after it receives an acknowledgment for all its own "Grant" messages (note that it will always happen).

In this way, the global termination of *Shout* will occur only after all the transmissions of "Grants" and "Grant-Acks" have taken place. Furthermore, the global termination of all activities coincides with the local termination of *Shout* at the initiator.

Summarizing, upon local termination of *Shout*, the initiator x_0 knows its status: It is not deadlocked if and only if it has received a "Grant" message from all its out-neighbors.

However, the other entities do not even know when their own local termination has occurred. For example, consider a nonsink entity that receives the first "Shout," forwards it to all its other neighbors, receives from each of them a reply, and then sends its own reply to its parent; in other words, all the *Shout* activities for x are terminated. Yet, it is still possible for x to receive a "Grant" message (it might come from its own parent: Exercise 8.6.3). Thus, it is necessary for the initiator to perform a "resolution" mechanism (e.g., it notifies all other entities of termination) even if the problem to be solved is only personal detection.

In the case of personal detection, the corresponding set of rules, called protocol *LockGrant*, is shown in Figures 8.5 and 8.6. In the protocol, the resolution mechanism is denoted by procedure RESOLVE (which is left unspecified); note that if the initiator is a sink, it will not even start the Shout because it already knows that it is not deadlocked.

Let us now prove the correctness of the protocol; first of all, let us focus on termination.

To terminate, the initiator must terminate its execution of *Shout*, that is, it must receive a "Reply" from all its neighbors. As described, if an entity sends "Grant" messages, it delays sending its "Reply" to its parent until it has received a "Grant-Ack" from all its in-neighbors. The following properties ensure that all these acknowledgments will arrive, the delayed Reply will be sent, and thus the initiator will terminate within finite time (Exercises 8.6.4 and 8.6.5).

Property 8.2.6 *If an entity sends a "Grant" message to a neighbor, it will receive an "Ack" from that neighbor within finite time.*

Property 8.2.7 *Every entity $y \neq x_0$ will send a "Reply" to its parent within finite time.*

Property 8.2.8 *If an entity sends a "Shout" message to a neighbor, it will receive a "Reply" message from that neighbor within finite time.*

From these properties, it follows:

Lemma 8.2.1 *The initiator x_0 will execute RESOLVE within finite time.*

Let us now examine the correctness of the protocol. We must show that when the initiator locally terminates the *Shout*, it knows whether or not it is deadlocked.

The following two properties indicate that when the initiator terminates, all other activities have terminated as well and that indeed the Grant mechanism embedded in the *Shout* works correctly (Exercises 8.6.6–8.6.8):

PROTOCOL LockGrant

- States: $\mathcal{S} = \{$INITIATOR, IDLE, ACTIVE$\}$;
  $\mathcal{S}_{\text{INIT}} = \{$INITIATOR, IDLE$\}$;

- Restrictions: **RI**, Single Initiator, Message Ordering.

```
INITIATOR
    Spontaneously
    begin
        if |outN(x)| > 0 then
            initiator:=true; INITIALIZE;
            send("Shout") to outN(x) ∪ inN(x);
            become ACTIVE;
        else
            alive:=true;
            RESOLVE;
        endif
    end

IDLE
    Receiving("Shout")
    begin
        INITIALIZE
        parent:= sender;
        send("Shout") to outN(x) ∪ inN(x) − {sender};
        if |outN(x)| = 0 then   /* I am a sink */
            alive:= sink:= true;
            send("Grant") to inN(x);
            waiting-for-ack:= true;
        else
            if all = 0 then   /* I am a leaf */
                send("Reply") to sender
                sent-last-reply:= true;
            endif
        endif
        become ACTIVE;
    end


Procedure  INITIALIZE
    begin
        granted:= count-reply := count-ack := 0;
        alive:= waiting-for-ack := sent-last-reply:= false;
        all:= |inN(x) ∪ ourN(x)| − 1;
        if initiator then all:= all +1 endif
    end
```

FIGURE 8.5: Protocol *LockGrant* (I).

Property 8.2.9 *If a "Grant" message has not been acknowledged at time t, the initiator x_0 has not yet received a "Reply" from all its neighbors at that time.*

Property 8.2.10 *An entity receives a "Grant" message from all its out-neighbors if and only if it is not deadlocked.*

Thus

Lemma 8.2.2 *The initiator x_0 is not deadlocked if and only if, when it executes RESOLVE, $alive(x_0) = $ **true**.*

```
ACTIVE
    Receiving("Shout")
    begin
        send("Reply") to sender;
    end

    Receiving("Grant")
    begin
        granted:= granted+1;
        if  granted < requests then
            send("Grant-Ack") to sender;
        else /* I am not deadlocked */
            alive:=true;
            grant-link:= sender;
            if  inN(x) ≠ ∅ then /* somebody is blocked on me */
                send("Grant") to inN(x);
                waiting-for-ack:= true;
            else
                send("Grant-Ack") to grant-link;
            endif
        endif
    end

    Receiving("Grant-Ack")
    begin
        count-ack := count-ack+1;
        if count-ack = |inN(x)| then /* received all acknowledgments */
            if not(sink) then
                send("Grant-Ack") to grant-link;
            endif
            if (count-reply=all and not(sent-last-reply)) then
                send("Reply") to parent;
            endif
        endif
    end

    Receiving("Reply")
    begin
        count-reply:= count-reply+1;
        if (count-reply=all and not(waiting-for-ack)) then
            if (initiator) then
                RESOLVE
            else
                send("Reply") to parent;
                sent-last-reply:= true;
            endif
        endif
    end
```

FIGURE 8.6: Protocol *LockGrant* (II).

From Lemmas 8.2.1 and 8.2.2 it follows:

Theorem 8.2.3 *Protocol LockGrant correctly solves the personal deadlock detection problem.*

To deal with the case of collective detection, it is sufficient to specify procedure RESOLVE accordingly.

The *cost* of protocol *LockGrant* is not difficult to analyze. There are two basic activities: the *shouting* and the *granting*. The shouting uses one "Shout" message on each link of the constructed tree and two shouts on all other links, and it uses a "Reply" per each "Shout"; so the total is at most $4|E(x_0)| - 2|N(x_0)| + 2$ messages, where $E(x_0)$ and $N(x_0)$ denote the number of bidirectional links and of entities, respectively, in the connected component $\vec{W}(x_0)$ of which x_0 is a part in $\vec{W}$. As for the granting process, there will be at most one "Grant" on each in-edge, each generating an "Ack," for a total is at most $2|E(x_0)|$ messages. Hence, the total, before final notification, is at most

$$6|E(x_0)| - 2|N(x_0)| + 2.$$

In the case of personal detection, the initiator has only to notify all other entities of termination; this can be done by broadcasting on the spanning tree constructed with shout, costing additional $|N(x_0)| - 1$ messages. Thus,

$$\mathbf{M}[LockGrant] \leq 6|E(x_0)| - |N(x_0)| + 1. \tag{8.1}$$

NOTE. The multiplicative constant 6 in the cost of protocol *LockGrant* can be reduced to 4 if *Shout+* is used instead of *Shout* (Problem 8.6.4).

In the case of *multiple* initiators, the strategy *AllGrant* of letting every initiator run its independent execution of *LockGrant* will indeed work. The bookkeeping at each entity becomes more involved but is still manageable. A better strategy would be to integrate into the protocol a leader-election process in each component among the initiators in that component (Problem 8.6.5).

8.2.5 Dynamic Wait-For Graphs

We have been examining the deadlock detection problem in the static case, that is, assuming that no other edges are added to the wait-for graph while the detection protocol is running.

In most systems applications, the wait-for graph is a *dynamic* graph: Each entity that is not waiting for permissions may at any time grant permissions to those entities (if any) waiting for it, or it might ask for permissions from one or more entities. In other words, the wait-for graph $\vec{W}(t)$ describes only the situation at time t; indeed $\vec{W}(t)$ might be different from $\vec{W}(t + 1)$. We do know, however, the following:

Property 8.2.11 *If an entity x is deadlocked in $\vec{W}(t)$, it will continue to be deadlocked also in $\vec{W}(t + 1)$.*

It is for this reason that "being deadlocked" is a *stable property*.

In this dynamic situation, a deadlock can be formed during (or after) the execution of a detection algorithm. So there can be no guarantee that if an entity is not deadlocked at the time of detection, it will remain so; indeed, "not being deadlocked" is *not* a stable property. This implies that when a detection protocol correctly reports that there *was* no deadlock, it does not mean that there *is* no deadlock. For these reasons, even the definition of the (personal and collective) deadlock detection problem must be refined.

We will say that a protocol P is a solution to the personal detection problem if it has the following properties: Let entity x start protocol P at time t. Then,

1. the execution of P terminates at x within finite time, say at time $t' \geq t$;
2. if x was deadlocked in $\vec{W}(t)$, then at time t' it determines so;
3. if x determines at time t' that it is not deadlocked, then x was not deadlocked in $\vec{W}(t)$.

Similarly, the definition for a solution to the collective deadlock determination problem must be modified (Exercise 8.6.9). Interestingly, the definition for system detection needs no changes.

Let us now consider solving the detection problem in this general case. We will first start with the single-request model and then consider the more general multiple-requests model.

Dynamic Single-Request Systems   Let us examine what events can take place in single-request systems. As an entity waiting for a permission is blocked, the only entities that can act are those that are not waiting: the roots of the rooted trees. What a root can possibly do is to grant a permission to one of its children (if any) or to request a permission from some other entity. Let us consider these two cases in some details.

If r grants a permission to a child x then, at the time $t' > t$ when x is notified, x is no longer waiting and becomes a root, and the edge (x, r) disappears from $\vec{W}(t')$.

If r asks an entity y for permission then, at the time $t' > t$ when y is notified, the edge (r, y) is added to $\vec{W}(t')$. This addition might have great consequences as it might create a deadlock. This can happen in two main cases:

- If y is in a crown, the entire tree rooted in r at time t is now part of a crown (see Figure 8.7(a)).
- If y is a descendent of r (i.e., node in the rooted tree of r), then that tree becomes a crown (see Figure 8.7(b)).

In addition to these two main cases, the request from r might cause a deadlock when happening concurrently with other requests from other roots creating an overall directed cycle (Figure 8.8). In discussing it, we can always think of this situation as happening not simultaneously but sequentially; for example, having the request from r to y occurring after the other requests have been issued.

Summarizing, rooted trees can change in size, new crowns can be created, and existing crowns can become larger in size. Therefore, the *deadlock detection* protocol in the dynamic case must be able to deal with the fact that while the detection messages

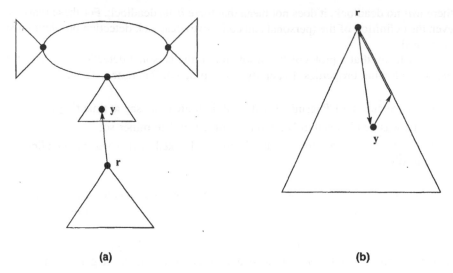

(a)   (b)

FIGURE 8.7: The request from r to y will transform the tree rooted in r into (part of) a crown.

are traveling along the links of the wait-for graph, new links are being added and some are possibly removed.

Fortunately, with simple modifications, strategy *SimpleCheck* will still be able to operate correctly in these more complex situations.

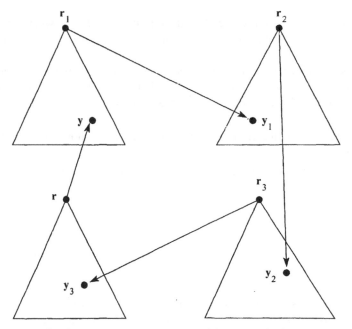

FIGURE 8.8: The concurrent requests of the roots will form a crown.

Let us consider first the case of a single initiator. In this case, protocol *SimpleCheck* works without any modifications. Let us examine the three possible scenarios:

1. We know that a deadlock will persist in time; thus, if an entity is involved in a deadlock at time t, it will continue to be so involved. In other words, if an entity x_0 starting protocol *SimpleCheck* is at that time in a crown, it will continue to be in a crown during all the executions of the protocol. During this time, the crown can grow; however, a crown grows only by making the fringes larger or by adding new fringes. In other words, its core will remain unchanged (Exercise 8.6.10). This means that when x_0 sends the "Check" message at time t, the path from x_0 to the closest entity y in the core at that time will not change; hence its message will reach y, travel along the core, and return to y, which will detect the existence of deadlock and notify x_0. In other words, the protocol will correctly report that there is a deadlock.

2. If x_0 is in a rooted tree that is *not* going to become (part of) a crown, then its message is eventually going to reach the root of the tree (Exercise 8.6.11); in other words, the protocol will correctly report to x that it is not involved in a deadlock at that time.

3. If x_0 is in a rooted tree that is going to become (part of) a crown at time $t'' > t$, there is a race condition. Until time t', x_0 is a part of a tree; if the message from x_0 is fast, it will reach the root at a time $t' < t''$ before a deadlock is being formed; in this case, the protocol will correctly report that at time t' x was not involved in a deadlock. By contrast, if the "Check" message from x_0 is slow, a crown will be formed while this message is traveling. Interestingly, if x_0 is not a part of the core of the new crown, then the message will reach the core of the new crown and travel along it, and the entity in the core closest to x_0 will receive this message again, detecting a deadlock. If x_0 instead is now part of the core, its "Check" message will eventually come back to it and x_0 will then detect that a deadlock exists. Therefore, in both cases, x_0 will detect that it is involved in a deadlock (Exercise 8.6.13).

With *multiple* initiators, protocol *SimpleCheck+* might have some problems owing to the fact that only the request with the smallest id is forwarded.

Example   Consider the following situation: A request is originated by x at time t while the component is a tree; the request reaches the root r at time $t_1 > t$; r sends a "No deadlock" message back to x, and then requests some other entity for a permission, creating a deadlock, say at time $t_2 > t_1$.

While this is happening, a child of x with larger id, say y, starts the deadlock detection protocol and sends a message to x at time $t_3 > t_2$. As $id(x) < id(y)$, x will add y to its checker list but will not forward the message.

When the "No deadlock" message arrives at time $t_4 > t_3$ at x, it will forward it to y because it is in its checker list. Thus y will be incorrectly notified that it was not involved in a deadlock when it started the detection process.

Observe that, in the case of multiple initiators, the strategy *AllCheck* of letting every initiator run its independent execution of *SimpleCheck* will indeed work. Although using many messages, the overall cost would not be more than $O(n)$ messages per initiator. The bookkeeping at each entity becomes more involved but is still manageable.

A more refined approach is provided by the strategy *DelayAllCheck* in which an initiator always forwards messages from other initiators with smaller ids, but it delays the decision on whether to forward a "Check" message with higher id until an answer to the previous one has arrived. Indeed, if a "Deadlock" message arrives, then there is no longer any need to forward that delayed "Check" message. By contrast, if a "No Deadlock" notification arrives, as the above example shows, it might not apply to the held "Check" message; in this case, it will then be forwarded. In order of magnitude, the worst-case cost is the same as the previous solution of always forwarding the "Check" messages: $O(n)$ messages per initiator.

Dynamic Multiple-Requests Systems   In the case of a *single* initiator, it is possible to modify protocol *LockGrant*, with subtle but simple changes, so that it works with the same cost also in the dynamic setting (Problem 8.6.6); we shall call the resulting protocol *DynamicLockGrant*.

In the case of *multiple* initiators, the strategy of letting every initiator run its independent execution of *DynamicLockGrant* will indeed work.

8.2.6   Other Request Systems

The multiple-requests system, of which the single request is a special case, is the most common request model in distributed applications, but not the only one, nor the more general one. In this section we will briefly describe the other systems and discuss deadlock detections in those systems.

OR-Request Systems   A request model very different from the ones we have considered so far is the one offered by the so-called *OR-request* systems. In these systems, an entity that is not currently waiting for any permissions (i.e., a sink) can issue several requests and it is blocked (unable to grant permissions or to issue other requests) until *one* of them is granted. In these systems, an entity is *deadlocked* if and only if it cannot reach any sink in $\vec{W}$.

This means that loops in the wait-for graph are not meaningful with respect to deadlock. For example, in the wait-for graph shown in Figure 8.9, entities b, c, and d are in a directed cycle but are not deadlocked because they can all reach a, which is a sink. What is meaningful is another type of structure.

Property 8.2.12   *In the OR-request model,*

(a) *all entities of a knot are deadlocked;*

(b) *if there is no deadlock, then $\vec{W}$ contains no knots.*

A *knot* $\vec{K}$ is a strongly connected subgraph of $\vec{W}$ where every node in $\vec{K}$ can only reach in $\vec{W}$ nodes of $\vec{K}$; informally, "once inside a knot, you cannot get out." For

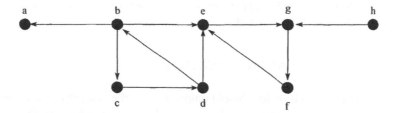

FIGURE 8.9: In the OR-request model, entities $a, b, c,$ and d are not deadlocked, while $e, f, g,$ and h are.

example, the wait-for graph shown in Figure 8.9 contains a knot $\{e, f, g\}$; the wait-for graph of Figure 8.1 has no knots and, thus, no entity there is deadlocked in the OR model.

In other words, in absence of deadlock, $\vec{W}(t)$ contains no knots. This means that to determine if there is deadlock in the system is equivalent to determine if there is a knot in the wait-for graph. For this reason, deadlock detection in the OR model is connected to the *knot detection* problem.

However, this is not enough for personal and component detection. In fact, being in a knot is a sufficient but not necessary condition to be deadlocked; for example, in Figure 8.9, h, which is deadlocked, is not a part of a knot. By contrast, reaching a knot is a necessary but not sufficient condition for being deadlocked; for example, in Figure 8.9, d can reach a knot but it is not deadlocked.

The personal and collective detection problems are somehow simpler in this model than in the AND-request model examined previously. Interestingly, protocol *Lock-Grant*, with very few modifications, solves the detection problems also in these systems (Exercise 8.6.14). Similarly, protocol *DynamicLockGrant* solves them in the case of a dynamic wait-for graph.

Generalized Request Systems   The AND- and the OR-request model are quite different from each other, but they are both special cases of a more general model called p-OF-q model. In p-OF-q systems, $p \leq q$, an entity that is not currently waiting for any permissions (i.e., a sink) can issue up to q requests and it is blocked (unable to grant permissions or to issue other requests) until p of them are granted. Notice that when $p = q$ (i.e., the entity must receive all permissions to become unblocked), we have the AND model, and when $p = 1$ (i.e., one permission is sufficient to unblock a waiting entity), we have the OR model.

An even more general request model, called *Generalized Requests*, is one where the condition allowing a waiting entity to become unblocked is expressed by a *predicate* (using "and," "or," and "p-of-q" connectors) on its outgoing links; examples of such predicates are as follows: "(two of l_1, l_2, l_3) or (l_1 and l_4)" and "(l_1 and l_2) or (l_3 and l_4)," where l_i refers to out-neighbors in the wait-for graph. Notice that different entities may be waiting on different predicates.

At a first glance, the solution to the detection problem would appear more difficult in these systems; this is, however, not the case. Indeed protocols *LockGrant* and *DynamicLockGrant*, with very few modifications, provide efficient solutions to the detection problem in the static and dynamic cases, respectively. See Exercises 8.6.16–8.6.19 and Problems 8.6.8 and 8.6.9.

8.3   GLOBAL TERMINATION DETECTION

Among the unique aspects of distributed computations is the difficulty of determining their *termination*. As we have seen throughout the book, we have to distinguish between *local* termination (i.e., termination of the execution of the protocol by a specified entity) and *global* termination (i.e., when the execution has ended in the entire system).

The importance of determining termination (local or global) derives from the fact that in real systems, entities execute not just a single protocol but several, and in some cases, there are precedence dependencies among them (i.e., the start of one cannot take place before the end of another). This occurs for example in *pipelined* (or multi-stages) computations: There is a sequence $C_1, C_2, \ldots, C_k$ of computations that must be performed by the system in order. To achieve this task, usually only local termination is really necessary: As soon as an entity determines the end of its participation in computation C_i, it can start C_{i+1}. There are, however, situations where global termination of C_i must be detected, at least by one entity, before the next computation may start. This for example happens when designers of multistages protocols do not want to deal with possible problems due to concurrency (e.g., because in this way the correctness is easier to prove).

Usually it is simple to design protocols so that each entity can determine when its participation in the computation is over. Indeed, almost all the protocols we have designed so far have a built-in local termination detection (e.g., the entity enters a terminal state). Global termination, on the contrary, is in general much more difficult to detect, even if there is in place a local termination detection; requiring global termination detection to be part of the protocol obviously increases the overall complexity of the design.

An approach has thus been to detach the task of global termination detection from the rest of the protocol and to handle it concurrently but separately. Indeed the problem itself can be viewed independently of the rest of the computation. This can be done as follows.

First of all, we need not know anything at all about the specifics of the *target* computation C (the computation whose termination we want to detect); indeed C might not even provide for *local* termination detection. We just need to be capable to know whether an entity is *active* (i.e., executing) or *passive* (i.e., not executing) and when a message is sent or received; all initiators will be initially considered *active*.

With this high-level view, the computation C will have the following simple properties:

- An *active* entity may become *passive* at any time.
- Only *active* entities may send messages.
- A *passive* entity can become *active* only if it receives a message.

The computation C is *globally terminated* if and only if all entities are *passive* and there are no messages in transit. The problem is to design a protocol that determines whether the computation C is globally terminated. We will distinguish two versions of this problem:

1. *personal detection*: An initiator must know, within finite time from the global termination of C, that this has occurred.
2. *collective detection*: All entities must know, within finite time from the global termination of C, that this has occurred.

First of all observe that once *personal* detection has been solved, *collective* detection is trivially achieved with an additional notification process; thus, we will focus on personal detection.

We will consider the problem under the standard assumptions: connectivity, Bidirectional Links, complete reliability, and unique identifiers. We will also assume *Message Ordering*, that is, the links are FIFO.

The messages sent by the detection protocol are clearly distinguishable from those of the computation C, and they are dealt with by each entity in a separate but overlapping way, that is, each entity will be handling simultaneously both the events for C and those for the termination detection; in the following, we will call C-messages the messages sent by the computation C. We will also assume that there is already available a subnetwork, specifically a spanning tree T, which will be used by the protocol.

8.3.1 A Simple Solution: Repeated Termination Queries

Termination Query   To develop our solution to the global termination detection problem, we will first consider a related simpler task, *Termination Query*, in which an initiator must know within finite time whether or not C is globally terminated at a given time. As we are not making any assumptions about time, let us be more specific.

A *termination query protocol Q* is an algorithm that has the following three properties:

1. The protocol terminates within finite time, and its result at the initiator is a Boolean value, *answer*.
2. If C was terminated when the protocol started, then $answer = \text{TRUE}$.
3. If $answer = \text{FALSE}$ then C was not terminated when the protocol started.

Answering a personal query is not difficult and can be achieved in many ways. Here is a simple way. Let us consider when there is a *single* initiator. The solution requires a control mechanism *CountAck*, which is run simultaneously with C during all the executions: in this mechanism, the reception of every C-message is acknowledged:

Control Mechanism *CountAck*:

- Every time an entity receives a C-message, it sends an acknowledgment.
- Each entity x keeps a counter *count(x)* of the number of C-messages it sent for which it has not yet received an acknowledgment.
- Each entity x keeps a Boolean variable *status(x)* that is set to 1 if and only if x is *active* in the computation C and/or *count(x)* > 0.

On the basis of the existence of this control mechanism, the solution protocol *TerminationQuery*, which can be started at any time, is as follows:

Protocol *TerminationQuery*:

1. The initiator x_0 broadcasts a "Color" message (on the spanning tree).
2. Every entity, upon receiving this message, will become *white* if *status(x)* = 0, *black* otherwise.
3. If a *white* entity receives a C-message, it becomes *black*.
4. Starting from the leaves, the AND of the colors (*white* = 0, *black* = 1) of all the entities is computed using a convergecast.

Note that *status*, *count*, *white*, and *black* are not defined in C but only in *TerminationQuery*. It is easy to verify (Exercise 8.6.20) that algorithm *TerminationQuery* is a correct personal query protocol, that is, regardless of time delays, an execution of *TerminationQuery* has the following property:

Property 8.3.1   *Let x_0 start* TerminationQuery *at time t and terminate it at time $t' > t$, and let $a(x)$ be the result of the AND at x_0 at time t'. Then,*

1. *if $a(x_0) = 0$, then C is globally terminated at time t';*
2. *if $a(x_0) = 1$, then C is not globally terminated at time t.*

The cost of *TerminationQuery* is also easy to determine: As it is just a broadcast followed by a convergecast on a tree, the total cost is simply $2(n - 1)$ messages.

To these costs we must, however, add the cost of the control mechanism, which uses one message (an acknowledgment) for each C-message. Hence, the total cost with multiple initiators is

$$M(C) + 2(n - 1),$$

where $M(C)$ is the number of messages sent during the execution of C being monitored.

The case of *multiple initiators* can be dealt with in two different ways: They can be treated independently, or they can be treated collectively. In the former case, using the fact that entities have unique ids, each initiator will start its own independent execution of the protocol, for a total of $2k(n - 1)$ messages, where k is the number of initiators.

If we treat the initiators collectively, then it is sufficient to use full saturation. Specifically, the Color messages are sent in the wake-up phase, and the AND is computed in the saturation phase; the notification phase will tell everybody the outcome. In this case, the saturated nodes become first aware of the result. In other words, Property 8.3.1 becomes

Property 8.3.2 *Let the wake-up phase start at time t and the saturation phase terminate at time $t' > t$, and let $a(x)$ be the result of the AND at the saturated nodes. Then,*

1. *if $a(x_0) = 0$, then C is globally terminated at time t';*
2. *if $a(x_0) = 1$, then C is not globally terminated at time t.*

The total cost will be at most $4(n - 1)$ messages, regardless of the number k of initiators. Also to this cost we must add the cost of the control mechanism, which uses one message (an acknowledgment) for each C-message. Hence, the total cost, with multiple initiators is

$$M(C) + 4(n - 1),$$

where $M(C)$ is the number of messages sent during the execution of C being monitored.

Repeated Queries   We have discussed, solved, and analyzed the simpler task of computing a personal query. The interest in this simpler problem is due to the fact that a solution to personal detection can be made by repeatedly executing a personal query protocol Q until global termination is detected. Consider first of all the following strategy:

Strategy *RepeatQuery*:   answer:=**false**; **while not**(answer) **do** Q.

The use of strategy *RepeatQuery* when Q is protocol *TerminationQuery* would lead to a global termination detection protocol whose total cost will be

$$M(C) + 4(n - 1)T,$$

where T is the number of times *TerminationQuery* is invoked before termination of C. As communication delays are unpredictable, T is unbounded. This means that the number of messages sent using this solution is unbounded.

Notice that for any solution protocol Q, its cost in terms of messages will always be of the form $A + B$, where A is the cost incurred to maintain the information needed by Q (e.g., the control mechanism used by *TerminationQuery*) and B is the cost of the actual execution of Q. This means that the cost of strategy *RepeatQuery* using Q is

$$A + BT,$$

which again is unbounded, regardless of A and B.

This means that regardless of how efficient is the employed solution Q to the personal query problem, the strategy *RepeatQuery* is a cost-wise unacceptable solution to the personal detection problem.

To make it bounded we need to exercise some additional control, restarting the query only if some necessary condition holds; namely, we will restart only if all entities have become or remained *passive* since last iteration. Notice that this condition alone is not sufficient as there might have been some messages in transit whose arrival has in the meanwhile transformed into *active* again some of these *passive* entities.

Let us consider again the single-initiator case and consider the first execution of Q; if successful, we are done. If unsuccessful, x_0 will wait for the next execution until it is first notified that all entities have become or remained *passive* since last query. In general, if an iteration is unsuccessful, the initiator will wait until it is first notified that all entities have become *passive* since that iteration and will only then start a new one. This is easily accomplished by the following strategy:

Strategy *RepeatQuery+*:

1. termination: = **false**;
2. **repeat until** termination:
   (a) x_0 waits until it becomes *passive* (if it is not already so) and then broadcasts a "Reset" message;
   (b) the broadcast is then followed by a delayed convergecast:
      • a leaf waits until it becomes *passive* and then sends a "Restart" message to its parent;
      • an internal node waits until it has received a "Restart" from all its children and it is itself *passive*; it then sends a "Restart" message to its parent;
   (c) when x_0 has received a "Restart" from all its neighbors, it waits until it is *passive* and then starts the execution of Q.

The advantage of this modified strategy is that the number of times the protocol Q is executed is at most $T \leq M(C)$; indeed it is possible that $T = M(C)$ (Exercise 8.6.21). This means that the total cost for solving the personal detection problem will be at most

$$A + B \, M(C),$$

which is bounded. In the particular case when $Q = TerminationQuery$, we will have a total cost

$$\mathbf{M}[RepeatQuery+] = 4n M(C), \tag{8.2}$$

which is bounded. The same approach with the same cost works also in the case of *multiple* initiators (see Exercise 8.6.22 and Problem 8.6.10).

8.3.2 Improved Protocols: Shrink

Let us now see how we can substantially reduce the cost of detecting global termination. As usual we will consider first the case of a computation when there is a *single* initiator.

We will dynamically construct and maintain a tree rooted in the initiator; the tree will grow and shrink during the computation until only the initiator is left: When this happens and the initiator is *passive*, termination of C has occurred. Let us describe the solution protocol in more details. The initiator x_0 will start the termination detection mechanism as soon as C starts. As before, we will have an acknowledgment for every C-message sent, and we will say that an entity is *white* if it is *passive* and has received an acknowledgment for all the C-messages it sent; otherwise, we will say that it is *black*. The strategy is simple:

Strategy *Shrink*:

- Whenever a *white* entity $y \neq x_0$ receives a C-message, it will become a child of the sender of the message; when y becomes *white* again, it will send an acknowledgment to its parent and have no longer any parent.
- Whenever a *black* entity receives a C-message, it will immediately send an acknowledgment to the sender.
- Whenever x_0 becomes *white*, global termination is detected.

To see why the corresponding protocol *Shrink* indeed works, first of all observe that the black nodes always form a tree rooted in the initiator, as indicated by the following properties (Exercise 8.6.23):

Property 8.3.3 *At any time t, if an entity is black, so is x_0.*

Property 8.3.4 *At any time t, the black nodes form a tree rooted in x_0 and the white nodes are singletons.*

Observe now that if x_0 becomes *white*, C has terminated, as indicated by the following properties (Exercise 8.6.24):

Property 8.3.5 *If all nodes are white at time t, C is globally terminated at that time.*

Finally, observe that if C terminates, x will indeed detect it within finite time (Exercise 8.6.25):

Property 8.3.6 *If C is globally terminated at time t, then there is a $t' \geq t$ such that all nodes are white at time t'.*

Summarizing, by Properties 8.3.3–8.3.6, protocol *Shrink* correctly solves the global termination detection problem when there is a single initiator.

What is the cost of protocol *Shrink*? Each C-message generates the transmission of an acknowledgment; no other messages are transmitted during the execution. Hence,

$$\mathbf{M}[Shrink] = M(C). \tag{8.3}$$

In other words, *Shrink* is not only simpler but also much more efficient than all solutions we have discussed so far for detecting global termination of single-initiator computations.

What happens if C has *multiple* initiators? With multiple initiators, protocol *Shrink* will create not one dynamic tree but rather a *forest* of dynamic trees, each one of them rooted in one of the initiators. Indeed Properties 8.3.5 and 8.3.6 still hold (Exercises 8.6.27 and 8.6.28), while Properies 8.3.3 and 8.3.4 become (Exercise 8.6.26) the following:

Property 8.3.7 *At any time t, if an entity is* black, *so is at least one of the initiators.*

Property 8.3.8 *At any time t, the* black *nodes form a forest of trees, each rooted in one of the initiators, and the white nodes are singletons.*

As a consequence,

Property 8.3.9 *At any time t, if all initiators are* white, *so is every entity.*

The problem is to detect when all initiators have become *white*; by Property 8.3.8, when this happens, all trees have shrunk and all initiators are singletons. Each initiator knows when its own tree has totally shrunk; so the problem is to determine when this has occurred at all initiators. The solution to this problem is simple; it is enough to perform a delayed full saturation on a predefined spanning tree of the network: A leaf waits until it becomes *white* and then starts the saturation (sending a message "Done"); an internal node waits until it is *white* and it has received "Done" from all neighbors but one and then sends "Done" to that neighbor. When a saturated node is *white*, it knows that indeed all initiators are *white* (Exercise 8.6.29):

Property 8.3.10 *If a saturated node is white at time t, then all nodes are white at that time.*

When this happens, by Properties 8.3.9 and 8.3.5, the computation C is globally terminated.

NOTE. In the delayed execution of the saturation technique, it is possible that only one entity becomes saturated (Exercise 8.6.30).

Let us call *MultiShrink* the corresponding protocol (see Problem 8.6.12), and let us analyze its costs. Again, each C-message will generate an acknowledgement, for a total of $M(C)$ message. In addition, *MultiShrink* uses a full saturation generating at most $4(n-1)$ messages. In other words,

$$\mathbf{M}[MultiShrink] = M(C) + 4(n-1), \tag{8.4}$$

a significant improvement over the cost of protocol *RepeatSimpleQuery*.

8.3.3 Concluding Remarks

Lower Bounds In the previous sections we have seen several protocols for global termination detection. For all of them, the number of messages was a function not only of the number n of entities in the network but also of the number $M(C)$ of messages of the computation C whose termination we want to detect. While n is a system parameter, $M(C)$ is not, and it could be arbitrarily large. Thus, it is important to know whether this factor is at all necessary or it is possible to substantially reduce it. In other words, it is important to establish a *lower bound* on the number of messages that any solution protocol must transmit to detect the global termination of a computation C.

In this regard, we have only a partial result; in fact we know only that there are computations such that to detect their global termination, any protocol needs to send at least as many messages as the computations (Problem 8.6.13):

Theorem 8.3.1 *For any $k \geq 0$, there is a computation C' such that*

1. $M(C') \geq k$;
2. to detect global termination of C', every protocol must send at least $M(C')$ messages.

As a consequence, protocol *Shrink* is worst-case optimal even constant-wise. In the case of multiple initiators, according to Theorem 8.3.1, protocol *MultiShrink* is optimal in the order of magnitude as long as $n = O(M(C))$ or smaller.

In reality, protocol *MultiShrink* is *always* optimal in the order of magnitude. This is because of the fact that having multiple initiators imposes a cost on solution protocols, as expressed by the following different lower bounds (Exercise 8.6.31):

Theorem 8.3.2 *With multiple initiators, for every computation C, every protocol must send at least $2n - 1$ messages in the worst case to detect the global termination of C.*

Garbage Collection There is an interesting correlation between the problem of global termination detection and the one arising in the context of *garbage collection*. Indeed, any garbage collection algorithm can be transformed into a global termination detection protocol (Problem 8.6.14). The resulting protocols are, however, not very efficient.

8.4 GLOBAL STABLE PROPERTY DETECTION

In the previous sections, we have examined the problems of detecting two important properties of a computation C: deadlock and global termination. Both properties have in common the fact that they are *stable*: Once they hold, they will continue to hold (unless some other computation is started). The solutions we have developed were quite specific to the particular nature of those two properties.

What we will discuss in this section is how to detect *any* stable property $\mathcal{P}$, regardless of its specific properties.

8.4.1 General Strategy

The goal is to develop a protocol that, for any stable property $\mathcal{P}$ and for any computation C, detects when $\mathcal{P}(C)$ holds.

Let us be more precise in terms of the requirements of the protocol, first of all the initiators: In termination detection they coincide with the initiators of C, while in deadlock detection it could be any entity. In this section, we will impose no restrictions: Any number of entities can independently initiate and they might not coincide with the initiators of C.

As before, we will distinguish between *personal* and *collective* detection:

1. *personal detection*: If $\mathcal{P}(C)$ holds, within finite time each initiator must know that this is the case.
2. *collective detection*: If $\mathcal{P}(C)$ holds, within finite time all entities must know that this is the case.

Observe that once *personal* detection has been solved, *collective* detection is trivially achieved with an additional notification process; thus, of the two, we will focus on personal detection. Further observe that for the personal (and thus collective) detection problem to be solvable, property $\mathcal{P}$ must eventually hold in C, otherwise no detection protocol will ever terminate.

We will consider the problem under the standard assumptions: connectivity, Bidirectional Links, complete reliability, and unique identifiers. We will also assume Message Ordering, that is, the links are FIFO.

As we did in the case of termination detection, our general solution strategy is based on the solution to a simpler problem:

personal query: An initiator must know within finite time whether or not $\mathcal{P}(C)$ holds.

More precisely, any solution Q to the personal query problem must have the following properties. Let x start Q at time t and terminate at time $t' > t$, and let q be the result of the query; then

1. if $\mathcal{P}(C)$ holds at time t; then $q = TRUE$;
2. if $q = FALSE$; then $\mathcal{P}(C)$ does not hold at time t.

Clearly a solution to personal and collective detection can be made by repeatedly executing a solution Q to the personal query problem.

Strategy *RepeatQuery*: **repeat Q until** $\mathcal{P}(C)$

NOTE. The cost of this strategy will be the cost of Q *times* the number of times Q is invoked; as we already observed in the case of termination detection, without any control, this cost is unbounded.

Let us not worry for the moment about the number of invocations, and let us focus instead on the design of a solution protocol Q to the personal query problem. What we need to do is to develop such a solution independently of the nature of property $\mathcal{P}$ (other than that it is stable).

Let us denote the status of the computation C at time t by $C[t]$, that is, $C[t]$ denotes the status of every entity as well as the status of every link at time t with respect to C. We will call $C[t]$ a *perfect snapshot* of C at time t.

Consider for the moment a single initiator (the following arguments actually hold, in the case of multiple initiators, for each of them). Let the initiator start at time t_0. If we could take a perfect snapshot $C[t']$ of C at any time $t' \geq t_0$ and collect this information at some entity (e.g., the initiator), then we could compute there if $\mathcal{P}(C)$ was holding at time t' and answer the personal query. Clearly, $C[t']$ is just the collection of the internal states $C(x)[t']$ of each entity x; so to collect $C[t']$ (which is unknown), we just need each entity x to send $C(x)[t']$ to the same place.

NOTE. To be able to do that, each entity must keep track of and remember all its internal states with respect to the computation C. Assume that this is the case (an expensive assumption storage-wise).

It would then appear that to solve the personal query problem, it is sufficient that the initiator x_0 at time t_0 broadcasts "Send me your internal state at time t_0"; every entity will then send its information to x_0 that will use it to reconstruct $C[t_0]$ and answer the query. Unfortunately, this approach not only is expensive but also does *not* work.

The problem is that even if an entity x knows its state at any time and remembers them all, it does not know what t_0 is. Recall, there are no global clocks, local clocks may sign different times and have different rates, and communication delays are unpredictable. As a consequence, *it is impossible to construct a perfect snapshot.*

Fortunately, we do not really need to take a perfect snapshot; an imperfect one will do, as long as it is "sharp" enough to provide consistent information.

8.4.2 Time Cuts and Consistent Snapshots

When we say that $C[t]$ denotes the status of C at "time" t, we are referring to "time" as seen by an observer *external* to the system, sometimes called "real time." Within the system, the actual value t of "real time" is not known: Each entity x has only access to its own local clock c_x, so the value $c_x(t)$ of x's clock at real time t might be different from that of other entities at the same time, and all of them different from t. Furthermore, unless the additional restrictions of full synchronicity hold, the local clocks might have different speeds, the distance between consecutive ticks of the same clock might change over time, there are no time bounds on communication delays, and so forth. In other words, within the system, *there is no common notion of time*. Fortunately, practically in all cases, although useful, a common notion of time is not needed.

To understand what is sufficient for our purposes, observe that "real time" gives a *total order* to all the events and the actions that occur in the system: We can say whether two events occur at the same time, whether an action is performed before an event takes place, and so forth. In other words, given any two actions or events that occurred in the system, we (external observers) can say (using real time) whether one occurred *before*, *at the same time* as, or *after* the other.

The entities in the system, with just access to their local clocks, have much less knowledge about the temporal relationships of actions and events; however, they do have some. In particular,

- each entity has a complete temporal knowledge of the events and actions occurring locally;
- when a message arrives, it also knows that the action of transmitting this message happened before its reception.

It turns out that this knowledge is indeed sufficient for obtaining a consistent snapshot. To see how, let us first of all generalize the notion of snapshot and introduce that of a cut.

Let $t_1, t_2, \ldots, t_n$ be instants of real time, not necessarily distinct, and let $x_0, x_2, \ldots, x_n$ be the entities; then $C(x_i)[t_i]$ denotes the state of entity x_i in computation C at time t_i. The set

$$T = \{t_1, t_2, \ldots, t_n\}$$

is called a time *cut*, and the set

$$C[T] = \{C(x_1)[t_1], C(x_2)[t_2], \ldots, C(x_n)[t_n]\}$$

of the associated entities' states is called the *snapshot* of C at time cut T. Notice that if all t_i are the same, the corresponding snapshot is perfect.

A cut partitions a computation into three temporal sides: *before* the cut, *at* the cut, and *after* the cut. This is very clear if one looks at the Time $\times$ Event Diagram (TED) (introduced in Chapter 1) of the computation C. For example, Figure 8.10 shows the TED of a simple computation C and three cuts (in bold) T_1, T_2, and T_3 for C. Anything before the cut is called *past*, the cut is called *present*, and anything after the cut is called *future*.

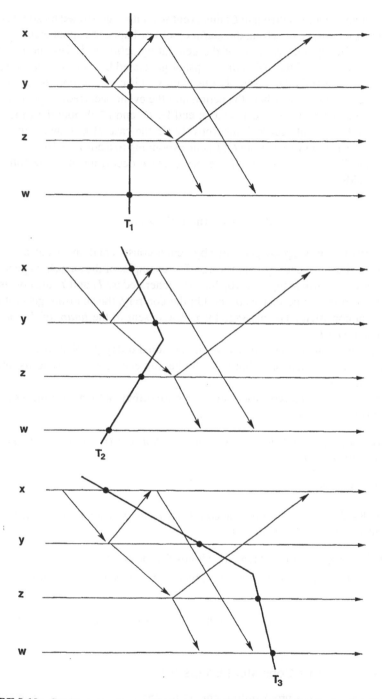

FIGURE 8.10: Cut T_1 generates a perfect snapshot; T_2 gives a consistent snapshot; T_3 generates an inconsistent snapshot.

Consider an event e occurring in C; this event was either generated by some action (i.e., sending a message or setting the alarm clock) or happened spontaneously (i.e., an impulse). Clearly, the real time of the generating action is *before* the real time of the generated event. Informally, the snapshot generated by a cut is *consistent* if it preserves this temporal relationship. Let us express this concept more precisely. Let x_i and x_j denote the entity where the action and the event occurred, respectively (in the case of a spontaneous event, $x_i = x_j$); and let t^- and t^+ denote the time when the action and the event occurred, respectively (in the case of a spontaneous event, $t^- = t^+$). Consider now a snapshot $C[T]$ corresponding to a cut $T = \{t_1, t_2, \ldots, t_n\}$; the snapshot $C[T]$ is *consistent* if for every event e occurring in C the following condition holds

$$\text{if } t^- \geq t_i \text{ then } t^+ > t_j. \tag{8.5}$$

In other words, the snapshot generated by a cut is consistent if, in the cut, a message is not received before sending that message. For example, of the snapshots generated by the three cuts shown in Figure 8.10, the ones generated by T_1 and T_2 are consistent; indeed, the former is a perfect snapshot. On the contrary, the snapshot generated by cut T_3 is not consistent: The message by x to w is sent in the *future* of T_3, but it is received in the *past*.

Summarizing, our strategy to resolve the personal query problem is to collect at the initiator x a consistent snapshot $C[T]$ by having each entity x_j send its internal state $C(x_j)[t_j]$ to x.

We must now show that consistent snapshots are sufficient for answering a personal query. This is indeed the case (Exercise **??**):

Property 8.4.1 *Let $C(T)$ be a consistent snapshot. If $\mathcal{P}(C)$ holds for the cut T, it holds for every $T' \geq T$.*

As a consequence,

Property 8.4.2 *Let $x = x_i$ start the collection of the snapshot $C[T]$ at time t and terminate at time $t', t \leq t_i \leq t'$; then*

1. if $\mathcal{P}(C)$ holds at time t, then $\mathcal{P}(C)$ holds for the cut T;
2. if $\mathcal{P}(C)$ does not hold for the cut T, then $\mathcal{P}(C)$ does not hold at time t.

Thus, our problem is now how to compute a consistent snapshot, which we will examine next.

8.4.3 Computing a Consistent Snapshot

Our task is to design a protocol to compute a consistent snapshot. To achieve this task, each entity x_i must select a time t_i, and these local choices must be such that the snapshot generated by the resulting cut is consistent. Specifically, each t_i must be such that if x_i sent a C-message to a neighbor x_j at or after t_i, this message must arrive at x_j *after* time t_j. The difficulty is that as communication delays are unpredictable, x_i does not know when its message arrives. Fortunately, there is a very simple way to achieve our goal.

Notice that as we have assumed FIFO links, when an entity y receives a message from a neighbor x, y knows that all messages sent by x to y before transmitting this one have already arrived. We can use this fact as follows.

Consider the following generalization of *WFlood* from Chapter 2:

Protocol WFlood+:

1. an initiator sends a wake-up to all neighbors;
2. a noninitiator, upon receiving a wake-up message for the first time, sends a wake-up to all its neighbors.

Notice that the only difference between *WFlood+* and *WFlood* is that now a noninitiator sends a wake-up message also to the entity that woke it up.

Let $\bar{t}_i$ be the time when x_i becomes "awake" (i.e., it initiates *WFlood+* or receives the first "wake-up" message). An interesting and important property is the following:

Property 8.4.3 *If x_i sends a C-message to x_j at time $t > \bar{t}_i$, then this message will arrive at x_j at a time $t' > \bar{t}_j$.*

Proof. Consider a "wake-up" message sent by an entity x_i to a neighbor x_j at time $t > \bar{t}_i$; this message will arrive at x_j at some time t'. Recall that x_i at time $\bar{t}_i$ sent a "wake-up" message to all its neighbors, including x_j; as links are FIFO, this "wake-up" message arrived to x_j at some time t'' before the C-message, that is, $t' > t''$.

When x_j receives the "wake-up" message from x_i, either it is already awake or it is woken up by it. In either case, $t'' \geq \bar{t}_j$; as $t' > t''$, it follows that $t' > \bar{t}_j$. ∎

This means that in the time cut $\overline{T} = \{\bar{t}_1, \bar{t}_2, \ldots, \bar{t}_n\}$ defined by these time values, no C-message is sent at T and every C-message sent after $\overline{T}$ also arrives after $\overline{T}$. In other words,

Property 8.4.4 *The snapshot $C[\overline{T}]$ is consistent.*

Thus the problem of constructing a consistent snapshot is solved by simply executing a wake-up using *WFlood+*. The cost is easy to determine: In the execution of *WFlood+* regardless of the number of initiators, exactly two messages are sent on each link, one in each direction. Thus, a total of $2m$ messages are sent.

8.4.4 Summary: Putting All Together

We have just seen how to determine a consistent snapshot $C[\overline{T}]$ (Protocol *WFlood+*) with multiple initiators. Once this is done, the entities still have to determine whether or not property $\mathcal{P}$ holds for $C[\overline{T}]$.

This can be accomplished by having each x_i send its local state $C(x_i)[\bar{t}_i]$ to some predefined entity (e.g., the initiator in case of a single-initiator, or the saturated nodes over an existing spanning tree, or a previously elected leader); this entity will collect these fragments of the snapshot, construct from them snapshot $C[\bar{T}]$, determine locally whether or not property $\mathcal{P}$ holds for $C[\bar{T}]$, and (if required) notify all other entities of the result of the local query.

Depending on the size of the local fragments of the snapshot, the amount of information transmitted can be prohibitive. An alternative to this centralized solution is to compute $\mathcal{P}(C)$ at $\bar{T}$ distributively. This, however, requires knowledge of the nature of property $\mathcal{P}$, something that we neither have nor want to require; recall: Our original goal is to design a protocol to detect a stable property $\mathcal{P}$ regardless of its nature.

At this point, we have a (centralized or decentralized) protocol Q for solving the personal query problem. We can then follow strategy *RepeatQuery* and repeatedly execute Q until the stable property $\mathcal{P}(C)$ is detected to hold.

As already mentioned, the overall cost is the cost of Q *times* the number of times Q is invoked; as we already observed in the case of termination detection, without any control, this cost is unbounded.

Summarizing, we have seen how to solve the global detection problem for stable properties by repeatedly taking consistent snapshots of the system; such a snapshot is sometimes called a *global state* of the system. This solution is independent of the stable property and thus can be applied to any. We have also seen that the cost of the solution we have designed can be prohibitive and, without some other control, it is possibly unbounded.

Clearly, for specific properties we can use knowledge of the property to reduce the costs (e.g., the number of times Q is executed, as we did in the case of termination) or to develop different ad hoc solutions (as we did in the case of deadlock); for example, see Problem 8.6.16.

8.5 BIBLIOGRAPHICAL NOTES

The problem of distributed *deadlock* detection has been extensively studied and a very large number of solutions have been designed, proposed, and analyzed. However, not all these attempts have been successful, some failing to work correctly, either detecting false deadlocks or failing to detect existing deadlocks, others exhibiting very poor performance. As deadlock can occur in almost any application area, solutions have been developed from researchers in all these areas (from distributed databases to systems of finite state machines, from distributed operating systems to distributed transactions to distributed simulation), many times unaware of (and sometimes reproducing) each other's efforts and results. Also, deadlocks in different types of request systems (single request, AND, OR, etc.) have oftentimes been studied in isolation as different problems, overlooking the similarities and the commonalities and sometimes proposing the same techniques. In addition, because of its link with cycle detection and with knot detection, some aspects of deadlock detection have also been studied by investigators in distributed graph algorithms.

Interestingly, one of the earliest algorithms, *LockGrant*, is not only the most efficient (in the order of magnitude) protocol for personal detection with a *single* initiator in a *static* graph but also the most general as it can be used (efficiently) in all types of request systems. It has been designed by Gabriel Bracha and Sam Toueg [2], and their static protocol can be modified to work efficiently also on *dynamic* graphs in all request systems (Problem 8.6.9). The number of messages has been subsequently reduced from $4m$ to $2m$ by Ajay Kshemkalyani and Mukesh Singhal [11].

In the presence of *multiple* initiators, the idea of integrating a leader-election process into the detection protocol (Problem 8.6.2) was first proposed by Israel Cidon [6].

The simpler problem of personal *knot detection* was first solved by Mani Chandy and Jayadev Misra [4] for a *single* initiator with $4m$ messages and later with $2m$ messages by Azzedine Boukerche and Carl Tropper [1]. A protocol for *multiple* initiators that uses only $3m + O(n \log n)$ messages has been designed by Israel Cidon [6].

The problem of detecting *global termination* of a computation was first posed by Nissim Francez [9] and Edsger Dijkstra and Carel Scholten [8].

Protocol *TerminationQuery* for the personal termination *query* problem was designed by Rodney Topor [21] and used in strategy *RepeatQuery* for the personal termination *detection* problem.

The more efficient protocol *Shrink* for single initiator is due to Edsger Dijkstra and Carel Scholten [8]; its extension to *multiple* initiators, protocol *MultiShrink*, has been designed by Nir Shavit and Nissim Francez [18].

The idea of message counting was first employed by Mani Chandy and Jayadev Misra [5] and refined by Friedmann Mattern [13]. Other mechanisms and ideas employed to detect termination include the following: "markers," proposed by Jayadev Misra [16]; "credits," suggested by Friedmann Mattern [14]; and "timestamps," proposed by S. Rana [17].

The relationship between the problems of *garbage collection* and that of *global termination detection* was first observed by Carel Scholten [unpublished], made explicit (in one direction) by Gerard Tel, Richard Tan, and Jan van Leeuwen [20], and analyzed (in the other direction: Problem 8.6.14) by Gerard Tel and Friedmann Mattern [19].

The fact that Protocol *WFlood+* constructs a consistent snapshot was first observed by Mani Chandy and Leslie Lamport [3]. Protocols to construct a consistent snapshot when the links are not FIFO were designed by Ten Lai and Tao Yang [12] and Friedmann Mattern [15]; they, however, require C-messages to contain control information.

The strategy of constructing and checking a consistent snapshot has been used by Gabriel Bracha and Sam Toueg for deadlock detection in dynamic graphs [2], and by Shing-Tsaan Huang [10] and Friedmann Mattern [13] for termination detection.

8.6 EXERCISES, PROBLEMS, AND ANSWERS

8.6.1 Exercises

Exercise 8.6.1   Prove that protocol *GeneralSimpleCheck* would solve the personal and component deadlock detection problem.

Exercise 8.6.2   Show the existence of wait-for graphs of n nodes in which protocol *GeneralSimpleCheck* would require a number of messages exponential in n.

Exercise 8.6.3   Show a situation where, when executing protocol *LockGrant*, an entity receives a "Grant" message *after* it has terminated its execution of *Shout*.

Exercise 8.6.4   Prove that in protocol *LockGrant*, if an entity sends a "Grant" message to a neighbor, it will receive a "Grant-Ack" from that neighbor within finite time.

Exercise 8.6.5   Prove that in protocol *LockGrant*, if an entity sends a "Shout" message to a neighbor, it will receive a "Reply" from that neighbor within finite time.

Exercise 8.6.6   Prove that in protocol *LockGrant*, if a "Grant" message has not been acknowledged at time t, the initiator x_0 has not yet received a "Reply" from all its neighbors at that time.

Exercise 8.6.7   Prove that in protocol *LockGrant*, if an entity receives a "Grant" message from all its out-neighbors then it is not deadlocked.

Exercise 8.6.8   Prove that in protocol *LockGrant*, if an entity is not deadlocked, it will receive a "Grant" message from all its out-neighbors within finite time.

Exercise 8.6.9   Modify the definition of a solution protocol for the collective deadlock detection problem in the dynamic case.

Exercise 8.6.10   Prove that in the dynamic single-request model, once formed the core of a crown will remain unchanged.

Exercise 8.6.11   Prove that in the dynamic single-request model, if the initiator x_0 is in a rooted tree that is not going to become (part of) a crown, then its message is eventually going to reach the root of the tree.

Exercise 8.6.12   Prove that in the dynamic single-request model, if a new crown is formed while the "Check" message started by x_0 is still traveling, the protocol will correctly notify x_0 that it is involved in a deadlock.

Exercise 8.6.13   Prove that in the dynamic single-request model, if a new crown is formed while the "Check" message started by x_0 is still traveling, the protocol will correctly notify x_0 that it is involved in a deadlock.

Exercise 8.6.14   Modify protocol *LockGrant* so that it solves the personal and the collective deadlock detection problem in the OR-Request model. Assume a single initiator. Prove the correctness and analyze the cost of the resulting protocol. Implement and throughly test your protocol. Compare the experimental results with the theoretical bounds.

Exercise 8.6.15   Implement and throughly test the protocol designed in Exercise 8.6.14. Compare the experimental results with the theoretical bounds.

Exercise 8.6.16   Modify protocol *LockGrant* so that it solves the personal and the collective deadlock detection problem in the *p-OF-q* Request model. Assume a single initiator. Prove the correctness and analyze the cost of the resulting protocol. Implement and throughly test your protocol. Compare the experimental results with the theoretical bounds.

Exercise 8.6.17   Implement and throughly test the protocol designed in Exercise 8.6.16. Compare the experimental results with the theoretical bounds.

Exercise 8.6.18   Modify protocol *LockGrant* so that it solves the personal and the collective deadlock detection problem in the *Generalized* Request model. Assume a single initiator. Prove the correctness and analyze the cost of the resulting protocol. Implement and throughly test your protocol. Compare the experimental results with the theoretical bounds.

Exercise 8.6.19   Implement and throughly test the protocol designed in Exercise 8.6.18. Compare the experimental results with the theoretical bounds.

Exercise 8.6.20   Prove that protocol *TerminationQuery* is a correct personal query protocol, that is, show that Property 8.3.1 holds.

Exercise 8.6.21   Prove that using strategy *RepeatQuery+*, protocol Q is executed at most $T \leq M(C)$ times. Show an example in which $T = M(C)$.

Exercise 8.6.22   Let Q be a multiple-initiators personal query protocol. Modify strategy *RepeatQuery+* to work with multiple initiators.

Exercise 8.6.23   Consider strategy *Shrink* for personal termination detection with a single initiator. Show that at any time, all *black* nodes form a tree rooted in the initiator and all *white* nodes are singletons.

Exercise 8.6.24 Consider strategy *Shrink* for personal termination detection with a single initiator. Prove that if all nodes are *white* at time t, then C is terminated at that time.

Exercise 8.6.25 Consider strategy *Shrink* for personal termination detection with a single initiator. Prove that if C is terminated at time t, then there is a $t' \geq t$ such that all nodes are *white* at time t'.

Exercise 8.6.26 Consider strategy *Shrink* for personal termination detection with multiple initiators. Show that at any time, the *black* nodes form a forest of trees, each rooted in one of the initiators, and the *white* nodes are singletons.

Exercise 8.6.27 Consider strategy *Shrink* for personal termination detection with multiple initiators. Prove that, if all nodes are *white* at time t, then C is terminated at that time.

Exercise 8.6.28 Consider strategy *Shrink* for personal termination detection with multiple initiators. Prove that if C is terminated at time t, then there is a $t' \geq t$ such that all nodes are *white* at time t'.

Exercise 8.6.29 Consider protocol *MultiShrink* for personal termination detection with multiple initiators. Prove that when a saturated node becomes *white* all other nodes are also *white*.

Exercise 8.6.30 Consider protocol *MultiShrink* for personal termination detection with multiple initiators. Explain why it is possible that only one entity becomes saturated. Show an example.

Exercise 8.6.31 (⋆) Prove that for every computation C, every protocol must send at least $2n - 1$ messages in the worst case to detect the global termination of C.

8.6.2 Problems

Problem 8.6.1 Write the set of rules of protocol *Dead Check* implementing the *simple check* strategy for personal and for collective deadlock detection in the single resource model. Implement and throughly test your protocol. Compare the experimental results with the theoretical bounds.

Problem 8.6.2 (⋆) For the problem of personal deadlock detection with multiple initiators consider the strategy to integrate into the solution an election process among the initiators. Design a protocol for the *single-request* model to implement efficiently this strategy; its total cost should be $o(kn)$ messages in the worst case, where k is the number of initiators and n is the number of entities. Prove the correctness and analyze the cost of your design. Implement and throughly test your protocol. Compare the experimental results with the theoretical bounds.

Problem 8.6.3 Implement protocol *LockGrant*, both for personal and for collective deadlock detections. Throughly test your protocol. Compare the experimental results with the theoretical bounds.

Problem 8.6.4 (⋆) In protocol *LockGrant* employ *Shout+* instead of *Shout*, so as to use at most $4|E(x_0)|$ messages in the worst case. Write the corresponding set of rules. Implement and throughly test your protocol. Compare the experimental results with the theoretical bounds.

Problem 8.6.5 (⋆⋆) For the problem of personal deadlock detection with multiple initiators consider the strategy to integrate into the solution an election process among the initiators. Design a protocol for the *AND-request* model to implement efficiently this strategy; its total cost should be $o(km)$ messages in the worst case, where k is the number of initiators and m is the number of links in the wait-for graph. Prove the correctness and analyze the cost of your design. Implement and throughly test your protocol. Compare the experimental results with the theoretical bounds.

Problem 8.6.6 (⋆⋆) Modify protocol *LockGrant* so that, with a single initiator, it works correctly also in a dynamic wait-for graph. Prove the correctness and analyze the cost of the modified protocol.

Problem 8.6.7 (⋆⋆) For the problem of personal deadlock detection with multiple initiators consider the strategy to integrate into the solution an election process among the initiators. Design a protocol for the *OR-request* model to implement efficiently this strategy; its total cost should be $o(km)$ messages in the worst case, where k is the number of initiators and m is the number of links in the wait-for graph. Prove the correctness and analyze the cost of your design. Implement and throughly test your protocol. Compare the experimental results with the theoretical bounds.

Problem 8.6.8 (⋆⋆) For the problem of personal deadlock detection with multiple initiators consider the strategy to integrate into the solution an election process among the initiators. Design a protocol for the *p-OF-q request* model to implement efficiently this strategy; its total cost should be $o(km)$ messages in the worst case, where k is the number of initiators and m is the number of links in the wait-for graph. Prove the correctness and analyze the cost of your design. Implement and throughly test your protocol. Compare the experimental results with the theoretical bounds.

Problem 8.6.9 (⋆⋆) For the problem of personal deadlock detection with multiple initiators consider the strategy to integrate into the solution an election process among the initiators. Design a protocol for the *Generalized* request model to implement efficiently this strategy; its total cost should be $o(km)$ messages in the worst case, where k is the number of initiators and m is the number of links in the wait-for graph.

Prove the correctness and analyze the cost of your design. Implement and throughly test your protocol. Compare the experimental results with the theoretical bounds.

Problem 8.6.10 (⋆)   Write the set of rules corresponding to strategy *RepeatQuery+* when Q is *TerminationQuery* and there are multiple initiators. Implement and throughly test your protocol. Compare the experimental results with the theoretical bounds.

Problem 8.6.11 (⋆)   Write the set of rules of protocol *Shrink* for global termination detection with a single initiator. Implement and throughly test your protocol. Compare the experimental results with the theoretical bounds.

Problem 8.6.12 (⋆)   Write the set of rules of protocol *MultiShrink* for global termination detection with multiple initiators. Implement and throughly test your protocol. Compare the experimental results with the theoretical bounds.

Problem 8.6.13 (⋆)   Construct a computation C_k, $k \geq 0$ such that $M(C_k) \geq k$ and to detect global termination of C', every protocol must send at least $M(C')$ messages.

Problem 8.6.14 (⋆⋆)   Show how to transform automatically a *garbage collection* algorithm GC into a termination detection protocol TD. Analyze the cost of TD.

Problem 8.6.15   Using the transformation of Problem 8.6.14, determine the cost of TD when GC is the *References Count* algorithm.

Problem 8.6.16   Consider a computation C that circulates k *tokens* among the entities in a system where tokens (but not messages) can be lost while in transit. The problem we need to solve is the detection of whether one or more tokens are lost. Adapt the general protocol we designed for detecting stable properties (i.e., strategy *RepeatQuery* using *WFlood+* for personal query resolution) to solve this problem. Use the specific nature of C to reduce the space and bit costs of each iteration, as well as the overall number of messages.

8.6.3 Answers to Exercises

Answer to Exercise 8.6.3
Consider the simple wait-for graph shown in Figure 8.11. When a receives the "Shout" message from the initiator x_0, it will forward it to b and, as it is a sink, it will also send a "Grant" message to both x_0 and b. Assume that the "Grant" message from a to b is very slow. In the meanwhile, b receives the "Shout" from a and forwards it to c and d, which will send a "Reply" to b; upon receiving these replies, b will send its "Reply" to its parent a, effectively terminating its execution of *Shout*. The "Grant" message from a will then arrive after all this has occurred.

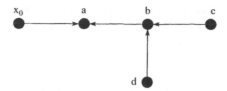

FIGURE 8.11: Entity *b* might locally terminate *Shout* before receiving "Grant" from *a*.

Answer to Exercise 8.6.5

Hint: First prove that in protocol *LockGrant*, within finite time, every entity but the initiator will send a "Reply" to its parent in the tree constructed by the *Shout*.

BIBLIOGRAPHY

[1] A. Boukerche and C. Tropper. A distributed graph algorithm for the detection of local cycles and knots. *IEEE Transactions on Parallel and Distributed Systems*, 9(8):748–757, August 1998.

[2] G. Bracha and S. Toueg. Distributed deadlock detection. *Distributed Computing*, 2: 127–138, 1987.

[3] K. M. Chandy and L. Lamport. Distributed snapshots: Determining global states of distributed systems. *ACM Transactions on Computer Systems*, 3(1):63–75, February 1985.

[4] K. M. Chandy and J. Misra. A distributed graph algorithm: knot detection. *ACM Transactions on Programming Languages and Systems*, 4:144–156, 1982.

[5] K. M. Chandy and J. Misra. A paradigm for detecting quiescent properties in distributed computations. In *K.R. Apt (Ed.), Logic and models of concurrent systems*, 1985.

[6] I. Cidon. An efficient distributed knot-detection algorithm. *IEEE Transactions on Software Engineering*, 15(5):644–649, May 1989.

[7] E. W. Dijkstra. *Selected writings on computing: A personal perspective*. Springer, 1982.

[8] E. W. Dijkstra and C.S. Scholten. Termination detection for diffusing computations. *Information Processing Letters*, 11(1):1–4, August 1980.

[9] N. Francez. Distributed termination. *ACM Transactions on Programming Languages and Systems*, 2(1):42–55, 1980.

[10] S. T. Huang. Termination detection by using distributed snapshots. *Information Processing Letters*, 32(3):113–120, 1989.

[11] A. Kshemkalyani and M. Singhal. Efficient detection and resolution of generalized deadlocks. *IEEE Transactions on Software Engineering*, 20(1):43–54, 1994.

[12] T. H. Lai and T. H. Yang. On distributed snapshots. *Information Processing Letters*, 25(5):153–158, 1987.

[13] F. Mattern. Algorithms for distributed termination detection. *Distributed Computing*, 2:161–175, 1987.

[14] F. Mattern. Global quiescence detection based on credit distribution and recovery. *Information Processing Letters*, 30(4):195–200, 1989.

[15] F. Mattern. Efficient algorithms for distributed snapshots and global virtual time approximation. *Journal of Parallel and Distributed Computing*, 18(4):423–434, August 1993.

[16] J. Misra. Detecting termination of distributed computations using markers. In *2nd Symposium on Principles of Distributed Computing*, pages 290–294, Montreal, 1983.

[17] S. P. Rana. A distributed solution of the distributed termination problem. *Information Processing Letters*, 17:43–46, 1983.

[18] N. Shavit and N. Francez. A new approach to detection of locally indicative stability. In *13th International Colloquium on Automata, Languages and Programming*, volume 226 of *Lecture Notes in Computer Science*, pages 344–358. Springer, 1986.

[19] G. Tel and F. Mattern. The derivation of distributed termination detection algorithms from garbage collection schemes. *ACM Transactions on Programming Languages and Systems*, 15(1):1–35, January 1993.

[20] G. Tel, R. B. Tan, and J. van Leeuwen. The derivation of graph marking algorithms from distributed termination detection protocols. *Science Of Computer Programming*, 10(2):107–137, April 1988.

[21] R. W. Topor. Termination detection for distributed computation. *Information Processing Letters*, 18(1):33–36, 1984.

CHAPTER 9

Continuous Computations

9.1 INTRODUCTION

When we have been discussing computations in distributed environments, we have always considered computations that once started (by some impulse), terminate within finite time. The termination conditions can be explicit in the protocol (e.g., the entities enter terminal states) or implicit (and hence a termination detection protocol must be run concurrently). The key point is that, implicit or explicit, the termination occurs.

There are, however, computations that never terminate. These are, for example, computations needed for the control and maintenance of the environment, and they are "on" as long as the system is "on": The protocols composing a distributed operating system, the transaction management protocols in a distributed transaction system, the network service protocols in a data communication network, the object management functions in a distributed object system, and so forth.

Because of this nature, these computations are called *continuous computations.*

We have already seen one such computation in Chapter 4, when dealing with the problem of maintaining routing tables; those protocols would never really terminate as long as there are changes in the network topology or in the traffic conditions.

Another example of continuous computation is the *heartbeat* protocol that provides a step-synchronization for the entities in the system: Each entity endlessly sends a "heartbeat" message to all its neighbors, waiting to receive one from all of them before its next transmission. Heartbeat protocols form the backbone of the management of most distributed systems and networks. It is, for example, used in most failure detection mechanisms: An entity decides that a failure has occurred if the wait for a heartbeat from a neighbor exceeds a timeout value.

In this chapter we will examine some basic problems whose solution requires continuous computations: maintaining logical clocks, controlling access to a shared resource or service, maintaining a distributed queue, and detecting and resolving deadlocks.

Design and Analysis of Distributed Algorithms, by Nicola Santoro
Copyright © 2007 John Wiley & Sons, Inc.

Some continuous problems are just the (endless) repetition of a terminating problem (plus adjustments); others could be solved in that way, but they also have unique nonterminating solutions; others yet do not have any terminating counterpart. In this chapter we will examine continuous problems of all these types.

Before we proceed, let us ask a simple but provocative question:

What is the *cost* of a continuous computation?

As the computation never ends, the answer is obviously *"infinite."* While true, it is not meaningful because then *all* continuous computations have the same cost. What this answer really points out is that we should not (because we cannot) measure the total cost of the entire execution of a continuous computation. Which measure is most appropriate depends on the nature of the problem. Consider the *heartbeat* protocol, whose total cost is infinite; The meaningful cost measure in this case is the total number of messages it uses *per* single beat: $2\ m$. In the case of the routing table maintenance protocols, a meaningful measure is the total number of messages exchanged in the system *per* change in the topology.

Summarizing, we will measure a continuous computation in terms of either its cost *per* basic operation it implements or its cost *per* basic event triggering its action.

9.2 KEEPING VIRTUAL TIME

9.2.1 Virtual Time and Causal Order

In a distributed computing environment, without additional restrictions, there is definitely no common notion of real (i.e., physical) *time* among the entities. Each entity has a local clock; however, each is independent of the others. In general this fact does not restrict our ability to solve problems or perform tasks; indeed, all the protocols we have designed, with the exception of those for fully synchronous systems, do not require any common notion of real time among the entities.

Still, there are cases when such a notion would be helpful. Consider, for example, the situation when we need to *undo* some operation a (e.g., the transmission of a message) that has been erroneously performed. In this case, we need to undo also everything (e.g., transmission of other messages) that was caused by a. In this context, it is necessary to determine whether a certain event or action b (e.g., the transmission of some other message by some other entity) was caused (directly or indirectly) by that original action a. If we find out that a happened after b, that is $t(a) > t(b)$, we can exclude that b was caused by a, and we need not undo it. So, although it would not completely solve the problem, having access to real time would be useful.

As we know, entities do not have access to real time t. They can, however, create, using local clocks and counters, a common notion of time T among them, that would allow them to approximate real time or at least exploit some useful properties of real time.

When we talk about a common notion of time we mean a function T that assigns a value (not necessarily unique) from a partially ordered set to each event in the system; we will denote by $<$ the partial order. To be meaningful, this function must satisfy two basic properties:

- *Local Events Ordering*: Let a and b two events occuring both at x, with $t(a) <$ $t(b)$. Then $T(a) < T(b)$.
- *Send/Receive Ordering*: Let a be the event at x whose reaction is the transmission of a message to neighbor y, and let b be the arrival at y of that message. Then $T(a) < T(b)$.

Any function T satisfying these two properties will be called *virtual time*.

The other desirable property is the one allowing us to simulate real time in the *undo* problem: If a "happened after" b in virtual time (i.e., $T(a) > T(b)$), then a did *not* cause b (directly or indirectly). Let us be more precise. We say that event a *causally preceeds*, or simply *causes* event b, and denote this fact by $a \rightarrow b$, if one of the following conditions holds:

1. both a and b occur at the same entity and $t(a) < t(b)$;
2. a is the event at x whose reaction is the transmission of a message to neighbor y, and b is the arrival at y of that message;
3. there exists a sequence $e_1, e_2, \ldots, e_k$ of events such that $e_1 = a$, $e_k = b$, and $e_i \rightarrow e_{i+1}$.

We will say that two events a and b are *causally related* if $a \rightarrow b$ or $b \rightarrow a$. Sometimes events are not causally related at all: We will say that a and b are *independent* if both $a \not\rightarrow b$ and $b \not\rightarrow a$.

We can now formally define the property we are looking for:

- *Causal Order*: For any two events a and b, if $a \rightarrow b$ then $T(a) < T(b)$.

Interestingly, the simultaneous presence of properties *Local Events* and *Send/Receive* ordering are enough to guarantee *Causal Order* (Exercise 9.6.1):

Property 9.2.1 *Let T be virtual time. Then T satisfies* Causal Order.

The problem is how can the entities create a virtual time T. This should be done if possible *without* generating additional messages. To achieve this goal, each entity x must create and maintain a *virtual clock* T_x that assigns an integer value to each event occurring locally; these virtual clocks define an overall time function T: For an event a occurring at x, $T(a) = T_x(a)$; hence, the clocks must be designed and maintained in such a way that the function T is indeed virtual time. Our goal is to design an algorithm that specifies how to create such virtual clocks and maintain them. Clearly, mantaining virtual time is a continuous computation.

As virtual clocks are mechanisms we design and construct, one might ask whether it is possible to design them so that, in addition to *Causal Order*, they satisfy some other desirable property. Consider again the case of the *undo* operation; *Causal Order* allows only to say that if $T(a) > T(b)$, then $a \not\rightarrow b$, while what we really need to know is whether $a \to b$. So, for example, it would be very useful if the virtual clocks satisfy the much stronger property

- *Complete Causal Order*: $a \to b$ if and only if $T(a) < T(b)$.

If we could construct virtual clocks that satisfy the *Complete Causal Order* property, then to identify what to undo would be easy: To completely undo a we must undo every b with $T(b) > T(a)$.

Notice that *real time* is *not complete* with respect to causal order; in fact, $t(a) < t(b)$ does not imply at all that a caused b! In other words, Complete Causal Order is *not* provided by real clocks. This suggests that creating virtual clocks with this property is not a trivial task.

Also notice that each local clock c_x, by definition, satisfies the Complete Causal Order property for the locally occurring events. This means that as long as an entity does not interact with other entities, its local clock generates a completely consistent virtual time. The problems clearly arise when entities interact with each another.

In the following we will design an algorithm to construct and maintain virtual clocks; we will also develop a system of virtual clocks that satisfy Complete Causal Order. In both cases, we will assume the standard restrictions **IR**: Connectivity, Complete Reliability, and Bidirectional Links, as well as Unique Identifiers. We will also assume *Message Ordering* (i.e., FIFO links).

9.2.2 Causal Order: Counter Clocks

As locally generated events and actions are already naturally ordered by the local clocks, to construct and maintain virtual clocks (i.e., clocks that satisfy Causal Order), we have to worry mostly about the interaction between different entities. Fortunately, entities interact directly only through messages; clearly, the operation a of transmitting a message generates the event b of receiving that message, that is, $a \to b$. Hence, we must somehow handle the arrival of a message not like any other event or local action but as a special one: It is the moment when the local times of the two entities, the sender and the receiver, come into contact; we must ensure that this causal order is preserved by the clocks we are designing. A simple algorithm for clock construction and maintenance is the following.

Algorithm *CounterClock*:

1. We equip each entity x with a local integer counter C_x of the local events and actions, that is, C_x is initially set to 0 and it is increased by 1 every time x reacts to an event other than arrival of a message; the increment occurs *at the beginning* of the action.
2. Let us consider now the interaction between entities. Whenever an entity x sends a message to a neighbor y, it encloses in the message the current value of its local counter. Whenever an entity y receives a message with a counter value *count*, it increases its local counter to $C_y := 1 + \max\{C_y, count\}$

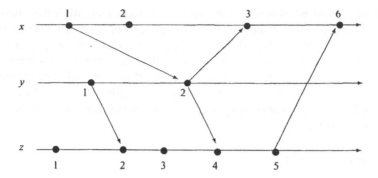

FIGURE 9.1: Virtual time generated by *CounterClocks*.

Consider, for example, the TED diagram shown in Figure 9.1; the message sent by z to y contains the counter value $C_z = 5$; just before receiving this message $C_x = 3$; when reacting to the message arrival, x sets $C_x = 1 + \max\{5, 3\} = 6$.

This system of local counters defines a global measure of time C; for any event a at x, $C(a)$ is just $C_x(a)$. Notice that each local counter is totally consistent with its local clock: For any two local events a and b, $C_x(a) < C_x(b)$ if and only if $c_x(a) < c_x(b)$; as local clocks satisfy the causal order property for local events, these counters satisfy *local events* ordering. By construction, if a is the transmission of a message and b is its reception, then $C(a) = C_x(a) < C_x(b) = C(b)$, that is, *send/receive* ordering holds.

In other words, algorithm *CounterClock* constructs and maintains *virtual clocks*:

Theorem 9.2.1   *Let C be the global time defined by the local counters of algorithm* CounterClock. *For any two actions and/or events a and b, if $a \to b$ then $C(a) < C(b)$.*

This algorithm achieves its goal *without* any additional communication. It does, however, require an additional field (the value of the local counter) in each message; the bookkeeping is minimal: limited to storing the counter and increasing its value at each event.

Notice that although the time function C created by algorithm *CounterClock* satisfies the causal order property like real time t, it may differ greatly from real time. For example (Exercises 9.6.2 and 9.6.3), it is possible that $t(a) > t(b)$, while $C(a) < C(b)$. It is also possible that two independent events, occurring at diffe rent entities at different times, have the same virtual time.

9.2.3 Complete Causal Order: Vector Clocks

With the virtual clocks generated by algorithm *CounterClock*, we are guaranteed that property Causal Order holds, that is, if $a \to b$, then $C(a) < C(b)$. However, the converse is not true. In fact, it is possible that $C(a) < C(b)$, but $a \not\to b$. This means that if $C(a) < C(b)$, it is impossible for us to decide whether or not a causes b. By contrast, as we mentioned earlier, it is precisely this type of knowledge that is the most helpful, for example, in the *undo* operation case.

It is natural to ask whether we can design virtual clocks that satisfy the much more powerful *Complete Causal Order* property. Let us point out again that real time clocks do *not* satisfy this property. Surprisingly, it is possible to achieve this property using solely local counters; however, we need *many* of them together; let us see how.

For simplicity, let us assume that we have established a total order among the entities, for example, by *ranking* them according to their ids (see Problem 2.9.4); thus, we will denote the entities as $x_1, x_2, ..., x_n$, where the index of an entity denotes its position in the total order.

Algorithm *VectorClock*:

1. We equip each entity x_i with a local integer counter C_i of the local events, that is, C_i is initially set to 0 and it is increased by 1 every time x_i reacts to an event; the increment occurs *at the beginning* of the action. We equip each entity x_i also with a n-dimensional vector V_i of values, one for each entity in the network. The value $V_i[i]$ is always the value of the local counter C_i; the value of $V_i[j], i \neq j$, is initially 0 and can change only when a message arrives at x_i, according to the rule 2(b) described next.

2. Let us consider now the interaction between entities.

    (a) Whenever an entity x_i sends a message to a neighbor x_j, it encloses in the message the vector of values V_i .

    (b) Whenever an entity x_j processes the arrival of a message with a vector *vect* of values, it updates its local vector V_j as follows: for all $i \neq j$, it sets $V_j[i] := \max\{vect[i], V_j[i]\}$.

As an example, in the TED diagram shown in Figure 9.2, when x_1 receives the message from x_2, its vector is [2 0 0], while the message contains vector [1 2 0]; when reacting to the message, x_1 will first increase its local counter transforming its vector into [3 0 0] and then process the message transforming its vector into [3 2 0].

Consider an event a at x_i. We define $V_i(a)$ as follows: If a is the reception of a message, then $V_i(a)$ is the value of the vector V_i after its updating when processing

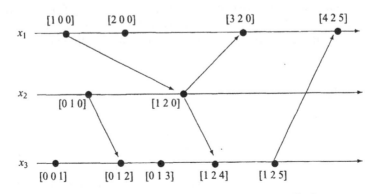

FIGURE 9.2: Virtual time generated by *VectorClocks*.

the message. For all other events (impulses and alarm clock ringing), $V_i(a)$ is just the value of vector V_i when event a is processed (recall that the local counter is increased as the first operation of the processing).

This system of local vectors defines a global time function V: For any event a at x_i, $V(a)$ is just $V_i(a)$. Notice that the values assigned to events by the time function V are vectors.

Let us now define the partial order we will use on vectors: Given any two n-dimensional vectors A and B, we say that $A \leq B$ if $A[i] \leq B[i]$ for all indices i; we say that $A < B$ if and only if $A \leq B$ and $A[i] < B[i]$ for at least an index i. So, for example, $[1\ 2\ 0] < [3\ 2\ 0]$.

Notice that from the definition, it follows that some values are not comparable; for example, $[1\ 3\ 0] \nleq [3\ 2\ 0]$ and $[3\ 2\ 0] \nleq [1\ 3\ 0]$.

It is not difficult to see that the global time V with the partial order so defined is a *virtual time*, that is, it satisfies the *Causal Order* property. In fact, by construction,

Property 9.2.2 *For any two events a and b at x_i, $V_i(a) < V_i(b)$ if and only if $t(a) < t(b)$.*

This means that V satisfies *local events* ordering. Next observe that these local vectors satisfy also *send/receive* ordering (Exercise 9.6.4):

Property 9.2.3 *Let a be an event in whose reaction a message is transmitted by x_i, and let b be the reception of that message by x_j. Then $V(a) = V_i(a) < V_j(b) = V(b)$.*

Therefore, these local vectors are indeed virtual clocks:

Lemma 9.2.1 *For any two events a and b, if $a \rightarrow b$, then $V(a) < V(b)$.*

Interestingly, as already mentioned, the converse is also true (Exercise 9.6.5):

Lemma 9.2.2 *For any two events a and b, if $V(a) < V(b)$, then $a \rightarrow b$.*

That is, by Lemmas 9.2.1 and 9.2.2, the local vectors satisfy the *Complete Causal Order* property:

Theorem 9.2.2 *Let V be the global time defined by the local counters of algorithm VectorClock. For any two events a and b, $V(a) < V(b)$ if and only if $a \rightarrow b$.*

Vector clocks have many other interesting properties also. For example, consider the vector clock when an entity x_i reacts to an event a; the value of each component of the vector clock $V_i(a)$ can give precise information about how many preceeding events are causally related to a. In fact,

Property 9.2.4   *Let a be an event occurring at x_i.*

1. $V_i(a)[j]$ *is the number of events e occurred at x_j such that $e \rightarrow a$.*
2. *The total number of events e where $e \rightarrow a$ is precisely $\sum_{j=1}^{n} V_i(a)[j] - 1$.*

It is also possible for an entity x_i to tell whether two received messages M' and M'' are causally related or independent;

Property 9.2.5   *Let $vect'$ and $vect''$ be the vectors included in messages M' and M'', respectively, received by x_i. If $vect' \langle vect''$ or $vect' \rangle vect''$, then the events that caused the transmission of those messages are causally related, else they are independent.*

This property is useful, for example, when we do want to discard obsolete messages: If two messages are independent, both should probably be kept; by contrast, if they are causally related, only the most recent (i.e., with the greater vector) needs to be kept.

Let us now consider the *cost* of algorithm *VectorClock*. This algorithm requires that an n-dimensional vector of counters is included in each message. By contrast, it ensures a much stronger property that not even real clocks can offer. Indeed, the dimension n is necessary to ensure *Complete Causal Order* using timestamps (Problem 9.6.1).

A way to decrease the amount of additional information transmitted with each message is to include in each message not the entire vector but only the entries that have changed since last message to the same neighbor.

For large systems with frequent communication, this approach can significantly reduce the total amount of transmitted data with respect to always sending the vector. The drawback is the increased storage and bookkeeping: Each entity x_i must remember, for each neighbor x_j and for each entry k in the vector, the last value of $V_i[k]$ that x_i sent to x_j. Another drawback is that Property 9.2.5 would no longer hold (Exercise 9.6.8).

9.2.4 Concluding Remarks

Hacking   In presenting algorithm *VectorClocks* we have assumed that there is an *a priori* total ordering of the entities, and that each entity knows both its rank in the ordering and the total number n of entities. This can be clearly obtained, for example, by performing a *ranking* protocol on the entities' ids. The cost for this operation is expensive, $O(n^2)$ messages in the worst case, even if there is already a leader and a spanning tree. However, this cost would be incurred only once, before the creation of the clocks takes place.

Interestingly, with simple modifications to algorithm *VectorClocks*, it is possible to achieve the goal (i.e., to construct a virtual clock satisfying the *Complete Causal Order* property) without any *a priori* knowledge and yet *without* incurring in any initial cost; even more interesting is the fact that, in some cases, maintaining the clocks requires much *less* information inside the messages.

We shall call this algorithm *PseudȯVectorClocks* and leave its specification and analysis as an exercise (Problem 9.6.2 and Exercise 9.6.9).

Bounding the Clocks   The major problem with both *CounterClocks* and with *VectorClocks* is that the values of the counters are monotonically increasing: They keep on growing. This means that these values and, hence, the bit complexity of the messages are *unbounded*.

This problem is quite serious especially with *VectorClocks*. A possible solution is to occasionally reset the vectors; the difficulty with this approach is clearly caused by messages in transit: The resetting of the virtual clocks will destroy any existing causal order between the arrival of these messages and the events that caused their transmission.

Any strategy to avoid this unfortunate consequence (Problem 9.6.3) is bound to be both expensive and intrusive.

9.3 DISTRIBUTED MUTUAL EXCLUSION

9.3.1 The Problem

In a distributed computing environment, there are many cases and situations in which it is necessary to give a single entity (or a single group of entities) exclusive control.

This occurs, for example, whenever computations require the presence of a central controller (e.g., because the coordination itself is more efficiently performed this way). During the lifetime of the system, this requirement will occur recurrently; hence, the problem is a *continuous* one. The typical solution used in these situations is to perform an *election* so as to select the coordinator every time one is needed. We have discussed and examined how to perform this task in details in Chapter 3. There are some drawbacks with the approach of repeatedly choosing a leader. The first and foremost is that it is usually *unfair*: Recall that there is no restriction on which entity will become leader; thus, it is possible that some entities will never assume such a role, while others (e.g., the ones with small ids) will always be chosen. This means that the workload is not really balanced within the system; this can also create additional bottlenecks. A secondary (but important) disadvantage of repeatedly electing a leader is its *cost*: Even if just performed on a (a priori constructed) spanning tree, at least $\Omega(n)$ messages will be required each time.

Another situation when exclusive control is necessary is when accessing a *critical resource* of a system. This is, for example, the case when only a single resource of some type (e.g., a printer, a bus) exists in the system and that resource cannot be used concurrently. In this case, any entity requiring the use of that resource must ensure that when it does so, it is the only one doing so. What is important is not the nature of the resource but the fact that it must be held in *mutual exclusion*: only one at the time. This means that when more than one entity may want to access the critical resource, only one should be allowed. Any mechanism must also clearly ensure that any request is eventually granted, that is, no entity will wait forever. The approach of using election, to select the entity to which access is granted, is unfortunately not a wise one. This is not (only) because of the cost but because of its unfairness: It does not guarantee that every entity wanting to access a resource will be allowed to do so (i.e., will become leader) within finite time.

This gives rise to a very interesting continuous problem, that of *distributed mutual exclusion*. We will describe it more precisely using the metaphor of *critical operations* in a continuous computation C. In this metaphor,

1. every entity is involved in a continuous computation C,
2. some operations that entities can perform in C are designed as *critical*,
3. an entity may need to perform a *critical* operation at any time, any number of times,
4. an entity required to perform a *critical* operation cannot continue C until that operation has been performed,

where an operation may be an action or even an entire subprotocol. A *distributed mutual exclusion* mechanism is any protocol that ensures the following two properties:

- *Mutual exclusion:* If an entity is performing a *critical* operation, no other entity is doing so.
- *Fairness:* If an entity wants to perform a *critical* operation, it will do so within finite time.

In the rest of this section we will see how to design efficient protocols with those properties. In the process, we will see that there is an interesting connection between the problem of distributed mutual exclusion and that of managing a distributed queue (another continuous computation). In particular, we will see how *any* protocol for fair management of a distributed queue can be used to solve the problem of distributed mutual exclusion. Throughout, we will assume restrictions **IR**.

9.3.2 A Simple and Efficient Solution

The problem of distributed mutual exclusion has a very simple and efficient *centralized* solution:

Protocol *Central*:

Initially, an entity is elected as leader; this entity will then coordinate the granting of permissions as follows:

1. each entity wanting to perform a critical operation sends a request to the leader; once granted permission, the entity performs its critical operation, and when finished, it informs the leader;
2. the leader grants permissions to one requesting entity at a time, ensuring that both mutual exclusion and fairness are satisfied.

The last point is achieved, for example, by having the leader keep the pending requests in a first in first out (FIFO) ordered list.

This very simple centralized protocol is not only correct but also quite efficient. In fact, for each critical operation, there is a request from the entity to the leader, a permission (eventually) from the leader to that entity, and the notification of termination from the entity back to the leader. Thus, there will be $3d(x, r)$ messages for each operation x wants to perform, where r is the leader; so, the operating cost of *Central* will be no more than

$$3 \operatorname{diam}(G)$$

messages *per* critical operation. This means that in a *complete graph* the cost will be only three messages per critical operation.

The drawbacks of this solution are those of all centralized solutions: The woarkload is not balanced; the leader might have to keep a large amount of information; the leader is a fault-tolerance bottleneck. As we are assuming total reliability, we will not worry for the moment about the issue of fault tolerance. The other two issues, however, are motivational enough to look for decentralized solutions.

9.3.3   Traversing the Network

To construct an efficient decentralized mutual-exclusion protocol, let us first reexpress the mechanism of the centralized protocol as follows: In the system there is a single "permission" *token*, initially held by the leader, and an entity can perform a critical operation only if in possession of such a token. It is this fact that ensures the *mutual exclusion* property within protocol *Central*. The *fairness* property is instead guaranteed in protocol *Central* because (1) the decision to which entity should the token be given is made by the leader, to whom the token is returned once a critical operation has been performed, and (2) the leader uses a fair decision mechanism (e.g., a FIFO list).

We can still enforce mutual exclusion using the idea of a permission token, and at the same time achieve fairness without having a leader, in a purely decentralized way. For example, we can have the token circulate among all the entities:

Protocol *EndlessTraversal*:

* A single token continuously performs a traversal of the network.
* When an entity x receives the token, if it needs to perform a critical operation, it will do so and upon completion, it will continue the circulation of the token; otherwise, it will circulate it immediately.
* If an entity needs to perform a critical operation, it will wait until it receives the token.

We have discussed at length how to efficiently perform a single traversal of a network (Section 2.3). Recall that a complete traversal can be done using a spanning tree of the network, at a cost of $2(n - 1)$ messages per traversal. If the network is Hamiltonian, that is, it has a spanning cycle, we can use that cycle to perform the traversal transmitting only n messages for a complete traversal. Indeed this is used in many practical systems.

What is the cost *per* critical operation of operating such a protocol? To answer this question, consider a period of time when all entities are continuously asking for the token; in this case, almost after each move, the token will be allowing an entity to perform a critical operation. This means that in such a situation of *heavy load*, the cost of *EndlessTraversal* is just $O(1)$ messages *per* critical operation. If the requests are few and infrequent, that is, with *light load*, the amount of messages *per* request is unpredictable as it depends on the time between successive requests and the speed of the token. From a practical point of view, this means that the management of a seldomly used resource may result in overcharging the network with messages.

Consider now a period of time where the entities have *no* need to perform any critical operations; during all this time, the token will continue to traverse the network, looking for entities needing it, and finding none. As this situation of *no load* can continue for an unpredictable amount of time, it follows that, in protocol *EndlessTraversal*, the number of messages *per* critical operation, is *unbounded*!

Let us see how this unpleasant situation can be improved. Let us consider the virtual ring R associated to the depth-first traversal of the network; in case the network is Hamiltonian, we will use the Hamiltonian cycle as the ring.

In a traversal, the token moves along R in one direction, call it "right." If a token reaches an entity that does *not* need to perform a critical operation (or just finished executing one), to cut down the number of message transmissions, instead of automatically forwarding the token along the ring, the entity will do so only if there are indeed requests for the token, that is, if there are entities wanting to perform a critical operation.

The problem is how to make the entity holding the token know if there are entities wanting it. This problem is fortunately easy to solve: An entity needing to perform a critical operation and not in possession of the token will issue a *request* for the token; the request travels along the ring in the opposite direction of the token, until it reaches the entity holding the token or an entity that has also issued a request for the token. There are many details that must be taken into account to transform this informal description into a protocol. Let us be more precise.

In our description, each link will have a color, and colors change depending on the type of message according to the following two rules:

- Links are either *white* or *black*; initially, all links are *white*.
- Whenever a *request* is sent on a link , that link becomes *black*; whenever the *token* is sent on a link, that link becomes *white*.

The resulting mechanism is then specified as follows:

Mechanism *OnDemandTraversal*:

1. When an entity needs to perform a critical operation and does not have the token, if its left link is white, it sends a *request* there and waits for the token.

2. When an entity receives a *request* (from the right link), if its left link is white, it forwards the *request* and waits for the token.

3. When an entity has received or receives the token, it will execute the following two steps:

   (a) if it needs to perform a critical operation, it performs it;

   (b) if its right link is black, it sends the token to the right.

In this way, instead of a blind endless traversal, we can have one that is fueled by requests for the token.

It is not difficult to verify that the corresponding protocol *OnDemandTraversal* is indeed correct, ensuring both mutual exclusion and fairness (Exercise 9.6.11). Unlike *EndlessTraversal*, the cost of protocol *OnDemandTraversal* is never unbounded. In fact, if there are no requests in the system, the token will not circulate. In other words, each traversal of the token satisfies at least a request, and possibly more. This means that in the worst case, a traversal satisfies exactly one request; in other words, the number of token movements *per* request is at most $\bar{n} - 1$, where $\bar{n}$ is the number of nodes on R. In addition to the token, the protocol also uses request messages. A request message, moving in the opposite direction of the token, moves along the ring until it finds the token or another entity waiting for the token. (NOTE: the token and a request never cross on a link (see Exercise 9.6.12).) This means that a request will cause at most $n - 1$ transmissions. Therefore, the total number of messages *per* critical operation in protocol *OnDemandTraversal* in the worst case is

$$2(\bar{n} - 1) \leq 4(n - 2).$$

Notice that although bounded, this is always worse than the cost obtained by *Central*. In particular, in a complete graph the worst case cost of *OnDemandTraversal* will be $2(n - 1)$, while in *Central*, as we have seen, three messages suffice.

The worst case does not tell us the whole story. In fact, the actual cost will depend on the frequency and the spread of the requests. In particular, like protocol *EndlessTraversal*, the more frequent the requests and the larger their spread, the more protocol will *OnDemandTraversal* have a performance approaching $O(1)$ messages *per* critical operation. This will be so, regardless of the diameter of the topology, even in networks where protocol *Central* under the same conditions could require $O(n)$ messages *per* request.

We have seen how to have the token move only if there are requests. The movements of the token, fueled by requests, were according to a perennial traversal of R, a cycle containing all the entities. If the network is Hamiltonian, we clearly choose R to be the Hamiltonian cycle; else we would like to construct the shortest such cycle. We do know that for any network we can always construct a spanning cycle R with $2(n - 1)$ nodes: The one obtained by a depth-first traversal of a spanning tree of the network.

9.3.4 Managing a Distributed Queue

In the previous section, we have seen mutual-exclusion solutions based on traversal of a ring. Notice that if starting from the token we move to the right (i.e., in the direction of movement of the token) along the ring, the order in which we encounter the entities needing the token is a total order; let us denote by $Q[t] = \langle x_1, x_2, \ldots, x_k \rangle$ the ordered sequence of those entities at time t.

We can think of the sequence $Q[t]$ as a single-ordered *queue*. Indeed, if no other entities request the token, those in the queue will receive the token precisely according to their order in the queue, and once an entity receives the token, it is removed from the queue. Any new request for the token, say from y at time $t' > t$, will have cause y to be inserted in the queue; its position in the the queue depends on its position in the ring R: If, among all the entities in the queue at time t', x_i (respective, x_{i+1}) is the closest to y on its left (respective right) in R, then y will be entered between x_i and x_{i+1}; that is, $Q[t'] = \langle x_1, x_2, \ldots, x_i, y, x_{i+1}, \ldots, x_k \rangle$. In other words, the execution of protocol *OnDemandTraversal* can be viewed as the management of a distributed ordered queue.

This point of view opens an interesting and surprising connection between the problem of distributed mutual exclusion and that of fair management of a distributed queue:

Any fair distributed queue-management technique solves distributed mutual exclusion.

The mutual-exclusion protocol is obtained from the queue-management protocol simply as follows (see Figure 9.3):

- every entity requesting the token is inserted in the queue;
- whenever an entity ends its critical operation and releases the token, an entity is removed from the queue and assigned the token.

Note that the queue does not need to be totally ordered; it is enough that every element in the queue is removed (i.e., receives the token) within finite time. Our goal is to use this approach to design a more efficient distributed mutual-exclusion protocol.

QUEUE   TOKEN

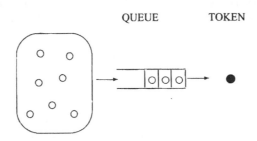

FIGURE 9.3: Mutual exclusion via queue management.

To this end we will examine a different fair management technique of a distributed ordered queue. This technique, called *Arrow*, maintains a *first-in-first-out* queue, that is, if the queue is $\langle x_1, x_2, \ldots, x_k \rangle$, and y makes a request for the token, the queue will become $\langle x_1, x_2, \ldots, x_k, y \rangle$, regardless of the location of y in the network. It uses a spanning tree of the network; it also requires the existence and availability of a correct *routing mechanism* (possibly, using only edges of the tree).

The strategy of *Arrow* is based on two ideas:

(i) the entity holding the token knows the identity of the first entity in the queue, and every entity in the queue knows the identity of the next one in the queue;

(ii) each link is logically directed toward the last entity in the queue.

The first idea allows an entity, once it has finished executing its critical operation, to know to which other entity it should send the token. The second idea, of making the tree rooted in the last entity in the queue, makes reaching the end of the queue very easy: Just follow the "arrow" (i.e., the direction of the links).

These two ideas can be implemented with a simple mechanism to handle requests and token transfers. Let us see how.

Assume that the needed structure is already in place, that is, (i) and (ii) hold. This means that every entity x knows which of its neighbors, last(x), is in the direction of the last entity in the queue; furthermore, if x is in the queue or holds the token, it knows the identity of the entity next(x) next in the queue (if any).

Let us consider first how to handle the token transfers. When the entity x currently holding the token terminates its critical operation, as it knows the identity of the first entity x_1 in the queue, it can send the token to it using the routing protocol; as we are assuming that the routing protocol is correct, this message will be delivered to x_1 within finite time. Notice that when x_1 receives the token, it is no longer in the queue, and it already knows the identity of the entity x_2 that should receive the token when it has finished. In other words, the handling of the token is done independently of the handling of the requests and is implemented using a correct routing protocol; thus, as long as every entity in the queue knows the identity of the next, token transfers pose no problems.

Consider now how to handle the requests. Let us consider an entity y, not in the queue, that now wants to access the queue (i.e., needs the token). Two things have to be accomplished to insert y in the queue: The last entity x_k in the queue must know the identity of y, and the tree must become rooted in y. It is easy for y to notify x_k: As the tree is rooted in x_k, y needs to just send a request message toward the root (i.e., to last(x)). To transform the tree into one rooted in y is also easy. As we have already seen many times before (e.g., in protocol *MegaMerger*), we need to "flip" the logical direction of the links on the path from y to x_k; thus, it is sufficient that each node receiving the request from y to x_k flips the direction of the link on which the message arrives. Summarizing, y sends a message requesting to enter the queue to the root of the tree (the last entity in the queue); this message will cause all the links from x to the root to flip their direction, transforming y in to the new root (the last entity in the queue). Notice that when the request message from y reaches the old root, that entity will know that y is now after it in the queue.

Summarizing, if the needed structure and information is in place, a single request for the token can be easily and simply handled, correctly maintaining and updating the structure and information.

If there are several concurrent requests for the token, the handling of one could interfere with the handling of another, for example, when trying to root the tree in the "last" entity in the queue: Indeed, which of them is going to be the last? Fortunately, concurrency is not a problem: The set of rules to handle a single request will correctly work for any number of them!

Let us first of all write down more precisely the set of rules:

Protocol *Arrow*:

- Initially, no entity is in the queue, next$(x) = x$ for every x, an entity r is holding the token, and the tree is rooted in r (i.e., all last$(\cdot)$ point toward r with last$(r) = r$).
- Handling requests
  - When entity x needs the token, it sends a "Request(x)" message containing its id to last(x) and sets last$(x) := x$.
  - When an entity y with last$(y) = w$ receives a "Request(x)" from z,
    1. it sets last$(y) := z$ (i.e., it flips the logical direction of the link (y, z));
    2. if $w \neq y$ (i.e., y is not waiting in the queue), then y forwards "Request(x)" to w,. otherwise,
       (a) y sets next$(y) := x$ (i.e., x is next after y in the queue);
       (b) if y holds the token and it is not in a critical operation, it executes *Token Transfer* (described below).
- Handling the token: An entity x holding the token, upon termination of a critical operation or, after termination, when prompted by the arrival of a request, executes the following:

Token Transfer

If next$(x) \neq x$ (i.e., the queue is not empty), using the routing protocol, x sends "Token(id)" to next(x), where id is the identity of next(x), and sets next$(x) := x$.

If two or more "Request" messages are issued concurrently, only one will reach the current root: The others will be diverted to one of the entities issuing one of the messages.

Example   Consider the situation shown in Figure 9.4. The token is at node d that is executing a critical operation, no entities are in the queue, and the tree is rooted in d. A request for the token is made by b and concurrently by c; both b and c set *last* to themselves and send their request following the direction of the arrow. The request

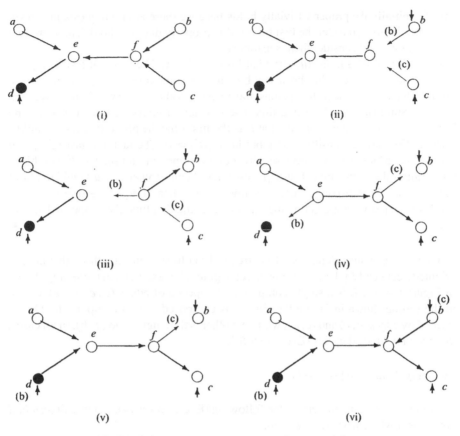

(i)

(ii)

(iii)

(iv)

(v)

(vi)

FIGURE 9.4: Two concurrent requests in protocol Arrow.

message from b arrives at f before that of c; f forwards the request to e (following the arrow) and flips the direction of the link to b setting last(f) = b. When f receives the request from c, it will forward it to b (following the arrow) and flip the direction of the link to c setting last(f) = c. In other words, the request from b is forwarded to d, while that from c is forwarded to b. As a result, at the end, next(d) = b and next(b) = c, that is, b is ahead of c in the queue. Had the message from c arrived at f before that of b, the outcome would have been reversed. Notice that at the end the tree is rooted in c.

The correctness of the protocol is neither obvious nor immediate. Let us see why it works. Observe that if there is a request in transit on a link, then the link is not directed toward any of the two entities connected by it. More precisely, let us denote by transit(u, v)[t] the set of messages in transit from u to neighbor v at time t; then,

Property 9.3.1   *If "Request" $\in transit(u, v)[t]$, then $last(u)[t] \neq v$ and $last(v)[t] \neq u$.*

Proof. Initially the property trivially holds because there are no requests in transit. By contradiction, consider the first time t' this property does not hold. There are two cases, and we will consider them separately.

Case 1: "Request" $\in$ transit$(u, v)[t']$ but last$(u)[t'] = v$. The fact that last$(u)[t'] = v$ implies that a "Request" has been sent by v to u at some time $t < t'$, but this in turn implies that at that time last$(v)[t]$ must have been u (otherwise v would not have sent it to u). Summarizing, there is a time $t < t'$ when "Request"$\in$ transit$(v, u)[t]$ and last$(u) = v$, contradicting the fact that t' is the first time the property does not hold.

Case 2: "Request"$\in$ transit$(u, v)[t']$, but last$(v)[t'] = u$. The fact that last$(v)[t'] = u$ implies that a "Request" has been sent by u to v at some time at time $t < t'$; but this in turn implies that at that time, last$(u)[t]$ must have been v (otherwise u would not have sent it to v). Summarizing, there is a time $t < t'$ when "Request"$\in$ transit$(u, v)[t]$ and last$(u)[t] = v$, contradicting the fact that t' is the first time the property does not hold. ∎

Consider now the orientation of the tree links at time t ignoring those that are not oriented; let us call $L[t]$ the resulting directed graph. For example, in the setting shown in Figure 9.4 (ii), L is a single component composed of edges (a, e), (f, e), (e, d); in the setting shown in Figure 9.4 (iii), L is composed of two components: One is formed by edges (a, e) and (e, d), while the other is the single edge (f, b). In all cases, there are no directed cycles (Exercise 9.6.13):

Property 9.3.2 $L[t]$ *is acyclic.*

Another important property is the following (Exercise 9.6.14). Let us call *terminal* any node u where $last(u) = u$; then,

Property 9.3.3   *In $L[t]$, from any nonterminal node there is a directed path to exactly one terminal entity.*

We will call such a path *terminal*. We are now ready to prove the main correctness property. Let us call an entity *waiter* at time t if it has requested a token and it has not yet received it at time t; then, using Properties 9.3.1, 9.3.2, and 9.3.3, we have (Exercise 9.6.15),

Theorem 9.3.1   *In $L[t]$ any terminal path leads to either the entity holding the token or a waiter.*

We need to show that, within finite time, every message will stop traveling. Call target$(v)[t]$ the terminal node at the end of the terminal path of v at time t; if a "Request" is traveling from u to v at time t, then the target of the message is target $(v)[t]$. Then (Exercise 9.6.16),

Theorem 9.3.2   *Every request will be delivered to its target.*

Let us now examine the *cost* of achieving distributed mutual exclusion using protocol *Arrow*. The request from x_i must reach x_{i-1} and eventually the token will be transferred from x_{i-1} to x_i; if the routing protocol uses the spanning tree, then the cost will be exactly $2\,d_T(x_{i-1}, x_i)$. This cost clearly depends on T and on the location of these entities on T; in the worst case, the cost *per* critical operation is

$$2\,\mathrm{diam}(T),$$

which is achievable. This means that the number of messages in the worst case is always better that that of protocol *OnDemandTraversal*.

In situations of high load (i.e., frequent requests from many entities), the improvement (if any at all) strongly depends on the structure of the spanning tree (see Exercise 9.6.17).

9.3.5 Decentralized Permissions

In the centralized solution, every entity needing to perform a critical operation would ask for permission to do so; as there was one entity capable of granting such a permission, the request would be sent just there.

We can still use the same idea, of asking for permission and waiting to obtain it, in a decentralized way: If an entity x needs to perform a critical operation, it asks *all* the other entities for their permission and it will perform the critical operation when it receives permission from *all* entities. An entity y, upon receiving such a request, will grant its permission if not performing a critical operation or waiting itself to receive permission.

In other words, if no other entity is currently performing a critical operation or waiting itself to receive permission, x will be allowed to perform its critical operation.

What happens, however, if some entity y is performing a critical operation or waiting for permissions? We must specify some rules that ensure that even in this case x will indeed receive permission from all entities within finite time.

This is done by first of all imposing a *total order* on the requests so that, given any two different requests r_1 and r_2, either $r_1 > r_2$ or $r_1 < r_2$. Assuming this is done, the general rulers are as follows:

Strategy *AskAll*:

- When an entity x needs to perform a critical operation, it sends a request $r(x)$ to *all* other entities asking for their permission; it will perform the critical operation when it receives permission from *all* entities.
- When an entity y receives a request $r(x)$ for permission,
    - if y is not executing a critical operation nor it is waiting for permission, it grants its permission to $r(x)$;
    - if y is executing its critical operation, it inserts $r(x)$ into a local FIFO queue $Q(y)$;
    - if y is waiting for permissions, it grants its permission to $r(x)$ immediately if $r(x) < r(y)$; otherwise (i.e., $r(x) > r(y)$) it inserts $r(x)$ into a local FIFO queue $Q(y)$.

- When an entity z finishes performing its critical operation, it removes from $Q(z)$ one request at the time and grants to it its permission.

The broadcasting of a request by x to all entities is easily and efficiently done by flooding on the spanning tree. The collection of the permissions can be performed as a delayed convergecast toward x on the tree: Think of the tree as rooted in x; starting from the leaves, a node transmits its permission to its "parents" only after it receives the permission from all its "children" and itself has granted the permission. This means that this strategy would cost $2(n - 1)$ messages *per* critical operation.

Unfortunately, this simple strategy does not always work. In fact, its correctness relies on the total order imposed on the requests, but not every total order will do. To understand what can go wrong, consider first the following example.

Example Consider the following total order. When x issues a request, the value associated to its request is the ordered couple $r(x) = (\mathrm{id}(x), t_x)$ composed of the id of x and of the value t_x of the local clock when the request is made. These couples are clearly totally ordered as the ids are unique. Unfortunately, in this total order, *all* the requests by x come before those of y if $\mathrm{id}(x) < \mathrm{id}(y)$; this means that it is possible for x, by continuously issuing requests, to forever prevent y from performing a critical operation, violating the *fairness* condition!

In the example we just examined, the problem was due to the nature of the specific total order. There might be problems also with other total orders.

Example Suppose that y sends its request and that no entity is performing a critical operation or is requesting a permission; thus, every entity receiving the request $r(y)$ will grant its permission. After it has granted permission to $r(y)$, entity x now needs to perform a critical operation; x then broadcasts its request $r(x)$. Assume $r(x) < r(y)$. It is indeed possible that $r(x)$ arrives at y *before* y has received all the permission for its request; in this case, as $r(x) < r(y)$, y will grant its permission to $r(x)$. As a consequence, within finite time both y and x will perform a critical operation, violating the *mutual exclusion* condition!

These two examples show that the total order imposed on the requests cannot be arbitrary; rather, it must satisfy some temporal constraints. Indeed, the property we need is the following:

- *Temporal Constraint*: If a request $r(x)$ is generated after x has granted its permission to a request $r(y)$ generated by y, then $r(x) > r(y)$.

In fact

Theorem 9.3.3 *Under* Temporal Constraint,

1. *at any time, at most one entity is executing a critical operation, and*
2. *every request receives permissions from all entities within finite time.*

Let us prove mutual exclusion. By contradiction, let two entities x and y perform a critical operation at the same time; this means that each must have granted permission to the request of the other. Without loss of generality, let $r(x) < r(y)$. Under this condition, the only reason why x would grant its permission to $r(y)$ is that $r(y)$ arrives *before* x issued $r(x)$ (otherwise, as $r(x) < r(y)$, x would not have granted the permission). In this case, however, according to the *Temporal Constraint*, $r(x) > r(y)$: a contradiction.

To prove fairness, we need to show that each convergecast is eventually completed; this is left as an exercise (Exercise 9.6.18).

Let us see now how to ensure *Temporal Constraint*. Observe that this property can be easily achieved using the *virtual clocks* discussed in Section 9.2.2. What an entity x needs to do is to advance the value of its virtual clock whenever it wants to issue a request and use that value as $r(x)$. The properties of virtual clocks ensure that *Temporal Constraint* holds (Exercise 9.6.19).

We will call *AskAllClocks* the resulting protocol employing logical clocks in its rules (Exercise 9.6.20).

9.3.6 Mutual Exclusion in Complete Graphs: Quorum

In the case of a complete network, the approaches that we have described so far become rather straightforward. New ones can actually be devised that would be not efficient in other networks. In the following we will consider how to render the permission-based approach of *AskAll* more efficient in the case of a complete network.

In protocol *AskAllClocks*, each request must be granted a permission from every entity. A way to reduce the amount of messages is to reduce the number of permissions needed before an entity can perform its critical operation. Clearly, we would need to change the permission-granting mechanism to ensure that two or more entities are *not* allowed to perform a critical operation concurrently.

To achieve this goal, let us examine protocol *AskAllClocks*. In this protocol, if an entity neither has issued a request nor is performing a critical region, it will "accept" (i.e., grant its permission to) *all* incoming requests, that is, it treats requests in a nonexclusive way. If the entity has made its own request, until it is granted permission from all entities, it will accept *all* incoming requests with smaller value, that is, it treats requests with smaller value in a nonexclusive way.

What we can do is to render the permission granting mechanism *exclusive*: If an entity grants permission to a request, it will not accept any other request until the first one has been resolved (i.e. the requesting entity has performed its critical operation).

Note that with such a rule, if an entity receives just $\lfloor n/2 \rfloor + 1$ permissions for its own request, it knows that no other request will be able to have so many permissions, and it can, therefore, perform its critical operation. All of this with half of the permissions. At a first glance it appears that with this approach we can ensure mutual exclusion with fewer permissions. There are, however, several problems.

First of all observe that the main goal of reducing the number of messages is not achieved: A request is still sent to all entities that, if there are no other requests, will all send their permissions, for a total of $2(n - 1)$ messages *per* request. To resolve this problem, we will have each entity ask for permissions not from all other entities but rather from a specific *subset*. In this way, the number of messages for a request by x will be twice the size of the subset associated to x. So what we would like to do is to select these sets as small as possible. However, we still must ensure that mutual exclusion is preserved; to do so, it is necessary that, for any two entities x and y, their subsets have at least an entity z in common; in this way, if z grants permission to x, it will not do so to y concurrently.

Specifically, let $S(x)$ denote the subset associated to x; then for all x and y,

1. $S(x) \cap S(y) \neq \emptyset$
2. not $S(x) \subset S(y)$.

The collection of such sets is called a *coterie*, and the set $S(x)$ is called the *quorum* of x.

Summarizing, each entity wanting to perform a critical operation will now send its request only to the members of its quorum and will start the operation only once it receives permission from all of them. Notice that when the quorum of each entity is composed of all other entities, that is, $S(x) = \mathcal{E} \setminus \{x\}$ for all x, we are exactly in the same situation we started with, in which every entity must request all other entities for permission.

The second problem is major and persists regardless of the size of the quorums: If there are concurrent requests, it is possible that none of them receives permissions from every member of its quorum; for example, consider three entities x, y, and z all asking for permission concurrently; the quorums of any two of them have at least an entity in common: Let $u \in S(x) \cap S(y)$, $v \in S(y) \cap S(z)$, $w \in S(x) \cap S(z)$, with u, v, and w distinct nodes. Let u receive first the request of x, v that of y, and w that of z; then u will grant its permission to x and put on hold the request for y, v will grant its permission to y and put on hold the request for z, and w will grant its permission to z and put on hold the request for x. Hence, none of x, y, and z will receive a permission from all its quorum, so none will ever be allowed to perform a critical operation; furthermore, all the incoming requests from other entities will also be put on hold. In other words, the system will be *deadlocked*.

To remedy this, we will make permissions "contestable" and "revocable", that is, an entity that has granted its permission, it might under some conditions to revoke its permission and grant it to some other request. Let us describe the entire new process.

Consider an entity z that is not executing a critical operation and that has not given permission to any request (still pending); if it receives a *request* $r(x)$, then it grants its permission to x (by sending a *grant* message). If x receives permissions from every entity in its quorum, it will start its critical operation; upon termination, it will notify its quorum that the request is no longer pending (by sending a *completed* message).

Consider the case when z has granted permission to a request $r(y)$ (still pending), and it receives a *request* $r(x)$. If $r(x) > r(y)$, then z will locally enqueue the request and notify x (by sending a *on hold* message).

If instead $r(x) < r(y)$, then z must decide whether or not to revoke the permission given to y and to transfer it to x. It does so by sending a *probe* message to y and waiting for an answer; during this time, z will not send any other *probe* to y. If the reply is that it is all right to revoke the permission (i.e., it receives a *revoke* message from y), then z will grant its permission to x.

Let us see under what conditions y will tell z that it is all right to revoke the granted permission. The general rule will be that if an entity receives an *on hold* answer to its request, then it must reply with *revoke* to any *probe* message it receives, that is, if its request is put on hold, an entity will give up on all permissions that are being contested. Therefore, when the *probe* from z arrives at y, if y has already received a *on hold* message, it will send a *revoke* message to z; otherwise, y waits to see what the replies to its request will be: Should one of them be *on hold*, y will send *revoke* to z. By contrast, if none of the replies to its request has been *on hold*, then y has received permission from everybody in its quorum; hence y will start its critical operation; upon termination, it will notify all its quorum (including z), that the request is no longer pending (by sending a *completed* message).

Summarizing, if $r(x) < r(y)$, then z will receive as a reply to its *probe* to y either a *revoke* or a *completed* message. In either case, z will then grant its permission to x.

Notice the similarity between the *probe* and that used in the election protocol *Complete* for complete graphs. The entire set of rules of the corresponding protocol *AskQuorum* must take into account several important details (e.g., how to enqueue and dequeue requests); proving its correctness in nontrivial but not overly difficult; see Exercises 9.6.21 and 9.6.22.

The *cost* of the protocol is not difficult to determine: Each *request* message can cause a *probe* message, replied by a *revoke* message that will cause a *grant* and (eventually) the corresponding *release*. Alternatively, each *request* can cause just an *on hold* reply followed eventually by a *grant* and eventually by the corresponding *release*. As the request of an entity x is sent to its quorum $S(x)$, the total number of messages *per* request by x is at most $5|S(x)|$. That means that, in the worst case, the number of messages *per* critical operation is

$$5 \max_x \{||S(x)||\}.$$

If we want just to minimize this quantity, we can choose the coterie where each quorum is composed of a single entity, the same for all quorums, that is, $S(x) = S(y) = r$ for all x, y. Notice that in this case, we have exactly the centralized approach to distributed mutual exclusion: r is the central controller ensuring both fairness and mutual exclusion; the cost will be just five messages *per* critical operation, which is actually worse than that of protocol *Central* when used in a complete graph.

The drawback with this choice of coterie is the same as with any centralized solution. In particular, the load is unbalanced: r receives and must handle almost all the traffic in the system. Indeed, a desirable requirement for a coterie is that it is balanced. To formalize this concept, let the load of x in a coterie C be the number $load(x)$ of quorums in which x appears. Let $load_{max}$ and $load_{min}$ denote the maximum

x_1	x_2	x_3	x_4
x_5	x_6	x_7	x_8
x_9	x_{10}	x_{11}	x_{12}
x_{13}	x_{14}	x_{15}	x_{16}

FIGURE 9.5: Constructing coterie *Square*.

and minimum among the loads of the entities, respectively. We say that a coterie is α-unbalanced, $1 \leq \alpha \leq n$, if

$$\frac{\text{load}_{\max}}{\max\{1, \text{load}_{\min}\}} \leq \alpha.$$

Clearly, the smaller the α, the more balanced the collective load. In particular, when $\alpha = 1$, the load is perfectly balanced. By contrast, the centralized coterie, $\{\{r\}, \{r\} \ldots, \{r\}\}$, is the most unbalanced with $\alpha = n$.

To minimize both quantities, $\max_x\{|S(x)|\}$ and α, we should choose the coterie so that each quorum has (approximately) the same size and each entity is (approximately) in the same number of quorums.

A simple method to achieve this goal is the following. Assume for simplicity that $n = p^2$. Arrange all entities in a $p \times p$ matrix; then the quorum $S(x)$ of x is composed of the entities in the row and in the column containing x.

In this coterie, each quorum contains exactly $2(p - 1) = 2(\sqrt{n} - 1)$ entities; as every entity is in exactly $2(p - 1) = 2(\sqrt{n} - 1)$ quorums, $\alpha = 1$. For example, using the matrix shown in Figure 9.5 where $n = 16$, entity x_7 will have quorum $\{x_3, x_5, x_6, x_8, x_{11}, x_{15}\}$, and it will be in the quorum of precisely those entities.

If n is not a perfect square, we can use a $\lceil \sqrt{n} \rceil \times \lceil \sqrt{n} \rceil$ array where some entities are necessarily repeated. The corresponding coterie, called *Square*, will yield a worst-case cost of

$$10(\lceil \sqrt{n} \rceil - 1)$$

messages per critical operation; its α is not far from 1 (Exercise 9.6.23).

Notice that coterie *Square* is not optimal among the balanced ones (Exercise 9.6.24). Further notice that to be usable, the coterie must be constructed before the mutual-exclusion protocol takes place.

9.3.7 Concluding Remarks

Performance We have employed different strategies to construct efficient protocols for distributed mutual exclusion and analyzed their cost in terms of number of messages *per* critical operation. We have seen how this cost sometimes depends on the load of the system, that is, how frequent and widespread the requests are (see Figure 9.6). In all these protocols the messages have normal size (i.e., contain only a constant number of data items); clearly and trivially, if the system allows very long

protocol	messages *per* critical operation	remarks	disadvantages
Central	$3d(T)$		unbalanced
Endless Traversal	∞ $O(1)$	light/no load heavy load	unbounded cost
OnDemand Traversal	$4(n-2)$ $O(1)$	light load heavy load	
Arrow	$2d(T)$		requires routing
AskAllClocks	$2(n-1)$		requires logical clocks

FIGURE 9.6: Protocols for distributed mutual exclusion.

messages (e.g., containing the list of all pending requests), the number of messages decreases. In those cases, to compare protocols , the *bit* complexity should be used instead.

The number of messages (or of bits) *per* critical operation is not the only factor to be taken into account. In particular, in addition to the amount of work (i.e., message transmissions), we are interested in how this work is distributed among the entities, on whether or not it is balanced. All decentralized protocols are better in this respects than protocol *Central*; they all, however, have drawbacks either in terms of poorer performance or because requiring additional tools and mechanisms.

Fault Tolerance The issue of fault tolerance is relevant not only for centralized solutions but also for decentralized ones as well. None of the protocols we have considered considers the possibility of faults, and indeed these protocols would not work correctly, should a failure occur.

The task of designing fault-tolerant protocols (e.g., of making the proposed ones fault tolerant) can be achieved, as we know, by adding capabilities to the system (e.g., synchrony, fault detection). The goal is in particular to ensure that the protocol satisfies the following consequence of the fairness requirement, which is explicit in the classical (i.e., nondistributed) mutual-exclusion problem:

Any entity not performing a critical operation must not prevent an entity wanting to perform a critical operation from doing so.

This means that if an entity fails when *not* performing a critical operation, this failure should not prevent other entities from performing their critical operations.

To achieve this goal we assume reliable fault detection and that if/when faults occur, there will be enough time for both detection and restorative action. For some protocols, the transformation into a fault-tolerant one is not difficult. Consider for example protocol *Central* and consider crash failures of entities. Should any entity other than the leader fail, or recover after a failure, then no action is necessary and no messages need to be transmitted. If the leader fails, on the other hand, a new leader must be elected and all entities must resubmit their requests to the new leader before normal functioning can resume. For other protocols, however, the requirement of being able to tolerate crash failures requires major modifications.

9.4 DEADLOCK: SYSTEM DETECTION AND RESOLUTION

9.4.1 System Detection and Resolution

We have examined the problem *distributed deadlock detection* in some detail in Section 8.2. There, we considered two *terminating* versions, the personal detection and the collective detection problems, both with static and with dynamic requests.

In real systems, however, the requests are only *dynamic* and the main problem, is a *continuous* one: Requests are continuously and unpredictably generated, possibly creating deadlocks, and every deadlock in the system must be *resolved* within finite time from its occurrence.

Resolving a deadlock means that some requests must be aborted so that the resulting wait-for graph is free of deadlock. Clearly, to be resolved, a deadlock must first be detected. The mechanism, specifying how to detect the occurrence of deadlock and how to decide which requests to abort, forms the core to the solution of this continuous problem that we will call *system detection and resolution*. Clearly, in this mechanism, we can employ the protocols for personal or collective detection we designed and discussed in Section 8.2.

To solve this problem, we will use the general strategy of repeatedly having one or more entities start a personal detection protocol; to work correctly, this strategy must ensure that if a deadlock occurs, at least one entity involved in it will sooner or later start a personal detection. Regardless of the type of requests are allowed in the system (e.g., single request, multiple requests, OR requests, etc.) we will use the same rule to decide by whom and when a personal detection should be started:

- Whenever an entity waits for a permission longer than a predefined *timeout* value, the entity will initiate the detection process.

Thus, any entity requesting a permission, after waiting "too long," will start a personal detection. Once a deadlock has been detected, in the strategy the resolution mechanism takes place, ensuring that only the necessary requests are aborted and that the deadlock is indeed resolved.

IMPORTANT. In this strategy, when using personal detection, we do not actually need the initiator to be notified of the result. In fact, if it is detected that there is no deadlock, then there is nothing to be resolved; hence, the entity making the discovery need not notify the initiator and the detection process can terminate. Similarly, if there is a deadlock, the entity making the discovery can start the resolution mechanism immediately, with no need to notify the initiator that a deadlock exists. Hence, in our strategy we will use this scaled down version of the personal detection protocols.

Notice that there might be several deadlocks in the system at the same time, some being formed while the computation is taking place, and that several entities can independently detect the presence of the same deadlock. Hence, efficiency is of paramount importance. Analogously to the other continuous computations, we will measure the cost of a solution as the total number of messages transmitted *per* request.

We will consider the problem under the standard assumptions: connectivity, Bidirectional Links, complete reliability, and unique identifiers. We will also assume message ordering, that is, the links are FIFO.

9.4.2 Detection and Resolution in Single-Request Systems

Let us consider the problem in systems where a nonwaiting entity can ask for only one permission at a time. In this case, we know that there is a deadlock in the system if and only if there is a cycle in the wait-for graph.

We can use protocol *SimpleCheck* for detection without the final notification to the initiator: The message will travel until it reaches the root of the component (if there is no deadlock in the component) or the closest entity in the crown (if there is deadlock in the component). In the first case, the root will just discard the message. In the second case, that entity in the crown will detect the existence of the deadlock when it receives the message for the second time; the resolution mechanism must be started now.

Notice that, to resolve a deadlock in the single-request model, it is necessary and also sufficient to abort a single request in the core (i.e., remove one edge from the cycle). This means that we must first of all know which edges in the wait-for graph form the cycle.

Further notice that, as mentioned earlier, it is possible that several entities in the same component start detection independently. In this case, the same deadlock (assuming one exists) will be detected by several entities. As we need to remove only one link, to decide which one, we will run an *election* among the entities of the core that have detected the deadlock: The leader will then abort its own request, destroying the cycle and resolving the deadlock. Observe that, once this is done, the component becomes a tree rooted in the leader.

To design protocol *SingleDetectResolve* implementing this strategy (Problem 9.6.4), several minor issues must be solved. For example, to run the ring-election protocol on the core, the entities initiating that protocol must know which of its possibly many links are those in the cycle (Exercise 9.6.25). Also, once the election process is started, any subsequent detection message should be stopped from circulating in the ring.

What is the cost of this protocol *SingleDetectResolve*? We will separate the costs of the detection from those of the resolution; this is because in our strategy, the detection cost is incurred for each request, while the resolution is performed only once a deadlock is detected.

The cost for detection are just those of protocol *SimpleCheck* minus the notification. In absence of deadlock, the message travels to the root and dies there, using at most $\bar{n} - 1$ transmissions, where $\bar{n}$ is the number of entities in the component of the initiator. In presence of deadlock, the message will travel also along the core; still, the entire process will cause a total of at most $\bar{n}$ transmissions. Hence, the detection component of *SingleDetectResolve* uses at most $\bar{n}$ messages *per* request.

Let us now consider the resolution process of protocol *SingleDetectResolve*. Once a deadlock is detected, the detecting agent will start an election protocol along the ring; using an efficient ring-election protocol, for example, *Stages*, the cost *per deadlock* is at most $2\bar{n} \log \bar{n}$ messages.

9.4.3 Detection and Resolution in Multiple-Requests Systems

In systems where a nonwaiting entity can ask for many permission at a time (i.e., AND, OR, p-OF-q, generalized systems), the solution strategy will be the same as for single-request systems:

Strategy *DetectResolve*:

1. Any entity after waiting too long for permission(s) starts a personal detection protocol for dynamic wait-for graphs.
2. Whenever an entity detects the existence of a deadlock, it becomes a *candidate* and starts an election process to elect a leader among the candidates in its component; during this process, further detection messages in the component are discarded.
3. Once elected, the leader chooses which link(s) must be removed (i.e., which request(s) must be aborted) and ensures that this is done.

The cost of this strategy clearly depends on the types of requests allowed in the system and on the protocols used for personal detection and for election. In the case of AND requests, for example, if we use protocol *DynamicDeadGrant* for personal detection and protocol *MegaMerger* for election in the component, the cost will be at most

$$6\bar{m} - \bar{n} + 1$$

messages *per* request, and at most

$$2\bar{m} + 5\bar{n} \log \bar{n}$$

messages *per* deadlock.

9.5 BIBLIOGRAPHICAL NOTES

The notions of virtual clocks and causal order were first explicitly stated and analyzed by Leslie Lamport to whom Algorithm *CounterClocks* is due. The idea of *vector time*, on which protocol *VectorClocks* is based, has been independently discovered by several people in distributed database management: by Douglas Parker, Gerald Popek, Gerard Rudisin, Allen Stoughton, Bruce Walker, Evelyn Walton, Johanna Chow, David Edwards, Stephen Kiser, and Charles Kline [24]; Gene Wuu and Arthur Bernstein [36]; and Robert Strom and Shaula Yemini [33]. The concept of vector time as an extension of virtual time was independently introduced by Colin Fidge [8] and by Friedemann Mattern [19]; they examined its properties and designed protocol *VectorClocks*. The mathematical structure of vector time has been extensively investigated by Reinhard Schwarz and Friedemann Mattern [29], and by Friedemann Mattern [20].

Protocol *VectorClocks+* (Exercise 9.6.6) is due to Mukesh Singhal and Ajay Kshemkalyani [31], while Exercise 9.6.8 is due to Sigurd Melda, Sriram Sankar, and James Vera [21]. Protocol *PseudoVectorClocks* (Problem 9.6.2) has been designed by Mark Wineberg [unpublished]. The fact that n-dimensional timestamps are needed to ensure *Complete Causal Order* has been proven by Bernadette Charron-Bost [5].

In the context of *distributed mutual exclusion*, circular token-based control (i.e., protocol *EndlessTraversal*) is the most commonly used mechanism in practical systems, ranging from token rings to bus networks and to hub polling systems; it is indeed at the basis of several IEEE standards. Although its cost is theoretically unbounded, an extensive amount of literature exists on the performance of the resulting system. The bounded-cost protocol *OnDemandTraversal* and other variants were designed and analyzed by Esteban Feuerstein, Stefano Leonardi, Alberto Marchetti-Spaccamela, and Nicola Santoro [7].

Most of the research work on distributed mutual exclusion has focused on *complete graphs*. In this context, the idea of using logical clocks to impose a total order satisfying the *temporal condition* was proposed by Leslie Lamport [16]; the improvement at the base of protocol *AskAllClock* was designed by Glenn Ricart and Ashok Agrawala [27]; a way of bounding the values of the timestamps was proposed by Ikiro Suzuki and Tadao Kasami [34]; further improvements in the constant were obtained by O.S.F. Carvalho and Gerard Roucairol [4].

The idea of using just a *majority* of (instead of all) the permissions had been introduced much earlier by Bob Thomas [35] together with the idea of using *timestamps* to tag requests. The notion of majority was extended by Dave Gifford, who proposed *weighted voting* [10]. The notions of *coterie* and of *quorum set* were first introduced by Daniel Barbara and Hector Garcia-Molina [2, 9]. Coterie *Square* is due to Mamoru Maekawa [18], whose protocol, however, suffered from deadlock (in the same way protocol *AskAll* does), as pointed out by Beverly Sanders [28]. Other quorum-based protocols have been developed by Divyakant Agrawal and Amr El Abbadi [1], Mukesh Singal [30], Toshihide Ibaraki and Tiko Kameda [13], and Mitchell Nielsen, Masaaki Mizuno, and Michele Raynal [23], among others. Always for complete graphs, the mutual exclusion of Mohamed Naimi, Michel Trehel, and Andre Arnold [22] is based on path reversal.

The basic structure of protocol *Arrow* was designed by Kerry Raymond [26]; some ideas of the protocol were also informally described by Jan van de Snepscheut [32]. The design has been further refined by Michael Demmer and Maurice Herlihy [6] who designed the version presented here and proved its correctness; a variant has been designed by David Peleg and Eilon Reshef [25]. An in-depth analysis of its complexity and performance has been carried out by Christian Lavault [17] and, more recently, by Fabian Kuhn and Roger Wattenhofer [15]. Another protocol for general graph is due to Jean-Michel Helary, Noel Plouzeau, and Michel Raynal [11].

We have reviewed the literature on *deadlock* detection in Chapter 8. The more general continuing problem of *system detection and resolution* is the one really occurring in systems. The solution strategy considered in this chapter has been extensively investigated and experimentally analyzed under all types of systems, for example by Natalija Krivokapic, Alfons Kemper, and Ehud Gudes [14]. The issue of how long an entity should wait before using timeout has been studied by Micha Hofri [12] and extensively discussed by Philip A. Bernstein and Eric Newcomer [3].

9.6 EXERCISES, PROBLEMS, AND ANSWERS

9.6.1 Exercises

Exercise 9.6.1 Let T be a virtual time, that is, it satisfies both *local events* ordering and *send/receive* ordering. Prove that for any two events a and b, if $a \to b$ then $T(a) < T(b)$. *(Hint: by induction on the length of any sequence of events.)*

Exercise 9.6.2 Let C be the virtual time constructed by algorithm *CounterClocks*. For each of the following situations, provide a small example showing its occurrence:

1. $t(a) > t(b)$ but $C(a) < C(b)$
2. $t(a) = t(b)$ while $C(a) < C(b)$
3. $t(a) < t(b)$ but $C(a) = C(b)$
4. $t(a) < t(b)$ while $C(a) > C(b)$

Exercise 9.6.3 Let C be the virtual time constructed by algorithm *CounterClocks*. For each of the following situations, provide a small example showing its occurrence:

1. $t(a) > t(b) > t(c)$ but $C(a) = C(b) > C(c)$
2. $t(a) = t(b) = t(c)$ while $C(a) < C(c) < C(b)$
3. $t(a) < t(b) < t(c)$ but $C(a) > C(b) > C(c)$

Exercise 9.6.4 Let V be the global time constructed by algorithm *VectorClocks*. Prove that V satisfies *send/receive* ordering.

Exercise 9.6.5 Let V be the global time constructed by algorithm *VectorClocks*. Prove that for any two events a and b, if $V(a) < V(b)$ then $a \to b$.

Exercise 9.6.6 Modify algorithm *VectorClocks* so as to include in each message not the entire vector but only the entries that have changed as last message to the same neighbor. Prove the correctness of the resulting protocol *VectorClocks+*.

Exercise 9.6.7 Implement and throughly test protocol *VectorClocks+* of question 9.6.6. Compare experimentally the amount of information transmitted by *VectorClocks+* with that of *VectorClocks*.

Exercise 9.6.8 Consider protocol *VectorClocks+* of Exercise 9.6.6. Prove that Property 9.2.5 no longer holds.

Exercise 9.6.9 (⋆) Implement and throughly test protocol *PseudoVectorClocks* of Problem 9.6.2. Compare experimentally the amount of information transmitted by *PseudoVectorClocks* with that of *VectorClocks*.

Exercise 9.6.10 Consider a complete network. Modify protocol *Central* so that with three messages per critical operation, the leader needs only to keep one item of information, instead of the entire set of pending requests. Prove correctness of the resulting protocol.

Exercise 9.6.11 Prove that protocol *OnDemandTraversal* is correct, ensuring both mutual exclusion and fairness.

Exercise 9.6.12 Prove that in protocol *OnDemandTraversal*, a request message and the token cannot cross each other on a link.

Exercise 9.6.13 Prove that at any time t during the execution of protocol *Arrow*, $L[t]$ is acyclic.

Exercise 9.6.14 Prove that at any time t during the execution of protocol *Arrow*, from any nonterminal node there is a directed path to exactly one terminal entity.

Exercise 9.6.15 An entity is said to be a *waiter* at time t if it has requested a token and it has not yet received it at time t. Prove that at any time t during the execution of protocol *Arrow*, in $L[t]$ any terminal path leads either to the entity holding the token or to a waiter.

Exercise 9.6.16 Prove that during the execution of protocol *Arrow*, every request will be delivered to its target within finite time.

Exercise 9.6.17 Compare experimentally the performance of protocols *Arrow* and *OnDemandTraversal* under different load conditions. Investigate the impact of the structure of the spanning tree on their performace.

Exercise 9.6.18   Prove that under *Temporal Constraint*, in protocol *AskAll* every request receives permissions from all entities within finite time.

Exercise 9.6.19   Show how to use using *virtual clocks* to ensure that property *Temporal Constraint* holds.

Exercise 9.6.20   ($\star$) Write the set of rules corresponding to Strategy *AskAll* using logical clocks to impose total order among requests. Implement and throughly test the corresponding protocol *AskAllClocks*. Compare the experimental results with the theoretical bounds.

Exercise 9.6.21   ($\star$) Write the set of rules of protocol *AskQuorum* and prove its correctness.

Exercise 9.6.22   ($\star$) Implement and throughly test protocol *AskQuorum* of Exercise 9.6.21. Compare the experimental results with the theoretical bounds.

Exercise 9.6.23   Calculate the coefficient α for the coterie *Square* when n is not a perfect square.

Exercise 9.6.24   ($\star$) Let $n = p^2$. Construct a coterie with $\alpha = 1$ where each quorum has size precisely p.

Exercise 9.6.25   Devise a method so that the entities in the core can execute the ring-election protocol *without* sending any message to noncore entities.

9.6.2   Problems

Problem 9.6.1   ($\star\star$) Prove that any timestamp-based virtual clock that satisfies property *Complete Causal Order* must use vectors of size at least n.

Problem 9.6.2   ($\star$) Modify algorithm *VectorClocks*, so as to construct and maintain virtual clocks satisfying the *Complete Causal Order* property without any *a priori* knowledge, without incurring in any initial cost, without any additional messages, and with no more information in each message that that required by *VectorClocks*.

Problem 9.6.3   ($\star\star$) Design an algorithm to occasionally reduce the values of the vector clocks. Your protocol should not destroy any causal relationship between the events occurring after the reduction. Prove its correctness and analyze its performance.

Problem 9.6.4   ($\star$) Write the rules of protocol *SingleDetectResolve* for deadlock detection and resolution in single-request systems. Implement it and throughly test it. Compare its experimental performance with the theoretical bounds.

9.6.3 Answers to Exercises

Answer to Exercise 9.6.13

As the undelying graph is a tree, it is sufficient to show that it is impossible that both last$(u)[t] = v$ and last$(v)[t] = u$. By contradiction, consider the first time t' when last(u) is set to v while last$(v)[t'] = u$. This can occur only if a "Request" message is sent at that time from u to v and last(u) was at that time equal to v, but by Property 9.3.1 this is impossible.

Answer to Exercise 9.6.15

At a given time t, any node x partitions the nodes into two sets: the set $A(x)[t]$ of those whose terminal paths include x and the set $B(x)[t]$ of those whose terminal path does *not* include x. Call target$(v)[t]$ the terminal node at the end of the terminal path of v at time t; then observe that for every $y \in A(x)[t]$, target$(x) =$ target(y). Consider the state of the system before flipping last(x) to y at time t'. By Property 9.3.2, $x \in B(y)[t']$. After the flipping, for every $w \in B(y)[t]$, target$(w)[t] =$ target$(w)[t']$, so target$(w)[t']$ remains the holder of the token or a waiter. For every $z \in A(x)[t']$, including x, target$(z)[t] =$ target$(y)[t] =$ target$(y)[t']$, so target$(z)[t]$ remains the holder of the token or a waiter.

BIBLIOGRAPHY

[1] D. Agrawal and A. El Abbadi. An efficient and fault-tolerant solution for distributed mutual exclusion. *ACM Transactions on Computer Systems*, 9(1):1–20, February 1991.

[2] D. Barbara and H. Garcia-Molina. Mutual exclusion in partitioned distributed systems. *Distributed Computing*, 1(2):119–132, 1986.

[3] P. A. Bernstein and E. Newcomer. *Principles of Transaction Processing*. Morgan Kaufmann, 1997.

[4] O. S. F. Carvalho and G. Roucairol. On mutual exclusion in computer network. *Communications of the ACM, 26(2)*, 26(2):146–147, 1983.

[5] B. Charron-Bost. Concerning the size of logical clocks in distributed systems. *Information Processing Letters*, 39(1):11–16, 1991.

[6] M.J. Demmer and M. Herlihy. The arrow distributed directory protocol. In *Int. Symposium on Distributed Computing*, pages 119–133, 1998.

[7] E. Feuerstein, S. Leonardi, A. Marchetti-Spaccamela, and N. Santoro. Efficient token-based control in rings. *Information Processing Letters*, 66(4):175–180, 1998.

[8] C.J. Fidge. Timestamps in message-passing systems that preserve the partial ordering. In *11th Australian Computer Science Conference*, pages 56–66, feb 1988.

[9] H. Garcia-Molina and D. Barbara. How to assign votes in a distributed system. *Journal of the ACM*, 32(4):841–860, 1985.

[10] D.K Gifford. Weighted voting for replicated data. In *7th ACM Symposium on Operating System Principles*, pages 150–162, dec 1979.

[11] J. M. Helary, N. Plouzeau, and M. Raynal. A distributed algorithm for mutual exclusion in an arbitrary network. *The Computer Journal*, 31(4):289–295, August 1988.

[12] M. Hofri. On timeout for global deadlock detection in decentralized database systems. *Information Processing Letters*, 51(6):295–302, 1994.

[13] T. Ibaraki and T. Kameda. A theory of coteries: Mutual exclusion in distributed systems. *IEEE Trans. Parallel Distrib. Syst.*, 4(7):779–794, 1993.

[14] N. Krivokapic, A. Kemper, and E. Gudes. Deadlock detection in distributed database systems: A new algorithm and a comparative performance analysis. *VLDB Journal: Very Large Data Bases*, 8(2):79–100, 1999.

[15] F. Kuhn and R. Wattenhofer. Dynamic analysis of the arrow distributed protocol. In *16th ACM Symposium on Parallelism in Algorithms and Architectures*, pages 294–301, June 2004.

[16] L. Lamport. Time, clocks, and the ordering of events in a distributed system. *Communications of the ACM*, 21(7):558–565, July 1978.

[17] C. Lavault. Analysis of an efficient distributed algorithm for mutual exclusion. In *2nd Joint International Conference on Vector and Parallel Processing*, pages 133–144, Lyon, sept 1992. Spronger.

[18] M. Maekawa. A $\sqrt{N}$ algorithm for mutual exclusion in decentralized systems. *ACM Trabsactions on Computer Systems*, 3(2):145–159, 1985.

[19] F. Mattern. Virtual time and global states of distributed systems. In Cosnard M. et al., editor, *Workshop on Parallel and Distributed Algorithms*, pages 215–226, North-Holland/ Elsevier, 1989.

[20] F. Mattern. Logical time. In P. Dasgupta and J. Urban, editors, *Encyclopedia of Distributed Computing*. Kluwer, 1999.

[21] S. Meldal, S. Sankar, and J. Vera. Exploiting locality in maintaining potential causality. In *10th ACM Symposium on Principles of Distributed Computing*, pages 231–239, 1991.

[22] M. Naimi, M. Trehel, and A. Arnold. A log *n* distributed mutual exclusion algorithm based on path reversal. *Journal of Parallel and Distributed Computing*, 34:1–13, 1996.

[23] M. L. Neilsen, M. Mizuno, and Michel Raynal. A general method to define quorums. In *12th International Conference on Distributed Computing Systems*, pages 657–664, 1992.

[24] D. Parker, G. Popek, G. Rudisin, A. Stoughton, B. Walker, E. Walton, J. Chow, D. Edwards, S. Kiser, and C. Kline. Detection of mutual inconsistency in distributed systems. *IEEE Transactions on Software Engineering*, 9(3):240–247, 1983.

[25] D. Peleg and E. Reshef. Low complexity variants of the arrow distributed directory. *Journal of Computer and System Science*, 63:474–485, 2001.

[26] K. Raymond. A tree-based algorithm for distributed mutual exclusion. *ACM Transactions on Computer Systems*, 7(1):61–77, February 1989.

[27] G. Ricart and A.K. Agrawala. An optimal algorithm for mutual exclusion in computer networks. *Communications of the ACM*, 24(1):9–17, 1981.

[28] B. A. Sanders. The information structure of distributed mutual exclusion algorithms. *ACM Transactions on Computer Systems*, 5(3):284–299, August 1987.

[29] R. Schwarz and F. Mattern. Detecting Causal Relationships in Distributed Computations: In Search of the Holy Grail. *Distributed Computing*, 7(3), mar 1994.

[30] M. Singhal. A class of deadlock-free Maekawa-type algorithms for mutual exclusion in distributed systems. *Distributed Computing*, 4(3):131–138, 1991.

[31] M. Singhal and A. Kshemkalyani. An efficient implementation of vector clocks. *Information Processing Letters*, 43(1):47–52, 1992.

[32] J. van de Snepscheut. Fair mutual exclusion on a graph of processes. *Distributed Computing*, 2:113–115, 1987.

[33] R.E. Strom and S. Yemini. Optimistic recovery in distributed systems. *ACM Transactions on Computing Systems*, 3(3):204–226, 1985.

[34] I. Suzuki and T. Kasami. A distributed mutual exclusion algorithm. *ACM Transactions on Computer Systems*, 3(4):344–349, nov 1985.

[35] R.H. Thomas. A majority consensus approach to concurrency control for multiple copy databases. *ACM Transactions on Database Systems*, 4(2):180–209, june 1979.

[36] G.T.J. Wuu and A. J. Bernstein. Efficient solutions to the replicated log and dictionary problems. In *3rd ACM Symposium on Principles of Distributed Computing*, pages 233–242, Vancouver, 1984.

A

action, 2, 14, 530
addition, 412, 474, 475, 478, 481, 484
agreement, 415–416
  communication fault, 469
  consensus, 416
  from Boolean to general, 438
  majority, 469
  unanimity, 416
arbitrary graph
  Byzantine agreement, 440
  election, 185
    lower bound, 209
ask your neighbours (Strategy), 53
asynchronous-to-synchronous transform,
  357

B

behaviour, 2
  homogeneous, 3
bidirectional links, 8
bit complexity, 129
bivalent configuration, 420
breadth-first spanning-tree, 240–249
broadcast, 10, 17, 29–35, 225
  fault tolerant, 415, 462, 476, 485
  mesh, 217
  by traversal, 51
  complete graph, 35
  hypercube, 32
  tree, 32
  with termination detection, 88
broadcast tree, 61
butterfly
  election, 221
  interval routing, 273

Byzantine fault, 412, 430–443
  impossibility of consensus, 435
  ubiquitous, 475

C

cardinal statistics, 77
causal order, 543–547
causal time, 10
cellular automata, 391
center finding, 81
chordal ring
  election, 183, 221
clocks
  synchronized, 333–406
common knowledge, 416, 460
communication center, 280
communication delays
  bounded, 9, 333, 424
  finite (Axiom), 5
  general, 5
  unitary, 9, 335
communication fault, 412,
  467–485
communicator, 342–352
  2-bit, 340, 345, 359
  3-bit, 346
  bit pattern, 352
  corruption tolerant, 351
  lower bound, 352
  monotonically increasing, 394
  optimal, 347
  size, 352
compact routing, 261
  interval, 262
complete causal order, 544

Design and Analysis of Distributed Algorithms, by Nicola Santoro
Copyright © 2007 John Wiley & Sons, Inc.

Printed and bound by CPI Group (UK) Ltd, Croydon, CR0 4YY

Printed and bound by CPI Group (UK) Ltd, Croydon, CR0 4YY

27/10/2024

14580261-0004